Lecture Notes in Computer Science

Lecture Notes in Computer Science

Edited by G. Goos and J. Hartmanis

303

J. W. Schmidt S. Ceri M. Missikoff (Eds.)

Advances in Database Technology – EDBT '88

International Conference on Extending Database Technology
Venice, Italy, March 14–18, 1988
Proceedings

Springer-Verlag

Berlin Heidelberg New York London Paris Tokyo

Editors

Joachim W. Schmidt
Fachbereich Informatik, Johann Wolfgang Goethe-Universität
Postfach 11 19 32, D-6000 Frankfurt am Main 11, FRG

Stefano Ceri
Dipartimento di Matematica, Università di Modena
Via Campi 213/B, I-41100 Modena, Italy

Michele Missikoff
IASI-CNR
Viale Manzoni 30, I-00185 Rome, Italy

CR Subject Classification (1987): D.3.3, E.2, F.4.1, H.2, I.2.1, I.2.4

ISBN 3-540-19074-0 Springer-Verlag Berlin Heidelberg New York
ISBN 0-387-19074-0 Springer-Verlag New York Berlin Heidelberg

Printing and binding: Druckhaus Beltz, Hemsbach/Bergstr.
2145/3140-543210

Preface

Within the last 20 years the database area has enriched computer science with a set of mutually related results of considerable practical importance and theoretical interest. This "database technology" covers a wide range of achievements, from conceptually rich and semantically well-defined abstract models down to the level of robust and efficient system implementations. Most of the basic issues are remarkably well understood within a framework of adequate and sound formalizations.

During these two decades database technology managed to develop appropriate solutions for a wide variety of commercial applications and its economic success can be taken as a proof of its relevance.

Currently, after a period of conceptual consolidation and implementational improvement, database technology is being challenged again. Pushed by the demands of novel application classes and new types of users, by the expanding complexity of data-based information systems and by the ever increasing amounts of data, as well as being pulled by new developments in hardware and systems architectures, database technology is having to adapt and extend rapidly.

Our intent in creating the EDBT Conference was to provide an international forum appropriate for the exchange of results in research, development, and applications which *extend* the scope of *database technology*. The EDBT Conference is designed to facilitate and stimulate communication among researchers and between academia and industry.

The scientific program of EDBT '88 flows in a single stream of presentations (a format we were close to giving up on when confronted with the overwhelming response of 168 submissions and only 27 slots available!). The papers originated from 28 countries and can be divided roughly into two broad areas. The figures in parentheses indicate the number of submissions which addressed this subject.

Extended Database Semantics (91):

> Complex Database Objects (19),
> Databases and Logic (30),
> Expert Systems and Databases (24),
> Extended Data Semantics and Data Types (18)

Extended Architectures and Systems Support (51):

> Transaction Models and Concurrency (16),
> Data Distribution (11),
> Efficient Data Access (17),
> Data Administration and Control (7).

Most of the remaining submissions concentrated on special database applications (22), in particular in the area of heterogeneous and multimedia databases.

In his invited paper Lucca Cardelli from DEC Systems Research, Palo Alto, presents "Type Systems for Data-Oriented Languages", a concern that is also addressed by the panel on the relationship between "Databases and Programming Languages: A Shotgun Marriage?"

An increasing amount of research and development in our field is done through international co-operation and within joint projects (ESPRIT, Alvey, EUREKA, various national and industrial programs). EDBT '88 reflects this aspect in specific project sessions based on submitted and reviewed short papers. One such session, chaired by Domenico Sacca (University of Calabria, Italy), presents projects that develop "Support for Data- and Knowledge-Based Applications". A second one, organized by Giuseppe Pelagatti (University of Brescia, Italy), concentrates on "Database Applications in Distributed Environments".

Two days of tutorials precede the Scientific Program. Research colleagues working in some of the most rapidly moving areas of database technology present the state-of-the-art in their particular field of interest:

Francois Bancilhon	Object-Oriented Databases
Carlo Batini, Dave Reiner	Database Design: Methodologies and Tools
Phil Bernstein	Transaction Processing Systems
Herve Gallaire	Logic and Databases
John Nestor	Database Technology for Software Engineering
David De Witt	Extensible Database Systems.

An Industrial Exhibition and a Book Fair running in parallel to EDBT '88 attracted the participation of about 25 different companies.

The program committee of EDBT '88 was chaired by Joachim W. Schmidt (Frankfurt University, FR Germany); the members were

S. Alagic (Yugoslavia)	H. Kangassalo (Finland)
A. Albano (Italy)	M. Missikoff (Italy)
P. Apers (Netherlands)	J. Mylopoulos (Canada)
M. Atkinson (G. Britain)	E. Neuhold (FR Germany)
F. Bancilhon (France)	J.M. Nicolas (FR Germany)
R. Bayer (FR Germany)	A. Pirotte (Belgium)
C. Beeri (Israel)	A. Reuter (FR Germany)
G. Bracchi (Italy)	G. Schlageter (FR Germany)
M.L. Brodie (USA)	A. Sernadas (Portugal)
J. Bubenko (Sweden)	A. Solvberg (Norway)
S. Ceri (Italy)	N. Spyratos (France)
Q. Chen (PR China)	P. Stocker (G. Britain)
P. Dadam (FR Germany)	K. Subieta (Poland)
R. Demolombe (France)	B. Thalheim (DR Germany)
D.J. De Witt (USA)	D.C. Tsichritzis (Switzerland)
A. Furtado (Brazil)	Y. Vassiliou (Greece)
G. Gardarin (France)	G. Wiederhold (USA)
G. Gottlob (Austria)	H. Williams (G. Britain)
L.A. Kalinichenko (USSR)	C. Zaniolo (USA)
Y. Kambayashi (Japan)	C.A. Zehnder (Switzerland)

We would like to give our sincere thanks to all program committee members as well as to all the other reviewers for their care in evaluating the submitted papers.

Our thanks are also extended to Professor U. Serafini, President of AICCRE, for his active role in promoting EDBT '88 within Europe and to Venetian authorities, and to Professor L. Bianco, Director of IASI-CNR, and the entire secretarial and technical staff of IASI-CNR for their confidence and support given to the conference right from the early stages of the organizational process.

We also acknowledge the continuous help of all the members of the organizational committee: P. Atzeni, A. D'Atri, H. Eckhardt, J. Elmore, G. Gardarin, K.G. Jeffrey, F.L. Ricci, G. Turco and C. Zaniolo.

Finally we would like to thank our secretaries and their assistants, A. Bambey, F. Fühler, U. Kasielke, M. Ritsert, I. Wetzel and A. Ziegler.

Springer-Verlag, in particular I. Mayer, was as always very helpful in preparing the proceedings.

EDBT '88 is being held on San Giorgio Island in Venice from March 14th to 18th, 1988. We would like to thank the Cini Foundation for the opportunity to profit from the stimulating and relaxing atmosphere of this unique setting.

Venice, March 1988   Joachim W. Schmidt   (Program Committee Chairman)
                       Stefano Ceri   (Conference Chairman)
                       Michele Missikoff   (Organizing Committee Chairman)

Contents

Special Data

Short Project Papers

Support for Data- and Knowledge-Based Applications

Distributed Database Applications

Types for Data-Oriented Languages
(Overview)

Luca Cardelli

Digital Equipment Corporation, Systems Research Center
130 Lytton Avenue, Palo Alto, CA 94301

1. Introduction

By the term *data-oriented language*, I mean a language whose *main* concern is in the structuring and handling of data. For contrast, procedure-oriented and process-oriented languages are mostly concerned with expressing algorithms and protocols. Other terms, such as the much abused *object-oriented*, can be used to indicate an integration of the above features. A useful and complete language should certainly integrate all of the above "orientations", but here we will mostly focus on data structuring.

Data orientation has traditionally been the main characteristic of information systems, but has also played an increasingly important role in general-purpose programming languages. While the first programming languages were mostly algorithmic, with little emphasis on data structures, more recent languages have seen a relative standardization of control-flow features and a large emphasis and experimentation in data structuring, including the packaging of procedures into abstract data types, objects, and modules (see [Cardelli Wegner 85] for a tutorial and bibliography).

At the same time, information systems have evolved towards more expressive ways of modelling reality, which has meant more complex data models and more flexible and integrated query languages. Many people have noted that powerful query languages tightly coupled with complex data models have all the characteristics of programming languages, and have suggested there should be a systematic integration. This has resulted in the development of systems such as Pascal/R [Schmidt 77], Adaplex [Smith Fox Landers 83], PS-algol [PPRG 85], Taxis [Mylopoulos Bernstein Wong 80] and Galileo [Albano Cardelli Orsini 85].

We now have a sufficient number of examples to justify looking for a broad framework. In order to integrate information systems and programming languages, it is first necessary to unify the information-system concept of *data model* with the programming-language concept of *type system*. We argue that *type theory* (the formal study of type, or classification, systems) is the correct framework within which to study and carry out such unification. In this framework we can analyze existing integrated data-oriented systems and to design better ones.

A nice step in unifying data models and type systems was the introduction of *orthogonal persistence* of data [Atkinson Bailey Chisholm Cockshott Morrison 83], which bridges the gap between ephemeral (programming-language) and persistent (information-system) data. But this is not sufficient; it has become increasingly evident that data models aim to be more expressive than ordinary type systems, and that the nature of information systems impose additional constraints such as the ability to evolve data schemas over time. Hence new concepts have to be developed, and a good general framework is required.

The prominent feature of data-oriented languages is the richness of their type structure. This may include various flavors of structured data (arrays, trees, sets, relations), abstract types, polymorphism, inheritance, computations over types, etc. In fact, the type structure may be so rich that the traditional distinction between values and types is insufficient to characterize it completely.

We shall talk about various uses of *kinds* [McCracken 79] which are the "types" of types, to organize such rich type structures. The main contention of this paper is that kind structures should be of benefit in understanding and developing data-oriented languages.

Richness of type structure seems necessary for world modeling, which is process of formalizing (pieces of) reality or abstract concepts. World modeling has conflicting goals: expressiveness is the most desirable feature, but it has to coexist with reliability, by which we mean the ability to check and maintain world models mechanically (through static typechecking) so that programs can be written and maintained reliably, and also with efficiency, which means that type structures must be easily typecheckable and should facilitate efficient computation.

If we wanted to emphasize expressiveness only, we would probably choose something like set theory as our description system; but this is not efficiently typecheckable and has no obvious relation to efficient computation. Efficiency, on the other hand, has been amply emphasized in the past, generally to the detriment of expressiveness. Here we mainly focus on reliability and, while keeping it fixed, strive for expressiveness with an eye on efficiency.

2. Polymorphism

Our aim is to design statically typed languages with much of the flexibility of untyped languages. We want the rigor of static typing for reliability and efficiency. We want the flexibility of untyped languages for expressiveness. The compromise is a difficult one; some dynamic typechecking may be ultimately required, but we aim to make it as rare as possible. If we can make typing largely static, then we will have largely reached our goals of reliability and efficiency.

A good combination of expressiveness and reliability is reached through various forms of *polymorphism* (sometimes called *genericity*) which is the ability of typed programs to operate on data of different, but related, types. (The ability to operate on data of unrelated types involves *overloading* and *coercions*, and will not be discussed here.)

To make the discussion more concrete, we introduce a simple untyped language, which we later extend and use as the basis of typed languages. Here we use x for variables, k for built-in constants (e.g. numbers and operations), t for tags (e.g. record field names), and a, b, and c for terms.

	introduction	*elimination*
variables	x	
constants	k	
functions	fun(x) b	b(a)
pairs	<a,b>	lft(c) rht(c)
records	$(t_1=a_1, ... , t_n=a_n)$	c.t
variants	$[t=a]$	case c of $[t_1=x_1] b_1$ ... $[t_n=x_n] b_n$
recursion	rec(x) a	

Under the *introduction* heading we list ways of building (introducing) entities: we have constructors for functions, pairs, records (which are unordered tagged tuples of values) and variants (tagged values). The *elimination* column lists ways of using and decomposing (eliminating) entities: application uses functions, left and right projections decompose pairs, field selection decomposes records, and the case statement analyzes a variant according to its tag (binding the appropriate variable x_i to the contents of the variant in the body b_i). Recursion can be eliminated by expanding a recursive definition.

Characteristic of untyped languages is that all the constructs described in the elimination column may *fail* during computation. Application fails if a non-function is applied; projections fail if a non-pair is decomposed, etc. These possible failures make untyped or dynamically typed programs unreliable: even if programs are carefully coded the first time, later changes may require manual inspection of the entire program to check against failure points; this is an unreliable process and the quality of software degrades.

In order to statically trap failure points, we want to impose a type system on our untyped language. We can do this in many different ways, but any static type system restricts the class of programs that can be written, and hence reduces the expressiveness of the language. The goal is then to preserve as much flexibility as possible through polymorphism. There are two main situations:

- In the untyped language, some functions can be applied to objects of different types without ever failing, since they do not examine objects too closely: this phenomenon is called *parametric polymorphism* (since it can be modeled in typed languages by type parameters):

    (fun(x) x) (3)   (fun(x) x) (true)

Here we have the identity function (which does not examine its argument, but simply returns it) applied to an integer and a boolean. Other parametric polymorphic functions are the length-of-a-list function, which does not examine the list elements but just counts them, and sorting functions, which do not examine the list elements except to compare them.

- In the untyped language, a function that can be applied to a record without failing can also be applied to any record having additional fields, because the additional fields will be ignored. This is called *subtype polymorphism* (since we can define a subtype relation on record types, based on the number, tags, and types of record fields):

(fun(x) x.t) (⟨t=3⟩)   (fun(x) x.t) (⟨t=3, u=true⟩)

Here we have a function extracting the t component of a record, which works on any record having at least a t component. A similar kind of subtype polymorphism can be detected in variants: a function correctly handling three classes of differently tagged variant objects, will not fail if only two classes of differently tagged variant objects ever occur.

Many type systems have been devised to deal with polymorphism. In the next section we examine some of the options.

3. Levels

We now examine a number of type systems that can be imposed on our untyped language, from the most restrictive to the most flexible ones. To get a glimpse of their features, we show how to define the identity function in each one of them.

These type systems differ in the number of *levels* they require to be described. Intuitively, values (i.e. the entities expressible in the untyped language) are all lumped together in a set of all values at *Level 0*. At *Level 1* we have types, intended as sets of values, and type operators, intended as functions mapping types to types (e.g. the List type operator is a function mapping the type Int to the type of lists of integer). These two levels are sufficient for most ordinary languages, but we will add *Level 2*, the level of *kinds*. Kinds are the "types" of types and operators; intuitively they are either sets of types or sets of operators.

Types classify data and computations, and kinds classify types and operators. Just as we have values and value computations at Level 0, that are classified by Level 1 entities (types), we also have types and type computations at Level 1 that are classified by Level 2 entities (kinds). We use the notation a:A to indicate that value a has type A, and the notation A::K to indicate that type A has kind K. We use lower case identifiers for Level 0, capitalized identifiers for Level 1, and all caps for Level 2.

We display the level structure of the various type systems by simple *level diagrams*, based on the intuition of types as sets of values and kinds as sets of types and operators.

One type

Our initial untyped language can be described by the following level diagram. There is a uniform set of values, and since there are no type distinctions we can imagine that there is a single type, the type of all values, called Value. Hence the type level is collapsed to a single point.

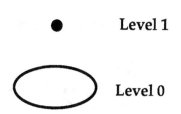

Level 1

Level 0

```
def id: Value =
      fun(x:Value) x
   id(3)
```

In this system, the identity function is defined and used as shown above; definitions have the general form "def x:A = a". (We could have simply written fun(x)x, as in the untyped language, since all variables have the same type.)

Many types

We now introduce type distinctions: our value set is partitioned into distinct regions of booleans, integers, boolean functions, integer functions, and so on, each identified by a distinct type (we drop the universal Value type). All program variables must now be annotated with their types. We obtain a *monomorphic* type system (each value having a single type) not much different from Pascal's.

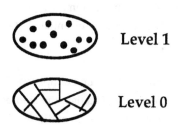

Level 1

Level 0

```
def id: Int→Int =
      fun(x:Int) x
   id(3)
```

The (integer) identity function is now strictly typed, and we have lost the ability to express polymorphic functions of any kind: for example, the boolean identity must be written separately. We have however gained a static type system, in which run-time failures can be detected at compile-time.

One kind

We are now ready to introduce our first kind: the kind of all types, called TYPE. In this system we can introduce variables ranging over types, and we can classify them by giving them the kind TYPE.

Level 2

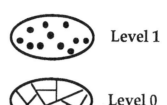

Level 1

Level 0

def id: All[A::TYPE] A→A =
    fun[A::TYPE] fun(x:A) x
id[Int](3)
id[Bool](true)

The above is the polymorphic identity function and two different uses of it (we use round brackets for entities at Level 0 and square brackets for entities at Level 1). We have a function taking a type as an argument, and a corresponding application of a type to such function. The type of a polymorphic function has the form All[A::TYPE]B; this is the type of a function taking a type A and returning a value in B. (We could have simply written fun[A] fun(x:A) x, since all type variables have the same kind.)

We now have a language supporting parametric polymorphism, through the notion of abstraction over type variables which can be instantiated at different types.

Many kinds

Finally, we can introduce more kinds. For example we can introduce all the kinds of the form K⇒L, for kinds K and L; TYPE⇒TYPE is then the kind of all one-argument type operators (such as List). Level 1 acquires type operators, in addition to types, and it is partitioned by the various kinds existing at Level 2 (note that type operators are functions, not types: there is no value whose type is a type operator).

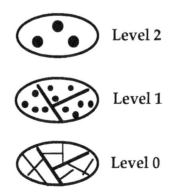

Def Endo:: TYPE⇒TYPE =
 Fun[A::TYPE] A→A
def id: All[A::TYPE] Endo[A] =
 fun[A::TYPE] fun(x:A) x
id[Int](3)

Here Endo(-morphism) is a type operator which given a type A returns the type of functions from A to A; its kind is TYPE⇒TYPE. The polymorphic identity is a function which given a type A returns an endomorphism on A, in particular the identity over A.

 Several other classes of kinds can be introduced, and we shall see later on.

Kinds are types (Type:Type)

 We should mention some "degenerate" type systems, which are obtained by collapsing the level structure we have just set up. We can collapse kinds and types by the simple assumption the there is a type of all types, including itself. We then lose the distinction between kinds and types (and also our syntactic distinction between "::" and ":", between square brackets and round brackets, etc.).

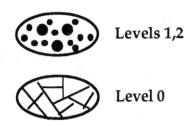

Levels 1,2

Level 0

def Endo: Type→Type =
 fun(A:Type) A→A
def id: All(A:Type) Endo(A) =
 fun(A:Type) fun(x:A) x
id(Int)(3)

The problem with this collapsed system is that, although we still have static typechecking, we lose the ability to perform what we might call *static levelchecking*. That is, it is not possible to determine the proper level of certain expressions. For example, in the expression:

 fun(A:Type) fun(x:A) x

is A a Level 2 or a Level 1 entity? And is x a Level 1 or a Level 0 entity? This cannot be determined because both the following applications are legal (the latter uses Type:Type):

 id (Int) (3) id (Type) (Int)

Lack of level distinctions causes problems in compilation, since compilation strategies are generally based on the idea the Level 0 entities are evaluated at *run-time*, and all the other levels are processed at *compile-time*.

Types are values

Finally, we can collapse all three levels, obtaining something similar to an untyped language. The difference is that there are now types and kinds in the value domain, which can be manipulated. Smalltalk, with its notions of classes and metaclasses, has some of these features.

 Levels 0, 1, 2

        def Endo: Type→Type =
            fun(A:Type) A→A
        def id : All(A:Type) Endo(A) =
            fun(A:Type) fun(x:A) x
        id(Int)(3)

In spite of all the type information we lose static typing; dubious programs such as id(3)(4), and failing programs such as 3(4), are now statically legal.

4. A three-level language

In the rest of the paper, we adopt the many-kinds (three levels) option, which seems to be a natural extrapolation of language evolution. The first procedural languages only had a fixed number of types. Recent languages have a multiplicity of types, and user-definable types. More advanced, polymorphic, languages have (often implicitly) a kind of all types, type operators, and other non-trivial level structures. Future languages will have a richer kind structure, with user-definable kinds.

Level 0: values

In this subsection we sketch the Level 0 (values) of a three-level data-oriented language. Basically, we have typed versions of the values in our initial untyped language, and we also add a few more.

We have basic data values such as "ok" (a trivial value), booleans, characters, strings, integers and reals.

We have records $(t_1=a_1, ... , t_n=a_n)$ with field selection. Record fields are unordered, must have disjoint tags, and can store arbitrary values, including functions.

We have variants, $[t=a]$ with a case statements. Enumerations are a special case of variants, when the data contents are trivial (e.g. "ok") and only the tags matter.

We have typed higher-order functions. These include ordinary functions taking values as arguments and returning values as results, such as

        def succ = fun(x:Int) x+1   succ(3)

and polymorphic functions, taking types as arguments, and returning values as results:

def id = fun[A::TYPE] fun(x:A) x   id[Int](3)

Note that polymorphic functions inhabit Level 0, although they take types as arguments.

We have tuples, including both tuples of values, such as <3,4> and mixed tuples of types and values, such as <Int, 0, succ>. In the latter case the type components of a tuple can only be handled in a limited way, so that these tuple represents elements of abstract types [Mitchell Plotkin 85].

We have sets {a, b, c} and set operations. Sets of records are relations, which admit generalized relational algebra operations [Buneman Ohori 87].

A value b=ref(c) is a modifiable reference to a value c; it can be dereferenced by deref(b) and assigned by b := c'.

Recursion is used to define recursive functions and other recursive values, such as data structures containing loops.

Exceptions can also be seen as special values which can be "raised" and "trapped" to interrupt and resume the normal flow of control.

Level 1: types and operators

At Level 1 we have the types of Level 0 entities, and operators among Level 1 entities. We also introduce a reflexive and transitive relation of *subtyping*, denoted by A<:B (A is a subtype of B) for types A and B. Subtyping is intuitively understood as set inclusion between types: if A<:B then any value of type A also has type B.

In correspondence with the basic values, we have the basic types Ok (whose only value is "ok"), Bool, Char, String, Int, Real, etc. There are no non-trivial subtyping relations among basic types.

A record type $(t_1:A_1, ... , t_n:A_n)$ is the type of a record value $(t_1=a_1, ... , t_n=a_n)$ if A_i is the type of a_i, for all i. Record types are identified up to reordering of their fields. Two record types are in the subtype relation A<:B, if all the tags of B appear in A, and the corresponding types are in the subtype relation. This subtyping relation between record types models some forms of multiple inheritance [Cardelli 84].

A variant type $[t_1:A_1, ... , t_n:A_n]$ is the type of a variant value $[t=a]$ if there is an index i such that $t=t_i$ and $a:A_i$. Variant types are identified up to reordering of their fields. Two variant types are in the subtype relation A<:B if the tags of B include the tags of A, and the corresponding types are in the subtyping relation.

The type of a function fun(x:A)b is A→B, if b has type B. The type of a polymorphic function fun[X::K]b is All[X::K]B, if b has type B (where B may have occurrences of X). Subtyping of function spaces is given by the following rule: A→B <: A'→B' if A' <: A (note the inversion) and B<:B'. Similarly, All[X::K]B <: All[X::K']B' if K'<::K (where <:: denotes a *subkind* relation, discussed later), and B<:B' under the assumption that X::K.

The type of a pair <a,b> is the cartesian product A×B, for a:A and b:B. The types of mixed tuples of types and values (abstract types) are discussed in [Mitchell Plotkin 85].

Set types $\{A_1, \ldots, A_n\}$, relation types, and relation algebra operators are discussed in detail in [Ohori 87]. For set types, A<:B if for each A_i in A there is a B_j in B with $A_i <: B_j$.

The type of an assignable object ref(a) is Ref(A), if a:A. The subtyping rule for Ref types cannot be simple subtyping of the domain types, because unsafe programs could then be written. Hence we require that Ref(A)<:Ref(A') if A<:A' and A'<:A.

Recursive types and operators are supported by the construct Rec(X::K)A, which we can use to define list types, tree types, etc. Subtyping of recursive types is determined by expanding the recursive definitions.

The most unusual feature of Level 1 is the presence of type operators, which perform computations over types in much the same way functions perform computations over values. The syntax is also very similar:

Fun[X::K]B   A[B]

The first expression denotes an operator which given an entity of kind K (e.g. a type if K=TYPE) returns the Level 1 entity B (e.g. a type, or another operator). The second expression denotes the application of an operator to a Level 1 object (e.g. a type, or another operator). We can then define, for example, an operator List such that List[Int] is the type of integer lists, and an operator Tree such that Tree[Int][Bool] is the type of binary trees with integer leaves and boolean nodes.

Since operators represent almost-ordinary computations (but one level "up"), we might want to write programs such as:

Def F = Fun[X::BOOL] if X then Int else Bool end

F[True]

but what are "True" and "BOOL" here? This "True" inhabits Level 1, hence it is different from the "true" value. We can think of "true" as a run-time boolean, and "True" as a compile-time boolean; "True" is a *lifted* version of the value "true". Similarly the conditional in the example is a lifted version of the conditional at the value level. Then the "BOOL" kind is a *lifted type* (from Level 1 to Level 2). The idea of lifted values and types may seem strange, but in a sense it is unavoidable: it can be shown that once operators are allowed, lifted booleans, integers, etc. can be defined purely in terms of higher-order operators. An important restriction is that all computations at Level 1 must be side-effect free, to preserve sound typing.

Level 2: kinds

The main novelty in this presentation is the richness of structure at the kind level. Most languages have no kinds at all, and even polymorphic languages may have only one: the kind of all types. Here we introduce many more classes of kinds.

TYPE is the kind of all types, i.e. it is the "type" of basic types, record types, variant types, function types, tuple types, etc. Its presence means that variables of kind TYPE, ranging over all types, can be introduced.

As we have seen in the previous section, we can introduce a kind BOOL, which is a lifted version of the Bool type, together with the Level 1 entities True::BOOL, False::BOOL, which are lifted versions of Level 0 booleans, and with the relevant operators such as conditional. Similarly for the INT kind, etc. This can provide a rich computational languages for defining complex type structures at compile-time.

ALL[A::K]L is the kind of operators from kind K to kind L, normally written K⇒L if A does not occur in L. For example, TYPE⇒TYPE is the kind of unary type operators, such as List, and TYPE⇒(TYPE⇒TYPE) is the kind of binary type operators, such as the function space operator "→". These kinds provide the mechanism for performing *static kindchecking* of type computations involving type operators. The kindchecking rules for operators are analogous to the typechecking rules for functions.

The idea of subtyping was introduced case by case in the previous section for each type construction, but it can also be captured uniformly by a new class of kinds. We can define POWER[A] to be the kind of all the subtypes of type A [Cardelli 88]. Hence B::POWER[A] means that B is a subtype of A. By introducing the binding fun[A<:B] as an abbreviation of fun[A::POWER[B]] (and similarly for All[A<:B]), we can express subtype polymorphism very precisely, including dependencies between input and output subtypes:

> def id: All[A<:B] A→A =
>
> fun[A<:B] fun(x:A) x

Here id is the polymorphic identity restricted to the subtypes of some type B. Given a subtype A of B and an object of that subtype, it returns an object of that same subtype.

A very speculative but interesting possibility is to introduce the equivalent of Ref types at the kind level. Suppose we indicate by MODIF the kind of modifiable types, i.e. types which may change in time, and by B::MODIF=Modif[Int] a modifiable type which is currently bound to Int (with the rule that Modif[B] has kind MODIF for any type B). Then the value b:B=modif(3) would be correctly typed at the present moment (with the rule that modif(b) has type Modif[B] if b has type B), but we risk breaking the type system by later assigning B := Bool (a Level 1 assignment) and extracting an integer as a boolean out of b.

This problem explains why type computations should generally be side-effect free, but the above situation is actually quite common in module systems, where version stamps are used to keep track of interfaces (types) which have changed, and of modules (values) which have to be reexamined. Hence we may imagine that modif(3) is a version-stamped integer, whose version stamp is invalidated when the assignment B := Bool is performed. Any following attempt to access the integer inside modif(3) will result in checking its version stamp against the current version stamp, and failing.

If we have subtypes, we must also have subkinds, because the subtype relation A<:B induces a natural reflexive and transitive subkind relation (indicated by "<::"), given by POWER[A]<::POWER[B]. More interestingly, POWER[A]<::TYPE must hold, since any collection of types (here, the subtypes of A) must be included in the collection of all types.

Some applications

Since kinds are collections of types, we can imagine introducing kinds such as RECORD, the collection of all record types, SET, the collection of all set types, RELATION, the collection of all set-of-record types, etc. In fact, we already have enough machinery to define them without taking them as primitives. For example, all record types are subtypes of the empty record type ⟨⟩, hence we can define RECORD = POWER[⟨⟩]:

Def Record::TYPE = ⟨⟩
DEF RECORD = POWER[Record]

We can now exhibit a kind for an "And" operator which takes two record types and returns a record type which contains the fields of both (we can assume that this operation fails or returns a trivial type if corresponding field types do not match):

And :: RECORD ⇒ RECORD ⇒ RECORD
⟨t=3, u=true⟩ : And[⟨t:Int⟩][⟨u:Bool⟩]

Although this operator (and others to follow) cannot be defined within the language, the fact that we can express its kind means that we can combine it freely with other operators.

Similarly, we can define relation kinds, together with natural join operations for relations (as defined in [Buneman Ohori 87]):

Def Relation::TYPE = {Record}
DEF RELATION = POWER[Relation]

Join :: RELATION ⇒ RELATION ⇒ RELATION
join : ALL[A::RELATION] ALL[B::RELATION] (A×B) → Join[A][B]

The "Join" type operator produces the result type of natural join operations; it is similar to "And", but works on sets of records (relations). The "join" operation is parameterized by two relation types A and B, and for each pair of relations it produces a relation (the natural join of the two) whose type is Join[A][B]. For example:

def r : Join[{⟨t:Int, u:Bool⟩}][{⟨u:Bool, v:String⟩}] =
    join[{⟨t:Int, u:Bool⟩}][{⟨u:Bool, v:String⟩}]
        (<{⟨t=3, u=true⟩}, {⟨u=true, v="xx"⟩}>)
    ≡ {⟨t=3, u=true, v="xx"⟩} : {⟨t:Int, u:Bool, v:String⟩}

Finally, we can view a database as a set of relations, and we can exhibit the kinds and types of database merge operators which perform simple set-theoretical unions of relations (database merge is actually more complex; this covers only one of the necessary steps):

Def DataBase::TYPE = {Relation}
DEF DATABASE = POWER[DataBase]

Merge :: DATABASE ⇒ DATABASE ⇒ DATABASE
merge : ALL[A::DATABASE] ALL[B::DATABASE] (A×B) → Merge[A][B]

def d : Merge[{{(t:Int, u:Bool)}}][{{(u:Bool, v:String)}}] =
   merge[{{(t:Int, u:Bool)}}][{{(u:Bool, v:String)}}]
       (<{{(t=3, u=true)}}, {{(u=true, v="xx")}}>)
   ≡ {{(t=3,u=true)}, {(u=true,v="xx")}} : {{(t:Int,u:Bool)}, {(u:Bool,v:String)}}

Here we have merged two simple databases containing one relation each, where each relation contains a single record (see [Ohori 87] for the precise type rules).

5. Formalization

Type systems can be precisely described as formal systems based on *judgements*. A judgement is a relation between environments and expressions, inductively defined by axioms and inference rules; for example: "in environment E, term a has type A" is a judgement.

Typical judgements found in most type systems, and in the system informally described in this paper, include the following. Here E is an *environment* specifying types for variables (of the form "x:A") and kinds for type variables (of the form "X::K"); "E ⊢ ..." reads "Given the environment E we can establish that ..."):

⊢ E env	E is a legal environment
E ⊢ K kind	K is a kind
E ⊢ A :: K	A has kind K
E ⊢ A type	A is a type (same as E ⊢ A::TYPE)
E ⊢ a : A	a has type A
E ⊢ K = L	K and L are equivalent kinds
E ⊢ A = B	A and B are equivalent types
E ⊢ K <:: L	K is a subkind of L
E ⊢ A <: B	A is a subtype of B (same as E ⊢ A::POWER(B))

Most type constructions are characterized by rules of Formation, Introduction, Elimination, and Subtyping. For example, the usual typechecking rules for functions can be expressed as follows (where "E, x:A" is the environment E extended with the assumption "x:A", and the horizontal line reads "implies"):

Formation	$$\frac{E \vdash A \text{ type} \quad E \vdash B \text{ type}}{E \vdash A \rightarrow B \text{ type}}$$
Introduction	$$\frac{E,\, x{:}A \vdash b{:}B}{E \vdash \text{fun}(x{:}A)\, b : A \rightarrow B}$$
Elimination	$$\frac{E \vdash b{:}A \rightarrow B \quad E \vdash a{:}A}{E \vdash b(a) : B}$$
Subtyping	$$\frac{E \vdash A'{<:}A \quad E \vdash B{<:}B'}{E \vdash A \rightarrow B <: A' \rightarrow B'}$$

In such a formalized framework, we say that a term b has a type B if it is possible to infer E ⊢ b:B according to the axioms and inference rules (given some environment E providing declarations for the free variables of b and B). See [Cardelli 88] for an example of a complete inference system.

6. Conclusions

Data-oriented languages may benefit from a rich kind structure. We have shown that kinds can provides a framework for relational and database-wide operations, for subtype relations, for schema computations, and perhaps even for schema evolution.

References

[Albano Cardelli Orsini 85] A.Albano, L.Cardelli, R.Orsini: **Galileo: a strongly typed, interactive conceptual language**, *Transactions on Database Systems*, June 1985, 10(2), pp. 230-260.

[Atkinson Bailey Chisholm Cockshott Morrison 83] M.P.Atkinson, P.J.Bailey, K.J.Chisholm, W.P.Cockshott, R.Morrison: **An approach to persistent programming**, *Computer Journal* 26(4), November 1983.

[Buneman Ohori 87] P.Buneman, A.Ohori: **Using powerdomains to generalize relational databases**, submitted for publication.

[Cardelli 84] L.Cardelli: **A semantics of multiple inheritance**, in *Semantics of Data Types*, G.Kahn, D.B.MacQueen and G.Plotkin Ed. Lecture Notes in Computer Science n.173, Springer-Verlag 1984.

[Cardelli 88] L.Cardelli: **Structural subtyping and the notion of power type**, *Proc. POPL 1988*.

[Cardelli Wegner 85] L.Cardelli, P.Wegner: **On understanding types, data abstraction and polymorphism**, *Computing Surveys*, Vol 17 n. 4, pp 471-522, December 1985.

[McCracken 79] N.McCracken: **An investigation of a programming language with a polymorphic type structure**, Ph.D. Thesis, Syracuse University, June 1979.

[Mitchell Plotkin 85] J.C.Mitchell, G.D.Plotkin: **Abstract types have existential type**, *Proc. POPL 1985*.

[Mylopoulos Bernstein Wong 80] J.Mylopoulos, P.A.Bernstein, H.K.T.Wong: **A language facility for designing database intensive applications**, *ACM Transactions on Database Systems* 5(2), June 1980.

[Ohori 87] A. Ohori: **Orderings and types in databases**, *Proc. of the Workshop on Database Programming Languages*, Roscoff, France, September 1987.

[PPRG 85] Persistent Programming Research Group: **The PS-algol reference manual - second edition**, *Technical Report PPR-12-85, University of Glasgow, Dept. of Computing Science*, Glasgow G12 8QQ, Scotland, 1985.

[Smith Fox Landers 83] J.M.Smith, S.Fox, T.Landers: **Adaplex: rationale and reference manual, second edition**, *Computer Corporation of America*, Four Cambridge Center, Cambridge, Mass. 02142, 1983.

[Schmidt 77] J.W.Schmidt: **Some high level language constructs for data of type relation**, *ACM Transaction on Database Systems* 2(3), pp. 247-281, September 1977.

Optimization in a Logic Based Language
for Knowledge and Data Intensive Applications

Ravi Krishnamurthy   *Carlo Zaniolo*

MCC, 3500 Balcones Center Dr., Austin, TX, 78759

Abstract

This paper describes the optimization approach taken to ensure the safe and efficient execution of applications written in LDL, which is a declarative language based on Horn Clause Logic and intended for data intensive and knowledge based applications. In order to generalize the strategy successfully used in relational database systems we first characterize the optimization problem in terms of its execution space, cost functions and search algorithm. Then we extend this framework to deal with rules, complex terms, recursion and various problems resulting from the richer expressive power of Logic. Among these is the termination problem (safety), whereby an unsafe execution is treated as an extreme case of poor execution.

1. Introduction

The Logic Data Language LDL, combines the expressive power of a high level logic based language (such as Prolog) with the non-navigational style of relational query languages, where the user need only supply a correct query, and the system is expected to devise an efficient execution strategy for it. Consequently, the query optimizer is given the responsibility of choosing an optimal execution --a function similar to that of an optimizer in a relational database system. A relational system uses knowledge of storage structures, information about database statistics and various estimates to predict the cost of execution schemes chosen from a pre-defined search space and to select a minimum cost execution in such a space.

A LDL system offers to a user all the benefits of a database language --including the elimination of the impedance mismatch between the language and the query language-- in addition, its rule based deductive capability and its unification–based pattern matching capability make it very suitable for knowledge based and symbolic applications. The power of LDL is not without a cost, since its implementation poses non trivial compilation and optimization problems. The various compilation techniques used for LDL were described in [BMSU85, SZ86, Za85, ZS87]. This paper concentrates on the optimization problem; i.e., the problem of devising an efficient execution strategy for the given query. The termination problem (safety) is also tackled in this context, since the lack of termination can be viewed as an extreme case of poor termination. Therefore, our optimization problem revisits the well–known problem of control in logic programs as per Kowalski's famous equation Algorithm = Logic + Control [Kw 79]. Several approaches to this arduous problems have been proposed in the past.

Prolog visits and expands the rule goals in a strictly lexicographical order; thus, it is up to the programmer to make sure that this order leads to a safe and efficient execution. Approaches, such as intelligent backtracking, eliminate some of the inefficiencies of Prolog without changing this basic control mechanism. However, there has been proposals for a more explicit control of logic programs-- e.g., by supporting several 'and' connectives, each eliciting different sequencing behavior from the interpreter [Per 82].

Of more direct interest to this paper are those approaches where the control of execution is exercised, at least in part, by the system. For instance, reasoning at the metalevel is proposed in [SG 85] as the best way for the system to determine which goal is to be expanded next. A second approach consists in freezing unsafe goals until a sufficient number of arguments become instantiated [Col 82, Nai 85, AN 86]. For instance, the evaluation of an arithmetic expression is delayed until its variables become instantiated. More general situations can be treated via mode declarations added to procedures. The execution of a goal is then postponed until some modes are satisfied, for the procedure unifying with the given goal. These modes, can either be given by the user, or automatically inferred by the system [Na 85]. Observe that, in all these approaches, the control is *dynamic*, i.e., exercised by the system at run time.

The approach explored in this paper is that of *static control*; the flow of the execution is predetermined at compile time and simply enacted at run time. The NAIL! system also follows a static strategy, which matches execution strategies with the given query and rule set by means of *capture rules* [Ull 85, MUV 86]. The test to determine whether a certain capture rule is applicable in a given situation is based upon the form of the rules and the patterns of argument bindings in the goal (adornments); for each applicable capture rule there exists a corresponding substantiation algorithm for materializing the captured goals. While the testing for capture rules can be organized in such a way that more specialized rules are tried before more general ones-- under the assumption that more specialized rules produce more efficient execution strategies -- the notion of cost driven optimization is not part of the NAIL! system. Thus it appears that this system is more effective in dealing with the safety problem than with the optimization problem. This is consistent with the fact that the NAIL! system does not handle directly simple conjunctive queries; these are passed to an underlying off-the-shelf relational database system for query optimization.

This paper describes a fully integrated compile-time approach that ensures both safety and optimization to guarantee the amalgamation of the database functionality with the programming language functionality of LDL. Therefore, the LDL optimizer subsumes the basic control strategies used in relational systems as well as those used in [MUV 86]. In particular for LDL programs that are equivalent to the usual join-project-select queries of relational systems, the LDL optimizer behaves as the optimizer of a relational system[Sel 79].

The technical challenges posed by the LDL optimizer follow from its expressive power extending far beyond that of relational query languages. Indeed, in addition non recursive queries and flat relational data, Horn Clauses include recursive definitions and complex objects, such as hierarchies, lists and heterogeneous structures. Beyond that, LDL supports additional constructs including stratified negation [BN 87], set operators and predicates [TZ 86, BN 87], and updates [NK

87]. Therefore, new operators are needed to handle complex data, and constructs such as recursion, negation, sets, etc.. Moreover, the complexities of data and operations emphasize the need for new database statistics and new estimations of cost. Finally, the presence of evaluable functions and of recursive predicates with function symbols give the user the ability to state queries that are *unsafe* (i.e., do not terminate). As unsafe executions are a limiting case of poor executions, the optimizer must guarantee that the resulting execution is safe.

In this we limit the discussion to the problem of optimizing the pure fixpoint semantics of Horn clause queries [Llo 84]. After setting up the definitions in Section 2, the optimization is character-ized as a minimization problem based on a cost function over an execution space in Section 3. The execution model is discussed in Section 4, using which the execution space is defined in Section 5. We outline our cost function assumptions in Section 6. The search strategy is detailed in Section 7 by extending the traditional approach to the nonrecursive case first; and then extended to include recursion. The problem of safety is addressed in section 8, where we extend the optimi-zation algorithm to ensure safety.

2. Definitions

The knowledge base consists of a *rule base* and a *database* (also known as fact base). An example of rule base is given in Figure 2-1 . Throughout this paper, we follow the notational

```
                    Query is P1(x,y)?
        R1 : P1(x,y) <-- P2(x,x1), P3(x1,y).
        R21: P2(x,y) <-- B21(x,x1), P2(x1,y1), B22(y1,y).
        R22: P2(x,y) <-- P4(x,y).
        R3 : P3(x,y) <-- B31(x,x1), B32(x1,y).
        R4 : P4(x,y) <-- B41(x,x1), P2(x1,y).
        Figure 2-1:  Rule Base
```

convention that Pi's, Bi's, and f's are *predicates, base predicates* (i.e., predicate on a base-rela-tion), and *function symbols*, respectively. The Bi's are relations from the database and the Pi's are the derived predicates whose tuples (i.e., in the relation corresponding to that predicate) can be computed using the rules. Note that each rule contains the *head* of the rule (i.e., the predicate to the left of the arrow) and the *body* that defines the tuples that are contributed by this rule to the set of tuples associated with the head predicate. A rule may be *recursive*, in the sense that the definition in the body may depend on the head predicate, either directly by reference or transitively through a predicate referenced in the body. An example of a recursive rule is R21.

In a given rule base, we say that a predicate P implies a predicate Q, written $P \rightarrow Q$, if there is a rule with Q as the head and P in the body, or there exists a P' where $P \rightarrow P'$ and $P' \rightarrow Q$ (tran-sitivity). Then a predicate P, such that $P \rightarrow P$, will be called *recursive*. Two predicates, P and Q are called *mutually recursive if* $P \rightarrow Q$ and $Q \rightarrow P$. Since this implication relationship is an equivalence relation, it can be be used to partition the recursive predicates into disjoint subsets, which we will call *recursive cliques*. A clique C1 is said to *follow* another clique C2 if there exists a recursive predicate in C2 that is used to define the clique C1. Obviously the follow relation is a partial order due the definition of clique.

In a departure from previous approaches to compilation of logic, we make our optimization query-specific. A query with indicated bound/unbound arguments (called binding) will be called a *query form*. Thus, P1(c,y)? is a query form in which c and y denote a bound and unbound argument respectively. Throughout this paper we use x,y to denote variables and c to denote a constant. We say that the optimization is query specific because the algorithm is repeated for each such query form. For instance, the query, P1(x,y)?, will be compiled and optimized separately from P1(c,y)?. Indeed the execution strategy chosen for a query P1(x,y)? may be inefficient for a query P1(c,y)? , or an execution designed for P1(c,y)? may be unsafe for P1(x,y)?.

In general, we can define the notion of a binding for a predicate in a rule body based on a given permutation of the literals in the body. This process of using information from the prior literals was called *sideways information passing (SIP)* in [Ull 85]. We note here that a given permutation is associated with a unique SIP.

3. The Optimization Problem

We define the optimization problem as the minimization of the cost over a given execution space (i.e., the set of all allowed executions for a given query). This is formally stated below.

Logic Query Optimization Problem:

Given a query Q, an execution space E and a cost function defined over E, find an execution pg in E that is of minimum cost; i.e.

$$\underset{pg \in E}{\text{MIN}} \left[\text{cost of pg(Q)} \right]$$

Any solution to the above optimization problem can then be described along four main coordinates, as follows:

i) the model of an execution, pg;

ii) the definition of the execution space, E, consisting of all allowable executions;

iii) the cost functions which associate a cost estimate with each point of the execution space; and

iv) the search strategy to determine the minimum cost execution in the given space.

The model of an execution represents the relevant aspects of the processing so that the execution space can be defined based on the properties of the execution. The designer must select the set of allowable executions over which the least cost execution is chosen. Obviously, the main trade-off here is that a very small execution space will eliminate many efficient executions, whereas a very large execution space will render the problem of optimization intractable, for a given search algorithm. In the next sections we describe the design of the execution model, the definition of the execution space, and the search algorithm. The cost formulae are in most cases system dependent. Thus we will consider the cost formulae as a black box, where the actual formulae are not discussed except for those assumptions that impact the global architecture of the system.

4. Execution Model

LDL's target language is a relational algebra extended with additional constructs to handle complex terms and fixpoint computations. An execution over this target language can be modelled as a rooted directed graph, called *'processing graph'*, as shown in Figure 4–1b for the example of

Figure 2–1. Intuitively, leaf nodes (i.e., the nodes with non-zero in-degree) of this graph correspond to operators and the results of their predecessors are the input operands. The representation in this form is similar to the predicate connection graph [KT 81], or rule graph [Ull 85], except that we give specific semantics to the internal nodes, and use a notion of contraction for recursion as described below.

In keeping with our relational algebra based execution model, we map each AND node into a *join* and each OR node into a *union*. Recursion is implied by an edge to an ancestor or a node in the sibling subtree. We restrict our attention to *fixpoint* methods for recursion, i.e., methods that implement recursive predicates by means of a *least fixpoint operator*. We assume that the fixed point operation of the recursive predicates in a clique is not computed in a piece-meal fashion (i.e., the fixpoint operation is atomic with respect to other operations in the processing tree). In order to model this property, we define the notion of a contraction. A *contraction* of a clique is the extrapolation of the traditional notion of an edge contraction in a graph. An edge is said to be *contracted* if it is deleted and its ends (i.e., nodes) are identified (i.e., merged). A clique is said to be *contracted* if all the edges of the clique are contracted. Intuitively, the contraction of a clique consists of replacing the set of nodes in the clique by a single node and associating all the edges in/out of any node in the clique with this new node, (as in Figure 4–1c), generically called *Contracted Clique node* (or *CC node*). As the structure of the rules in the clique will be needed for optimization, we associate the set of rules in the clique to this CC node. Intuitively, a CC node correspond to the fixpoint operation for the clique, whose operands are the results of the predecessors.

It is easy to see that a contracted processing graph is acyclic (a DAG). Moreover, for ease of exposition we also assume that this graph is converted into a tree by replicating the children with multiple successors. In the rest of the paper we assume that the processing graph has been contracted and due the above stipulation, we interchangeably use the terms processing graph and processing tree.

Associated with each node is a relation that is computed from the relations of its predecessors, by doing the operation (e.g., join, union) specified in the label. We use a square node to denote materialization of relations and a triangle node to denote the pipelining of the tuples. A pipelined

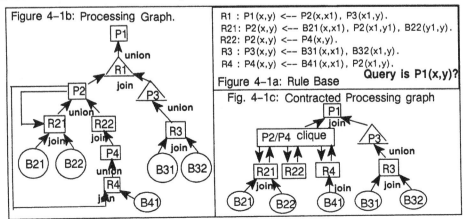

Figure 4–1b: Processing Graph.

R1 : P1(x,y) <-- P2(x,x1), P3(x1,y).
R21: P2(x,y) <-- B21(x,x1), P2(x1,y1), B22(y1,y).
R22: P2(x,y) <-- P4(x,y).
R3 : P3(x,y) <-- B31(x,x1), B32(x1,y).
R4 : P4(x,y) <-- B41(x,x1), P2(x1,y).

Figure 4–1a: Rule Base   Query is P1(x,y)?

Fig. 4–1c: Contracted Processing graph

xecution, as the name implies, computes only those tuples for the subtree that are relevant to the ·peration for which this node is an operand. In the case of join, this computation is evaluated in a azy fashion as follows: a tuple for a subtree is generated using the binding from the result of the ubquery to the *left* of that subtree. This binding is referred to as *binding implied by the pipeline.* Note that we impose a *left to right* order of execution. Subtrees that are rooted under a material- zed node are computed bottom–up, without any sideways information passing; i.e., the result of he subtree is computed completely before the ancestor operation is started.

Each interior node in the graph is also labeled by the method used (e.g., join method, recursion nethod etc.). The set of labels for these nodes are restricted *only* by the availability of the tech- niques in the system. Further, we also allow the result of computing a subtree to be filtered/pro- ected through a selection/restriction/projection predicate. We extend the labeling scheme to en- :ode all such variations due to filtering and projecting. The label for a CC node is to specify the :hoices for the fixpoint operation, which are the choices for SIPs and recursive method to be used.

The execution corresponding to a processing tree proceeds bottom–up left to right as follows: The leftmost subtree whose children are all leaves is computed and the resulting relation replaces he subtree in the processing tree. The computation of this subtree is dependent on the type of the ·oot node of the subtree –- pipelined or materialized –- as described above. If the subtree is ·ooted at a contracted clique node, then the fixed point result of the recursive clique is computed, either in a pipelined fashion or in a materialized fashion; the former (i.e., pipelining) requires the ·se of techniques such as Magic Sets or Counting [BMSU 85, SZ 86].

5. Execution Space

Note that many processing trees can be generated for any given query and a given set of rules. These processing trees are logically equivalent to each other, since they return the same result; however very different costs may be associated with each tree, since each embodies critical decisions regarding the methods to be used for the operations, their ordering, and the intermediate relations to be materialized. The set of logically equivalent processing trees thus defines the *execution space* over which the optimization is performed using a cost model, which associates a cost to each execution. We define this space by the following equivalence preserv- ing transformations:

1) **MP:** *Materialize/Pipeline:* A pipelined node can be changed to a materialized node and vice versa.

2) **FU:** *Flatten/Unflatten:* Flattening distributes a join over an union. The inverse transformation will be called unflatten. An example of this is shown in Figure 4–2.

3) **PS:** *PushSelect/PullSelect:* A select can be piggy backed to a materialized or pipelined node and applied to the tuples as they are generated. Selects can be pushed into a nonrecursive operator (i.e., join or union that is not a part of a recursive cycle) in the obvious way.

4) **PP:** *PushProject/PullProject:* This transformation can be defined similar to the case of select.

5) **PR:** *Permute:* This transforms a given subtree by permuting the order of the subtrees. Note that the inverse of a permutation is defined by another permutation.

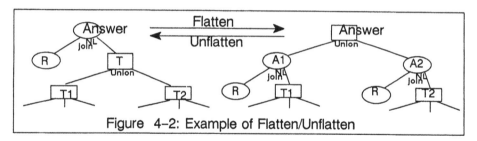

Figure 4-2: Example of Flatten/Unflatten

6) **PA:** *Permute & Adorn:* The recursive methods such as Magic Sets and Counting, require a SIP for each rule in the clique to be specified and an adornment to be chosen for each recursive predicate. As we shall see in Section 7, a given permutation for each rule determines the SIPs for the clique as well as an adorned program. For each adorned program there is a set of applicable recursive methods (e.g., Semi-naive, Magic Sets, Counting).

7) **EL:** *Exchange Label:* Change the label of a join/union operation to another available method.

Each of the above transformational rules map a processing tree into another equivalent processing tree and is also capable of mapping vice versa. We define an equivalence relation under a set of transformational rules T as follows: a processing tree p1 is equivalent to p2 under T, if p2 can be obtained by zero or more application of rules in T. The equivalence class (induced by said equivalence relation) defines our execution space. As an equivalence class (and therefore an execution space) is uniquely determined by a set of transformational rules, an execution space is referred to by a set notation: {Ti | Ti is a transformational rule defined above}. For example, {MP, PR}, {MP, PR, PS, PP} are execution spaces.

As mentioned before, the choice of proper execution space is a critical design decision. By limiting ourselves to the above transformations, we have excluded many other types of optimizations like peep-hole optimizations (as used in traditional optimization phase of a programming language compiler), semantic optimizations, etc. This is a reflection of the restrictions posed in the context of relational systems from which we have generalized and is not meant to imply that they are considered less important. As in the case of relational systems, these supplementable optimizations can also be used. Even in the realm of above transformations, we were unable to find an efficient strategy for the entire space. Consequently, we limit our discussion in this paper to the space defined by {MP, PS, PP, PR, PA, EL} (i.e., Flattening and Unflattening are not allowed). As discussed in Section 8, programs can be constructed for which no safe (and therefore, no efficient) executions exists without flattening. Our experience with rule based systems, however, has been that these are artificial situations which the user can be expected to avoid without any additional inconvenience.

6. Cost Model:

The cost model assigns a cost to each processing tree, thereby ordering the executions. Typically, the cost spectrum of the executions in an execution space spans many orders of magnitude, even in the relational domain. We expect this to be magnified in the Horn clause domain. Thus "it s more important to avoid the worst executions than to obtain the best execution", a maxim widely assumed by the query optimizer designers. The experience with relational system has shown that he main purpose of a cost model is to differentiate between good and bad executions. In fact, it is known, from the relational experience, that even an inexact cost model can achieve this goal reasonably well.

The cost includes CPU, disk I/O, communication, etc., which are combined into a single cost that is dependent on the particular system. We assume that a list of methods is available for each operation (join, union and recursion), and for each method, we also assume the ability to compute the associated cost and the resulting cardinality. For the sake of this discussion, the cost can be viewed as some monotonically increasing function on the size of the operands. As the cost of an unsafe execution is to be modeled by an infinite cost, the cost function should guarantee an infinite cost if the size approaches infinity. This is used to encode the unsafe property of the execution.

Intuitively, the cost of an execution is the sum of the cost of individual operations. This amounts to summing up the cost for each node in the processing tree.

7. Search Strategies

We first outline the generic strategies that are known based on the experience with the relational systems. As a typical relational query is a conjunctive query, we discuss these strategies in the context of conjunctive queries. Then we generalize these strategies to the case of nonrecursive queries (i.e., AND/OR tree) and then to the complete Horn clause queries where we tackle the case for recursion.

7.1. Generic Strategies:

An important lesson learnt from the implementation of relational database systems is that the execution space of a conjunctive query can be viewed as the orderings of joins (and therefore relations) [Sel 79]. The gist of the relational optimization algorithm is as follows: For each permutation of the set of relations, choose a join method for each join and compute the cost. The result is the minimum cost permutation. Note that for a given permutation, the choice of join method becomes a local decision; i.e., the EL label is unique. Further, a selection or a projection can be pushed to the first operation on the relation without any loss of optimality, for a given ordering of joins. Thus the choice of preselect, preproject, etc. are incorporated in the choice of the join method. Consequently, the actual search space used by the optimizer reduces to {MP, PR}, yet the chosen minimum cost processing tree is optimal in the execution space defined by {MP, PR, PS, PP, EL}. (Note that PA is inapplicable as there are no recursions.) Further, the binding implied by the pipelining is also treated as selections and handled in a similar manner.

This above exhaustive enumeration approach, taken in the relational context, essentially enumerates a search space that is combinatoric on n, the number of relations in the conjunct. The dynamic programming method presented in [Sel 79] only improves this to $O(n*2^n)$ time by using $O(2^n)$ space. Naturally, this method becomes prohibitive when the join involves many relations.

Consequently, database systems (e.g., SQL/DS, commercial INGRES) must limit the queries to no more than 10 or 15 joins. As an alternative to exhaustive search, we consider two other methods.

In [KBZ 86], we presented a quadratic time algorithm that computes the optimal ordering of conjunctive queries when the query is acyclic and the cost function satisfies a linearity property called the Adjacent Sequence Interchange (ASI) property. Further, this algorithm was extended to include cyclic queries and other cost models. The resulting algorithm has proved to be heuristically effective for cyclic queries as well as other cost models [Vil 87]. The comparison was made by randomly picking queries and states of the database and then comparing the results of the quadratic time and exhaustive algorithms. The results showed that the quadratic algorithm chooses the optimal permutation in most cases and in more than 90% of the cases, it produces no worse than twice/thrice the optimal. These results have been shown to have a statistical confidence of 95% with a 3% error.

Another approach to searching the large search space is to use a stochastic algorithm. Intuitively, the minimum cost permutation can be found by picking, randomly, a "large" number of permutations from the search space and choosing the minimum cost permutation. Obviously, the number of permutations that need to be chosen approaches the size of the search space for a reasonable assurance of obtaining the minimum. This number is claimed to be much smaller by using a technique called Simulated Annealing [IW 87]. We use this technique to the optimization of conjunctive queries as follows. For any given permutation, define a neighbor to be any permutation that differs in exactly two places (i.e., two positions in one permutation is interchanged to get the other). It is easy to prove that the closure of the neighbor (equivalence) relation is indeed the set of all permutations (i.e., the execution space for conjunctive queries). The simulated annealing can then be viewed as a "random" walk of the execution space using this neighbor relation. If we ignore the annealing parameters, then the neighbor relation completely characterizes the simulated annealing process. We shall use this notion to characterize the strategy using simulated annealing.

In short, we have summarized three generic strategies: exhaustive, quadratic and stochastic. The main trade-offs amongst these strategies is between efficiency (i.e., time complexity) and flexibility. Note that the quadratic strategy is the most efficient, whereas it is least flexible in terms of the possible modifications to cost functions, query structure, etc. Our goal is to present a design for the search strategy that is capable of using multiple strategies interchangeably. The main reason for requiring the system to be flexible is that the system is initially intended as an experimental vehicle since there is no prior experience in the design of an optimizer for a logic language and the field of logic languages is still in its infancy; thus new ideas will be forthcoming that the design should be capable of incorporating into the system.

7.2. Nonrecursive Queries

Initially, we extend the exhaustive strategy that was used in the case of conjunctive queries to the nonrecursive case, which is then extended to the other two strategies. Extrapolating from the conjunctive case, selects/projects are always pushed down any number of levels for non-recursive rules by simply migrating to the lower level rules the constraints inherited from the upper rules.

imple compile–time rule–rewriting techniques can be used to push selection/projection down into on–recursive rules.

Let us first consider the case when we materialize all the temporary results for each predicate in the rule base. As we do not allow flatten/unflatten transformation, we can proceed as follows: optimize a lowest subtree in the AND/OR tree. This subtree is a conjunctive query, as all children in this subtree are leaves (e.g., base relations) and we may use the exhaustive strategy. After optimizing the subtree we replace the subtree by a "base relation" and repeat this process until the tree is reduced to a single node. It is easy to show that this algorithm exhausts the search space {PR} and finds an optimal execution over {PR, PS, PP, EL}. Further, as in the relational systems, such an algorithm is *reasonably efficient* if number of predicates in the body does not exceed 10–15.

In order to allow the execution to use the side ways information by choosing pipelined executions, we make the following observation. Because all the subtrees were materialized above, the binding pattern of the head of any rule was uniquely determined. Consequently, we were able to outline the above bottom-up algorithm using this unique binding for each subtree. If we do allow pipelined execution, then the subtree may be bound in different ways, depending on the ordering of the siblings of the root of the subtree. Consequently, the subtree may be optimized differently. Observe that the number of binding patterns for a predicate is purely dependent on the number of arguments of that predicate. So, the extension to the above bottom-up algorithm is to optimize each subtree for all possible binding and to use the cost for the appropriate binding when computing the cost of joining this subtree with its siblings. Obviously, the maximum number of bindings is equal to the cardinality of the power set of the arguments. In order to avoid optimizing a subtree with a binding pattern that may never be used, a top-down algorithm can be devised. Such an algorithm has been shown in Figure 7–1.

This algorithm guarantees that each subtree is optimized exactly ONCE for each binding. The worst case time complexity can be computed as follows: Suppose that there are k variables per predicate, N total predicates in the rule base, and n be the number of predicates per conjunct, then we have the following worst case estimates:

$2^k * n! =$ worst case cost of reducing one AND–subtree.

$N/n =$ number of AND–subtrees.

Thus, the total worst case complexity of this algorithm is $O(N * 2^k * n!)$. However, using the dynamic programming approach for the enumeration of the conjunctive search [Sel 79], we reduce the $n!$ permutations to 2^n choices. Thus the worst case complexity becomes $O(N * 2^k * 2^n)$. Normally, the number of arguments per predicate (k) is usually less than five and number of predicates per conjunct (n) is usually less than 10. For these values of k and n, we conclude the feasibility of this approach based on the experience from commercial database systems.

NR–OPT: Compute a processing tree for a nonrecursive logic query.
Input is a processing tree rooted at a node N.
Output is an optimized processing graph.

1) Node N is an AND node, say As:
    I) For each permutation of the sequence of subtrees,
       Using the binding implied by the permutation do:
         a) For each OR–subtree Os of As do: Compute NR–OPT(Os).
         b) Compute the cost for this permutation using the cost model.
         c) Maintain the minimum cost permutation.

    II) Return cost, cardinality, and the graph for the minimum cost processing graph.

2) Node N is an OR node say Os:
    1) IF this subtree, Os, has NOT already been optimized for this binding
       THEN do:
         a) For each AND–subtree As of Os : Compute NR–OPT(As).
         b) Compute the cost of the union of the children.

         c) record the cost, cardinality, graph, etc., for Os, indexed by the binding.
    2) ELSE read cost, cardinality, graph, etc., for Os, based on the binding.

Figure 7–1:   NR–OPT algorithm for non–recursive query.

The algorithm of Figure 7–1 becomes impractical for large values of k and/or n. The main practical concern is n since the number of arguments in recursive predicates is either small, or reducible to a small number by the use of complex terms. We discuss below how the algorithm in Figure 7–1 can be easily modified to take advantage of the quadratic strategy [KBZ 86] or of simulated annealing.

Note that the step 1) of the algorithm NR–OPT is responsible for the exponential behavior w.r.t. n. This step is a generalization of the optimization search for conjunctive query. Consequently, replacing the exhaustive strategy with the stochastic strategy is straightforward, whereas the incorporation of quadratic strategy is little more involved requiring the generalization of the ASI property. As this involves more detail discussion of the ASI property, we omit this discussion in this paper for reasons of brevity. In either case, the resulting algorithm is capable of optimizing rule bases that have large n. Also note that the choice of strategies may be made per rule. That is, the more efficient strategies are used only if the rules actually has a large number of literals in the body of the rule. The optimizer for LDL currently has all three strategies implemented whereas only the exhaustive strategy is integrated into the system.

Even though we do not expect k to be very large, it would be comforting if we could find an approximation for this case too. This remains a topic for further research.

.3. Recursive queries

In the last two sections we have seen that pushing selection and projection is a linchpin of non–recursive optimization methods. This was used to reduce the search space from {MP, PR, PS, PP} to {MP, PR}. Unfortunately, this simple technique is frequently inapplicable to recursive predicates [AU 85]. Therefore a number of specialized implementation methods have been proposed to allow recursive predicates to take advantage of constants or bindings present in the goal. (The interested reader is referred to [BR 86] for an overview.) Further, the same techniques are used to incorporate the notion of pipelining (i.e., side ways information passing). We use the *magic set method* [BMSU 85] and *generalized counting method* [SZ 86] that have been shown to produce some of the most efficient [BR 86] and general algorithms to support recursion in the LDL optimizer. Moreover, they are compatible with the optimization framework used in this paper, since we can now map a recursive Horn clause query into an equivalent expression of extended relational algebra operators and least fixpoint operators.

Consider the recursive predicate plus the binding used in the operation corresponding to the successor node to the CC node. This recursive predicate plus the binding can be viewed as a *'subquery"* for the CC node. We replicate the recursive rules in the clique as follows: for each rule (say with head predicate P) and for each binding pattern, a, the rule is replicated by renaming the head as 'P.a'. An adornment is a binding pattern that is associated with a literal.

Given a subquery for the CC node and a SIP per (replicated) rule (i.e., the permutation for the literals in the body for each rule), then we can adorn the program, similar to the adornment of rules in [BMSU 86, Ull 85] as follows: We construct the adorned version of the program *Pgm'* for the original program *Pgm* by replacing the derived predicates in the body by the adorned versions. The process starts from the given subquery whose adornments determine an adorned version of the predicate. For each adorned predicate, P.a, and for each rule that has P.a in the head, we generate an adorned version for the rule as described below and add it to *Pgm'*. We then mark P.a. Note that the adorned version of a rule may generate additional predicates that are adorned. The process terminates when no unmarked adorned predicates are left.

The adornment for a recursive predicate in the body is assigned as follows: an argument is bound if the variable(s) in the argument occurs either in a bound argument of the head literal or in a goal that precedes it in the chosen permutation. All other arguments of this literal are adorned as free. Each literal P that is associated with a binding a is renamed as 'P.a'. We present below, the adorned programs for the query forms sg.bf and sg.bb, in which the chosen SIP for all replicated rules is self evident.

Original Rule: sg (X,Y) <– up(X,X1), sg(Y1,X1), dn(Y1,Y)

Adorned clique for the query sg.bf: ('bf' is the binding)
sg.bf (X,Y) <– up(X,X1), sg.fb(Y1,X1), dn(Y1,Y)
sg.fb (X,Y) <– dn(Y1,Y), sg.bf(Y1,X1), up(X,X1)

Adorned clique for the query sg.bb:

    sg.bb (X,Y) <- up(X,X1), sg.fb(Y1,X1), dn(Y1,Y)
    sg.fb (X,Y) <- dn(Y1,Y), sg.bf(Y1,X1), up(X,X1)
    sg.bf (X,Y) <- up(X,X1), sg.fb(Y1,X1), dn(Y1,Y)

Note that for a given subquery and a permutation for each rule in the clique, the resulting adorned program is unique. Further, for a given adorned program, the transformed program by Magic Sets or Counting is also unique. As a result, the execution (and the associated cost) is uniquely determined, for a given cost and size estimates for all the literals (in the rules of the clique) that are not in the clique. From this we can conclude that the space of executions that are to be enumerated is defined by the different permutations of the rules in the clique. In other words, if there are *nc* rules in the clique, then each possible cross product of *nc* permutations defines a *c-permutation*. For each c-permutation, and a subquery there is an adorned program. Note that all of them are not distinct, but collectively they exhaust the possible adorned programs.

We extend the algorithm presented in the previous section to include the capability to optimize a recursive query. When a subtree rooted at a CC node is to be optimized, the choice is in adorning

---

OPT: Compute a processing tree for a recurrsive logic query.
  Input is a processing tree rooted at a node N.
  Output is an optimized processing graph.

1) Node N is an AND node, say As:
    I) For each permutation of the sequence of subtrees,
        Using the binding implied by the permutation do:
        a) For each OR-subtree Os of As do: Compute OPT(Os).
        b) Compute the cost for this permutation using the cost model.
        c) Maintain the minimum cost permutation.

    II) Return cost, cardinality, and the graph for the minimum cost processing graph.

2) Node N is an OR node say Os:
    1) IF this subtree, Os, has NOT already been optimized for this binding
        THEN do:
        a) For each AND-subtree As of Os : Compute OPT(As).
        b) Compute the cost of the union of the children.

        c) record the cost, cardinality, graph, etc., for Os, indexed by the binding.
    2) ELSE read cost, cardinality, graph, etc., for Os, based on the binding.

3) Node N is a CC node, say Cs:
    I) For each c-permutations of the rules in Cs do:
        i) Adorn relevant rules
        ii) For each adorned literal, Os, NOT in the clique Cs do: Compute OPT(Os).
        iii) For each applicable recursive method do:
            Compute cost of the clique Cs and maintain the minimum cost solution.

    II) Return the minimum cost soulution

Figure 7-2:   OPT algorithm for recursive queries.

he node with the proper label. We have to enumerate all the c-permutations for the clique. For each such assignment of c-permutations, the rules are adorned and the literals not in the clique are optimized for the respective adornment. Then the cost of the fixpoint operations is computed or each applicable recursive method (e.g., Magic Sets, Naive, Counting) and the minimum cost execution is chosen. This algorithm is shown in Figure 7–2. Note that the optimization for the clique s, once again, dependent only on the adornment of the subquery. Therefore, the result of the optimization can be saved and used to avoid recomputation as it was done in the OR–subtree case. This has been omitted for brevity of the algorithm.

It is easy to show that the algorithm finds the optimal execution in the execution space {MP, PR, PS, EA, PA} while searching the space {MP, PR, PA}. Note that the recursive techniques such as Magic Sets and Counting can only handle pushing selections. In order to push projections we use the techniques proposed in [RBK 87], which is used as a preprocessing step to the optimizer. It is easy to see that enumeration of all the permutations for the rules in the clique is impractical even or small number of rules in the clique. It is conjectured by many researchers that the mutual ecursions are not common and complicated ones are used even less. So if this conjecture is true then exhaustive search may not be impractical.

Nevertheless, we are interested in being able to optimize larger class of queries. For this we present the use of the stochastic strategy. Note that if the enumeration of the search space consisting of all possible c-permutations of a clique (in case 3 of the algorithm) is improved, then the algorithm can be used for a larger class of queries. Further note that we observed that by specifying the neighbor relation for a given execution, such that the closure of this relation defines the space to be searched, we can characterize the simulated annealing process. We present such a neighbor relation here. Let us define a neighbor of a c-permutation, CP1, to be another cross product of nc permutations, CP2, such that all but one of these nc permutations in CP2 are identical to the ones in CP1 and the one that differs, is obtainable by interchanging exactly two literals in the permutation. Obviously, the closure of this (equivalence) relation is the space that we set out to search. Consequently, we have characterized the simulated annealing process and the iterative loop choosing the c-permutations in the algorithm OPT can be replaced by the simulated annealing process.

An interesting open question is the incorporation of a polynomial time algorithm by superimposing some linearity property on the cost function for a recursive clique, as it was done for the conjunctive case in [KBZ 86].

Safety Problem:

Safety is a serious concern in implementing Horn clause queries. Any evaluable predicates (e.g., comparison predicates like x>y, x=y+y*z), and recursive predicates with function symbols are examples of potentially unsafe predicates. While an evaluable predicate will be executed by calls to built–in routines, they can be formally viewed as infinite relations defining, for example, all the pairs of integers satisfying the relationship x>y, or all the triplets satisfying the relationship x=y+y*z [TZ 86]. Consequently, these predicates may result in unsafe executions in two ways: 1) the result of the query is infinite; 2) the execution requires the computation of a rule resulting in an infinite intermediate result. The former is termed the lack of *finite answer* and the latter the lack of *effective computability or EC*. Note that the answer may be finite even if a rule is not effectively computable. In this section we outline our approach with the emphasis on the interaction with the optimizer. For a more complete treatise on this topic see [KRS 87].

8.1. Checking for safety:

Patterns of argument bindings that ensure EC are simple to derive for comparison predicates. For instance, we can assume that for comparison predicates other than equality, all variables must be bound before the predicate is safe. When equality is involved in a form *"x= expression"*, then we are ensured of EC as soon as all the variables in *expression* are instantiated. These are only sufficient conditions and more general ones – e.g., based on combinations of comparison predicates – could be given (see for instance [M 84]). But for each extension of a sufficient condition, a rapidly increasing price would have to be paid in the algorithms used to detect EC and in the system routines used to support these predicates at run time. Indeed, the problem of deciding EC for Horn clauses with comparison predicates is undecidable even when no recursion is involved [Za 86] . On the other hand, EC based on safe binding patterns is easy to detect. Thus, deriving more general sufficient conditions for ensuring EC that is easy to check is an important problem facing the optimizer designer.

If all rules of a nonrecursive query are effectively computable, then the answer is finite. However, for a recursive query, each bottom-up application of any rule may be effectively computable, but the answer may be infinite due to unbounded iterations required for a fixpoint operator. In order to guarantee that the number of iterations are finite for each recursive clique, a well-founded order based on some monotonicity property must be derived. For example, if a list is traversed recursively, then "the size of the list is monotonically decreasing with a bound of an empty list" is a well-founded order. This forms the well-founded condition for termination of the iteration. Some methods to derive the monotonicity property are discussed in [Nai 85, UV 85, SZ 86]. A general algorithm to ensure the existence of a well-founded condition is outlined in [KRS 87]. As these are only sufficient conditions, they do not necessarily detect all safe executions. Consequently, more general monotonicity properties must be either inferred from the program or declared by the user in some form. These are topics of future research.

8.2. Searching for Safe Executions:

As mentioned before, the optimizer enumerates all the possible permutations of the goals in the rules. For each permutation, the cost is evaluated and the minimum cost solution is recorded. All that is needed to ensure safety is that EC is guaranteed for each rule and well founded order(s) is associated with each recursive clique. If both these tests succeed, then the cost of this particular execution is estimated and the optimization algorithm proceeds as usual. If the tests fails, the permutation is discarded. In practice, this can be done by simply assigning an extremely high cost to unsafe goals and then let the standard optimization algorithm do the pruning. If the cost of the end-solution produced by the optimizer is not less than this extreme value, a proper message must inform the user that the query is unsafe.

.3 Comparison with Previous Work

The approaches to safety proposed in [Col 82, Nai 85, AN 86] is also based on reordering the oals in a given rule; but that is done at run-time by delaying goals when the number of instanated arguments is insufficient to guarantee safety. This approach suffers from run-time overhead, nd cannot guarantee termination at compile time or otherwise pinpoint the source of safety probms to the user -- a very desirable feature, since unsafe programs are typically incorrect ones. ur compile-time approach overcomes these problems and is more amenable to optimization.

The reader should, however, be aware of some of the limitations implicit in all approaches ased on reordering of goals in rules. For instance a query

$p(x, y, z), y = 2 * x$?

n the rule

$p(x, y, z) <-- x=3, z=x*y$

obviously finite since the only answer is $<x=3, y=6, z=18>$. However, this answer cannot be omputed under any permutation of goals in the rule. Thus both the approach given in [Col 82, lai 85, AN 86] and the above optimization cum safety algorithm will fail to produce a safe execuon for this query. Two other approaches, however, will succeed. One, described in [Za 86], letermines whether there is a finite domain underlying the variables in the rules using an algoithm based on a functional dependency model. Safe queries are then processed in a bottom up ashion with the help of "magic sets", which make the process safe. The second solution consists n flattening, whereby the three equalities are combined in a conjunct and properly processed in he obvious order referred to earlier.

his example clarifies the drawbacks that follow from our expedient decision of not pursuing lattening in the first version of the optimizer. Some flattening is being considered for later verions of the optimizer. Observe that, unlike previous approaches to control where such strategic lecisions were wired-in into the system, an extension of the LDL optimizer to support flattening only requires adding another equivalence-preserving transformation.

9. Conclusion

This paper has explored the new and challenging problem of optimizing a Logic based language or data intensive applications. Thus the first contribution of the paper consists in providing a formal statement of the problem and in clarifying the main design issues involved. The second contribuion is the solution approach proposed, which (i) cleanly integrates the search for a minimum cost execution with the safety analysis and (ii) is solidly rooted in the experience and know-how acquired in optimizing relational systems. Therefore the LDL optimizer includes both the conjunctive query optimization technique of relational systems [Sel 79] and the safety-oriented techniques described in [MVU 86]. Finally the paper has introduced two new algorithms, one for optimizing non-recursive Horn Clauses, the other for recursive ones, and proposed three search strategies as the vehicle for implementing these algorithms. The first one is an exhaustive search that, because of its complete nature, supplies the basis for assessing the soundness of the overall approach and the effectiveness of the two alternative algorithms (quadratic strategy and simulated annealing) which are to be used to tame the computational complexity of the problem. The results of early experiments were also reported that confirm the heuristic effectiveness of the more efficient algorithms.

Common subexpression elimination[GM 82], which appears particularly useful when flattening occurs, is one of the optimization aspects not covered in this paper. A simple technique using a hill-climbing method is easy to superimpose on the proposed strategy, but more ambitious technique provide a topic for future research. Further, an extrapolation of common subexpression in logic queries can be seen in the following example: let both goals P(a,b,X) and P(a,Y,c) occur in a query. Then it is conceivable that computing P(a,Y,X) once and restricting the result for each of the cases may be more efficient.

Acknowledgments:
We are grateful to Shamim Naqvi for inspiring discussions. We are also grateful to an anonymous referee for a very detailed comments.

References:

[AN 86]   Ait–Kaci, H. and R. Nasr, "Residuation: a Paradigm for Integrating Logic and Functional Programming," submitted for publication.

[AU 79]   Aho, A. and J. Ullman, Universality of Data Retrieval Languages, *Proc. POPL Conf.,* San Antonio, TX, 1979.

[BMSU85]   Bancilhon, F., D, Maier, Y. Sagiv and Ullman, Magic Sets and other Strange Ways to Implements Logic Programs, *Proc. 5–th ACM SIGMOD–SIGACT Symposium on Principles of Database Systems,* pp. 1–16, 1986.

[BR 86]   Bancilhon, F., and R. Ramakrishan, An Amateur's Introduction to Recursive Query Processing Strategies, *Proc. 1986 ACM–SIGMOD Intl. Conf. on Mgt. of Data,* pp. 16–52, 1986.

[BN 87]   Beeri, C., S. Naqvi, R. Ramakrishnan, O. Shmueli, S. Tsur, Sets and Negation in a Logic Database Language, *Proc. 6–th ACM SIGMOD–SIGACT Symposium on Principles of Database Systems,* 1987.

[Col 82]   Colmemauer, A. et al., Prolog II: Reference Manual and Theoretical Model, Groupe d'Intelligence artificielle, Faculte de Sciences de Lumin, 1982.

[GM 82]   Grant, J. and Minker J., On Optimizing the Evaluation of a Set of Expressions, *Int. Journal of Computer and Information Science, 11, 3 (1982), 179–189.*

[IW 87]   Ioannidis, Y. E, Wong, E, Query Optimization by Simulated Annealing, *Proc. 1987 ACM–SIGMOD Intl. Conf. on Mgt. oof Data,* San Francisco, 1987.

[Kw 79]   Kowalski, R.A., "Algorithm = Logic + Control", *CACM,* 22, 7, pp. 424–436, (1979).

[KBZ 86] Krishnamurthy, R., Boral, H., Zaniolo, C. Optimization of Nonrecursive Queries, *Proc. of 12th VLDB,* Kyoto, Japan, 1986.

[KRS 87] Krishnamurthy, R., R. Ramakrishnan. O. Shmueli, "A Framework for Testing Safety and Effective Computability", MCC Report 1987 and also submitted for external publication.

[KT 81]   Kellog, C., and Travis, L. Reasoning with data in a deductively augmented database system, in *Advances in Database Theory: Vol 1,* H.Gallaire, J. Minker, and J. Nicholas eds., Plenum Press, New York, 1981, pp 261–298.

[Llo 84] Lloyd, J. W., *Foundations of Logic Programming,* Springer-Verlag, 1984.

[M 84]   Maier, D., *The Theory of Relational Databases,* (pp. 553–542), Comp. Science Press, 1984.

[MUV 86]   K. Morris, J. D. Ullman and A. Van Gelder, Design Overview of the Nail! System, *Proc. Third Int. Symposium on Logic Programming,* pp. 127–139, 1986.

[Nai 85] Naish, L., Negation and Control in Prolog, Ph. D. Thesis, Dept. of CS, Univ. of Melbourne, Austr., 1985.

[NK 87]   Naqvi Shamim and R. Krishnamurthy, Semantics of Updates in Logic Programming, Workshop on Database and Programming Languages, Roscoff, France 1987.

[Per 82] Pereira Luis Moniz, Logic Control with Logic, UNL Report 2/82 (1982).

[RBK 87] Ramakrishnan, R, C. Beeri, R. Krishnamurthy, Optimizing Existential Queries, MCC Technical Report, 1987, (also submitted for external publication).

[Sel 79] Sellinger, P.G. et. al. Access Path Selection in a Relational Database Management System., *Proc. 1979 ACM-SIGMOD Intl. Conf. on Mgt. of Data,* pp. 23–34, 1979.

[SG 85]   Smith, D. E. and M. R. Genesereth, Ordering Conjunctive Queries, *Artificial Intelligence* **26**, pp. 171–185, 1985.

[SZ 86]   Sacca', D. and C. Zaniolo, The Generalized Counting Method for Recursive Logic Queries, *Proc. ICDT '86 —Int. Conf. on Database Theory,* Rome, Italy, 1986.

[TZ 86]   Tsur, S. and C. Zaniolo, LDL: A Logic–Based Data Language,*Proc. of 12th VLDB,* Kyoto, Japan, 1986.

[Ull 85] Ullman, J. D., Implementation of logical query languages for databases, *TODS,* 10, 3, (1985), 289–321.

[UV 85]   Ullman, J.D. and A. Van Gelder, Testing Applicability of Top–Down Capture Rules, Stanford Univ. Report STAN-CS-85-146, 1985.

[Vil 87] Villarreal, E., "Evaluation of an $O(N^{**}2)$ Method for Query Optimization", MS Thesis, Dept. of Computer Science, Univ. of Texas at Austin, Austin, TX.

[Za 85]   Zaniolo, C. The representation and deductive retrieval of complex objects, *Proc. of 11th VLDB,* pp. 458–469, 1985.

[Za 86]   Zaniolo, C., Safety and Compilation of Non–Recursive Horn Clauses, *Proc. First Int. Conf. on Expert Database Systems,* Charleston, S.C., 1986.

[ZS 87]   Zaniolo C. and D. Sacca', "Rule Rewriting Methods for Efficient Implementations of Horn Logic," MCC Technical Report 1987, submitted for publication.

A PROLOG INTERFACE TO A FUNCTIONAL DATA MODEL DATABASE

Peter M D Gray, David S Moffat and Norman W Paton

Department of Computing Science
University of Aberdeen
Scotland

ABSTRACT

This paper describes a new database architecture for the manipulation of objects, based on an extended version of Prolog with modules. The modules permit the entity classes of the Functional Data Model to be viewed as Abstract Data Types to which methods stored in the modules can be applied. The database is stored as linked structures in a persistent heap. This architecture facilitates the use of Prolog as a navigational query language which can explore relationships in an object-oriented database.

1. INTRODUCTION

In recent years there has been considerable interest in the relationship between logic and databases [Gallaire 84, Warren 81] which has led to a more specific interest in the use of Prolog as a database language [Maier 84]. Prolog as a language has certain features which recommend it as a database system. Prolog is a concise and powerful query language [Zaniolo 84], is well suited to query parsing and optimisation [Warren 81, Gray 85], can easily be used for defining views [Gray 87] and need not be embedded in a conventional algorithmic language. Conventional Prolog systems do however have a number of serious limitations as database systems, such as the absence of secondary storage management and the lack of a schema. In an effort to overcome these limitations, a number of researchers have implemented Prolog interfaces to relational databases [Bocca 86], but there has also been some interest in interfacing Prolog to other data models [Zaniolo 84, Gray 85].

This paper describes a new database architecture based on Perlog, an extended version of Prolog with modules [Moffat 88a]. In Perlog, modules are used to partition the clause base, as a basis for implementing abstract data types and as the unit of commitment.

Perlog is tightly coupled to PS-algol and its persistent data management system [Atkinson 83, Moffat 86]. PS-algol is a strongly typed database programming language which allows one to store arbitrary pointer structures on disc and access them transparently. It also has the computational features of a language like Pascal. Call-outs are made from Perlog to low-level PS-algol routines which implement the storage of the entity classes and functions of the Functional Data Model (FDM) [Shipman 79].

An earlier implementation of the FDM without modules was written entirely in PS-algol [Atkinson 84]. Our implementation uses the extensions to Prolog provided by Perlog. In Perlog, variables can be bound to pointers to entities stored as PS-algol structures on disc. Indeed, Prolog procedures are themselves stored on disc in their semi-compiled form along with the PS-algol structures to which they contain references. These procedures persist over long periods in modules which are shared by various applications, instead of being bound directly into the application program. Thus procedures can be defined which serve as methods in an object-oriented database for Prolog.

Object-oriented databases are of interest because they are inherently extensible to include new data types and are suitable for representing complex networks of objects and the relationships between them. These networks can be searched using AI search techniques expressed in Prolog [Bratko 86].

Relational databases are appropriate for applications which require an exhaustive search to find all the answers to a query. For example, the *join* operator of relational algebra is used to find all instances of a relationship between sets of objects. By contrast, the object-oriented paradigm is better suited to following a chain of relationships associated with a single object. Our system uses the full recursive facilities of Prolog to define methods which compute relationships and which are themselves stored in the database along with entities. Thus it is both structurally and behaviourally object-oriented, in the sense used by [Dittrich 86].

In this paper we give an overview of Perlog, outline an example database, describe the Prolog used in the implementation and discuss possible applications.

2. PERLOG - A PROLOG WITH MODULES AND PERSISTENCE

Many recent implementations of Prolog make use of modules for partitioning the clause base (e.g. DEC-10, BIM, Quintus, MPROLOG) each of which has its own syntax and approach to handling visibility. Modules in Perlog were designed for storing persistent data and notably make use of local declarations for atoms and terms as well as for predicates. The issues involved in introducing modules to Prolog are discussed elsewhere [Szeredi 82, Moffat 88]; here we simply describe the approach taken in Perlog.

2.1. Modules In Perlog

In Perlog there is the concept of a *top* or *current* module. When Perlog is first entered, *user* is the top module. Modules are created using the built-in predicate (BIP) *create_mod(ModName)*. The easiest way to add code to a module is by *consult(File,ModName)* which reads the file *File* of Prolog into module *ModName*.

By default all names beginning with a $ are local while all others are global. All predicates with global names need an explicit *export* of the form

    :- export Name.

All global calls that do not have a definition within the same module need an explicit *import* of the form

> :- import Name.

The command *link* is used to associate the exports of one module with the imports of another. Consider the following files:

f1:

> :- export parent.
>
> parent(john, mary).
> parent(mary, jane).
> parent($fred, $mike).

f2:

> :- import parent.
>
> gparent(X,Y) :- parent(X,Z), parent(Z,Y).

A possible Perlog session is:

> ?- create_mod(m1), consult(f1,m1), % create and populate
>   create_mod(m2), consult(f2,m2), % modules m1 and m2
>   link(m1), link(m2).
>   yes
>
> ?- ch_top(m2).   % make m2 the top module
>   yes
>
> ?- gparent(X,Y).
>   X = john
>   Y = jane
>   yes
>
> ?- parent(john,X).
>   X = mary
>   yes
>
> ?- parent($fred,X).
>   no

The call of parent with *$fred* as an argument fails because the input argument is local to module *m2* and will not unify with the *$fred* which is local to m1.

Local names can also be used as functors to form local terms such as *$obj1(X)*. These can be used to represent instances of Abstract Data Types (ADT) if all the methods for an ADT are in the one module, and the term representing the ADT occurs only within the head of its methods. In this situation no other predicates will be able to unify with the term structure in order to de-struct it, thereby ensuring its privacy.

Suppose that objects *$obj1(Obj)* and *$obj2(Obj)* which belong to different classes which are stored in different modules are to be displayed by a predicate *display/1*. Modules *m1* and *m2* contain the following declarations:

m1:

    :- method display, weight.

    display($obj1(Obj)) :- write(Obj), nl.

    weight($obj1(Obj)) :- ...

m2:

    :- method display.

    display($obj2(Obj)) :- ps_apply(writeout,[Obj],[]).

When a call is made to *display*, the interpreter will look at the private term given as its first argument and select the definition of *display* from the module to which this term belongs.

The BIP *ps_apply/3* is used to call out from Perlog to PS-algol. The first argument to *ps_apply* is the name of the PS-algol function to be called, the second is a list of input parameters and the third is a list of results.

2.2. Modular Commitment

In Perlog there is a built-in predicate *commit(Module)* which writes the updated contents of *Module* to a database. The module which has been committed can be opened later for read or write access by the built-in predicate *restore(Module,Mode)*. When a restored module is in use, the clauses it contains are read from disk into main memory as they are referenced [Moffat 86]. The *commit* predicate can also take a list of modules, all open in write mode, and the *commit* will either succeed or fail in its entirety.

During a Perlog session, several things could take place to alter the contents of a database module. Predicates could be consulted into the module which define views on entity classes, answer complex queries or manage the graphical display of objects. These predicates may call out to routines written in PS-algol for calculation or I/O. A load utility can be used to read files of data, populating the database with new entity instances through calls to *newentity* and *addfunction-val* (see section 3.4.3). All the predicates and entity data are then committed at the end of a session, using Prolog's atom hash table as a source of protection. At any time the Prolog built-in predicate *listing_mod(Module)* can be used to display the predicates and entity types stored in the module. Cross module references may occur, for example to objects in another module shared among multiple users, and the commitment algorithm [Moffat 88b] handles this transparently.

3. USING THE PROLOG/FDM SYSTEM

The database is an extension of the Functional Data Model of [Shipman 79], which is a form of semantic data model. Entity types (which are arranged in a generalisation hierarchy) have functions declared over them which may return scalar values representing attributes, or entity values representing relationships. The functions can be multi-valued to permit direct modelling of 1:many and many:many relationships. The FDM is easily implemented in Perlog by treating entity types as ADTs (represented by local terms) and the functions over them as methods (for example, see *getfnval* below).

3.1. Example Schema

The schema for part of a university database in FDM notation is given below. The schema is parsed by a Prolog parser which creates new modules or extends existing modules, asserts type information into the module and consults default methods into the module as explained in section 4. Some of the schema meta-data is held in PS-algol structures which are constructed by call-outs through *ps_apply/3*.

The schema associates entity classes and related functions with database modules and describes the key of each entity class. The statement

    declare staff ->> person

can be read as "create a new entity class staff which is a subtype of the entity class person". Single-valued functions are represented in the schema by single-headed arrows (->) and multi-valued functions are represented by double-headed arrows(->>).

Keys can be compound and are defined in the schema using key_of. The statement

    key_of x is key_of(f), g

can be read as "the key of an entity of class x is obtained by concatenating the key of the entity which is returned by f(x) onto the scalar value returned by g(x)".

    create module persondb in persondb.

    declare person ->> entity.
    declare staff ->> person.
    declare student ->> person.

    declare research ->> staff.
    declare teaching ->> staff.

declare undergrad ->> student.
declare postgrad ->> student.

declare cname(person) -> string.
declare sname(person) -> string.
declare parent(person) ->> person.

declare position(staff) -> string.
declare room(staff) -> string.

declare year(student) -> integer.
declare faculty(student) -> string.
declare birth_year(student) -> integer.

key_of person is sname,cname.

create module coursedb in coursedb.

declare course ->> entity.

declare level(course) -> integer.
declare code(course) -> string.

declare staff_runs_course ->> entity.

declare section_name(staff_runs_course) -> string.

declare has_course(staff_runs_course) -> course.
declare has_lecturer(staff_runs_course) -> teaching.

key_of course is code.
key_of staff_runs_course is key_of(has_lecturer), key_of(has_course).

extend module persondb.

declare takes(undergrad) ->> course.

3.2. Modifying The Schema

Entity classes and the functions over them can be created and removed at any time in the life of a database. To add new entity classes and functions to an existing database it is only necessary to parse the new declarations using the *extend module* option of the parser illustrated above. The parser is invoked by the *declare_database(FileName)* predicate. The Prolog routines *entity_class_delete(EName, Password)* and *function_delete(FName, ArgType, ResType)* are used to remove entity classes and functions. It is not possible to delete a function which is used in the key of an entity.

3.3. Querying The Database

The predicates *getentity* and *getfunctionval* are used to extract data from the database. There are three versions of *getentity:*

1. getentity(EntityClass, Instance). Given the name of an EntityClass, return its instances one at a time by backtracking.

2. getentity(EntityClass, Key, Instance). Given the name of an EntityClass and a Key, return the entity instance with that key.

3. getentity(EntityClass, StartKey, StopKey, Instance). Given the name of an EntityClass and two strings as keys, return each instance of the entity with key >= StartKey and key <= StopKey.

There are two versions of getfunctionval:

1. getfunctionval(FunctionName, Arg, Res). Given the name of a function and its argument, return its result(s) one at a time by backtracking.

2. getfunctionval(FunctionName, Arg1, Arg2, Res). As above for functions of arity 2. While we do not often use functions of arity2, they are sometimes of value. For example, when modelling protein sequences, the relationship between the protein and its residues can be represented by the function *residue_at(protein,pos) -> residue* which permits direct accesses to the residue at position *pos* in the sequence.

Some implementations of the FDM permit stored functions of arity greater than 2 [Atkinson 84]. This is not necessary however, since relationships between more than 2 entity classes can be expressed by introducing extra entity classes. Alternatively, where such functions represent views rather than updateable relationships, Prolog can be used to write such a function as shown in section 4.2.2. This provides a more powerful view language than Daplex alone.

Unlike the original FDM, we allow functions on scalars to return entities. This is useful for providing secondary indexes.

3.4. Updating The Database

3.4.1. Inserting Entity Instances

The predicate *newentity(EntityClass,KeyInst,Instance)* is used to create instances of an entity class. KeyInst is the key of the new entity and is used to populate all functions from which the key is derived. e.g. The command

newentity(teaching,['Gray','Peter'],Instance).

will create a new entity of type *teaching* with key 'Gray|Peter' and will populate the functions *cname* and *sname* on the new entity instance. A load utility has been written which populates the database from a file of key and attribute values.

3.4.2. Deleting Entity Instances

The predicate *deletentity(EntityClass,Instance)* is used to delete instances of an entity class. All references to the deleted entity are removed from the database as are all *key dependent* entity instances. e.g. If a member of the *teaching* staff is removed from the university database, then so are the *staff_runs_course* entity instances associated with the deleted member of staff.

3.4.3. Changing Function Values

The following routines are used for adding, modifying and deleting function values from the database:

addfunctionval(FName,Arg,Res)
modifyfunctionval(FName,Arg,OldRes,NewRes)
deletefunctionval(FName,Arg,Res)

There are similar routines for functions of arity 2. These routines may contain their own integrity constraints and are not undone by backtracking. All updates performed in a session are aborted if the new state of the module is not committed.

When a function of arity one which represents a relationship between two entity classes is declared, its inverse is automatically declared. All modifications to the value of a function result in appropriate modifications to the value of its inverse. The name of the inverse is the name of the function suffixed by *_inv* and it can be used in calls to *getfunctionval*. The inverse can be used in the definition of two-place Prolog predicates such as *takes(Student,Course)* which, when given one of its arguments returns the other.

There are three categories of function; *optional*, *mandatory*, and *total*. The following table indicates their properties:

Category	Delete	Modify	Empty
Total	No	Yes	No
Mandatory	No	Yes	Yes
Optional	Yes	Yes	Yes

The *Delete* column indicates whether function values can be deleted, the *Modify* column indicates whether function values can be modified, and the *Empty* column indicates whether the value *EMPTY* (see below) can be assigned to the function.

The default value of all functions is *nil*, (i.e. 'undefined') which causes the Prolog goal trying to return the value of the function to fail. When the last/only value of a function is removed the value of the function becomes *nil*. However, if it is known that there is no value for the function, get-functionval can be made to return the special pseudo-value *EMPTY*, for which the programmer must test.

Total functions are used in the construction of keys. Once a value has been assigned to a function declared to be *total* the value can be replaced with another value, but cannot be deleted or replaced with *EMPTY*. When a *total* function is used in the construction of a key, population of the function takes place in the same transaction as the creation of the entity, so it is not possible for a *total* function used in the construction of a key to return *EMPTY* or *nil*. *Mandatory* functions are the same as total functions except that they can return the value *EMPTY*. There are no restrictions imposed on updates to functions declared to be *optional*.

The default classification of functions not involved in the construction of keys is *optional*. Functions used in the construction of keys are automatically declared to be *total*.

3.5. Integrity And Type Checking

Prolog is not a strongly typed language, so all type checking must be performed at run time.

Integrity constraints written in Prolog can be incorporated in method declarations. Referential integrity is guaranteed in the FDM as references are not by value, and the consistency of keys is managed by update routines described above. However, strong constraints are not enforced on new methods and the system is deliberately open-ended to allow the addition of new entity classes and control structures. Prolog is its own meta-language, and we value the ability to treat method definitions as data. In the light of this, we do not want prematurely to constrain the development of the system by over enforcing rigid constraints.

3.6. Changing The Class Of An Entity Instance

It is possible for one entity instance to belong to more than one subtype of an entity class. For example, it is reasonable for a member of the research staff to be registered for a second degree as a postgraduate student. To permit the inclusion of an existing entity in another subtype the predicate *include* is used. e.g. to indicate that David Moffat, a member of the research staff is also a postgraduate student the following Prolog is typed:

        getentity(research,'Moffat|David',Dave_As_Researcher),
        include(research,Dave_As_Researcher,postgrad,Dave_As_PostGrad).

The predicate *exclude(EntityClass,EntityInst)* removes an entity instance from an entity class.

3.7. Example Prolog Queries and Updates

1. "Which room is Norman Paton's?"

        getentity(staff,'Paton|Norman',Norm),   % get staff entity by key
        getfunctionval(room,Norm,Room),   % get room of staff entity
        write(Room).

2. "Which courses are taught by Peter Gray?"

        getentity(staff,'Gray|Peter',PGray),   % get staff entity by key
        getfunctionval(has_lecturer_inv,PGray,SRC),   % use inverse of has_lecturer
        getfunctionval(has_course,SRC,Course),   % find course from SCL
        getfunctionval(code,Course,Code),
        getfunctionval(section_name,SRC,Section),
        write([section,Section,having,Code]), nl,
        fail;   % force Prolog to backtrack
        true.

3. "Increase the year of all undergraduates by 1"

        getentity(undergrad,Undergrad),
        getfunctionval(year,Undergrad,OldYear),
        NewYear is OldYear + 1,
        updatefunctionval(year,Undergrad,OldYear,NewYear),
        fail;
        true.

4. "Given a person entity, find the ancestors of that person"

        ancestor(Person,Ancestor) :-
                getfunctionval(parent,Person,Temp),
                (Ancestor = Temp; ancestor(Temp,Ancestor)).

3.8. Alternative User Interfaces

There are two alternatives to writing queries directly in Prolog:

1. A parser for a version of *DAPLEX* [Shipman 79] has been written in Prolog which generates Prolog queries (such as those in section 3.7) and also permits updates.

2. An interactive *database browser* has been implemented on a micro using GEM windows.

4. IMPLEMENTATION

In this section we describe the implementation of a FDM database in the Perlog environment.

4.1. Module Interaction

When the FDM interface is being used, two system modules are always present, *fdm_sys* and *linkmod*. The module *fdm_sys* contains a lexical analyser, a parser, a load utility, high and low level interface predicates and some utility routines. The low level interface routines handle the process of calling out from Prolog to PS-algol.

The *linkmod* module, which is never committed, stores links between the textual name of a function or entity class and the module in which it is stored. This is used by the high level interface routines of *fdm_sys* to obtain the private term necessary for use with the method declarations held in the database modules. Effectively it is a kind of cached dictionary providing a fast lookup of entity class descriptor by entity class name. The descriptors identify the module in which the methods are stored.

4.2. Database Module Contents

Each FDM database is associated with one or more modules. The allocation of entity classes to modules is specified in the schema (section 3.1). If there are two or more modules associated with a database they can be restored independently, and functions on entity classes in one module can return entities from another module. Each database module contains descriptors for entity classes and associated functions. These descriptors in turn reference and protect the PS-algol structures used to store the instances.

The PS-algol structure used to hold entity instances is a *table* which is an extensible associative structure permitting direct or sequential access to its contents. The results of functions of arity 1 on entities are stored in an extensible vector of lists attached to the entity instance. Functions on scalars are represented by tables indexed by the argument, and functions of arity 2 are represented by tables of tables.

Data stored on disc is read into main memory if and only if a pointer to it is dereferenced. This is efficient where a search follows relationship pointers deep into a network of objects, but is less suitable for scanning the instances of a single entity class.

4.2.1. Function and Entity Descriptors

When a new entity or function is declared, its description is asserted into the appropriate module. The entity class descriptor is:

$edesc(EntStr, EName, Is-A, KeyType, KeyDesc).

EntStr: A reference to the PS-algol table used for the storage of the entity class (wrapped in a private term).

EName: The name of the entity class.

Is-A: The immediate supertype of the entity class.

KeyType: The type of the key of the entity - *integer* or *string*.

KeyDesc: A description of the derivation of the key of the entity.

e.g. The entity descriptor for the entity class *student* in the university database is:

$edesc($eterm(PS-obj),student,person,string,[sname,cname]).

The function descriptor is:

$fdesc(FunStr, FName, Arg1, Arg2, Res, Type, Status).

FunStr: A reference to the PS-algol function descriptor.

FName: The name of the function.

Arg1: The type of the first argument.

Arg2: The type of the optional second argument.

Res: The result type.

Type: One of *single* or *multi*, indicating whether or not the function is restricted to returning only one value.

Status: One of *total*, *mandatory* or *optional* (section 3.4.3).

e.g. The function descriptor for the function *takes* in the university database is:

$fdesc($fterm(PS_fun),takes,undergrad,undef,course,multi,optional).

4.2.2. Methods

When a module is created by parsing a schema, the default methods for database access are read into it. These methods can later be modified to permit non-standard storage of and access to entity instances and function values. For example, the Prolog for the function *age* which derives the (approximate) age of a student from his year of birth is:

```
% derive the age of a student from his year of birth
getfnval($fterm(age),Arg1,Age) :-
        getfunctionval(birth_year,Arg1,BirthYear),
        $current_year(Year),
        Age is Year - BirthYear.

% warn user that age is not a stored value
modifyfnval($fterm(age),_,_) :-
        write('ERROR: Cannot update age - it is derived from birth_year'),
        nl,
        fail.


$current_year(88).


% let system know of new function
:- assert($fdesc($fterm(age),age,student,undef,integer,single,total)).
```

To associate new methods such as this with an existing database module, the user modifies the methods file for that module and uses the BIP *reconsult(File,Module)* to update its clause base. User defined methods can be written in Prolog as above or can call out to PS-algol using *ps_apply/3*.

Note that *getfunctionval* is a generic function defined in *fdm_sys* and not a method. It uses the clauses stored in *linkmod* to obtain the private term needed to invoke the method *getfnval* in the appropriate module.

4.3. Current Position

The Perlog system which is an amalgamation of CProlog [Pereira 83] and PS-algol [Atkinson 83] runs on a VAX 11/750 under UNIX. The FDM interface and associated utilities as described above consists of 4000 lines of Prolog and 2000 lines of PS-algol.

4.4. Future Directions

There is clearly scope for experimentation with query optimisation [Gray 83], view definitions and integrity constraints in the Prolog/FDM environment. We are using the system to store protein structure data [Rawlings 85, Paton 88] from the Brookhaven databank, and hope to use it as one component in an information management system for protein chemists. In the longer term we hope to make use of persistent storage hardware [Cockshott 87] to reduce the overhead of the current implementation which is based on an object management system written in C.

5. CONCLUSIONS

A system has been built which gives tight coupling from Prolog to a semantic net database. While there are several implementations which couple Prolog to relational databases, this is the first we know which links Prolog to a database suitable for the storage of objects along with methods, as required for CAD and AI frame structures. The system permits the use of Prolog with a schema based on that of DAPLEX, and the modules facilitate incremental updates to both function definitions and data without dumping and restoring the entire Prolog clause base. Subschemas, view definitions and parsers are concisely and cost-effectively implemented in Prolog rather than by cumbersome routines in the database kernel.

6. ACKNOWLEDGEMENTS

This work is supported by grant GR/D/32765 from the UK Science and Engineering Research Council. We are grateful for continued support from the Alvey Directorate and for discussions with our Alvey partners.

7. REFERENCES

[Atkinson 83] Atkinson, M.P., Bailey, P.J., Chisholm, K.L., Cockshott, W.P. & Morrison, R.. "An Approach to Persistent Programming", The Computer Journal, 26, 4.

[Atkinson 84] Atkinson, M.P. & Kulkarni, K.G.. "Experimenting With The Functional Data Model" in "Databases - Role and Structure", Stocker, Gray & Atkinson (eds), Cambridge University Press.

[Bocca 86] Bocca, J.. "On the EvaluationStrategy of EDUCE", Proc. ACM SIGMOD 86, Zaniolo (ed).

[Bratko 86] Bratko, I.. "Prolog Programming for Artificial Intelligence", Addison-Wesley.

[Clocksin 81] Clocksin, W.F. & Mellish, C.S.. "Programming in Prolog", Springer-Verlag.

[Cockshott 87] Cockshott, W.P.. "Persistent Object Store Hardware and Software Interfaces", Proc. 2nd Workshop of SIGKME, Brunel University.

[Dittrich 86] Dittrich, K.R.. "Object-oriented Database Systems: the Notion and the Issues", Proc. International Workshop on Object-Oriented Database Systems, Dittrich & Dayal (eds).

[Gallaire 84] Gallaire, H., Minker, J. & Nicolas, J-M.. "Logic and Databases: A Deductive Approach"; ACM Computing Surveys, Vol 16, No.2.

[Gray 83] Gray, P.M.D. & Moffat, D.S.. "Manipulating Descriptions of Programs for Database Access", Proc. Eighth International Joint Conference on Artificial Intelligence, IJCAI-83 (Karlsruhe), A. Bundy (ed.), 21-24.

[Gray 85] Gray, P.M.D.. "Efficient Prolog Access to Codasyl and FDM Databases", Proc. ACM SIGMOD 1985, ed. S. Navathe, pp 437-443.

[Gray 87]   Gray, P.M.D.. "Integration of Databases and Expert Systems Through Prolog", presented at AI Conference, San Sebastian (Sept 87).

[Maier 84]   Maier, D.. "Databases in the Fifth Generation Project: Is Prolog a Database Language?", in "New Directions For Database Systems", Ariav & Clifford (eds), Abtex.

[Moffat 86]   Moffat, D.S. & Gray, P.M.D.. "Interfacing Prolog to a Persistent Data store", 3rd International Conf. on Logic Programming, London, ed. E.Shapiro, 1986.

[Moffat 88a]   Moffat, D.S. & Gray, P.M.D.. "Perlog: A Prolog with Persistence and Modules", To be published in The Computer Journal.

[Moffat 88b]   Moffat, D.S., "Modular Commitment in Persistent Prolog", to be published in "Prolog and Databases: Implementation and Applications", Gray & Lucas (eds), Ellis Horwood.

[Paton 88]   Paton, N.W. & Gray, P.M.D.. "An Object-Oriented Database for Storage and Analysis of Protein Structure Data", to be published in "Prolog and Databases: Implementations and Applications", Gray & Lucas (eds), Ellis Horwood.

[Pereira 83]   Pereira, F., Warren, D., Bowen, D., Byrd, L. & Pereira, L.. "C-Prolog User's Manual", EdCAAD, Dept of Architecture, Univ. of Edinburgh.

[Rawlings 85]   Rawlings, C.J., Taylor, W.R., Nyakairu, J., Fox, J. & Sternberg, M.J.E., "Using Prolog To Represent and Reason about Protein Structure", Proc. 3rd International Conf. on Logic Programming, Shapiro (ed).

[Shipman 79]   Shipman, D.. "The Functional Data Model and the Data Language DAPLEX", SIGMOD 79 Conf, revised version, ACM TODS, 6, 140-173.

[Szeredi 82]   Szeredi, P.. "Module Concepts for Prolog", SZKI, 1251 Budapest P.O.B. 19.

[Warren 81]   Warren, D.H.D.. "Efficient Processing of Interactive Relational Database Queries expressed in Logic", Proc. 7th VLDB conference, Cannes, 272-281, 1981.

[Zaniolo 84]   Zaniolo, C.. "Prolog: A Database Query Language For All Seasons" in Proc. First International Workshop on Expert Database Systems, L. Kerschberg (ed).

The Processing and Evaluation of Transitive Closure Queries

Jiawei Han
Simon Fraser University, British Columbia, CANADA

Ghassen Qadah and **Chinying Chaou**
Northwestern University, Illinois, U.S.A.

ABSTRACT *A transitive closure operator will be an important new operator in future deductive database systems. We discuss the compilation of recursive rule clusters into formulas containing transitive closure operations and study three promising algorithms for the processing of transitive closure queries: the wavefront algorithm, the δ-wavefront algorithm and the level-relaxed δ-wavefront algorithm. The relative processing efficiency of these algorithms are analyzed and compared based on different database structures and accessing methods. Our study shows that the δ-wavefront algorithm performs consistently better than the wavefront algorithm, and the level-relaxed δ-wavefront algorithm has high potential of further reducing I/O accessing cost on the databases with clustered derivation paths. The study also provides some interesting heuristics on the database structures and implementation techniques in the processing of recursive database queries.*

1. Introduction

Recursion enhances the expressive power of relational database systems but the efficient evaluation of recursive queries poses challenges to most researchers. Although complex recursions may demand great skill and efforts in compiling and processing, a scan of current literature reveals that most recursive queries in practical applications can be processed by conventional relational operations plus a new transitive closure operation. Therefore, the efficient evaluation of transitive closure queries becomes an important issue in recent database research.

Like most researchers, we assume that a deductive database contains an **extensional database (EDB)** (a set of base relations) and an **intensional database (IDB)** (a set of deduction rules) [14]. Each deduction rule is a *safe* and *function-free* Horn-clause of the form (in Prolog-like syntax),

$$R :- P_1, ..., P_k. \tag{1}$$

where the predicate R is the head of the rule and $P_1, ..., P_k$ is the body. Each predicate contains a list of arguments, e.g., $R(x_1, x_2, ..., x_n)$, where each argument x_i is a variable or a constant.

In our discussion, we use upper case letters to denote relations, with R, S and T indicating virtual relations, and others indicating base relations, and we use lower case letters to denote attributes, with a, b, c,... near the start of the alphabet indicating constant vectors, and u, v, .., z near the end of the alphabet indicating variable vectors.

A rule is **linearly recursive** if the predicate in the head appears exactly once in the body and all the other predicates in the body are not directly or indirectly defined by the head predicate. A linear recursive rule is a **transitive closure rule** if its definition contains only one-sided join with the recursive predicate. For example, the following rule is a transitive closure rule.

$$R(x,y) :- A(x,u), R(u,y). \tag{2}$$

For each recursive predicate R, we assume that there is at least one non-recursive definition (the **exit rule**), such as

$$R(x,y) :- E(x,y). \tag{3}$$

The rules in *IDB* which directly or transitively define a predicate form a **rule cluster** for the predicate. The rule cluster is a **recursive cluster** if it contains one or more recursively defined rules. Obviously, the two rules (2) and (3) define a recursive cluster. If the variables among the predicates in the body of a rule form a chain, such as the above, we do not have to write the variables explicitly because they are implied. Therefore, the two rules can be written as

$$R :- A, R. \qquad R :- E. \tag{4}$$

The compilation of the R-cluster derives a sequence of expanded formulas,

$E.$
$A, E.$
$A, A, E.$
$A, A, ..., E.$
......

or simply written as $A^* E$ where A^* is the transitive and reflexive closure of A. Since such a formula represents the complete result of compilation, it is called the **compiled formula**.

In general, a transitive closure operator refers to A^* or A^+ ($A^+ = AA^*$). We discuss the efficient implementation of the transitive closure operation in large databases. There are some interesting studies on the evaluation of the *total transitive closure*, such as the naive and semi-naive evaluation [4], the logarithmic algorithm [23], the adapted Warren's algorithm [17], and the direct algorithm [1]. However, it is very expensive and rarely necessary to evaluate the *total* closure for a query because most inquiries are to find the portion of a closure related only to a small number of query constants, such as *"find John's ancestors"*. Therefore, what we need to compute is the *query-related* transitive closure (σA^*). An obvious heuristic that we should adopt is to *perform selection first using the query constants and evaluate only the portion of the transitive closure related to those constants*. An interesting algorithm in this direction is the Henschen-Naqvi algorithm [14] (also proposed in [2] for some transitive closure queries) which uses one more heuristic, *using the intermediate results derived from the last iteration in* *the processing of the current iteration*, therefore it is called *the wavefront algorithm* [9]. Further optimization has been explored in [9, 10] where *the δ-wavefront algorithm* and *the level-relaxation method* have been proposed to reduce redundancy at the levels of tuple processing and file accessing, respectively.

This paper studies these three methods and it is organized as follows. In Section 2, we demonstrate that many complicated recursions can be compiled into formulas which require transitive closure algorithms rather than more complicated recursive query evaluation algorithms. In Section 3, we study three promising algorithms in the implementation of a transitive closure operator: *the wavefront algorithm, the δ-wavefront algorithm* and *the level-relaxed δ-wavefront algorithm*. Section 4 is on the performance study of the three algorithms based on two models, an analytical model and a simulation model, and three different implementations: *B-tree, hashing, and hashing with bit-vector filtering*. The performance results are also analyzed there. We conclude our discussion in Section 5.

2. Compiling Recursive Clusters into Formulas Involving Transitive Closure Operators

Many recursive rules in practical applications are transitive closure rules, such as ancestor, component, supervisor and connected flight. Many other recursive rules, though not in the simple form of transitive closure rules, are compilable to the form where the transitive closure processing strategies are applicable. We study some interesting cases.

2.1. Compiling the Single Recursive Rule of a Cluster

The predicate connection graph analysis [16] has been popularly used in the compilation of deductive databases. However, the variables within the predicates and their relationship play an important role in the compilation of recursive rules. Therefore, many researchers study the compilation of recursive rules by the analysis of variable connection graphs [13, 15, 18].

Ioannidis [15] developed a method for the analysis of the bounded recursion using a hybrid graph, the α-graph. Each recursive rule has a corresponding α-graph in which vertices represent variables in the rule, direct edges connect vertices (variables) at the same argument position in the head and the body of the recursive predicate, and undirected edges connect vertices (variables) in the same non-recursive predicates.

Naughton [18] built a similar graph, the A(argument)/V(variable) graph, which registers more detailed information than the α-graph. Moreover, he discovered that a recursion which adopts the transitive closure processing strategy (*the one-sided recursion* according to his term) has an intersting property: *the A/V graph of its recursive rule forms a cycle of unit length* [19]. This property can also be derived in the analysis of α-graphs.

To compile general linear recursion, the α-graphs is modified to the V-graph in [13] by adding labels to vertices representing unary relations. The study shows that the transitive closure processing strategies can be applied to more complicated V-graph connections which covers a great portion of the general linear recursion [13].

We illustrate in the following example the idea of compiling linear recursive rules using the V-graphs.

Example 1. Suppose the recursive cluster R consists of a recursive rule

$$R(x, y, z, w) :- A(x_1, t, t_1), B(x, x_1), R(x_1, y, z_1, w), C(t_1, x, t),$$

$$D(z, x_1), F(z, t_2, z_1), G(w, y). \tag{5}$$

and an exit rule

$$R(x, y, z, w) :- E(x, y, z, w). \tag{6}$$

The V-graph for the recursive rule a) and its simplified graph b) is shown in Figure 1.

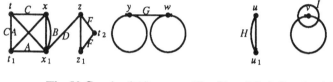

The V-Graph of (6) The Simplified Graph of (6)

Figure 1. The Variable Connection Graph of (6) and Its Simplification

By combining the non-recursive components and removing isolated variables, the rule (5) becomes

$$R(x, y, z, w) :- H(x, z, x_1, z_1), R(x_1, y, z_1, w), G(w, y).$$

where

$$H(x, z, x_1, z_1) :- A(x_1, t, t_1), B(x, x_1), C(t_1, x, t), D(z, x_1), F(z, t_2, z_1)$$

The rule can be further simplified to (7) by vectorizing the connected components, i.e., using vector u for x and z, vector u_1 for x_1 and z_1, and vector v for y and w.

$$R(u, v) :- H(u, u_1), R(u_1, v,), I(v). \tag{7}$$

where $I(v) :- G(w, y)$. Therefore, the cluster can be compiled to $H*EI$ which contains a transitive closure operator.

Note that the vectorization of the variables in the head predicate should still allow users asking flexible queries, such as $?-R(a, ?y, ?z, b)$. Similar questions exist even in simple transitive closure recursion where people may ask queries like $?-R(a, b)$. A detailed study in [13] finds that they can be processed using the variations of the methods studied here.

It is not the goal of this paper to have a complete study on the processing of different forms of queries and the compilation of complex linear recursive clusters by the variable connection graph analysis. We simply assume that the queries are in simple form, and each recursive rule has been appropriately compiled to the form where the variables inside the predicates are not have to be written explicitly, i.e., to the form like $R :- A, R$ or $R :- R, A$. A detailed study of processing different forms of queries and compiling complex linear recursive clusters is in [13].

2.2. Compiling Multiple Recursive Rules and Multiple Exit Rules of the Recursive Cluster

Multiple rules in a recursive cluster may contain complex connections among predicates. The indirect non-recursive rules can be easily resolved by predicate connection graph analysis in compilation. For example, in R-cluster

$$R :- T, R. \qquad R :- S, B. \qquad S :- T, B, C.$$
$$S :- A, D. \qquad T :- A, E.$$

S can be first resolved to $A(D \cup EBC)$, then R is compiled to

$$(AE)^* A (D \cup EBC) B. \qquad (8)$$

A recursive cluster containing multiple transitive closure rules and multiple exit rules can be compiled by sharing common sub-expressions. For example, the R-cluster

$$R :- A_1. \qquad \cdots \qquad R :- A_k.$$
$$R :- B_1, R. \qquad \cdots \qquad R :- B_i, R.$$
$$R :- R, C_1. \qquad \cdots \qquad R :- R, C_j.$$

can be compiled into $B^* A C^*$, where $A = A_1 \cup \cdots \cup A_k$, $B = B_1 \cup B_2 \cup \ldots \cup B_i$, and $C = C_1 \cup C_2 \cup \ldots \cup C_j$.

2.3. Multiple Levels of TC Rules in the Cluster

For a cluster containing multiple levels of transitive closure rules, the compilation proceeds from the deep-most level to the top-most level and the compiled formulas are still transitive closure operations plus conventional relational operations. For example, the R-cluster

$$R :- S, R. \qquad R :- E. \qquad S :- S, B. \qquad S :- C.$$

where S is recursion at a lower level than R, can be compiled by first compiling S to CB^*, then compiling R to $(CB^*)^* E$.

2.4. Some Special Non-linear Recursive Clusters

There are some special non-linear recursive cluster where the transitive closure processing strategies are also applicable. A typical example is the R-cluster

$$R :- E. \qquad R :- R, R, \ldots, R. \qquad (9)$$

where there are k ($k \geq 2$) occurrences of R on the right hand side of the rule. It can be compiled to $(E^{k-1})^* E$.

Another special non-linear recursive cluster is

$$R :- E. \qquad R :- R, A, R, A, \ldots, R. \qquad (10)$$

where the right hand side of the rule contains k ($k \geq 2$) occurrences of R separated by the same A for each pair, which can be compiled to $((EA)^{(k-1)})^* E$. Note that the cluster (9) can also be thought as a special case of (10) with all the A-predicates missing.

2.5. From Transitive Closure to General Linear Recursion

One step beyond transitive closure recursion is the general linear recursion. For example, the popularly discussed *same-generation* example [21] is a recursion which consists of two synchronized compiled chains. It is essentially

$$R(x,z) :- A(x,y), R(y,w), B(w,z). \tag{11}$$

and

$$R(x,z) :- E(x,z). \tag{12}$$

which defines a linear recursive cluster whose compiled formula is $\overset{n}{\underset{k=0}{\cup}} A^k EB^k$. People might have tried to directly apply the transitive closure processing strategy to process it by shifting the non-recursive predicates B and C in rule (11) to one side, such as

$$R(x,z) :- A(x,y), B(w,z), R(y,w). \tag{13}$$

However, the grouping of A and B together results in iterative joins on the cross-product of two EDB relations A and B, which is very expensive in processing. A better method is to adopt the counting method, the magic set method [5], or the level-cycle merging algorithm in the case of cyclic databases [11], which has been discussed in many papers and is not the theme of this paper.

A further generalization of the same-generalization example is the multi-chain recursion [12] which consists of multiple synchronized compiled chains in the formula. A multi-way counting method has been studied in the processing of such recursive queries [12].

Nevertheless, the transitive closure processing strategy still strongly influences the algorithms for the processing of linear recursive queries. For example, the counting method is essentially the processing of two synchronized transitive closures. Therefore, many techniques developed in transitive closure processing are transferable to the processing of other recursive queries.

3. Three Query Evaluation Algorithms

Since most compiled formulas discussed above contain A^* operations, our study focuses on the efficient evaluation of queries in the form of σA^*. We discuss three query evaluation algorithms: *the Wavefront Algorithm, the δ-Wavefront Algorithm*, and *the Level-Relaxed δ-Wavefront Algorithm*.

All the three algorithms are unary algorithms, that is, the intermediate relation is unary. Thus we introduce a **quarter-join** operator, ∇, whose function is equivalent to the natural join of a unary relation with a binary relation followed by projecting off the join attribute(s), i.e., $C = A \nabla B$ indicates $C(y) :- A(w), B(w,y)$, which is equivalent to $\pi_{(y)}[A(w) \bowtie B(w,y)]$. We call ∇ the *quarter-join* because the result is a single attribute, which costs even less than a *semi-join*. For other notations we follow the conventional relational databases, i.e., σ denotes the selection on a predicate in the form of *column = value*; $\cup$ denotes the union of two relations with redundant tuples eliminated; and $-$ denotes the difference of two relations.

3.1. The Wavefront Algorithm

The Wavefront Algorithm is essentially the Henschen-Naqvi algorithm in the case of transitive closure recursions [14]. We rewrite it in terms of relational operations and add a temporary relation *CLOSURE* to collect results and facilitate the termination on cyclic data relations.

Two temporary unary relations, *WAVE* and *CLOSURE*, are used in derivation. At first, they are initiated to query constant a. At the k-th iteration, the algorithm uses the temporary unary *wavefront* relation *WAVE*, the intermediate results derived at the (k−1)-th iteration, to (quarter-)join with relation A. All the results are accumulated in *CLOSURE* as the answer to the query. The process terminates when *WAVE* becomes empty or *CLOSURE* stabilizes. Since the algorithm uses immediately previous values to generate new waves, it is called the *Wavefront Algorithm*.

Algorithm 1. The Wavefront Algorithm.

Begin

        WAVE := a;

        CLOSURE := a;

        Repeat

                WAVE := *WAVE* ∇ A;

                CLOSURE := *WAVE* $\cup$ *CLOSURE*;

        Until (*WAVE* = ϕ) **or** (*CLOSURE* does not change);

End.

The proof of the termination and the correctness of the algorithm is in [10]. This algorithm has been shown in [6] to be the best performing algorithm among many competitive algorithms for processing transitive closure queries. The good performance is due to (i) starting from the early binding of the query constant, (ii) using only values generated in the (k−1)-th iteration to derive the k-th iteration, and (iii) using unary intermediate relations instead of binary ones. However, redundant processing has not been eliminated in the algorithm, as can be seen in the following example.

Example 2. Suppose the base relation $A(x,y)$ contains the following tuples, and its database digraph is shown in Figure 2.

    (a b), (a c), (a d), (b e), (b c), (c a), (d f), (d b), (e g), (g d), (g h), (i k).

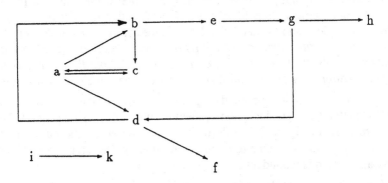

Figure 2. The Database Digraph of Relation A

The process in the derivation of *WAVE* and *CLOSURE* is shown in Table 1 and Figure 3. (Note: NTA in the table means the Number of Tuples Accessed.)

Iteration	Old-*WAVE*	New_*WAVE*	*CLOSURE*	NTA
1	a	b, c, d	a, b, c, d	3
2	b, c, d	a, b, c, e, f	a, b, c, d, e, f	5
3	a, b, c, e, f	a, b, c, d, e, g	a, b, c, d, e, f, g	7
4	a, b, c, d, e, g	a, b, c, d, e, f, g, h	a, b, c, d, e, f, g, h	11
5	a, b, c, d, e, f, g, h	a, b, c, d, e, f, g, h	a, b, c, d, e, f, g, h	11

Table 1. Redundancy Still Exists in the Wavefront Algorithm

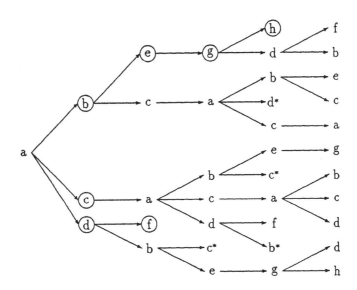

Figure 3. The Derivation of σA* Using the Wavefront Algorithm

In a database digraph, an edge represents a tuple in the database relation. For a derivation using an edge e, the tail of the edge e is called the *driver* and the head of e the *result*. Example 2 shows that redundancy comes from two sources: (1) *cyclic data: the data directly or transitively rederived by itself*, e.g., (a, c) and (c, a) forming a cycle; (2) *asynchronous data: the data which do not form cycles but the same data are derived in different iterations*, e.g., (a, c) and (b, c) generating the same c at different iterations.

Both cyclic and asynchronous data produce values which have been processed in some previous iteration. The inclusion of them in future processing generates nothing but redundant results. In Figure 3, the third iteration is based on the output of the second iteration: *a, b, c, e,* and *f*. Since *a, b,* and *c* are already used in a previous iteration, the reprocessing of them is redundant.

In Figure 3, a circled driver indicates a (real) new driver contribute to the answer, and "*" indicates that the value redundantly derived at the same iteration are automatically eliminated by conventional relational operators. Such notations are used throughout the paper.

3.2. The δ-Wavefront Algorithm

To eliminate redundant processing, we introduce the δ-*Wavefront Algorithm* which is an improvement of the Wavefront Algorithm by excluding any drivers which have been previously used from re-entering *WAVE*.

The algorithm proceeds as follows. Two temporary relations, *CLOSURE* and *WAVE*, are, respectively, used to collect results and active drivers, and are initialized to the query constant *a*. At each iteration the query processor checks every newly generated value in *WAVE* against those generated in previous iterations and accumulated in *CLOSURE*. If it is already in *CLOSURE*, we simply exclude it from *WAVE*. The processing terminates when *WAVE* becomes empty, and the final results are all the values in *CLOSURE*.

Algorithm 2. The δ-Wavefront Algorithm
Begin
    $WAVE := a$;
    $CLOSURE := a$;
    While $WAVE <> \phi$ **Do**
    Begin
        $WAVE := WAVE \nabla A$;
        $WAVE := WAVE - CLOSURE$;
        $CLOSURE := WAVE \cup CLOSURE$
    End
End.

The proof of the termination and the completeness of the algorithm is also in [10]. According to the algorithm, any driver used in deriving new values is included in *CLOSURE*, thus excluded from *WAVE* and will not be used in deriving new values in future iterations. Hence there is no redundant tuple processing.

Example 3. Data relation *A* of Example 2 is processed using the δ-Wavefront Algorithm. The iterations and the results are presented in Figure 4 and Table 2.

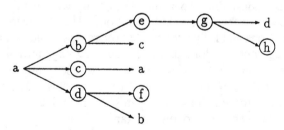

Figure 4. The Processing of σ*A** Using the δ-Wavefront Algorithm

Iteration	CLOSURE	Old WAVE	New WAVE	NTA
1	a	a	b, c, d	3
2	a, b, c, d	b, c, d	e, f	5
3	a, b, c, d, e, f	e, f	g	1
4	a, b, c, d, e, f, g	g	h	2
5	a, b, c, d, e, f, g, h	h		0

Table 2. Tuple Processing Redundancy Is Eliminated in the δ-Wavefront Algorithm

The δ-wavefront algorithm has two advantages:

(1) Redundancy has been eliminated because of the exclusion of the already-processed drivers from *WAVE* for future derivation.

(2) It usually takes less number of iterations to terminate, and the termination test is simplified, i.e., *terminating when WAVE is empty*, even for cyclic databases, which is obviously simpler than examining whether the *CLOSURE* does not grow in the Wavefront Algorithm although the latter may also be implemented efficiently by some "tricks", such as examining the last update time or checking the "dirty" bits of the *CLOSURE* pages.

3.3. A Level-Relaxed δ-Wavefront Algorithm

The wavefront algorithm eliminates redundant processing at the *iteration level* by using only those derived at the last iteration to avoid the reprocessing of the portion of the previous iterations. The δ-wavefront algorithm improves it at the *tuple level* by excluding processed drivers from re-processing, thus each driver is used only once in derivation. Since the processing is examined as low as at the tuple level, it seems that there is not much room for further optimization. However, by examining a more detailed level, the *database accessing level*, we find that further optimization is still possible.

In relational databases, tuples are stored on different pages (or segments) on disks. In the derivation of a single transitive closure, a data page may have to be fetched and accessed many times at different iterations. Such repeated fetching and accessing of the same data pages is undesirable. To avoid doing this, we develop a *level-relaxed δ-wavefront algorithm* to further reduce I/O operations. The idea is to relax the restriction on the levels of iterations and fully explore the drivers accessible in main memory before swapping a data page out. As long as the current data page in main memory contains tuples accessible by active drivers, it is not to be swapped out. Thus some costly I/O operations can be saved if there are some derivation paths clustered in current main memory, and we may proceed along these paths for many iteration levels without page swapping. This can be seen in the following example.

Example 4. We first observe a tiny example (which may not a realistic one in real computers). Suppose the main memory holds only one page of the data relation A, and the base relation A is in two data pages as follows:

Tuples	Page_No.
(a c), (a d), (a b), (b e), (b c), (e g)	1
(c a), (d f), (d b), (g d), (g h), (i k)	2

Table 3. Only One of the Two Pages of Relation A Resides in Main Memory.

Suppose the level relaxation is not applied. Based on the δ-Wavefront Algorithm, Page 1 is accessed by driver a at the first iteration; Pages 2 and 1 are accessed by drivers c, d and b at the second iteration; Page 1 is accessed by driver e at the third iteration; and Page 2 is accessed by driver g at the fourth iteration. Since the main memory can hold only one page of A, we need at least 4 pages of I/O's in the transitive closure processing, even if we know where each data is stored beforehand (possibly by sorting, indexing or hashing) and choose the best order to access tuples in each $WAVE$.

However, if we relax the restriction on iteration level, accessing on Page 1 will derive a, b, c, d, e, g in $CLOSURE$ and leave drivers c, d, g in the $WAVE$. The accessing of Page 2 will derive f, b, a, d, h. Tuples a, b, d are used before thus eliminated; and f and h cannot generate any new result. Thus further derivation makes $WAVE$ empty and the process terminates. The total number of I/O's on data page accessing is only 2. Here we assume that all the drivers with the same value are stored in the same page. Since data or indices are sorted or clustered in most databases, such assumption is true in most cases. Therefore, by relaxation of the level-oriented calculation, we can exploit the data clustering property to reduce the total number of I/O operations.

We present the level-relaxed version of the δ-Wavefront algorithm below.

Algorithm 3. A Level-Relaxed δ-Wavefront Algorithm for the Processing of σA^*.

Begin
  $WAVE := a$;
  $CLOSURE := a$;
  Repeat
    WHILE drivers in $WAVE$ can fire in main memory **DO**
    Begin
      $New\_CLOSURE := drivers \nabla the\_drivable\_portion\_of\_A$;
      $live\_drivers := New\_CLOSURE - CLOSURE$;
      $WAVE := WAVE \cup live\_drivers - drivers$;
      $CLOSURE := CLOSURE \cup live\_drivers$;
    End;
    If $WAVE <> \phi$
    Then Fetch drivable data pages to main memory
  Until $WAVE = \phi$
End.

Note: (1) ∇ is implemented as a main memory algorithm; (2) live_drivers are those newly derived but not already in $CLOSURE$; (3) the accessed drivers are excluded from $WAVE$ based on the assumption that the drivers of the same value reside at the same page. □

Based on this algorithm, the processing of the previous example is as follows.

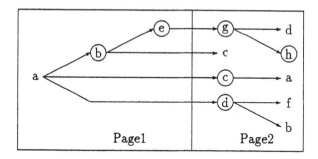

Figure 5. The Processing Using the Level-Relaxed δ-Wavefront Algorithm

Accessing Page No.	*CLOSURE*	*WAVE*
1	a, b, c, d, e, g	c, d, g
2	a, b, c, d, e, g, f, h	φ

Table 4. Only Two I/O's Are Needed By Level Relaxation

By level-relaxation, the paths traversible in main memory are fully explored. Therefore, the chances of refetching and reaccessing of the same data page are reduced. Nevertheless, it does not indicate that a page will be fetched to main memory at most once. Bridges linking a derivation path may not reside fully in main memory, the page may have to be swapped out and re-entered into main memory when the required bridge is built-up later.

Clearly, the improvement of level-relaxation is significant when a driver has many successors in the database digraph or when the ratio of pages stored in main memory over the total number of pages in the relation is high. However, such improvement may not be significant for uniformly distributed data with relatively sparse number of successors in the database digraph, as shown in our performance study, because there are fewer chances that the newly generated drivers can be fired directly in main memory. Nevertheless, the level relaxation is still quite attractive because many real databases have relatively clustered derivation paths for recursive queries. For example, it is more likely that one's recent ancestors or supervisors being "clustered" in one's local area rather than uniformly distributed in the world.

Level-relaxation may also be very useful in distributed databases where a relation is divided into disjoint horizontal fragments which are allocated at different sites of a computer network. A typical example, where level relaxation works better than level observation is the following: Assume that there exists a demographic database of the U.S. population containing a relation with schema (PERSON, PARENT, ...) which is horizontally fragmented and distributed over the statistic centers in the capitals of the single states. Assuming that on the average, five or six consecutive generations of a family stay in the same state before the branch moves to another state, it is easy to see that level-relaxation leads to a drastic reduction of the number of messages necessary to answer the query about all ancestors of a given individual. The performance study of the level-relaxed recursive query processing in distributed databases is to be reported in another paper.

The level relaxation method can also be used in the Wavefront algorithm and the algorithms for the processing of other linear and nonlinear recursive queries as long as the processing is independent of the derivation level and the relative processing order [11]. Many popularly studied recursive query processing algorithms have such property, such as the counting method [5], the level-cycle merging algorithm, and the multi-formula merged processing of nonlinear recursive queries [11], where the level information is correctly registered for each intermediate tuple in the processing. Therefore, we claim that level-relaxed processing is important for the processing of general recursive queries.

4. A Comparative Study of the Performance of the Three Algorithms

Based on the discussion of Section 3, it is easy to predict that the relative performance (in terms of execution speed) of the three presented transitive closure algorithms will be

the level-relaxed δ-Wavefront > the δ-Wavefront > the Wavefront

where $A > B$ indicates that A executes faster than B. Despite this, a quantitative evaluation for the performance of the three algorithms is still needed to verify our prediction and, moreover, to provide us with a quantitative estimate for the performance of one algorithm relative to another. In addition, such a detailed study would allow us to investigate the effect of the physical database structures and accessing methods on the behavior of these algorithms.

Two models, an analytical model and a simulation model, have been constructed to compute the performance measure, the *total execution time (Time) for each algorithm. Note within a single processor environment the measure Time* is defined as the time required to execute a given algorithm assuming there exists no overlap between the CPU and I/O. Experimentation with both types of models shows that although the analytical model gives somewhat more conservative estimates for the performance measure than the simulation one, both models generate close enough results, which validates our performance study and provides us with some insights about the behavior of the studied algorithms.

For a given algorithm, we consider two implementation techniques, a *B-tree-based* and a *hash-based*. The former builds a B+-tree index on top of the base relation A, and most accesses to the relation go through such an index. In our performance evaluation, we assume that the amount of memory allocated to the relation A is large enough to keep all of the non-leaf pages of the B-tree stored in main memory. The latter builds a hash table for relation A, and the number of entries in such a hash table is equal to the number of pages available in main memory to buffer relation A. That is, at any time there exists only one page from each of the buckets of the hash table in memory.

The hash-based and the B-tree-based implementations can be *with* or *without a bit-vector filtering mechanism*. The bit-vector [3] have been successfully used to speed up the processing of the traditional join operation on a single-processor and multiprocessor machines [8, 20, 22]. In this study, we investigate the benefit of using the bit-vector to speed up the execution of the transitive closure algorithms.

In our performance analysis, we assume that the relation A is binary. A real data relation may not be binary, but for most transitive closure queries, only two attributes are involved in the iterative processing. Therefore, it is beneficial to project the relation on these two attributes first, and then process this much smaller binary relation iteratively.

In constructing our models, we have used two sets of parameters, the relation-related and the hardware-related, both of which are presented in Table 5. The relation-related parameters characterize the base relation A, the hardware-related parameters characterize the hardware resources available to the processing of the algorithms. Table 5 also presents some typical values for the parameters assumed in our study, where we use R and ΔR to represent *CLOSURE* and *WAVE*, respectively. We assume that ΔR fits in the main memory, and R is stored in the structure of B-tree or hash table according to its corresponding implementation.

Parameter	Definition	Typical Value(s)
A_{size}	the cardinality of A	1000–10000
W_{tuple}	the size of a tuple in bytes	40
W_{driver}	the size of a driver in bytes	20
DR	initial driver ratio	var
BF	average branching factor	var (1.61)
DF	average duplication factor	≈ 0
OVF	average overlapping factor	var (0.068)
$P_{deaddriver}$	probability of a driver generates nothing	var (0.39)
P_{max}	average maximum length of recursion	10
P_A	number of pages in memory allocated to A	var
P_R	number of pages allocated to R	var
$P_{\Delta R}$	number of pages allocated to ΔR	var
P_{size}	page size in bytes	1000
T_{comp}	time to compare two drivers in memory	3 µs
T_{move}	time to move a tuple in memory	20 µs
T_{hash}	time to compute a hashing function	9 µs
T_{io}	time to perform a random page I/O	15 ms

Table 5. Parameters

In Table 5, the initial driver ratio, DR, is the number of distinct query constants (initial drivers) over the number of distinct values in the driver attribute in relation A. The average branching factor, BF, is the average number of tuples derived by one driver in one iteration. The average duplication factor, DF, is the average of the number of duplicates generated at one iteration over the total number of generated values at the same iteration. The average overlapping factor, OVF, is the average of the number of values generated at one iteration but already in $CLOSURE$ over the total number of values generated at the same iteration. Note in the table, *var* indicates that the corresponding parameter is a variable in our performance study, while *var(val)* indicates that in some test it is a var while in others val is assumed to be the typical value in the table.

4.1. The Analytical Models

Analytical models for the various implementations of the *wavefront* and the δ *wavefront* algorithms have been developed. The formulas developed to compute the performance measure for these algorithms are presented in Tables 6 to 8. The first two tables present the general formulas which compute *Time* for the *wavefront* and the δ-*wavefront* algorithms without using bit-vector filtering. Table 8, on the other hand, presents the same formulas when the bit-vector filter is used. In these formulas, R_j is the number of drivers in $CLOSURE$ after the j-th iteration, Gross ΔR_j is the number of tuples derived during the j-th iteration, and ΔR_j is the number of distinct and non-overlapped drivers generated during the j-th iteration. We use $|X|$ to indicate the number of pages occupied by relation X, and $\|X\|$ to indicate the cardinality of the relation X.

Generally speaking, *Time* for a given algorithm is the summation of the time spent at all the iterations (from 1 to P_{max}). The execution time of a given iteration can be decomposed into two components, namely, the time to compute the Quarter_Join operation (Quarter_Join_Time) and the time to compute the Union operation (Union_Time). The Quarter_Join_Time is calculated based on the size of the intermediate relation and the base relation A. The detailed calculations of the time for the Quarter_Join and the Union are based on the implementation techniques (B-Tree or Hashing) and are presented in Appendix A.

The major difference between the formulas in Tables 6 and 7 is that (i) in the wavefront algorithm, all the intermediate results ($Gross\,\Delta R_j$) are used in the next iteration, while in the δ-wavefront algorithm, only the non-overlapped portions of the intermediate results (ΔR) are used in the Quarter_Join, and (ii) the δ-wavefront algorithm implements a difference operation to remove the drivers in ΔR which is already in R.

Table 8 presents the formulas for the two algorithms with bit-vector filtering. When the bit-vector is available, a driver in an intermediate relation T may not have to access the base relation A to decide whether it can derive new results. Only those which survive the bit-vector testing should access the relation. Using an ideal filter, all the dead drivers in a given iteration can be detected and filtered out, and therefore, the number of the surviving drivers should be $T \times (1 - P_{deaddriver})$. However, in a real filter, some of the dead drivers go undetected. To accommodate this fact, we introduce a *Fudge* factor, F, $(F \leq 1)$, and the number of the surviving drivers becomes $T \times (1 - F \times P_{deaddriver})$.

Time_of_Wavefront_Algorithm =

$$\sum_{j=1}^{P_{max}} \text{Quarter\_Join\_Time}(\text{Gross } \Delta R_j, A) +$$
$$\text{Union\_Time}(\text{Gross } \Delta R_j, \Delta R_j, R_{j-1})$$

where

$$\| \text{Gross } \Delta R_1 \| = DR \times \| A \| \times (1 - P_{deaddriver}) \times BF$$

$$\| \text{Gross } \Delta R_j \| = \| \text{Gross } \Delta R_{j-1} \| \times (1 - DF) \times (1 - P_{deaddriver}) \times BF \quad (j > 1)$$

$$\| \Delta R_0 \| = DR \times \| A \|$$

$$\| \Delta R_j \| = \| \Delta R_{j-1} \| \times (1 - P_{deaddriver}) \times BF \times (1 - DF) \times (1 - OVF) \quad (j \geq 1)$$

$$\| R_0 \| = DR \times \| A \|$$

$$\| R_j \| = \sum_{i=0}^{j} \| \Delta R_i \|$$
$$= DR \times \| A \| \times (1 + \sum_{i=1}^{j} [(1 - P_{deaddriver}) \times BF (1 - DF) \times (1 - OVF)]^i)$$

Table 6. Execution Time for the Wavefront Algorithm
(Without the Bit-Vector Filtering)

Time_of_δ-Wavefront_Algorithm =

$$\sum_{j=1}^{P_{max}} \text{Quarter\_Join\_Time}(\Delta R_j, A) +$$
$$\text{Union\_Difference\_Time}(\text{Gross}\Delta R_j, \Delta R_j, R_{j-1})$$

where

$$\| \Delta R_0 \| = DR \times \| A \|$$

$$\| \text{Gross } \Delta R_j \| = \| \Delta R_{j-1} \| \times (1 - P_{deaddriver}) \times BF$$

$$\| \Delta R_j \| = \| \text{Gross } \Delta R_j \| \times (1 - DF) \times (1 - OVF)$$

$$\| R_j \| = \sum_{i=0}^{j} \| \Delta R_i \|$$

Table 7. Execution Time for the δ-Wavefront Algorithm
(Without Bit-Vector Filtering)

Time_of_Wavefront_Algorithm =

$$\sum_{j=1}^{P_{max}} \text{Quarter\_Join\_Time}(\text{Gross} \| \Delta R_j \| \times (1 - F \times P_{deaddriver}), A) +$$

$$\text{Union\_Time}(\text{Gross} \| \Delta R_j \| \times (1 - F \times P_{deaddriver}), \Delta R_j, R_{j-1})$$

Time_of_δ-Wavefront_Algorithm =

$$\sum_{j=1}^{P_{max}} \text{Quarter\_Join\_Time}(\| \Delta R_j \| \times (1 - F \times P_{deaddriver}), A) +$$

$$(\text{Union\_Difference\_Time}(\text{Gross} \| \Delta R_j \| \times (1 - F \times P_{deaddriver}), R_{j-1}))$$

Table 8. Execution Time for the the Wavefront_Algorithm and
the δ-Wavefront_Algorithm (With Bit-Vector Filtering)

4.2. The Simulation Model

The performance of the three algorithms has also been evaluated by means of simulation. Our simulator consists of two parts, a synthetic database generator and an algorithm simulator. The synthetic database generator generates synthetic tuples for a binary base relation A. The two attributes of the relation are defined on a common domain of arbitrary size. The values in a tuple are drawn in random from the common domain, which is simulated using a random number generator with range equal to the size of the common domain. The algorithm simulator takes the generated relation and simulates the various implementations of the transitive closure algorithms.

For the *hash-based* implementations, tuples are stored in a hash table using a simple hash function "driver *mod* number_of_entries" and a simple overflow chaining method to handle collision. The number_of_entries of the hash table is equal to P_A. The *CLO-SURE* relation is handled similarly.

For the *B-tree based* implementations, tuples in the base relation are sorted based on the driver attribute and structured as a B+ tree, and the *CLOSURE* relation is structured as a B-tree.

The *bit vector filtering mechanism* [3] is implemented by allocating a bit vector of size equal to the number of tuples in the relation multiplied by some integer constant. A hash function is used to set the bits in the bit-vector according to the values in the driver attribute of the base relation A. Whenever a value is generated, it is hashed to the bit-vector and discarded if the corresponding bit is not set.

4.3. The Analysis of the Performance Results

In our simulation study, we have experimented with a base relation of 1000 tuples. The values of the tuples are uniformly distributed in the range of 1 to 1000. The statistics collected from the simulator shows that the average branching factor in the generated relation is 1.61, and $P_{deaddriver}$ is 0.39. We randomly select 10 initial drivers, and based on these initial drivers, the average P_{max} is 10, OVF is 0.068, and DF is almost 0. In our analytical study, we have used these statistics as a pivot settings for our experimentation with the analytical models.

Figures 6 — 11 present some of the results of our experimentation with the analytical models, whereas Figures 12 and 13 present those of the simulation models. These figures plot the total execution time of the modeled implementations verses some important parameters.

The results of analytical modeling show that some important facts which are consistent throughout all the experiments: (i) *the δ-wavefront algorithm* performs consistently better than *the wavefront algorithm*; (ii) the hash-based implementation performs better than the B+ tree-based implementation; and (iii) when the bit-vector filter is used, the execution time of all of the algorithms decrease dramatically.

Figure 6 shows the effect of the overlapping factor on the total execution time. When the overlapping factor increases, the relative performance of the δ-wavefront dramatically increases over that of the wavefront. Figure 7 shows that the total execution time of all the algorithms increases exponentially when the branching factor increases. Therefore, it is important to control the branching factor. Figure 8 shows that the effect of increasing the percentages of pages of the base relation in memory will dramatically decrease the total execution time. We can observe a saturation point in the hash based implementation, e.g., 0.7 in Figure 8, beyond which the total execution time changes very little. Such a saturation point occurs when all the pages which store the hash table can be buffered in the main memory. It also indicates that hash-based implementation has lower memory requirement than the B-tree-based implementation. Figure 9 shows that for a fixed branching factor the total execution time increases linearly when the initial driver ratio increases. Figures 10 and 11 are similar to Figures 8 and 9 except the size of the relation is 10000 rather than 1000. They simply confirm the results presented in the case of smaller relations.

The results of the simulation test (Figure 12 and Figure 13) support our analytical modeling. Moreover, it shows that *the level-relaxed δ-wavefront algorithm* performs slightly better than its non-level-relaxed version in all the cases. We believe that the reason that the level-relaxed version does not show much improvement is because that it was tested against a uniformly distributed database. From our discussion in Section 3, we can see that the level-relaxed processing benefits more when data in a database are clustered rather than uniformly distributed. We believe that it is necessary to test the level-relaxed versions on differently clustered databases later.

The performance testing validates the important heuristics discussed in the previous section: *performing selection first, using intermediate processing results (as the new drivers), excluding processed drivers from re-processing,* and *exploring accessible drivers at different iterations.* Moreover, it shows that some implementation technique may further improve the performance, such as hashing and bit-vector based filtering. Those results are consistent with most of the previous studies on join techniques for non-recursive queries [8, 20, 22].

5. Conclusions

We have studied the efficient processing and evaluation of transitive closure database queries. A large class of recursive clusters can be compiled into formulas which require transitive closure operations. To efficiently process a transitive closure operation, we have studied three algorithms, *the wavefront, the δ-wavefront*, and *the level-relaxed δ-wavefront algorithms*. Analytical and simulation models have been developed for the different implementations of these algorithms. Our performance study shows that the δ-wavefront algorithm performs consistently better than the wavefront algorithm, and furthermore, the hash-based implementation of the δ-wavefront algorithm augmented with a bit-vector filter attains a considerable improvement over other implementations.

The philosophy of the *δ-wavefront* and *the level-relaxed δ-wavefront algorithms* is to eliminate redundant processing at the lowest possible level to reduce the cost of database accessing. Similar ideas have been explored for more complex linear and nonlinear recursions in [11] and more performance study should be done on those proposed algorithms.

Acknowledgements

The work was supported by the U.S. National Science Foundation under Grant DCR-860-8311 and by the Simon Fraser University under the President's Research Grant and the Research Grant of Centre for System Science. The authors would like to express our thanks to Larry Henschen for his helpful discussions and to the anonymous reviewers for their helpful comments on the paper.

References References

1. R. Agrawal and H. Jagadish, Direct Algorithms for Computing the Transitive Closure of Database Relations, *Proceedings of the 13th International Conference on Very Large Data Bases*, Brighton, England, Sept. 1987.

2. A. Aho and J. D. Ullman, Universality of Data Retrieval Languages, *Proceedings of the 6th ACM Symposium on Programming Languages*, San Antonio, Texas, Jan. 1979.

3. E. Babb, Implementation of Relational Database by Means of Specialized Hardware, *ACM Transactions on Database Systems 6(2)*, , 1979.

4. F. Bancilhon, Naive Evaluation of Recursively Defined Relations, *On Knowledge Base Management Systems (M. Brodie and J. Mylopoulos eds.), Springer-Verlag*, , 1986.

5. F. Bancilhon, D. Maier, Y. Sagiv and J. D. Ullman, Magic Sets and Other Strange Ways to Implement Logic Programs, *Proceedings of 5th ACM Symposium on Principles of Database Systems*, Cambridge, MA, 1986.

6. F. Bancilhon and R. Ramakrishnan, An Amateur's Introduction to Recursive Query Processing Strategies, *Proceedings of 1986 ACM-SIGMOD Conference on Management of Data*, Washington, DC, May 1986.

7. D. J. DeWitt, et. al., Implementation Techniques for Main Memory Database Systems, *Proceedings of 1984 ACM-SIGMOD Conference on Management of Data*, , June 1984.

8. J. R. Goodman, An Investigation of Multiprocessor Structures and Algorithms for Database Management, *Mem No. UCB/ERLM81, University of California-Berkeley*, , May 1981 .

9. J. Han, Pattern-Based and Knowledge-Directed Query Compilation in Recursive Data Bases, *Computer Science Department Technical Report No. 629 (Ph.D. Dissertation)*, University of Wisconsin at Madison, Dec. 1985.

10. J. Han and L. J. Henschen, Compiling and Processing Transitive Closure Queries in Relational Database Systems, *EECS Tech. Rep. 86-06-DBM-02*, Northwestern University, 1986, submitted for publication.

11. J. Han and L. J. Henschen, Handling Redundancy in the Processing of Recursive Database Queries, *Proceedings of the 1987 ACM-SIGMOD Conference on Management of Data*, San Fransisco, CA, May 1987.

12. J. Han, Multi-Chain Recursion and Its Query Processing Methods, *submitted for publication*, , 1987.

13. J. Han, Compiling Single-Chain Recursion by Variable Connection Graph Analysis, *submitted for publication*, , 1987.

14. L. J. Henschen and S. Naqvi, On Compiling Queries in Recursive First-Order Databases, *J. ACM 31(1)*, , 1984.

15. Y. E. Ioannidis, A Time Bound on the Materialization of Some Recursively Defined Views, *Proceedings of the 11th International Conference on Very Large Data Bases*, Stockholm, Sweden, Aug. 1985.

16. R. Kowalski, *Logic for Problem Solving*, American Elsevier, 1979.

17. H. Lu, K. Mikkilineni and J. Richardson, Design and Evaluation of Algorithms to Compute the Transitive Closure of a Database Relation, *Proceedings of 1987 Data Engineering Conference*, Los Angeles, CA, Feb. 1987.

18. J. F. Naughton, Data Independent Recursion in Deductive Databases, *Proceedings of 5th ACM Symposium on Principles of Database Systems*, Cambridge, MA, 1986.

19. J. F. Naughton, One-Sided Recursion, *Proceedings of 6th ACM Symposium on Principles of Database Systems*, San Diego, CA, 1987.

20. G. Z. Qadah, The Join Operation on a Multiprocessor Database Machine: Algorithms and the Evaluation of their Performance, *Proceedings of 4th International Workshop on Database Machines*, , 1985.

21. J. D. Ullman, Implementation of Logical Query Languages for Databases, *ACM Transactions on Database Systems 10(3)*, , 1985.

22. P. Valduriez and G. Gardarin, Join and Semijoin Algorithms for a Multiprocessor Database Machine, *ACM Transactions on Database Systems 9(1)*, , 1984.

23. P. Valduriez and H. Boral, Evaluation of Recursive Queries Using Join Indices, *Proceedings of the 1st International Conference on Expert Database Systems*, Charleston, SC, April 1986.

Appendix A

More Formulas for the Computation of the Execution Time

We present more formulas for the computation of execution time of the operations in Section 4.1 based on two implementation techniques, $B+$ *tree* and *hashing*. These formulas include the Union_Time, the Union_Difference_Time and the Quarter_Join_Time.

1. The Hash-Based Model

Union_Time(Gross ΔR , ΔR , R) = T(Gross ΔR , ΔR , R, C) when C = 1.

Union_Difference_Time(Gross ΔR , ΔR , R) = T(Gross ΔR , ΔR , R, C) when C = 2.

T(Gross ΔR , ΔR , R, C) =
(1) $\|Gross\,\Delta R\| \times (T_{hash} + \|R\| / P_R \times T_{comp})$
(2) $+ C \times \|\Delta R\| \times T_{move})$
(3) $+ (\max(|R| - P_R, 0) / P_R) \times Expect(P_R, \|Gross\,\Delta R\|) \times T_{io}$

Table A.1. The Union_Time and the Union_Difference_Time of the Hash-Based Model

Table A.1 computes the Union_Time and the Union_Difference_Time of the hash-based model which is the accumulation of (1) the time to hash each driver to a specific bucket in the hash table and search for a match in the bucket, (2) the time to move tuples to R and/or ΔR , and (3) the time to fetch referenced pages of R that are not in memory. $Expect(M, N) = N \times (1 - e^{-M/N})$ is the expected number of entries of the hash table of size M examined by the number of tuples, N.

Quarter_Join_Time(ΔR , A) =
(1) $T_{hash} \times \|\Delta R\|$
(2) $+ Expect(A_{datapage}, \|\Delta R\|) \times (1 - P_A / A_{datapage}) \times T_{io}$
(3) $+ T_{comp} \times (\Delta R \times .5 \times P_{size} / P_{tuple})$
(4) $+ T_{move} \times BF \times (1 - P_{deaddriver}) \times \|\Delta R\|$

Table A.2. Quarter_Join_Time of Hash-Based Data Model

Table A.2 computes the Quarter_Join_Time of the hash-based model which is the summation of (1) the time to hash each driver into a bucket in the hash table of relation A , (2) the time to fetch the referenced pages that are not in memory, (3) the time for each driver to search one pages of tuples, and (4) the time to move the results to ΔR .

2. The B+ Tree Model

To computer the various parameters of the *B+ tree*, we have adopted the model present in [7]. Table A.3 presents equations to compute some of the basic parameters for such model.

F_{fanout}	$0.69 \times P_{size}/(W_{driver} + 4)$
$A_{datapage}$	$A_{size} \times Wtuple /0.69 \times P_{size}$
$A_{totalpage}$	$A_{datapage} \times F_{fanout}/(F_{fanout} - 1)$
$A_{indexpage}$	$A_{totalpage} - A_{datapage}$
$A_{iotimecoef}$	$T_{io} \times (1 - (P_A - A_{indexpage})/ A_{datapage})$
$A_{searchtimecoef}$	$T_{comp} \times \log_2(F_{fanout}) \times \log_{F_{fanout}} A_{datapage}$

Table A.3. Parameters of the B+ Tree Model

F_{fanout} means number of drivers in one index page. $A_{datapage}$ is the number of leaf pages which contain the tuples of relation A. $A_{indexpage}$ is the number of pages of the intermediate nodes in the B+ tree (assumed to be in the main memory). $A_{iotimecoef}$ is the expected time to reference a page. $A_{searchtimecoef}$ is the time to find the leaf page referenced by a driver.

Union_Time(Gross ΔR , ΔR , R) = T(Gross ΔR , ΔR , R, C) when C = 1.

Union_Difference_Time(Gross ΔR , ΔR , R) = T(Gross ΔR , ΔR , R, C) when C = 2.

T(Gross ΔR , ΔR , R, C) =
(1) $\| Gross\Delta R \| \times T_{comp} \times \log_2 \|R\|$
(2) $+ C \times \| \Delta R \| \times T_{move}$
(3) $+ \max(| R | - P_R, 0)/| R | \times \text{Expect}(| R | , \| Gross \Delta R \|) \times \log_{F_{fanout}} | R | \times T_{io}$

Table A.4. The Union_Time and the Union_Difference_Time of the B+-Tree-Based Model

Table A.4. computes the Union or the Union_Difference_Time for the B+ tree model which is the summation of (1) the time to check whether each newly derived result is in R, (2) the time to move each newly derived value into R (and ΔR for the δ-wavefront algorithm), and (3) the time to fetch all the pages in R which are not in the main memory.

Quarter_join_Time(ΔR, A) =
(1) $+ A_{searchtimecoef} \times \|\Delta R\|$
(2) $+ \text{Expect}(A_{datapage}, \|\Delta R\|) \times A_{iotimecoef}$
(3) $+ T_{comp} \times \|\Delta R\| \times .5 \times P_{size} \times P_{tuple}$
(4) $+ T_{move} \times BF \times (1 - P_{deaddriver}) \times \|\Delta R\|$

Table A.5. Quarter_Join_Time of B+ Tree

Finally, Table A.5 computes the Quarter_Join_Time of the B+ tree model which is the summation of (1) the time for each driver to search the B+ tree, (2) the time to fetch the reference data pages that are not in the main memory, (3) the time for each driver to search inside a referenced page, and (4) the time to move the results to ΔR. When the B+ tree based implementation is augmented with a bit-vector filter, expression (4) should be modified to $T_{move} \times BF \times \|\Delta R\|$. This is also true when computing the Quarter_Join_Time for the hash-based implementation.

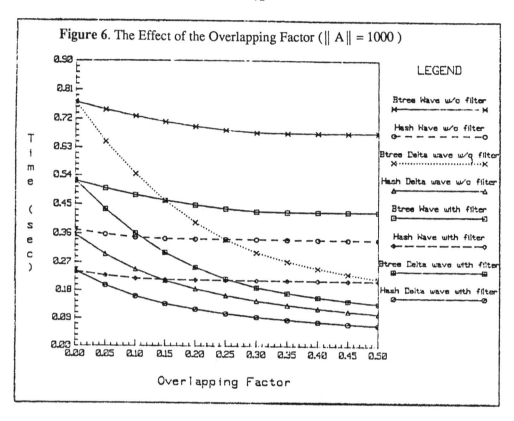

Figure 6. The Effect of the Overlapping Factor (‖ A ‖ = 1000)

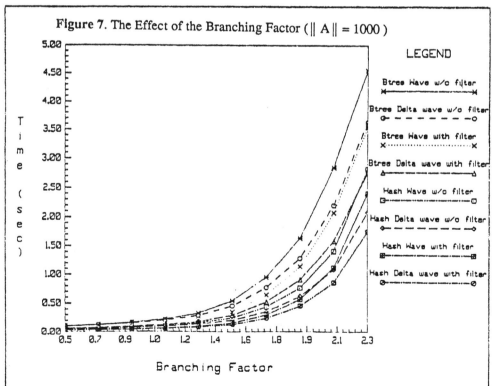

Figure 7. The Effect of the Branching Factor (‖ A ‖ = 1000)

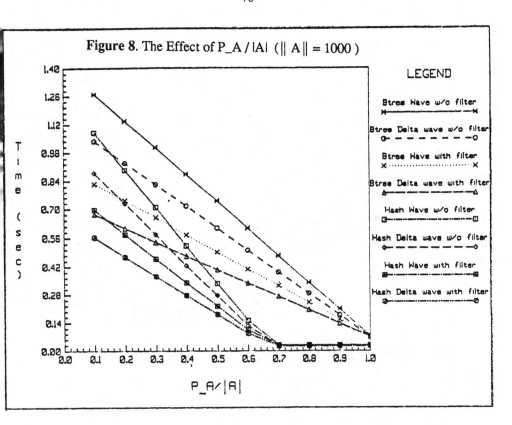

Figure 8. The Effect of P_A / |A| (‖ A ‖ = 1000)

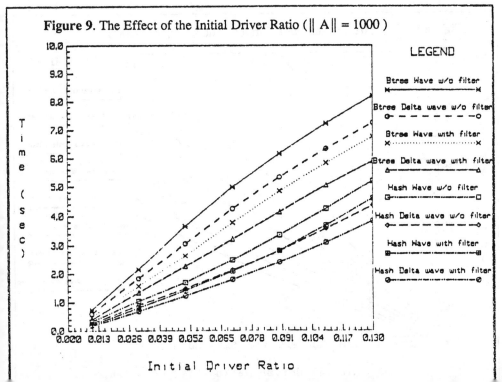

Figure 9. The Effect of the Initial Driver Ratio (‖ A ‖ = 1000)

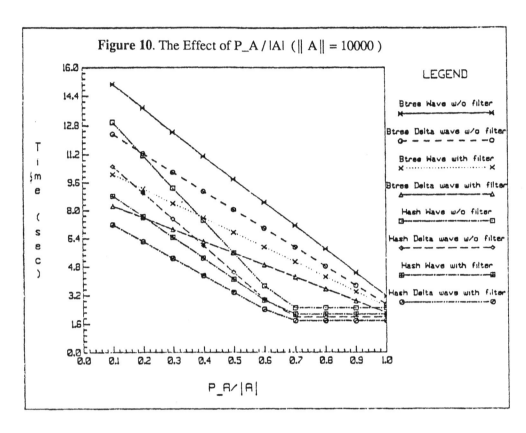

Figure 10. The Effect of P_A / |A| (‖ A ‖ = 10000)

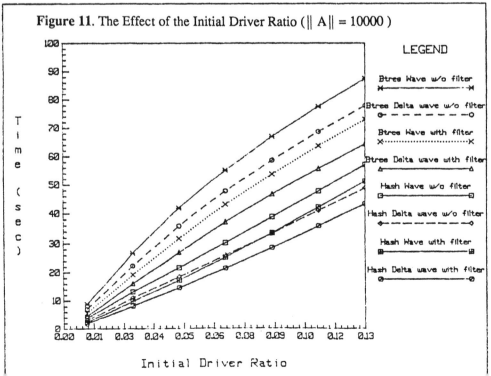

Figure 11. The Effect of the Initial Driver Ratio (‖ A ‖ = 10000)

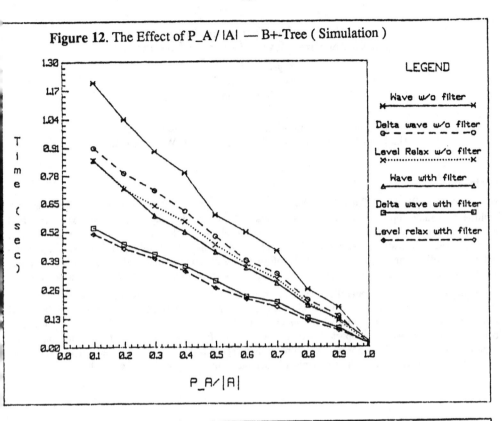

Figure 12. The Effect of P_A / |A| — B+-Tree (Simulation)

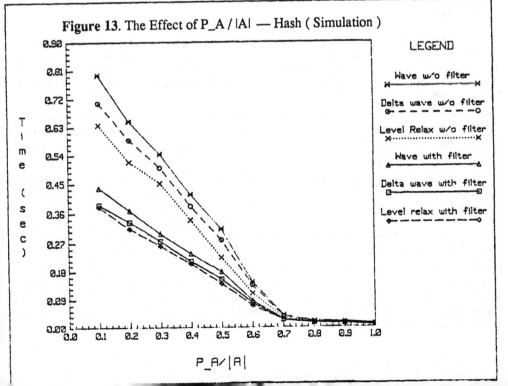

Figure 13. The Effect of P_A / |A| — Hash (Simulation)

Supporting Semantic Rules
by a Generalized Event/Trigger Mechanism

Angelika M. Kotz
Klaus R. Dittrich
Jutta A. Mülle

Forschungszentrum Informatik an der Universität Karlsruhe
Haid-und-Neu-Str. 10 -14, D-7500 Karlsruhe 1, West Germany

Abstract

Non-standard applications like CAD/CAM, image processing and AI require database systems with facilities to handle sophisticated semantics. Advanced data models supporting complexly structured objects, abstract data types and the like have been developed to this end. However, any data model remains necessarily restricted to rather static and global semantics, not taking into account individual and dynamically changing issues. It is therefore necessary to formulate additional semantic rules, which may be rather complex and pose a variety of checking as well as enforcement requirements.

In this paper we present a generalized event/trigger concept as a basic support mechanism for semantic rules, which allows for flexible checking times and arbitrary actions in case of rule violation. If necessary, the user is able to control the supervision of semantic rules dynamically. Several levels of local and global rules are supported, existing algorithms for rule checking/enforcement can be integrated, and specific rules governing complex engineering processes (so-called action plans) can be dealt with. The usefulness of the mechanism is demonstrated by a number of examples.

1. Motivation

Recent efforts in database technology have focused on better supporting advanced application areas like computer-aided design and manufacturing, artificial intelligence, geography, image processing etc. A considerable number of new database management systems (DBMS) and extensions to existing ones have been and are currently being developed trying to provide concepts that are of specific usefulness for these areas.

One of the foremost issues is to cover application semantics in sufficient detail which allows the DBMS to enforce consistency in a broader sense, relieves users and application programs (i.e. software tools in advanced integrated environments) from repeatedly caring themselves for this task, and can even lead towards better performance of the overall system.

The data model of a DBMS is traditionally the prime framework to represent application semantics, and certainly the object-oriented approaches that are currently en vogue ([DD86], [Zdo85]) are much more powerful in this respect than e.g. the pure relational model. However, by its very nature, any data model is restricted to capture those structural and operational semantics that are rather global and static in the sense that they e.g. pertain to all instances of a type, apply uniformly over a longer period of time, and similar.

Further semantics are conveniently expressed as consistency and derivation rules which we shall collectively call *semantic rules*. As will be shown in the next section, these rules have to be conceived in a very broad sense in engineering applications. They are rather complex and pose a variety of checking and enforcement requirements. Nevertheless, for the reasons stated above, as many of these rules as possible should be represented within and exploited by the DBMS.

Section 3 summarizes what mechanisms have been proposed to date to deal with semantic rules in database systems. Based on the shortcomings detected, we propose a general basic framework called *event/trigger mechanism (ETM)* in section 4 and demonstrate its usefulness by a number of examples in section 5. Finally, section 6 gives some ideas on how we implemented the ETM.

2. Semantic rules in engineering applications

When regarding sematic rules in the broad sense as required for engineering applications, various issues have to be considered:

- Semantic rules relate to the typical objects appearing in engineering applications as well as to the way these objects are dealt with. These objects are *structured in a highly complex way* and take part in arbitrary relationships. The semantic rules applicable to these objects are equally complex and a large number of them exists. One rule may involve numerous objects from many different types. Think of design data for instance. These data have to satisfy technological constraints, physical laws, national or international standards, customers' requirements etc. A composite object has to be built from many subobjects in a controlled manner. Specification or interface have to be in accordance with their appropriate implementation.

- There are semantic rules that may be deliberately violated over long periods of time. *Global consistency* of data is reached stepwise along different stages of *local consistency*. In these intermediate stages, some part of the database is semantically correct while other data are inconsistent or even still missing. Long-term inconsistencies on different levels must be tolerable without loosing the semantic correctness already existing in an uncontrolled way.

- The point in time when consistency has to be assured cannot be fixed once and for all. Very often it is the application program or the user himself who has to decide whether the point has been reached. Attaching consistency checking invariably to the end of a transaction is by far not sufficient here.

- *Reactions in case of violation* of semantic rules have to be *flexible and under outside control*, too. In traditional DBMS transactions are just backed out when inconsistency is detected at their end. This cannot be accepted in applications where typical transactions may last for hours or even days and involve a lot of work on large data volumes. Therefore, other ways of reaction must be provided for. Just notifying the user will be one possible way to deal with the situation, eventually giving him some additional help and explanations where and why data are inconsistent. Another possible way is to repair inconsistency by deriving dependent data automatically, thereby guaranteeing semantic rules by construction. In this case the rules are used as derivation rather then consistency rules. Arbitrary definitions of data dependencies and the corresponding actions (generally in a high-level language including database operations) are needed for this purpose.

- Many semantic rules are not handled explicitly − i.e. in a declarative manner − but are *embodied algorithmically in checking and derivation programs*. These programs have to be executed at certain times to ensure the semantic correctness for subsequent work. Think for instance of simulation programs, design rule checkers in electronic circuit design or the calculation of statics for a new building. Though hidden within programs, those semantic rules should not remain unknown to the database system. While the DBMS in these cases is not explicitly aware of their contents, it can still enforce their execution and ensure correct reactions depending on the results.

- A special semantic problem with technical DBMS applications, especially in CAD, is that there are *predefined action plans*, specifying which action (or program) should be executed at which stage. There may be action sequencing, conditional execution or iteration in this plan. Enforcing a well-defined action plan is one way to the stepwise provision of global semantic correctness. Note that the action plan comprises checking actions as well as actions 'doing the real work'.

● New DBMS applications prove to be rather *dynamic areas*. The set of semantic rules to be managed changes by far more frequently than in traditional applications. It varies according to technology, the development of new tools, management decisions, design procedures used in specific projects and design teams, and the personal habits of individual designers.

From the requirements explained above, we sum up the following features of semantic rules in non-standard database applications:

1. Large number of complex rules.
2. Several levels of local and global rules.
3. Checking and/or enforcing rules at arbitrary points in time, often under external control.
4. Arbitrary reactions in case of rule violation.
5. Declarative and algorithmical rule definition.
6. Integration of existing programs and action plans.
7. Dynamic definition of rules.

We will now briefly review which present-day mechanisms are around that meet these requirements. *Note that we are not dealing with questions of how to formulate consistency rules, which inference mechanisms to use for derivation rules etc. However, our concern are flexible underlying control mechanisms to support semantic rules in database systems.*

3. Existing mechanisms

Current DBMS use *transactions* not only as the units of atomicity, isolation, and persistency, but also as the units of consistency. Every transaction has to guarantee invariably the whole set of consistency rules, otherwise it is rolled back. Even if more elaborate mechanisms to define consistency rules were offered, the rigidness is in contrast to requirements 2, 3, and 4 above.

There are various proposals to extend the transaction concept to capture more semantics, like nested transactions for consistency checking [EL82], individual pre- and postconditions for transactions [KE83] or transactions working according to a directed dependency graph [Neu83]. However, such extensions are able to support requirement 2 only. Furthermore, they tend to overload the transaction concept. Rather complex transaction structures are necessary which are difficult to apply and understand. Furthermore, it is not possible to adapt to new semantic rules once a transaction has been programmed.

To conclude, while the traditional way of consistency checking at the end of transactions remains *one possibility* to assure data semantics, it is by far not sufficient.

The main idea of incorporating *active elements* is to have the DBMS administer not only the static data structures, but also arbitrary actions on and behaviour of them. A rather general mechanism to manage actions has been proposed for POSTGRES [Sto86]: arbitrary procedures may be 'registered' as database objects and stored for later execution. These procedures can be applied for many different purposes like user commands, database procedures etc. More specific approaches to combine static and dynamic database capabilities are presented by Melkanoff and Chen. Actions are represented in terms of virtual relations [MC83] or in a more formal way by rule-based method and task descriptions [Che86]. Thus deductive queries, behavioral simulations, explicit representation of control knowledge and integrity control are supported.

Derived data are a means of ensuring semantic correctness automatically. These data are calculated from others by some sort of functional dependency. A simple form of derived data is already found in the CODASYL data model (data fields with IS RESULT clause). An example for a more advanced way to derive complex functionally defined data can be found in CACTIS [HK86]. In the 'active semantics' concept of CACTIS, objects are assigned a behavioral specification according to which they react actively to changes in other parts of the database. The most far-reaching concept of deriving data is realized by deductive database systems, where data can be derived from the extensionally defined 'facts' by applying additional knowledge (rules). This guarantees semantic rules by construction. In the case of derived data as well as in the approaches to integrate static and dynamic capabilities as were mentioned above, there is no way to deviate from semantic rules and react flexibly or in a local context, and thus requirements 2, 3, 4 are not met.

A special concept to integrate 're'actions into the DBMS are *triggers*. Compared to mere actions, a reaction also comprises the reason why or the information when it takes place. Trigger concepts in DBMS allow for DB-operations that — conditionally or unconditionally — succeed other DB-operations. In [Esw76] a trigger is defined as a block consisting of a condition and a body, with the meaning that the body is executed whenever the condition arises. So the trigger associates an action with the cause of its execution. Note the similarities to exception handling in programming languages. The trigger body may comprise program control structures as well as DB-operations (at least in theory, though in rarely any real system). Furthermore, triggers can be dynamically defined during runtime. Building upon Eswaran's general idea, several special trigger mechanisms have been developed for DBMS (e.g. for System R [Cha76] and POSTGRES [Sto86a]). [RR82] introduces a methodology for information systems design including dynamic aspects whose terminology (but not its contents) is similar to our approach. For all existing trigger concepts, however, the set of triggering conditions is limited to

- the begin or end of a DB-operation and/or
- the occurence of a certain DB state or state transition,

and thus requirement 3 is severely violated. Furthermore, checking algorithms for semantic rules have not been integrated into the trigger concept so far.

To sum up, the concepts of active elements in DBMS are useful for enhancing the database by application-specific knowledge. Triggers are particularly suitable to define flexible reactions which can be used to insure semantic correctness. However, neither of the concepts existing so far can cope with all the requirements stated above. This is why we extended and generalized existing trigger concepts to the so-called *event/trigger-mechanism (ETM)*. In the ETM, actions can be defined and associated with arbitrary events. Especially, the events do not have to correspond to any predefined state in the database.

Note that the ETM will *not* replace transactions, but will coexist with them. Transactions (possibly in an extended form like nested transactions) are still necessary for concurrency control and some basic sort of recovery. The ETM does, however, allow to go beyond the tight coupling of consistency enforcement to transactions.

4. The event/trigger-mechanism

We will now present the ETM starting with its basic features and operations, and then discuss related issues as nested triggers, recovery, synchronization etc. Subsequently we will explain how the ETM is used in the context of database systems.

4.1 Basic features

The ETM is based on three components

- events
- actions
- triggers

Every event, action, and trigger can be individually and dynamically defined, with semantics as described in the sequel.

An *event* is an indicator to signal that a specific situation has been reached to which reactions may be necessary. The kind of situation to be indicated is not limited in any way. However, the event itself does not carry any information about that, but is just described by a unique identifier. The identifier of an event (actually of an event type) represents a class of situations that are equivalent with respect to subsequent reactions. The declaration of an event type is done by giving the event identifier $<E\_id>$ and eventually some formal parameters $<fep_i>$ to pass context information from event to action.

```
event <E_id> (<fep₁>: <fep_type₁>, . . ., <fepₐ>: <fep_typeₐ>);
```

An event type can be instantiated an arbitrary number of times by 'raising the event'. This is done by calling the operation

```
raise <E_id> (aep₁, . . ., aepₐ);
```

with actual parameters aep_i. Note that there are only input parameters.

An *action* is an arbitrary program module to be executed. It may be defined in some high-level language including database operations. An action is declared by giving its unique identifier $<A\_id>$, the formal parameters $<fap_i>$ and the action body

```
action <A_id> (<fap₁>: <fap_type₁>, . . ., <fapₐ>: <fap_typeₐ>)
             = <action_body>
```

Actions may be executed explicitly by calling

```
exec <A_id> (aap₁, . . ., aapₐ);
```

but are mainly thought for triggered execution. A *trigger* serves to associate an event with an action. It is a pair

$$T = (E, A)$$

with the meaning that raising of event E implies the execution of action A (graphically depicted as in fig.1).

Fig.1: Graphial representation of T = (E, A)

Triggers are defined by

```
trigger <T_id> = on <E_id>
                    do <action> (tap₁, . . ., tapₐ)
with
tapᵢ ∈ {expr (fepⱼ: fepⱼ formal parameters of event <E_id>)}
```

$<E\_id>$ has to identify an event that has already been declared. $<action>$ can be either the identifier of a predefined action or an action body specified right in place. The actual parameters of the action are calculated from the actual event parameters according to the expressions tap_i, every time the event is raised.

Triggers may be activated and deactivated dynamically by

```
activate <T_id>;
deactivate <T_id>;
```

If deactivated, a trigger does not cause any reaction when the corresponding event is raised. After definition, a trigger has to be activated explicitly.

Of course, there are operators to delete each of the three constructs:

```
delete_event    <E_id>;
delete_action   <A_id>;
delete_trigger  <T_id>;
```

The basic mechanism described so far is an easy to use, yet powerful instrument for defining all sorts of execution flows where a dynamic coupling of situations and activities is desired. Events may be raised with arbitrary (even without any) actions associated to them. On the other hand the predefined actions can be executed in reaction to any event. By activating and deactivating triggers, reactions can be switched on and off deliberately.

4.2 Related issues

There may be an arbitrary number of actions triggered by the same event (*multiple trigger definition*) to allow for the easy modification and extension of the set of reactions to a situation class independent of each other. The sequencing of actions that has to be done in this case is handled by a priority scheme, i.e. an action priority is specified with the trigger definition.

A triggered action may itself raise events to initiate further actions. In this case we talk about *nested triggers*. They are especially useful for dealing with hierarchical and even recursive data structures which are rather frequent in non-standard applications. The problem with nested triggers is how to handle termination. We propose straightforward runtime methods like timeout, combined with action analysis to detect cycles (reject unconditional cycles at definition time, supervise conditional cycles at runtime) where applicable.

For *synchronization and recovery* purposes, triggered actions are handled by mechanisms similar to nested transactions. Each action may be backed out separately, raising a special event that indicates the abort situation. For this event, appropriate reactions can be defined by just another trigger. Synchronous as well as asynchronous execution of triggered actions is possible, the latter being useful in order to make use of parallel hardware resources.

4.3 The ETM in the context of database systems

As seen so far, the ETM provides an interface to define and to delete events, actions and triggers as well as to raise events and to execute actions. When using the ETM as a component of a DBMS, there are two ways to exploit this interface:

- to make it available for users/application programs at the DBMS interface,
- to use it from within other DBMS components.

Often the user knows when a situation occurs in the working environment, so he wants to raise events explicitly. On the other hand, there are a number of standard situations within the DBMS where the corresponding event can be raised implicitly (i.e. by the DBMS programmer). Typical situations of this kind are the execution of a DML-operation, the checkin or checkout of an object and the like. The DBMS will use the ETM interface to predefine a set of so-called *standard events* for these cases.

In some cases, the user may wish to raise an event whenever a certain database state or state transition occurs. To this end, a language to define some sort of demons (for demons in AI compair e.g. PLANNAR [Hew71]) is provided, called the *event definition language (EDL)*. Note that we do not regard this as a task of the event/trigger mechanism itself but of an additional component in the DBMS that is put on top of the ETM-interface. The EDL depends on the data model and thus has to be developed individually for every database system. Internally the EDL will be mapped to actions triggered by standard events.

Similarly we provide for a language to define classical concistency constraints. Again this is not part of the ETM, but of an additional DBMS-component using the ETM operations. The *constraint definition language (CDL)* allows for the declarative as well as algorithmical definition of consistency rules. The checking routines generated from the constraint definitions may be triggered like any other action. At its end, every checking procedure raises an event indicating whether inconsistency has been stated or not, i.e.

```
event <constraint>.FAIL        or
event <constraint>.SUCCESS
```

Various flavors of EDLs and CDLs may be defined for the ETM, partially depending on the data model used in the DBMS in question.

Fig.2 shows the overall system architecture.

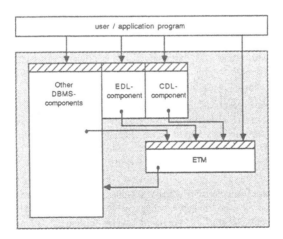

Fig.2: System architecture

5. Examples

In the sequel we will give evidence that the ETM is suited to the requirements stated above by discussing a number of examples. Note that by necessity our examples encorporate rather elaborate semantics that at least partially have to be expreesed by DBMS-dependent syntax. As we do not have the space to introduce all necessary environment details, we rely on an intuitive notation.

Example 1:

During the design process, objects are constructed by combining instances of lower-level objects (we assume that each object can be identified by its surrogate, the object_id). Each object will consist of an interface and an implementation part. There is a semantic rule stating that for a complete object both parts have to exist. During the design work, however, this rule does not have to hold. An object can be used in constructing other objects if its interface is defined, even if the implementation is still missing (fig.3).

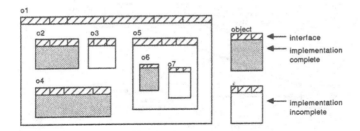

Fig.3: Objects using incomplete subobjects

This is a typical case where a semantic rule cannot be checked at the end of a number of transactions, but only when some specific operation (in this case the release-operation) takes place. In addition, the user may wish to have the rule checked explicitly from time to time to find out which implementation parts are still missing.

Using the ETM, these requirements can be fulfilled as follows:

```
EVENT release (release_object: object_id);
EVENT intermediate_checkpoint (object: object_id);
EVENT completeness.FAIL (incomplete_subobjects: list of object_id);
ACTION check_completeness (check_object: object_id) =
        BEGIN
        ok :=
        <∀ objects o₃ₐ where subobject(o₃ₐ, check_object)
         ∃ implementation(o₃ₐ)>
        IF not ok
        THEN RAISE completeness.FAIL (o₃ₐ where not ∃ implementation(o₃ₐ));
        END;
TRIGGER t_ro   = ON release
                 DO check_completeness (release_object);
TRIGGER t_icp  = ON intermediate_checkpoint
                 DO check_completeness (object);
TRIGGER t_cfail = ON completeness.FAIL
                 DO <list incomplete_subobjects>; <reject_release>;
```

The events used within the triggers t_ro and t_icp are raised as standard event within the release-operator (**RAISE release**) and by the user (**RAISE intermediate_checkpoint**) respectively. The binary predicate "subobject (o1, o2)" (object o1 is used within o2) which appears in the action **check_completeness** is assumed to be evaluatable within the data model used.

The implementation of subobjects may have been delegated to team colleagues. In this case, an additional action required on completeness.FAIL may be to inform the responsible persons that their implementations are still missing. On the other hand, changing the interface of an object should trigger messages to all persons currently using the object (change notification).

```
TRIGGER t_cfail1 = ON completeness.FAIL
                      DO <send messages to implementors of incomplete_subobjects>;
EVENT change_of_interface (changed_object: object_id);
TRIGGER t_int = ON change_of_interface
                   DO <send messages to implementors of all objects o where
                       subobject(changed_object, o)>;
```

The set of events, actions and events for example 1 is shown in fig.4.

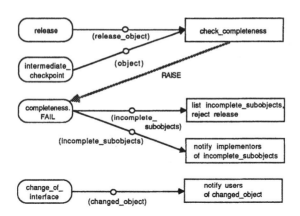

Fig.4: ETM-graph of example 1

The example shows that the ETM allows for the individual and independent definition of application specific situations and reactions to be taken when the situations occur. The application programs and/or the code of the DBMS-operations are not 'blown up' or subjected to frequent changes by integrating all the checks and succeeding activities.

Example 2:

Design objects often have a global structure like the one shown in fig.5. There are a number of representations which are input and/or output of different design steps. For each representation, there may be alternative developments (here called variants) each of which has in turn its design history (linear sequence of states). When a variant is 'released', its last state is frozen, i.e. the variant cannot be modified any more, unless it is explicitly thawed. When forming a configuration, one released variant is taken from every representation.

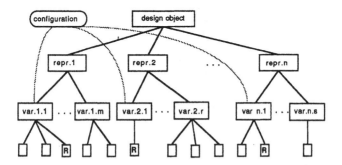

Fig.5: Global structure of a design object

Within this structure, there are several levels of local and global semantic rules. Within each representation, there are rules which have to be met locally. A special variant may add further rules with respect to performance data, space restrictions etc. These rules have to be checked at the latest when the variant is released (we do not consider here the rules that are checked immediately during each design step):

```
TRIGGER t_rrules_1 = ON release_repr_1
                     DO <check_repr_1_rules>;
TRIGGER t_vrules_1 = ON release_repr_1
                     DO <check_var_1_rules(var_no)>;
```

If inconsistency is detected with respect to one of the rules, the release operation is rejected or — if possible and meaningful — automatic derivation of dependent data is triggered.

```
TRIGGER t_rej_1 = ON check_repr_1_rules.FAIL
                  DO reject;
TRIGGER t_rep_2 = ON check_repr_2_rules.FAIL
                  DO <derivation_action>;
```

When a configuration is built, several global rules have to be checked. It has to be assured that exactly one variant is chosen from every representation, the variants must have been released and they have to match each other according to the inter-representation rules.

```
EVENT create_configuration(vaiant_list: var_list_type);
ACTION configuration_check(variant_list: var_list_type) =
       BEGIN
       ok1 :=
       <∀representations r ∃variant v(r):
           v(r) in variant_list and released(v(r))>;
       ok2 :=
       <check inter_representation_rules for corresponding variants>;
       IF not ok1 or not ok2
       THEN raise configuration_check.FAIL;
       END;
TRIGGER t_creconf = ON create_configuration(variant_list)
                    DO configuration_check(variant_list);
TRIGGER t_rejconf = ON configuration_check.FAIL
                    DO reject;
```

The overall ETM-structure of this example is sketched in fig.6.

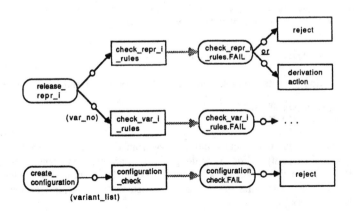

Fig.6: ETM-graph of example 2

Example 3:

The third example stems from the area of integrated circuit design. It shows the integration of existing (very complex) check programs as well as an action plan. The semantic rules are given in algorithmic form, hidden within verification and simulation programs. When developing a VLSI chip from a behavioral specification, the designer has to follow a certain design procedure like the one of fig.7. The action plan as well as the complex checking programs contained in it (system level simulation, RT-simulation etc.) can be handled by the ETM as follows.

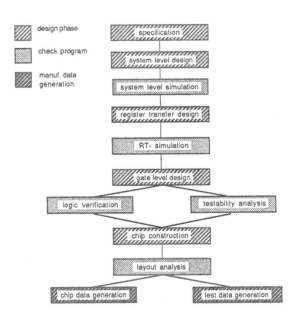

Fig.7: Design procedure in VLSI design

Each checking tool is defined as an action:

```
ACTION system_level_sim = <system level simulator>;
ACTION RT_sim          = <register transfer simulator>;
       .
       .
ACTION layout_analysis = <layout analyzer>;
```

At the end of these actions, events are raised, indicating the (boolean) result of the checking:

```
EVENT system_level_sim.SUCCESS
EVENT system_level_sim.FAIL        . . .
```

In the case of simulations, this may require interference from the human user to decide whether the result can be considered successful. For every design level, there are two events signalling the begin and the end of the work on this level. These events are raised from within the design tools or — in case a design level does not possess its specific tools — when the user declares explicitly to have entered or left a phase of work.

```
EVENT enter_specification;
EVENT leave_specification;
EVENT enter_system_level_design;
            .
EVENT leave_chip_construction;
EVENT enter_manufacturing;
```

At the end of each design level, the corresponding checking tool is triggered, i.e. executed automatically as soon as the event **leave_....** is raised:

```
TRIGGER t_sl = ON leave_system_level_design
               DO system_level_sim;
        .
        .
TRIGGER t_cc = ON leave_chip_construction
               DO layout_analysis;
```

To indicate the design step which is to be executed next, a state variable is used which may assume one of the following values:

```
state ∈ {system_level, RT_level, gate_level, layout_level, manufact_level}
```

When the specification is finished, the state is set to **system_level**. After each successful check, the state is upgraded to the succeeding level. To cope with multiple checks at the same level (e.g. logic verification and testability analysis at the gate level), the set of actions triggered by the same event is treated as a separate backout sphere. The state variable is locked until all the check actions have finished and the set of actions may be rolled back as is expressed by the action **reject_to_event**.

```
TRIGGER t_ls_state = ON leave_specification
                     DO state := system_level;
TRIGGER t_slssuc   = ON system_level_sim.SUCCESS
                     DO state := RT_level;
                .
                .
TRIGGER t_lvsuc    = ON logic_verification.SUCCESS
                     DO state := layout_level;
TRIGGER t_tasuc    = ON testability_analysis.SUCCESS
                     DO state := layout_level;
TRIGGER t_lvfail   = ON logic_verification.FAIL
                     DO reject_to_event;
TRIGGER t_tafail   = ON testability_analysis.FAIL
                     DO reject_to_event;
                .
TRIGGER t_lasuc    = ON layout_analysis.SUCCESS
                     DO state := manufact_level;
```

Entering a design step also triggers an action. This action reads the state and reacts accordingly if the state is lower or higher than the one needed:

```
TRIGGER t_esld = ON enter_system_level_design
                 DO IF state < system_level
                    THEN <bad design level, react accordingly>
                    ELSE IF state > system_level
                         THEN state := system_level;
```

The conventional solution without the ETM would be to update and read the state variable within the tools (programmed into the tool code). Thus, the design levels would not be made explicit by independent rule definitions, but hidden within each tool. If the design procedure changed, tool recompilation would be necessary. Another advantage of using the ETM is that the reactions to the events

enter_.... can easily be modified to enforce the sequence of design levels with varying degrees of rigidness (in case of bad design level prevent tool execution, just inform the user or similar).

The actions, events, and triggers presented above can be generated automatically from a structural description of any action plan with arbitrary levels and checking tools, with the additional advantage of having action plans explicitly represented in the database. Fig.8 shows the ETM-graph generated for an arbitrary design level i.

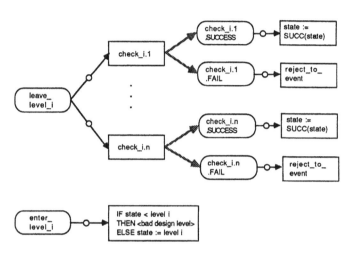

Fig.8: ETM-graph of design level i

Example 4:

We will now show how the traditional method of assuring consistency at the end of transactions can be described by the ETM as a special case. The checking of all consistency rules is triggered by a standard event that is raised whenever the end of a transaction is reached.

```
EVENT end_of_transaction;
TRIGGER t_rule_1 = ON end_of_transaction
                DO check_rule_1;
        .
        .
TRIGGER t_rule_n = ON end_of_transaction
                DO check_rule_n;
```

If the action **check_rule_i** detects an inconsistency, it raises the event **check_rule_i.FAIL**. In this case the transaction has to be rolled back, which is done by the predefined action **reject**.

```
TRIGGER t_rej_1 = ON check_rule_1.FAIL
                DO reject;
        .
        .
TRIGGER t_rej_n = ON check_rule_n.FAIL
                DO reject;
```

The ETM-graph for end_of_transaction is shown in fig.9. Note that the outside appearance of classical transactions need not be changed. If so desired for implementation purposes, the above ETM-operations can be generated automatically.

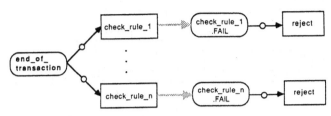

Fig.9: ETM-graph of example 4

3. Implementation

The ETM in its basic form has been implemented as part of DAMASCUS, a prototype DBMS for VLSI design currently operational at the Forschungszentrum Informatik at Karlsruhe [DKM85]. The system is built on top of the UNIX V operating system, using the UNIX concepts of process communication. The underlying hardware is a workstation environment.

In the implementation, runtime efficiency was given high priority as is generally necessary for advanced database applications that deal with huge data volumes. A central requirement was to cause only *minimal overhead for raising an event that does not have any action associated with it*. Thus the mechanism as such is very cheap with respect to runtime cost, only the actions really executed have to be paid for (which would be the case with *any* other mechanism providing the same service).

The data structures used for representing and accessing the ETM constructs make use of large (at least virtual) main memory capacities currently available for workstations. The ETM elements are accessed via hash tables kept in main memory during runtime. There are three hash tables for events (ET), actions (AT) and triggers (TT) respectively. Actions are compiled into an executable form and stored in the so-called action code pool, while the source code is kept in the action source pool. Fig.10 sketches the access structures (omitting details about the table entries). For all three tables, access is via the construct's ID. There are pointers between the different tables to speed up (de-)activation of triggers as well as deletion. The structure of the event table entries is tailored to the efficient management of events. In each event table entry, there is a list of the triggers currently associated with this event. This list is ordered by priority and contains direct pointers to the executable code of the actions to be triggered. The field ACTIV_IND is set to FALSE if there is no activated trigger associated with the event, thus no further searching has to be done.

To reduce the size of the main memory access tables, we are exploiting an additional scope concept which restricts the set of elements to be held at a time according to the local environment of the object currently being worked on, the person doing the work and the like. The scope concept is detailed in [Kot88].

When executed, the action is run in a child process communicating with the DBMS process. Presently, for portability reasons, we use UNIX pipes for process communication, though shared memory would be preferable for performance reasons. To further speed up execution, actions should also be available as linkage modules and run within the DBMS process. Because actions may be created and deleted at runtime, a dynamic linker would be required (which our system does not currently provide).

We are presently developing an EDL as well as a CDL for our data model (the internal object model of the DAMASCUS system) and mapping these onto the ETM.

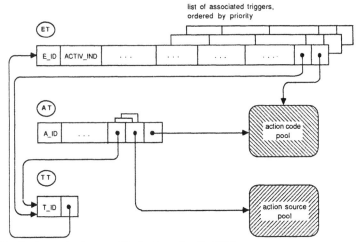

Fig.10: Access structures used for implementing the ETM

As correspondingly general and powerful mechanisms have not been implemented in DBMS so far, a quantitative comparison of performance is currently not very meaningful. Qualitatively, the following arguments apply. In our implementation, raising an event — the most critical operation — has the complexity of a main memory hash algorithm. The execution of an action requires a procedure call, combined with process switching and communication if the non-linked-in version of actions is used. Remember, however, that actions are only executed if explicitly desired and thus do *not* cause overhead that would be avoided by conventional solutions. The transformation of EDL- and CDL-statements requires the same methods as consistency rules in conventional DBMS and so performance is not affected. In summary, implementing semantic rules by the ETM is only marginally more costly than with 'hardwired' solutions, but provides by far more flexibility.

7. Conclusion

In this paper we have shown how a generalized trigger concept, the event/trigger mechanism, is suited to the problem of semantic rules in advanced database applications. It supports consistency as well as derivation rules in a very flexible, user-controllable way and thus enhances the DBMS by more application specific active semantics. The basic mechanism consists of a very concise set of concepts and operations. On top of it, semantics may be coded in user-defined events and actions or made more explicit by means of the event and constraint definition languages.

Note that beside the enforcement of semantic rules, the ETM may also be used for other purposes within a DBMS, including e.g.

- triggering of database snapshots,
- collection of statistical information,
- initiation of data reorganization,
- alarm handling,
- setting arbitrary safepoints for recovery,
- initiation of actions on other nodes within a distributed DBMS.

Further investigations will deal with applying the ETM to these tasks.

References

[Cha76]   D.D. Chamberlin et al.: *SEQUEL 2: A Unified Approach to Data Definition, Manipulation and Control.* IBM Journal of Research and Development, Nov.1976, pp.561-575.

[Che86]   Q. Chen: *A Rule-Based Object/Task Modelling Approach.* Proc. ACM SIGMOD 1986, pp.281-292.

[DD86]   K.R. Dittrich; U. Dayal (eds.): *Proc. Int. Workshop on Object-Oriented Database Systems.* Pacific Grove, Sept.1986. IEEE Computer Society Press 1986.

[DKM85]   K.R. Dittrich; A.M. Kotz; J.A. Mülle: *A Multilevel Approach to Design Database Systems and its Basic Mechanisms.* Proc. IEEE COMPINT, Montreal 1985.

[EL82]   C. Eastman; G. Lafue: *Semantic Integrity Transactions in Design Databases.* in: J. Encarnacao, F.L. Krause (eds.): File Structures and Data Bases for CAD, North Holland Publ. Comp. 1982, pp.45-54.

[Esw76]   K.P. Eswaran et al.: *The Notions of Consistency and Predicate Locks in a Database System.* Comm. of the ACM, Vol.9, No.11, Nov.1976, pp.624-633.

[Hew71]   C.E. Hewitt: *PLANNAR: A Language for Proving Theorems in Robots.* Proc. Int. Joint Conf. on Artificial Intelligence, London, Aug.1971.

[HK86]   S.E. Hudson; R. King: *CACTIS: A Database System for Specifying Functionally-Defined Data.* in [DD86], pp.26-37.

[Kot88]   A.M. Kotz: *Triggermechanimen zur Wahrung der Konsistenz von Entwurfsdaten in Datenbanksystemen.* Dissertation, University of Karlsruhe, to appear 1988.

[KE83]   A.R. Kutay; C.M. Eastman: *Transaction Management in Engineering Databases.* Proc. Database Week 1983, IEEE Computer Society Press, pp.73-80.

[MC83]   M.A. Melkanoff; Q. Chen: *An Experimental Database which combines Static and Dynamic Capabilities.* Engineering Design Applications, Proc. Data Base Week 1983, IEEE Computer Society Press, pp.53-61.

[Neu83]   T. Neumann: *On Representing the Design Information in a Common Database.* Proc. Database Week 1983, IEEE Computer Society Press, pp.81-87.

[RR82]   C. Rolland, C. Richard: *The REMORA Methodology for Information Systems Design and Management.* in: T.W. Olle et al. (eds.): Information Systems Design Methodologies: A Comparative Review. North-Holland Publ.Comp. 1982, pp.369-426.

[Sto86]   M. Stonebraker: *Object Management in POSTGRES using Procedures.* in [DD86], pp.66-72.

[Sto86a]   M. Stonebraker: *Triggers and Inference in Database Systems.* in: M.L. Brodie, J. Mylopoulos (eds.): On Knowledge Base Management Systems. Springer Verlag 1986, pp.297-314.

[Zdo85]   S.B. Zdonik: *Object Management Systems for Design Environments.* IEEE Database Engineering, Vol.8, No.4, 1985, pp.23-30.

Optimal plan search in a rule-based query optimizer

Ming-Chien Shan

Hewlett-Packard Laboratories
1501 Page Mill Road, Palo Alto, CA 94303

Abstract

This paper describes an optimal plan search strategy adopted in a rule-based query optimizer. Instead of attempting to search for the optimal plan directly, an initial plan is first generated based upon a set of heuristic rules. Depending upon the application, the initial plan may be used either as the final plan or as a base in a subsequent search. A new concept – clustering degree of an index – is introduced to better model the I/O costs of index scans. This new statistical information facilitates the formulation of the rules. An exhaustive search based upon the A* algorithm is then invoked to guarantee the optimal property of the plan. A lower bound value is derived and used as the estimation of "remaining distance" required in the A* algorithm. Noteworthy features of our approach include the capability for dynamic control of exhaustive search for an optimal plan, and on-line performance monitoring/tuning. The preliminary results lead us to believe that the rule-based approach is a promising one to face the new challenges of the optimizer, as created by the requirements of supporting diversified applications.

1 Introduction

In most database management systems, various ad hoc mechanisms are used for query processing, so that different cases of queries are not handled in a uniform way. This makes enhancements and extensions of the system very difficult. The issues of maintainability and extensibility had been ignored until recently, when they started gaining overdue interest [2, 15, 16, 27]. The approaches vary over a wide spectrum, from just recoding the optimization procedures in conventional rule format and employing traditional AI production systems for query processing, to the building of DBMS generators capable of supporting any data model.

The Iris database management system [14] developed at Hewlett-Packard Laboratories is a research prototype of a next-generation database management system. It is intended to meet the needs of new and emerging database applications, including software engineering, computer-aided design and manufacturing, office information and knowledge-based systems.

One of our objectives is to provide "extensibility" of the system in a general sense. In other words, we aim at the design of a system which can be dynamically tuned, with reasonable effort, to support different system configurations and/or functional requirements for various new applications. To facilitate the support of this capability, a rule-based approach to query optimization is adopted. The query optimization process is driven by a set of rules which are applied to the query tree during several recursive scans.

The design of the query optimizer plays a key role in the success of a database management system. A query optimizer evaluates a number of strategies for processing a given query and selects one that minimizes some cost measure. One problem in query optimizer design is how to search a large space of potential query execution plans efficiently. In this paper, issues related to optimal plan search in a rule-based optimizer are investigated and a new solution is proposed.

Most conventional systems, such as system R [28], make an exhaustive search using a breadth-first algorithm. Another search algorithm widely adopted in DBMSs is the hill-climbing algorithm [4, 16, 18, 33]. However, systems adopting the hill-climbing search algorithm risks choosing a suboptimal plan, due to such problems as the local maximum, plateau, and ridge problems [32]. It is not easy to enhance this kind of algorithm to correct this deficiency. Therefore, we feel that the adoption of an exhaustive search type of algorithm is still necessary for certain applications.

During the past decade, many researchers have written about query optimization, but none uses the A* algorithm [32] for optimal plan search. In order to apply the A* algorithm, one must be able, at any point within the search, to estimate the remaining distance to reach the goal. In the context of query optimization, this means that, given a current partial plan, a reasonable estimate of the cost of the additional work required to obtain a complete plan must be provided. One reason that the A* algorithm has not been widely adopted in query optimization is the difficulty of estimating this value.

We need a heuristic function that estimates the merits of each node generated in the query tree. It will enable unpromising paths to be pruned at an early stage when applying the A* algorithm. This is the essence of the A* search and the place where good heuristics should be exploited. Since an accurate value cannot be easily derived, a lower bound of the "remaining costs" is computed and used in the A* algorithm.

In our approach, a set of basic rules is first applied to produce an initial candidate plan. In general, the initial plan generated is a reasonable one and good for certain categories of applications such as ad hoc queries or queries compiled in a PC environment. However, if an optimal plan is required, as for queries in repeatedly executed applications, an exhaustive search of the entire plan space will be performed. During the search, the cost of the initial plan supplies an upper bound on the cost of the optimal plan. Additional information is also used for speeding up the pruning of unpromising plans.

2 An overview of Iris query processing

The Iris prototype consists of:

1. A Query Processing Manager.

   The data model supported by Iris falls into the general category of object-oriented models [12]. The query language supported is an object-oriented extension to SQL [10], called OSQL [3]. The Query Processing Manager compiles Iris queries into an internal relational algebra format, which is then interpreted against the stored data. OSQL, as presently implemented, does not support a nested query construct because its powerful functional capabilities obviate the need for SQL-like nested queries.

2. A Relational Storage Manager.

   This is a conventional relational storage manager and very similar to the Relational Storage Subsystem in System R. The capabilities provided by the storage manager include support for various access methods, concurrency control, logging and recovery, and buffer management.

3. A collection of interactive and programmatic interfaces.

   These currently include interactive OSQL, C and C++ with a call interface, and Common LISP with embedded OSQL statements.

Iris rule-based query compilation is detailed in [13]. Basically, the original query statement expressed in OSQL is translated into a query tree of extended relational algebra operators. As in [15], we use an extended relational algebra since the operators go beyond those of traditional relational algebra. Subsequently, the query tree undergoes a sequence of transformations through the judicious application of a set of rules, which results in an equivalent tree with a lower execution cost.

The optimizer uses a set of catalogued rules to produce an equivalent query tree by examining the node configuration of the query tree and invoking the appropriate rules. An indexing technique [29] is used to facilitate the search of relevant rules during the transformation. The rules to be applied are classified into two general categories, based upon their characteristics. They are *relational transformation rules* and *access plan computation rules*. These two kinds of rules are not applied in completely distinct stages. Their applications may be intermixed.

The *relational transformation rules* refine the query tree by applying rules based on relational algebra laws or semantic calculus. The query optimization process starts with transformations that are based upon relational algebra laws and generally felt to be useful. It continues by applying semantic deduction rules using semantic transformation or relational calculus to deduce more information which gives the optimizer more options for subsequent phases.

On the other hand, the *access plan computation rules* describe the correspondence between logical operators and physical access methods and associated cost formulas. The rules for initial plan generation described below also fall into this category.

Actually, the rules in each category are further divided into mini, midi, and maxi groups so that the mini group contains the basic ones and the maxi group contains the most sophisticated ones which require more comprehensive information (e.g., detailed statistical data). The latter perform some complicated computation, and may not always result in a major improvement of the tree.

During the last phase of query optimization, the minimization of some cost objective is sought. However, if the search starts at an arbitrary point, the number of execution plans explored could be staggeringly high. Thus, it is very important to reduce the number of execution plans evaluated by providing a good starting point in the search. That is, a reasonable execution plan for the query should be available and used as a base for cost comparison in subsequent searches for the optimal plan. In Iris, an initial plan is generated by applying a set of rules as described in section 3. In addition, heuristics are employeed to prune the search space. Otherwise, if the number of relations increases in a query, the search space becomes so large that the optimizer would be unacceptably slow.

In summary, the optimal plan search process consists of two phases: (1) the generation of an initial plan; (2) a thorough search of the potential execution plan space.

3 Initial plan generation

During the initial plan generation, it is necessary to avoid searching the combinatorial explosion of alternative plans, and at the same time it is necessary to generate a plan with acceptable performance. It is essential to have a simple, yet reasonably effective, mechanism for plan generation in which only a few clearly effective strategies are considered. Therefore, a rule-based approach is adopted to perform this task. This section describes the rules and supporting heuristics used by the query optimizer for generating the initial plan.

Most of the statistical information we use is of a kind generally available in existing database management systems. We use a hash sampling technique similar to [1] to compute a close approximation to the number of distinct values in the columns of a table. A slightly modified version of the formulas in [28] is used to compute the filter factors. For unclustered indexes, the usual assumption is that they are totally unclustered. This represents only the worst case of unclustered indexes. Its simplicity and vagueness cause problems in the modeling of unclustered indexes in cost formulas [22]. Since there is at most one clustered index allowed per table, most indexes will be unclustered and hence need to be modeled more accurately. This is because, in reality, each unclustered index still possesses some clustering which will vary from one unclustered index to another. No single value will ever be universally good for all unclustered indexes. Therefore, a new kind of statistical data – Index Clustering Degree (ICD) – is introduced. It provides a better understanding of the behavior of an index scan in terms of I/O cost, and enables us to model the cost more accurately. It roughly reflects the physical clustering of the data according to the logical key order of the index. It assumes the value 1 for a clustered index. For unclustered indexes, it is defined as the ratio of the number of disk data page fetches necessary to read the entire table with an index scan to the number of data pages occupied by the table. It can be measured by performing an index scan on the table and counting the number of data page I/Os actually incurred. Note that the buffering factor consideration will be naturally incorporated into the computation of the ICD if data are collected during normal system operation time. For systems in which the number of buffers allocated to an index scan is known in advance, the value of the ICD can be easily computed via a scan on the leaf pages in the index only. In our cost formulas, the number of data page I/Os for an index scan is then computed as the product of the number of pages in the table and the ICD of the index being used. A default value of 5 is initially assigned to the ICD of each index.

In general, a query execution plan associated with higher I/O cost is likely to cause higher CPU cost too. Because ICDs allow us to more accurately predict I/O costs, the correlation of CPU cost to I/O cost is stronger in our cost model than in conventional cost models [22, 28]. These models usually assume one I/O operation per tuple retrieved through an unclustered index, and they consequently overestimate I/O costs. Our heuristics are based on the assumption that an execution plan associated with less I/O cost will incur less CPU cost, and hence, less total cost. Therefore, the number of page I/Os is taken as the primary concern during the development of the rules. The principle that I/O cost is mainly dominated by the access path chosen is applied in single-table rules as well as multi-table rules.

Throughout this paper, the following notations will be used:

Let P denote the number of pages occupied by table T,

P_i denote the number of pages occupied by table T_i,

$\|T\|$ denote the cardinality of table T,

$\|T_i\|$ denote the cardinality of table T_i,

$\|T_i'\| = \|T_i\|$ * (filter factors of all predicates),

$\|T_i''\| = \|T_i\|$ * (filter factors of all *local* predicates),

fp_i be the filter factor of predicate i on table T,

fp_{ij} be the filter factor of predicate i on table T_j,

FP_j be the product of all filter factors of *local* predicates associated with table T_j,

ICD_i denote the clustering degree of index i on table T,

ICD_{ij} denote the clustering degree of index i on table T_j,

$\|D_{ij}\|$ denote the number of distinct values of column C_j in table T_i,

C_p denote the composite of previously joined tables, and

$\|C_p\|$ denote the the estimated cardinality of the composite C_p.

We say an index matches a predicate when the columns mentioned in the predicate are an initial substring of the set of columns of the index key. The GROUP-BY or ORDER-BY clause or join column matching indexes are defined in a similar way.

3.1 Single-table query rules

Roughly speaking, query execution plans are chosen based upon the costs of different applicable access paths for the table. For single-table queries, the basic rules used for computing execution plans are described in the following:

1. The default access path for a table is a sequential relation scan, and sorting is used to support any grouping or ordering requirement in queries with a GROUP-BY or ORDER-BY clause.

   (At this moment, hashing will not be considered in our prototype for supporting grouping requirements, even though the hashing tactic is a clear-cut winning strategy in many cases.)

   However,

2. If there exists a unique index matching an equal predicate, the index is used to access the table. Otherwise,

3. If there exists a clustered index matching an equal predicate, the index is used to access the table.

   (Usually, table key columns are designated as clustering columns. If the clustered index has a very high duplicate rate on key column values, we would like to consider it as a database design issue for the DBA.)

   Otherwise,

4. If there exist indexes matching an equal predicate or range predicate or the GROUP-BY clause, the one with the least I/O cost is used to access the table, provided its I/O cost is still less than a relation scan.

   (Let MI = $\{I_j\}$ be the set of indexes matching an equal or range predicate. If the GROUP-BY clause matching index has an ICD less than 10, this index is added into MI, provided it is not in the set yet. In addition, a new ICD value is assigned to the GROUP-BY clause matching index and used in subsequent cost computations. The new ICD value is computed as its original value divided by 2. Now, assume that $C_i = min\{P*fpj*ICDj$ for all Ij in MI$\}$. If $C_i < P$ then the corresponding index is used to access the table. Otherwise, the relation scan is used.

   The heuristics of choosing the values 10 and 2 used in the above computation are described as follows. First, consider a query of the form: SELECT * from T ORDER BY f1. Assume that there exists an index I with an ICD of K on the column f1. The sort cost for table T is approximated by $2*P*\log_n P$ when an n-way merge sort is utilized. Therefore, the costs of executing the query via the index scan or a relation scan plus sorting are $P*K$ and $2*P*\log_n P$ respectively. To favor the index scan, we must have $P*K < 2*P*\log_n P$. Let us assume that the average number of pages in a table is 100 and a 4-way merge sort is used. This implies $K < 10$.

   Secondly, consider a query of the form: SELECT * FROM T WHERE T.f1 < const1 ORDER BY f2. Assume that there exists an index I1 with clustering degree K1 and I2 with clustering degree K2 on columns f1 and f2 respectively. In this case, the execution costs for the query will be $(P*fp1*K1+P') + 2*P'*(\log_n P'-1)$ or $P*K2$, where $P' = P*fp1$, depending upon the use of index I1 or I2. We further assume that $fp1 = 0.5$. It follows that the two plans are "equal" when $K1 \approx 2*K2$.)

Otherwise,

5. If the ORDER-BY clause is present, a similar adjustment is performed on the values of the clustering degrees for relevant matching indexes.

(If no GROUP-BY clause is present in the query, the ICD of the matching index will be divided by 2 as in case 4 above. Otherwise, if ORDER-BY columns and GROUP-BY columns are matched, the ICD of the matching index will be further adjusted by dividing by 2 again. Note that if both GROUP-BY and ORDER-BY clauses are present but on different columns, the ORDER-BY matching index will not be included in the set MI.)

In addition,

6. If aggregate functions MAX or MIN are present without a GROUP-BY clause, the clustering degree will be further adjusted to favor the matching index.

In our system, since a single page contains records of one table only, the index scan is never used for sequential retrieval of all records in a table, as could be done in systems where records of multiple tables are stored in one page to avoid the scanning of irrelevant pages.

3.2 Multi-table query rules

For queries involving multiple tables, rules are needed to determine the join order and methods among tables. The relationships between tables are analyzed to divide tables into groups, called join groups. The query process then takes place at two levels: the inter-group level and the intra-group level. Basically, each join group is the unit for optimization in selecting the join order and methods.

3.2.1 Inter-group rules

During this phase of multi-table query processing, the join groups are first established by the following procedure:

1. Draw the join connection graph. Each table is a node, and an edge between two nodes exists if there is an equijoin predicate between the corresponding tables.

2. Make each connected subgraph in the join graph a join group. In addition, each isolated table forms a separate join group by itself.

Usually, there is only one join group per query. The most common cases for queries being decomposed into more than one join group are those having no equijoin predicate, but other kinds of join predicates between tables.

Within each join group, the join order and methods among tables will be computed based upon the rules described in the next section.

Since there exists no equijoin predicate between join groups, a Cartesian product must be performed among the join groups. The Cartesian product will be implemented by the nested-loop join method. Note that there is no advantage to considering merge-scan join or hash join methods for implementing the Cartesian product operation.

For the ordering between join groups, we put all multi-table join groups at the beginning of the total join chain, and push all single-table join groups towards the end of the chain. This is based upon the assumption that the generation of a join group's results is usually costly and therefore it is a good heuristic to reduce the time of its generations. Furthermore, the join groups in each category (i.e., single-table or multi-table join groups) are ordered according to their cardinalities. The smaller the estimated cardinality of a join group, the earlier it occurs in the sequence of the final join chain. The reasons for choosing smaller cardinality join groups to participate in the Cartesian product operation earlier (i.e., to play the outer table role in a nested-loop join) are an expected reduction in the number of OPEN/RESET/CLOSE scan costs incurred during the process, and the desire to keep intermediate join results small.

Note that the size of a join result does not depend upon the access path used, but rather on the filter factors of predicates on the joined tables. Therefore, the join group's cardinality is approximated by the following formula, which is a generalized version of [24]. The cardinality of a join group consisting of m tables is computed as:

$$(\,|\,|T1''\,|\,|/\,|\,|Dmax1\,|\,|) \, * \, (\,|\,|T2''\,|\,|/\,|\,|Dmax2\,|\,|) \, * \, . \, . \, * \, (\,|\,|Tm''\,|\,|/\,|\,|Dmaxm\,|\,|) \, * \, MIND$$

$$\text{where MIND} = \min(\,|\,|Dmin1\,|\,|, \, |\,|Dmin2\,|\,|, \, .., \, |\,|Dminm\,|\,|), \text{ and}$$
$$\text{Dmaxi} = \max(\,|\,|Dij\,|\,| \text{ for all join columns } cj \text{ on table } Ti), \text{ and}$$
$$\text{Dmini} = \min(\,|\,|Dij\,|\,| \text{ for all join columns } cj \text{ on table } Ti).$$

Informally, the formula is derived by considering the model that tables T1 and T2 are joined in a hierarchical way having the one with the smaller $||Dij||$ at the top as shown in Figure 1.

T1.c1 = T2.c2

```
+---------------+
|      T1       |    Assume that T1 has 22 distinct values in join column c1.
+---------------+    Each single column value of c1 is assumed by  ||T1''||/22 records.
        |
        |
        V
+---------------+
|      T2       |    Assume that T2 has 50 distinct values in join column c2.
+---------------+    Each single column value of c2 is assumed by  ||T2''||/50 records.

                    There are at most 22 distinct values of column c2 in the join.
                    Cardinality of (T1 join T2) =
                      ( ||T1''||/22) * ( ||T2''||/50) * min(22,50).
```

Figure 1.

3.2.2 Intra-group rules

After the order among join groups is determined, the join order and methods on tables within each join group is chosen. Basically, the same heuristics that are appled to single-table query rules are extended to deal with multi-table query rules.

An Eligible Join Set (EJS) is defined as the set consisting of all tables not joined yet, but reachable from a joined table in the join graph. Based upon the commonly used heuristic that Cartesian products should be performed as late as possible, only tables contained in the EJS are considered to be joined next.

The general principle is to use the nested-loop join method as much as possible. In addition, even though the access path for inner tables during the join process is dictated by the join column, the same rules as for a single-table query are exercised, whenever applicable, on access path selection for each individual table being accessed for another purpose.

Three join methods will be considered, namely, nested-loop join, merge-scan join, and partition-hash join [7]. The nested-loop join method with index access is designated as the default one. The other two join methods are considered only when no appropriate index is available.

We do not consider temporary index creation in the first phase of our prototype implementation, but plan to explore it in the future to increase the usefulness of the nested-loop join method. Buffering and memory issues are not yet fully considered either. For tables small enough to fit entirely in memory, hashing is cheaper than creating a temporary index in a nested-loop join.

Additional heuristics used to develop the multi-table query rules are as follows:

1. Usually, scans on inner tables are iterated more often than those on outer tables. Proper access paths on inner tables are desired for reducing total I/O cost. Therefore, tables with "cheaper" access paths tend to be pushed toward the end in the join chain.

2. Among tables with no proper access path, the one with smaller cardinality tends to be pushed toward the front of the join chain (i.e., to play the outer table role in the join process), for the purpose of saving OPEN/RESET/CLOSE scan costs.

3. The number of join predicates and the cardinality of a table are used to break a tie in our design. That is, in the case of more than one table having the same values for all relevant attributes in a rule, the table having more join predicates would be chosen as the one to be joined next. Potentially, it could introduce more tables into EJS and therefore increase the number of tables eligibly joined next. In addition, the table with smaller cardinality of qualified records is chosen to further break any potential tie.

To choose the first table in the join, the following rules are used:

1. Check if there exist tables with unique indexes matching any local predicate of the form "column = constant". If so, the one with the largest value of $\|T"\|$ is chosen. In addition, all other table(s) having this property will be joined next too.

2. Check if there exist tables with no matching index on the join column. If so, the one with the smallest value of $\|T"\|$ is chosen.

3. Check if there exist tables with no clustered index on the join column. If so, the one with the smallest value of $\|T"\|$ is chosen.

4. Otherwise, the table with the smallest value of $\|T"\|$ is chosen.

The actual access path for the first table is selected using the same rules as for a single-table query as described in section 3.1.

For the join methods and order among the remaining tables, the following rules are used:

1. Compute the value of the EJS.

2. If $\|EJS\| = 1$, i.e., only one table holds an equijoin predicate to tables joined already, this table is chosen as the one to be joined next.

   a. If the table has a clustered index matching the join column, then the nested-loop join method with index scan via this index is chosen.

   (Due to the clustering of the index key values, for each outer table record's value, the matching inner table records are expected to be clustered around one data page or few data pages. In this case, the major reason causing the usual high cost of nested-loop join – scanning an entire inner table for every outer table record – does not hold. In addition, there is no sorting cost on either outer or inner tables. Actually, for this case, the nested-loop join mimics a merge-scan join in the pattern of record accessing.)

   Otherwise,

   b. If the table has no matching index on the join column, then the hash join method or merge-scan join method is chosen, depending upon the existence of an ORDER-BY clause in the query.

   (Note that, due to the way that the access path to the first table is chosen, it is unlikely that it will be a join column matching index. Therefore, we assume that no useful order is generated on the join composite during previous joins. This is not always a true assertion. However, in order to produce the initial plan in an efficient manner without recording/comparing the orderings of intermediate results, it is believed to be a reasonable assumption in general.

   As indicated in [5], the nested-loop join is usually prohibitive for large tables with no index on the join columns. In addition, [7] claimed that hash join always performs better than merge-scan join with an average page I/O cost ratio of merge-scan join vs. hash join equal to 1.5. Therefore, the hash join is chosen as the default method.

The merge-scan join method will be considered only when an ORDER-BY clause is present in the query. (Note that the GROUP-BY clause is supported equally well by both hash and sort methods.) Furthermore, although the buffer pool size factor is not considered in the initial plan generation process, if a large buffer pool is allocated as it is in most production systems, it makes the hash join method more favorable since the merge-scan join method is usually not clever enough to take advantage of large buffer pool [7].

Since ordering among column values can be preserved through a series of joins consisting of nested-loop joins only, the merge-scan join method is chosen only when: (i) the ORDER-BY columns form a subset of the set of all join columns (note that, if more than one join predicate exists, all join columns are used in the hash or sort process), and (ii) an index of clustering degree less than 5 exists on all tables which have not been joined yet. The second condition is to guarantee that only the nested-loop join method is used in subsequent joins, so that the order established by the current merge-scan join will not be destroyed in subsequent joins. The heuristics for choosing the value 5 will be explained later.

We assume that all tables in queries are reasonably large in most applications. If this is not always the case, a rule can be added to choose the nested-loop join method if T is the table under consideration and $\|T\|$ < buffer pool size or 10.)

Otherwise,

c. If the table has a matching index with an ICD K less than 5 on the join column then the nested-loop join method is chosen. Otherwise, the hash join method or merge-scan join method is chosen, depending upon the existence of an ORDER-BY clause as described in rule (b) above.

(This is because the performance of the nested-loop join method is expected to degenerate as K becomes larger. It is better to consider other join methods to avoid repeating scans of the entire inner table when K is large.

The costs of the index scan and the sort for the inner table in either a nested-loop join or a merge-scan/hash join are $P*K$ and $2*P*\log_n P$ respectively. Based on the same assumptions on average statistical data used for single-table query rules, this leads to the necessary condition that K < 10 for the nested-loop join method to be the winner. In addition, the consideration that multiple scans on inner table are usually required in the nested-loop join method leads us to further reduce this value by half, i.e., to 5.)

3. If $\|EJS\|$ > 1, i.e., more than one table holds equijoin predicates to tables joined already, then:

   a. If table(s) with clustered index(es) on the join columns exist, then the table with the smallest $\|T''\|/\|Dj\|$ is chosen to be joined next, and the nested loop join method with index access is used.

(It is expected that, by choosing the table with smallest $\|T"\|/\|Dj\|$, the sizes of intermediate join results will be kept as small as possible.)

Otherwise,

b. If table(s) with matching indexes of ICD less than 5 on join columns exist, the table having an index with the smallest $\|T"\|/\|Dj\|$ is chosen and the nested loop join method is used, where Dj is the number of distinct values in the join column. Otherwise,

c. The table with the smallest $\|T"\|/\|Dj\|$ is chosen and, depending upon the existence of an ORDER-BY clause, either the hash join method or the sort merge join method is used.

For GROUP-BY or ORDER-BY clauses, the default support is sort. However, if the required order is generated and preserved in the join process, no additional sort is performed. This is detected by the following rules:

1. For a query execution plan involving hash join or merge-scan join, if the GROUP-BY column is the join column of the last table in the join chain, no additional sort is required.

2. The procedure is similar for ORDER-BY, but only merge-scan joins are considered.

3. For a query execution plan involving nested-loop joins only, if the order supported by the access path chosen on the first table matches the GROUP-BY or ORDER-BY requirement, no additional sort is needed.

In addition, the single-table query rules are used to select the access path for retrieving qualified records from tables as input to sort/hash routines.

Let us consider the six-way join query shown in figure 2 and assume that there is a clustered index on T1.f1, a unique index on T2.f11, an unclustered index of ICD 9 on T3.f4, an unclustered index of ICD 3 on T4.f6, and a clustered index on T6.f10.

```
SELECT * FROM T1, T2, T3, T4, T5, T6
WHERE T1.f1 = T2.f2 and T2.f3 = T3.f4 and T2.f5 = T4.f6 and T3.f7 = T5.f8
      and T5.f9 = T6.f10 and T2.f11 = 100 and T3.f12 <= 7 ORDER BY f7;
```

The execution plan generated by the rules is as follows:

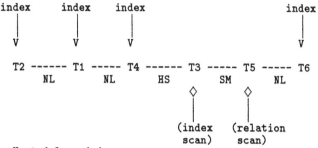

NL: Nested-loop join
HS: Hash join
SM: Merge-scan join

Figure 2.

Another way of generating the initial plan is to start an exhaustive search, but on a limited query execution plan space. Some heuristics are usually used to limit the scope of the search space dramatically. For example, always choose the most restricted table to be joined next in order to keep the size of each intermediate result small, or exclude some expensive operations from consideration. By doing this, it is expected that it is necessary only to augment the original query plan search algorithm to perform the initial plan generation, as in the approach taken in [25], rather than to come up with a set of rules to build the initial plan. However, one objective for the Iris prototype is to explore the possibility of incorporating artificial intelligence techniques into database management systems. We would like to evaluate, at the same time, how well rule-based query optimization works. This is done by comparing the initial plan and final plan generated by our system. By analyzing the results, we can verify and tune the set of rules for generating the initial plan. In addition, we hope to be able to learn the cost behavior of new access methods and join algorithms so that these new methods can be included in the basic rule set.

4 Optimal plan search

After the initial plan with cost V_o is generated, an exhaustive search for the optimal plan is started. During this phase, instead of exercising a breadth-first search as adopted in system R, a depth-first search strategy is used. The cost V_o of the initial plan supplies an upper bound for the optimal plan and is used to avoid a thorough search of the entire query plan space.

The actual algorithm used in the search is very similar to the A* search algorithm widely used in artificial intelligence. The difficulty in using the A* algorithm is that while the cost of tables already joined in the composite can be assumed known, the cost of joining the remaining tables must be estimated. The situation becomes even more difficult to analyze when more than one join group exists.

Consider a query involving a join of n tables. Let V_c be the total cost of the current candidate plan. Initially, it is set equal to V_o. During the probing of alternative plans, if, at step m, the accumulated cost V_m is already equal to or greater than the value V_c before a complete plan is generated, then the current path need not be pursued any further and can be pruned. In addition, to be able to prune suboptimal plans from the search tree at an even earlier stage, we compute a lower bound V_e on the cost of joining the rest of the tables. If $V_m + V_e >= V_c$, the current path is pruned and we switch to another path as shown in Figure 3.

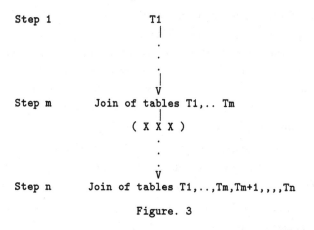

Figure. 3

In our current design, the computation of V_e is kept simple. A lower bound v_j on the cost of joining a table Tj to other table(s) is computed for each table Tj. The value of V_e is then computed as the sum of all v_j's for tables Tj not being joined yet, i.e., $V_e = v_{m+1} + v_{m+2} + ... + v_n$.

Based upon the usual statistical information kept in the database catalog, the value of v_j is computed as a rough estimate of the cost of joining table Tj to other table(s) under the ideal situation. In order to guarantee that we will not prune a good plan due to the miscomputing of value v_j, we adopt a very conservative approach.

Besides, the value of v_j is computed only once at the beginning of the search and is used through the entire process. We could compute the value v_j more accurately in a dynamic way. That is, the value of v_j could be recomputed at each step during the search so that it incorporates additional information into its computation, such as the ordering produced and the estimated cardinality of the intermediate result. The former approach saves the work of recomputing the value of v_j, but may lead to probing a larger search space. We realize that the degree of sophistication which gets into the formulation of the lower bound will critically affect the performance of the search for the optimal plan. However, for simplicity, we chose the former to implement and leave the exploration of the dynamic approach as a future project.

The value v_j for table Tj is computed according to the following rules:

1. If there exists only one join group, then,

   a. If table Tj has a clustered index matching a join column Ci, then $v_j = Pj * (\min\{1, (\min\{ICDij*fpij\})*Cpc\_min\})$, where Cpc_min is the minimal one among all possible $\|Cp\|$ values.

   This is because the ideal situation in which this table Tj being joined with previously joined table(s) is via a merge-scan join, assuming tuples in the composite Cp of previous joined table(s) are already in the join column order and the clustered index on Tj is used in the join to provide the required merge-scan join order. In this case, the join process will scan table Tj only once, and lead to $v_j = Pj$.

   On the other hand, when the cardinality of composite Cp is very small, the nested-loop join method might become the winner. This is because only a few scans on the inner table are required and only a fraction of the inner table is accessed during each scan if an index scan matching a local or join predicate is chosen. For example, if a unique index matches an equal predicate, there will be only one page I/O on table Tj during each scan of it. Therefore, the minimal I/O cost will be equal to $\min\{Pj*ICDij*fpij$ for matching predicates on table Tj$\} * Cpc\_min$.

   For the value of Cpc_min, a lower bound, i.e., $\min\{\|Tj'\|\}$, for it is used. If the dynamic approach of computing v_j were adopted, the estimate of Cpc_min could be improved, since tables joined in Cp were known.

   b. If the table Tj has no matching index on any join column, then $v_j = \min\{Pj*\min\{1, \min\{ICDij*fpij\}\}*Cpc\_min, Pj'(1+2*\log_n Pj')\}$, where $Pj' = Pj*FPj$.

   In this case, the minimal I/O cost for joining Tj via the nested-loop join method will be equal to $\min\{Pj, \min\{Pj*ICDij*fpij$ for predicates on table Tj$\}\} * Cpc\_min$, due to the fact that a relation scan or an index scan matching a predicate will be used to access table Tj.

   Since there is no existing access path supporting the required join order on table Tj's tuples, table Tj has to be sorted or hashed, depending upon whether the merge-scan join or hash join method is actually chosen. Both processes will cause $2*Pj'*\log_n Pj'$ page I/Os. In addition, at least the sorted/hashed Tj has to be scanned once during the join process. This adds another Pj' to the total I/O cost of the merge-scan/hash join method. Note that, as in case (a), tuples in the composite Cp are assumed to be in the join column order already.

   If the dynamic approach of computing v_j were adopted, a better knowledge of cardinality and ordering for Cp would be available and would replace our conservative assumptions.

   c. If the table Tj has a matching index of clustering degree K on a join column, then $v_j = \min\{Pj*\min\{1, \min\{ICDij*fpij\}\}*Cpc\_min, Pj'(1+2*\log_n Pj'), Pj*ICDij'\}$, where $Pj' = Pj*FPj$ and ICDij' is ICD for index matching a join column.

In this case, all join methods and table access methods are optimal candidates. During a nested-loop join, the choice between relation scan and index scan on table Tj will be determined by the clustering degrees and filter factors of matching predicates of indexes. The ordering on tuples of table Tj required by a merge-scan join could be provided via sorting or an index scan with a cost of $2*Pj' \log_n Pj'$ and $Pj*ICDij$ respectively.

2. If more than one join group, say q join groups, exist, then the value $Cnp = Rjp * \min\{Pj, Pj*ICDij'*fpij\}$ will be included in the computation of minima in the above rules, where $Rjp = \min\{Rjg1, Rjg2, ..., Rjgq\}$ and $Rjgi$ is the product of $\|T'\|$ for all tables T in i-th join group.

This is because, for the case of multiple join groups per query, table Tj might be chosen to join a table in a different join group. This is unknown at the time when v_j is computed. Therefore, the cost for joining Tj to a table in different join groups must be considered in the "betting" for the lower bound value v_j. Note that the only way of joining tables in different join groups is to perform the Cartesian product which can be implemented by the nested-loop join method only.

If the dynamic approach were adopted, it would become clear, at any step in the search, whether table Tj could be joined to a table within the same join group or not.

If a complete plan with a smaller cost is generated, this new plan will replace the original one as the current candidate plan in subsequent search steps. In addition, we also improve our plan incrementally in the following way. At each step m during the probing of a new plan, its current accumulated cost V_m is compared with the corresponding cost in the candidate plan. If V_m is cheaper and all other characteristics of the intermediate results of these two plans are "equal", then this segment of the plan is going to replace the corresponding segment in the candidate plan to form a new candidate plan. Here, "equal" means that both plan segments involve the same set of tables, have the same result cardinalities and ordering, etc. The new value for V_m will propagate to the remaining portion of the candidate plan to generate a new value of V_c.

In the exhaustive search phase, a general heuristics – keeping intermediate results as small as possible at each step during the entire query process – is applied for choosing an alternative plan to be explored next. It starts with the table with the least $\|T'\|$. Then, the table with next smaller $\|T'\|$ is considered for joining, etc. In addition, during the exploration of different access paths to a table, the single-table query rules are applied plus other commonly used heuristic pruning techniques [28]. This establishes the branching rule for choosing alternatives in the A* algorithm. An alternative for the branching rule could be based upon the lower bound value v_j of each table Tj. That is, first consider the plan in which the table with the least v_j is going to be joined next.

If the cost V_o of the initial plan is equal to or less than the sum of v_j for all tables Tj, there is no need for an exhaustive search since no improvement could be carried out on the initial plan. The initial results on most common cases of join queries show that the basic set of rules performs well and eighty percent of initial plans generated turn out to be the optimal plan and no exhaustive search is needed.

5 Conclusions

Various requirements raised by new and emerging applications have forced us to review current query optimization techniques. Even though the optimal plan chosen by an optimizer can be precisely determined only by actual calculation of the cost of various access paths, we believed that some general guidelines would be appropriate in many cases to quickly determine an execution plan for a query. These considerations led to a rule-based query optimizer which appears to be a promising approach to these problems.

In this paper, we have presented an optimal plan search strategy in a rule-based query optimizer. Our strategy provides several advantages over conventional approaches. Among them, four are particularly worth mentioning here:

1. *Dynamic control of the optimal plan search process.*

   Depending upon system environments and application types, the exhaustive search of optimal plans can be dynamically enabled or disabled. This is a very important feature from a performance point of view. In some cases, generating a reasonable plan heuristically is good enough; in other cases, an exhaustive search is required to guarantee the quality of the plan.

   There also exist certain cases in which an exhaustive search cannot be afforded or is not plausible. Examples are PC databases with limited memory, or new applications, such as expert database systems, with a search space that is several orders of magnitude larger than those currently handled by conventional DBMSs.

   To the best of our knowledge, no existing system generates query plans completely based upon heuristic rules. Our initial plan generation is the first one to explore this direction.

2. *Incorporation of A.I. techniques into DBMS.*

   The well-known search algorithm A* is used in the exhaustive search for an optimal plan. An estimate, i.e., a lower bound, of the "remaining cost" is computed to make the A* algorithm applicable.

3. *On-line performance monitoring/tuning.*

   By comparing the final plan with the initial plan, we are able to detect any anomalies and tune the basic rule set. The performance evaluation need not be done in an "off-line" style as is usually the case in DBMSs.

   In addition, it is expected that, by adding or removing appropriate rules, we will be able to explore new join algorithms, access methods, or data types and operations. Initially, new methods will not be considered by the rules for initial plan generation, but they are fully investigated during the exhaustive search phase. However, based upon information gleaned from empirical analysis, some useful heuristics can be found, and these new methods can be incorporated into the basic rule set later on.

4. *Less resource consumption.*

Compared with breadth-first search type processes [28], our optimal plan search process uses less memory and CPU resources. On the average, only two query execution plans will be kept in place during the search. In addition, the lower bound V_e is introduced to cut down the search time of the A* algorithm.

On the other hand, the breadth-first search algorithms require much more space to store the collection of all potential plans. As in [16], the search will terminate when the system runs out of memory. In lieu of this problem, our approach is able to guarantee the optimal plan for a query.

The way of computing the lower bound V_e might look pessimistic at first glance. However, in our experimental prototype, it seems to serve the purpose well. Of course, the current formulas provide us with an approximation only and could be improved by incorporating additional parameters in the formulas for V_e, e.g., including statistical information on intermediate results. It is expected that more pruning will occur earlier with improvements on the lower bound estimation V_e.

Our initial results [26] with a partially-implemented prototype show that this approach, compared with a more conventional one, adds negligible additional overhead but providing a lot of flexibility. For most common cases of queries, the initial plans generated by the basic rules are very close to the optimal ones. The scale of the experiments performed is far from complete. We intend to continue the validation and evaluation of the basic set of rules with a large variety of complex queries.

We plan to run a set of queries taken from the Iris benchmarks set. Whenever the optimizer (basic rules) chooses a poor plan, the pertinent rules will be examined and enhanced. Over time, the optimizer is expected to become reasonably good, and Iris' query processing can rely on it without performing exhaustive searches even for complicated queries.

An alternative under consideration for improving the speed of exhaustive search is to compute a lower bound (TLB) for the total cost of the query, based upon statistical information. During the exhaustive search, whenever the cost of the current candidate plan falls in a range calculated based upon the TLB value, the search is terminated and the current plan is used. For example, if the difference between the cost of current candidate plan and TLB is less than a predetermined (or dynamically determined based on the query's characteristics, e.g., the number of tables joined) figure, say 10% of TLB, then terminate the search. This approach is very useful in handling ad hoc queries or very large execution plan search space, especially when the selection of alternative plans to be explored next is also guided by heuristic rules to avoid exhaustive search on the entire plan space.

A simplified version [30] of the basic set of rules which does not use the statistical information D_{ij} is under design, being aimed at database applications in the PC environment. We also plan to improve the cost formulas to better conform to reality. In our current design, we still assume that column values are linearly and uniformly distributed. However, as is often the case, the distribution is neither linear nor uniform. We plan to collect statistical information in the style of "distribution steps" [23] to improve the accuracy of the estimates for the values of filter factors and clustering degrees of indexes. In addition, a simple buffering strategy – even allocation among tables [17] – will be adopted in our prototype. A dynamic buffer allocation policy based upon heuristic rules is worth exploring. These will be topics for future research.

6 Acknowledgements

The author would like to give his sincere thanks to Marie-Anne Neimat for her encouragement and valuable suggestions. In particular, the introduction of the unique index rule for multi-table queries is due to her suggestion.

The author is also grateful to David Beech. His careful reading of an earlier draft of this paper improved the presentation in many ways.

7 References

1. Astrahan, M., Schkolnick, M., and Whang, K., "Counting unique values of an attribute without sorting", IBM Research Report RJ4960, December, 1985.

2. Batory, D., et al., "GENESIS: A Reconfigurable Database Management System", Technical Report 86-07, Dept. of Computer Science, The University of Texas, Austin, 1986.

3. Beech, D., "A Foundation for Evolution from Relational to Object Databases", Proc. of Int. Conf. on EDBT, Venice, Italy, March, 1988.

4. Bernstein, P., et al., "Query Processing in a System for Distributed Databases(SDD-1)" ACM Trans. on Database Systems, Vol.6, No. 4, December, 1981.

5. Bitton, D., DeWitt, D., and Turbyfill C., "Benchmarking database systems - A systematic approach", Proc. of 9th Int. Conf. on VLDB, 1983.

6. Bloom, B., "Space/Time Trade-offs in Hash Coding with Allowable Errors", Comm. ACM, Vol. 13, No. 7, July, 1970.

7. Bratbergsengen, K., "Hashing methods and relational algebra operations", Proc. of 10th Int. Conf. on VLDB, August, 1984.

8. Carey, M., and Lu, H., "Some Experimental Results on Distributed Join Algorithms in a Local Network", Proc. of 11th Int. Conf. on VLDB, Sweden, August, 1985.

9. Christodoulakis, S., "Estimating Block Transfers and Join Sizes", Proc. ACM-SIGMOD, May, 1983.

10. Date, C., "A guide to the SQL standard", Addison-Wesley Publishing Company, 1987.

11. Dayal, U., and Smith, J., "PROBE: A Knowledge Oriented Database Management System", Proc. of the Islamorada Workshop on large scale knowledge base and reasoning systems, February, 1985.

12. Derrett, N., et al, "An object-oriented approach to data management", Proc. Compcon 31th IEEE Computer Society Int. Conf., San Francisco, March, 1986.

13. Derrett, N. and Shan, M., "Rule-based Query Optimization", Hewlett-Packard Lab. Research Report STL-87-07, December, 1987.

14. Fishman, D., et al., "Iris: An Object-Oriented Database Management System", ACM Trans. on Office Information Systems, Vol. 5, No. 1, January, 1987.

15. Freytag, J., "A Rule-based View of Query Optimization", Proc. ACM-SIGMOD, San Francisco, CA., May, 1987.

16. Graefe, G., and Dewitt, D., "The EXODUS Optimizer Generator", Proc. ACM-SIGMOD, San Francisco, CA., May, 1987.

17. Hagmann, R., "An Observation on Database Buffering Performance Metrics", Proc. of 12th Int. Conf. on VLDB, Tokyo, August, 1986.

18. Ioannidis, Y., and Wong, E., "Query Optimization by Simulated Annealing", Proc. ACM-SIGMOD, San Francisco, CA., May, 1987.

19. Jarke, M., and Koch, J.,"Query Optimization in Database Systems", ACM Computing Surveys, Vol. 16, No. 2, June, 1984.

20. Kitsuregawa, M., et al., "Application of Hash to Data Base Machine and its architecture", New Generation Computing, No.1, 1983.

21. Mackert, L., and Lohman, G., "Index scan using a finite LRU buffer: A validated I/O model", IBM Research Report RJ4836, September, 1985.

22. Mackert, L., and Lohman, G., "R* Optimizer validation and Performance Evaluation for Local Queries", Proc. ACM-SIGMOD, Washington, D.C., May, 1986.

23. Piatetsky-Shapiro, G., and Connell, C., "Accurate estimation of the number of tuples satisfying a condition", Proc. ACM-SIGMOD, May, 1984.

24. Rosenthal, A., "Note on the expected size of a join", SIGMOD record, July, 1981.

25. Rosenthal, A., Dayal, U., and Reiner, D., "Fast Query Optimization over a Large Strategy Space: The Pilot Pass Approach", Unpublished manuscript, 1986.

26. Ryan, T., and Cate, H., "Performance evaluations of Iris/OSQL and HP-SQL", Unpublished manuscript, December, 1987.

27. Schwarz, P., et al., "Extensibility in the Starburst Database System", Int. Workshop on Object-Oriented Database Systems, Pacific Grove, CA., September, 1986.

28. Selinger, P. et al., "Access path selection in a relational database management system", Proc. ACM-SIGMOD, Boston, MA., June, 1979.

29. Shan, M., "Rule management in Database Systems", Proc. 6th Advanced Database Symposium, Tokyo, Japan, August, 1986.

30. Shan, M., "Rule-based Query Optimization in PC environment – A heuristic approach", Hewlett-Packard Lab. Research Report, In preparation.

31. Stonebraker, M., and Rowe, L., "The Design of POSTGRES", Proc. ACM-SIGMOD, Washington, D.C., May, 1986.

32. Winston, P., "Artificial Intelligence", 2nd Edition, Addison-Wesley Publishing Company, 1984.

33. Wong, E., and Youssefi, K., "Decomposition: A Strategy for Query Processing", Proc. ACM Trans. on Database Systems, Vol. 1, No. 3, September, 1976.

34. Yu, C., and Chang, C., "Distributed Query Processing", ACM Computing Surveys, Vol. 16, No. 4, December, 1984.

Information Systems Design: An Expert System Approach

C. Cauvet, C. Proix and C. Rolland

University of Paris 1, 12 Place du Pantheon
75231 Paris Cedex 05, France

ABSTRACT

We present in this paper some aspects of an expert design
tool so-called OICSI. The scope of OICSI is to generate the IS
conceptual schema from a description of the application domain given
with a subset of the french natural language.
The tool starts, in a first step with an interpretation of natural
language descriptions leading to a descriptive network which
corresponds to a first version of the conceptual schema. Then in the
second step, OICSI uses design rules in order to complete and
transform the descriptive network into a normalized network which
describes all the elements of the final conceptual schema.
The paper focusses on the second step. It presents the
representation and validation rules included in the OICSI knowledge
based as a formalization of design rules issued from our own
practice and experience of Information System design.

1 INTRODUCTION

1.1 The state of the art in information systems design

Information systems (IS) design is a complicated task
which people have sought to master by using methodology. A
methodology can be defined as a consistent set of elements: **models**
(a set of concepts and rules governing their use), **languages**
(constructions allowing us to describe the results of modelling), a
methodological approach (operating process by which the design is
actually carried out) and **tools** (software supporting the approach).

The oldest methods stressed the methodological approach,
i.e the way in which the design process was conducted. In the
perspective of these methods, to design an information system is to
accomplish a set of tasks, which the method should list and organize
one with respect to the other. These methodologies are based on top-
down decomposition of the design process. They show this process as
developing in a linear manner and present themselves as guides for
each stage of the process. They are more aids to description of the
results of design than tools to be used for the designing itself.
SADT [ROS 77], SSA [GAN 79], ISAC [LUN 82] are examples of this
family of methodologies.

The most recent methods have stressed the models used for
designing, and the languages used to specifying. They recommend a
systemic approach in which the information system is seen as a

system, i.e a set of interconnected elements which are images, in
the form of data, of entities and associations of entities in the
real world.

In this approach, information systems design is related to
the activity of modelling, the result of which is an abstract
representation of the real world (so-called schema) elaborated by
means of the concepts of a model.

Initially the models aimed at describing the structure of
implementation of data. They have progressively evolved towards
conceptual models, the object of which is to show the semantic of
the contents of the information system. Many semantically rich
models are now available [CHE 76], [ABR 74], [SMI 77] ...
They constitute a contribution at the level of help to information
systems design, which are all the more useful since they include the
concepts of representation of the dynamic aspects of the real world.
[ROL 82], [BRO 82], [GUS 82],...

But it is not enough to dispose of pertinent models in
order to facilitate the task of design of a complex information
system. The models supply concepts by which one can define
consistent and readable schemas, but they do not help the designer
in the creative work of producing these schemas.

The choice of a schema is empirical. The richness of a
schema depends on the designer's own aptitude to perceive, select,
and classify similar individual phenomena into classes of
phenomena, to generalize the association between individual
phenomena into classes of associations between classes of phenomena
and to define the rules of behaviour and the restrictions to which
these phenomena are subjected. The notion of a "good schema" is not
formal, and more often than not the designer will chooze a solution
according to personal criteria forged by his own experience.

Thus, by using models, the result of the design process is
formalized, but the process that the designer carries out in order
to reach a schema remains manual and empirical.

1.2 Our approach

We believe that a step forward in the design of
information systems requires an effort of formalization of the
intellectual process of construction of schemas. Such formalization
should enable us to define a software tool which brings an effective
help to design.

The idea of supporting design by software tools is not new
[DBE 84], [CER 83], [BRA 83]. The fonctionalities of this software
are useful for helping the design team to memorize the results of
modelling, to control them and to restitute them in different forms.
They help in the management of schemas, but little in their
production. Our aim is to formalize the process of design so as to
allow it to be controlled by the tool.

We are conscious of the fact that design is a non-
algorithmic activity. It is a complex task, long and iterative
which is not very formal, and is full of uncertainty. The
experienced designer manages to master the task of design because
he uses on the one hand his formal knowledge of the models, and on

the other hand his experience which enables him to recognize
typical cases and to treat them by analogy, and to be attentive to
certain delicate aspects.

The nature of the task of design, therefore requires an
effort of formalization of, on the one hand the algorithmic part of
the design (for example algorithm of normalization) and on the
other, the heuristic part (experimental rules of designers).

In addition, if we wish to support the design process by a
tool, it must be able to include both formal knowledge and
experimental knowledge.

For all these reasons an expert system approach seems
appropriate.

This approach will allow us to reproduce the expert's
attitude, to exploit experimental knowledge necessary to the
mastering of design by combining it with more formal knowledge.

Our hypothesis was to define an expert system for aid to
the design process. The help supplied by the tool relies on a
knowledge base where the concepts and the formal rules governing
their use are grouped together with the rules of experimental know-
how of design experts. The quality of the expert system depends on
the richness of its knowledge base.

To define this knowledge base we have sought to analyse
the reasoning processes carried out by the designer during the
design process in order to reproduce them in the expert system.

Section 2 of this article concerns this aspect. The
knowledge base is a couple (base of facts, base of rules) that we
present successively in section 3 and 4.

In this article emphasis is placed on the knowledge base,
and not on the inference process by which OICSI progressively
generates the conceptual schema of an information system. Interested
readers will find a description of these aspects in [ROL 86]

2.   ANALYSIS OF CONCEPTUAL REASONING

2.1 Analysis and representation activities

Independently of the method used, any conceptual reasoning
includes, in our opinion, two complementary and interconnected
activities of design, namely:

- analysis activity
- representation activity

(a) At the origin of any design process, there is
observation of the real world, analysis of real phenomena,
regrouping these phenomena into classes, and description of these
classes by using the types of a model. This initial activity is
descriptive:

This is well illustrated by the NIAM method [VER 82] in which the designer is asked to begin by forming <u>descriptive sentences of the real facts</u> which reveal lexical objects, and to generalize them by introducing lexical object types (LOT) and non-lexical object types (NOLOT) to which the LOTs are attached. For example begining with the sentence:

"Pieters lives in Amersfoort"

and the lexical objects (Pieters,Amersfoort), the designer must generalize the sentence to form:

"The person with surname Pieters lives in the town with town name Amersfoort".

By carrying out this generalization, two NOLOTs are revealed (Person and Town), along with two LOTs (given names and town name) and the links which connect them. This leads finally to the NIAM schema in figure 1.

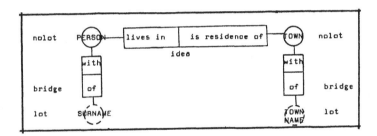

Figure 1: NIAM schema

(b) Unlike the preceding one,the second design activity is normative. It consists of an activity of representation which aims at allowing the designer to find a "good" representation of the classes of phenomena listed in the first stage through a formal structure. The criteria of a "good " representation are not always formal. This may be the elimination of redundancy, the search for elementarity, completeness, etc... Each method has its own criteria which are translated in general by <u>norms</u> with which the designer must conform in the elaboration of the schema. These norms are often included in the definition of the concepts. This aspect is clearly illustrated by relational normalization.

Lets assume that the designer starts with a relation:

CAR(numcar,trade-mark,power,color,owner's name,type)

which describes the object class "cars" identified during the first stage. The designer who wants a non-redundant representation has to break down this relation into two relations in third normal form:

CAR(numcar,color,owner's name,type)
CAR-TYPE(type,trade-mark,power)

Respecting the norm "elimination of redundancy" has led him to a data base schema which, he can assert, has the quality of being non-redundant.

But, in addition, it has allowed the designer to increase his knowledge of the real world by showing that in this problem there was not one single class of objects ("cars"), but two ("cars" and "car-types").

In general, normative representation leads to increased understanding of the real world. In addition it allows us to improve evaluation of the quality of the conceptual schema.

Both activities, descriptive and normative, are carried out in an iterative way.

Looking for a "good" representation of classes of phenomena which are perceived, the designer detects lacks, ambiguities and errors, and therefore reshapes and completes his analysis.

For example, in the previous case, the normalization leads the designer to find a new object "car-type", not initially perceived and to represent it in the conceptual schema.

2.2 Typology of facts and of knowledge

The preceding analysis of the conceptual reasoning process leads us to classify into types the facts and the knowledge manipulated by the designer during the conceptual phase in the following manner:

(a) There are three levels of facts:

- Initial facts as they exist in the application domain considered

- Classes of facts as the designer perceives them and which he describes by the types in the descriptive model.

- Elements of the conceptual schema finally retained as normalized representation of the previous classes of facts and expressed by means of normalized types in the conceptual model.

(b) Each one of the activities (analysis and representation) requires specific knowledge on the part of the designer.

- The first activity requires a good capacity for abstraction in order to pass from perception of concrete facts to a description in terms of classes.

- The second activity assumes a mastering of the model and of its associated norms. The designer must structure the classes of phenomena perceived so as to achieve a canonical conceptual representation. To do this, he employs rules for structuring which are either formally defined (eg relational normalisation) or forged by experience.

- In parallel with this, in order to test the quality of the conceptual schema he applies rules for <u>validation</u>.

- Finally when he comes across ambiguity or when he finds himself unable to comply with norms, he must imagine the reasons for this and then <u>question</u> the experts in the application domain so as to increase his knowledge and correct or complete the conceptual schema.

Thus, there are four types of knowledge needed to master the four types of tasks described here. We call them:

- abstraction type knowledge
- structuration type knowledge
- validation type knowledge
- interrogation / dialogue type knowledge

2.3 Organisation of OICSI

In order to reproduce the intellectual process accomplished by a designer during the design phase , we have organised the knowledge base of OICSI in the following way:

(a) The <u>base of facts</u> includes three levels of fact:

- Initial facts are sentences expressed in a sub-set of the French language

- Classes of facts are described in a semantic network referred to as "descriptive" including three basic types (entity, action, event) and their associations.

- Elements of the conceptual schema are described in a semantic network called "normalized semantic network". The nodes and the arcs of the network allow structured representation of the three basic types previously mentioned; by means of the abstraction forms of the semantic models, i.e aggregation, generalisation and association. These forms are applied to entity types, action types and event types.

(b) The <u>base of rules</u> includes five types of rules associated to the four types of knowledge previously indicated.

- Analysis rules
- Interpretation rules
- Structuration rules
- Validation rules
- Dialogue rules

Analysis and interpretation rules are the formalisation of abstraction type knowledge, the other rules correspond respectively to structuration type knowledge, to validation type knowledge and to the dialogue type knowledge.

These rules are used by OICSI's inference motor in an imbricated way. For example a validation rule can lead the tool to request the designer to provide supplementary information by applying dialogue rules which in turn, will lead to the application of structuration rules...

3. OICSI'S BASE OF FACTS

As mentioned previously OICSI's base of facts describes the knowledge acquired concerning the particular application domain during the design process. The state of the base evolves progressively towards a structured and canonical representation of the universe of discourse. Each initial fact goes successively through the three levels of representation indicated in paragraph 2.2. The design process is complete when the knowledge originally acquired on the application domain is fully represented by elements in the conceptual schema.

We present the base of facts by the different levels of fact.

3.1 Initial facts

Initial facts make possible the transfer of knowledge from the application domain to the designer.

Knowledge, thus acquired is informal, incomplete and not precise.

The major part of the application knowledge acquired is human knowledge. It is what is in the manager's brains. Such people transmit their knowledge by means of speech rather than documents. This explains why designers generally use interviews and pick up their knowledge from talking.

In OICSI the initial description of the universe of discourse provided by users of the future information system is made via sentences in French.

This choice creates certain problems: the richness of natural language complicates the analysis and interpretation tasks. In order to reduce these difficulties we have limited the use of the French language (these restrictions are summarized in figure 2).

> . Sentences must be in the present indicative tense, in the third person the singular or the plural.
> . The use of metaphors is forbidden.
> . Sentences including inversion of the subject group with regard to the verbal group are excluded.
> . Sentences which compose the text must be, so far as possible independent of each other.

Figure 2: Restriction of French language use

However these limits are sufficiently broad so as to not excessively restrict the system's users. In addition , we have developed tutorial software which explains to the user what kind of knowledge the system requires, in order to reduce "background noise" in discourse and to eliminate so far as possible all information which is not relevant from the design point of view. For example this tutorial software encourages users to describe classes of facts rather than facts themselves. Figure 3 illustrates sentences accepted by OICSI.

> . A client is described by a unique number, a name, an address.
> . An order is composed of a set of order lines, a number, and a client's name
> . When an order arrives, if the stock is sufficient, one makes delivery and updates the stock.
> . a client who has a turnover upper than $10 000, has a special status
> . an order line associated to a product which is out of stock is postponed

Figure 3: Examples of initial sentences

3.2 Classes of facts

We have chosen a descriptive model in which the static aspects and the dynamic aspects of the real world are represented simultaneous and in a complementary manner.

The model follows the perspective of the models included in the methods Remora [ROL 82], ACM/PCM [BRO 82], TAXIS [MYL 80] and CIAM [GUS 82]. It enables a causal description of the behaviour of the real system to be made (illustrated in figure 4): events trigger off actions which modify the state of entities; these state changes can in turn be events...

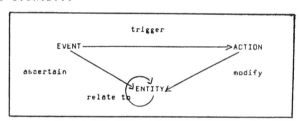

Figure 4: Causal description of the behaviour

The model involves three types of class: entity, action, event and four types of association between these classes.

. **An entity class** (having the meaning which is usual in data models) represents a set of concrete or abstract objects possessing analogous properties. The class "ORDER" and the class "CLIENT" are examples of the entity class.

. **An action class** represents a set of actions of the same type carried out in the real world. The class "DELIVERY" is an action class which describes all deliveries of orders.

. **An event class** is a set of similar state changes in the real world which effectively trigger off actions belonging to one or several action classes. For example the set of "ARRIVAL OF ORDER" forms an event class.

. **An association of type "relate to"** represents a link between two entity classes. This relation can express a link "is a" or "part of" between these two entity classes.
For example the relation "has ordered" defined between the two entity classes ORDER and CLIENT is of the type "relate to".

. An association of type "modify", defined between an action class A and an entity class E, expresses the fact that the actions of A modify the entities of E. For example, such a relation is defined between the action class "UPDATING OF STOCK" and the entity class "PRODUCT".

. An association of type "trigger" defined between an event class EV and an action class A expresses the fact that an event of EV triggers off an action of A. Several relations of the type "trigger" can be defined on the same event class.
For example two relations of this type exist between the event class "ARRIVAL OF ORDER" and the action classes "DELIVERY" and "UPDATING STOCK" expressing that the arrival triggers off the actions of delivery and updating.

. An association of type "ascertain" defined between an event class EV and an entity class expresses the fact that an element of EV is a state change of an entity of E. For example a relation of this type exists between the event class "STOCK BREAKING" and the entity class "PRODUCT".

This level of facts is represented by a semantic network. Each type of class is represented in it by a node type in the network (entity node, action node, event node). Any association between classes is expressed by an arc between the nodes associated with the class. One example of a descriptive network is given in figure 5

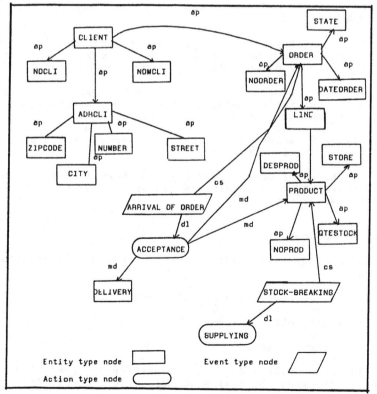

Figure 5: Descriptive network

NOTE: the network includes a fourth type of node: the node condition type. This node enables us to insert a predicate which completes the description of an action, an entity or an event.

3.3 The elements of the conceptual schema

The underlying model at this level corresponds to a normalized version of descriptive model.

The three basic types and the four association types are structured by means of three abstraction structures namely aggregation, generalization and association.

. Aggregation [SMI 77a] is used to manipulate as a complete whole (aggregate class) the regrouping of several different classes (component classes). For example: the class "STUDENT" can be considered as the aggregate class of the classes "NAME", "ADDRESS", "COURSES"...

. Generalization [SMI 77b] allow us to consider a group of specialised classes as a unique class which is the generic class. For example: the class STUDENT and the class TEACHER can be considered as a single class PERSON.

. Association [BRO 82] is used to manipulate as a block (set class) several instances of the same class (member class). For example: the class "TEAM" can be considered as a set class of the class "PLAYER".

The three forms apply to the three types: ENTITY, ACTION, and EVENT. The resulting conceptual schema is a hierarchy of entities, a hierarchy of actions and a hierarchy of events.

The use of norms (figure 6) in the representation of the three types by means of a hierarchy leads to a conceptual schema which is non-redondant, coherent and complete.

Figure 7 is the design conceptual schema corresponding to the classes of facts in figure 5.

The nodes of domain type (striped boxes) allow us to detail the representation of classes by associating each class property to a value domain.

4 THE BASE OF RULES

As already mentioned, the base of rules includes five types of rule:

- natural language analysis rules
- interpretation rules
- structuration rules
- validation rules
- dialogue rules.

These rules correspond to the different types of design activities. They allow the system to move progressively from initial facts to the conceptual schema.

CONSTRAINTS : The model is normative in the sense that the construction of complex objects is constrained in the following way:

N1: Identification of objects

Any complex object must have an identifier which is indicated on the network by the [id] symbol.
Example (figure 9): NOCLI is the identifier of the aggregate object CLIENT.

N2: Aggregation norm

The relationship between an aggregate object and one of its component object is a function that must be total and monovalued; the reverse "part of" relationship can be a multivalued and partial function.
Example: an ORDER has only one number (NOORDER), only one date (DATEORDER), one set DETAIL and refers to only one CLIENT. Conversely a CLIENT can have 0,1,n ORDERS.

N3: Set norm
The relationship between a set object and the corresponding member object must be a total and multivalued function; the reverse relationship "member of" must be a total and monovalued function.
Example: DETAIL is a set of LINE instances. Any LINE instance belong to one and only one instance of DETAIL.

N4: Generic norm

N4.1: An "is a" relationship between a specialized object and the corresponding generic object must be a total and monovalued function.

N4.2: Any instance of a generic object is at least one instance of a specialized object.

Example: any instance of respectively POSTPONED-ORDER and ACCEPTED-ORDER are instances of ORDER. The ORDER population is the union of POSTPONED-ORDER and ACCEPTED-ORDER populations.

N5: Event atomicity and completness norm

N5.1: An event is atomic: it is defined as the noticeable state change of only one entity.
Example: The STOCK-BREAKING event refers to the entity STOCK.

N5.2: The predicate specifying the noticeable state change must be present in the conceptual schema and introduced as a condition type node.
Example: The P1 predicate is a component object of the STOCK-BREAKING aggregate.

Figure 6: The Norms

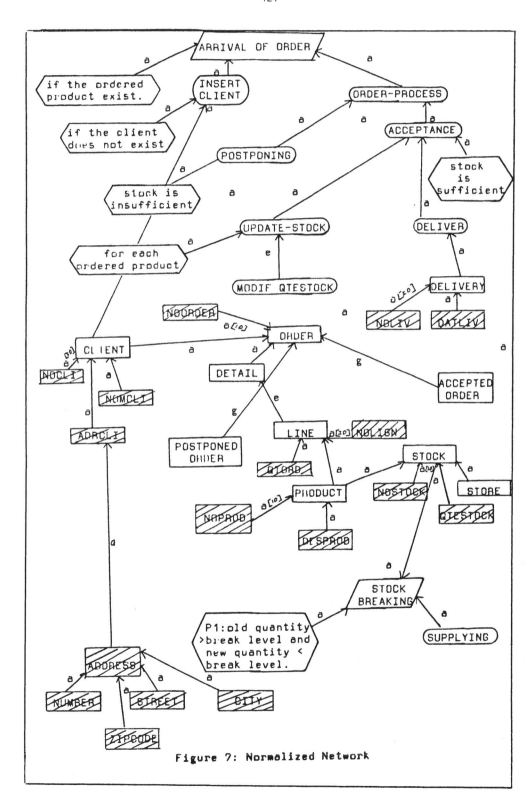

Figure 7: Normalized Network

They are all of the type production rules and are at present programmed in Prolog. We will analyse them in turn.

4.1 Natural language analysis rules

We use solutions proposed in the field of natural language recognition [BRU 75], [COR 79] and [KAY 81], in order to represent natural language statements by means of syntactic trees. The tree elaborating process uses two types of rules: lexical rules and syntactic rules.

The role of <u>lexical rules</u> is to determine the grammatical nature of each word and to associate semantic values to the word. The lexical rules use a dictionary which contain information about the grammatical nature of words and about verb meanings.

The <u>syntactic rules</u> allow the system, on the one hand, to verify that a sentence belongs to the authorized language, and, on the other hand, to build up syntactic trees as internal representation of this sentence. These rules are based on the use of a generative grammar [CHO 65] and they correspond to the system's grammatical knowledge.

4.2 Interpretation rules

These rules are the formalization of the knowledge used in the activity of abstraction. These rules operate on initial facts and generate fact classes.

The formalisation of the abstraction type knowledge is the most difficult. The abstraction task is the most creative and generally the designers are not able to explain how they perform it. Our option is based on the hypothesis that particular words or set of words, or particular grammatical structures are systematically used to describe particular situations. For example, event situations are described by means of sentences which begin with the word "when" or synonim; the verbs which are derived from "to be" and "to have" are used in the objects characterizations... Thus we have formalized the designer's knowledge in the abstraction area with two types of rules named:

    - analysis rules
    - interpretation rules.

(a) The analysis rules are of a grammatical type. They are used to determine the nature of circumstancial propositions, the nature of verbs etc...

For example:

R1: IF the first word of a circumstancial proposition is "when" or a synonim
    AND the verb of the proposition expresses an appearence
    THEN it is a time circumstancial proposition.

R2: IF the verb of a circumstancial proposition expresses a state (as to be, to stay,...)
    THEN it is a conditional circumstancial proposition.

(b) The interpretation rules perform the abstraction task. They mapp sentences and concepts, using the grammatical structure and the nature od sentence elements which have previously been determined.

For example:

R3: IF in the sentence, there is a time circumstancial proposition
   AND the main proposition verb expresses an action
   THEN - the time circumstancial proposition describes an event
        - the main proposition expresses an operation.

R4: IF there is only a main proposition, and one subject and one predicate
   AND the verb expresses a possession
   THEN - the subject describes an entity
        - the predicate describes an entity
        - the entity described by the predicate is an attribute of the subject entity

4.3 Structuration rules

The structuration rules operate on fact classes and generate elements of the conceptual schema. They offer a structuring of fact classes by taking into account of the three following criteria:

   - the model's norms
   - the necessity to represent the evolution over time for real phenomena
   - habits resulting from experience.

Each structuration rule associates alternative situations with an initial situation taken in the base of facts.

The context of a structuration rule can lead the inference motor to trigger off:

   - dialogue rules which enable the system to acquise complementary information from the designer, and which help the designer to choose the most adequate structure.

   - validation rules which enable the system to eliminate incorrect or ambiguous structures.

We will illustrate the structuration rules, of which there are thirty, and which can be grouped into three classes:

   - rules for structuring classes
   - rules for structuring associations between entity classes
   - rules for structuring dynamic aspects of entity classes.

4.3.1 Rules for structuring classes

They enable the system to complete the specification of
different classes present in the base of facts. They guide the
acquisition of class identifiers, the definition of value domains
for each class property, or otherwise carry out the typing of entity
nodes. These rules are mainly based on the model's norms.

We may illustrate this type of rule by the following
example.

Initially, the situation in the base of facts is that of
figure 8a

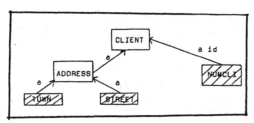

Figure 8a

Application of a validation rule requests correction of
the situation since each entity node must have an identifier.

In this context a dialogue rule is activated in order to
allow the designer to provide an identifier for the node "ADDRESS".

If he does not wish to identify the elements of the
population represented by the node "ADDRESS", the role of the
structuration rule is to propose an alternative solution illustrated
by figure 8b in which the "ADDRESS" node has become a domain node.

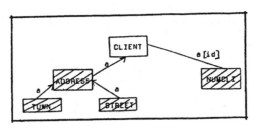

Figure 8b

4.3.2 Rules for structuring associations between entity classes

These rules allow the system to complete the
specification of associations between entity classes.

to do this:

- they use three characteristics (valuation, totality and permanence) of the association supplied by the user for each association. The definition of these three criteria is synthetized in figure 9.

- They offer the user different possible representations according to the three characteristics and the three elementary structures (aggregation, association and generalization).

---

totalness

An association of "relate to" type f between two entities A and B is <u>total</u>, if and only if each instance of A is associated with at least one instance of B, at any point of time, f is <u>partial</u> if not.
more formally:

f is total (t) $\longleftrightarrow \forall t \in T \ \forall a \in A \ \exists g \in Gt(f): \pi_1(g)=a.$

f is partial (pa) $\longleftrightarrow \exists t \in T \ \exists a \in A \ \not\exists g \in Gt(f): \pi_1(g)=a.$

where T=[points of time which are ordered]
Gt(f)={(a,b)∈ A×B / f(a)=b at t}
π_1(a,b): first component projection.

valuation

An association of "relate to" type f between two entities A and B is <u>simple</u> if and only if each instance of A is associated with at most one instance of B at any point of time, else f is <u>multiple</u>.
more formally:

f is simple (s) $\longleftrightarrow \forall t \in T \ \forall a \in A \ \exists g,g' \in Gt(f) \ \pi_1(g)=a \ \pi_1(g')=a \longrightarrow$

$g=g'$

f is multiple (m) $\longleftrightarrow \exists t \in T \ \exists a \in A \ \exists g,g' \in Gt(f) \cdot g \neq g' \ \pi_1(g)=a \wedge$
$\pi_1(g')=a$

permanency

An association of "relate to" type f between two entities A and B is <u>permanent</u> if and only if the set of the images of an instance of A at t is included in the set of the images of this instance at t' (t'>t), if not, f is <u>variable</u>.
more formally:

f is permanent (p) $\longleftrightarrow \forall t,t' \in T \ t<t' \ \forall a \in A \ $ we have:
{g∈ Gt(f), π_1(g)=a} ⊆ {g∈ Gt'(f), π_1(g)=a}

f is variable (v) $\longleftrightarrow \exists t,t' \in T \ t<t' \ \exists a \in A \ $ we have:
{g∈ Gt(f), π_1(g)=a} ⊄ {g∈ Gt'(f), π_1(g)=a}

Figure 9: Characterization of 'relate to' arcs

We can illustrate the rules of this type by the following example:

Initially, the situation is that of figure 10a.

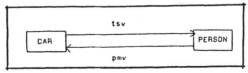

Figure 10a

This represents:

- an association <CAR-PERSON>. It is total (every car has an owner), simple (at any time a car has only one owner) and variable (a car can change owners).

- an association <PERSON-CAR>. It is partial (there are people who are not owners), multiple (a person can have several cars) and variable (a person can change cars).

In this context the role of the structuration rule is to propose two alternative structures (figure 10b and 10c).

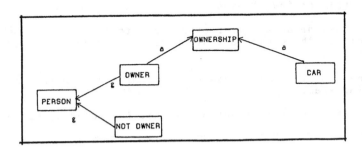

Figure 10b

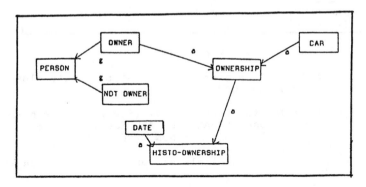

Figure 10c

The representation in figure 10b is an instantaneous representation of the association <PERSON-CAR>: any instance of the class "OWNERSHIP" expresses a current association between an owner and a car.

The representation in figure 10c is an extension of the one in figure 11b so as account for evolution of the association <PERSON-CAR>. The class "HISTO-OWNERSHIP" represents the whole set of associations <PERSON-CAR> over the course of time.

4.3.3 Rules for structuring dynamic aspects

These rules enable the system to represent the life cycle of entity classes (birth, death, modification...).

To do this:

- they detail the description of action classes and event classes present in the base of facts,

- they complete the description of the behaviour of entity classes (with action classes and event classes) so as to cover the whole life cycle of the classes,

- they propose different representations of this behaviour with the help of the elementary structures: aggregation, association and generalization.

We can illustrate this category of structuration rules by the following example:

Initially, the situation is that indicated by figure 11a.

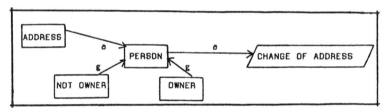

Figure 11a

This represents a hierarchy "IS A" of entity classes "PERSON", "OWNER" and "NON-OWNER".

The structuration rule suggest (figure 11b) a hierarchy "IS A" of the event classes "CHANGE OF ADDRESS", "CHANGE OF ADDRESS OF OWNER" and "CHANGE OF ADDRESS OF NON OWNER".

The specialised event classes are ascertained on the specialised entity classes.

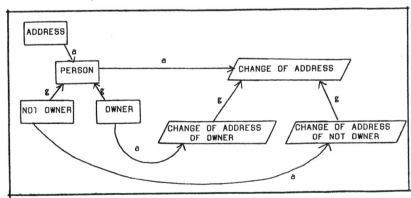

Figure 11b

In this contexte, the inference motor triggers off a dialogue rule to allow the designer to confirm or to refuse this proposition.

4.4 Validation rules

These rules result from formalisation of the activity of validation. They control and ensure the coherency of the base of facts.

They are grouped into:

- <u>conformity</u> rules which ensure conformity with the model's norms (identifier norm, norm of atomicity of action)

- <u>semantic coherency</u> rules which test adequation of the chosen representation with real phenomena.

These rules are based on the following principles:

- They detect incorrect situations (incoherency, ambiguity, lack...)

- The inference motor triggers off dialogue rules to allow the designer to correct such situations.

We can use several examples to illustrate this type of rule.

(a) Consider the following initial situation:

This situation is ambiguious, two plausible interpretation exist:

Either both arcs represent the same association written twice or both arcs represent different associations.

In this case the inference motor triggers off a dialogue rule asking the designer to remove the ambiguity.

If the second interpretation is chosen by the designer the two associations must be named differently (renting and owning) for example).

(b) Some rules of this type detected situations which have been shown by experience to be frequent sources of error.

b1: Given the following initial situation:

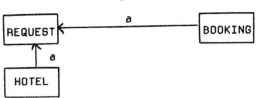

Though correct with respect to the norms of the model this situation can be bad representation of the real world since the hotel where the booking was made is not necessarily the hotel which was requested.

Such a situation leads to the inference motor's triggering off dialogue and structuring rules aiming at clarifying the description.

b2: Consider the following initial situation:

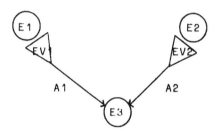

This situation describes two events EV1 and EV2 which trigger off actions modifying the same entity E3. In this context the dialogue rules will enable the system to ensure that both events EV1 and EV2 are independent (one can occur independantly with respect to the other).

6. CONCLUSION

In this paper we have presented an expert design tool for conceptual modelling of information systems.

Motivation for this work is an increasing need of effective and easy to use design support tools in any system development environment, and in particular in databases applications which become more and more large and semantically complex and where the development costs should be limited.

The knowledge base of OISCI is the basis of the tool. We mention that it includes both a base of facts and a base of rules. The base of facts allows to describe at different levels of abstraction the facts of the application domain that must be <represented in the information system. The base of rules is a step forward in the formalization of both formal design rules and experimental design rules.

Our futur works deal with the relational mapping of the normalized network, and the connection with the Proquel language and Rubis DBMS [LIN 87] which supports an automatic control of the dynamic aspects of information systems, i.e event recognition, and action triggering.

REFERENCES

[ABR 74] Jr. Abrial: Data Semantics in Data Management Systems
Klimbie and Koffman (eds) North Holland 1974.
[BRA 83] R.P. Bragger, A. Dudler, J. Rebsamen, C.A. Zehnder:
"GAMBIT: An interactive Database Design Tool for Data Structures,
Integrity Constraints and Transactions" in Database Techniques for
Professional Workstations, ETH Zurich 1983.
[BRO 82] M.L Brodie, E. Silva: Active and Passive Component
Modeling: ACM/PCM in IFIP WG8.1 working conference on "Information
systems design methodologies: a comparative review" 1982.
[BRU 75] B. Bruce: Case Systems for Natural Language, Artificial
Intelligence Nb 6 1975.
[CER 83] S. Ceri: "Methodologies and Tools for Database Design" ed,
North Holland Publ Co 1983.
[CHE 76] P.P. Chen: "The entity Relationship Model - Towards a
Unified View of Data" ACM TODS V1, N1, 1976.
[CHO 65] Chomsky Aspects of the theory of syntax MIT Press 1965
[COR 79] M. Cordier: Connaissances semantiques et pragmatiques en
comprehension du langage naturel 2ème congrés AFCET-INRIA
Reconnaissance des formes et Intelligence Artificielle, Toulouse
1979.
[DBE 84]: Data Base Engineering review vol 17 n°4. Special issue on
Data design aids methods and environment Dec 84
[FIL 68] :"Case for case" in Universal theory in linguistic Bach
(ed) 1968.
[GAN 79] C. Gane T. Sarson: Structured systems analysis Prentice
Hall 1979
[GUS 82] M.R. Gustafsson, J.A. Bubenko T. Karlsson: "A Declarative
Approach to Conceptual Information Processing" in IFIP WG8.1 Working
Conference on "Information Systems Design Methodologies: a
comparative review" 1982.
[KAY 1981] Kayser: les ATN sémantiques, 3ème Congrés Reconnaissance
des formes et Intelligence Artificielle AFCET 1981.
[LIN 87]: JY Lingat, P. Nobecourt, C. Rolland: Behaviour Management
in Data Base applications in Proceedings of VLDB 87 Brigthon UK.
[LUN 82]: Lundeberg: The ISAC approch to specification of IS and its
application to the organization of an IFIP working conference in
IFIP WG8.1 working conference on "Information systems design
methodologies: a comparative review" 1982.
[MYL 80] J. Mylopoulos,H. Wong: Some features of the TAXIS model
Proc. 6th Int conf. on VLDB 1980.
informatiques Masson 1983.
[ROLLAND 82] C. Rolland, C. Richard: The Remora methodology fo
information systems design and management in IFIP WG8.1 working
conference on "Information systems design methodologies: a
comparative review" 1982
[ROL 86] C. Rolland, C. Proix: An expert system approach to
information system design in Proc. IFIP Congress 86 North Holland
1986.
[ROS 77] Dt. Ross, Kl Schaum: Structured systems analysis for
requirements definition IEEE Transaction on software engineering
1977
[SMI 77a] J.M Smith, C.P. Smith: Database Abstractions :
Aggregation. Communications of ACM. June 1977.
[SMI 77b] J.M. Smith, C.P. Smith: Database Abstractions :
Aggregation and Generalization. ACM TRANSACTIONS on Database
Systems. June 1977.
[VER 82] G.M.A. Verheijen, J. VAN Bekkum: "NIAM: An Information
Analysis Method.

Multi-Level Transaction Management, Theoretical Art or Practical Need?*

C. Beeri[1], H.-J. Schek[2], G. Weikum[2]

[1] Hebrew University at Jerusalem
Israel

[2] Technical University of Darmstadt
West Germany

Summary

A useful approach to the design and description of complex data management systems is the decomposition of a system into a hierarchically organized collection of levels. In such a system, transaction management is distributed among the levels. This paper presents the fundamental theory of multi-level concurrency control and recovery. A model for the computation of multi-level transactions is introduced by generalizing from the well known single-level theory. Three basic principles, called commutation, reduction, and abstraction are explained. Using them enables one to explain and prove seemingly "tricky" implementation techniques as correct, by regarding them as multi-level algorithms. We show how the theory helps to understand and explain in a systematic framework techniques that are in use in today's DBMSs. We also discuss how and why multi-level algorithms may achieve better performance than single-level ones.

1. INTRODUCTION

Many operational and proposed database systems use quite sophisticated algorithms for transaction management. These algorithms often combine several techniques for concurrency control and recovery. Although transaction management has been thoroughly investigated, and is now considered to be well understood [BHG87], these algorithms do not seem to fit into the accepted framework - they cannot be proven correct, nor easily explained in it.

In this paper, we present multi-level transactions, an extension of the classical transaction model, as a framework in which transaction management algorithms for large and complex systems can be designed, explained and proven to be correct. Nested transactions have received much attention recently, particularly for use in distributed systems and in object-oriented programming environments [Mo85, Li85, Wa84, BKK85, HR87]. Multi-level transactions, sometimes referred to as "open nested transactions" [Tr83, cf. also Gr81b], are a special case, in which transaction management takes place on a fixed set of levels simultaneously. It is particularly suited to the design and description of transaction management in complex systems. (Object oriented systems are an exception. A framework as the one presented here for multi-level systems can probably be developed for object oriented systems as well; this is a subject for future research.)

A fair number of recent publications deals with the theory of nested and multi-level transactions [BBGLS83, BBG87, LM86, MGG86, Wei86a]. These papers are quite technical. We aim to provide in this paper an introduction to the model, to explain the underlying principles, and to present the arguments for its suitability as a framework for dealing with transaction management in complex systems.

The following points are considered. First, in generalizing from single-level to multi-level transactions, how are the paradigms of concurrency control and recovery affected, in particular what are the correctness criteria? Second, given the new model, what are the proof techniques that can be used for proving the correctness of algorithms. Proving correctness is not a purely academic exercise. Synchronization protocols, as well as techniques for enhancing system reliability, are quite complex, and therefore error prone. Subtle changes in a recovery algorithm may have

---

* This research was supported by a grant from the State of Hessen, provided under an agreement for cooperation with the Hebrew University.

disastrous effects on the reliability of a system. A thorough and methodical analysis, aimed at producing a correctness proof, helps to discover such bugs. Furthermore, a well structured proof methodology is an excellent guide for a well structured algorithm design.

The third point concerns performance. Multi-level algorithms are often used to obtain better performance than is achievable with single-level algorithms. However, a multi-level approach also incurs higher overhead. Thus, a performance gain is not a necessary consequence of a multi-level architecture, but rather it depends on many factors; these include a proper choice of levels and a careful evaluation of the cost/benefit tradeoff of various algorithms. We explain why and how is the multi-level approach related to performance. We do not however, provide a detailed analysis of issues relating to cost/benefit analysis; such an analysis is outside the scope of this paper.

The outline of the paper is as follows: In Section 2 we describe implementation practices of concurrency control and recovery that are used in various systems. We do not describe all techniques in use, nor provide a detailed discussion of the techniques that we do describe. Our goal is to convince the reader, by considering the plethora of techniques (or possibly "tricks") of the need for a unifying and simplifying framework. Section 3 presents the model of multi-level transactions. Sections 4 and 5 then deal with concurrency control and recovery, respectively. In Section 6, we use the model and the concepts developed in previous sections to explain some of the combinations of techniques mentioned in Section 2. We also discuss how our framework may be applied in systems that store and manipulate complex objects, which is typically the case in the new generation of experimental database systems. For illustration purposes we use the DASDBS prototype [PSSWD87], currently under implementation at Darmstadt.

2. IMPLEMENTATION PRACTICES

It is well known that simple user requests usually involve considerable activity below the user interface. For example, a request to delete or insert a tuple in a relational system involves the manipulation of several physical records, some representing the tuple, others in various indices, the manipulation of the pages containing these records, and the manipulation of internal tables, such as the free space map. Concurrency control and recovery mechanisms need to deal with this complex activity, to guarantee consistency and reliability. A simple, page oriented, approach to transaction management, that treats all data uniformly, is correct. However, it results in a degradation of performance that is intolerable for many applications. To guarantee an acceptable level of performance, more sophisticated solutions have been proposed and implemented. In this section we describe some of these ideas and techniques. Our discussion is couched in terms of the relational model. However, it applies equally well to other data models.

2.1 Concurrency Control

Consider the following three transactions, that insert, delete, and read tuples of relations R and S.

(T1) insert into R(col1 = a, col2 = b)

insert into S(col1 = d, col2 = e)

(T2) delete from R
where col1 = a and col2 = c

(T3) select *
from R
where col1 = a and col2 = b

Note that there is a conflict between T1 and T3. There is no conflict, however, between T1 and T2, and between T2 and T3. Each of these two pairs can in principle be executed concurrently.

The simple textbook approach to concurrency control is to use strict two phase locking (2PL) on the database entities. This is a one-level algorithm. Since pages are the units of information passed between the database system and the operating system, a straightforward implementation is to use 2PL on pages. This solution is correct. However, a page often contains several records, and a page lock held by one transaction may unnecessarily block another transaction that needs to access another record on the page. For example, if the records of R are organized by the values of col1, if T3 locks the page(s) containing the records it needs, it probably prevents T2 from accessing some of the records it needs, until T3 releases its locks. Thus, page level locking does not achieve the level of concurrency that is potentially possible.

One can use record locks instead of page locks. This by itself, however, is insufficient to guarantee correctness. To access or update a record, one needs also to access or update access paths and data structures on the page(s) that contain the record. Concurrent accesses may corrupt these structures. (Simply stated, record operations are not atomic.) The solution, employed in System R [As76], and later by many other systems, is to use, in addition to record based 2PL, also "short" page locks. Each page lock is held only for the duration of a record operation, called RSS operation in System R. These locks serve to guarantee the consistency (i.e. atomicity) of record operations. Serializability is guaranteed by the record based locking protocol.

The scenario above is actually simplified. In reality, in addition to data records, transactions also need to access index records and internal tables. Assume, for example, that both T2 and T3 use an index on col1 for accessing R. If T3 first locks the pages of the index containing the index records for col1 = a, then surely T2 will be blocked. Further, if the index is a B-tree, internal nodes need to be locked as well to guarantee consistency. A transaction that locks the root in update mode blocks all other transactions from accessing the index until it terminates. Similar, or even worse, effects are caused by locks on internal tables, since these are accessed by all transactions. Finally, there is the well known phantom problem. In our example, locks held by T3 on the records it reads, do not necessarily block T1 from inserting a new record that qualifies for retrieval by T3. These and similar problems have been extensively discussed in the literature.

Replacing page locks by record locks is a good solution for accesses to the data records. It does not solve the other problems. The solutions that have been proposed all break the concurrency control mechanism into components. The index is accessed using one of the special purpose tree oriented protocols that guarantee that nodes are locked only for short durations [Sh85]. Data records are locked instead of data pages, with auxiliary "short" page locks, as described above. "Short" locks are also used for "hot spot" internal tables (these are often called latches). Several solutions have been offered for the phantom problem. One is a simple form of predicate locking: key intervals are locked. This solution is easily implemented by locking index leaf entries. Note that in this solution, if T3 locks the index entry for col1 = a, T2 is blocked. In order to overcome this, the usage of more sophisticated predicates for locking has been proposed in [BJS86], or the utilization of signatures for locking, not only for searching, has been recommended in [DPS83].

2.2 Recovery

Probably the most well known and popular recovery method is logging. Here again, the textbook method is appropriate for a one-level system, hence it is natural to consider page level logging. Optimizations such as logging byte intervals rather than complete pages enhance the performance of this simple method. However, the recovery mechanism must be compatible with the concurrency control mechanism being used. It is well known that if locks on pages are released before end of transaction then using page before-images for rollback is incorrect: rolling back the effects of an aborted transaction may destroy some of the effects of a committed transaction. That is, strict 2PL needs to be used on the pages. However, if record locking is used, then page locks are "short" and are released before the end of transaction. To prevent "domino" effects, more sophisticated solutions are necessary. System R uses a two-component recovery scheme. A shadow pages technique is used to guarantee a certain degree of consistency for record operations [Gr81a].

Record level logging, using abstract representations of operations and their inverses is used as a complementary technique. It is stated in [Gr81a] that the shadow page mechanism has been found to be inefficient, and in retrospect it should not have been implemented. However, in that case another mechanism would have been needed to bridge the uncompatibility gap between concurrency control and recovery. For example, the Synapse system also uses a two-component scheme, but logging is used in both components [Ong84].

2.3 Some Questions

As we have demonstrated, to achieve acceptable performance, database systems need to use sophisticated and quite complex transaction management mechanisms, combining various techniques and protocols. The following questions naturally arise. The correctness of concurrency control protocols is traditionally defined in terms of serializability. The early release of "short" locks violates the 2PL property; furthermore, it is easy to find interleaving of operations of transactions that are allowed, e.g., by the protocol used by System R, that are not serializable. Have we lost serializability as the correctness criterion, and if so, what is the correctness criterion that is being used? Similarly, have we abandoned the idea of strict 2PL as a basis for recovery? Many of the techniques we have mentioned can be explained on an ad-hoc basis. However, systems that are radically different from the systems of the previous generation are now being developed. Can such techniques be adapted for systems that support new applications, with more complex data and transaction types? Phrased differently, are we dealing with techniques applied in the framework of an engineering discipline, or simply with a set of clever, but ad-hoc, tricks.

We postulate that these and many other techniques can be explained and related to each other by regarding transaction management as taking place at several levels of abstraction, and by regarding higher level transactions as consisting of subtransactions. In terms of the discussion above, we may identify pages, records and tuples, or tuple predicates, as levels of abstractions. Accesses to indices, to data records and to internal tables can be viewed as subtransactions. The different components of transaction management algorithms are used for synchronization at different levels of abstraction. In short, we offer multi-level transactions as the right framework for designing, understanding and proving the correctness of transaction management mechanisms in real-life database systems. This approach is elaborated in the following sections.

3. A MODEL

We introduce here a model for multi-level transactions, and briefly consider some of its features. The model is presented as a special case of a nested transactions model.

In the classical transaction model, a transaction invokes operations. In a system that allows nesting, a transaction may also invoke subtransactions. Since these subtransactions may also invoke subtransactions, the computation generated by one transaction can be viewed as a *tree*. The interleaved computation of several transactions is a *forest*. Each leaf of the forest corresponds to an operation, each internal node corresponds to a (sub)-transaction; from its parent's viewpoint, the node is considered as an (abstract) operation. The roots correspond to the transactions. In addition to the caller-callee relationship, a computation contains a *partial order* on the nodes of the forest. The order is defined on the leaves – these are the operations that are actually executed. The ordering of internal nodes is derived from that of the leaves; a node x precedes a node y if all the leaves under x precede all the leaves under y.

A structure $(F, <)$, consisting of a forest, and of a partial order on its nodes (that satisfies the constraint that the order on internal nodes is derived from that of the leaves) is called a *nested history*. It is a generalization of the concept of history, used in classical serializability. In this paper, we use nested history instead of history. *

---

* In the following we use history and computation interchangeably.

In a *general (unstructured) nested system*, subtransaction invocation is determined by the application or system programmer. There is no constraint on the structure of computations, in particular on their depth. Also, the system state is the same at all stages of a computation - there is no concept of state abstraction. This is in contrast to the situation in a typical data management system. In such a system, transactions invoke high level operations. But these operations are not executed directly; rather, there is a program associated with each operation, and the program is invoked to carry out the operation. The execution of the program is a subtransaction that implements the operation. In such a system, there are constraints on the structure of computations – all the forests are similarly structured, and in particular have a predetermined number of levels. The views of the system's state associated with the levels may differ - higher levels are associated with more abstract views of the states. We refer to this special case of nested transaction systems as *multi-level* transaction systems. In object oriented systems, where operations on (messages to) an object may cause it to send messages to other objects, the restrictions on depth do not exist. However, a structure, defined by the relationships between objects is still imposed on the computations, and the concept of state abstraction plays a significant role. Such systems may be refered to as *general structured* nested transaction systems. In this paper we deal with multi-level systems. We believe that our approach can be extended to general structured systems, but we do not pursue this direction here.

An operation of a transaction is implemented by a program. However, is it justified to regard a computation of this program as a subtransaction? When dealing with concurrency control, we assume that the code for the transaction is written so that it correctly implements the specification of the transaction. However, the code is written under the assumption that the operations are carried out atomically *, and without interleaving with operations of other transactions, so the correctness of the code holds only when this assumption is valid. This assumption certainly makes sense when the transaction is user code – users need not be aware of the facts that other transactions are being run concurrently. It is also reasonable when the transaction is actually a subtransaction at a higher level of the system – this is a consequence of the principle of information hiding. If operations are atomic, then the fact that operations are in reality interleaved with those of other transactions is taken care of by concurrency control. If operations are not really atomic, but rather are implemented as sequences of lower level operations, then, to preserve the correctness of the system, the computations that implement operations must guarantee virtual atomicity of the operations, with respect to both isolation from the partial effects of other operations and recovery. Thus, these computations must behave as subtransactions.

We assume the following properties of histories. First, leaf operations are executed atomically. The order on the leaves does not need to be total. In a distributed system it will in general be partial. As explained above, the order on the internal nodes is derived from that of the leaves under them

Both transactions and subtransactions may abort. When a transaction is aborted its computation is terminated. When a subtransaction is aborted its parent must be notified; however, the parent continues its execution. The ability to abort subtransactions and continue the computation increases the power and flexibility of the transaction paradigm beyond that of classical transactions.

Let us consider the differences between general (unstructured) nesting and multi-level nesting. The first, and most obvious difference, is that in a multi-level system we have a fixed number of levels. We may regard each adjacent pair of levels as defining a *layer* of the system, and we may use layer specific concurrency control and recovery mechanisms. This appraoch opens the way to modular transaction management techniques, and combines nicely with a top-down approach to system design. In contrast, in a general unstructured nested system there is no predefined notion

---

* 'Atomically' is used here in the intuitive sense – indivisible.

of layers, so a single global mechanism needs to be used.

The other major difference is that of *state abstraction*. We have not disussed states of the system so far – they are not part of the history. However, obviously the computation represented by a history changes the state of the system. In a multi-level system it is usually the case that the system's states are viewed differently on each level. The higher the level, the more abstract the state. In a general nested system, there need not be abstraction. The concept of state abstraction is significant in both concurrency control and recovery. As we will show in the sequel, performance gains achieved by multi-level transaction management can in often be attributed to the use of state abstractions.

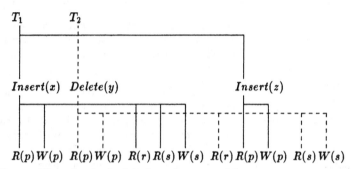

Fig. 1: Three-level schedule (running example)

We use the computation shown in fig. 1 as a running example. It is based on the following scenario. The two transactions T1 and T2 from our introductory example execute the record operations $Insert(x)$, $Insert(z)$, and $Delete(y)$ respectively. For sake of simplicity we did not include the execution of T3 here.

The record operations, in turn, are executed as sequences of page reads and writes in an interleaved manner. We assume that all three records are stored in the page p, and that the insertion and deletion of tuples from R requires index entry maintenance on page s. The page r is the index root page to be read only. Insertion of tuple z into relation S does not require index maintenance. Note that this execution is still an oversimplified presentation af a real execution in that e.g. catalogue access and free space administration is not considered. The sequence of the page operations shown in fig. 1 corresponds to the actual execution sequence. It is easy to observe that the serialization graph for T1 and T2 with respect to page operations has a cycle. So, the contents of the pages p and s obtained by the computation in fig. 1 most probably may not be obtained by executing first T1 and then T2 or vice versa, i.e. by a serial execution. In spite of that we are going to prove correctness for this computation. The solution consists in regarding record operations as (sub-)transactions and in abstracting from details within pages as we will show in the following.

4. CONCURRENCY CONTROL

In this section we deal with concurrency control. We disregard the possibility of aborts or crashes.

4.1 The Paradigm

Consider first non-nested transactions. Each transaction executes atomic operations, but transaction executions are not atomic. The goal of concurrency control is to ensure this property also for interleaved computations. Concurrency control ensures that an interleaved execution is *serializable*, i.e., is equivalent to some serial execution. Transactions in a serializable execution are *isolated*: each transaction observes none or all the effects of any other transaction. Serializability implies more than isolation. Given the equivalent serial order, a transaction sees all the effects of the transactions that precede it in that order, and none of the effects of the transactions that follow it. In addition, the final state reflects the effects of all transactions, executed in that order. In a serializable computation, the executions of transactions take place in possibly overlapping time intervals, but their effect is as if they took place in non-overlapping intervales.

Now assume nesting is allowed. A subtransaction corresponds to an (abstract) operation. The parent transaction expects the operation to be executed atomically. Hence it needs to be isolated from partial effects of concurrent transactions and subtransactions. In particular, if concurrency within transactions is allowed, the subtransactions of each transaction need to be isolated from each other as well. Thus, a nested execution defines a hierarchy of isolation scopes. An interleaved execution should have the same effect as one in which transaction executions occur in disjoint intervals, and within each transaction, the subtransactions execute in disjoint intervals, and so on.

A nested computation is *serial* if it defines a total order on the root transactions, and on the children of each transaction and sub-transaction. Correctness for an interleaved computation is defined as being equivalent to a serial computation. This is a natural extension of the classical *serializability* concept.

A transaction is an execution of a program, and executions of the program in different circumstances may differ. Classical serializability allows an interleaved computation only if it has an equivalent computation in which each transaction has the same operations as in the interleaved computation. This restriction is the key to the simplicity of the theory – no program transformation techniques are involved. We extend this assumption to nested transactions. We only consider equivalence of computations in which the orderings are different, but the operations of each transaction and the parent-child relations are the same.

4.2 Correctness

In principle, one may adopt a *uniform* approach to concurrency control in a multi-level system – a single scheduler is applied to all (sub-)transactions. A more flexible and modular approach that offers better support for structured system design is the *layer-oriented* approach - a different scheduler is used for controlling concurrency at each layer. (Recall that a layer is an adjacent pair of levels. A one-layer scheduler regards the top level nodes as transactions, and the bottom level nodes as operations. All classical schedulers are one-layer.) We concentrate here on the latter approach.

The simplest approach to designing a layer-oriented concurrency control mechanism is to use one of the well known protocols of the classical theory for each of the schedulers. Different schedulers may use the same or different protocols. Unfortunately, not all combinations are correct. To understand why, let us consider how multi-layer protocols can be proven correct.

The basic tool in correctness proofs is equivalence preserving transformations on computations. As in classical serializability, we rely on commutativity of operations. If two adjacent operations commute, then their order can be changed. In the classical theory, this transformation cannot be applied to operations of the same transaction; the ordering imposed by a transaction on its operations needs to be preserved. In a multi-level system the restriction is inherited – if the order of two subtransactions (viewed as operations) cannot be changed because of this restriction, the same is true for any two of their operations. Therefore, we allow to change the order of adjacent commuting operations provided that their least common ancestor (if it exists) does not impose an order on their execution. (This issue is extensively discussed in [BBG87]. In particular, it is explained there that the order imposed by a parent need not be total.) *

Current protocols base their decisions only on commutativity information. Their decisions may be based on the order in which requests for operations arrive, but they do not use other information on orders. Therefore, it is convenient to use an approximation to the restriction

---

* This restriction is actually too strict. See the discussion below.

above. If a transaction "wants" child x to precede child y, then it will not issue the request for y until after x has finished. As a consequence, in the computation, $x < y$ holds. Furthermore, every descendent x precedes every descendent of y. Thus, we restrict the application of commutativity based order changes to pairs of adjacent operations that have distinct, unordered parents. Note that if a (one-layer) computation $c1$ can be transformed by a sequence of such transformations to a serial computation $c2$, then whenever transaction $T1$ precedes transaction $T2$ in $c1$, then the same holds in $c2$. We say that $c1$ is *order-preserving serializable*. A one-layer protocol that allows only order-preserving serializable computations is called *order preserving*.

Commutativity based transformations do not suffice to serialize nested computations, as witnessed by our running example. A second type of transformation is obtained by considering subtransactions as implementations of (abstract) operations. Given a nested computation, let us consider the sub-computation rooted at the parents of the leaf operations. Assuming that by using commutativity we have serialized this sub-computation. Considering it as sub-computation as a one-layer computation, each of its roots is now executed atomically. We can, therefore, prune the subtree rooted at each such root, and replace the subtransaction label of that root with the corresponding operation. This transformation is called *reduction*. By using it we have reduced the number of levels by one. If originally we had an n-level computation, we now have an equivalent (n-1)-level computation.

This process, using alternatively commutativity and reduction, can be continued until only the root level remains, and then we have a serial computation, equivalent to the one from which we started.

As an illustration, we show that the computation in our running example is serializable. We may first commute the $R(p)$, $W(p)$ pair form the $Insert(z)$ operation with the $R(s)$, $W(s)$ pair from the $Delete(y)$. Next, we commute the $R(p)$, $W(p)$ of $Delete(y)$ with the $R(r)$, $R(s)$, $W(s)$ actions of $Insert(x)$. Note that we did not commute actions between the $Insert(x)$ and $Insert(z)$ since they belong to the same transaction. So the order has been preserved. As a next step we apply reduction, i.e. we prune the third level and apply commutations again. E.g. we may commute $Delete(y)$ with $Insert(z)$ ending up with an equivalent serial execution T1 before T2.

There is another, possibly more significant, reason for requiring the one-layer schedulers to use order-preserving protocols. Before presenting it, let us first consider how to prove correctness of protocols, rather than correctness of computations. For that we extend the techniques used in classical serialiazbility. For the sub-computation with roots at level n-1 and leaves at level n (i.e., the computation of layer n-1), consider the *(n-1)-to-n serialization graph*. If that serializtion graph is acyclic then that sub-computation is serializable, and we can apply reduction. It would now seem that if each of the (i-1)-to-i serialization graphs in a given computation is acyclic, then it is serializable. However, in general, this argument fails. When we use the acyclicity of the (n-1)-to-n serialization graph to prune level n, we are in effect changing the execution order. The new order is obtained from any topological ordering of the serialization graph. It imposes an order on the nodes of level n-1, which after pruning is the new leaf level. The important point to observe now is that the execution order on the new (n-1)-level computation is different from the original execution order, restricted to the top n-1 levels. The fact that the (n-2)-to-(n-1) serialization graph in the original computation is acyclic may not imply that the (n-2)-to-(n-1) serialization graph for the new computation is acyclic.

There is a need for some coordination, or handshake, between the schedulers for their combination to be correct. It is needed in order that the nice properties that each scheduler guarantees for its slice of the computation are preserved by the other schedulers. The handshake need not be explicit; it may simply be a property of the protocol used by each scheduler that guarantees the preservation of the effects of other schedulers. It turns out that order preservation is such a property. Consider a conflict based scheduler, say $S1$, that is used between levels n-2 and n-1. It allows only computations in which conflicting operations are ordered. The ordering is determined by the scheduler - this is how it guarantees an acyclic serialization graph. Now assume that the scheduler, say $S2$, used between levels n-1 and level n is order preserving. The scheduler $S2$ guarantees that level n can be pruned, and furthermore, in doing so the new order that is obtained preserves whatever ordering that was imposed on level n-1 by $S1$. This suffices to guarantee that all pairs of conflicting operations on level n-1 are now ordered as in the original order. Since the (n-2)-to-(n-1) serialization graph is defined only in terms of conflicting pairs, we immediately obtain that this serialization graph is preserved when level n is pruned. This line or reasoning leads to the following fundamental theorem.

Theorem [BBG87, cf. also Wei86a]: A combined scheduler for an n-level system, consisting of n-1 order preserving conflict based schedulers, used between the pairs of adjacent levels, is correct.

Fortunateley, many classical protocols are order preserving. These includes the popular two phase locking protocol, optmistic concurrency control and time stamp methods that use monotonically increasing time stamps.

Order preservation has not received a lot of attention in the classical theory of serializability. The previous discussion sheds light on its fundamental role in multi-level systems. (A similar conclusion, regarding the significance of order preservation, has been reached by Lamport, following quite a different route [La86].) A user of an interface regards the operations its sends for execution as atomic. It is rarely the case that they are really executed atomically. Rather, the interface "seen" by that user is supported by software that often executes operations concurrently. The atomicity "seen" by the user is actually serializability guaranteed by that software. As the previous discussion shows, serializability is too weak. The property that is needed is *order preserving* serializability. We postulate that concurrent systems should in general support the property of order preserving serializability for their interfaces.

Despite the discussion above, order preservation is only a sufficient condition for a proper handshake between schedulers. Other, weaker, conditions can be used. We briefly consider one possibility. Given a multi-level computation, with n levels, consider the layer consisting of the two bottom levels, i.e., levels $n-1$ and n, as an independent computation. We may change the order of two commuting operations of level n that belong to different subtransactions of level $n-1$, even though the order imposed by a higher level ancestor is invalidated. This is an equivalence preserving transformation only for that independent computation, not for the complete n-level computation. Following a sequence of applications of commutativity, we may then perform reduction, obtaining a one level computation on the operations of level $n-1$. The ordering on this computation may again be changed by applying commutativity. If, by doing that, we reinstall on that computation an order that is compatible with the order imposed by the subtransactions of levels 1 to $n-2$ on level $n-2$, then we can attach the computation we have obtained as a new $n-1$th level to the given multi-level computation (removing first the original levels n, $n-1$, of course). We have thus obtained an $n-1$ levels computation that is equivalent to the given n-level computation, by going through a sequence of computations that were not equivalent to it.

The crucial issue now is to find a condition that guarantees that such an equivalence transformation exists. Further, we still need a handshake between the schedulers of the different layers. We note that from the discussion of order preservation above it follows that a scheduler needs only to preserve the order of conflicting operations of the top level of its layer - this suffices for the ordering constraints imposed by the scheduler above to be preserved. A condition that guarantees such restricted order preservation is that if two subtransactions on a given level are in conflict, then there exists a pair of their children on the next level that is also in conflict. The reason is that the serialization graph "pulls up" the ordering of such a conflicting pair of children to their parents, and the scheduler preserves the partial order embedded in the graph. But now observe that the ordering imposed by higher level ancestors on conflicting subtransactions of the top level of the layer of that scheduler is also preserved - for the same reason. As for the ordering constraints on commuting subtransactions, these can be reinstalled after reduction by applying commutativity transaformations.

Theorem [Wei87a]: Assume that, in all computations in an n-level system, if two subtransactions conflict then there exists a pair of their children on the next level that are also in conflict. Then a combined scheduler consisting of $n-1$ conflict based schedulers, used between the pairs of adjacent levels, is correct.

According to this theorem, the 3-level schedule shown in fig. 3 is correct, though it is not order preserving serializable from level 2 to level 3.

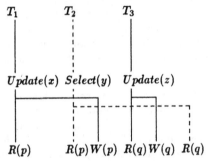

Fig. 2: Three-level schedule that is not order preserving serializable from level 2 to level 3

In this scenario, you may think of x, y, and z as tuples in a hashed file, where y is located on an overflow page. The only existing serialization order between levels 2 and 3 is $Update(z)$ - $Select(y)$ - $Update(x)$, and does not preserve the original order of the two $Update$ subtransactions. However, as there is no conflict between these level 2 operations, we can change the order once more after appying the reduction step, thus obtaining the original order again.

As an application of the order preservation theorem, consider a protocol which uses 2PL twice: Transactions use 2PL on records; to execute a record operation, the page containing it is locked for the duration of the record operation only. On the surface, this looks like a violation of 2PL, since transactions release page locks, then obtain other locks. However, let us consider the system as a three level system. The protocol used between the transactions and the record operations is 2PL. The protocol used between the record operations and the page operations is also 2PL. In a multi-level system, concepts like 2PL are relative. The 2-to-3 scheduler regards the record operations as transactions; its goal is only to ensure serializability of the sub-computation rooted at the record operations. Since 2PL is order preserving, the theorem applies and we obtain that the combined protocol is correct.

In proving the correctness of our running example, and of the iterated application of the 2PL, we have actually cheated. For certain record placement strategies, our protocol allows computations that have no equivalent serial computation. Assume, for example that a computation contains on the record level the operations insert1(x) followed by insert2(y), and that both records were inserted into the same page, x first and then y. The operations commute, and in serializing the computation we may need to change their order. However, the positions of x and y in the page are different if x is inserted before y. Why can we claim then that the operations commute, if the results of executing them in different orders may be different?

The answer lies in the concept of *state abstraction*. While performing page operations, the position of every byte counts. On the record level, we have a more abstract view of states. We want pages to be consistent, and we regard two states as being the same if the pages contain the same records. Details such as record placement become irrelevant at this level of abstraction. Commutativity for the record level is defined in terms of these abstract states, and is more permissive than if it were defined in terms of the page contents. In particular, if a given computation transforms the system from state s1 to state s2, and by changing the order of two record operations we obtain a computation that transforms s1 to s3, we consider the record operations as commutative if s2 and s3 represent the same abstract state. It is shown in [BBG87] that the concepts and techniques of multi-level serializability, namely commutativity and reduction, can be generalized to accomodate state abstractions. When state abstraction is used, transactions can use locks on the entities that are represented in the abstract states - the records. A subtransaction needs the coarser page lock, but that lock is held only for a short duration, since the parent does not need it.

The discussion above illustrates one source for a performance gain that can be achieved by adopting a multi-level protocol – only fine-grained entities are locked for long periods. Note that if each record occupied a page, there would be no real performance gain. Of course, this reasoning isnot restricted to locking based protocols, and state abstraction is not the only source for a performance gain. By breaking a computation of a transaction into subtransactions, interference between transactions is converted into interference between subtransactions, and this often reduces the undesirable effects of such interference, e.g., blocking.

It is interesting to note that our running example with three levels may not be obtained by two 2PL schedulers. However, we may transform it into a four-level computation by introducing another "internal record" layer as shown in fig. 2 with operations like $i(.)$, $d(.)$, $u(.)$, and $r(.)$ which insert, delete, update, and read a stored record or an index leaf entry. The resulting computation can be obtained by 2PL schedulers for each layer. This, again, shows the central importance of abstraction: A rather sophisticated scheduler allowing the three-level computation in fig. 1 is replaced by simple 2PL schedulers on the four-level computation of fig. 3. Generally, it seems that sophisticated schedulers on few layers can be replaced by simple 2PL schedulers on more levels of abstraction. This aspect deserves further investigation.

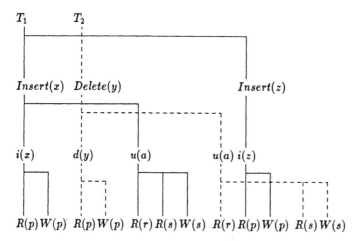

Fig. 3: Four-level schedule, equivalent to fig. 1 obtained by 2PL schedulers

5. RECOVERY

The study of recovery in multi-level systems is still going on. We restrict ourselves to informally presenting basic ideas and principles. Material on multi-level recovery can be found in [MGG86, WS84, DeL87, Wei87a].

5.1 The Paradigm

The goals of the recovery mechanism in a multi-level system are, in principle, quite close to those in a single-level system. However, nesting creates a hierarchy of recovery scopes. This leads to two differences. First, a commit of a subtransaction has a somewhat different semantics than the commit of a transaction. Transaction commit cannot take place unless redo data is safe on stable storage, for otherwise durability cannot be guaranteed. The commit of a subtransaction is only relative to its parent. If a crash occures before the root ancestor of the subtransction committed, that root will be aborted. Thus, subtransaction commit notifies the parent that the subtransaction has terminated successfully, but there is no need for a guarantee of permanence, hence log ahead is not required.

The second difference is that a subtransaction may abort, yet its parent may continue to execute. Aborting a (sub-)transaction implies that all its effects, including those of its subtransactions must be rolled back. The parent may choose to restart the subtransaction, or try another computation path. In this aspect, nesting allows for flexibility and can provide savepoints to the user [Mo85].

5.2 Correctness

It is well-known that recovery protocols must not be designed independently of the concurrency control method. To achieve persistency and failure atomicity, in addition to serializability, requires a well-defined cooperation of these system components. The following key observations are crucial to understanding the interrelation between recovery and concurrency control:

- Recovery actions access shared data just as normal operations do, and therefore

- actions that are issued to undo or redo (parts of) transactions or subtransactions must preserve the serializable behaviour of successfully completed transactions.

From these observations, we derive the following. Recovery actions must participate in the concurrency control protocols, just like ordinary actions. To reason about recovery, we propose that all the activity that takes place to abort a (sub-)transaction or to redo part of a transaction is represented explicitly in the computation. This is important since it allows us to reason about concurrency control and recovery in the same framework. The effect of a subtransaction may be rolled back either by executing suitable inverse operations for each of its operations, or by a compensating subtransaction. (Note that a compensating subtransaction may perform operations that are not directly related to the operations of the original transaction, and in particular are not inverses.) A compensating subtransaction can simply be viewed as an inverse operation on the next level of abstraction. Recovery oriented operations may be issued by a parent, or by the system. For reasons to be explained, we connect abort operations to the subtransaction being aborted, and a compensating transaction to the parent of the subtransaction being aborted, even if they are initiated by the system. Thus, the tree structure represents a relationship that is more general than the caller-callee relationship.

Now, the paradigm for proving that a computation, involving concurrency and recovery actions, is correct, is the following. Using regular serializability arguments, we first try to show that the computation is equivalent to a serial computation. If recovery actions participate in the concurrency control protocol, as we have required above, then this claim follows from the correctness of the concurrency control protocol. Now, if a subtransaction was aborted by a sequence of operations, then as we agreed above, these operations appear in the subtree rooted at the node representing the subtransaction. In the equivalent serial computation, this subtree is separated from the other parts of the computation. All that remains is to show that the total effect of the subtree is "null" using the specific knowledge we have on the semantics of the abort operations, and using sequential reasoning. Usually, the abort operations are inverses of operations executed by the subtransaction, so we argue that the operations nullify each other in pairs. Note that this is essentially the way we prove that page level logging, using before-images for undo, correctly implements transaction abort. We have just replaced before-images by the more general and abstract concept of inverse operation.

If a subtransaction is aborted by a compensating subtransaction, a similar argumemnt applies, except that now we need to consider the subtree rooted at the parent. For crash recovery, the issues are considerably more complex, since we also need to find a suitable representation in the history for the event of the crash. The principle, however, is the same. In the following, we will expand and illustrate on this appraoch, considering aborts first, and then crashes.

5.3 Transaction Aborts

Database systems that rely on conventional page locking often perform transaction aborts by means of page before-images. This straightforward method of rollback no longer works correctly in the case of multi-level transactions that use short page locks. Simply restoring before-images to undo a transaction may result in illegal side effects such as unintentionally backing out updates of a second, possibly already committed transaction, as well.

In our running example, assume that T_2 aborts after T_1 has committed. If we were using page before-images for undo, we would restore the state of page p to that before T_2's first access to it, thereby removing record z that was inserted by T_1. Applying before-images is essentially a write operation on the page. The scenario is shown in fig. 3, with recovery actions underlined. It is quite obvious that the history shown is not serializable, since the low-level conflicts form a cycle in the 2-to-3 serialization graph.

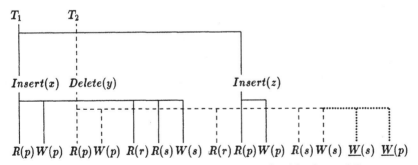

Fig. 4: Non-serializable schedule resulting from page-level backout of T_2

Clearly, the kind of domino effect that is observed in the above example, is due to the early release of page locks, which is the intended purpose of multi-level concurrency control. So, separation between uncommitted transactions is only guaranteed at the record level. The conclusion is that subtransaction aborts, without dealing with cascading aborts, must be performed at a level where concurrent transactions are prevented from viewing uncommitted results. If, in a computation, completed subtransactions have already made visible their changes to the other subtransactions, the activity of aborts must move one level up, until an ancestor is found that has not yet committed, so (assuming a strict execution) the effects of its subtransactions are visible only inside its computation tree. The abort is then performed by issuing an inverse operation by that ancestor, which can also be viewed as a compensating subtransaction.

In our example, a completed record operation cannot be rolled back by using inverses at the page level, but it can be rolled back by an inverse at the record level. The following figure shows the correct execution of T_2's abort. Particularly, note that record y need not necessarily be reinserted at its former location.

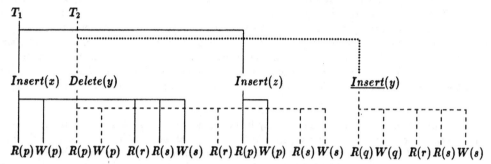

Fig. 5: Transaction abort through compensation of subtransactions

If locking is used for concurrency control, compensating subtransactions have to reacquire low-level locks. This entails no violation of serializability – these locks are requested in separate subtransactions which are handled just like normal subtransactions. Further note that the higher level itself, which still holds all of its locks, does not usually need any additional locks to perform an inverse operation, provided that a lock that permits the execution of an action also permits the execution of its inverse. More generally, this means that we require the underlying conflict relation to be symmetrical: If two actions commute, necessarily their inverses must commute too. Otherwise we have to introduce a conflict for both of them.

To determine the inverse operation of an action a, it is not sufficient to know the name of the operation a has performed and the affected object. For example, undoing a $Delete(x)$ tuple operation requires information on the value of x to construct the appropriate $Insert(x)$ action. For this purpose, in a multi-level architecture each level has to record enough information about its update actions on a log, so as to be able to perform the corresponding inverse actions. Note, that on page level inverse operations of *Write* accesses essentially are *Write* actions again, and the necessary log may well be organized like a conventional before-image file.

5.4 Crash Recovery

The well-known paradigm of recovery after a system failure, demands that uncommitted transactions be aborted, and that effects of committed transactions be redone if some of their updates have been lost [Gr78, HR83, BHG87]. These fundamental rules, of course, are still valid for multi-level systems. In addition, however, undo and redo steps must be aware of state abstractions, as well as the precise effect of the crash.

In order to consider correctness, we need to represent crashes in histories. The effect of a crash is a state change – before it happened, the database state was defined in terms of both stable storage and buffer pool; after the crash, the state is defined in terms of the stable storage only. (By stable storage we mean here the database stored on stable storage, but not the recovery related data, such as the log. This is not part of the state, rather it is used to correct the state.) However, storage types are not part of our model. The basic idea is that the effect of a crash is equivalent to a sequence of inverse operations. Some of these inverses destroy the effects of committed transactions, and these need to be redone. Others destroy the effects of active transactions, hence these effects need not be undone during recovery. The contents of the database after the crash, and the contents of the log, allow the crash recovery mechanism to find out what needs to be redone or undone, and in what order.

To illustrate this idea, consider a single-level, page based system. When the system is up, the state is a collection of page values. For each page, its value is the value in its location in stable storage, unless it has an image in a buffer, in which case, its value is that image. A crash destroys the current values of the pages that have images in the buffers. For each such page, there is a sequence of page writes that were executed on it since it was copied to the buffer, and the crash has the effect of executing the sequence of inverse operations, in inverse order. (The interleavings of inverses for different pages are irrelevant). A sequence of writes on a page that was thus inverted may contain the writes of committed transactions, and these have to be redone. It may contain the writes of uncommitted transactions, and these need not be undone. Assuming that transaction use strict 2PL with page locks, the situation is simpler - either a page contains only writes of committed transactions, or only writes of committed transactions followed by writes of a single active transaction.

In a multi-level system, the situation may be much more complex. A key issue is the level at which we can describe the crash as a sequence of inverse operations, which can be characterized in terms of *propagation*, namely the level at which the propagation of updates from the buffer pool to stable storage can be described [HR83]. A crash can always be described as a sequence of inverses on the lowest level; however, appropriate mechanisms can guarantee that it is actually a sequence of inverses on a higher level. System R uses such mechanisms – see next section. Given the level at which the crash can be described, the restart can then be executed in terms of inverse operations of that level and of levels above it. Note that inverse operations of that level must in general be used; using only higher level inverses is not enough. When an inverse operation is to be processed during system restart, we face the problem, that its execution is only well-defined in a state which satisfies certain consistency constraints. To perform a record operation, for example, access paths on the pages must be consistent with primary data. If the crash can be described on the record level, then it is guaranteed that these structures are always consistent after a crash, then recovery can be performed in terms of inverse record operations only. If not, then page level inverses need to be performed to bring pages to consistent states, and only then can inverse record operations be applied.

More details on realisation strategies and performance aspects of multi-level crash recovery are contained in [Wei87a]. We will illustrate the ideas sketched above in section 6, in the context of particular example systems.

6. MULTI-LEVEL TRANSACTIONS IN PRACTICE

It is quite astonishing that there are still people who doubt that multi-level transaction management really works, though its main ideas have actually been implemented in several commercial database systems. For many classical applications, record level locking is crucial to obtain satisfactory throughput rates, whereas just dealing with page locks would result in an intolerable number of conflicts. However, this seemingly straightforward approach to concurrency control is only correct under the assumption that single record operations are atomic and isolated from each other. A simple solution to make this condition hold is to schedule record operations in a strictly sequential way. Thus, every system which applies concurrency control on the record level, or even exploits semantic knowledge on a still higher level, actually is based on (some form of) multi-level transactions. The full power of this paradigm is realized in systems which process several (non-conflicting) record operations in parallel. In general, this possibility is highly desirable, since each record operation may typically comprise 5 to 10 page accesses (including access paths, catalog data, and free place administration tables). In order to take care of low-level (pseudo) conflicts on the involved pages, additional short-term locks are needed. Since they are used only for isolating single record operations from each other, short locks can be released at the end of each record level action without violating serializability.

If the system is implemented in such a way that no deadlocks can ever arise on the page level, e.g. because of a specific order in which pages are accessed during a record operation, th' short-term locks can be implemented by so-called *latches* . For every single page a latch is used to serialize parallel accesses, i.e. to prevent critical sections in which the page is accessed from being entered by more than one record operation at the same time. As seizing and freeing a latch can be done with just a few machine instructions, such a special implementation of low-level concurrency control may save a great deal of locking overhead.

One well-known example of a system which applies record level concurrency control is the relational prototype System R [As76, Ch81]. Basically, System R locks records and index keys that are accessed by the RSS, the storage system of System R, on behalf of a user transaction. In addition, short locks on pages are acquired during the execution of single record operations, i.e. RSS calls. As we have shown in section 5, releasing page locks prematurely inevitably requires a multi-level recovery approach. Since details of the System R recovery manager are well documented in [Gr81a] , we only sketch its crucial steps. (Along similar lines we would also outline a correctness proof, by the way.)

(1) Shadow storage provides for atomic propagation of all page updates between two successive checkpoints.

(2) As checkpoints do not interleave with RSS actions, single record operations are thereby made atomic.

(3) RSS actions are recorded on a log file for undo and redo of transactions after a crash, and for transaction abort.

Because of (2), a crash can always be described as a sequence of inverse record operations. Thus, there is no need for additional page level recovery, and record level recovery, implemented by a log protocol, as described in (3) is sufficient. It is important to notice that though shadowing on the page level may be replaced by a different technique (for it has been considered, in retrospect, as a bad design decision [Gr81a]), for correctness reasons some recovery mechanism is indispensable to guarantee atomicity of RSS actions. An alternative to realize step (1) has been implemented in the Synapse DBMS [Ong84]. Instead of shadowing, this system is based on logging page before-images to make checkpoint intervals atomic.

Multi-level transactions obviously are useful to explain performance-related tricks within a general framework. The other way round, this means that they are a good starting point to build well-structured modular systems without disregarding performance. A system which has been strongly motivated by this paradigm is the Darmstadt Database System called DASDBS [PSSWD87]. The goal of DASDBS is to support a variety of advanced applications dealing with complex objects by a common kernel which offers two well-defined levels of storage services: a complex record-oriented and a page-oriented interface. Various application-specific data management extensions on top of the kernel have been designed and are under implementation [Sch87]. Since DASDBS pursues the idea of an extensible multi-level interface system, modularity of transaction management is a crucial issue; nevertheless each layer must provide reasonable performance.

The DASDBS kernel offers retrieval and update operations on hierarchically structured records of arbitrary length, which we call *complex records*. A complex record in general consists of some elementary fields and a set of subrecords each of which may again contain sets of subrecords, and so on. Records and subrecords are addressed via hierarchical names which are immutable. To control clustering and to provide efficient access to entire complex records as well as subrecords, a suitable storage structure has been developed. On an internal storage level, complex records are divided into bytestring *fragments*, each of which fits entirely within a single page. A record's hierarchical structure is reflected in its *record directory* which contains pointers to the fragments of each subrecord. Details of the DASDBS storage structure are described in [DPSW88]. We expect every system that supports complex objects to use similar concepts at some level (see for example [Ca86]).

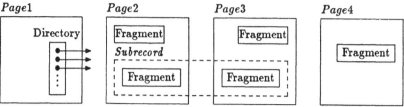

Fig. 6: Storage structure of a complex record (simplified)

As in the figure, complex records typically span several pages. Therefore, at a first glance there seems to be no need for a sophisticated multi-level concurrency control protocol. Just locking the record seems to be sufficient, for it implicitly locks all the underlying pages. However, there is still the case where records may share a page. Even more important within the context of DASDBS, we expect transactions to access subrecords quite often, a case that is efficiently supported through the record directory. If we were using page level concurrency control instead of record locking to allow concurrent access on disjoint subrecords, the directory page would obviously become a hot spot. Moreover, as fragments may be moved within pages or can even migrate across page boundaries when subrecords are enlarged, every page potentially causes pseudo conflicts. A typical update operation on a complex (sub-) record leads to the following execution steps:

- read one or more directory entries,

- read and write one or more fragments, possibly shifting fragments around,

- if necessary update the directory entry or entries.

The following figure illustrates these steps with concurrent transactions T_1 and T_2, operating on disjoint subrecords $R.X.Y.A$ and $R.X.Z.B$.

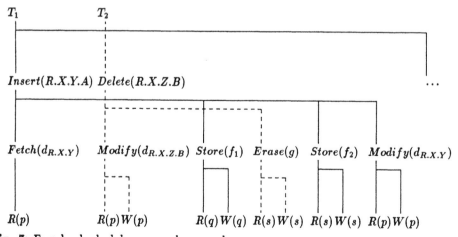

Fig. 7: Four-level schedule on complex records

Clearly, there is no conflict on the level of complex record operations in our example. Since on the storage structure level DASDBS accesses only those directory entries and data fragments which belong to the referenced subrecords, there is no conflict on that level either. On the page level, finally, conflicts do arise due to the actions on p and s. The whole schedule from level 1 to level 4 is obviously not serializable because of these page conflicts, nor is the schedule from level 2 to level 4 for the same reason. In contrast to this, the schedule from level 3, that is the level of storage structure operations, to level 4 is serializable, and therefore multi-level serializability of the entire schedule is guaranteed according to the theorems of section 4.2. The explicit introduction of the storage structure level as part of the multi-level transaction model leads to enhanced concurrency of complex record operations.

We can now utilize these considerations in the design of a multi-level locking protocol for the DASDBS kernel. The lock manager we have developed allows to acquire locks on sets of items to cope with variable granularities. In the case of records and subrecords conflicts are detected by comparing hierarchical names. A conflict is signaled if and only if two subrecords are non-disjoint, that is if one name is a prefix of the other, and the operations do not commute. Locking the hierarchical name of a complex subrecord has the nice side effect that the directory entry and all fragments belonging to that subrecord are implicitly locked too. In other words, there is no need to acquire any locks whatsoever on the storage structure level, saving us a lot of overhead. In addition to the subrecord locks we just have to obtain "short" locks on pages (possibly implemented as latches) for the duration of a single action on a directory entry or a fragment. While this design allows very high concurrency on complex records, eliminates hot spots and yet keeps the number of necessary lock request blocks fairly small, the current implementation of the DASDBS transaction manager so far makes only partial use of these considerations. To simplify the implementation of recovery on the page level, by logging complete pages instead of storage structure entries, locks on modified pages are held until the corresponding record operation terminates. Furthermore, note that in the realized strategy the storage structures of complex records are completely transparent, so that the implementation of record operations might be changed without invalidating the correctness of the locking protocol. In this sense, we made a compromise between modularity and performance. After having gained some experience with the current sub-optimal approach, we will reconsider the more sophisticated protocol described above.

The DASDBS kernel has a two-level transaction management: While the two-level concurrency control strategy of the kernel is pretty close to the System R use of "long locks" and "short locks", a quite different approach is pursued for its two-level recovery scheme. In contrast to the checkpoint-oriented low-level mechanism of System R, its basic recovery component is (sub-) transaction-oriented. Therefore, it may either be directly used for the application level as a page-based recovery method (provided page locks are held until EOT), or combined with the high-level recovery mechanism in the more interesting case of multi-level concurrency control. Crash recovery can be roughly characterized by the following steps:

(1) The Cache/Safe technique [EB84] executes page modifications of subtransactions atomically and persistently, viz by keeping before-images in the cache, and writing after-images atomically to a sequential log file, the so-called "safe".

(2) Thus, single record level operations appear atomic and persistent, so that

(3) the record level recovery component only needs to log undo information, viz inverse record operations.

Note that the record level recovery manager need not care about redo steps, since the page level already provides all higher level clients with the abstraction of "stable memory", i.e. makes buffer volatility transparent as far as single record operations are concerned. We expect future operating systems to provide this sort of functionality [Wei86b] which then could substitute the bottom layer of our multi-level architecture. So we deliberately decided to make changes of committed subtransactions persistent, although this is not necessary in principle. For cases where this may turn out as a serious performance bottleneck, we also investigate an alternative which only provides non-persistent atomic subtransactions on the page level by deferring after-image writes until the top level commit.

While first prototype versions of the kernel itself and the corresponding multi-level transaction manager have been implemented and the integration of both is underway, we also considered concurrency control for a flat relational front-end on top of our nested relational kernel. (This extension aims at clustering tuples from different but related relations in a single hierarchical record, in order to materialize frequent joins [SSP87].) It turned out that if we were directly using kernel transactions for this high-level interface, we would get pseudo-conflicts, e.g. on index keys. Consider, for instance, transactions T2 and T3 of section 2.1. T2 would block T3, or vice versa, by locking the index entry for key 'a' of col1, which is implemented as an internal record at the kernel interface. To get rid of such pseudo-conflicts as soon as possible, we have investigated the feasibility of a restricted form of predicate locking [Wei87a] and more sophisticated implementation techniques thereof [DPS83] to be applied in the front-end. T2 and T3 are conflict-free under this protocol. Each single predicate-oriented tuple operation should in turn be implemented as a subtransaction on the kernel level.

More details on the ongoing implementation and a preliminary performance analysis of the DASDBS multi-level transaction management approach are contained in [Wei87a]. Besides the described approaches, a variety of further strategies on two or more layers is conceivable. To realize such sophisticated concurrency control and recovery protocols in a layered architecture, it is not only tempting but really helpful to use multi-level transactions as a framework for understanding strategies and developing correctness proofs. The discussion in this section has shown that a multi-level approach to transaction management can enhance throughput, provided it is carefully implemented. Crucial factors that determine whether there is really a gain of performance or not are the number of levels, the characteristics of operations on these various levels, the overhead of concurrency control protocols that are used, and the costs of more sophisticated multi-level recovery algorithms.

7. CONCLUSION AND FURTHER QUESTIONS

Starting with a summary of implementation techniques in existing systems and of proposals to further improve the degree of parallelism, we pointed out the need for a more general model in which one can describe and reason about such protocols. Our objective, therefore, was to show that the theory of multi-level transaction management is a powerful, albeit simple, framework to fill that gap. Using a simple running example we presented a model and explained how correctness of multi-level concurrency control and, closely related, multi-level recovery can be proven. Our presentation aimed at an intuitive understanding and at an insight into its practical importance, rather than at a complete formal treatment which is contained elsewhere. We presented order-preserving serializability as the key "hand-shaking" mechanism between the layer-specific schedulers. The model allows to consider intra-transaction parallism. We did not discuss this aspect nor did we consider further issues of multi-level transaction management which have been addressed already in our previous work [BBG87, WS84, Wei86b, Wei87a, Wei87b] such as

Existence of Inverses: Deleting a (possibly large) object first and then inserting it again may be impossible if the space is used already by another transaction. The "simple undo" fails.

Deadlocks: In current systems the execution of an inverse operation may cause a deadlock if locking is used. In order to avoid the undo of an undo, systems have introduced the notion of a "golden" transaction and only one aborting transaction gets this "golden latch" at one time (cf. [Gr81a]). It turns out that under our assumptions the action and its inverse can be executed. There is no deadlock at the level of the inverse operation. However, deadlocks at a lower level may occur, since locks on pages have been released at the time when the subtransaction committed and must be acquired again for the undo. In such a case we restart an undo.

Crash Recovery: The system may crash during the execution of an inverse operation. Is the property of idempotency used? If log writes at higher layers are written with standard operations at the next deeper layer, how is logging of log-writes avoided?

Operating System Transaction Management: A further property of our multi-level approach is that we can easily exploit transaction management, if offered by the operating system. The operating system then is the lowest layer upon we build our DBMS transaction management.

Further investigations on questions like these and more evaluations are necessary. However, as it stands now, many questions can already be answered in a satisfactory manner by multi-level transaction management developed so far.

Acknowledgement

We would like to thank the anonymous referees for their unexpectedly detailed and really helpful comments.

References

[As76]   Astrahan, M.M., et al., System R: Relational Approach to Database Management, ACM TODS Vol.1 No.2, 1976

[BBG87]   Beeri, C., Bernstein, P.A., Goodman, N., A Model for Nested Transactions Systems, Technical Report, Hebrew University, 1987

[BBGLS83] Beeri, C., Bernstein, P.A., Goodman, N., Lai, M.-Y., Shasha, D.E., A Concurrency Control Theory for Nested Transactions, Proc. 2nd ACM Symp. on Principles of Distributed Computing, 1983

[BHG87]   Bernstein, P.A., Hadzilacos, V., Goodman, N., Concurrency Control and Recovery in Database Systems, Addison-Wesley Publ., 1987

[BJS86]   Böttcher,S., Jarke, M., Schmidt, J.W., Adaptive Predicate Managers in Database Systems, Proc. 12th VLDB Conference, 1986

[BKK85]   Bancilhon, F., Kim, W., Korth, H.F., A Model of CAD Transactions, Proc. 11th VLDB Conference, 1985

[Ca86]   Carey, M.J., DeWitt, D.J., Frank, D., Graefe, G., Muralikrishna, M., Richardson, J.E., Shekita, E.J., The Architecture of the EXODUS Extensible DBMS, Proc. Int. Workshop on Object-Oriented Database Systems, 1986

[Ch81]   Chamberlin, D.D., et al., A History and Evaluation of System R, Communications of the ACM Vol.24 No.10, 1981

[DeL87]   DeLeon, M., Sequential Correctness, Atomicity and Persistency in Database Systems - A Model and a Proof Paradigm, M.Sc. Thesis (in Hebrew), The Hebrew University at Jerusalem, 1987

[DPS83]   Dadam, P., Pistor, P., Schek, H.-J., A Predicate Oriented Locking Approach for Integrated Information Systems, Information Processing'83, North-Holland, 1983

[DPSW88] Deppisch, U., Paul, H.-B., Schek, H.-J., Weikum, G., Managing Complex Objects in the Darmstadt Database Kernel System, in: A. Buchmann, U. Dayal, K. Dittrich (eds.), Object-Oriented Database Systems, Springer, to appear

[EB84]   Elhardt, K., Bayer, R., A Database Cache for High Performance and Fast Restart in Database Systems, ACM TODS Vol.9 No.4, 1984

[Gr78]   Gray, J.N., Notes on Data Base Operating Systems, in: Operating Systems - An Advanced Course, LNCS 60, Springer, 1978

[Gr81a]   Gray, J., McJones, P., Blasgen, M., Lindsay, B., Lorie, R., Price, T., Putzolu, F., Traiger, I., The Recovery Manager of the System R Database Manager, ACM Computing Surveys Vol.13 No.2, 1981

[Gr81b]   Gray, J., The Transaction Concept: Virtues and Limitations, Proc. 7th VLDB Conference, 1981

[HR83]   Haerder, T., Reuter, A., Principles of Transaction-Oriented Database Recovery, ACM Computing Surveys Vol.15 No.4, 1983

[HR87]   Haerder, T., Rothermel, K., Concepts for Transaction Recovery in Nested Transactions, Proc. ACM SIGMOD Conference, 1987

[La86]   Lamport, L., On Interprocess Communication - Part I: Basic Formalism, Distributed Computing Vol. 1, 1986

[Li85]   Liskov, B., Overview of the Argus Language and System, in: Distributed Systems, LNCS 190, Springer, 1985

[LM86]   Lynch, N., Merritt, M., Introduction to the Theory of Nested Transactions, Proc. Int. Conf. on Database Theory, Springer, 1986

[MGG86] Moss, J.E.B., Griffeth, N.D., Graham, M.H., Abstraction in Recovery Management, Proc. ACM SIGMOD Conference, 1986

[Mo85] Moss, J.E.B., Nested Transactions: An Approach to Reliable Distributed Computing, MIT Press, 1985

[Ong84] Ong, K.S., Synapse Approach to Database Recovery, Proc. 3rd ACM Symp. on PODS, 1984

[PSSWD87] Paul, H.-B., Schek, H.-J., Scholl, M., Weikum, G., Deppisch, U., Architecture and Implementation of the Darmstadt Database Kernel System, Proc. ACM SIGMOD Conference, 1987

[Sch87] Schek, H.-J., DASDBS: A Kernel DBMS and Application-Specific Layers, IEEE Database Engineering, Special Issue on Extensible DBMS, 1987

[Sh85] Shasha, D., What Good are Concurrent Search Structure Algorithms for Databases Anyway?, IEEE Database Engineering Vol. 8 No. 2, 1985

[SSP87] Scholl, M.H., Schek, H.-J., Paul, H.-B., Supporting Flat Relations by a Nested Relational Kernel, Proc. 13th VLDB Conference, 1987

[Tr83] Traiger, I.L., Trends in Systems Aspects of Database Management, Proc. 2nd Int. Conf. on Databases (ICOD-2), 1983

[Wa84] Walter, B., Nested Transactions with Multiple Commit Points: An Approach to the Structuring of Advanced Database Applications, Proc. 10th VLDB Conference, 1984

[Wei86a] Weikum, G., A Theoretical Foundation of Multi-Level Concurrency Control, Proc. 5th ACM Symp. on PODS, 1986

[Wei86b] Weikum, G., Pros and Cons of Operating System Transactions for Data Base Systems, ACM/IEEE Fall Joint Computer Conference, 1986

[Wei87a] Weikum, G., Principles and Realisation Strategies of Multi-Level Transaction Management, Technical Report DVSI-1987-T1, Technical University of Darmstadt

[Wei87b] Weikum, G., Enhancing Concurrency in Layered Systems, 2nd Int. Workshop on High Performance Transaction Systems, 1987

[WS84] Weikum, G., Schek, H.-J., Architectural Issues of Transaction Management in Layered Systems, Proc. 10th VLDB Conference, 1984

Views and Security in Distributed Database Management Systems

E. Bertino (*)(+) and L.M. Haas (**)

(*) IEI-CNR Pisa (Italy)
(**) IBM Almaden Research Center, San Jose, California (USA)

ABSTRACT

Views are used in database systems to present data to different applications in a form reflecting their individual needs. The view mechanism contributes to data protection, independence, and isolation. In this paper we first discuss some issues concerning Distributed Database security and then the design of distributed views providing security features. The following issues concerning views are discussed: represention, change, authorization, and usage.

1. Introduction

As automation increases and our reliance on computer systems grows, it becomes important to ensure that the information entrusted to these systems is protected. In fact, the increasing sophistication of users makes business and individuals more vulnerable to abuse by computer experts. A number of cases of misuse involving computers have been described [PERR84], [KRAU79[. Examples of misuse include the theft of money by interception of electronic-funds-transfer messages among banks, access of confidential information which is then used for illegal purposes, such as blackmail or espionage, and disruption of operations such as chemical process control or computer-aided manufacturing.

The increased usage of databases to store large amounts of data has created new security problems. Typically a database contains data of various degrees of importance and levels of sensitivity. This data is shared among a wide variety of users with different responsibilities and privileges. It is therefore necessary to restrict users of the database to those portions of the total data that are necessary for their activities. Additionally, more control is needed over changes a user can make to data because of the many ways these changes can affect other users of the database. There are three kinds of safeguards concerned with ensuring data privacy and security in databases: access controls, inference controls and information flow control. Access control mechanisms regulate the reading, changing, and deletion of data. Modern database management systems (DBMS), like the relational DBMS's [SQL81] and [STON76] provide authorization capabilities that allow selective sharing of data among users. Inference controls protect statistical databases by preventing questioners from deducing confidential information by posing carefully designed sequences of statistical queries and correlating the answers [DENN83]. Flow controls prevent users, authorized to access some data, from making such data available to unauthorized users, for instance by making copies of sensitive data [DENN76].

It should be stressed, however, that the security measures provided by DBMS's alone are not sufficient. The underlying systems, such as the operating systems and the computer hardware, must also be secure and reliable. Security procedures external to the computer system are also needed, such as locks on the computer-room door and fireproof safes for storing copies of the database. As pointed out in [DOWN77] to support a secure DBMS, an operating system should at least provide facilities (1) to prevent modifications of the DBMS and the user programs; (2) to protect data in memory; (3) to prevent any programs other than the DBMS from accessing the

---

(+)The work reported in this paper was carried out while the author was visiting the IBM San Jose Research Center in summer 1984

database; (4) to perform correct physical I/O; and (5) to authenticate DBMS users. Examples of secure operating systems are KSOS [MCCA79], the UCLA secure Unix [POPE79], [WALK80], and IBM's KVM/370 [GOLD79].

The introduction of Distributed DBMS's (DDBMS) has alleviated some of these problems by providing the possibility of physically separating sensitive data [RUSH83]. Such data could be stored at trusted sites, that is, sites with computers running secure software and with external security procedures. However, with the distribution of a database over a computer network new threats to data security arise. In a distributed database data may flow among the various sites. Therefore the controls at a specific site become irrelevant if data stored at that site is readily available to other sites that do not have effective security controls. Also data may be exposed to various types of attack while in transit across the network links. Some of these types of attack are: spurious message injection, message reception by unauthorized receivers, transmission disruption, and rerouting data to fake nodes.

It is clear that secure communications among the system components is essential to provide data security by means of physical isolation. However, secure communication alone is not enough to ensure data security. Security also depends on the implementation of the software managing the data. In this paper, we discuss this issue in the framework of the design of a view mechanism for a Distributed DBMS. Section two provides a very brief overview of distributed databases, including R* [HAAS82], which we will use to illustrate our discussion in Section three of the view mechanism's implementation.

2. Distributed DBMSs

2.1. Requirements and goals

A DDBMS can be defined as a system that allows uniform, integrated management of data distributed across a computer network of database sites. Uniform and integrated management of distributed data means that the applications must be provided with: (1) a common global view of all the data (Global Schema) and a unified data dictionary; (2) a common, uniform language for data access and manipulation; and (3) transparency of data's physical location. These requirements are also often referred to as **transparency**.

Another important goal of a DDBMS is to maintain the **autonomy** of the system's sites. This requires that:

1. The local operations of each DBMS site must be unaffected by the addition of new sites, so that reprogramming of user applications is unnecessary. This facilitates the expansion of the DBMS network as new DBMS nodes are added.

2. Local DBMS operations must be unaffected by global operations, and global operations must not cause database reorganization.

3. Each local DBMS must keep control over its own local data even when there are remote applications using this data. In particular [HAAS82] this means that each site must be able to drop, change and create new data as well as grant and revoke authorization privileges on local data without accessing or consulting other sites.

4. Each DBMS must be able to "stand-alone", that is, to access and perform any operations on its local data even in the presence of faults which disconnect it from all other DBMS sites.

It is clear that these goals may conflict. For instance, a Global Schema, while enhancing transparency, can limit site autonomy, since a site is not able to change a local data object without broadcasting the changes to other sites. Integrating a new DBMS into the DDBMS might also require a redefinition of the global schema. The opposite approach to this is to have a distributed schema. In this case the degree of transparency is reduced, but more robustness and potential for autonomy are obtained. As we will see in the following sections these two objectives have different impacts on the design of a view mechanism.

2.1.1. An example: R*

R* is an experimental prototype which extends the architecture of System R [ASTR76] to a distributed environment. Three main goals have affected the design of R* [HAAS82]: site autonomy, ease of use and performance.

```
The examples in this paper will be drawn from a
database consisting of three relations at two sites:

  EMPLOYEE (EMP#,NAME,SALARY,ADDRESS,MANAGER,DEPARTMENT) at site A

  PLANNED_TRIP (EMP#,DESTINATION,COST,DATE,APPROVAL) at site A

  DEPARTMENT (DEPT#,NAME,LOCATION,BUDGET) at site B
```

Figure 1: Database example

Autonomy is achieved by decentralization. All services, such as deadlock detection, recovery, locking, catalog management, and query compilation are performed either locally or in a fully distributed manner. No service is centralized. In this way, users at a site are never prevented by any other site from performing any action they wish on purely local data.

Ease of use is a broad goal, encompassing everything from data transparency to a high level interface. In R*, the SQL language is the user interface. SQL is a non-procedural query language that was also used as the interface to System R. User comments indicated [CHAM80] that System R was considered easy to use. This provides the basis for a single-system image, as the same commands are used to perform both local and remote actions. R* also provides location transparency (the user does not have to know where data is located in order to use it) but does not provide a Global Schema or a common data dictionary.

Finally, performance is improved by using compilation techniques. Compilation means that the queries contained within an application program are processed before the actual program execution takes place. This allows efficient code for query execution to be produced and allows the steps of query preparation to be bypassed at run time (e.g., parsing, catalog access, query optimization, authorization checking). In R*, query compilation is a distributed operation which involves all the sites participating in the execution of a multi-site query.

Compilation, while increasing the runtime efficiency, introduces some complexity into the system as well. When a query is compiled, the system checks that the objects referenced in a query exist and are valid, and that the user is authorized to perform the operations specified by the query on those objects. However, since execution may be separated in time from compilation, it is necessary to ensure that these objects and authorizations still exist when the query is executed. If all the objects and authorizations needed by queries in the program exist, the program is said to be **valid**.

To keep track of a program's validity, R* records in special system catalogs at compilation time the set of privileges needed and the set of objects which must exist and be valid. These records are known as **authorization dependencies** and **existence dependencies**. Authorization dependencies are of the form: **<program owner>** *grants* **<privilege>** *to* **<program>** *on* **<object>**. Existence dependencies are of the form: **<program>** *depends on* **<object>**. When a privilege is revoked or an object is dropped or invalidated, these records are searched to find programs that depend on that privilege and those programs are marked invalid. In R*, these records are stored in a distributed fashion with the data objects to which they refer [NG82]. If a change occurs to the data object, the program which depends on it can be invalidated locally (necessary for site autonomy) and when the program is next executed it can be revalidated if possible by recompiling. Otherwise an error can be returned.

2.2. Issues in Distributed Database Security

Two types of control are very important for data security in a (Distributed) DBMS. **Data access controls** define and enforce the security policy of the system. **Information flow controls** define the channels (both physical and logical) along which information is allowed to move (1). Few general purpose DBMSs provide information flow controls. This type of control is very hard to provide; some approaches which can be taken are described in [DENN79]. We will briefly discuss information flow in DDBMSs in one of the following subsections.

Access controls are common, and several types of access controls can be distinguished. They can be classified as either external access controls (data-independent), object-dependent access controls (content-independent), or content-dependent access controls. We will also refer to the last two types of controls as data-dependent access controls. There are several ways to support these access controls in a distributed environment. In the present paper we will limit the discussion to the data-dependent access controls since this has a major impact on the view design.

2.2.1. Data-dependent Access Controls

Information regarding data-dependent access controls can be easily modelled by means of **access rules** [FERN81]. An access rule is a quadruple (s,o,r,p), where s is the subject holding the right r on the object o under the conditions expressed by the predicate p.

This is very natural for a system like R^* in which access to objects within the database is controlled by privileges. The database objects consist of stored tables, virtual tables (views, see below), and their attributes. The owner of the object controls the privileges on that object. These privileges vary, depending on the type of the object. For example, the only explicit privilege a user may have on an attribute is the UPDATE privilege, while he may have SELECT, INSERT, UPDATE and/or DELETE privileges on the records of a stored table or view.

The owner of a stored table has all possible privileges on that table and its attributes. He can grant any or all of those privileges to another user. He may also grant that user the right to further grant access rights on the object to other users, thereby sharing his control of the object. Grants of privileges on an object may occur at any time during the existence of that object. Likewise, privileges may be dynamically revoked at any time. This is not always a simple operation. For example, if the owner of an object, O, chooses to revoke a privilege from a user, U, to whom he had previously granted access with the right to make further grants, then any users to whom U had granted access to O must lose their privilege as well – unless the privilege had also been granted to them by another source. An efficient algorithm for revoking privileges is described in [GRIF76].

In a DDBMS we are concerned with two key questions: Where to store (and apply) access rules, and where to define access rules. Two approaches can be devised for each question. For **storing** access rules, one approach is to have a **global repository**, containing the access rules for all the objects existing within the DDBMS. The global repository could in turn be stored at one or more sites (possibly at every site in the DDBMS). The second approach consists of storing the access rules together with the objects to which they refer. The solution chosen will have a great impact on data security, since access rules are enforced at the site(s) where they are stored. A global, fully replicated repository would imply that access rules can be enforced at any site. This allows authorization to be checked once, at the user's site, improving system performance. However, malicious users at unsecure sites could then bypass the access rules. On the other hand, if the rules are applied at every site (the other option), performance may be degraded by the "extra" checking. Another problem is that site autonomy would be limited because each site must modify the global repository when access rules for local objects are modified.

In R^* a table may be created at any site [LIND81]. This site is known as the birth site. It may be stored at some other site, which we refer to as the table store site. The birth site of a table plays a central role since it maintains the information about the actual store site for that table. This allows tables to migrate to different sites, without affecting the existing application programs. The table store site is in charge of storing and managing all catalog information about the tables it stores. Among this information are the access rules, which define the set of local and

---

(1) This list it is not exhaustive. Other controls, including inference controls, history-dependent controls, data ownership and administration, are also important

non-local users authorized to access the tables stored at that site. In other words, authorization information is distributed together with the data to which it refers. If a table migrates to another site, the authorization information related to this table is moved to the table's new store site. Because the access rules are stored with the data, grant and revoke of access privileges on locally stored data are local operations. The participation of other sites is not required to perform such requests. Therefore, as pointed out in [WILM81], site autonomy is preserved as there are no global authorization tables.

The second question concerns where to **define** access rules, in other words where access rights can be granted. We can distinguish several possibilities:

1. Access privileges on an object can be granted from any site, regardless of where the access rules for that object are stored.

2. Access privileges on an object can be granted only at the site where the access rules for that object are stored.

The first approach ensures complete transparency, because the user does not need to know where the access rules for an object are stored. However, this approach does not ensure data security because access rules could be perverted either at the sites where they are defined, when such sites are unsecure, or on the network when being transmitted to the site(s) where they are to be stored. The second approach does not guarantee transparency. A user, trying to grant access privileges from a site, could have his request refused if that site is not the store site for the access rules. R* follows a hybrid approach in this case. A grant can be initiated from any site, but will automatically be shipped to the store site, where it will be performed. Since R* only stores access rules at the site storing the data, the rules can only be perverted during definition by a system programmer at the store site, or someone with the ability to interfere with the communication system.

2.2.2. Information Flow in DDBMSs

In a database management system, a flow occurs from data object X to data object Y when a transaction that reads from X writes a value into Y. Illegal flows occur in one of two ways. In one, which we will refer to as "copy violations", protected data is copied to a less protected location, either another relation, a VDT screen, or even a piece of paper. In the other type, "in transit" violations, data moving from one protected state to another (equally protected) state within the system is "tapped" in transit. Some protection against the first kind of illegal flow is available, but is not implemented in most database management systems.

Both types of illegal flow can occur in Distributed DBMS, and in fact the problems can be more severe. For example, DDBMS provide the potential for isolating sensitive data in one database. But if any users of the sensitive database have the right to connect to other databases and access remote data, then there is the potential for data to flow out of the sensitive system. Again, this can happen if the information is copied out, which can be attacked using mechanisms similar to those proposed for single-site systems. In addition, if a user wishes to view some of the sensitive data in combination with data from another database, in a join, for example, a query optimizer interested only in performance might choose to send the sensitive data to the less protected (less trusted) site to do the operation before returning the result. This would expose sensitive data both on the wire and in transit at the less trusted site. Encrypting data on the wire will alleviate but not eliminate this risk, if data must be decrypted at the less trusted site in order to do the join operation. Infact in most cases performing joins on encrypted data would be more costly and some joins may be impossible.

A query such as that in Figure 2 could cause this sort of problem, if site B does not trust site A with the attribute BUDGET. One join strategy the optimizer might consider for this query is to send the necessary information from DEPARTMENT to site A, to be joined with EMPLOYEE and PLANNED_TRIP, with the result forwarded to the query site (C). This plan is illustrated in Figure 3. This would mean sending the sensitive BUDGET information to site A, which is not trusted by B. Alternative strategies that do not expose the BUDGET column at site A can easily be found, but may be more expensive. For example, PLANNED_TRIP could be sent to B, joined with DEPARTMENT, the result sent back to A to be joined with EMPLOYEE and the final result returned to C. Note that this plan is only allowable if B trusts A with the other fields of the DEPARTMENT table. Otherwise, execution strategies which would conform to security constraints would force sending the entire EMPLOYEE and PLANNED_TRIP tables to B, doing the join there and sending the result to C, or sending all the data to C and doing the joins there.

```
Query Site: Site C

Select   EMPLOYEE.EMP#, NAME, DEPARTMENT, DESTINATION, DATE
   from  EMPLOYEE,PLANNED_ID,DEPARTMENT
   where EMPLOYEE.EMP# = PLANNED_TRIP.EMP#
   and   EMPLOYEE.DEPARTMENT = DEPT#
   and   COST > BUDGET

This query finds all employees who plan business trips whose cost
may exceed the budget of the department where the employees work.
```

Figure 2: Distributed Query example

Depending on the data size, those may not to be efficient plans.

The notion of a trusted site can be fairly restrictive. In an environment such as that of R* site B trusts site A with a set of data values V if (1) all system programmers at A are trusted, (2) all users at A who are authorized to see V are trusted, and (3) all Database Administrators (DBAs) of A are trusted. A user is trusted if there is an extremely high probability that he will be a good citizen and follow the security policy of the system. Depending on the "units" of trust – fields, relations or a whole database – factoring security requirements into the query optimizer could add a great deal of complexity and severely constrain the choice of execution strategy. This could lead to a real degradation in query performance at execution.

3. Distributed Views

Views can be an important seturity mechanism for a (D)DBMS. Views are virtual tables derived (directly or indirectly) from one or more stored "base" tables, using the relational operators (restrict, project, join) and/or statistical summary. In R* the semantics of a view are given by an SQL SELECT statement. Several examples of view definitions are presented in Figure 4. The "contents" of a view are not stored, but are derived dynamically when the view is referenced in a query. As pointed out in [DENN84], the view approach has several advantages. Views provide a high level of abstraction corresponding to the users' views of the database. They can incorporate access predicates in their definition and allow the authorization rules to remain static even when the data is dynamic.

Views are a powerful means of access control. This power is derived from the fact that users who have privileges on a view can access the information defined by that view regardless of whether they have any rights on the underlying objects. Thus it is not necessary to give a user SELECT access to the EMPLOYEE table if some of the data in that table is sensitive; instead, a view may be defined on top of EMPLOYEE which hides the sensitive information, and the user may be granted SELECT access to the view. Views may be used to provide attribute-level control of data, content-dependent control, or to hide particulars by giving statistical summaries of data. They are even being used to implement security levels in multilevel secure database management systems [DENN86], [CLAY83].

They can also reduce the risks of data flow violations, as they restrict the data which is "passed" to the users, thus restricting what can be copied or tapped. Since view queries are queries where security is known to be important, it might be reasonable to pay a potential performance penalty for these queries and optimize them subject to security constraints as suggested above.

Although views can be a powerful tool for security, they pose some threats to the security

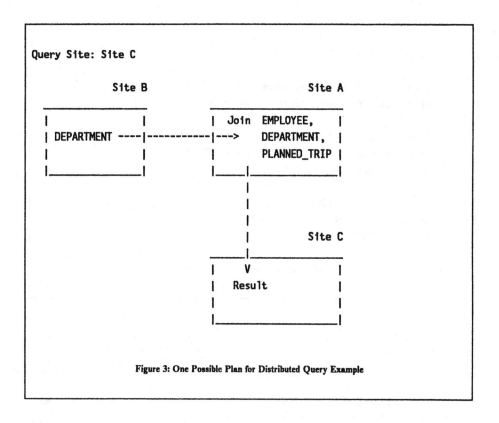

Figure 3: One Possible Plan for Distributed Query Example

system as well. The owner of a relation containing some sensitive data who would never let users from a certain site see that relation may decide that it is safe to allow them access through a view (which might exclude the sensitive columns). However, if the optimizer is not conscious of the security requirements as previously discussed, this may result in sensitive data being exposed at an untrusted site. Furthermore, the view definition is data, stored in the database, and hence, subject to corruption like any other piece of data. Corruption of a view definition could have severe effects on security – for example, dropping a restrictive predicate could cause the system to expose much more data than the owner intended, and, in a distributed system, this might occur at a site where users would not normally have rights to any of the data. Thus the view definition must be carefully protected.

Some of the questions a design for the view mechanism must answer are:

o **Representation:** What is it? Where is it stored? How is it protected?

o **Change:** How are changes to the view definition or the base objects tracked?

o **Authorization:** Who gets what rights on a view? Where is this information stored? How are rights granted and revoked?

o **Usage:** When and where is a view definition composed into a query? How is this operation protected?

These questions and some possible solutions are discussed in more detail below.

3.1. Representation

A (D)DBMS must construct and store an internal representation for each view that it supports. This occurs at view definition time. In systems such as R*, this internal representation is a parse tree for the view definition statement [BERT83]. This parse tree, after the view definition

```
View creator: UserA

At A: Create view VEMP (VEMP#, VNAME, VSALARY)
       as select EMP#, NAME, SALARY from EMPLOYEE

At B: Create view SAL (A_SAL,DNO)
       as select avg(SALARY),DEPARTMENT from EMPLOYEE
       group by DEPARTMENT

At A: Create view EMP_FLOOR (E_NAME,E_FLOOR)
       as select NAME,FLOOR from EMPLOYEE, DEPARTMENT
       where DEPARTMENT=DEPT#
```

Figure 4: Examples of view definition.

processing, is stored in a special system catalog. When a view is later referenced in a query, a view composition operation is performed to combine the view's parse tree with the query parse tree. The result is a composite parse tree which contains only references to real stored tables. When a view definition references another view, the "lower" (referenced) view's parse tree is composed with that of the new view during view definition, so that the stored representation of the view only references stored tables.

To discuss views and queries on views, some terminology is needed to describe the roles which different sites must play. The *view definition site* is the site from which the view is defined. Since the view can be defined on tables stored at remote sites, these sites are also important. We call sites that store a physical table which is referenced directly or indirectly by the view definition *view glue sites*. Note that the view definition site is a view glue site if the view references some table stored at the definition site. Finally, a view can be referenced from sites other than the definition site; we call the site where a query referencing the view is initiated the *query site*.

The internal representation of a view could be stored at the view definition site, the view glue sites, or both. If it is stored at the view definition site only, then every query which uses the view will have to access the view definition site – even if the view definition references no tables at that site. However, this may enhance security by isolating the view definition. Storing the internal representation at the glue sites can reduce the overhead on those queries which reference no data at the view definition site, at the cost of redundantly storing (and maintaining) the representation. Since the glue sites store the (sensitive) base data the view protects, they must be trusted sites. In any case, in a system characterized by autonomy such as R*, view definition will have to be a distributed operation, so that the view definer's access rights on the underlying tables can be checked. Furthermore, it is useful to have some representation of the view at the glue sites to facilitate handling changes to the base tables which affect the view (see below). Likewise it is useful to have a representation of the view at the view definition site for locating the view and handling changes to the view itself. Thus R* stores the view parse tree at both view definition and glue sites.

3.2. Change

To use the view mechanism as a means of access control, the system must guarantee that when a user tries to perform an operation on a view (1) he has the right to perform that operation on that view and (2) the view is *valid*. A view is valid if (1) it exists, (2) all objects that it references exist and are valid, and (3) the view owner still has the necessary privileges to define the view and grant the right to perform that operation on the view. This last is necessary because the view user gains his rights to access the view contents only through the view owner (whether directly or indirectly). If the owner of a view does not have the right to execute the query which defines the

---

Authorization dependencies:

At site A:

UserA grants Select with grant to VEMP on EMPLOYEE

UserA grants Delete to VEMP on EMPLOYEE

UserA grants Update with grant to VEMP on EMPLOYEE

UserA grants Select with grant to SAL on EMPLOYEE

UserA grants Select to EMP_FLOOR on EMPLOYEE

At site B:

UserA grants Select to EMP_FLOOR on DEPARTMENT

Existence Dependencies:

At site A:

VEMP depends on EMPLOYEE

SAL depends on EMPLOYEE

EMP_FLOOR depends on EMPLOYEE

At site B:

EMP_FLOOR depends on DEPARTMENT

Figure 5: Authorization dependencies

---

view, neither should any other user.

Thus when a view is defined, the system determines a set of objects and authorizations which must exist for the view to be used. The view is said to be *bound* to these objects and authorizations. When a change occurs which disrupts these bindings it must be detected, and the view must be invalidated. (This may set off a chain of invalidations if other views or programs depend on the validity of this view). When a view has been invalidated, further use of the view must be precluded. Continued use of an invalid view would be a severe breach of security. This binding is identical to that which takes place during program compilation, and can be solved similarly, using dependency records, which again are stored with the base object. The dependency records needed for the views in Figure 4 are shown in Figure 5.

Again, the method to be used for invalidation will vary depending on the database architecture. R* takes a distributed approach [NG82] to invalidating programs, in which a piece of the access plan for executing the queries in the program is stored at each site that stores a physical table referenced by a query. Since dependency records are stored with the physical tables, it is possible to determine locally which programs are affected by changes to the table (e.g., table migration, or index deletion) or to the user's authorization for that table (update privilege is revoked), and this can be recorded by marking the local piece of the access plan invalid without involving any other sites.

This approach has been extended to handle views. As mentioned above, R* stores the parse tree representation of the view at each of the view glue sites. If one of the tables is altered, or if a critical authorization is dropped, this parse tree can be marked invalid locally, and again, no other site needs to be informed. The next time the view is used, the glue site will be accessed (because it stores a physical table that is needed) and will check that the view is valid before proceeding. If

Privileges on base tables		Resulting privileges on views		
EMPLOYEE	DEPARTMENT	VEMP	SAL	EMP_FLOOR
Select with Grant	Select	Select with Grant	Select with Grant	Select
Delete	-	Delete	-	-
Update	-	Update	-	-

Figure 6: Resulting privileges on the views in Figure 4

the view is invalid the glue site will reject the query and try to inform the view definition site that the view is invalid. The view definition site can attempt to revalidate the view by redefining it.

This approach preserves site autonomy, as each site can modify its own data and/or revoke access rights on its own data without notifying other sites. However, with this approach the view definition site (and the sites that record who is authorized to use the view, if different) may not know that a view is invalid. Thus, it is possible in R* to grant a user rights on an invalid view. It is important to distinguish between grantability and usability of an object in distributed systems, as grantability need not imply that an object is usable.

3.3. Authorization

There are two different aspects of authorization for views. During view definition, the system must check the owner's right(s) to define the view, and infer the privileges the owner should be given on the view. Then the system must record and track the privileges the owner and other users have been given.

Though a view is not stored, it is a database object, and has an owner (normally the view definer) like any other database object. The owner can grant another user any or all of the privileges which he, the owner, has the right to grant on the view. Unlike the owner of a stored table, the owner of a view may only have a subset of the possible privileges. The owner's privileges depend on two things: the view semantics and the owner's privileges on the base objects.

Certain operations may not be legal depending on the semantics of a given view. For example, although UPDATE is normally a legal operation on a table or view, it is not legal when applied to the view SAL in Figure 4, because of the aggregate function in the view definition. Therefore, the owner of SAL would not have the UPDATE privilege on SAL, and hence, could not grant UPDATE on SAL to any other user. This is true regardless of whether the owner has the UPDATE privilege on the base table EMPLOYEE.

The owner's privileges on the underlying objects (base tables or views) also affect his privileges on the view. In particular, the owner will not have more privileges on the view than he has on the underlying objects. For example, if the owner of VEMP in Figure 4 has SELECT, DELETE and UPDATE privileges on EMPLOYEE, but not INSERT, then he will only have SELECT, DELETE and UPDATE privileges on VEMP.

To take a slightly more sophisticated example, if the owner of EMP_FLOOR has the SELECT privilege on EMPLOYEE, with the right to grant that privilege to others, and also has the SELECT privilege on DEPARTMENT, but without the right to grant that privilege, then he will have the SELECT privilege on EMP_FLOOR but without the right to grant that privilege. Hence no other user (except a DBA, of course) will be able to read from this view. These examples are summarized in Figure 6.

To check the owner's rights on the base objects, the system will use whatever security mechanisms it has defined for base objects. In a system like R*, this will be done in a decentralized fashion. Then each glue site, having checked that the view definer has the appropriate rights on the locally stored base objects, sends a "vote" back to the view definition site, which tells the definition site what type of privileges this glue site thinks the view definer has on this view. The definition site can use the votes to deduce the actual privileges the definer should receive.

Once the owner's privileges have been determined, they must be remembered, by storing them somewhere. Further, as other users are granted rights on the view, these must also be recorded. There are several possibilities:

Record at the view definition site. This implies that only the view definition site must be accessed to perform grant and revoke operations. This enhances site autonomy and the performance of grant and revoke operations. However, there is performance penalty for queries using a view when none of the base tables referenced in the view are stored at the view definition site, as the view definition site must be accessed to check the authorization at compile time, and again at runtime to ensure that the authorization is still there. Thus, if the view definition site is down, the query may not be executed, even though no real data requested by the query are stored at this site.

Record at all glue sites. This approach has the disadvantage that grant and revoke are distributed operations. In particular, it is not possible to revoke a privilege if one of the glue sites is down. Thus autonomy is reduced. However, there is no problem in invalidating a program when access rights are revoked from the program, as this invalidation can be performed at the view glue sites, which are accessed by the program in order to get the data. Also, there is no need to access the view definition site at execution time if there are no tables stored at that site.

Record at a particular glue site. This glue site, which we will call the *authorizer* glue site, is chosen in the following way. If the view definition site stores one of the tables referenced in the view definition, then the view definition site is the authorizer, else the authorizer is the site storing the first table referenced in the view definition. This approach has the advantage that no extra accesses are needed when running or compiling a program, if the view definition site does not store any table. When granting and revoking access rights on the view, we need to access at most two sites. This is the main advantage of this approach against the second.

In the design of views in R*, we have adopted the third solution. When a view is referenced in a query, the authorization checking on the view is performed at the authorizer site which must be visited during distributed query planning because a table of the query (via the view) is stored there. Granting and revoking privileges, as well, are performed at the view authorizer. When a request to grant some privileges is issued from a site other than the view definition site, a remote catalog lookup is performed [LIND81], which first tries the view definition site and then the authorizer if different. However, when cached information about the view is present, the request can be forwarded directly to the view authorizer. This mechanism maps easily to that used in managing tables, and hence can be implemented with a minimal amount of additional code, enhancing uniformity within the system.

3.4. Usage

When a view is used in a query, the view definition must be retrieved, and merged with the query. This step is called view composition, and in R* it is done by merging the internal representations (parse trees). View composition can be performed at the view definition site, the query site, or some or all of the glue sites. The choice that is made will affect both security and performance.

For security, it is attractive to compose the view definition into the query at the view definition site. This provides the potential to control information flow for views. The view definition site is a trusted site, so we can assume the merge takes place correctly, with no perversion of the view definition. Further, since this is a view, where security is known to be important, the optimizer at the view definition site could choose a secure execution strategy for materializing the view. This strategy could then be "merged" with the strategy for the rest of the query (typically defined by the query site). In a system like R*, the view could in fact be "pre-compiled", so that the access plan for a query using the view would invoke the access plan for the view.

Unfortunately, this approach leads to very poor performance [BERT83]. To the performance penalty incurred by considering data flow constraints during optimization, are added penalties which arise from not being able to plan the entire query at one site (no global optimization) and from having to funnel data through the view definition site even if no data is stored there. In R*, these penalties were considered large enough to effectively rule out this option.

If view composition is performed at the query site, there is no performance penalty from using the view, but there are several security risks. The potential for data flow control is lessened, as once the view is merged in the optimizer is faced with a normal query. The view definition itself is exposed at the query site, where it could be perverted during the composition operation. If the view definition is cached at the query site it is even more at risk, but speed and availability for query compilation are greatly enhanced.

Alternatively, the view could be composed into the query at some subset of the glue sites. These sites would then jointly assume responsibility for query planning. This can lead to inefficiencies both in the planning process and in the execution plan [DANI82], because if multiple views are involved no one site may be able to plan the entire query execution.

In R*, view composition takes place at the query site for simplicity and performance. To improve the security, during distributed compilation the glue sites check that view composition occurred correctly. This prevents a compile-time change to the query, and restricts possible exposures to the unlikely execution-time "in transit" violations.

Thus, when a view is used from sites other than the view definition site, the view definition statement is retrieved by the query site. At the query site, this statement is reparsed to obtain the view parse tree, which is cached locally. After view composition is performed, a composed parse tree for the query is obtained, referencing only base tables. If any of these base tables is stored at remote sites, a distributed query compilation take place [DANI82]. This involves formulating a global plan for query execution and distributing this plan to all the sites involved. Among the information contained in the plan is the query statement, into which the view definition(s) has been composed. (This statement can be derived by unparsing the composed parse tree). The plan also contains a list of the views used in the composition.

Each glue site for a view referenced in the query checks that the predicates appearing in the view are also present in the composed query statement. The glue sites perform this activity by comparing the parsed representation of the view which is stored in their catalogs to the parsed representation of the composed query. If a glue site determines that some predicate is missing or changed the query is rejected and an error message is sent back to the query site.

Thus R* has opted to ignore the potential views provide for data flow control, but to exploit their value as access control mechanisms. Views can be used to provide even stronger security depending on the implementation approach taken. However, stronger security will be achieved at the expense of performance in most cases. For a general purpose DDBMS, it is not clear that the incremental gain in security is worth the potentially large cost in performance and complexity.

4. Conclusions

We have discussed the design of a view mechanism for a DDBMS, and have shown that the implementation of such a mechansim must consider a number of tradeoffs among security, autonomy, and performance.

Views have been implemented as part of the DDBMS R*. R*'s major design goal, autonomy of individual sites, is compatible with the goal of a secure system; thus, R* provides fairly strong protection of data. If R* were enhanced to use encryption when transmitting data and requests for data, it would be secure against attacks on the networks. Flow control is needed to make the system fully secure, but seems unnecessary and expensive for a general purpose system.

REFERENCES

[ASTR76] Astrahan M.M., et Al., "System R: A Relational Approach to Database Management", *ACM Trans. on Database Systems*, **1:2** (June, 1976) pp.97-137.

[BERT83] Bertino E., Haas L.M., Lindsay B.G., "View Management in Distributed Database Systems", *Ninth International Conference on Very Large Data Bases* (Florence, November 1983).

[CHAM75] Chamberlin D.D., Gray J.N., and Traiger I.L., View, Authorization and Locking in Database System", *Proc. AFIPS NCC* 44 (1975).

[CHAM80] Chamberlin D., "A Summary of User Experience with the SQL Data Sublanguage" IBM Research Report RJ2767 (San Jose, CA, March 1980).

[CLAY83] Claybrook H., "Using Views in a Multilevel Secure Database Management System", *Proc. 1983 IEEE Symposium on Security and Privacy* (April, 1983) pp.4-17.

[COMP83] Special Issue on Data Security in Computer Networks, *IEEE Computer* 16:2 (February 1983).

[DANI82] Daniels, D., "Query Compilation in a Distributed Database System", IBM Research Report RJ3423 (San Jose, CA, March 1982).

[DENN86] Denning D.E., Akl S.G., Morgenstern M., Neumann P.G., Schell R.R., Heckman M. "Views for Multilevel Database Security", *Proc. 1986 IEEE Symposium on Security and Privacy* (Oakland (CA), April, 1986) pp.156-172.

[DENN84] Denning D.E., "Database Security: Access Controls" in *Security and Privacy, Proc. of the Joint IBM/Newcastle upon Tyne Seminar* (B.Randell, ed.), (Newcastle upon Tyne, September, 1984) pp.29-31.

[DENN83] Denning D.E., Schlorer J., "Inference Controls for Statistical Databases", *IEEE Computer* 16:7 (July, 1983) pp.69-81.

[DENN79] Denning D.E., and Denning P.J., "Data Security" *ACM Computing Surveys* 11:3 (September, 1979) pp.227-249.

[DENN76] Denning D.E., "A Lattice Model of Secure Information Flow", *Communications of the ACM* 20:7 (July, 1977) pp.504-513.

[DOWN77] Downs D., and Popek G.J., "A Kernel Design for a Secure Data Base Management System", *Proc. 3rd Int. Conf. on Very Large Data Bases* (Tokyo, October, 1977) pp.507-514.

[FERN81] Fernandez E.B., Summers R.C., Wood C., "Database Security and Integrity", Addison-Wesley (1981).

[GOLD79] Gold B.D. et al., "A Security Retrofit of VM/370", *AFIPS Conf. Proc. 48, 1979 NCC*, AFIPS Press (1979) pp.335-344.

[GRIF76] Griffiths P., Wade B., "An Authorization Mechanism for a Relational Database System", *ACM Trans. on Database Systems* 1:3 (September, 1976) pp.242-255.

[HAAS82] Haas L.M., et al., "R*: A Research Project on a Distributed Database System", *Database Engineering Bulletin (IEEE Computer Society)* 5:4 (December, 1982).

[KRAU79] Krauss L.I., and MacGahan A., "Computer Fraud and Countermeausures", Prentice-Hall, Inc., Englewood Cliffs, NJ (1979).

[**LAND84**] Landwehr C.E., Heitmeyer C.L., and McLean J., "A Security Model for Military Message System", **2:3** (August, 1984) pp.198-222. *ACM Trans. on Computer Systems*

[**LIND84**] Lindsay B.G., Haas L.M., Mohan C., Wilms P.F., Yost R.A., "Computation and Communication in R*: A Distributed Database Manager", *ACM Trans. on Computer Systems* **2:1** (February) 1984. Also in *Proc. 9th ACM Symposium on Operating Systems Principles* (Bretton Woods, October, 1983)

[**LIND81**] Lindsay B.G., "Object Naming and Catalog Management for a Distributed Database Manager", *Proc. 2nd International Conference on Distributed Computing Systems* (Paris, France, April, 1981).

[**LOHM85**] Lohman G.M., Mohan C., Haas L.M., Daniels D. Lindsay B.G., Selinger P.G., Wilms P.F., "Query Processing in R*", In *Query Processing in Database Systems* (W. Kim, D. Reiner, and D. Batory, Eds.), Springer-Verlag, (1985).

[**MCCA79**] McCauley E.J., and Drongowski P.J., "KSOS-The Design of a Secure Operating System", in *AFIPS Conf. Proc. 48, 1979 NCC*, AFIPS Press (1979) pp.345-351.

[**MURR84**] Murray W.H., "Security Considerations for Personal Computers", *IBM Systems Journal* **23:3** 1984.

[**NEED78**] Needham R.M., and Schroeder M.D., "Using Encryption for Authentication in Large Networks of Computers", *Communications of the ACM* **20:12** (December, 1978).

[**NG82**] Ng P., "Distributed Compilation and Recompilation of Database Queries", IBM Research Report RJ3375 (San Jose, CA, January, 1984).

[**PERR84**] Perry T.S, and Wallich P., "Can Computer Crime be Stopped?", *IEEE Spectrum* **21:5** (May, 1984) pp.34-45.

[**POPE79**] Popek, G. et al., "UCLA Secure UNIX", in *AFIPS Conf. Proc. 48, 1979 NCC*, AFIPS Press (1979) pp.355-364.

[**RUSH83**] Rushby J., and Randell B., "A Distributed Secure System", *IEEE Computer* **16:7** (July, 1983) pp.55-67.

[**SQL81**] IBM Corporation, "SQL/Data System: Application Programming", SH24-5018 (1981).

[**STON76**] Stonebraker M., Wong E., Krep P., and Held G., "The Design and Implementation of INGRES", *ACM Trans. on Database Systems* **1:3** (September, 1976).

[**TRUE83**] Trueblood R.P, Hartson H.R., and Martin J.J., "MULTISAFE - A Modular Multiprocessing Approach to Secure Database Management", *ACM Trans. on Database Systems* **8:3** (September, 1983) pp.382-409.

[VOYD83] Voydock V.L., and Kent S.T., "Security Mechanisms in High-Level Network Protocols", *ACM Computing Surveys* **15:2** (June, 1983) pp.135-171.

[WALK80] Walker B.J., Kemmmerer R.A., and Popek G.J., "Specification and Verification of the UCLA Unix Security Kernel", *Communications of the ACM* **23:2** (February, 1980) pp.118-131.

[WILL81] Williams R., Daniels D., Haas L.M., Lapis G., Lindsay B.G., Ng P., Obermark R., Selinger P.G., Walker A., Wilms P.F., Yost R.A., "R*: An Overview of the Architecture", in *Improving Database Usability and Responsiveness*, (P.Scheuermann, ed.), Academic Press (New York, 1982) pp.1-27.

[WILM81] Wilms P.F. "A Database Authorization Mechanism Supporting Individual and Group Authorization", in *Distributed Data Sharing Systems*, (van de Riet and Litwin, Eds.), North-Holland Publishing Company (1982).

[ZIMM80] Zimmermann H., "OSI Reference Model - The ISO Model of Architecture for Open System Interconnection", *IEEE Trans. on Communications* **28:4** (April, 1980) pp.425-432.

An Overview of the Distributed Query System DQS

V. Belcastro, A. Dutkowski, W. Kaminski, M. Kowalewski,
C.L. Mallamaci, S. Mezyk, T. Mostardi, F.P. Scrocco,
W. Staniszkis, G.Turco

CRAI
Contrada S. Stefano, 87036 Rende (CS), Italy.

ABSTRACT

DQS is a multidatabase system integrating heterogeneous distributed databases in a SNA network of IBM mainframes. It is a relational system with SQL implemented as the data language. DQS architecture and software organization are presented. Principal implementation problems, such as distributed query processing and optimization are discussed.

1. INTRODUCTION

While reaching its maturity, the evolving database management technology has left a residue of a large number of database systems representing a substantial investment both in application software and stored data. On the other hand, the growing information requirements, in particular the Information Center concept, have created a strong demand for integration of existing data resources.

Two possible approaches may be used to meet the requirements of information system users. An obvious one is to develop new database systems, utilizing either a centralized or a distributed database management system, based on a completely new database and application design catering for the required integration of data resources. The alternative solution is to provide the users with a software tool to access and manipulate data residing in preexisting, heterogeneous databases.

The first solution, although technically sound and based on a well proven technology, would in most cases be considered as prohibitively expensive. The constantly growing application backlog would further discourage investment of the scarce human resources in redevelopment of already existing applications.

Hence, the alternative solution, i.e. application of new database management tools providing means to access the preexisting databases without disturbing the already operational applications, has in the last five years been gaining increasing popularity.

An important class of new systems, called multidatabase management systems, has emerged, represented mostly by research prototypes, to provide facilities for integration of preexisting, heterogeneous databases distributed in a computer network. By heterogeneous databases we mean databases representing diverse data models, or at least supported by different database management systems.

A multidatabase management system may be defined in terms of the following characteristics:

1. Integration of heterogeneous databases - this implies that the underlying databases, accessible through the system, are managed by different DBMSes and may represent diverse logical data models.

2. Distribution - the fact that data are not resident at the same site and that all sites are linked via a wide or local network.

3. Logical correlation - the fact that data have some properties that tie them together, so that they may be represented by a meaningful, common data model.

Distribution may not always be a necessary condition to justify an application of a multidatabase management system. Clearly, there exist cases, where different centralized database management systems are present at a single site, and a multidatabase system may be used to provide for the required integration of data. However, the lack of distribution capabilities would be a serious limitation with respect to most applications.

Logical correlation implies existence of a common logical data model with its corresponding data language. Since many different data models already exist, corresponding to the various centralized databases accessible in the realm of a multidatabase system, the necessary mappings between those data models and the common data model must be provided. This is the major distinguishing factor between the multidatabase and the distributed database management systems. In the latter case, a common logical data model is applied and the data are physically distributed.

The state-of-the-art survey of the distributed database management technology has been given in [CER84, MOH84, STA85]. Both types of systems, namely the distributed database and the multidatabase systems, have been presented. We shall briefly summarize information regarding the most important developments in the area of multidatabase management systems.

A representative sample of the current research and development work includes such systems as ADDS [BRE84, BRE86], MERMAID [BRI84, TEM83, TEM86a], MULTIBASE [SMI81, LAN82], NDMS [STA84a], SIRIUS-DELTA [LIT82], AIDA [TEM86b], and MULTI-STAR [BEL87]. A survey of the current multidatabase management systems is presented in [STA86].

Most of the above multidatabase management systems, with exception of MULTIBASE, have been based on the relational data model as the global schema representation. Some systems do not support heterogeneous data models of the underlying databases. They are still considered multidatabase management systems, because integrated access to databases managed by diverse DBMSes is supported.

In most cases, distributed transaction processing is not supported. This is due to unresolved problems of concurrency control in the multi-DBMS environment. The difficulty results from the fact that multidatabase management systems utilize the host DBMSes on the level of user interfaces, that is on the query language or the data manipulation language level. Hence, it is impossible to apply most of the concurrency control algorithms developed for the distributed database management systems.

The lack of cooperation between local and global locking mechanisms may, for example, lead to undetectable global deadlocks. A detailed presentation of concurrency control problems in multi-DBMS environment may be found in [GLI84a, GLI84b].

In the following section we discuss the architecture of DQS, presenting both the DQS network architecture and the DQS node software structure. Subsequently we present the distributed query processing covering both the distributed query representation and execution as well as distributed query optimization.

2. DQS ARCHITECTURE

Distributed Query System (DQS) provides a retrieval-only relational interface, via SQL, to heterogeneous databases residing in a SNA network of IBM (or IBM-compatible) mainframes. Currently the system supports access to IMS/VS, IDMS, ADABAS, and RODAN databases, as well as to standard operating system data sets. The modular system design facilitates easy extension to interface with new DBMSes.

The local terminal support (within a DQS node) is provided by CICS/VS. The CICS/VS has been selected in order to provide for easy integration of DQS into the existing TP environments. The remote data communications are handled by the DQS data exchange protocol superimposed on the ACF/VTAM data communication functions.

The architecture is presented both in terms of the global view of the system and its required software environment, as well as in terms of the DQS software structure constituting an operational DQS node. In both of the above aspects of the system architecture only those features that are directly relevant to the multidatabase management functions are discussed.

2.1. DQS Network Architecture

The DQS network comprises a collection of IBM (or IBM-compatible) mainframes controlled by the MVS operating system connected via the SNA network. Each of the network nodes must host the DQS control region comprising the DQS software as well as the DQS Data Dictionary.

The DQS data communication functions assume that there exists a path between all nodes of the network. The actual physical routing is handled by the corresponding ACF/VTAM facilities. Since the physical path selection is transparent to DQS, the uniform data transmission cost between nodes is assumed for distributed query optimization.

The overview of the DQS network architecture is presented in Figure 1. The principal components of the architecture are the preexisting databases, with the corresponding database management systems, and the DQS node environment, comprising the DQS user interfaces, the DQS control software and the DQS Data Dictionary.

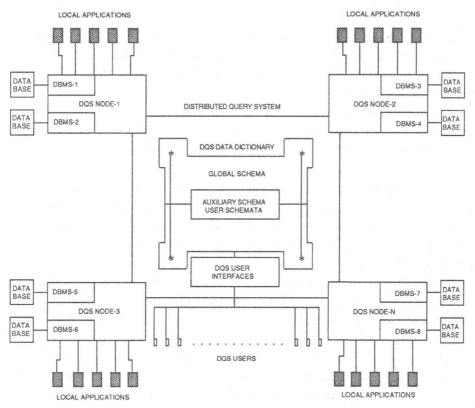

Figure 1. Overview of the DQS network architecture.

The preexisting databases, or the operating system data sets, function independently supporting their applications and user communities. Execution of DQS functions against a database is completely transparent, apart from additional processing workload generated by the distributed queries, to the local applications.

It is appropriate to stress at this point that no replication of data, apart from user defined and controlled snapshots, is necessary. The existing databases serve as the data repository of the DQS source data. All the required transformations are performed on intermediate data during the distributed query execution.

The principal end-user interface is provided by SQL data definition and manipulation functions. Data administration tools comprise languages to define the DQS node environment, and to describe mappings between the source database data models and the global schema relations. We discuss the user interfaces in the following subsection dealing with the DQS node structure.

The DQS Data Dictionary is a distributed meta-database comprising all necessary data description and control information. The DDD information is partially replicated among the DQS nodes. Replication of the control information may create serious data dictionary integrity problems and it requires, with the current DQS version, coordination of data administration work undertaken within individual DQS nodes.

The Global Schema represents the DQS *relational database*. We use the quotes to indicate that the schema represents a virtual database in the sense that relations represented by the Global Schema descriptions are only materialized as required during the distributed query processing.

Two principal types of relational schemes are comprised in the Global Schema, namely the base relation schemes and the derived relation schemes. It is worth noting that the 1NF is sufficient for all relation schemes since DQS does not allow update operations.

The base relation schemes, defined with the use of DEFINE TABLE SQL statement, are coupled with the corresponding mapping definitions comprised in the Auxiliary Schema. The base relations produced by arbitrary mappings, within the bounds of mapping definition language conventions, provide the data model independence within the system.

However, since a base relation must be associated, via the mapping definition, with a specific local database, the distribution transparency is not achieved on the base relation level. In order to resolve this deficiency we allow derived relations, defined with the use of DEFINE VIEW SQL statement, within the Global Schema.

Views defined on base relations are the principal data abstraction mechanism utilized within DQS. Aggregation abstractions are defined as joins over two or more base relations. Generalization abstractions may either be exclusive IS A hierarchies, thus conforming to the definition of generalization abstraction given in [SMI77], or non-exclusive IS A hierarchies. In the latter case, all of the well-defined relation rules, given in [SMI77], hold but the rule that requires the sets of lower level generic objects to be disjoint. Utility of non-exclusive generalization abstractions in the multidatabase systems has been demonstrated in [DAY83].

The exclusive generalizations are materialized as a union of projections of the underlying relations. Since relations participating in the UNION operation must be union-compatible, i.e. must agree on all attribute types and formats, the appropriate conversions must be defined within the base relation mapping specification.

The non-exclusive generalizations may be defined as a projection of the outer equi-join [COD79, DAT83] on the prime keys of the underlying relations. The MEAN function, defined on a list of attributes, may be used to resolve attribute value conflicts within tuples representing the same objects.

Considering the DQS data abstraction mechanism from the point of view of data distribution we notice that the former case, i.e. the exclusive generalization, corresponds to the horizontal partitioning of data, and the latter case corresponds to the vertical partitioning.

The Global Schema is replicated within the entire DQS network. This is required because of the centralized query translation and optimization mechanism that makes reference to the Global Schema relation schemes.

User schemata represent further abstractions: aggregations, restrictions, and generalizations, defined according to application and/or individual end-user requirements. The SQL view definition mechanism is used throughout the system as the data definition facility.

The Auxiliary Schema contains two major types of control information: the quantitative data description and the mapping definitions.

The quantitative data description characterizes the value distributions of selected base relation attributes. The statistical information is kept in the form of distribution histograms obtained on request by the UPDATE STATISTICS support function. If no statistical information is available for an attribute, meaning that the corresponding histogram has never been requested, the default value distribution is assumed. The statistical information is replicated in all DQS nodes to be available for distributed query optimization.

The mapping definitions, pertaining to individual base relations, are distributed among DQS nodes according to the location of the source database. Mapping definitions may be created and updated only by the authorized user (data administrator) defined within the local node. Mapping definitions are neither accessible nor known to other DQS nodes.

Additional information contained in the DQS Data Dictionary pertain to the environment definition. The environment definition comprises the user characteristics, including their names, locations, authorization levels, and resource restrictions. The user may access the system only via the native DQS node, hence no replication of user definitions is required.

DQS control software is replicated in all nodes of the DQS network. Communication among the DQS nodes is based on the appropriate functions of the DQS Intermediate Language that either pass the control information or trigger transfer of intermediate results.

Two classes of DQS nodes, according to availability of DQS control software facilities, may be set up. Active DQS nodes provide the entire range of DQS functions comprising both the user interfaces and the distributed data management functions. In such case active CICS/VS region is required to support the user interface. Passive DQS nodes do not support local users and comprise only the distributed data management functions. In such case only local mapping definitions are stored in the DDD.

The example shown in Figure 2 illustrates the data abstraction mechanism: data model transparency is achieved by application of proper mapping definition. Once created according to specified mapping rules, the base tables SALES_LON, SALES_PAR and INSTORE no longer depend on any particular data model.

SALES OFFICE IN NODE LONDON: IMS DATA BASE

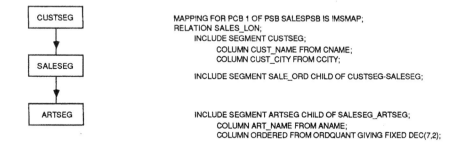

MAPPING FOR PCB 1 OF PSB SALESPSB IS IMSMAP;
RELATION SALES_LON;
    INCLUDE SEGMENT CUSTSEG;
        COLUMN CUST_NAME FROM CNAME;
        COLUMN CUST_CITY FROM CCITY;

    INCLUDE SEGMENT SALE_ORD CHILD OF CUSTSEG-SALESEG;

    INCLUDE SEGMENT ARTSEG CHILD OF SALESEG_ARTSEG;
        COLUMN ART_NAME FROM ANAME;
        COLUMN ORDERED FROM ORDQUANT GIVING FIXED DEC(7,2);

SALES OFFICE IN NODE PARIS: IDMS DATA BASE

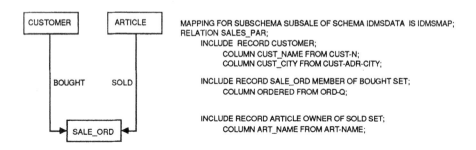

MAPPING FOR SUBSCHEMA SUBSALE OF SCHEMA IDMSDATA IS IDMSMAP;
RELATION SALES_PAR;
    INCLUDE RECORD CUSTOMER;
        COLUMN CUST_NAME FROM CUST-N;
        COLUMN CUST_CITY FROM CUST-ADR-CITY;

    INCLUDE RECORD SALE_ORD MEMBER OF BOUGHT SET;
        COLUMN ORDERED FROM ORD-Q;

    INCLUDE RECORD ARTICLE OWNER OF SOLD SET;
        COLUMN ART_NAME FROM ART-NAME;

HEADQUARTERS IN NODE ROME: VSAM FILE.

MAPPING FOR SUBSCHEMA VSAMFILE IS VSAMMAP;
RELATION INSTORE;
    INCLUDE RECORD VSAMREC;
        COLUMN STORE_CITY   FROM   1-16 CHAR (16);
        COLUMNSTORE_ART   FROM 22-41 CHAR (20);
        COLUMN STORE-QUANT FROM 50-53 FIXED DEC (7,2);

Figure 2. Data model independent data abstraction.

Data distribution transparency is provided by definition of the following view:

DEFINE VIEW SALES (CUST_NAME, CUST_CITY, ART_NAME, ORDERED) AS
SELECT CUST_NAME, CUST_CITY, ART_NAME, ORDERED FROM
SALES_LON
UNION
SELECT CUST_NAME, CUST_CITY, ART_NAME, ORDERED FROM
SALES_PAR;

Another level of data abstraction represents the following sample query:

SELECT CUST_NAME, CUST_CITY, ART_NAME, STORE_QUANT
FROM SALES, INSTORE
WHERE CUST_CITY= STORE_CITY;

2.2. The DQS Node Structure

The principal components of the DQS node are the control software, namely the user interface software and the distributed data management software, the DQS Data Dictionary, the Working Storage, and the local DBMS(es) with the corresponding local databases. The DQS node structure is shown in Figure 3.

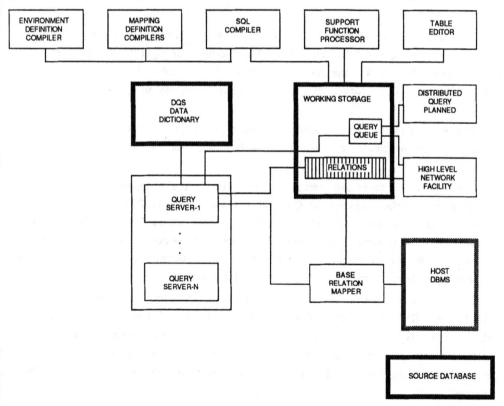

Figure 3. DQS node structure.

The user interface software comprises all DQS language compilers and the associated support functions. The SQL compiler produces a query tree that is subsequently transformed into an optimized query program by the Query Planner. We discuss our query optimization approach in the following section.

The distributed data management software consists of the data communication functions and the data manipulation functions.

The data communication functions implement the DQS data communication protocol representing the application level with respect to the ACF/VTAM protocol.

The data manipulation functions are serviced by an arbitrary number of Query Servers executed as independent subtasks in the DQS region. The actual number of active Query Servers may be specified during DQS initiation by the data administrator. The number should be selected as a function of the expected query processing workload and the DQS region memory size.

The Query Server executes the DQS Intermediate Language commands selected from the Query Queue according to the query program synchronization rules. We discuss the parallel execution and synchronization of query programs in the following section.

DIL provides a vehicle for implementation of relational algebra operations comprised in the query tree. The actual data manipulation algorithms are determined by the Query Planner and the resulting query program consists of a sequence of DIL commands and the precedence matrix representing the query program synchronization rules.

The summary of the DIL commands is presented in table 1. Most of the commands provide standard distributed data manipulation functions that may be encountered in any DDBMS.

The CREATE command actually implements the multidatabase function of DQS providing an interface between the Query Server and the source DBMS. The command invokes a Base Relation Mapper corresponding to the source DBMS, which in turn materializes base relation tuples from the underlying database records. The actual navigation in the source database is based on the materialization algorithm determined by the mapping rules specified for the target base relation.

It is worth noting that our materialization approach differs from that proposed in MULTIBASE [DAY82]. The base relation materialization algorithm implemented in MULTIBASE is based on dynamic construction of materialization algorithms by the local query optimizer. A general class of tree materialization algorithms has been defined and a heuristic algorithm is used to synthesize an efficient materialization program.

The major advantages of our approach are the possibility to define arbitrary materialization algorithms, i.e. plex materialization algorithms, as well as enhanced control over data extraction operations from any of the local databases.

DIL command	Options	Function
CREATE (map-id/rel-id→rel-id)	mapping select	Materialization of base tables from local data bases/files. Creation of new table by projection and/or restriction of input table.
DROP (rel-id→free space)		Releases working storage occupied by the table.
HASH (rel-id,col-id→bm-filt-id)		Maps hash indexes obtained by hashing values of column into the bit vector.
INTERSECT (rel-id1,rel-id2→rel-id)	hash sort	Creates an intersection of two input tables using hash or sort method.
JOIN (rel-id1,rel-id2→rel-id)	hash sort cart.prod.	Joins locally two input tables using hash, sort or cartesian product method.
MINUS (rel-id1,rel-id2→rel-id)	hash sort	Creates a difference of two input tables using hash or sort method.
RANGE (rel-id,col-id→r-filt-id)		Searches the minimum and maximum value of table column giving range filter.
RESTRICT (rel-id,col-id,filt-id→rel-id)	bit-map range	Creates a new restricted table using bit-map or range filter applied to specified column.
SEND (re-id/filt-id/plan-id,node-id)	table range filt bitmap filt subplan	Sends the table, bit-map filter, range filter or the subplan to the specified site (node).
SORT (rel-id,col-id,ord[,...]→rel-id)		Sorts the input table according to specified criteria: sort keys and sort sequence orders.
UNION (rel-id1,rel-id2→rel-id)		Creates the table being the sum of all rows of both input tables.

Table 1. DQS Intermediate Language commands

The Base Relation Mappers are constructed as mapping language interpreters for each DBMS integrated into the DQS environment. This implementation approach allows for easy extension of DQS to handle new DBMSes and data set organizations.

Storage and manipulation of DQS relations, both the base as well as intermediate result relations, is performed in the Working Storage. The WS is a two level memory hierarchy with the transient storage implemented in the main memory and the persistent storage implemented on disk. The use of persistent memory for intermediate results is necessary in order to cater for arbitrary size of query results as well as to provide the basis for the query recovery mechanism.

The snapshot relations as well as query results are also stored in the persistent storage. Since both the query results as well as the snapshot relations may subsequently be used as query arguments, the WS facility closely resembles a relational database management system.

3. DISTRIBUTED QUERY PROCESSING

DQS users may pose an arbitrary number, subject to resource restrictions imposed by the data administrator, of concurrent queries. Each query is processed by the query acceptance procedures validating the query scope against the user authorization as well as performing a syntactic and semantic check on the query statement.

If accepted, the query is appended to the query queue for further processing. The user may utilize the system support functions to look up query results and query status information stored in the Working Storage.

The asynchronous query execution prevents user terminals from being blocked by long queries, thus permitting the user to perform other work. This leads to the query optimization algorithm oriented towards the overall query execution cost rather than towards the response time.

We present two principal aspects of DQS distributed query processing, namely the distributed query representation and execution synchronization rules, as well as the distributed query optimization algorithm.

3.1. Representation of Distributed Queries

A user query, expressed in SQL, is subject to a number of transformations prior to the actual execution. The subsequent forms of distributed query representation are schematically shown in Figure 4.

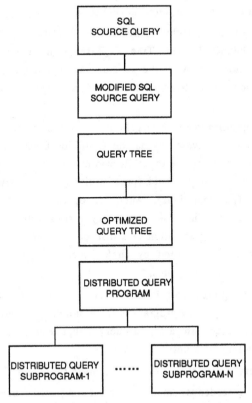

Figure 4. Distributed query representations.

The SQL query submitted in the source version is queued in the user's native DQS node. The SQL compiler processes outstanding queries in the following steps:

1. Syntactic analysis

2. Query modification

3. Query Tree generation

4. Algebraic transformation of the Query Tree

The query modification function recursively substitutes all view names with the SELECT statements specified in the corresponding view definitions.

The Intermediate Query Tree is generated as the N-ary tree where the root represents the query result, the leave nodes represent base relations comprised in the Global Schema, and the intermediate nodes represent partial results produced during query execution.

The Intermediate Query Tree is algebraically transformed into the N-ary Query Tree (QT). The algebraic transformation moves the restriction predicates and the projection lists down the Query Tree, if possible, until the corresponding leave nodes are reached. The objective of the algebraic transformation is to reduce the size of intermediate relations represented by the QT nodes. A detailed specification of the algebraic transformation rules may be found in [FOR82].

The query optimization algorithm processes the N-ary Query Tree and produces a binary tree called the Optimized Query Tree. OQT represents the scheduling of binary relational algebra operations, namely the join, union, intersection, and set difference operations. The location of operation results and the operation algorithms are also determined.

The final query optimization step is generation of the query program. The query program may be logically represented as the Condition-Event Petri net. Each query program operation, corresponding to the DIL command, is determined exactly by those conditions which cease to hold (preconditions), and by those conditions which begin to hold (postconditions), when the operation producing the transition is done. We can associate the intermediate query results with the conditions of our representation. A Petri net representation of a distributed query is shown in Figure 5. Graphically, conditions are represented by circles, operations by bars, and connections between conditions and operations by arcs.

The C-E Petri net representation facilitates query scheduling exploiting the inherent intra-query parallelism. The query program is fragmented, according to processing site of the specific DIL commands, into a set of query subprograms. The subprograms are shipped to the corresponding DQS network nodes.

Internally the query program is represented as a triple $< A,F,S>$, where:

A   is a dynamic precedence matrix representing the operation dependencies expressed by the query Petri net representation.

F   is a sequence of DIL operations

S   is the symbol table providing linkage between symbolic DIL command arguments and their physical locations.

A is a square matrix of order n over a domain $(0,1)$, where n is the number of operations comprised in the query program. An element $a_{i,j}=1$ means that the j-th operation involves postconditions which are also the preconditions of the i-th operation. Hence, the execution of the i-th operation is conditioned on termination of the j-th operation. Elements of the dynamic precedence matrix are updated appropriately by the Query Servers. The matrix A is locked for the duration of the control information update by the Query Server.

Concurrent Query Servers independently process DIL commands taking the arguments from and storing the results in the Working Storage. The scheduling algorithm of a Query Server looks for the first unlocked dynamic precedence matrix A, locks it and selects the i-th row such that For All $[1< k< n]$ $a_{i,k}=0$, sets $a_{i,i}=1$, unlocks the matrix, and executes the corresponding DIL command.

The above scheduling algorithm supports parallel execution of DIL commands contained in a query subprogram, as well as provides the required synchronization between the distributed query subprograms.

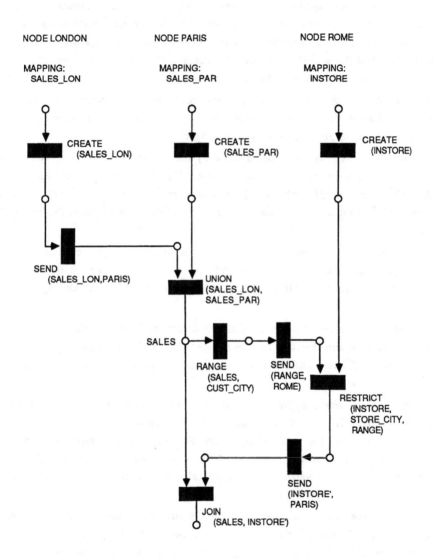

Figure 5. The Petri net representation of the query presented in section 2.1.

4. DISTRIBUTED QUERY OPTIMIZATION

The goal of our query optimization algorithm is to minimize the overall distributed query processing cost expressed as the linear combination of the CPU, I/O, and data transmission costs. The cost-oriented approach reflects our opinion that most of the multidatabase system users will be more interested in the real query processing cost rather than in the response time.

Additionally, the system administrator may require means to control query processing workload distribution in order to meet the specific constraints imposed on the multidatabase system within a given network configuration.

Arbitrary cost weights may be defined by the system administrator, being either the relative weights representing the relative value of a given resource (e.g. a particular CPU or an I/O subsystem) or values representing the real accounting costs. Data transmission cost is considered to be uniform throughout the entire DQS network.

The output of the query optimization algorithm is the schedule of binary relational algebra operations, namely join and the set theoretical operations, represented as a binary tree. Location of intermediate results as well as the operation algorithms are also selected.

The distributed query processing sites are determined by the selected location of intermediate results and by the relational operation implementation algorithm. Note, that the location of base relations is fixed and the result is always located in the query originating site.

The relational algebra operation implementation is predefined as an extensible set of algorithms, logically defined as Petri nets of DIL commands, characterized by cost equations. Selection of the optimal algorithm depends on the location of operation arguments, the required result location, and the cost weights associated with processing resources. The variation of the join algorithm presented within the query of Figure 5 is shown in Figure 6.

Note, that the value of cost equations is strongly dependent on the operation argument and result size. Relation size is a product of the relation cardinality and width. The centralized optimization approach precludes the use of feed back information regarding cardinalities of intermediate results. Hence, a statistical evaluation approach is used to establish the expected cardinalities of the intermediate results.

The statistical evaluation, based on distribution histograms constructed for base relation attributes and maintained in the DDD, establishes selectivity factors of the restriction, join, as well as the set theoretic operations. The selectivity factors are established for each QT level to be subsequently used for expected cardinality estimation. The detailed description of the relational operation selectivity evaluation in DQS is presented in [KAM87].

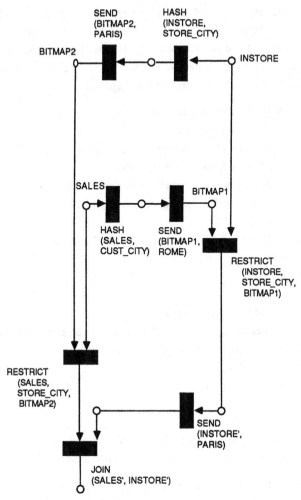

Figure 6. Petri net representation of a join algorithm.

A heuristic algorithm is used to produce the Optimized Query Tree. The algorithm traverses the Query Tree in the left-to-right, top-down fashion locating the nodes that have not yet been scheduled. The node selected for scheduling must have all its children already scheduled. Note, that this condition causes the algorithm to commence always from the leaf nodes.

The partial schedule is constructed by selecting pairs of relations and adding them to the partial schedule produced within the previous iteration of the algorithm presented in Figure 7. The final partial schedule represents the complete binary tree for the object N-ary node. Partial schedules are produced for each eligible result site.

The eligible result sites may be all DQS network sites, or a subset selected according to the dynamically established heuristics level. The eligible source sites are either the actual sites, in the case of base relations, or the result sites from the lower Query Tree level.

The last QT node to be scheduled is the root node. Again partial schedules are constructed for each eligible result site. The least global cost, plus transmission cost to ship result to the query originating site, is selected at the root node. Note, that selection of the root node schedule automatically determines the Optimized Query Tree. The outline of the QT node optimization algorithm is presented in Figure 7.

```
For i= N Step -1 Until i= 1 Do
    For Each partial-schedule Do
        For Each pair of i-ary partial-schedule-relations Do
            For Each eligible-result-site Do
                For Each pair of eligible-source-sites Do
                    Select the least costly DIL-algorithm
                End
                Select the least costly pair of eligible-source-sites
            End
        End
        For Each eligible-result-site Do
            Construct the (i-1)ary partial-schedule by Selecting the least
            least costly pair for this eligible result site
        End
    End
End
```

Where:
    N - is the number of Query Tree node argument relations
    K - is the number of eligible DQS network sites

Figure 7. Heuristic optimization algorithm for the Query Tree node.

The time complexity of the heuristic optimization algorithm for a single QT node is approximately $O(N^2 \times K^4)$. The heuristics are introduced by substituting the $i(i-1)K/2$ partial schedules, that would be generated for each iteration of the exact algorithm, with K partial schedules by selecting the ones containing the least costly relation pair for each of K result sites.

Additional heuristics are dynamically introduced by restricting the set of eligible sites, i.e. making K smaller. The coarseness of the heuristics depends on the dynamic parameter that varies according to the actual optimization time and the optimization level parameter defined for a DQS site.

The important characteristic of our distributed query optimization approach is the extensible set of algorithms implementing the relational algebra operations. New algorithms may be defined with the use of DIL commands by the system administrator and they may be stored in the DDD with the use of appropriate support functions.

A more detailed description of distributed query optimization in DQS may be found in [DUT87].

CONCLUSIONS

The present version of DQS has been used to develop pilot multidatabase systems and the resulting experience has suggested the following principal development directions:

1. Extending the system to cope with heterogeneous hardware environments. Integration with the UNIX environment is already underway.

2. Extending DQS SQL to incorporate embedded features and to handle update operations.

3. Development of advanced, logic programming based query system.

4. Development of advanced, knowledge-based user interface [SAC85].

Preliminary work on multidatabase system design methodology has been stimulated by the pilot application experience and the initial results are presented in [MOS87].

Further experimentation with the query optimization subsystem is to be undertaken in order to gain more insight into the distributed query optimization heuristics and to refine the selectivity estimation.

ACKNOWLEDGMENTS

We are grateful to G. Paletta for his collaboration in the distributed query optimization. His work on the optimization algorithms has provided valuable input to our heuristic solution.

REFERENCES

BEL87   Bell, D., Fernandez Perez De Talens A., Gianotti, N., Grimson, J., Hutt, A., O'Sullivan, D., Turco, G., MULTI-STAR: A Multidatabase System for Health Information Systems, Proc. of the 7th Int. Congress on Medical Informatics, Rome, September, 1987.

BRE84   Breitbart, Y.J., Tieman, L.R., ADDS - Heterogeneous Distributed Database System, Proc. of the 3rd Int. Seminar on Distributed Data Sharing Systems, F.A. Schreiber and W. Litwin (Eds), Parma, Italy, March, 1984, North Holland, 1985.

BRE86   Breitbart, Y., Olson, P.L., Thompson, G.R., Database Integration in a Distributed Heterogeneous Database System, Proc. of the Int. Conference on Data Engineering, February 5-7, 1986, Los Angeles, USA, IEEE Computer Society, 1986.

BRI84   Brill, D., Templeton, M., Yu, C., Distributed Query Optimization in MERMAID: a Frontend to Data Management Systems, Proc. of the Int. Conference on Data Engineering, Los Angeles, April 1984.

CER84   Ceri, S., Pelagatti, G., Distributed Databases - Principles and Systems, McGraw-Hill, 1984.

COD79   Codd, E.F., Extending the Database Relational Model to Capture More Meaning, ACM TODS, Vol. 4, No. 4, December 1979.

DAT83   Data, C.J., The Outer Join, Proc. of the Second Int. Conference on Databases, September 1983, Cambridge, England, Wiley Heyden Ltd, London, 1983.

DAY82   Dayal, U., Goodman, N., Query Optimization for CODASYL Database Systems, Proc. of the ACM/SIGMOD 82 Int. Conference on Management of Data, 1982.

DAY83   Dayal, U., Processing Queries over Generalization Hierarchies in a Multidatabase System, Proc. of the 9th Int. Conference on Very Large Data Bases, Florence, Italy, October-November 1983.

DUT87   Dutkowski, A., Kaminski, W., Kowalewski, M., Staniszkis, W., Distributed Query Optimization in DQS, CRAI Research Report 87-19, Rende, Italy, 1987.

FOR82   Forker, H.J., Algebraical and Operational Methods for the Optimization of Query Processing in Distributed Relational Database Systems, Proc. of the 2nd International Symposium on Distributed Data Bases, H.-J. Schneider (Ed.), Berlin, September 1-3, 1982, West Germany.

GLI84a   Gligor, V.D., Luckenbaugh, G.L., Interconnecting Heterogeneous Database Management Systems, IEEE Computer, Volume 17, Number 1, 1984.

GLI84b   Gligor, V.D., Popescu-Zeletin, R., Concurrency Control Issues in Distributed Heterogeneous Database Management Systems, Proc. of the 3rd Int. Seminar on Distributed Data Sharing Systems, F.A., Schreiber, W. Litwin (Eds.), Parma, Italy, March 1984, North-Holland 1985.

KAM87   Kaminski, W., Staniszkis, W., Probabilistic Cardinality Evaluation of Relational Operation Results, Proc. of the 10th Int. Seminar on DBMS, October 1987, Cedzyna, Poland.

LAN82   Landers, T., Rosenberg, R.L., An Overview of Multibase, Proc. of the 2nd Int. Symposium on Distributed Data Bases, H.-J. Schreiber (Ed.), Berlin, September 1982, North-Holland, 1982.

LIT82   Litwin, W., Boudenant, J., Esculier, C.,Ferrier, A., Glorieux, A.M., La Chimia, J., Kabbaj, K., Molinoux, C., Rolin, P., Stangret, C., SIRIUS Systems for Distributed Data Management, Proc. of the 2nd Int. Symposium on Distributed Data Bases, H.-J. Schreiber (Ed.) Berlin, September 1982, North-Holland, 1982.

MOH84   Mohan, C., Recent and Future Trends in Distributed Data Base Management, Proc. of the NYU Symposium on New Directions in Database Systems, May, 1984.

MOS87   Mostardi, T., Staniszkis, W., Multidatabase System Design Methodology, Proc. of the 10th Int. Seminar on DBMS, October 1987, Cedzyna, Poland.

SAC85   Sacca', D., Vermeir, D., D'Atri, A., Liso, A., Pedersen, G.S., Snijders, J.J., Spyratos, N., Description of the Overall Architecture of the KIWI System, ESPRIT '85: Status Report of Continuing Work, The Commission of the European Communities, North-Holland, 1986.

SMI77   Smith, J.M., Smith, D.C.P., Database Abstractions: Aggregation and Generalization, ACM TODS, Vol. 2, No. 2, June 1977.

SMI81   Smith, J.M., Bernstein, P.A., Dayal, U.,Goodman, N., Landers, T.A., Lin, W.-T.K.,Wong, E., MULTIBASE -- Integrating Heterogeneous Distributed Database Systems, Proc. AFIPS NCC, Volume 50, 1981.

STA83   Staniszkis, W., Kowalewski, M., Turco, G., Krajewski, K., Saccone, M., Network Data Management System - General Architecture and Implementation Principles, Proc. of the Third International Conference on Engineering Software, Imperial College of Science and Technology, London, England, April, 1983.

STA84   Staniszkis, W., Kaminski, W., Kowalewski, M., Krajewski, K., Mezyk, S., and Turco, G., Architecture of the Network Data Management System, Proc. of the 3rd Int. Seminar on Distributed Data Sharing Systems, F.A. Schreiber and W. Litwin (Eds.), Parma, Italy, March, 1984, North-Holland, 1985.

STA85   Staniszkis, W., Distributed Database Management, State-of-the-Art and Future Trends, Proc. of the 8th Int. Seminar on Database Management Systems, October, 1985, Piestany, Cechoslovakia.

TEM83   Tempelton, M., Brill, D., Hwang, A., Kameny, I., Lund, E., An Overview of the MERMAID System -- A Front-end to Heterogeneous Databases, Proc. of the 16th Annual Electronics and Aerospace Conference, Washington D.C., September, 1983.

TEM86a   Tempelton, M., Brill, D., Chen, A., Lund,E., MERMAID - Experiences with Network Operation, Proc. of the Int. Conference on Data Engineering, February 5-7, 1986, Los Angeles, USA, IEEE Computer Society, 1986.

TEM86b   Tempelton, M., Brill, D., Chen, A., Dao, S., Lund, E., MacGregor, R., Ward, B., Introduction to AIDA - A Front-end to Heterogeneous Databases, to appear in a IEEE publication.

TAILOR, A Tool for Updating Views

Amit P. Sheth
UNISYS West Coast Research Center
2400 Colorado Avenue
Santa Monica CA 90406 USA
amit@sm.unisys.com

James A. Larson and Evan Watkins
Honeywell CSDD
1000 Boone Avenue North
Golden Valley, MN 55427 USA

ABSTRACT

TAILOR is a tool for updating views. It interacts with the database *administrator* at view definition time to capture syntactic knowledge, structural constraints, and application semantics. It also interacts with the database *user* and consults the *database* at view update time to capture additional application semantics and database semantics, respectively. TAILOR uses this information to select from among several alternative update translations against the base relations when the user updates a view. This paper describes an overview of the algorithms used by TAILOR and its implementation using a comprehensive example of a view update and how TAILOR performs it.

Key Words: view update, relational views, semantic knowledge, database semantics, application semantics, semantic integrity constraints, translations, semantic ambiguity problem, rule based approach.

1. Introduction

Given a view of a relational database, a database user would like to execute queries and updates on that view. The operation of query can be performed against a view using a method called query modification [Stonebraker 75]. However, the operation of executing an update against a view is more difficult because in some cases the update can be translated into several alternative candidate "translations", sets of updates against the base relations stored in the database.

This work was partially supported by NSF grant DMC-84-12085 and Honeywell CSDD and was performed at Honeywell CSDD.

TAILOR is a tool which solves the "semantic ambiguity problem" [Masunaga 84], that is, the problem of choosing from among these candidate translations. To perform this selection, TAILOR uses several types of syntactic and semantic knowledge which is obtained at view definition time and at view update time.

The literature describes much work in the area of updating views [Osman 79, Dayal 78, Dayal 82, Carlson 79, Bancilhon 79, Bancilhon 81, Cosmadakis 84, Hegner 84, Furtado 85, Date 86]. Keller [Keller 85, Keller 86] suggests that for certain types of views, all the semantics required to solve the ambiguity in the view update problem can be collected at view definition time. Masunaga [Masunaga 84] argues that the database semantics captured at view definition time are not sufficient, and that the translation must ultimately be guided by the user's intention when the update is issued.

Our work was influenced by [Keller 85] and [Masunaga 84]. We believe that both database semantics and application semantics are required. Some semantics can be obtained at view definition time, and the remaining semantics must be obtained at view update time. The examples discussed in this paper and [Larson 87] show the need for this approach.

TAILOR extends previous work in view updates along three dimensions. (1) It handles a larger set of view types, including views defined by set difference, union, intersection, select, project, and join. (2) It considers a larger number of possible translations for each of the view types. As a result, however, it must deal with more ambiguities in translation. (3) It uses more information to resolve ambiguities. This information can be provided at view definition time as well as view update time. A more detailed description of TAILOR and the theoretical basis for its rules are found in [Larson 87].

Section 2 of this paper motivates the need for solving the semantic ambiguity problem by describing an example view and the resulting candidate set of translations that can occur due to a single update against the view. This example will be used throughout the paper. Section 3 describes the types of information needed by TAILOR to solve the semantic ambiguity problem. Section 4 presents the algorithm used by TAILOR to solve the semantic ambiguity problem. We also give a simplified presentation of the implementation and discuss the interface used by the database administrator (DBA) and the database user. Section 5 describes our choice of implementation environment for TAILOR. In Section 6 we give our conclusions about the feasibility and applicability of TAILOR in a real DBMS.

2. An Example

Consider the base relations UNDERGRAD, which contains information about students in an undergraduate school, and GRAD, which contains information about students in a graduate school. Both base relations have the same domains: ID# is the unique identifier of each student, NAME contains a character string representing the student's name, EFA indicates if the student is eligible for financial aid, and AID indicates the amount of financial aid received.

The STUDENT view is derived by forming the UNION of GRAD and UNDERGRAD relations. Given the above base relations, the STUDENT view follows:

The DELINQUENT view is derived from the STUDENT view by selecting all of the tuples from STUDENT such that EFA = "NO" and AID > 0. The DELINQUENT view contains information about students who have received some financial aid, but who have become ineligible since receiving the aid. For example, many federal student loans require the recipient to maintain a full-time student status for the entire period for which the loan was issued, usually two semesters. This view is used by the Financial Aid Office.

UNDERGRAD			
ID#	NAME	EFA	AID
1	SMITH	NO	500
2	JONES	NO	0

GRAD			
ID#	NAME	EFA	AID
3	WATSON	YES	1000

STUDENT			
ID#	NAME	EFA	AID
1	SMITH	NO	500
2	JONES	NO	0
3	WATSON	YES	1000

DELINQUENT			
ID#	NAME	EFA	AID
1	SMITH	NO	500

Figure 2-1 shows the schematic of the database relations and the views used in our example. TAILOR's window facility shows a screen similar to that shown in this figure when a user works with the DELINQUENT view.

We illustrate the *semantic ambiguity problem* of a view update with the following example, which has three *candidate translations*.

Example: Suppose Smith regains his eligibility for financial aid, then the Financial Aid Office deletes < 1, SMITH, NO, 500> from the DELINQUENT view. There are at least three candidate translations that can change the UNDER-GRAD base relation to reflect this change:

(1) Replace < 1, SMITH, NO, 500> with < 1, SMITH, YES, 500> in UNDERGRAD, or

(2) Replace < 1, SMITH, NO, 500> with < 1, SMITH, NO, 0> in UNDER-GRAD, or

(3) Delete < 1, SMITH, NO, 500> from UNDERGRAD.

Since only one translation should be used to update the base relations, additional semantics are necessary in order to select the correct translation. In this example, the following semantics lead to deleting the third choice. Personnel in the Financial Aid Office may update the DELINQUENT view to reflect the changes in eligibility and amount of aid. However, personnel in the Financial Aid Office may not enroll or disenroll students, so updates against the DELINQUENT may result only in a modification to GRAD or UNDERGRAD relation; insertion or deletion against GRAD or UNDERGRAD relations are

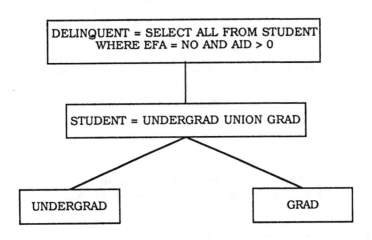

Figure 2-1. Schematic of the Base Relations and the Views

not allowed as a result of updates to the DELINQUENT view. This semantics can be used to delete the third translation from the set of three candidate translations. The choice between candidate translations 1 and 2 can only be made by the Financial Aid Office personnel submitting a view update on DELINQUENT.

As the above example illustrates, additional knowledge may be necessary to solve the semantic ambiguity problem. The next section describes the various types of knowledge that may be needed to trim the choices and select a single translation for execution.

3. Knowledge Needed for Solving the Semantic Ambiguity Problem

Figure 3-1 shows a taxonomy of knowledge we apply in solving the semantic ambiguity problem. We believe that both syntactic and semantic types of knowledge are necessary.

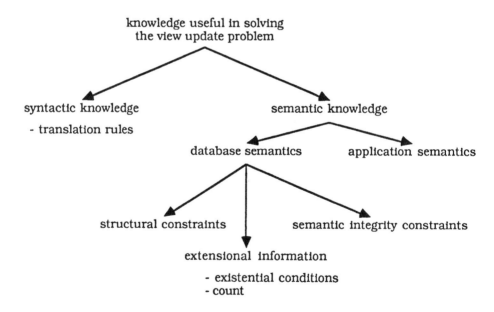

Figure 3-1. Taxonomy of Knowledge
Useful in Solving the View Update Problem

Syntactic knowledge is represented by the structural aspects (syntax) of a database schema. It is used to derive **translation rules,** which describe syntactically allowed translations of the update against a view to updates against underlying relations on which the view is defined. A translation is used to derive the commands to be performed against the underlying relations in order to accomplish an update against a view.

Semantic knowledge consists of database semantics and application semantics.

Database semantics include **structural constraints** (e.g., ID# is the unique identifier of an undergraduate student), **extensional information** including **existential conditions** (e.g., there is an undergraduate student with ID# equal to "1") and **count** (e.g., there is exactly one tuple in relation STUDENT with value of ID# equal to "1"), and **semantic integrity constraints** (e.g., the functional dependency from ID# to NAME, EFA, and AID in the UNDERGRADUATE relation).

Application semantics provide information about the application of a view that is useful in solving semantic ambiguity problems. Knowing that updates against the DELINQUENT view can never result in insertions or deletions against the underlying GRAD and UNDERGRAD base relations is useful in making choices about how to translate insertions and deletions against the DELINQUENT view. Application semantics may include pragmatic rules (e.g., it is preferable to modify the location of an airplane rather than the location of an airport) and historic default rules (e.g., if the previous deletion on a view was translated as modify, use modify again).

Our view update algorithm described in the next section uses all of the above forms of knowledge.

4. TAILOR's View Update Algorithm

After defining several terms, we give an overview of the view update algorithm used by TAILOR and then discuss the three important modules of TAILOR that perform the three steps of the algorithm given in the overview.

A *simple* view (e.g., STUDENT) relation V can be defined in terms of the underlying database relations A and B by using one of the operations of the relational algebra,

$$V := f(A,B)$$

where f is one of the relational algebra operators. (If the operation is unary, e.g., project or select, then only one of the two input operands is used.) A *nested* view (e.g., DELINQUENT) has at least one of its operands as a view. An update (insert, delete or replace) against a view V must be translated into a sequence of updates against the underlying relations A and B. There may be several candidate sequences corresponding to a single update against V. Each of these sequences is called a *translation*. A *translation rule* consists of a set of *candidate translations* applicable to a view update. A *translation rule table* is a collection of all the translation rules applicable to a view type.

If the translation rule corresponding to a view update contains no translation, then the view update cannot be performed, and an error message is generated. If the translation rule has a single translation, then the translation can be performed on the underlying relations in response to the view update. If the translation rule has multiple candidate translations, then it is termed a *semantic ambiguity problem* (SAP), and the semantics collected at various stages of the algorithm are used to trim the candidate translation to a single translation (hence *solving the SAP*), which is eventually executed. Table 4-1 shows some of the SAPs that TAILOR can resolve. A complete description of SAPs is given in [Larson 87].

View Name View Definition	Operation	Database State	SAP
Set Difference: $V := A - B$	delete v	$v \in A$ and $v \notin B$	SAP-DIFFERENCE: {insert v into B} or {delete v from A} or {insert v into B ; delete v from A}
Set Union: $V := A \cup B$	insert v	$v \notin A$ and $v \notin B$	SAP-UNION: {insert v into A} or {insert v into B} or {insert v into A ; insert v into B}
Set Intersection: $V := A \cap B$	delete v	$v \in A$ and $v \in B$	SAP-INTERSECT: {delete v from A} or {delete v from B} or {delete v from A ; delete v from B}
Selection: $V := select (A, f(v))$ ($f(v)$ is the select condition)	delete v	$v \in A$ and $f(v)$ true in A	SAP-SELECT: {delete v from A} or {make f(v) false in A}
Projection: $V := A[v_1,...,v_m]$	insert v where $v = <v_1,...,v_m>$	$v \notin A[v_1,...,v_m]$	SAP-PROJECT: {determine $v_{m+1},...,v_n$; insert $<v_1,...,v_m,...,v_n>$ into A}

Table 4-1. Some of the SAPs resolved by TAILOR

4.1. Overview

In very simplified terms, TAILOR's approach to updating views and solving the semantic ambiguity problem can be described as using syntactic information to generate the set of possible translations, using semantic information to trim this set to a unique translation, and then performing the updates to the underlying base relations as specified by the unique translation. TAILOR's view update algorithm can be summarized as follows:

Step 1a: Define view.

This step is performed once for every new view before any update is performed on the view. The actions performed in this step are (1) collect a view definition (i.e., syntactic knowledge and structural constraints), and (2) collect the application semantics that the DBA can provide at this time.

Step 1b: Determine the relevant translation rules.

A translation rule table is associated with each view based on the type of the view defined in the previous step. A translation rule table consists of a set of rules relevant to the type of the view (see section 4.2.2).

Step 1c: Apply semantic knowledge to attempt to solve SAP in the view.

The actions performed in this step are (1) use semantic integrity constraints, associated with the underlying relations on which the view is defined, to attempt to solve a SAP, and (2) use the application semantics collected in step 1a to attempt to solve a SAP.

Step 2: Accept a view update and apply appropriate translation rule.

Choose a translation rule from the translation rule table which is appropriate for the given view update. If the chosen translation rule is not a SAP or if it is a SAP which was solved in step 1, there is a single translation corresponding to the given view update. Perform the updates specified in the translation on the underlying relations. Otherwise, perform step 3.

Step 3: Solve the SAP at view update time.

Collect additional application semantics from the user or database semantics from the database and solve the SAP. Perform updates on the underlying relations corresponding to the chosen translation.

Steps 1c uses semantic information collected at view definition time, while step 3 uses semantic information collected at view update time.

Figure 4-1 shows the major TAILOR modules. We now describe how different modules of TAILOR are used to perform the above steps. The DBA uses a TAILOR module called the View Definition Assistant (VDA) to define the views, and provides semantic knowledge known to the DBA at view definition time. This is step 1 described above and is discussed further in Sub-section 4.2. A database user submits the update on the views using a TAILOR module called the Translator. This is step 2 described above and is discussed further in Subsection 4.3. The user often provides additional application semantics when asked by the TAILOR module called the Semantic Ambiguity Solver (SAS). This is step 3 described above and is further discussed in Sub-section 4.4. For simplicity and brevity, we use examples to demonstrate the functioning of TAILOR modules and do not provide complete theoretical and algorithmic details.

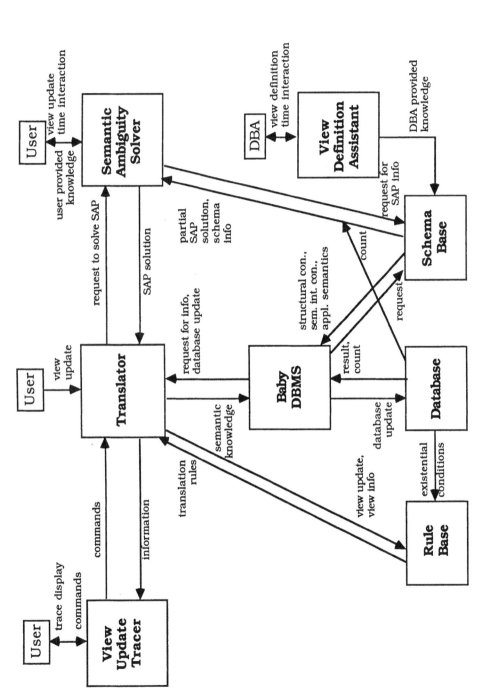

Figure 4-1. Structure of TAILOR

4.2. View Definition Assistant

The VDA is a tool invoked by the DBA to define a new view. It performs steps 1a, 1b and 1c of the view update algorithm as follows.

4.2.1. Define the view

The VDA provides a window interface to allow the DBA to enter the name of the view, the view type, the view operands (underlying relations), the view condition (e.g., the select condition for a select view, join attributes for a join view, or other view dependent information) and the view attributes. For example, to define the STUDENT view, the DBA provides the following information in an interactive session with the VDA:

        Name of the view -- STUDENT
        Type of the view -- UNION
        Operands -- UNDERGRAD, GRAD
        View condition -- none
        View attributes -- ID# ,NAME,EFA,AID

Similarly, DELINQUENT can be defined as:

        Name of the view -- DELINQUENT
        Type of the view -- SELECTION
        Operands -- STUDENT
        View condition -- EFA = "NO" and AID > 0
        View attributes -- ID# ,NAME,EFA,AID

We will use the DELINQUENT view to demonstrate how TAILOR's algorithm works for the rest of the paper.

4.2.2. Determine Relevant Translation Rules

The translation rules for a view type are stored in a corresponding *translation rule table*. For example, Appendix 1 shows translation rule tables for two view types, union and select,
for update types insert and delete. Thus, when the view DELINQUENT is defined, the VDA associates a rule table for select with the view. As explained in subsection 4.3, it is the Translator's job to associate a particular rule from the rule table to a given update by using the information on update type (e.g., insert, delete) and existential condition (e.g., $v \in A$; see subsection 4.3.2). Next we discuss how knowledge available at the view definition time can be used to partially or fully resolve a SAP.

4.2.3. Use Semantic Knowledge at View Definition Time to Resolve Ambiguity

Two types of semantic knowledge are useful to resolve semantic ambiguity in the translation rules (i.e., trim the set of candidate translations in a SAP) for a view: semantic integrity constraints associated with the underlying relations and application semantics provided by the DBA.

The types of semantic integrity constraints the VDA can use currently are inclusion dependency, disjoint dependency, functional dependency and cardinality. In our example of DELINQUENT view, no semantic integrity constraint is available to trim the set of candidate translations in the SAP discussed below. Use of semantic integrity constraints to solve a SAP is summarized in Appendix 2.

We now describe how the application semantics can be used to resolve semantic ambiguity. In the case of a select view (e.g., DELINQUENT), the following SAP is present:

SAP-SELECT: if the tuple v is to be deleted from V and if v is present in A then
either (1) delete v from A, or
(2) replace v such that the select condition is false for v.

The VDA interacts with the DBA to collect the application semantics for the view and applies them to trim the number of candidate translations. The interaction consists of asking pertinent questions (for a dialog-based interface) or presenting alternatives corresponding to each of the remaining candidate translations in the SAP (in a menu-based interface) to the DBA and recording his/her choice.

Now let us look at how the SAP for DELINQUENT is trimmed. The VDA informs the DBA of the candidate translations in the view and asks the DBA to supply any application semantics that can be useful to eliminate each of the candidate translations from the SAP. In the case of DELINQUENT, when the VDA asks the DBA for application semantics corresponding to the option (1) of SAP-SELECT, the DBA uses the following application semantics: deleting a student from DELINQUENT should not result in deleting the student from STUDENT. The DBA can apply this semantics to eliminate option (1) from the possible solutions of the SAP-SELECT. Assume that the DBA does not provide any further application semantics for DELINQUENT. Note that SAP-SELECT is not yet completely solved because option (2) contains multiple translations, one for each way to make the select condition "EFA = "NO" and AID > 0" false.

Since option (2) was not deleted from the SAP-SELECT, information must be provided on how to "make select condition false". The DBA should try to provide this information at view definition time if possible, otherwise the user will have to provide the information at view update time. In our example, the DBA may specify that the select condition can be made false by making the student eligible, i.e., replacing EFA equal to "NO" to EFA equal to "YES", or by making the aid given to the student zero, i.e., replacing AID by value "0". Thus option (2) of this SAP represents two translations. This information is stored in the schema base for later use by the SAS.

4.3. Translator

The translator is the front end module of TAILOR for updating views. It accepts a view update and processes it. It performs three steps : (1) accepts the view update from the user, (2) determines existential conditions and determines the translation rule, and (3) applies the translation if possible. These steps are discussed in more detail below.

4.3.1. Accept the view update

In this step, the user specifies the view update. For example, the user may give the following view update.
Delete < 1, SMITH, NO, 500> From DELINQUENT.

4.3.2. Determine existential conditions and the translation rule

Each translation rule has a premise and an action. Existential conditions and the update type are used to evaluate the premise of translation rules associated with the view on which the update is submitted. In other words, a translation rule whose premise evaluates to true using the existential conditions is selected for the given view update. For updating a tuple v in a view V defined using a binary operator (e.g., union) the existential conditions can be one of the following: (1) v in A ($v \in$ A) and v in B ($v \in$ B); or (2) v not in A ($v \notin$ A) and v in B ($v \in$ B); or (3) v not in A ($v \notin$ A) and v in B ($v \in$ B); or (4) v not in A ($v \notin$ A) and v not in B ($v \notin$ B). For a view defined using a unary operator (e.g., select), the existential conditions can be one of the following: (1) $v \in$ A; or (2) $v \notin$ A. For a given view update, the existential values are determined by querying the database. Once the existential conditions are determined, the premise of every translation rule associated with the view is evaluated. Only one translation rule will fire for the given existential conditions at the view update time. For example, in the SAP-SELECT translation rule, the premise is "if the tuple v is to be deleted from V and if v is present in A". For the view update "Delete < 1, SMITH, NO, 500> From DELINQUENT", this premise will evaluate to true if the tuple $v \in$ STUDENT. Since STUDENT is itself a view, the Translator will decide this by first determining existential conditions for STUDENT (in our example, $v \in$ STUDENT if (1) $v \in$ UNDERGRAD, or (2) $v \in$ GRAD, or (3) $v \in$ UNDERGRAD and $v \in$ GRAD).

Determining existential conditions requires one or more retrievals. For the reason of performance, it may be desirable to avoid finding existential conditions. This is possible in *some cases* as follows. Assume the following semantics of an insert: insert a in relation A if a $\notin$ A, otherwise, error. Similarly assume for delete: delete a from A if a $\in$ A, otherwise, error. Then, existential conditions need to be explicitly found from the database only for those updates which may result in a SAP, e.g., insert in a union view (see example 4-1). They need not be found explicitly in the updates which can not result in a SAP, e.g., delete from a union view (see example 4-2). Let us look at two examples to illustrate this.

Example 4-1: Consider view update "insert v into V" where $V := A \cup B$. From table 4-1 (or table A1-1 in Appendix 1), we see that this is a SAP with three candidate translations:

1. {insert v into B}
2. {insert v into A}
3. {insert v into A; insert v into B}

We must use existential conditions to select from among these three translations because no one of the three translations always suceeds.

Case 1: Use translation {insert v into B}.
This case works if $v \notin$ B, but fails if $v \in$ B even though it may be possible to accomplish insert v into V by inserting v into A.

Case 2: Use translation {insert v into A}.
Similar to case 1.

Case 3: Use translation {insert v into A and insert v into B}.

Subcase 3-1: $v \in A, v \in B$.
Both operations of the candidate translation will abort, so the view update will be aborted.

Subcase 3-2: $v \notin A, v \in B$.
Operation "insert v into A" will succeed, but "insert v into B" will abort, so the view update will be aborted. Operation "insert v into A" should be undone.

Subcase 3-3: $v \in A, v \notin B$.
Similar to case 2.

Subcase 3-4: $v \notin A$, $v \notin B$.

    Both operations of the candidate translations will be performed. But we loose the power of SAP2 since two possible translations are not considered and the candidate translation used in this case may not be the most appropriate translation.

Subcases 3-2 and 3-3 illustrate that the third translation also does not always suceed.

Example 4-2: Consider view update "delete v from V" where V:= $A \cup B$. This is not a SAP. Executing translation {delete v from A; delete v from B} will always cause deletion of v from V as desired.

Case 1: $v \in A$, $v \in B$

    Operations "delete v from A" and "delete v from B" will suceed.

Case 2: $v \notin A$, $v \in B$

    Operation "delete v from B" will suceed but "delete v from A" will fail. However, the desired effect of deleting v from V will be accomplished.

Case 3: $v \in A$, $v \notin B$

    Similar to case 2 above.

Case 4: $v \notin A$, $v \notin B$

    Both the operations, "delete v from A" and "delete v from B" will fail, so v will not be deleted from V because it was not there to start with. This is the desired result.

    In general, in cases when the view update can result in a SAP, not using existential conditions will result in need for undoing the operations and loss of the power of SAPs. For simplicity, we describe the algorithm as if the existential conditions are explicitly determined.

4.3.3. Apply the translation if possible

    If the translation rule that fires in the previous step consists of only one translation, then the corresponding updates are performed on the underlying relations. If the translation rule is a SAP then the Translator queries the schema base to find out if the candidate translations were reduced to one (i.e., if the SAP was solved) by the VDA. If so, it will perform the corresponding translation. Otherwise, the SAP is not yet completely solved. In this case, the Translator invokes the Semantic Ambiguity Solver to solve the SAP.

    Let us continue with our view update, "Delete < 1, SMITH, NO, 500> From DELINQUENT". To delete v from a select view V = select(A), the translation rule SAP-SELECT applies if $v \in A$. Because that the existential condition is < 1, SMITH, NO, 500> $\in$ STUDENT, the translation rule SAP-SELECT applies. In section 4.2.3, we also show how the first translation of the

SAP-SELECT was dismissed using application semantics provided by the DBA. Hence, when Translator evaluated the delete, it found that the appropriate translation in this case is "replace v such that the select condition is false for v". For our example, this translates to "replace < 1, SMITH, NO, 500> " with the result of evaluating "make the select condition false". Since there are multiple ways to make the select condition false, a semantic ambiguity still exists, hence Translator invokes the SAS.

4.4. Semantic Ambiguity Solver

The Semantic Ambiguity Solver (SAS) is invoked if the previous steps are unable to trim down the candidate translations to one. SAS interacts with the user to collect application semantics and uses them to trim the candidate translations. Conceptually this is similar to using application semantics provided by the DBA as discussed in subsection 4.2.3.

Let us continue with our example after the SAS is invoked by the Translator as discussed at the end of subsection 4.3.3. The update, "Delete < 1, SMITH, NO, 500> From DELINQUENT", is translated into the update, "Replace < 1, SMITH, NO, 500> in STUDENT", by the Translator. In subsection 4.2.3, we discussed the two choices given by the DBA to do the above replace. The SAS consults the schema base to retrieve the information stored by the VDA as discussed in subsection 4.2.3, and presents the user with the choices replace < 1, SMITH, NO, 500> with < 1, SMITH, YES, 500> or with < 1, SMITH, NO, 0> . If the user wants to delete SMITH from DELIN-QUENT because SMITH has become eligible again by registering for the minimum required course work, then user will choose < 1, SMITH, YES, 500> . On the other hand, if the user wants to delete SMITH from DELIN-QUENT because SMITH has repaid his loan, then user will choose < 1, SMITH, NO, 0> . Note that this choice can not be made at a view definition time. Thus it is necessary for a view update algorithm to have an update time component. For our example, suppose that SMITH regains his eligibility. The SAS collects the user's response and instructs the Translator to apply corresponding updates on the underlying relations. In this case, "Delete < 1, SMITH, NO, 500> From DELINQUENT" is translated into "Replace < 1, SMITH, NO, 500> With < 1, SMITH, YES, 500> in STUDENT". In the next iteration, the latter update will be translated into "Replace < 1, SMITH, NO,

500> With < 1, SMITH, YES, 500> in UNDERGRAD".

4.5. Other Modules

We now briefly describe other modules of TAILOR.

Rule base-- The rule base consists of the translation rule tables for all view types. When provided with a view update and existential conditions, the rule base returns the appropriate translation rule.

Database-- The database consists of the extensional component (attribute values) of the database relations.

Schema base-- The schema base consists of the intensional components of the database relations (i.e., descriptions of database relation schemas) and descriptions of view relations schemas. This includes all the semantic integrity constraints associated with each of the relations and the semantic information collected by the VDA at view definition time. Appendix 3 shows a part of a schema base for the example we discussed earlier.

Baby DBMS-- The baby DBMS provides the three update functions: insert a tuple in a relation in the database, delete a tuple from a relation in the database, and initialize a database relation in the database. It provides four retrieval functions: find a tuple in a relation in the database, get a tuple in a relation in the database, print a relation in the database, and retrieve schema information from schema base.

View Update Tracer-- The view update tracer provides a window-based interface using Lisp flavors to the user for easy use of TAILOR. This is a non-essential component of the tool but makes experimentation fun.

5. Implementation Environment

We had the following requirements for the implementation environment.

(1) Because TAILOR is a research tool, the implementation environment must lend itself to experimentation and modifications. This requires a good development environment with good interface facilities.

(2) Because we are using a rule-based approach, the environment must have good rule representation and manipulation facilities.

(3) The environment must support a database management system and database.

(4) The environment must support flexible string manipulation and error handling facilities.

Our choice for an implementation environment was the Symbolics Common Lisp environment. The Symbolics meets the development requirements in the following manner.

(1) An integrated editor, compiler, interpreter, and debugger provide an excellent development environment. A comprehensive windowing system provides the tools needed to develop a good interface.

(2) Lisp is historically the most common language for rule representation and manipulation.

(3) Lisp is as suitable as other languages for implementing a toy database management system.

(4) Lisp provides better string manipulation capabilities than most other languages. Symbolics Common Lisp allows a program to handle any software errors or program exceptions that may occur.

5. Conclusion

TAILOR has been operational since December 1986. It was used to prototype the various types of knowledge needed to resolve the semantic ambiguity problems for several small databases. As an experimental vehicle, TAILOR has already been useful in that it enabled us to discover errors in the basic set of translation rules that can be associated with the various view types. The rule-based approach used by TAILOR enabled us to quickly correct the translation rules in error.

In this paper, we have not given all the details of the algorithm used by TAILOR. Our approach in this paper was to present how TAILOR works using a comprehensive example. However, TAILOR is capable of performing updates on set difference, union, intersection, select, project and join views. The views can be nested (defined on other views), as in case of the DELINQUENT view, or simple (defined on base relations only), as in case of the STUDENT.

TAILOR has demonstrated that it is possible to solve the view update problem for a large set of views by using syntactic and semantic information collected at view definition time and at view update time. We show that some information can only be supplied at the view update time but not at the view definition time. However, our approach is to minimize the information to be provided at view update time and maximize the information that can be gathered at view definition time.

The more semantic ambiguity problems which TAILOR must solve, the more semantic information that must be captured and maintained and the more time-consuming TAILOR processing becomes. Before implementing TAILOR with a production DBMS, we recommend a careful analysis of the types of updates, the amount of semantic information that the database administrator can supply at view definition time, and the amount of semantic information that the database user can or will supply at view update time. After an understanding of these requirements, we believe that the relevant portions of the algorithms in TAILOR can be reimplemented in an efficient form compatible with the target DBMS.

7. References

[Bancilhon 79] F. Bancilhon, "Supporting View Updates in Relational Databases,"in Data Base Architecture, Bracci and Nijssen, eds., North Holland, June 1979.

[Bancilhon 81] F. Bancilhon and N. Spyratos, "Update Semantics and Relational Views," *ACM Trans. on Database Systems*, 6:4, December 1981.

[Cosmadakis 84] S. Cosmadakis and C. Papadimitriou, "Updates of Relational Views," *Journal of ACM*, 31:4, October 1984.

[Date 86] C. J. Date, "Updating Views," Chapter 17 in Relational Database: Selected Writings, Addison-Wesley, 1986.

[Dayal 78] U. Dayal and P. A. Bernstein, "On the Updatability of Relational Views," *Proc. of the Fourth VLDB Conference*, Berlin, West Germany, October 1978.

[Dayal 82] U. Dayal and P. A. Bernstein, "On the Correct Translation of Update Operations on Relational Views," *ACM Trans. on Database Systems*, 7:3, September 1982.

[Furtado 85] A. L. Furtado and M. A. Casanova, "Updating Relational Views," in Query Processing in Database Systems, W. Kim, D. S. Reiner, and D. S. Batory, eds., Springer-Verlag, 1985.

[Hegner 84] S. J. Hegner, "Canonical View Update Support through Boolean Algebra of Components," *Proc. of the Third ACM SIGACT-SIGMOD Symp. on Principles of Database Systems*, April 1984.

[Keller 82] A. M. Keller, "Updates to Relational Databases Through Views Involving Joins," in Improving Database Usability and Responsiveness, Peter Scheuermann, ed., Academic Press, New York, 1982.

[Keller 85] Arthur M. Keller, "Algorithms for Translating View Updates to Database Updates for Views Involving Selections, Projections, and Joins," *Proc. of the Fourth ACM SIGACT-SIGMOD Symp. on Principles of Database Systems*, March 1985.

[Keller 86] Arthur M. Keller, "Choosing Translator at the view definition time," *Proc. of the 12th VLDB*, Kyoto, Japan, August 1986.

[Larson 87] J. Larson and A. Sheth, "Updating Relational Views Using Knowledge at View Definition and View Update Time," Honeywell Technical Report, 1000 Boone Ave No., Golden Valley, MN 55427.

[Masunaga 84] Y. Masunaga, "A Relational Database View Update Translation Mechanism," *Proc. of the 10th VLDB*, Singapore, August 1986.

[Osman 79] I. M. Osman, "Updating Defined Relations," *Proc. of NCC 48*, 1979.

[Stonebraker 75] M. Stonebraker, "Implementation of Integrity Constraints and Views by Query Modification," *Proc. of the ACM SIGMOD International Conference on Management of Data*, San Jose, June 1975.

APPENDIX 1: Translation Rules Tables

This appendix translation rule tables for union and selection view types. Tables for other view types are given in [Larson 87]. Translation rule tables for all view types are stored in the Rule Base module of TAILOR in rule form.

$V := A \cup B$			
	$v \in A$ $v \in B$	$v \notin A$ $v \in B$	$v \in A$ $v \notin B$	$v \notin A$ $v \notin B$
insert v	Error: already in underlying relation	Error: already in underlying relation	Error: already in underlying relation	SAP-UNION: {insert v into A} or {insert v into B} or {insert v into A ; insert v into B}
delete v	{delete v from A; delete v from B}	{delete v from B}	{delete v from A}	Error: tuple not in underlying relation

Table A1-1. Translation Rule Table for Set Union View

$V := A[v \mid f(v) = $ true $]$, where $f(v)$ is the select condition		
	$v \in A$ $f(v)$ in A	$v \in A$ $\neg f(v)$ in A	$v \notin A$
insert v	Error: already in underlying relation	{make f(v) true in A}	{insert v into A}
delete v	SAP-SELECT: {delete v from A} or {make f(v) false in A}	Error: tuple not in underlying relation	Error: tuple not in underlying relation

Table A1-2. Translation Rule Table for Selection View

APPENDIX 2: Use of Semantic Integrity Constraints

This appendix briefly discusses the use of semantic integrity constraints in solving the SAPs shown in table 4-1. Table A2-1 shows the definitions of some of the semantic integrity constraints in terms of the constraints they impose on the base relations. Table A2-2 is a continuation of Table 4-1. It shows how a semantic integrity constraint shown in the top row may be used to partially resolve a SAP shown in the first column. For example, SAP-DIFFERENCE (row 1) has three candidate translations:

1. {insert v into B}
2. {delete v from A}
3. {insert v into B; delete v from A}

The inclusion constraint (column 2) restrict the candidate translations to {insert v into B} and {delete v from A}, while the disjoint constraint restricts the candidate translations to {delete v from A} and {insert v into B; delete v from A}.

Use of semantic integrity constraints to solve SAPs, including SAPs for join views, is discussed in detail in [Larson 87].

Semantic Integrity constraint	Constraint
Inclusion Dependency: A[x] INCLUDES B[x]	$\neg (x \notin A \wedge x \in B)$
Disjoint Dependency: A[x] DISJOINT B[x]	$\neg (x \in A \wedge x \in B)$
Functional Dependency: FD: $a_i \rightarrow a_j$	For all $a, a' \in A \wedge a \neq a'$, $a.a_i = a'.a_i \Rightarrow a.a_j = a'.a_j$
Cardinality Constraint	$n \leq count(A) \leq m$

Table A2-1. Definition of Semanitc Integrity Constraints

	Constraints			
SAP description (see Table 4-1)	inclusion	disjoint	functional dependency	cardinality
SAP-DIFFERENCE: 1. insert v into B 2. delete v from A 3. insert v into B; delete v from A	if A includes B, then 1 or 2;	if A & B are disjoint, then 2 or 3	no effect	if cardinality(A) equals min, then 1; if cardinality(B) equals max, then 2
SAP-UNION: 1. insert v into A 2. insert v into B 3. insert v into A; insert v into B	if A includes B, then 1 or 3; if B includes A, then 2 or 3	if A & B are disjoint, then 1 or 2	no effect	if cardinality(A) equals max, then 2; if cardinality(B) equals max, then 1
SAP-INTERSECT: 1. delete v from A 2. delete v from B 3. delete v from A; delete v from B	if A includes B, then 2 or 3; if B includes A, then 1 or 3	empty view	no effect	if cardinality(A) equals min, then 2; if cardinality(B) equals min, then 1
SAP-SELECT: 1. delete v from A 2. make f(v) false in A	not applicable	not applicable	if $\neg f(v)$ violates f.d. then 1	if cardinality(A) equals min, then 2
SAP-PROJECT: determine $v_{m+1},...,v_n$ insert $<v_1,...,v_m,...,v_n>$ into A	not applicable	not applicable	use the f.d. to fill in unknown values	if cardinality(A) equals max, then error

Table A2-2. Applying Semantic Integrity Constraints to Solve SAPs

APPENDIX 3: A Sample Schema Base

Schema base entry format:
(name of view or relation
 RELATION or VIEW
 (property_name property_value)
 (property_name property_value)

 .
 .

 (property_name property_value))

Examples of property names:
ATT_LIST - a list of attribute names.
NUM_TUPLES - the number of tuples (an integer).
CONSTRAINT_LIST - a list of the constraint identifiers associated with the view
          or relation. A constraint identifier has the following form:
          (constraint_name operand(s)).
VIEW_TYPE - one of UNION, INTERSECTION, SELECTION, DIFFERENCE,
          PROJECTION, or JOIN.
OPERAND_LIST - a list of the relation(s) and/or view(s) which are the operands of
          the view.
SAP_X_SOLUTIONS - a list of integers. Each integer indicates an option number
          for one of the options available for the SAP associated with
          a view of type X.
MAKE_SELECT_CONDITION_FALSE - a lambda function (LISP) that will take a tuple
          and transform it to make the select condition
          for a particular selection view false.

UNDERGRAD and GRAD: We will assume that the relations UNDERGRAD
and GRAD already exist. Their schema base entries are, respectively:
(UNDERGRAD
 RELATION
 (ATT_LIST (ID# NAME EFA AID))
 (NUM_TUPLES 2)
 (CONSTRAINT_LIST (DISJOINT GRAD)))

(GRAD
 RELATION
 (ATT_LIST (ID# NAME EFA AID))
 (NUM_TUPLES 1)
 (CONSTRAINT_LIST (DISJOINT UNDERGRAD)))

STUDENT: Schema base entry after view definition.
(STUDENT
 VIEW
 (VIEW_TYPE UNION)
 (ATT_LIST (ID# NAME EFA AID))
 (OPERAND_LIST (UNDERGRAD GRAD))
 (SAP_UNION_SOLUTIONS (1 2))
 (CONSTRAINT_LIST ((DISJOINT UNDERGRAD GRAD))))

DELINQUENT: Schema base entry after view definition.
(DELINQUENT

```
VIEW
(VIEW_TYPE SELECTION)
(OPERAND_LIST (STUDENT))
(ATT_LIST (ID# NAME EFA AID))
(SAP_SELECT_SOLUTIONS (2))
(MAKE_SELECT_CONDITION_FALSE (VALUES-LIST
                (LAMBDA (TUPLE)
                  (CHANGE_ATT TUPLE 'EFA 'YES))
                (LAMBDA (TUPLE)
                  (CHANGE_ATT TUPLE 'AID '0)))))
```

An Intelligent Information Dictionary
for Semantic Manipulation of Relational Databases[1]

Stephanie J. Cammarata
The RAND Corporation
1700 Main Street
Santa Monica, CA
90406-2138

ABSTRACT

This paper describes an intelligent information dictionary (IID) which serves as a knowledge-based interface between a database user and the query language of a relational database management system. IID extends the traditional roles of a data dictionary by enabling a user to view, manipulate, and verify semantic aspects of relational data. Our use of IID focuses on the interactive creation of simulation-specific databases from large "public" databases in the domain of military simulation and modeling. We have identified classes of database-related activities performed by a simulation developer when preparing databases as input to simulation models. Three categories of IID capabilities supporting these activities are *explanation and browsing, customized data manipulation,* and *interactive consistency checking.* In this paper we detail specific features of these categories and present examples of their use.

1. Introduction

An intelligent information dictionary extends the traditional roles of a data dictionary by enabling the user to view, manipulate, and verify semantic aspects of data not expressed in a relational database. In the past, data dictionary systems have served as an interface between the database management system (DBMS) and the application programs that access the data. This close coupling of data dictionary, DBMS, and application programs excludes facilities for interactive access by a casual user. With the advent of workstation environments, interactive software, and public domain databases, the use of DBMS is no longer limited to database administrators (DBAs), operations managers, and application programs. Researchers and practitioners in many disciplines are experimenting with DBMS for organizing, maintaining, and sharing databases [McCa82]. Unfortunately, the DBMS tools and languages currently in

[1] This research was sponsored by the Defense Advanced Research Projects Agency under the auspices of RAND's National Defense Research Institute, a Federally Funded Research and Development Center sponsored by the Office of the Secretary of Defense.

existence do not have facilities to aid these users in understanding and accessing the information they need [Curt81].

In this paper we discuss an intelligent information dictionary (IID) system which we developed as a knowledge-based interface between an interactive user and the query language (QL) of a relational DBMS. IID aids a user in understanding the organization of a relational database by providing application-specific explanations of relations, domains, attributes, and constraints. This facility combines knowledge of the domain with knowledge of relational database concepts to produce interactive tools for browsing, customized data manipulation, and interactive consistency checking. IID encourages users to interact with a relational database by manipulating semantic entities and relationships which are implicit in the relational representation.

In the next section we present a scenario that motivates this research within the domain of military simulation and modeling. We describe three categories of database related activities performed by a simulation developer when preparing databases as input to simulation models. Section 3 discusses IID capabilities supporting these interactive database "preparation" activities and presents examples of their use. The architecture of IID is outlined in Section 4, and Section 5 discusses related research. In Section 6 we conclude with some directions for future work.

2. Motivation and rationale

National security policy research and analysis depends on the heavy use of military modeling and simulation, such as battle management, and command and control studies. It is imperative that these models use large quantities of real-world data which is valid and consistent. Therefore, many classified and unclassified databases are maintained at RAND as input to simulation models. As part of our research, we observed and analyzed the use of these "public" databases as input to specific simulation models.

When simulation developers attempt to use these databases, they face some major obstacles. Most of the public databases are acquired from federal agencies which distribute data to a wide variety of clients and customers. When the databases arrive at a client's site, they are generally organized as record-oriented flat files that are subsequently "relationized" and loaded into a DBMS. However, the resulting relational schema is not designed using established database design or modeling principles and is not developed with the assistance of any domain experts. Consequently, semantic integrity constraints that should apply to the public databases are rarely expressed in the relational schema organization or reflected in the data instances. In addition, little documentation is provided with the public databases, and many data values are missing, inconsistent, and erroneous.

At RAND, these public databases are maintained in Ingres. Upon closer examination of database usage, we discovered that the relationship between the Ingres databases and their simulation-specific counterparts is not at all isomorphic. Most of the public databases contain more data than is necessary for a particular study; therefore, it is common for a simulation builder to extract a subset of the Ingres databases for use as input to a specific simulation model. Furthermore, modelers and analysts require data which is tailored to their own specific simulation needs. Their requirements usually entail a combination of transformations to the Ingres databases to derive a database with the desired profile.

During this derivation process, the semantics of the data play a major role in the integration and abstraction operations performed by the simulation builder. Unfortunately, DBMS query languages cannot easily or directly express these transformations. The database manipulations are usually performed through the joint efforts of an application expert and a database specialist. The application expert uses his or her domain expertise to decide how data records should be integrated and abstracted; the database specialist contributes by providing knowledge about database operations to achieve the desired view. Furthermore, many of the required operations cannot be performed within the DBMS query language and also require the services of an applications programmer.

2.1. Database preparation activities

By observing modelers interacting with relational databases, we have identified three distinct cognitive phases that are critical in composing simulation databases: *mental modeling and synthesis*, *conceptual retrieval*, and *semantic validation*. In the following subsections, we discuss the limitations of interactive DBMS facilities and how they hamper each phase of database interaction. Our objective was to remedy these deficiencies by providing an interactive environment supporting database preparation processes.

2.1.1. Mental modeling and synthesis

When users are presented with the task of browsing through a database, they tend to preview the data in a fashion which helps them mentally abstract major concepts and relationships. The first phase of this process is usually scanning the relational tables and attribute names to arrive at a central organizing theme. For someone unfamiliar with the specific relational database, this activity is difficult because attribute names are non-intuitive acronyms listed in a data dictionary with no description of meaning or usage. After a user tries to glean an overall organization of the relational structure, he or she begins looking at rows of values in the relational tables. The relational model does not naturally represent hierarchical concepts; therefore, users frequently search through data and schema hoping to find some hierarchical organization as a basis for abstracting the flat relational tables. Furthermore, most data is encoded and unformatted, providing little evidence that their mental model of the structural organization is valid and consistent. By iteratively looking at the relational structure and selected data values, a user begins to synthesize a conceptual image of the entities and relationships represented in the database and how they map to the necessary simulation concepts.

Although query languages allow flexibility in searching and selecting records based on syntactic pattern matching and efficient indexing techniques, they do not provide an overview or general presentation of the data. If a potential user is familiar with a database and is an experienced DBMS user, then it is much easier to browse through a database in search of specific concepts and entities. However, for the casual user there are few tools or friendly environments to support this modeling and synthesis process. For example, if a simulation builder needs information about the 67th Armor Division, he or she may approach this query by searching all tables for the string "67th Armor Division". It is unlikely that this query will retrieve any useful information. First, "67th Armor Division" is probably abbreviated or encoded so a syntactic search may not produce any matches. Second, there are many different kinds of information that a user may desire about an armor division, such as the general characteristics of the 67th Division, or the subordinate units which are commanded by the 67th Division. A simple text search, however, would not provide any explanation of what is retrieved, only specific data values.

2.1.2. Conceptual retrieval

After a user has gained some familiarity with the organization, structure, and content of a particular database, he or she must determine what data to retrieve for deriving a specific simulation database. The user compares his or her mental model of what is in the database with a conceptual profile of the desired data. Based on this comparison, the user must retrieve those relational entities which map onto the desired conceptual profile. A significant factor which simulation builders consider is the granularity or resolution of the information. Most often, the public databases represent a finer resolution than is needed for the resulting database. Integrating and aggregating data elements play a major role in composing a simulation database.

Users would like to access and retrieve data from public databases whose values collectively represent conceptual entities or relationships. However, query languages provide only a microscopic view of data entities and elements. To derive an entity with the desired profile, a user must translate the profile into standard DBMS selection, projection and join operations. For example, if a user wants to retrieve all "reconnaissance" aircraft, he or she must mentally compose a semantic description for the concept of reconnaissance. Next, the user must map the semantic description onto the attributes and data available in the public databases. Finally, a DBMS query is constructed which integrates data from various sources, retrieving those items which correspond to the concept of reconnaissance. Similarly, to derive a value for "firepower" associated with an airbase, it is necessary to access and aggregate a number of variables upon which firepower is dependent.

Although many of these capabilities can be performed by programs using an embedded data manipulation language, we should not expect casual DBMS users to become DBMS experts simply to browse through the data and retrieve relevant conceptual entities. View mechanisms and embedded data manipulation languages are similarly geared toward interfacing application programs with the database and ignore the needs of interactive users.

2.1.3. Semantic validation

The final activity performed when constructing a simulation database is to validate the correctness of the structure and content of the derived database. In many cases, the data which has been selected may not be consistent or correct. Numeric cross tabulations may be incorrect if only a subset of the database is retrieved. Existence dependencies between entities may also need to be verified. For instance, a user may want to enforce a constraint stating that if long range bombers are located at an airfield, then the airfield must have at least one concrete runway. In addition, the simulation developer may want to add additional constraints on the derived database which did not hold for the public databases.

We have observed this validation process being carried out jointly by a database and domain expert. This task is usually performed by manually searching through data records, looking for suspect or errorful values. Often, simply the presence of a data record will trigger, in the mind of the domain specialist, a condition or constraint which should be considered in the simulation database. Augmenting the resulting database is also common when necessary data is not available from the public databases.

3. IID capabilities

Traditional data dictionaries are used for defining DBMS entities, generating reports, and expressing transactions, but are not suitable as an interface between an interactive user and a DBMS [Alle82]. Our intelligent information dictionary fills this need by addressing the three phases of database preparation discussed above. IID supports *explanation and browsing, customized data manipulation*, and *interactive consistency checking* by combining domain knowledge with relational DBMS knowledge. Object-oriented knowledge bases in IID represent both the constructs of a relational database and domain specific knowledge acquired from an application specialist. IID is implemented in Franzlisp Flavors running on a Sun Microsystems workstation. The dictionary communicates with the Ingres relational DBMS, also resident on a Sun machine. The application database we are utilizing to test IID is an air order of battle (AOB) database representing air resources such as airbases, runways, and aircraft. The examples shown in the following sections are derived fron this database and other similar military databases. Details of the IID architecture are presented in Section 4.

3.1. Explanation and browsing

Explanation and browsing is enabled in IID by presenting an extensive collection of metadata to users to guide them through the maze of relations and attributes. Metadata in our information dictionary does not refer strictly to information needed by the DBMS, such as data type and field length. Rather, it refers to semantic information about the data which users rely on when making decisions about how entities relate to each other, and whether the data is relevant to their application. Figure 1 shows the user interface for browsing through relations and columns. Much of the information show in Figure 1 is maintained strictly within the information dictionary without accessing the relational databases. In this example the user is viewing the column names for the "aircraft" relation, and the column "btype" is further described. The allowable values for btype are expressed as "Value constraints". The items in this enumerated list are mouse sensitive and can be further described as we have shown for the value "BC".

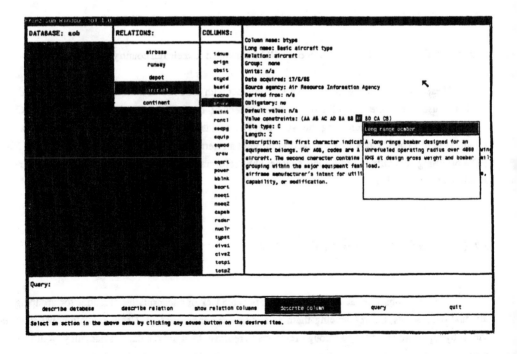

Figure 1: IID explanation and browsing

Values for column descriptors such as "Date acquired", "Source agency", and "Derived from", are represented and maintained in the information dictionary. Therefore, when a new version of the AOB database is loaded, the "Date acquired" field reflects this new information. The descriptors "Obligatory", "Default value", and "Value constraints" not only provide explanatory information but also have associated procedures which interactively validate data instances. These capabilities are further discussed in the section describing consistency checking.

Another feature useful for browsing through an unfamiliar database is IID's *verbose* mode. When verbose mode is enabled, encoded DBMS output is expanded into its full textual name or identifier. Similarly, input to the DBMS through IID can contain fully expanded abbreviations. For example, in a traditional query language, a user must know the country code for France in order to retrieve all aircraft located in France. With IID's verbose mode, a user can submit the query:

retrieve (aircraft.idnum) where country = "france"

Although "country" is not a valid column name and "France" is not an allowable value for the column name "ctycd", IID preprocesses the input and submits to Ingres the query:

retrieve (aircraft.idnum) where aircraft.ctycd = "fr"

Similarly during output, any country codes will be expanded to their full country name.

These browsing capabilities help a user interact with a DBMS in a more natural fashion and distance the user from the unintelligible *codified* aspect of databases maintained by a DBMS. Other research efforts are also addressing the issue that DBMS interfaces are unsuitable for casual users. The Rabbit system [Tou82] aids user interaction through an iterative process of *query reformulation*. Both IID's browsing capabilities and Rabbit's retrieval by reformulation attempt to facilitate the user's understanding of instance data.

3.2. Customized data manipulation

One major obstacle facing interactive users is the lack of encapsulation facilities for grouping individual data values and referencing them as a single semantic concept. Users emulate conceptual retrieval by repeatedly navigating through relations to retrieve the desired data. Instead, they would like to express a combination of attributes and values as a *customized conceptual package* and subsequently refer to that concept as a single entity. Three IID features encourage customized data manipulation: *view templates*, *smart joins*, and *aggregation functions*.

3.2.1. View templates

View templates allow a DBMS user to build a template or profile for a particular concept, and refer to that template for data access. IID translates a view template into an acceptable query and submits it to the DBMS. In Figure 2, we show the template describing a *reconnaissance* aircraft. Although the concept of *mission* is not explicitly represented in this database, the user's notion of a reconnaissance mission translates into characteristics represented in the database such as aircraft capabilities and radar equipment. In this example, "mission" can be regarded as a *virtual* column for aircraft and "reconnaissance" can be viewed as a virtual value for the column.

The retrieve command shown in the "Query:" window of Figure 2 indicates how the user would express a *templated* query. With this capability, domain specialists can refer to database entities in their own terminology and can customize the meaning of application-specific concepts and relationships. The window interface also allows a user to view the template description as we have shown in the "TEM-PLATE:" window of Figure 2.

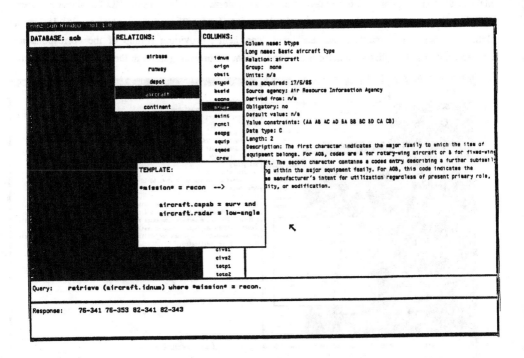

Figure 2 A view template for reconnaissance

3.2.2. Smart join operator

Expressing a join in a relational query language requires a user to navigate through foreign key attributes. In IID, a smart join operator uses the information stored in the dictionary to recognize implicit links between relations. For instance, in Figure 3 a user wishes to retrieve all aircraft of a certain type that are located in Europe. However, aircraft are not recorded by continent; rather, they are organized by country. In Quel, this query would be expressed as:

$$\textit{retrieve (aircraft.idnum) where aircraft.btype = "AC" and}$$
$$\textit{aircraft.baseid = airbase.baseid and}$$
$$\textit{airbase.ctycd = continent.ctycd and}$$
$$\textit{continent.name = "europe"}$$

Using IID's join feature, the user need only submit the retrieve command shown in the "Query:" window of Figure 3. During IID query preprocessing, the dictionary refers to its domain specific knowledge about aircraft and airbases, and to its knowledge of relational joins. Join fields may be specified with the database dictionary information or may be expressed interactively by a user. IID translates the user's query into the equivalent Quel command and submits it to Ingres. The window interface also depicts the relationship between "aircraft", "airbase", and "continent", providing a map of the correspondence between relations. This display feature is also convenient for browsing through the network of relations.

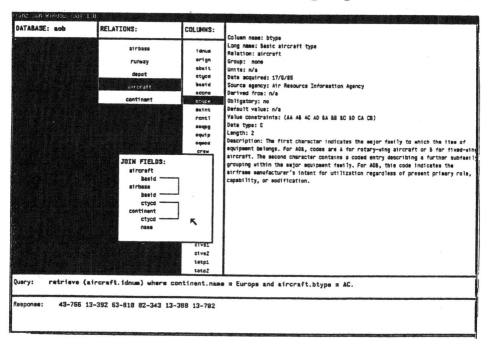

Figure 3 A smart join operation

3.2.3. Aggregation functions

Aggregation functions are useful for abstracting a detailed database and retrieving data at the desired level of granularity. Built-in DBMS aggregate functions are limited to operations such as count, sum, and average. IID's aggregation functions allow a user to express a domain-specific aggregation and use that specification for interactive queries. Consider the query shown in Figure 4. In this example, the user is interested in computing the *firepower* associated with airbases. In the AOB database, however, firepower is not recorded for airbases but rather it is stored with *missile depots*. An IID aggregation function allows a user to specify how firepower should be computed, and to subsequently invoke the pre-specified declaration. In this way, the user has the flexibility to interactively derive appropriate data. Aggregation functions, like view templates, enable users to construct virtual columns which are automatically expanded by IID. The interactive query in Figure 4 is translated into a Quel query of the form:

$$\textit{retrieve (airbase.baseid, firepower=avg (depot.firepower}$$
$$\textit{by depot.baseid))}$$
$$\textit{where airbase.baseid = depot.baseid}$$

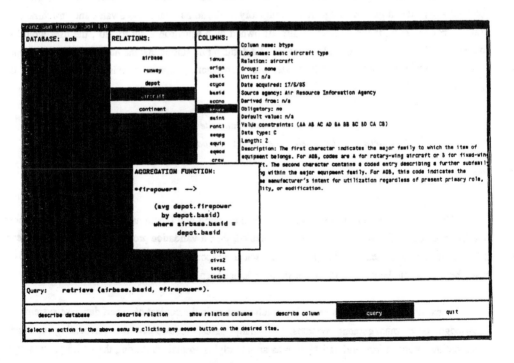

Figure 4 An aggregation function for firepower

Aggregation functions, view templates, and a smart join operator supply the user with a more comprehensible view of the database without forcing the user to review the details of each record. We envision users constructing libraries of view templates and aggregation functions. These stored declarations can be accessed and viewed by other users thereby creating multiple perspectives. *Soft selection criteria* [Mart86] is another area which relaxes the rigidity of DBMS query languages by allowing subjective or varying selection qualifications. Similar research has been conducted for statistical databases where aggregation is a predominate function in database queries [Chan81].

3.3. Interactive consistency checking

Many knowledge base management systems and intelligent database systems are providing facilities to automatically verify semantic constraints through the use of triggers and allerters [Ston85]. For interactive database users who are deriving *personal* databases from large public databases, conventional methodologies for constraint specification and enforcement do not apply. Conventional constraints must be built into the data dictionary by a database administrator and data modeler. Instead, users would like to express new value and structural constraints, and modify those declared for the public databases. The semantic validation capabilities available in IID allow interactive "scrubbing" of data values in the public databases which may be incorrect or inconsistent with the resulting derived database. The information dictionary maintains knowledge about obligatory fields, default values, and value and structural constraints. For instance, if the number of aircraft owned by a squadron is set to "20", the user would be notified that "20" is an incorrect value because of a domain rule stating that the number of aircraft owned by squadron must be a multiple of 6. A user may also want to express an existence constraint of the form:

> *If there is a nuclear launching site on an airbase,*
> *then there must be at least one nuclear weapons depot on that airbase.*

Validation mode in IID supports both value constraints and functional dependencies. If the above rule has been entered and validation mode is enabled, then a validation procedure is invoked whenever the user retrieves a nuclear launching site. If a nuclear weapons depot does not exist in the derived database, the user would be notified that a constraint rule has been violated.

Constraint management is receiving much attention in the context of expert database systems and knowledge base management systems. In many cases, researchers are advocating constraint specification, propagation, and satisfaction as an underlying formalism driving the entire processing of the system [Shep86]. In IID, however, consistency checking is approached from a very localized perspective, that is, a user's derivation of application specific databases. IID's validation procedures report invalid data but currently make no attempt to correct inconsistencies.

4. IID architecture

The IID software system is comprised of three major processing components: the Lingres interface, IID object-oriented dictionary framework, and user interface. These components are shown as shaded modules in Figure 5. Domain dependent information reside in at least three data and knowledge bases: the relational database maintained in Ingres, the "public" knowledge base, and one or more "private" knowledge bases. Figure 5 depicts these "domain specific" entities as dotted modules. Explanation and browsing, verbose mode, and validation mode are currently operational in IID. Limited functionality for aggregation functions, smart joins, and user templates has been tested and general versions are currently under development. Design and implementation of an extended user interface is also underway.

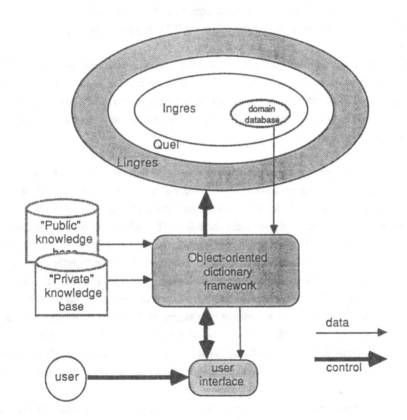

Figure 5 IID system architecture

We implemented IID's user interface on top of a Sun View windows package in Franzlisp. Our initial version of the user interface was designed to give the user the full range of functionality provided by IID at the expense of overloading the user with too many options. We are experimenting with various designs and organization of windows, menus, and input procedures to maximize the capabilities of IID while minimizing the cognitive overhead incurred by hierarchies of menus and windows.

Commands issued to IID through the user interface are passed on to IID's object-oriented dictionary framework. We implemented this module as a domain-independent and DBMS-independent environment for reasoning about relational database entities. The dictionary framework incorporates general knowledge about DBMS concepts such as relations, attributes, and joins. In addition, the framework accesses domain-specific information necessary for IID processing. During IID user interaction, the dictionary framework combined with domain information, such as AOB data and knowledge bases, enables facilities like verbose mode, consistency checking, and automatic join operations by reasoning about database structures and domain entities.

Much of IID's processing translates a user's query into a syntactically and semantically valid Quel query. This translation is similar to the programming language concept of *macro expansion* where a succinct declarative expression is replaced by a detailed procedural expression. IID constructs a Quel command (semantically equivalent to the user's input query) and submits it to Ingres through the Lingres interface. Data instances are returned to the user following IID query postprocessing.

Three separate sources of information comprise the domain dependent components of IID. One data repository is the public relational database maintained in Ingres. The AOB database we are utilizing to develop and test IID contains three main relations of approximately 2000, 7700, and 11000 tuples, and the number of fields per relation ranges from 25 to 36. This database is the source of value data retrieved in response to IID queries.

A "public" knowledge base corresponding to a domain database is one of two knowledge sources representing the semantics of the relational database. The information retained in this knowledge base can be regarded as the *default* semantics applicable to the domain database. Development of this component for the AOB database resulted from a data modeling effort which proceeded in parallel with the design and implementation of IID's processing components. The knowledge base is organized as objects relevant to AOB entities such as aircraft and airbases. Extensive descriptional information to support IID's explanation facilities was acquired from AOB domain specialists and extracted from various sources of documentation. The second knowledge source, a private knowledge base, represents semantic information derived by a user. This knowledge base augments the public knowledge base and stores aggregation functions and view templates for a particular simulation model or user. We envision many private knowledge bases representing different views of the domain database. During our initial developement effort, however, we have been experimenting with a single private knowledge base.

The Lingres facility we developed allows access to an Ingres database from Flavors and Lisp, and offers the full functionality of Quel's retrieve, create, delete, destroy, and append commands. Lingres maintains only the schema and dictionary data that Ingres itself supports. These capabilities are similar in functionality to those offered by Kee Connection, an expert system tool interface [Inte87]. For the purposes of modularity and future development, our goal for Lingres was merely to mimic the functionality of Ingres, i.e.,"Ingres in Lisp". In the future, changing to Common Lisp (or another Lisp) will affect only the "Lisp to C" connection; supporting SQL will only require new parsing routines in

Lingres; and changing to another relational DBMS, e.g., Oracle, would simply mean replacing Ingres system calls with calls to Oracle system routines. One of the most time consuming operations of IID is communicating with Ingres; therefore, Lingres also improves IID efficiency by duplicating Ingres metadata, thereby reducing communications with Ingres.

5. Related research efforts

Similar work addressing browsing and explanation is often refered to as *metadata management*. Mark and Roussopoulos [Mark86, Mark87] approach metadata management through *self-describing* data models. They are developing capabilities, similar to IID, to initially browse through the schema to learn about the database and then proceed to access the data. They are applying their model to facilitate standardized information interchange. In this application, however, they are not dealing with semantic aspects of the data, and therefore have not incorporated domain specific knowledge for explanation and validation.

Information Resource Dictionary Systems (IRDS) have also been the subject of a considerable amount research [Dolk87, Kers83, Nava86]. In the past, IRDS were considered primarily as a design tool for information modeling and database design. Only *active* data dictionaries were utilized during batch DBMS operation or real-time transaction processing. In [Gold85] Goldfine describes the National Bureau of Standards specifications of an IRDS system. This standard specifies a kernel set of basic data dictionary capabilities plus a collection of independent optional modules. So far, three additional modules have been specified dealing with security, application program interface, and documentation. The emphasis on program interfaces, and neglect of interactive tools is evident in the specification. However, we are seeing efforts extending the kernel IRDS specification to support interactive environments [Koss87].

The scope of an IRDS system embodies the major activities, processes, information flows, organizational constraints, and concepts of an "Enterprise Model". Because interactive use of a DBMS and data dictionary have not been feasible until recently, traditional information management processes do not include casual users exploring a database, deriving new databases, or sharing *personal* databases. We expect that the functionality offered by IID will become necessary as the use of interactive information systems proliferates.

6. Conclusions and future work

In this paper we have discussed a development effort and resulting software for improved interactions between a database user and a relational DBMS. IID is targeted to aid a casual database user who is familiar with the database domain but is not an experienced DBMS user. One of our research goals was to extract domain-specific information from a simulation expert and incorporate it as knowledge in the information dictionary. Another goal was to represent knowledge about relational database operations, such as join operations, to support query construction. Explanation and browsing, customized data manipulation, and consistency checking are the main processes supported by the IID interactive environment. Our initial studies indicate that IID facilities augmented with domain and database knowledge will significantly streamline the interactive preparation of simulation databases.

Development of IID grew out of a larger project which is addressing the use of large heterogeneous databases in object-oriented simulation systems. We have recognized that the preparation phases of mental modeling and conceptual data manipulation stem from attempts to view a flat relational database as an object-oriented hierarchy of simulation entities. IID strives to present the mapping between relations and domain entities more explicitly.

In the short term, we will be expanding IID's facilities to include spatial presentation and aggregation. In many public databases, location of entities is a major determinate in whether or not the entity is included in a simulation database. We plan to extend the explanation facilities so that spatial data can be quickly plotted on a geographical map, and data points on the map can be easily accessed and aggregated.

Configuration management of both public and simulation databases is another desirable feature. Users would like to be notified if any of their simulation data has been invalidated by a new version of the public databases. Furthermore, they hope to be able to pose queries about the changes that were enforced by a new version, such as: What is the difference between the old and new versions of the F-14 aircraft data? To support this feature, it is necessary to track and log the derivation of any simulation database and reason about operations which produced the resulting data.

In parallel with IID development, we will be augmenting our simulation knowledge base with metadata and constraint information related not only to the relational aspects of the data, but also to the object-oriented schema of the data. Our long term objective is the use of IID as an active information dictionary within an object-oriented simulation language. In this role it will provide a dynamic communication channel between a object-oriented semantic schema and the corresponding relational instances of many diverse public databases.

References

[Alle82]   Allen, F. W., Loomis, M. E., and Manning, M. V., "The integrated dictionary/directory system," *ACM Computing Surveys* **14**(2), pp.245-286 (June 1982).

[Chan81]   Chan, P. and Shoshani, A., "Subject: A directory driven system for organizing and accessing large statistical databases," pp. 553-563 in *Proceedings of the seventh international conference on very large Data Bases*, Cannes, France (1981).

[Curt81]   Curtice, R.M., "Data dictionaries: An assessment of current practice and problems," pp. 564-570 in *Proceedings of 7th conference on very large data bases*, Cannes, France (September 1981).

[Dolk87]   Dolk, D. and II, R. Kirsch, "A relational information resource dictionary system," *Communications of the ACM* **30**(1), pp.48-61 (January 1987).

[Gold85]   Goldfine, A., "The information resource dictionary system," pp. 114-122 in *Proceedings of the fourth international conference Entity-Relationship approach*, Chicago, IL (October 1985).

[Inte87]   *Intellinews* **3**(2), Intellicorp (January 1987).

[Kers83]   Kerschberg, L., Marchand, D., and Sen, A., "Information system integration: A metadata management approach," pp. 223-239 in *Proceedings of the fourth international conference on Information Systems*, Houston, TX (1983).

[Koss87]   Kossman, R., "An active information resource dictionary," in *Proceedings of Ingres user association meetings*, San Francisco, CA (April 1987).

[Mark86]   Mark, L. and Roussopoulos, N., "Metadata management," *Computer* **19**(12), pp.26-35 (December 1986).

[Mark87]   Mark, L. and Roussopoulos, N., "Information interchange between self-describing databases," *Data Engineering* **10**(3), pp.46-52 (September 1987).

[Mart86]   Martin, D., *Advanced database techniques*, The MIT Press, Cambridge, MA (1986).

[McCa82]   McCarthy, J.L., "Metadata management for large statistical databases," in *Proceedings of 8th conference on very large databases* (September 1982).

[Nava86]   Navathe, S. and Kerschberg, L., "Role of dictionaries in information resource management," *Information and Management* **10**(1), pp.21-46 (January 1986).

[Shep86]   Shephard, A. and Kerschberg, L., "Constraint management in expert database systems," pp. 309-331 in *Expert database systems*, ed. L. Kerschberg, Benjamin/Cummings Publishing Company, Inc., Menlo Park, CA (1986).

[Ston85]   Stonebraker, M. and Rowe, L.A., "The design of POSTGRES," Memorandum No. UCB/ERL 85/95, University of California, Berkeley, Berkeley, CA (November 15, 1985).

[Tou82]   Tou, F. N., Williams, M. D., Fikes, R., Henderson, A., and Malone, T., "Rabbit: An intelligent database assistant," pp. 314-318 in *Proceedings of the third annual national conference on artificial intelligence*, Pittsburg (1982).

A Model of Authorization for Object–Oriented and Semantic Databases

Fausto Rabitti, Darrell Woelk, Won Kim

Microelectronics and Computer Technology Corporation
3500 West Balcones Center Drive
Austin, Texas 78759

Abstract

This paper presents a formal model of authorization for use as the basis for an authorization mechanism in ORION, a prototype database system which directly supports the object–oriented paradigm and a number of semantic data modeling concepts. The model extends in two significant ways the existing models of authorization, which have been designed for database systems supporting the relational, network, or hierarchical models of data. First, it fully develops the concept of implicit authorization, introduced in an earlier paper [FERN75b], to help solve the storage requirement of representing all authorizations in a system by allowing the system to deduce authorizations from explicitly stored authorizations, and to provide a basis for detecting authorization definitions which conflict with existing authorizations. Second, it provides a formal basis for accommodating a number of modeling concepts which the existing models of authorization cannot address: the IS–PART–OF relationship between an object and its containing object, and versions of an object.

1. Introduction

In a multi–user environment with a large shared database, it is necessary to restrict access rights (authorizations) to different parts of the database to different users. In database systems, an authorization is a specification of an authorization type (read, write, create) on a database entity (the entire database, a relation, a tuple) for a user [GRIF76, FERN81, DATE84]. An authorization mechanism, that is, the specification and enforcement of authorization, is a key function in most commercial database systems. Authorization was an area of research in databases briefly in the mid–seventies, when researchers attempted to understand the consequences of the relational model of data on the database system architecture, in particular the authorization component. The research during that period resulted in such (then) novel concepts as specifying individual columns (attributes) of a relation or a relational view as a unit of authorization, recursive granting and revoking of authorizations, and distribution of authorization–checking overhead to compile time and run–time [GRIF76].

Once relational database systems have been successfully introduced in the market, authorization in database systems has ceased to be an active area of research. In attempting to understand the consequences of the object–oriented (and semantic) data model on the database system architecture, in particular, in the context of the ORION object–oriented databse system [BANE87], however, we have discovered that the model of authorization developed for relational databases requires some fairly significant or interesting extensions. There are two fundamental reasons for the extensions. One is the shortcomings in existing models of authorization (which remain under richer data models). Another is that the object–oriented (and semantic) data model is much richer than the relational model. These points are discussed below.

[FERN81] defines the authorization model in terms of three domains: the subjects (users), objects (database entities), and types (read, write, create, etc.). A naive implementation of the model would be a st of triplets (subject, object, type) for all subjects, objects, and types in the system. The storage requirements of such an implementation would be prohibitive. In practice, systems have used either the capability sts (in which the authorized objects and types are recorded for each subject) or the access–control lists (in which the authorized subjects and types are recorded for each object).

The existing models of authorization suffer from at least three shortcomings. The first is the lack of a systematic approach to reduce the storage requirements for maintaining valid authorization definitions. [FERN75b] proposes an approach which can be the basis for systematically reducing the storage requirements. It defines a partial order for a set of authorization objects, such that an explicit authorization of a certain type on an object for a certain subject implies the same authorization type on some other objects for the same subject. However, this proposal does not provide a complete treatment of implicit authorization along all three domains of authorization.

The second shortcoming is the lack of a formal basis for specifying exceptions to an authorization on all three domains of authorization. That is, they do not have the authorization primitives that can be used to specify exceptions to a group of authorized users (e.g., authorize all but Smith), exceptions to a set of entities (e.g., authorize access to all classes but the class Confidential–Documents), and exceptions to a set of authorization types (e.g., all authorization types except Create–Class).

The third shortcoming of the existing models of authorization is that they do not capture the authorization semantics inherent in richer semantic data models. A richer data model makes life easier for the users of a database system, but complicates implementation of the database system. The data modeling concepts which complicate the semantics of authorizations include the IS–A relationship between a pair of class objects, the IS–PART–OF relationship between a pair of instance objects, an abstract object consisting of a hierarchy of versioned instance objects, and the object–oriented notion that a class object is an object rather than just a template for the structure of its instances [GOLD81, BOBR85].

This paper presents our solutions to the above–mentioned problems. Our research has proceeded in three stages. First, we refined the concept of implicit authorizations on authorization hierarchies of [FERN75b], especially those on the subject and type domains of authorization. We then introduced the concept of a negative authorization to allow an explicit distinction between a prohibition and the absence of authorization, and the concept of a weak authorization to admit the possibility of overriding an authorization with a negative authorization at a lower level of an authorization hierarchy along any domain of authorization. Third, we extended the concept of implicit authorizations on the authorization hierarchy to incorporate the semantics of the IS–A relationship and inheritance of object properties, the IS–PART–OF relationship, and versions. Because of space limitation, we will defer discussions of implicit authorizations for the IS–A relationship and inheritance to a sequel to the present paper. Further, again, because of space limitations, we will not provide detailed algorithms for the authorization operations, grant and revoke, in this paper.

In Section 2 we motivate and formalize the concepts underlying our authorization mechanism. We also define the operations on the model. Sections 3, 4 and 5 develop rules for deducing authorizations for authorization subjects, authorization types and authorization objects. In Section 6, we explain the implicit authorizations for authorization objects in a database system which supports composite objects, and versions of objects. We summarize the paper in Section 7.

2. Basic Concepts for our Authorization Model

In this section, we introduce and motivate the concepts which form the basis for our model of authorization, and provide formal definitions for them.

2.1 Concepts

Earlier research in authorization [LAMP71, GRAH72, FERN81] has formalized an authorization as a 4-tuple (s,o,a,p) where

> $s \in S$, is the set of subjects (i.e. users) in a system,
> $o \in O$, is the set of objects in a system,
> $a \in A$, is the set of types of authorization, and
> p is a predicate which evaluates to True iff s has authorization a on o.

To evaluate p, we need a function

$$f: S \times O \times A \rightarrow \left\{\text{True, False}\right\}$$

such that, given a triplet (s,o,a), f determines whether subject s has authorization type a on object o.

Implicit Authorizations

The easiest way to implement the function f is to list explicitly all the triplets (s,o,a) for which f is True. Often, however, a value of f may imply other values along any of the S, O, A domains of f. For example, a manager should be able to access any information which the employees of the manager may access; if a user s has the delete authorization on the class, then s should have the same authorization on any instance of the class; and if a user s has the write authorization on an object, s should also have the read authorization on the object.

A systematic approach for deducing authorizations from those explicitly defined will obviate the need to specify all values of f, and will also allow detection of conflicts between values of the function f.

Positive / Negative Authorizations

The authorization mechanism in database systems generally assumes that the default authorization, when nothing is specified, is null (system closure assumption). This means that a subject has null authorization on every object until authorized [FERN81]. That is, an authorization is inherently positive, i.e. the subject is granted access to the specific object. The fact that the subject has no access to the specific object is described only by the lack of authorization.

We introduce the concept of a negative authorization to complement the positive authorization. A subject s may be denied access to an object o either because s has no authorization on o or because s has a negative authorization on o. For example, in the authorization object hierarchy shown in Figure 1, the absence of a positive write authorization on the class[Auto] is different from a negative write authorization on class[Auto]. In the first case, there may be a positive write authorization on an instance of the class[Auto].

Strong / Weak Authorizations

An authorization in existing models is a strong authorization, in the sense that an authorization on a node implies authorizations, at lower levels of the authorization hierarchy, which cannot be overridden. A weak

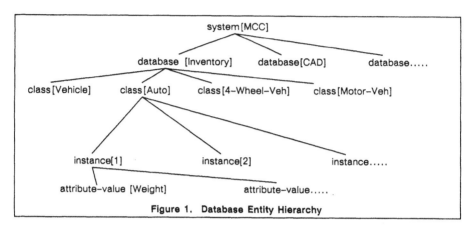

Figure 1. Database Entity Hierarchy

authorization can be overridden by other authorizations, strong or weak, at lower levels of the authorization hierarchy; thus it allows exceptions in the implicit authorizations.

Combining the Concepts

The combination of the concepts of positive/negative authorizations and strong/weak authorization allows a more concise and flexible representation of diverse authorization requirements. It helps to alleviate the storage requirements. Further, combining one weak negative authorization with a few strong positive authorizations has the effect of allowing a few exceptional positive authorizations to override a negative authorization at a higher level. Similarly, combining one weak positive authorization with a few strong negative authorizations allows singling out a few exceptional negative authorizations from a positive authorization at a higher level. This is illustrated in the following example.

Suppose that the class [Auto] in Figure 1 has 1000 instances, and that we wish to grant a read authorization to user S on all instances of the class except one instance, say instance[2]. The conventional approach would require us to specify a read authorization on 999 individual instances of class[Auto], except instance[2]. With a combination of one weak positive authorization and one strong negative authorizations, we can accomplish the same operation simply. We specify a weak read authorization on class[Auto] for S, and grant to S a negative strong read authorization on instance[2].

2.2 Formal Definitions

We now define formally the authorization concepts introduced in Section 2.1.

2.2.1 Positive and Negative Authorizations

Definition 1:
    A positive authorization is a triplet (s,o,a), with $s \in S$, $o \in O$, $a \in A$.

Definition 2:
    A negative authorization is a triplet $(s,o,\neg a)$, with $s \in S$, $o \in O$, $a \in A$.

An authorization (s,o,a), with a positive or negative, can be True or False according to the value of the function f on (s,o,a).

For notational simplicity, we use the following definitions:

Definition 3:

   The notation $'(s,o,a)$, with $s \in S$, $o \in O$, $a \in A$ and a positive or negative, means:
   $f(s,o,a)$=True.

   The notation $\neg'(s,o,a)$, with $s \in S$, $o \in O$, $a \in A$ and a positive or negative, means:
   $f(s,o,a)$=False.

2.2.2 Strong Authorizations and the Authorization Base

Definition 4:

   A strong authorization is a triplet (s,o,a), with $s \in S$, $o \in O$, $a \in A$ and a positive or negative. (Throughout this paper, we will use the term authorization to mean a strong authorization, positive or negative, unless it is necessary to distinguish it from a weak authorization.)

Definition 5:

   An Authorization Base (AB) is a set of strong authorizations (s,o,a), with $s \in S$, $o \in O$, $a \in A$ and a positive or negative:
   $$AB \subseteq S \times O \times A$$
   Authorizations in the AB are explicit strong authorizations and are defined to be True:
   if $(s,o,a) \in AB$, then $'(s,o,a)$.

Definition 6:

   Function $i(s,o,a)$:
   $$i: S \times O \times A \rightarrow \Big\{\text{True, False, Undecided}\Big\}$$
   If $(s,o,a) \in AB$, then $i(s,o,a)$=True;
   else:
       if there exists an $(s._1,o._1,a._1) \in AB$ such that $'(s._1,o._1,a._1) \rightarrow '(s,o,a)$
           then $i(s,o,a)$=True;
       else if there exists an $(s._1,o._1,a._1) \in AB$ such that $'(s._1,o._1,a._1) \rightarrow \neg'(s,o,a)$
           then $i(s,o,a)$=False;
       else $i(s,o,a)$=Undecided.

The function $i(s,o,a)$ computes the value of an authorization from the explicit authorizations in the AB. $i(s,o,a)$ returns either True or False if either the authorization (s,o,a) or $(s,o,\neg a)$ can be deduced from some $(s._1,o._1,a._1)$ in the AB. If neither conclusion can be deduced from the AB, $i(s,o,a)$ returns Undecided. For any authorization $(s,o,a) \in AB$, we can define the *scope* of an explicit authorization (s,o,a) to be the set of implicit authorizations $(s._1,o._1,a._1)$ such that $'(s,o,a) \rightarrow '(s._1,o._1,a._1)$, that is, the set of implicit authorizations which can be deduced from (s,o,a).

We define two invariants of the AB. Any operation on the AB must always leave the AB in a state satisfying the invariants.

Consistency of the AB:

   For any $(s,o,a) \in AB$,
   if there exists an $(s._1,o._1,a._1) \in A$ such that $'(s._1,o._1,a._1) \rightarrow '(s,o,a)$,
   then there must not exist any $(s._2,o._2,a._2) \in AB$ such that $'(s._2,o._2,a._2) \rightarrow \neg'(s,o,a)$.

Non-Redundancy of the AB:

   If $(s,o,a) \in AB$ and $'(s,o,a) \rightarrow '(s._1,o._1,a._1)$ then $(s._1,o._1,a._1) \notin AB$.

2.2.3 Weak Authorizations and the Weak Authorization Base

Definition 7:

A weak authorization is a triplet $[s,o,a]$, with $s \in S$, $o \in O$, $a \in A$ and a positive or negative.

Definition 8:

A Weak Authorization Base (WAB) is a set of weak authorizations $[s,o,a]$, with $s \in S$, $o \in O$, $a \in A$:

$$WAB \subseteq S \times O \times A$$

Weak authorizations in WAB are explicit weak authorizations.

Definition 9:

Function $d(s,o,a)$:

$$d: S \times O \times A \rightarrow \{\text{True, False}\}$$

Suppose $[s_{.1},o_{.1},a_{.1}] \mapsto [s,o,a]$: (The notation $\mapsto$ will be explained shortly.)

if $'(s_{.1},o_{.1},a_{.1}) \rightarrow '(s,o,a)$,

then $d(s,o,a)=$True;

else if $'(s_{.1},o_{.1},a_{.1}) \rightarrow \neg'(s,o,a)$,

then $d(s,o,a)=$False.

The function d determines if the value of a weak authorization $[s,o,a]$ is True or False in the WAB. While $i(s,o,a)$ computes implicit authorizations in the AB, $d(s,o,a)$ computes implicit authorizations in the WAB. The WAB complements the AB to enable the computation of function f, which gives the value of an authorization. The function $d(s,o,a)$ is used to determine the value of a weak authorization $[s,o,a]$, when the value of (s,o,a) cannot be computed by $i(s,o,a)$.

For notational simplicity, we use the following definitions:

Definition 10:

The notation $'[s,o,a]$, with $s \in S$, $o \in O$, $a \in A$ and a positive or negative, means:

$d(s,o,a)=$True.

The notation $\neg'[s,o,a]$, with $s \in S$, $o \in O$, $a \in A$ and a positive or negative, means:

$d(s,o,a)=$False.

We define the scope of an explicit weak authorization $[s,o,a]$ to be the set of implicit authorizations which can be deduced from $[s,o,a]$. However, the scope of a weak authorization must be defined using the *weak implication*, which we will indicate with the symbol "$\mapsto$", rather than the implication "$\rightarrow$". Athough we introduce the concept of weak implication here to complete the formal basis of our authorization model, because of space limitations, we will not elaborate on it in the remainder of this paper.

Definition 11:

The scope of a weak authorization $[s_{.1},o_{.1},a_{.1}] \in WAB$, denoted with $P[s_{.1},o_{.1},a_{.1}]$, is the set of weak authorizations $[s,o,a]$, with $s \in S$, $o \in O$, $a \in A$ and a positive or negative, such that:

$d(s,o,a)=$True iff $'(s_{.1},o_{.1},a_{.1}) \rightarrow '(s,o,a)$ or

$d(s,o,a)=$False iff $'(s_{.1},o_{.1},a_{.1}) \rightarrow \neg'(s,o,a)$.

Definition 12:

We define weak authorization implication to mean that $[s_{.1},o_{.1},a_{.1}] \in WAB$ and $[s,o,a] \in P[s_{.1},o_{.1},a_{.1}]$.

We denote this by $[s_{.1},o_{.1},a_{.1}] \mapsto [s,o,a]$.

Below we define three invariants of the *WAB*.

Completeness of the WAB:
For any authorization (s,o,a), there must exist an $[s_1,o_1,a_1] \in WAB$ such that $[s_1,o_1,a_1] \mapsto [s,o,a]$.

Consistency of the WAB:
For any authorization (s,o,a), if there exists an $[s_1,o_1,a_1] \in WAB$ such that:
$[s_1,o_1,a_1] \mapsto [s,o,a]$ and $'(s_1,o_1,a_1) \to '(s,o,a)$,
then for any $[s_2,o_2,a_2] \in WAB$, such that $[s_2,o_2,a_2] \mapsto [s,o,a]$,
$'(s_2,o_2,a_2) \to '(s,o,a)$.

Non-Redundancy of the WAB:
If $[s_1,o_1,a_1] \in WAB$, then there cannot be any $[s_2,o_2,a_2]$ in *WAB* such that:
for any authorization (s,o,a),
if $[s_2,o_2,a_2] \mapsto [s,o,a]$ and $'(s_1,o_1,a_1) \to '(s,o,a)$.
then $[s_1,o_1,a_1] \mapsto [s,o,a]$, and $'(s_2,o_2,a_2) \to '(s,o,a)$.

The only exception to this rule is the case in which $[s_2,o_2,a_2]$ is entered in the *WAB* to ensure the consistency of the *WAB*.

The completeness invariant requires that the entire space $S \times O \times A$ be covered by some scope of weak authorization definition, so that the function d is completely defined on $S \times O \times A$.

The consistency invariant requires that where the scopes of different weak authorizations overlap, these weak authorizations must imply the same authorizations. This implies that the definition of a new weak authorization in the *WAB* may modify the scope of another weak authorization already in the *WAB*. In fact, while the scope of an authorization in *AB* is not modified by the presence of other authorizations in the *AB*, the scope of a weak authorization in the *WAB* can be modified by the presence of other weak authorizations in the *WAB*. For example, suppose that a weak read authorization is defined for a certain user on system [MCC], and that the same user is later granted a weak write authorization on the class [Auto]. The scope of the former weak authorization is modified (i.e subtracted) by the latter.

The non-redundancy invariant requires that in the *WAB* there are no "useless" weak authorization. A weak authorization $[s_2,o_2,a_2]$ is useless if its scope is completely contained within the scope of another weak authorization $[s_1,o_1,a_1]$ and the values of all weak authorizations implied by $[s_2,o_2,a_2]$ are also implied by $[s_1,o_1,a_1]$. For example, suppose that a weak read authorization is defined for a certain user on system [MCC], then granting the user the same weak read authorization on class [Auto] would be useless.

However, a weak authorization with these characteristics is not useless, if it ensures the consistency of the *WAB*, that is, $[s_2,o_2,a_2]$ resolves conflicts of weak authorizations on a part of the scope of $[s_1,o_1,a_1]$ which overlaps the scope of a conflicting authorization in *WAB*.

2.2.4 Interactions between Strong and Weak Authorizations

We need to define two invariants which apply simultaneously to the *WAB* and the *AB*. Any operation on both the *AB* and the *WAB* must always leave both the *WAB* and the *AB* in a state that satisfies these invariants.

Consistency of WAB with respect to AB:

For all $[s,o,a] \in WAB$, there must not exist any $(s_{.1},o_{.1},a_{.1}) \in AB$ such that:
$'(s_{.1},o_{.1},a_{.1}) \rightarrow \neg'(s_{.2},o_{.2},a_{.2})$ for all $[s_{.2},o_{.2},a_{.2}]$ such that $[s,o,a] \mapsto [s_{.2},o_{.2},a_{.2}]$ and $'(s,o,a) \rightarrow '(s_{.2},o_{.2},a_{.2})$.

Non-Redundancy of WAB with AB:

For all $[s,o,a] \in WAB$, there must not exist any $(s_{.1},o_{.1},a_{.1}) \in AB$ such that:
$'(s_{.1},o_{.1},a_{.1}) \rightarrow '(s_{.2},o_{.2},a_{.2})$ for all $[s_{.2},o_{.2},a_{.2}]$ such that $[s,o,a] \mapsto [s_{.2},o_{.2},a_{.2}]$ and $'(s,o,a) \rightarrow '(s_{.2},o_{.2},a_{.2})$.

The consistency invariant requires that the weak authorizations in the scope of a weak authorization do not conflict. The non-redundancy invariant requires that they are not the same as those of the authorizations in the AB. For example, suppose that a write authorization is defined for a user on database[Inventory]. It is not possible to define a negative weak write authorization for that user on the class[Auto], since it would contradict the implicit write authorization on the class[Auto]. Also it is useless to grant the same user a weak read authorization on the class[Auto], since he has an implicit write authorization on the class[Auto].

We do not require the AB to be consistent with the WAB, since we use the WAB only to complement the AB in the computation of the function f when no value can be deduced from the AB alone. The state of the WAB must always be consistent with the state of the AB (not vice-versa); we always require the former to conform to the latter. That is, a change in the WAB is allowed only if the new state of the WAB is consistent with the state of the AB. If instead, a change in the AB brings it to a state not consistent with the WAB, then the WAB must be changed to conform to the new state of the AB.

Now we can define the function $f(s,o,a)$ in terms of the functions $i(s,o,a)$ and $d(s,o,a)$ on the AB and the WAB. To evaluate the function $f(s,o,a)$ is to check the authorization (s,o,a). First, $i(s,o,a)$ is applied to the AB to determine the authorization (s,o,a). If it cannot be determined from the AB, $d(s,o,a)$ is applied to the WAB to determine the corresponding weak authorization $[s,o,a]$.

```
Function f(s,o,a):
    if i(s,o,a)= Undecided,
        then f(s,o,a)=d(s,o,a);
    else
        f(s,o,a)=i(s,o,a).
```

3. Implicit Authorizations for Authorization Subjects

A database environment often has a large number of users, who may be grouped into a limited set of roles (functions) they perform. The first of the three ways to reduce the number of authorization definitions which must be explicitly maintained in the system is to reduce the number of authorization subjects. The approach proposed in [FERN75a] groups subjects into user classes. Similarly, our approach is to assign users to roles and to associate authorizations with the roles. A user may belong to any number of roles. However, unlike [FERN75a], we structure the roles into a rooted directed acyclic graph, which we call a Role Lattice (RL). A node of the RL represents a role, and a directed arc from role A to role B indicates that the authorizations for role A include the authorizations for role B. A role can have multiple children roles, subsuming all authorizations of all the children roles. Further, a role can have multiple parent roles, so that all users who belong to the ancestors of a role share all the authorizations of that role. The role lattice has a single root, the super-user role.

An example role lattice is shown in Figure 2. In the figure, if object A is accessible to the role **mgr** and user–1 belongs to role **mgr**, then user–1 can access object A. Further, if user–2 belongs to role **accounts-recv-mgr**, user–2 can also access object A.

The rule for checking authorization on users can be stated as follows:

A user has the authorization a on an object O if there exists a role r such that $f(r,o,a)=True$ and the user belongs to r.

We use the links between roles in the RL to deduce implicit authorizations for authorization subjects.

Definition 13:
The notation $S.i \rightarrow S.j$, where $S.i \in S$ and $S.j \in S$, indicates that there is a link from $S.i$ to $S.j$ in the RL.

Definition 14:
The notation $S.i \Rightarrow S.j$, where $S.i \in S$ and $S.j \in S$, means that:
either $i = j$, or $S.i \rightarrow S.j$
or there exist $S.1, ..., S.n$ in S, such that $S.i \rightarrow S.1 \rightarrow ... \rightarrow S.n \rightarrow S.j$.

We have the following rule and corollary for the implicit authorizations on roles connected in the RL:

Rule 1:
For any $o \in O$ and $a.n \in A$,
if $S.i \rightarrow S.j$ then $'(S.j,o,a.n) \rightarrow '(S.i,o,a.n)$, or
if $S.i \Rightarrow S.j$ then $'(S.j,o,a.n) \rightarrow '(S.i,o,a.n)$

Corollary 1: (This corollary is derived from rule 1 and applies to negative authorizations)
For any $o \in O$ and $a.n \in A$,
if $S.i \rightarrow S.j$ then $'(S.i,o,\neg a.n) \rightarrow '(S.j,o,\neg a.n)$, or
if $S.i \Rightarrow S.j$ then $'(S.i,o,\neg a.n) \rightarrow '(S.j,o,\neg a.n)$

Rule 1 impacts the assignment of users to roles. Suppose that $S.i \Rightarrow S.j$. If the user U already belongs to role $S.i$, it is not necessary to assign U to role $S.j$. However, if the user belongs to role $S.j$, and if U is assigned to role $S.i$, U must be deleted from role $S.j$.

4. Implicit Authorizations for Authorization Types

The second way to reduce the number of explicit authorization definitions in the system is to exploit implicit authorizations which can be deduced from the authorization types. To accomplish this, we define a

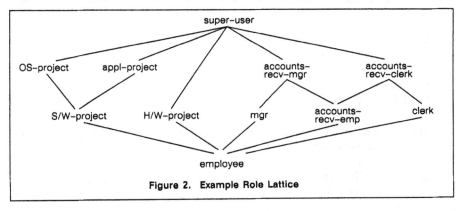

Figure 2. Example Role Lattice

total ordering of all authorization types in A; that is, we arrange the authorization types in decreasing order of strength.

Definition 15:

The set A of authorization types is: $\{a._1, a._2, \ldots, a._z\}$
For any $s \in S$ and $o \in O$, if $i < j$ then
$'(s,o,a._i) \rightarrow '(s,o,a._j)$ and $'(s,o,\neg a._j) \rightarrow '(s,o,\neg a._i)$

One important extension we introduce to authorization types is the distinction between a *total* and *partial* authorization (t and p) for each authorization type a in A with respect to an authorization object. In general, an authorization object is a logical database entity which consists of a set of lower-level database entities. For authorization purposes, we distinguish an authorization object from the set of lower-level authorization objects that constitute that object; and associate with the object the aggregate properties of the set of lower-level objects, as well as the definition of the lower-level objects. Then a total authorization on an object is an authorization on the object and the set of lower-level objects that constitute that object; while a partial authorization on an object is an authorization on the object only. For example, a total read authorization on a class is an authorization to read all information about the class, including the definition and the aggregate properties of the instances of the class. A partial read on a class is an authorization to read only the definition and aggregate properties of the instances of the class.

A total authorization implies the corresponding partial authorization and the total and partial authorizations for all weaker authorization types. A partial authorization implies only the partial authorizations for the weaker authorization types.

Definition 16:

The extended set of authorization types AX is: $\{t._1, p._1, t._2, p._2, \ldots, t._z, p._z\}$
All properties defined for $(s,o,a._i)$, with $a._i \in A$, are also valid for both $(s,o,t._i)$ and $(s,o,p._i)$, with $t._i \in AX$ and $p._i \in AX$.

For any $s \in S$ and $o \in O$:
$'(s,o,t._i) \rightarrow '(s,o,p._i)$ and $'(s,o,\neg p._i) \rightarrow '(s,o,\neg t._i)$.

In the following, we use the notation $a._i \in A$ when it is not necessary to distinguish between total and partial authorizations, and $t._i \in AX$ or $p._i \in AX$ when this distinction is necessary.

The following rule and corollary define implicit authorizations which can be deduced from the total ordering of authorization types.

Rule 2:

For any $s \in S$ and $o \in O$, if $i \leq j$ then:
$'(s,o,t._i) \rightarrow '(s,o,t._j)$
$'(s,o,p._i) \rightarrow '(s,o,p._j)$
$'(s,o,t._i) \rightarrow '(s,o,p._j)$.

Corollary 2: (This corollary is derived from Rule 2 and applies to negative authorizations)
For any $s \in S$ and $o \in O$, if $i \leq j$ then:
$'(s,o,\neg t._j) \rightarrow '(s,o,\neg t._i)$
$'(s,o,\neg p._j) \rightarrow '(s,o,\neg p._i)$
$'(s,o,\neg p._j) \rightarrow '(s,o,\neg t._i)$

5. Implicit Authorizations for Authorization Objects

The third way of reducing the number of authorization definitions which must be maintained in the system is to organize the authorization objects in a hierarchical structure and define implicit authorizations for all descendants of a node for which an explicit authorization is specified. This is in principle similar to the approach proposed in [FERN75b] for implicit authorizations for authorization objects. Implicit authorizations for authorization objects has in general a greater potential for reducing the authorization definitions than those for authorization types and authorization subjects, simply because the number of objects in a database is in general much larger than the number of subjects or authorization types.

5.1 Authorization Object Schema and Authorization Object Lattice

In an object-oriented data model, any database entity is modeled as an object with a unique identifier [GOLD81, GOLD83, BOBR83, BOBR85, STEF86]. In particular, a class is an object which holds the definition, behavior, and aggregate properties of the set of instances that belong to it; and a meta-class is an object which holds the definition, behavior, and aggregate properties of the set of classes that belong to it. Since an object holds the behavior and aggregate properties of the set of lower-level objects that belong to it, an operation on the object does not always imply the same operation on any of the lower-level objects that belong to it. This is an important difference between an object-oriented data model and conventional data models. Under a conventional data model, an operation on a data entity (e.g., change the definition of a relation) implies the same operation on the lower-level entities that belong to it (e.g., tuples of the relation).

The above consideration has led us, in a significant departure from [FERN75b], to separate an abstract object type into two explicit authorization objects, the object type and the set of instances of that object type. The resulting directed hierarchy of authorization object types, called the Authorization Object Schema (AOS), is shown in Figure 3. In our examples in this section, we will use write and read as the only authorization types. We note that if we did not separate an abstract object type into two authorization objects, we would have to introduce additional authorization types. For example, if we did not separate the class into the class authorization object and setof-instances authorization object, we would need four authorization types for the class node: write class object, read class object, write all instances of the class, and read all instances of the class.

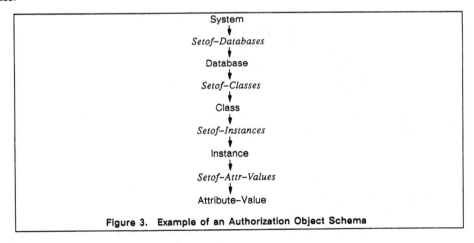

Figure 3. Example of an Authorization Object Schema

An instance of the AOS is a structure called the Authorization Object Lattice (AOL), shown in Figure 4. An AOL is a rooted directed acyclic graph in which each node is an authorization object. Each directed arc from node A to node B is called an *Implication Link* (IL), which indicates that an authorization on node A implies the same authorization on node B. The *setof* nodes in Figure 4 may each have Implication Links to a number of nodes at the next lower level. For example, the *setof-instances* [Auto] authorization object may have Implication Links to many instance authorization objects. Other nodes shown are restricted to one Implication Link to a node at the next lower level. For example, the class [Auto] authorization object may have an Implication Link to only one *setof-instances* authorization object.

5.2 Implication Links between Authorization Objects

In this section, we describe the authorizations implied in the Implication Links.

Definition 17:
The notation $O.i \rightarrow O.j$, where $O.i \in O$ and $O.j \in O$, means that there is an Implication Link from $O.i$ to $O.j$ in the AOL.

Definition 18:
The notation $O.i \Rightarrow O.j$, where $O.i \in O$ and $O.j \in O$, means that
either $i = j$ or $O.i \rightarrow O.j$
or there exist $O.1, ..., O.n$ in O, such that $O.i \rightarrow O.1 \rightarrow ... \rightarrow O.n \rightarrow O.j$.

The authorizations implied in the Implication Links between authorization objects are defined in the following rule and corollary.

Rule 3:
For any $s \in S$ and $a.n \in A$.

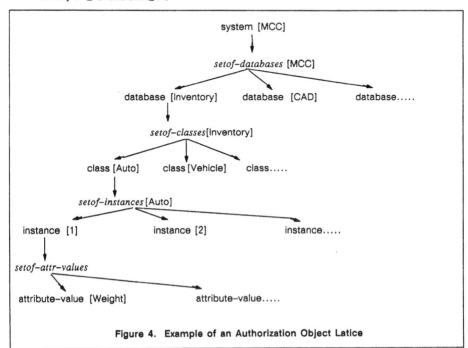

Figure 4. Example of an Authorization Object Latice

if $O.i \rightarrow O.j$ then:
$$'(s,o.i,t.n) \rightarrow '(s,o.j,t.n)$$
$$'(s,o.j,p.n) \rightarrow '(s,o.i,p.n).$$

For any $s \in S$, $a.n \in A$ and $a.m \in A$,
if $O.i \Rightarrow O.j$ and $n \leq m$ then:
$$'(s,o.i,t.n) \rightarrow '(s,o.j,a.m)$$
$$'(s,o.j,a.n) \rightarrow '(s,o.i,p.m).$$

Corollary 3: (This corollary is derived from Rule 3 and applies to negative authorizations)
For any $s \in S$ and $a.n \in A$,
if $O.i \rightarrow O.j$ then:
$$'(s,o.i,\neg p.n) \rightarrow '(s,o.j,\neg p.n)$$
$$'(s,o.j,\neg t.n) \rightarrow '(s,o.i,\neg t.n).$$

For any $s \in S$, $a.n \in A$ and $a.m \in A$,
if $O.i \Rightarrow O.j$ and $n \leq m$ then:
$$'(s,o.i,\neg p.m) \rightarrow '(s,o.j,\neg a.n)$$
$$'(s,o.j,\neg a.m) \rightarrow '(s,o.i,\neg t.n).$$

Figure 5 is a graphical representation of the implicit positive authorizations between authorization objects connected by Implication Links: $O.a \rightarrow O.b \rightarrow O.c$. In the figure, the nodes at the same horizontal level indicate the different authorization types ($t.1, p.1, t.2, p.2$) for an authorization object ($O.a$ or $O.b$ or $O.c$). The shaded boxes in Figure 5 show authorization objects and authorization types which will be used as examples in the following discussion. There are three authorization objects in this example. The *setof-classes* [Inventory] object represents all of the classes in the Inventory database; the class [Auto] object represents the definition of the class Auto; and the *setof-instances* [Auto] object represents all instances of the class [Auto]. The authorization types are total write (TW), partial write (PW), total read (TR), partial read (PR). The directed arcs in the figure represent implicit authorizations which can be deduced.

Figure 6a shows that a positive TW authorization on the class [Auto] implies a PW authorization on that class and a TW authorization on all Auto instances. In Figure 6b it is shown that a PW authorization on the class Auto does not imply any (positive) write authorizations on any of the Auto instances.

A partial authorization is more meaningful when used as a negative authorization. In Figures 6c and 6d, we show that the information content of a negative partial authorization, $(s,O.b,\neg p.2)$, is higher than that of a

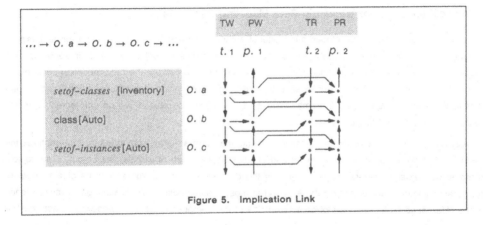

Figure 5.   Implication Link

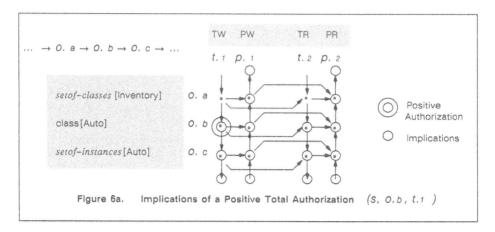

Figure 6a.   Implications of a Positive Total Authorization $(S, O.b, t.1)$

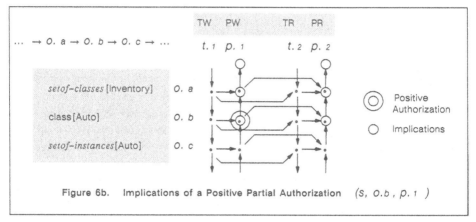

Figure 6b.   Implications of a Positive Partial Authorization $(S, O.b, p.1)$

negative total authorization, $(S, O.b, \neg t.2)$. Figure 6c shows that a negative PR on the class [Auto] implies that a TR authorization on the class is False and any read authorizations on all Auto instances are False. Figure 6d shows that a negative TR authorization does not imply any (negative) read authorizations on the class Auto or its instances.

6.   Implication Links for Semantic Data Modeling Concepts

In previous sections, we developed our model of authorization which can be used as a formal basis for an authorization component in a database system which supports an object-oriented or semantic data model. In this section, we will describe extensions to the model to capture the data modeling concepts of composite objects and versions. Our extensions consist of the definition of additional authorization object types in the Authorization Object Schema. These new authorization objects will be connected using the Implication Links defined in the previous section.

A *composite object* is a collection of related objects that form a hierarchical structure that captures the IS-PART-OF relationship between an object and another object which references the object. The objects belong to a number of different classes; that is the composite object schema consists of a number of component classes. Each object can be a part of at most one composite object, although it may reference and be referenced by any number of objects outside of the composite object. Composite objects can be

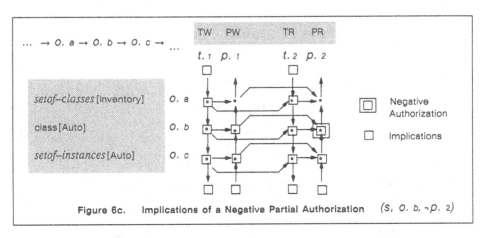

Figure 6c.   Implications of a Negative Partial Authorization $(S, O. b, \neg p. 2)$

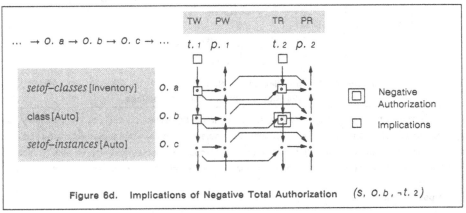

Figure 6d.   Implications of Negative Total Authorization $(S, O. b, \neg t. 2)$

used as units for locking, clustering, and deletion as described in [KIM87]. An instance object which has references to other instance objects can be thought of as both a simple object or as the aggregation of all of its component objects. In a multi-user environment, different users may create and access different component objects.

Users of computer-aided design or office information systems often need to generate and experiment with a number of versions of an object. A database system for such application systems must directly support the concept of versions. [CHOU86] provides a model of versions in which any number of versions may be derived by any user from any version of an object. The model supports two ways to bind an object with another versioned object: *static* and *dynamic*. In static binding, the first object directly references the second object. In dynamic binding, the first object does not directly reference the second object, but instead references a *generic object*, which maintains the history of derivation of versions of the second object, and the default version for dynamic binding.

Our approach to extend the notion of implicit authorization to composite objects and versions is to augment the AOS defined in the previous section with two additional types of authorization objects: composite objects and versions, as shown in Figure 7. The bold arcs represent the Implication Links between authorization objects in the authorization object lattice defined in the previous section. The non-bold arcs represent Implication Links for the new authorization objects in the augmented authorization object lattice.

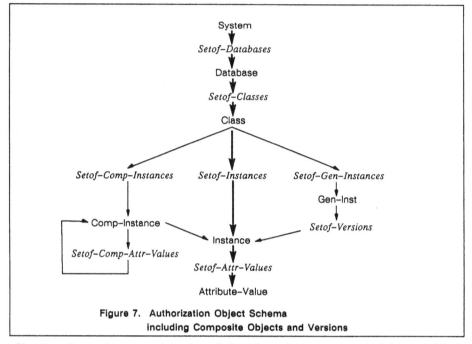

System

Setof–Databases

Database

Setof–Classes

Class

Setof–Comp–Instances   *Setof–Instances*   *Setof–Gen–Instances*

Gen–Inst

Setof–Versions

Comp–Instance

Setof–Comp–Attr–Values

Instance

Setof–Attr–Values

Attribute–Value

Figure 7. Authorization Object Schema
including Composite Objects and Versions

The alternatives to this approach are to explicitly define authorization on each of the potentially many component objects of a composite object, versions of an object, or on each of the classes on the composite object schema. The implicit authorization mechanism on composite objects must also be able to recognize authorization conflicts which may arise when authorization is defined on individual component objects.

6.1 Composite Objects

Our approach to implicit authorizations for composite objects is to define an explicit authorization on the root of a composite object to imply authorizations on the component objects. Figure 8 is an AOL with a composite object. The composite Auto object is composed of an Auto instance which contains an Autobody instance which, in turn, contains a Fender instance. The Auto instance in the database is represented by the instance[1] node in the AOL. Note that the comp–inst[1] node in the AOL can be used for authorization on the Auto composite object. Authorization on the *setof–comp–instances* node below the class[Auto] node is used to grant authorization on all Auto composite objects. Authorization on the comp–inst[1] node implies authorization on the instance[1] node. Authorization on the comp–inst[1] node also implies authorization on the comp–inst[2] node (which represents a composite instance of the class Autobody in the database). Finally, authorization on the comp–inst[2] node implies authorization on the comp–inst[3] node, which then implies authorization on the instance[3] node (which represents an instance of the class Fender).

Figure 9a shows the implicit authorizations resulting from a positive TW authorization on the Autobody composite object. In this example, we can see how a positive TW authorization is then implied for comp–inst[3] and then for instance[3] of the class Fender. We can also see that a PR authorization is implied for the comp–inst[1] of the class Auto.

Figure 9b shows the implicit authorizations resulting from a negative PR authorization on the set of all composite objects of the class Auto. In this example, we can see that this implies a negative TW authoriza-

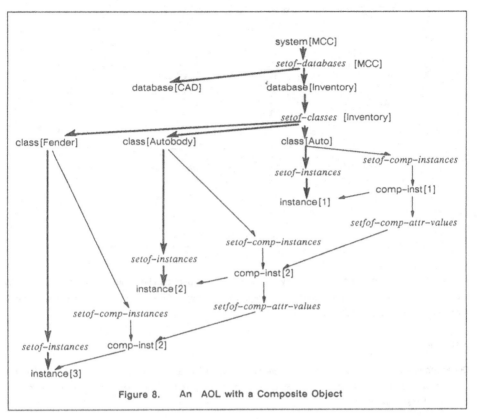

Figure 8.   An AOL with a Composite Object

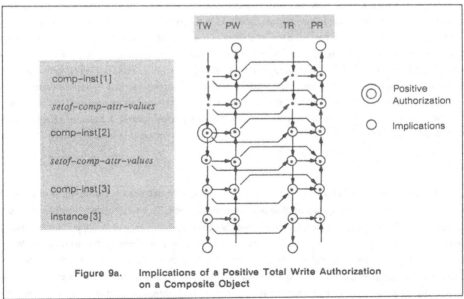

Figure 9a.   Implications of a Positive Total Write Authorization
on a Composite Object

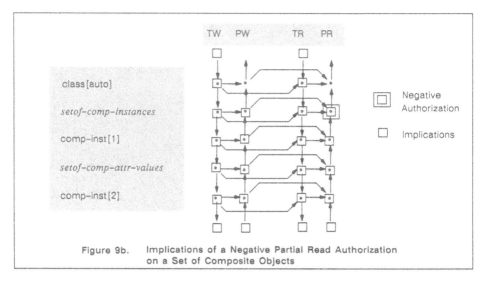

Figure 9b. Implications of a Negative Partial Read Authorization
on a Set of Composite Objects

tion on the comp-inst[2] of the class Autobody. In other words, a user can be denied authorization to modify any of the components of any Auto instance by a negative authorization on the *setof-comp-instances* authorization object for the class Auto.

6.2 Versions

Our approach for implicit authorizations for versions is to define an authorization on the generic object to imply authorizations on versions of the object, while also allowing explicit authorization definitions on individual versions of the object.

Figure 10 illustrates an AOL with versioned objects. In this example, two generic objects have been created in the database and each generic object describes two version objects. The nodes gen-inst[1] and gen-inst[2] in the AOL represent the two generic objects in the database. Authorization on the gen-inst[1] node allows a user to modify the generic object itself and also will imply authorization on the two version objects referenced by gen-inst[1]. Authorization on the *setof-gen-instances* node will imply authorization on all of the generic instances of the class Auto. Authorization on the *setof-versions* node referenced by the gen-inst[1] node will imply authorization on the two version objects referenced by gen-inst[1]. In this way, we are able to specify instance level authorization over a potentially large number of selected instances using a single explicit authorization.

7. Summary

In this paper, we presented a formal model of authorization for database systems which extends the existing models. The model was developed to provide a formal basis for an authorization mechanism for a future version of ORION, a prototype object-oriented database system which also supports a number of semantic data modeling concepts. It incorporates two significant extensions to the existing models of authorization. One is a more complete framework for implicit authorizations along the three domains of authorization, the subjects (users), objects (database entities), and types (read, write, create, etc.). The concept of implicit authorization helps solve the storage requirement of representing all valid authorizations in a system, by allowing the system to deduce authorizations from those explicitly stored in the system. It also

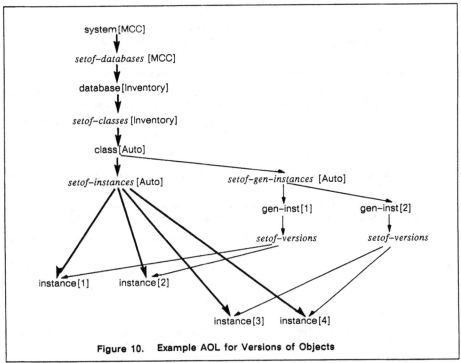

Figure 10. Example AOL for Versions of Objects

serves as the basis for detecting authorization definitions which may conflict with explicitly stored or implicit authorizations. Another extension is the formal basis for capturing, for purposes of authorization, the semantics of a number of data modeling concepts for which the existing models of authorization were not designed. These data modeling concepts include the IS-PART-OF relationship in a composite object between an object and another object which contains the object, and versions of an object.

In this paper, first we introduced the basic elements of our model of authorization, as discussed above. Next, we developed rules for computing implicit authorizations from the representations of the three domains of authorization; directed acyclic graphs for authorization subjects and objects, and a linear sequence for authorization types. Then we described the semantics of implicit authorization in semantic data modeling concepts. The semantics of authorization implication for a hierarchy of database objects apply directly to the IS-PART-OF relationship in a composite object and versions.

Because of space limitations, we could not include a number of additional important results in this paper. First, we did not discuss implicit authorizations for the IS-A relationship and inheritance. Second, we did not elaborate the notion of implicit weak authorizations for the authorization objects. Third, we did not provide detailed algorithms for the authorization operations, grant and revoke. We will report these results in a sequel to this paper.

REFERENCES

[BANE87] Banerjee, J., H. T. Chou, J. Garza, W. Kim, D. Woelk, N. Ballou, and H. J. Kim. "Data Model Issues for Object–Oriented Applications," *ACM Trans. on Office Information Systems*, April 1987.

[BOBR83] Bobrow, D.G.. and M. Stefik. *The LOOPS Manual*, Xerox PARC, Palo Alto, CA., 1983.

[BOBR85] Bobrow, D.G. et al. *CommonLoops: Merging Common Lisp and Object–Oriented Programming*, Intelligent Systems Laboratory Series ISL–85–8, Xerox PARC, Palo Alto, CA., 1985.

[CHOU86] Chou, H.T. and W. Kim, "A Framework for Versions in a CAD Environment," *Proc. 12th Int. Conf. on Very Large Data Bases*, August 1986, Kyoto, Japan.

[DATE84] Date, C. J. "A Guide to DB2," Addison–Wesley (1985).

[FERN75a] Fernandez, E. B., R. C. Summers, C. D. Coleman. "An Authorization Model for a Shared Database," *Proc. 1975 ACM–SIGMOD Int. Conference*, ACM, New York (1975).

[FERN75b] Fernandez, E. B., R. C. Summers, T. Lang. "Definition and Evaluation of Access Rules in Data Management Systems," *Proc. 1st Int. Conf. on Very Large Data Bases*, Boston (1975).

[FERN81] Fernandez, E. B., R. C. Summers, C. Wood, "Database Security and Integrity," Addison–Wesley (1981).

[GOLD81] Goldberg, A. "Introducing the Smalltalk–80 System," *Byte*, vol. 6, no. 8, August 1981, pp. 14–26.

[GOLD83] Goldberg, A. and D. Robson. *Smalltalk–80: The Language and its Implementation*, Addison–Wesley, Reading, MA 1983.

[GRAH72] Graham, G.S. and P.J. Denning, "Protection: Principles and Practice," *AFIPS Conf. Proc. 40*, 1972 SJCC, pages 417–429. AFIPS Press, Montvale, N.J., 1972.

[GRIF76] Griffiths, P.P. and B.W. Wade, "An Authorization Mechanism for a Relational Database System," *ACM Transactions on Database Systems*, Volume 1, Number 3, September 1976), pages 242–255.

[KIM87] Kim, W., et al. "Composite Object Support in an Object–Oriented Database System," in *Proc. Object–Oriented Programming Systems, Languages, and Applications*, October 1987, Orlando, Florida.

[LAMP71] Lampson, B.W. "Protection," *Proc. of the 5th Annual Princeton Conf. on Information Sciences and Systems*, (1971).

[STEF86] Stefik, M., and D.G. Bobrow. "Object–Oriented Programming: Themes and Variations," *The AI Magazine*, January 1986, pp. 40–62.

A Foundation for Evolution
from Relational to Object Databases

David Beech

Hewlett-Packard Laboratories
1501, Page Mill Road
Palo Alto
CA 94304

ABSTRACT *Object models have an important part to play in the future of database systems, but progress is hampered by lack of agreement on their essential characteristics. Strong constraints on the design of a common model are exercised by the need to interface well with object models in programming languages, and the desirability of a smooth evolution from existing database technology.*

This paper briefly reviews some salient features of database and language object concepts, and then draws attention to a correspondence between relational and object database models. It shows how this can be exploited in defining Object SQL (OSQL), which reinterprets and extends SQL to define object types and instances, together with functions which relate and manipulate objects. OSQL has been implemented as an interface to the Iris Object DBMS.

1. Introduction

Object models have an important part to play in the future of database systems. No lengthy justification of this view will be given here, since it is becoming widely accepted [IEEE 85, Dayal & Dittrich 86, Maier *et al.* 87, Bancilhon *et al.* 87], the main reasons being the suitability of object models for treating complex and irregular objects (e.g. in engineering systems), their conceptual naturalness (e.g. for multi-media office systems), and their consonance with strong trends in programming languages and software engineering.

Progress seems to be hampered at the moment by confusion as to exactly what is meant by "object models", and it appears that a proposal for a common Object Data Base (ODB) model is needed, to provide a focus for the database community analogous to that provided earlier by the relational model. Such a model could also serve as the basis for sharing of objects between different programming languages—it is undesirable, even if it were economically feasible, for each object-oriented language to have its own database system. However, the situation is more constrained than was the case with the introduction of the relational model, since several programming languages are already developing object models, and this is clearly a fleeting opportunity to minimise the impedance mismatch between the data structures of databases and of programming languages.

Therefore the approach that we took was first to make a top-down review of requirements for an ODB model, in order to determine the essential ingredients and the extensions needed when compared to programming language models. This work will be briefly summarized below.

Next we considered the relationship to existing database technology. Just as the practical impact of object-oriented programming is coming largely through extensions of existing languages, as in C++ [Stroustrup 86], Objective-C [Cox 86] and the Common Lisp Object System [Bobrow *et al.* 87], it would be advantageous, if possible, to offer smooth progress from relational [Codd 70] to object database systems rather than requiring a revolution.

The main contribution of this paper is to describe the surprisingly positive outcome of an investigation of the evolutionary possibilities. It turns out that a foundation can be laid in a way which exploits a natural mapping between relational and object models. This will be illustrated by introducing Object SQL (OSQL), which reinterprets and extends existing SQL [ANSI 86] to work with objects and functions.

The success of an approach like this depends on the extent to which it can gain the advantages of evolution without seriously compromising its ideal goals. Experience so far is promising, in that an initial version of OSQL has already been implemented for the Iris Object DBMS [Fishman *et al.* 87], and appears to be quite attractive. Of course, SQL has some infelicities, but so does every language which actually exists. The faults are not nearly as severe as sometimes claimed [Date 87], and they are compensated by some pragmatic virtues which make the end result competitive with what might realistically be achieved by a brand new language. It will also be seen later that the proposed evolution can produce considerable improvements in SQL.

2. Object Model

The specific database influences on an object model may be classified into three main groups:

- the need for a general treatment, not merely of isolated objects, but of large collections of objects and relationships between them, with powerful and efficient retrieval and update facilities, including view mappings;

- requirements arising from the long-term persistence and sharing of objects, e.g., evolutionary change to the definitions of objects, types, and type graphs; version management; concurrency and access control; and transaction management and recovery;

- the desirability of increasing the semantic content of databases, so that more information can reside in usable form in the databases rather than being scattered unintelligibly among programs that access them, and so that databases can grow into knowledge bases and support inferential retrieval without requiring another revolution.

2.1 Summary of the Model

A comprehensive treatment of the groundwork for an ODB model at the level of abstract data types may be found in [Beech 87a], with an expanded discussion of intensional aspects in [Beech 87b]. For present purposes, we will concentrate on some basic notions proposed for objects, types, functions and aggregate constructors.

2.1.1 Objects

The primary characteristic of an *object* is that it has an identity which persists through time, however the properties of the object may change [Khoshafian & Copeland 86]. This identity may be considered to be represented by a system-generated object identifier (oid). Objects may be explicitly created and destroyed. Snapshots of objects may be captured by versions, which are objects with their own identity, and which form the version set of their generic object [Landis 86, Beech & Mahbod 88].

2.1.2 Types

Every object is an instance of one or more *types*. There is the usual notion of a type semi-lattice, i.e., the possibility of multiple inheritance, although we shall not discuss the details of this here. Types may also be added to and removed from objects dynamically, to reflect the need to retain the identity of long-lived objects in a database even while their nature may change considerably. Types are themselves modelled as objects, and like other objects may be alterable and versionable.

2.1.3 Functions

Functions are also objects, defined to take arguments of certain types and return a result (possibly an aggregate) of a certain type. Functions are *applied* to their arguments—"apply" is not itself a function, but a meta-action of the model. Functions may produce truth-values or results of any other type, and may be defined *intensionally* by specification of formulae, or *extensionally* without any formula but solely by explicit setting and updating of their values for particular arguments. Formulae in the model provide recursive computability. Functions may also be defined by algorithms with side-effects—thus the "function" terminology follows that of many programming languages rather than that of mathematics. Functions may also be *foreign functions* written in programming languages, provided that their argument and result interfaces are consistent with this model, which of course implies some mutual understanding of types.

Functions which take only one argument may be grouped with the definition of the type of that argument, and are then known as *properties* of the type. By default, they correspond to instance variables in the representation of instances of the type, but the model also allows for different representations of a type to be specified beneath the same function interface.

2.1.4 Aggregates and Iteration

Aggregate type constructors include *set, multiset, list* and *tuple*. Here again, a terminological question arises, and we choose to retain the familiar words and issue the caveat that we treat extensional collections such as sets differently from pure mathematical sets. A set in the model is itself an object, and obeys the usual rules for object identity. Objects may be inserted and removed explicitly, and it is thus possible for two sets to have the same members without being identical. This corresponds to the semantic situation in a time-varying world where the objects being modelled are distinct, although at a given level of abstraction and at a given time they cannot be distinguished by their components. Other ODB models have similar constructs [e.g. Bancilhon *et al.* 87].

Iteration is possible over the members of an aggregate, being introduced into the abstract model as a function which passes the body of the iteration to the aggregate object, as in Smalltalk [Goldberg & Robson 83]. Of course, a language interface can represent this by any syntax it chooses, such as a `for each` ... construct.

2.2 Comparison with Language Models

In this necessarily brief comparison with object models in programming languages, we will take C++ and Objective-C as representatives of the Simula [Dahl, Myrhaug & Nygaard 70] and Smalltalk schools respectively, and the Common Lisp Object System (CLOS) as a contributor of other original ideas.

2.2.1 Objects

Each of the languages has the concept of object identity, and offers explicit object creation. C++ also provides for explicit object destruction. None of these languages has a version concept.

2.2.2 Types

The abstract data type concept occurs in each of the three languages slightly differently, although in each case called *class*, probably to ease the pain of grafting it onto existing type systems in the base languages. ("A class is a user-defined type." [Stroustrup 86]) The main ingredients of a class definition are a class name, an optional superclass name (or multiple superclass names in CLOS), a set of instance variables defining a representation for instances of the class, and (except in CLOS) a set of functions (or "methods") comprising the interface to the class. The pure interface and the representational aspects are not well separated in these languages, and they differ in the ways in which they support encapsulation, i.e., hiding of the representation from *public* as distinct from *private* use in implementing functions. (None supports authorization schemes, restricting access to certain users, as in database systems and operating systems.)

CLOS adds a *metaclass* concept, so that class objects themselves can be instances of different metaclasses, and may thus be differently implemented.

2.2.3 Functions

C++ and CLOS use normal function notation to apply functions or methods to object arguments. Both languages take advantage of this to offer *generic* functions, where the function name is overloaded and corresponds to a family of functions from which an appropriate member is selected, based on the argument types. Functions and generic selection thus appear to treat their arguments symmetrically. C++ further supports symmetry by allowing its *member* functions to be defined separately from the classes of which they are members (as required in CLOS), and to be made *friends* of other classes.

Objective-C retains a sharp distinction between C functions, and *messages* which specify an object, a method name, and any additional arguments. The message syntax is asymmetrical, and overloading of method names can only be performed on the type of the "distinguished argument", the object to which the message is sent.

CLOS has a convenient way of creating property functions in the interface to a class, by means of **reader** and **accessor** options attached to the instance variables.

2.2.4 Aggregates and Iteration

There is no direct support for sets or multisets in these languages, although all have bounded arrays. C++ and Objective-C have tuples (structs), and CLOS has lists (!). Iteration involves lower-level manipulation of subscripts, pointers, etc., or is achieved by recursion.

3. Correspondence between Object and Relational Models

There are some strong conceptual correspondences between the ODB model outlined above and the relational model. Whereas the relational model uses tables to represent not only Employees and Departments, but also the EmpDept relationship between them, the object model allows for discrimination between these, much as in the entity-relationship model [Chen 76]: Employee and Department become entity types, and EmpDept becomes a function. Thus the first step in the correspondence is that a relational table corresponds to either (i) a type or (ii) an extensional function in the ODB. The second step is that a column name and type in the relational table correspond in case (i) to the name and result type of a property function of the ODB, or in case (ii) to the name and type of a function parameter or result. (Similarly, relational views and their column definitions correspond to intensional functions and their parameter and result definitions.)

In case (ii), comparing a function to a table, each parameter and result position corresponds to a column in the table. However, in case (i), the essential difference is that the table corresponding to a type implicitly contains another column for the object identifiers of the instances.

Thus in the ODB it is no longer necessary for the user to generate and manage unique keys for objects. Moreover, the referential integrity problem cannot arise during object creation, and the system can perform appropriate control of dangling references due to deletion.

The presence of functions as first-class constituents is a great part of the strength of any object model. The user need no longer specify joins by matching keys to navigate between objects. The use of functions for navigation, the ability to nest functions, and the availabiity of user-defined functions in search predicates, will frequently lead to simpler and more efficient queries. For update, the value of user-defined functions is even greater, e.g., in permitting specification of semantics for view updates which would otherwise be ambiguous or beyond the powers of the system.

3.1 Language Design Considerations

One linguistic approach that was examined in the Iris project was to design a new language to exhibit the benefits of the object and function model described above. In particular, we sought inspiration from languages which have emphasized functional navigation such as Daplex [Shipman 80], GORDAS [Elmasri & Wiederhold 80], and IDM [Beech, Feldman & Johnson 82].

Another approach that seemed worth considering was to take SQL as a base, for the following reasons:

- It is socially irresponsible to invent new languages if an existing language is a good approximation to what is required;

- It is possible to stand on the shoulders of the SQL designers—many of the features of SQL are solutions to problems which would have to be solved again in a new language;

- An extension of the SQL interface embedded in programming languages becomes another possibility, together with reuse of existing language preprocessors;

- Some of the extensions may also be improvements to be considered for relational SQL;

- Migration from relational to object databases should be facilitated.

The adaptation of SQL was surprisingly smooth, and the result was OSQL (for Object SQL, or Oh! SQL). The disadvantages of this approach, such as occasional syntactic awkwardness, or the possibility of misunderstanding due to reinterpretation of familiar constructs, were judged to be relatively slight.

As a general principle, OSQL includes identical syntax to SQL, where the semantics carry over according to the correspondences described earlier. Optional alternative keywords are offered where the existing keywords would be too misleading for human users under the reinterpretation.

A key feature of SQL is the triple role of the FROM clause in a SELECT, which determines the quantification over tuples to be tested by the WHERE clause, introduces bound variables for the quantification (or allows the table name to stand also for the bound variable where there is no ambiguity), and controls name scope for these variables and for the implicit qualification of those column names which are unique among the tables mentioned in the FROM clause. All of these features can usefully be carried over to an ODB interface, where **for each** reads better than FROM since it is being applied to instances of a type rather than to a table (for clarity of exposition, we shall use a different font for OSQL examples to distinguish them from SQL):

```
Select name, address
for each supplier
where city = 'Palo Alto';
```

Here **supplier** represents both the type and a bound variable, and the latter is implicitly the operand of name(supplier), address(supplier) and city(supplier). Again as in SQL, although the **for each** clause comes after the **Select** clause, its name scope includes the **Select** clause; and although the **Select** clause comes first, its functions are semantically the last to be applied, after the bound variables satisfying the **where** clause have been determined.

There are some interesting implications of being able to refer directly to objects in an ODB model. In SQL, one might SELECT * FROM S to select all columns, and OSQL retains the notation **Select * for each S** with a similar meaning, of selecting all properties defined for the type. On the other hand, where SQL might SELECT S# FROM S to extract the key, OSQL allows the object itself to be retrieved by **Select S for each S**, which may be abbreviated to **Select each S**. The full form would be required only for queries which had more than S alone in the **select** or **for each** clauses.

Other SQL statements carry over quite directly to the ODB model, and have useful features such as the optional list of column names on an INSERT to correspond to the list of values provided (extending to the insertion of multiple tuples without repeating the column names). The syntax for defining a table is a suitable foundation for both the definition of a type together with its properties, and the definition of a function with its parameters.

More strongly functional query languages sometimes gain from being more flexible syntactically than the deliberately rigid SELECT ... FROM ... WHERE ... pattern of SQL, but if user-defined functions are admitted into the **select** and **where** clauses, the differences are slight. Furthermore, it would seem easy to allow the SQL pattern to be optionally permuted into FROM ... WHERE ... SELECT ... to fit the SQL semantics and scope rules, with obvious potential for further improvements, in the style of Daplex or QUEL [Held, Stonebraker & Wong 75].

Another important aspect of the functional languages is that they are not obliged to produce normalized relations as their results, and this freedom could be beneficial in various ways. Instead of one-to-many relationships being expressed in rectangular tables with the first value being repeated alongside each related value, the result would conceptually be a list structure corresponding to a report format in which, for example, each supplier's name would occur only once although multiple phone numbers might be shown alongside. Besides the intelligibility of such hierarchical structures, there is also the prospect of more compact representation of information of this kind. Nested structures of function applications (some returning sets of values) used in functional languages can be introduced into the select clause of OSQL with similar effects.

3.2 Summary of Results

The main extensions included in order to adapt SQL to the object and function model are:

- System-generated invisible unique object identifiers, and the use of direct references to objects rather than the use of their keys in where clauses;

- Interface variables which may be bound to objects, e.g., in a Select:

```
Select into bestsession
each Session s
where p8 in sPaper(s);
```

The variable bestsession is bound to the object, not to its properties, and may thereafter be used to refer to the object (just as p8 refers to a Paper here), where in SQL the user must retrieve and work with the visible key value;

- User-defined functions in where and select clauses, and in updates.

The main keyword alternatives are:

- CREATE TABLE becomes either Create type or Create function, and DROP TABLE becomes Delete type or Delete function since it deletes an object;

- INSERT INTO T ... VALUES ... becomes Create T ... instance[s] ... for creating one or more instances if T is a type, or Add T(...) = ... if T is a function.

- FROM becomes each or for each;

- UPDATE for functions becomes Set or Add, to distinguish between single-valued and aggregate-valued cases;

- DELETE for functions becomes Remove, since it does not delete an object;

- NOT NULL becomes required, to avoid phrases like not null unique.

Some further extensions have been made, and many more will be needed and have been considered, such as the treatment of complex objects and recursive queries, and the use of authorization to support selective encapsulation of objects, but discussion of these is beyond the scope of this paper which concentrates on establishing the viability of the SQL-compatible foundation.

4. Object SQL

We will illustrate the use of OSQL in a simple application to the work of the program committee for a conference. The database will record information such as the details of papers submitted, the assignment of reviewers to the papers, the grades given, acceptance status, and notifications to the authors. We choose and comment on a few representative statements, with the goal of demonstrating (to those who are familiar with SQL) the smooth transition to OSQL, and (to those who may not be) the reasonably natural and concise interface which results, often reflecting quite closely the formulation of the requests in English.

4.1 Types and Extensional Functions

Information about various kinds of people will be recorded, so we first introduce the generic type of object Person together with some property functions applicable in principle to all persons (even though they may not actually have values for all persons):

```
Create type Person
(
        name char(20) required,
        address char(40),
        netaddress char(30),
        phone char(14)
);
```

Now define Reviewer as a subtype of Person. Notice that in defining a subtype, property functions like **expertise** may be introduced which are applicable to any Reviewer object. Since the same object also has the Person type, property functions of Person are applicable too. The new property function is set-valued. (Assume that a type Topic has already been created.)

```
Create type Reviewer subtype of Person
(
        expertise set of Topic
);
```

We may also want to introduce the concept of an Author for stronger typing, even without any additional properties:

```
Create type Author subtype of Person;
```

The type Paper is introduced as follows:

```
Create type Paper
(
        title char(50) required,
        papno integer unique required,
        prim Topic,
        sec Topic,
        status char(10) required,
        authors set of Author required
);
```

The user-defined types Topic and Author are now being specified as result types for properties of a Paper, i.e., objects can conceptually 'refer to' other objects.

Already in making *bundled* type definitions, we have been creating function objects corresponding to the properties, as well as creating the type objects themselves. However, just as it is possible to define a type without mentioning any functions applicable to its instances, so it is possible to create functions separately from types:

```
Create function reviewersOf(Paper) -> set of Reviewer;
```

This function could have been specified as a bundled property of the Paper type, but maybe it was overlooked at the time; or maybe it is not considered to be an inherent property of a paper as to who referees it, so that it may be more lucid to show this separately in the schema; or perhaps the type definition of Paper exists inviolable in a library and just requires an additional local function to be defined on it.

To create a predicate, omit any result type:

```
Create function Relevant (Topic);
```

The reviewersOf and Relevant functions, like the bundled property functions above, are extensionally defined—they will rely on being given values to store for all arguments for which they are to be defined. Separately created functions can also have two or more arguments, and this provides a strong motivation for using them to obtain symmetrical modeling of relationships between several types of object. For example, if responsibility for tracking accepted papers is assigned to individual committee members, this may be thought of as a predicate involving AccPaper and ComMember types:

```
Create function Tracking (AccPaper, ComMember);
```

If it would also be convenient to have functions TrackerOf (AccPaper) -> ComMember and TrackedBy (ComMember) -> AccPaper, these may then be defined intensionally, as we shall show later.

If reviewers assign grades to papers, the preferred model may be to define a stored function of two arguments with a result, rather than a 3-place predicate:

```
Create function grade (Paper, Reviewer) -> integer;
```

Tuple-valued functions may also be created, but it is probably more usual for these to be defined intensionally rather than as the extensional base.

4.2 Object Instantiation and Update

Just as it is possible to bundle property functions with types when defining them, so the initialization of property values may be bundled with the creation of instances, if desired. Since Reviewer is a subtype of Person, properties of either of these types may be selected for initialization of a reviewer:

```
Create Reviewer (name, expertise)
instances einstein ('Albert Einstein', null),
        newton ('Isaac Newton', (physics, mathematics)),
        turing ('Alan Turing',
                    (cs, mathematics, logic, philosophy));
```

A variable name such as einstein will be known to the OSQL processor only for the duration of the session, and need only be given if it is likely to be useful. If the user wishes to associate a variable name with an object which does not have one, this may be done with Select ... into ... (see below).

Maybe Einstein and Turing also submit papers, and at this point VonNeumann (already, say, a Person with variable name vonneumann) agrees to become a reviewer:

```
Add type Author to einstein, turing;
Add type Reviewer (expertise)
  to vonneumann ((physics, mathematics, philosophy,
                    psychology, cs, logic));
```

Here is some information about Einstein's paper:

```
Create Paper
            (papno, title, prim, sec, status, authors, reviewers)
instance p1 ( 1,
            'A Unified Field Theory - A Persistent Dream',
            physics,
            mathematics,
            'A',
            einstein,
            (newton, vonneumann) );
```

Grades may be assigned to papers as follows:

```
Set grade(p1, newton) = -4,
    grade(p1, vonneumann)  = 5;
```

Functions created within type definitions can be set in this way as well as by the bundled initialization illustrated earlier:

```
Set expertise(einstein) = mathematics,
    phone(einstein) = '(609)452-EMCC',
```

```
netaddr(einstein) = 'albert@ias.EDU';
```

For set-valued functions, it is possible to add a value to an existing set of values (or to an empty set):

```
Add expertise(einstein) = physics;
```

Removal of values has similar generality to setting and adding of values:

```
Remove expertise(einstein) = physics,
       grade(p1, vonneumann) = 5;
```

Where all results for a given argument tuple are to be removed, without the need for checking against what they are assumed to be currently, the results to be removed can be omitted:

```
Remove expertise(vonneumann);
```

Another form of update is to remove a type from an object. If the type also has functions involving it, then any values involving the given object will be removed also. For example, removal of the Reviewer type from an object will also affect the expertise property of that object:

```
Remove type Reviewer from turing;
```

It is likewise possible to delete an object completely, where the cascading deletion will remove all function values and types from the object first:

```
Delete newton;
```

If the object to be removed is a type or function, the coup de grace is equally simple, with the type being removed from all its instances first as above, or all values being removed from the function:

```
Delete type Reviewer;
Delete function grade;
```

The Set, Add and Remove statements may also be applied to simple derived functions. Work is in progress on user-defined specification of more ambitious view updates.

4.3 Queries

The simplest way of introducing OSQL queries is to assume an interactive interface with the possibility of displaying sets of results directly. The usual cursor mechanisms are also available for retrieving results one at a time.

To retrieve the titles of all papers:

```
Select title
for each Paper;
```

The use of title in the Select clause here is an abbreviation for title(Paper) (or Paper.title as in SQL). Any valid function may be applied here to the variables bound in the for each clause. Tuples may be returned, and functions may be nested, and functions may also be used in the where clause:

```
Select name, phone
for each Reviewer;

Select name(authorOf(p))
for each Paper p
where  name(prim(p)) = 'Philosophy';
```

To find the title of paper p1, no iteration is required:

```
Select title(p1);
```

If the Select clause is vacuous, the objects determined by the for each and where clauses will be returned without application of any functions to them. This means that their object identifiers will be returned, and is best used with the into option to associate them with variable names (one at a time, using a cursor with fetch ... into ... if the query is set-valued, as in SQL):

```
Select into p2
each Paper p
where papno(p)=2;
```

Set operations are permitted in predicates, and functions may be used instead of nested queries. Thus to find the titles of all the papers Russell is reviewing:

```
Select title
for each Paper p
where russell in reviewersOf(p);
```

It is possible to iterate over more than one type at a time, where each distinct tuple of instances of the types specified after for each will be considered once. So to get the numbers and topics of all papers such that their primary area is among the areas of expertise of one of their reviewers, we also need to exclude duplicates by requesting distinct results:

```
Select distinct papno, name(t)
for each Paper p, Reviewer r, Topic t
where t = prim(p) and r in reviewersOf(p)
                      and t in expertise(r);
```

4.4 Intensional Functions and More Updates

Functions may currently be intensionally defined with the help of Select. (Later extensions to provide more power in defining function bodies are obviously possible and, within limits, desirable. More general capability can be provided by importing foreign functions written in programming languages.)

For example, to derive the directional function TrackerOf from the symmetrical predicate Tracking introduced earlier:

```
Create function TrackerOf (AccPaper a) -> set of ComMember
   as  Select
       each  ComMember c
       where Tracking (a, c) ;
```

Or to make it convenient to return the grades of a given paper:

```
Create function GradesOf (Paper p) -> set of integer
   as  Select g
       for each Reviewer r, integer g
       where grade(p, r) = g ;

Select GradesOf(p2);
```

To return the reviewer's name along with each grade:

```
Create function ReviewerGrade (Paper p)
                  -> set of <char(20), integer>
   as  Select name(r), g
       for each Reviewer r, integer g
       where grade(p, r) = g ;
```

As was mentioned earlier, it is possible to update simple derived function values, for example:

```
Add TrackerOf(p1) = russell;
```

Having shown above how Select can be used for intensional definition of functions, we will illustrate the way in which very similar constructs can be used to define iterative updates. The Set, Add, and Remove statements can allow for each and where clauses to be appended to them—for example, to replace all negative grades by zero:

```
Set grade(p, r) = 0
for each Paper p, Reviewer r
where grade(p, r) < 0;
```

or to have every reviewer process the controversial paper p1:

```
Add reviewersOf(p1) = r
for each Reviewer r;
```

or to remove several values from a function:

```
Remove expertise(r) = physics
for each Reviewer r
where expertise(r) = mathematics;
```

4.5 SQL Comparison

This section shows how selected parts of the conference example can be expressed in SQL. This will illustrate both the similarity of OSQL to SQL, and some of the advantages of OSQL.

In creating the Person table, notice that the column person_no is introduced in order to provide a unique key:

```
CREATE TABLE Person
(
        person_no INTEGER NOT NULL UNIQUE,
        name CHAR(20) NOT NULL,
        address CHAR(40),
        netaddress CHAR(30),
        phone CHAR(14)
);
```

Create a new table called Reviewer. Note that the creation of separate tables for Person and Reviewer raises the *referential integrity* problem—the user is responsible for each Reviewer containing valid person_no and expertise keys:

```
CREATE TABLE Reviewer
(
        person_no INTEGER NOT NULL,
        expertise INTEGER
);
```

Similarly, in the type Paper, the set-valued property authors will require an additional table to be created, which must contain valid papno and author_no fields:

```
CREATE TABLE Paper
(
        title CHAR(50) NOT NULL,
        papno INTEGER NOT NULL UNIQUE,
        prim  INTEGER,
        sec   INTEGER,
        status CHAR(10) NOT NULL
);

CREATE TABLE P_Author
(
        papno INTEGER NOT NULL,
        author_no INTEGER NOT NULL );
```

Extensional functions carry over more directly, merely using keys rather than object references:

```
CREATE TABLE reviewersOf
(
      papno INTEGER NOT NULL,
      reviewer_no INTEGER
);
```

To find the titles of all the papers Russell is reviewing, the mechanism of the relational joins has to be spelled out in the relational query. For example, using the IN construct as before:

```
SELECT title
FROM Person, Paper
WHERE name = 'Russell' AND
      person_no IN
         (SELECT reviewer_no
          FROM reviewersOf
          WHERE reviewersOf.papno = Paper.papno
         );
```

5. Programming Language Interfaces

A result of adopting a language based on SQL would be that embedded OSQL could readily be used as a possible programming interface which would be uniform across several programming languages. For the longer term, we expect some languages to develop their own native interfaces to object databases. Indeed, the object concept is important enough that it transcends individual languages and is likely to become very widely used, and to be the cornerstone of inter-language communication with its definitions of shared types and functional interfaces.

Since a database system is the classic means of managing sharable information, there is a great need for language and database people to combine to agree on some common denominator among the variants of the object concept before it is too late. Apart from the management of shared persistent storage, including transaction management, concurrency control, and recovery, database systems have traditionally offered optimized means of accessing and manipulating large quantities of data in certain interrelated data structures, in ways not directly provided in programming languages. Thus in our view the long-term task of language design goes far beyond the support of database object references as though they were memory pointers, and needs to include the higher-level functionality of database systems such as a general treatment of collections of objects and relationships between objects, retrieval specified by predicates, multiple views of objects, and (in the future, to achieve acceptable performance) inferencing within the database system. This again calls for a sharing of the experience and creative ability of database and language people to give us a hope of a workable solution.

6. Conclusion

The search for a suitable interface for a common Object Data Base model yielded the previously unsuspected result that a reinterpretation and extension of SQL offered as good a solution as any, besides having evolutionary advantages. The foundations of the proposed language OSQL have been described, and illustrated with examples and comparisons which show some improvements over SQL.

OSQL also suggests a potential evolutionary growth path for SQL. It is possible to use a subset of OSQL which is very similar to SQL, or to begin to make sparing use of new features such as the implicit keys, or to move to a style which takes full advantage of intensional and nested functions in queries. Some of the new features of OSQL could be supported in a straightforward way on a relational system, while others would require a more ambitious object manager. Migration is never easy, but the OSQL approach should smooth the path for migration of both users and programs from SQL to the object world.

Acknowledgements

The contributions of Tim Connors, Peter Lyngbaek, Thomas Ryan, and Ming-Chien Shan to the design of OSQL for Iris are gratefully acknowledged. Charles Hoch implemented OSQL embedded in Lisp. Thomas Ryan had also implemented an earlier interactive interface to Iris in C, and I borrowed freely from his code in implementing interactive OSQL. The example application was originally written for the previous Iris interface by Rafi Ahmed.

References

[ANSI 86]

American National Standards Institute.   Database Language SQL. ANSI X3.135-1986.

[Bancilhon et al. 87]

Bancilhon, F., Briggs, T., Khoshafian, S., and Valduriez, P. FAD, a Powerful and Simple Database Language. Proc. 13th VLDB, Brighton. 1987.

[Beech, Feldman & Johnson 82]

Beech, D., Feldman, J.S., and Johnson, M.S. A Database Language for the Integrated Data Model. Computer Science Laboratory, HP Laboratories. December, 1982.

Beech 87a]

Beech, D. Groundwork for an Object Database Model. In: Shriver, B. and Wegner, P. (eds.) Research Directions in Object-Oriented Languages. MIT Press, 1987.

Beech 87b]

Beech, D. Intensional Concepts in a Database Programming Language. Proc. Roscoff Workshop on Database Programming Languages. Altair, Le Chesnay. 1987.

Beech & Mahbod 88]

Beech, D., and Mahbod, B. Generalized Version Control in an Object-Oriented Database. Proc. 4th Intl. Conf. on Data Engineering. IEEE, 1988.

[Bobrow *et al.* 87]

Bobrow, D.. DeMichiel, L.G., Gabriel, R.P., Keene, S.E., Kiczales, G., and Moon, D.A. Common Lisp Object System Specification. (87-002 Draft). Sept. 1987.

[Chen 76]

Chen, P.P.-S. The Entity-Relationship Model—Toward a Unified View of Data. ACM Trans. on Database Systems. March, 1976.

[Codd 70]

Codd, E.F. A Relational Model of Data for Large Shared Data Banks. *Comm. ACM* 13:6 (1970 June), 377-387.

[Cox 86]

Cox, B. Object-Oriented Programming—An Evolutionary Approach. Addison-Wesley, 1986.

[Dahl, Myrhaug & Nygaard 70]

Dahl, O.-J., Myrhaug, B., and Nygaard, K. SIMULA Common Base Language. Norwegian Computing Centre S-22. Oslo, 1970.

[Date 87]

Date, C.J. A Guide to the SQL Standard. Addison-Wesley, 1987.

[Dayal & Dittrich 86]

Dayal, U. and Dittrich, K.R. (eds.) Proc. Intl. Workshop on Object-Oriented Database Systems, Asilomar, CA. Sept. 1986.

[Elmasri & Wiederhold 81]

Elmasri, R. and Wiederhold, G.: GORDAS: A Formal High-Level Query Language for the Entity-Relationship Model. In Chen, P.P.S. (ed): *Entity-Relationship Approach to Information Modeling and Analysis*, ER Institute, 1981.

[Fishman *et al.* 87]

Fishman, D.H., Beech, D., Cate, H.P., Chow, E.C., Connors, T., Davis, J.W., Derrett, N., Hoch, C.G., Kent, W., Lyngbaek, P., Mahbod, B., Neimat, M.A., Ryan, T.A., and Shan, M.C. Iris: An Object-Oriented Database Management System. *ACM Transactions on Office Information Systems* 5:1 (January 1987), 48-69.

[Goldberg & Robson 83]

Goldberg, A. and Robson, D. *Smalltalk-80: The Language and its Implementation*. Addison-Wesley (1983).

[Held, Stonebraker & Wong 75]

Held, G., Stonebraker, M.R., and Wong, E. INGRES—A Relational Data Base System. Proc AFIPS NCC, 1975.

[IEEE 85]

IEEE. Database Engineering, 8:4. Special Issue on Object-Oriented Systems. December, 1985.

[Khoshafian & Copeland 86]]

Khoshafian, S., and Copeland, G. Object Identity. Proc. OOPSLA, Portland, OR. Sept. 1986.

[Landis 86]

Landis, G.S. Design Evolution and History in an Object-Oriented CAD/CAM Database. Proc. IEEE Compcon86. March 1986.

[Maier et al. 86]

Maier, D., Stein, J., Otis, A., and Purdy, A. Development of an Object-Oriented DBMS. Proc. OOPSLA, Portland, OR. Sept. 1986.

[Shipman 81]

Shipman. D. W. The Functional Data Model and the Data Language DAPLEX. ACM Transactions on Database Systems, Vol 6, No 1, March, 1981.

[Stroustrup 86]

Stroustrup, B. The C++ Programming Language. Addison-Wesley, 1986.

COL: A LOGIC-BASED LANGUAGE FOR COMPLEX OBJECTS[1]

Serge Abiteboul, Stephane Grumbach

I.N.R.I.A.

78153 Le Chesnay, FRANCE

abitebou@inria.inria.fr

grumbach@bdblues.inria

Abstract: A logic-based language for manipulating complex objects constructed using set and tuple constructors is introduced. A key feature of the language is the use of base and derived data functions. Under some stratification restrictions, the semantics of programs is given by a canonical minimal and causal model that can be computed using a finite sequence of fixpoints. Applications of the language to procedural data, semantic database models, heterogeneous databases integration, and datalog query evaluation are presented.

INTRODUCTION

Two approaches have been followed for defining manipulation languages for complex objects: (1) an algebraic approach [AB,ABi,FT,SS and many others], and (2) a calculus approach [J,AB,RKS]. Recently, there has been some interest in pursuing a so-called logic programming approach [BK,AG,Be+,K]. This is the approach followed here.

The *Complex Object Language* (COL) based on recursive rules is presented. This language is an extension of datalog (Horn clauses without function symbols) which permits the manipulation of complex objects obtained using tuple and (heterogeneous) set constructors. The originality of the approach is that besides the base and derived relations, base and derived "data functions" are considered. As we shall see, data functions are either defined extensionally (base data functions) or intentionally (derived data functions).

Data functions are natural tools to manipulate complex objects. Data functions present other advantages as well:

(i)   Since queries can be viewed as data functions, the inelegant dichotomy between data and queries of the relational model disappear. In particular, queries can be stored in the database as data functions. The model therefore permits the manipulation of procedural data [S].

---

[1] This research was supported in part by the Projet de Recherches Coordonnees BD3.

(ii)   In COL, data can be viewed both in a functional and in a relational manner. As a consequence, the language can be used in a heterogeneous database context (e.g., relational view on a functional data base; integration of a relational database with a functional one).

(iii) COL can also be used as a kernel language for semantic database models like SDM [HM], IFO [AH1] or Daplex [Sh].

(iv)   Some evaluation techniques for datalog queries like Magic Sets or others [B+,GM] make extensive use of particular functions. These functions can be formalized using our model.

The language COL is based on a clausal logic. The database consists of facts concerning both the predicates, and the data functions. New facts can be deduced using rules. The use of monovalued data functions in COL yields consistency problems which are studied in [AH3]. To simplify the presentation, we restrict here our formal presentation of the language to multivalued data functions. (However, some of the examples that are presented also use monovalued data functions.)

The present paper is devoted essentially to an informal presentation of the language. A detailed description of the theoretical foundations can be found in [AG]. The treatment of monovalued data functions is the object of a separate paper [AH3].

A COL program consists of facts and rules. Its semantics is given in terms of minimal models as it is standard for instance in datalog, or in datalog with negation. Unfortunately, because of sets and data functions, some programs may have more than one minimal models. A stratification in the spirit of the stratification introduced by [ABW,G,N and others] is used. It is shown in [AG] that for stratified programs, a canonical *causal* [BH] and *minimal* model of a given program can be computed using a sequence of fixpoints of operators. We briefly sketch here the stratification, and the fixpoint semantics.

Like in [ABW,G,N...], we allow negations in the body of rules. The stratification is necessary to handle such negations. We shall see that negation can be simulated using data functions.

As mentioned above, two other approaches have been independently followed to obtain a rule-based language for complex objects [Be+,K]. In [Be+], they do not insist on a strict typing of objects. In [K], only one level of nesting is tolerated. However, both approaches could easily be adapted to the data structures considered in this paper. Furthermore, in [AB], it is argued that all these approaches yield essentially the same power (i.e., the power of the safe calculus of [AB]). The points (i-iv) above clearly indicate advantages of our approach.

The paper is organized as follows. In the first section, types and typed objects are described. Motivations and examples of programs are given in Section 2. Advantages of the language are considered in a third section. The fourth section is devoted to a brief presentation of the formal basis of the language. Section 5 deals with stratification and the fixpoint semantics. Conclusions are given in a last section.

1. PRELIMINARIES

In this section, types and typed objects are described.

The existence of some *atomic types* is assumed. A set of *values* is associated with each type A. This set is called the *domain* of A, and denoted dom(A). To simplify the presentation, we assume that for each types A and B distinct, $dom(A) \cap dom(B) = \emptyset$. More complex types and objects are obtained in the following way.

Definition: if $T_1,...,T_n$ are types ($n \geq 1$), then

(i) $T=[T_1,...,T_n]$ is a (tuple) *type*, and $dom(T) = \{ [a_1,...,a_n] \mid \forall\ i,\ 1 \leq i \leq n,\ a_i \in dom(T_i) \}$.

(ii) $T=\{T_1,...,T_n\}$ is a (set) *type*, and $dom(T) = \{ \{a_1,...,a_m\} \mid m \geq 0,\ \forall\ i,\ 1 \leq i \leq m,\ \exists\ j,\ 1 \leq j \leq n,\ a_i \in dom(T_j) \}$.

Note that objects of a given type can be seen as particular trees of bounded depth. Most of the results of the paper would still hold if the strict typing policy is replaced by a weaker condition which guarantees the boundedness of object trees. Note also that the language allows the manipulation of heterogeneous sets. For instance, if CAR and PLANE are two types, then, for instance, {747, Concorde, Le Car, Mustang} is an object of type {CAR, PLANE}. However, our types are more restricted than types in [AH2,HY,KV] which use a "union of types" constructor. For instance, pairs with atomic first coordinate of type CAR, and second coordinate of type PLANE or CAR, are not considered. On the other hand, the type corresponding to sets of such pairs (i.e., {[CAR,PLANE], [CAR,CAR]}) can be used. Since we are mainly interested in sets of objects, this limitation is not too severe. Furthermore, the language COL could be extended in a simple way to handle such types.

For each type T, the existence of an infinite set $\{x_T,\ y_T...\}$ of *variables* of that type is assumed. When the type of a variable x_T is understood, or when this type is not relevant to the discussion, the variable is simply denoted x.

2. INFORMAL PRESENTATION AND EXAMPLES

In this section, we informally introduce the language COL. We present motivations, and illustrate various aspects of the language with examples.

As mentioned in the introduction, the two main approaches that have been followed for developing languages for complex objects, are an algebraic approach and a calculus one. Systems are now available (see, [D] or [V]). However, from our experience, the access languages that they provide are very hard to use. Furthermore, we do not believe that SQL extensions along the lines of [Pi] or [RKB], although quite inspiring, could be practical to use. It is therefore interesting to investigate alternatives. Three independent proposals for using a logic programming approach have been recently made [K,Be+,AG]. We elaborate here on one of these proposals [AG].

The first question is probably: why a logic programming approach? The recursion does not seem to be central to applications requiring heavy use of complex objects. Indeed, the major advantages of this approach are probably the use of constructed terms (conventional in logic programming). We will try to convince the reader that the logic-programming style fits naturally the context of complex objects. Furthermore, logic programming offers a sound mathematical ground.

Besides this logic programming aspect that is shared by [K,Be+], we emphasize the use of data functions. Functions play a crucial role in functional data models like [BF,Sh] and in many semantic database models (see [HK]). Their absence from the relational model together with their natural importance lead to the introduction and heavy use of functional dependencies. We believe that functions are essential in a complex objects context. Indeed, set grouping in [Be+] is introducing functions in some hidden ways. In COL, data functions (based or derived) are first class citizens.

Predicate and data functions are in capital letters. To distinguish them, data functions are in italic. (For instance, SPOUSE may denote a binary relations, and *SPOUSE* a data function.)

A COL program consists of an *extensional* part and an *intentional* one. The extensional part, also called the *database*, contains *facts*:

PARENT("toto","lulu");
ADDRESS("toto","paris","france");
FRIENDS("lulu") ∋ "zaza";
FRIENDS("lulu") ∋ "mimi";
BEST_FRIEND("lulu") = "dede".

The first two facts concern the relations PARENT and ADDRESS. The next two relate to the multivalued data function *FRIENDS*, and the last one to the monovalued data function *BEST_FRIEND*. Note that a fact about a multivalued data function gives a member of the image of the function for some value, whereas a fact about a mono-valued data function gives the image for some value.

The intentional part is formed of rules which permit the deduction of new facts:

FRIEND(x,y) ← *FRIENDS(y)* ∋ x;

FRIENDS(x) ∋ *BEST_FRIEND(x)* ←;

CHILDREN_FRIENDS(y) ∋ x ← PARENT(y,z), *FRIENDS(z)* ∋ x.

The first rule defines the predicate FRIEND. The second rule states that the best friend of somebody is also a friend of that person. Finally, the last one intentionally defines the data function *CHILDREN_FRIENDS*. For instance, the fact

FRIENDS("lulu") ∋ "dede";

CHILDREN_FRIENDS("toto") ∋ "zaza"

can be deduced from the facts and the rules above. If nothing else is in the database, then we can deduce that

$$CHILDREN\_FRIENDS(\text{"toto"}) = \{\text{"zaza"},\text{"mimi"},\text{"dede"}\}.$$

Similarly, we will deduce that *CHILDREN_FRIENDS*("zaza") is the empty set.

The semantics of a program will define extensions to the base and derived predicates and data functions. Examples of queries to the above program are FRIEND(x,"toto")?. Intuitively, the answer to such a query is the set of x such that FRIEND(x,"toto") holds. Similarly, one can ask the same query using *FRIENDS*("toto") ∋ x? which can be abbreviated to *FRIENDS*("toto")?.

We next present motivating examples of COL programs. One of the two object constructors of the language is a set constructor. The language therefore allows the manipulation of sets.

Example 2.1 (sets):

The predicates ∋ and = belong to the language. It is possible to define other predicates like ⊆, DISJOINT, DISJOINT-UNION and UNION, or functions like ∪, ∩ and *DIFFERENCE*. The following rules define the functions ∩, ∪, and *DIFFERENCE*:

var x: int; X,Y: {int};

∩(X,Y) ∋ x ← X ∋ x, ∋ x Y; ·

∪(X,Y) ∋ x ← X ∋ x;

∪(X,Y) ∋ x ← Y ∋ x;

DIFFERENCE(X,Y) ∋ x ← X ∋ x, ¬(Y ∋ x).

Intuitively, the functions ∩, ∪ and *DIFFERENCE* define sets by stating explicitly what are the elements of each set. Thus the term ∩(X,Y) for instance is interpreted as the set of all the elements x such that X ∋ x and Y ∋ x. Using these functions, the predicates ⊆, ⊂, DISJOINT, UNION and DISJOINT-UNION are now defined:

⊆(X,Y) ← ∪(X,Y) = Y,

⊂(X,Y) ← ⊆(X,Y), *DIFFERENCE*(Y, X) ∋ x,

DISJOINT(X,Y) ← ∩(X,Y) = ∅,

UNION(X,Y,∪(X,Y)) ←,

DISJOINT-UNION(X,Y,∪(X,Y)) ← DISJOINT(X,Y).

The language allows the manipulation of complex objects, and also of "nested relations" [ABi,FT,JS,...] which are special cases of complex objects. Our next example illustrates the manipulation of such objects.

Example 2.2 (nested relations):

Consider the predicate R(int,int,int) and the three predicates S(int,{[int,int]}), S'(int,{[int,int]}), S''(int,{[int,int]}). (The first field of S, S' and S'' contains an integer, and the second a binary relation.) Let F and TC be functions of the appropriate types.

> var Z: {[int,int]}; y, y', z: int;

Unnest:

> R(x,y,y') ← S(x,Z), Z ∋ [y,y'];

Nest:

> F(x) ∋ [y,y'] ← R(x,y,y');
>
> S'(x,F(x)) ← R(x,y,y');

Transitive closure of the second field of S':

> TC(Z) ∋ [x,z] ← Z ∋ [x,z];
>
> TC(Z) ∋ [x,z] ← Z ∋ [x,y], TC(Z) ∋ [y,z];
>
> S''(x,TC(Z)) ← S'(x,Z).

The language allows the manipulation of heterogeneous sets. This is illustrated in the next example:

Example 2.3 (heterogeneous sets):

Consider the following typed symbols:

• P({{int,string}}) (i.e., P is a unary predicate, and its unique field contains a set of sets of integers and strings).

- F is a function of type $\{int,string\} \rightarrow \{int\}$;

- $Q(\{\{int\}\})$; and

- H a function of type $\{\{int,string\}\} \rightarrow \{\{int\}\}$.

The following program filters the integers from P:

var V: $\{\{int,string\}\}$; W: $\{int,string\}$;
$F(W) \ni x \leftarrow P(V), V \ni W, W \ni x$;
$H(V) \ni F(W) \leftarrow P(V), V \ni W$;
$Q(H(V)) \leftarrow P(V)$.

To conclude this section, we present two simple examples to illustrate the use of recursion and of data functions.

Example 2.4 (ancestors):

Let PARENT(string,string) be a predicate. Let *ANCESTOR* be a function of type: string $\rightarrow \{string\}$. Then we can use the following rules:

var u, v, w: string;
$ANCESTOR(v) \ni u \leftarrow PARENT(u,v)$
$ANCESTOR(v) \ni u \leftarrow ANCESTOR(v) \ni w, PARENT(u,w)$.

Example 2.5 (father of wife of somebody's best friend):

Suppose that we are in a purely relational context. Then, we have, for instance, relations PARENT, MALE, SPOUSE, and BEST_FRIEND. We can use the following derived relations:

WIFE(u,v) $\leftarrow$ SPOUSE(u,v), MALE(v);
FATHER(u,v) $\leftarrow$ PARENT(u,v), MALE(u).

To obtain the father of the wife of joe's best friend, we have

(i)   to define the predicate

$$RESULT(w) \leftarrow FATHER(w,u), WIFE(u,v), BEST\_FRIEND(v,"joe").$$

(ii)   to ask the query RESULT(w)?.

Now suppose that we have data functions, *BEST_FRIEND*, *SPOUSE*, and relations PARENT and MALE. The following data functions can been defined:

$WIFE(u) = SPOUSE(u) \leftarrow MALE(u);$

$FATHER(u) = v \leftarrow PARENT(v,u), MALE(v).$

To obtain the father of the wife of joe's best friend, it suffices to ask the query

$$FATHER(WIFE(BEST\_FRIEND("joe")))?.$$

As shown in this last example, join can sometimes be replaced by function composition. This presents the following advantages:

- it is easier to formulate certain queries, and understand them at a logical level,

- the answer to the query can be evaluated more easily since the query compiler can use the extra information provided by data functions, and

- it is known that the result is unique.

To illustrate a subtlety in the manipulation of monovalued functions, suppose that the wife function is derived from the SPOUSE relation instead of a *SPOUSE* function. The following rule can be used:

$$WIFE(y) = x \leftarrow MALE(y), SPOUSE(x,y).$$

However, this supposes that each male has at most one spouse (which is some sort of weak monogamy since this is not required to females). In databases which violate the monogamy rule, the function *WIFE* is not well-defined, and the program is not consistent. This type of phenomena is studied in [AH3]. In particular, it is shown there that consistency of COL programs with monovalued data functions is undecidable. However, some decidable restrictions which cover most interesting cases are exhibited.

3. MORE MOTIVATIONS

In this section, we briefly consider advantages of the language. More precisely, we illustrate the following points:

(i)   procedural data;
(ii) heterogeneous databases;
(iii) semantic database models; and
(iv) evaluation techniques for datalog queries.

3.1 Procedural Data

One of the reasons for considering a functional database model versus a relational one is to remove the inelegant dichotomy between data and queries present in the relational model. The removal of that dichotomy is also the motivation for introducing procedural fields in Postgres [S]. However, if the procedural fields solution is interesting as being an extension of the popular relational model, it certainly lacks the elegance of the functional solution. We believe that COL presents the advantages of both approaches by first being a relational extension, and also by making explicit use of functions to handle procedural-like data. The purpose of this section is to briefly investigate this issue.

Procedural data is introduced in [S] in order to blur the dichotomy between data and queries. Queries can be stored in the database in particular fields (called procedural fields). When the corresponding data is needed, the queries are activated.

Consider the database schema:

R(employee, manager, {hobby}),.

S(employee, {phone}).

Suppose that the company policy is that managers can also be reached at their employees phone numbers. The relation S can be defined intentionally using a function PHO, the facts:

$PHO(John) \ni 5555, PHO(Peter) \ni 6666, PHO(Tom) \ni 7777...$

and using the rules:

$PHO(z) \ni w \leftarrow R(y,z,X), PHO(y) \ni w,$

$S(y,PHO(y)) \leftarrow.$

To continue with the same example, some facts are known on relation R:

R(John, Peter, {chess,football}), R(Peter, Max, {bridge})...

Suppose that it is also known that employee Tom is managed by Peter, and does not have any hobby but the ones of his boss. Then one might want to store the fact:

R(Tom, Peter, HOB(Peter))

where the *HOB* function is defined by:

$HOB(y) \ni x \leftarrow R(y,z,X), X \ni x.$

The data functions therefore brings a lot of flexibility. The query R(John,Peter,X)? is answered by a simple access to the database, whereas the query R(Tom,Peter,X)? can be translated to the query HOB(Peter) $\ni$ x? (if a lazy evaluation strategy is chosen). Furthermore, an update of Peter's hobbies will implicitly modify Tom's ones.

To conclude with this example, assume that it is known that Tom always has for hobbies the hobbies of his current boss. Then one might store the fact:

R(Tom, Peter, $BOSS\_HOB$(Tom))

where the *BOSS_HOB* function is defined by:

$BOSS\_HOB(y) \ni x \leftarrow R(y,z,X), HOB(z) \ni x.$

3.2 Heterogeneous databases

We show how to integrate a relational database, and a functional one into a COL database. It is also possible to use a similar approach to define heterogeneous views when relations and functions are considered, and to restructure a relational database into a functional one, or conversely. We present an example with multivalued functions only since monovalued data functions are not covered in the formal development below. Note that, in general, monovalued functions play a crucial role in this context. Consider the following two databases:

(a) *A RELATIONAL DATABASE:*

SHOW(film,theater,time)
PLAYS(actor,film)
LOCATION(theater,address)

(b) *A FUNCTIONAL DATABASE*

CASTING: film $\rightarrow\rightarrow$ actor
LOCATED: theater $\rightarrow\rightarrow$ address
EXHIB: film $\rightarrow\rightarrow$ theater, time
THEATER: $\rightarrow\rightarrow$ theater
FILM: $\rightarrow\rightarrow$ film

The two database can be integrated, for instance, in the following COL database:

(c) *THE INTEGRATING COL DATABASE*

The schema consists of the following:
GLOB_THEA(theater, address)
*GLOB*_INFO: theater $\rightarrow\rightarrow$ film, time
GLOB_FILM(film,{actor})

The integrating program is as follows:

GLOB_THEA(t,a) $\leftarrow$ LOCATION(t,a)
GLOB_THEA(t,a) $\leftarrow$ *THEATER*( ) $\ni$ t, LOCATED(t) $\ni$ a

ACTSIN(f) $\ni$ a $\leftarrow$ PLAYS(a,f)
ACTSIN(f) $\ni$ a $\leftarrow$ *CASTING*(f) $\ni$ a
GLOB_FILM(f,*ACTSIN*(f)) $\leftarrow$ PLAYS(a,f)
GLOB_FILM(f,*ACTSIN*(f)) $\leftarrow$ *FILM*( ) $\ni$ f

GLOB_INFO(t) $\ni$ [f,h] $\leftarrow$ SHOW(f,t,h)
GLOB_INFO(t) $\ni$ [f,h] $\leftarrow$ *EXHIB*(f) $\ni$ [t,h]

3.3 Semantic Database Modelling

The field of semantic database models (see, [HK] for a survey) has been primarily concerned with structures and semantics, and with notable exceptions like Daplex [Sh], language aspects have not been studied in depth. The COL language presents the advantages of dealing with complex objects, and of handling both data functions, and data relations. A consequence is that the language is quite suited to semantic database models.

In this section, we consider an example taken from the IFO model [AH1], and investigate what is still missing in the COL language to make it a language for the IFO model. The IFO model has been chosen here because it incorporates most structural aspects of semantic database models: it is an object-based model, with aggregation (tuple constructor), classification (set constructor), functions, specialization and generalization. Furthermore, the IFO model has been formally defined, which simplifies the investigation.

A first difficulty that is encountered comes from IFO nested functions. In IFO, the result of a function can itself be a function. Since this is a very peculiar aspect of IFO, we do not consider this feature here. We concentrate on an example given in [AH1] without nested function. The schema is shown in Figure 3.1. We present a corresponding COL database. We then discuss extensions of the language that need to be considered, and the limitations of the COL representation:

ABSTRACT TYPES are represented by basic domains:

    hull

    car

    person

    motor

    manufacturer

CONSTRUCTED TYPES are represented by base predicates:

    MOTORBOAT(hull,motor)

    CAR-ID(car,integer)

FUNCTIONS:

    OWNS: person $\rightarrow$ {[hull,motor],car}

    C-ID: car $\rightarrow$ [string,integer]

    M-ID: motor $\rightarrow$ [manufacturer,string]

    H-ID: hull $\rightarrow$ string

    PASSENGER-CAPACITY: [hull,motor] $\rightarrow$ integer

    PASSENGER-CAPACITY: car $\rightarrow$ integer

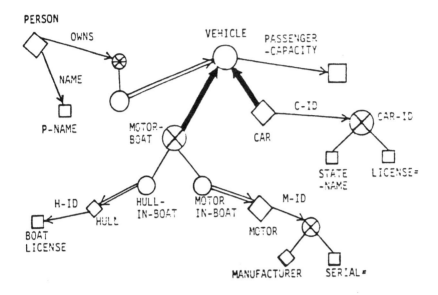

Figure 3.1: an IFO schema

NAME: person → string

A problem is posed by limitations of COL that were already mentioned: the type VEHICLE (i.e., either a MOTOR-BOAT or a CAR) can not be described, which yields a typing problem for the function *PASSENGER-CAPACITY*. As mentioned above, this problem can be overcome by considering simple extensions of the COL language. The introduction of *names* instead of the use of the numbering of tuple fields would be a simple modification of the language that would bring it closer to the IFO model.

Perhaps a more fundamental issue is that there is no explicit way of formulating ISA relationships. An extension of the language in that direction should be considered.

3.4 Evaluation of Datalog Queries

It is not our purpose here to explain yet another technique for evaluating datalog queries. We only want to hint that the COL language provides a nice formalism for studying such questions. We briefly consider the method of [GM]. Their proposal is to rewrite the relational system of equations used in a datalog query as a functional system of equations. Consider the famous Ancestor example:

$$ANC(x,y) \leftarrow PAR(x,y);$$
$$ANC(x,y) \leftarrow PAR(x,z), ANC(z,y).$$

Let us introduce the following three rules:

$$F_{PAR}(y) \ni x \leftarrow PAR(x,y);$$
$$F_{ANC}(y) \ni x \leftarrow F_{PAR}(y) \ni x;$$
$$F_{ANC}(y) \ni x \leftarrow F_{PAR}(z) \ni x, F_{ANC}(y) \ni z.$$

Now if the query ANC(x,Tom)? is given, one can compute instead F_{ANC}(Tom) (i.e., answer the query F_{ANC}(Tom) $\ni$ x?). In other words, a relational equation has been transformed into a functional equation:

$$F_{ANC} = F_{PAR} + F_{PAR} \circ F_{ANC}$$

where "+" stands for union and "$\circ$" for the composition of multivalued functions.

In another proposal for evaluating datalog queries [B+], namely the magic sets approach, particular terms called "grouping terms" are used. It is easy to see that these terms correspond to particular derived data functions.

4. A BRIEF FORMAL PRESENTATION

In this section, the complex object language is defined. We assume standard knowledge of logic programming such as in [L].

The *language L* of the underlying logic is first defined. This language is based on a typed alphabet containing: typed constants and variables; connectors and quantifiers $\wedge$, $\vee$, $\neg$, $\Rightarrow$, $\exists$, $\forall$; typed equality ($=_T$), and ownership ($\ni_{T,S}$) predicate symbols; typed predicate symbols; and typed function symbols of three kinds:

- data functions,
- tuple functions $[]_{T1,...,Tn}$,
- set functions $\{\}_{T1,...,Tn}$.

Terms of the form $[]_{T1,...,Tn}(a_1,...,a_n)$, will be denoted by $[a_1,...,a_n]$; and terms of the form $\{\}_{T1,...,Tn}(a_1,...,a_m)$ by $\{a_1,...,a_m\}$. The set function has an arbitrary (but finite) number of arguments. Clearly, that function could be replaced by a binary function set-cons and a particular symbol, say $\varnothing$, for the empty set. For instance, $\{\}_{T1,...,Tn}(a_1,...,a_m)$ would stand for

$$\text{set-cons}_{T1,...,Tn}(a_1,\text{set-cons}_{T1,...,Tn}(a_2,\text{set-cons}_{T1,...,Tn}(a_m,\varnothing))).$$

In the remainder of the paper, the word "function" will only refer to data functions, and not to tuple or set functions. It is assumed that all the functions that are considered in the following are set-valued, i.e., an image by a data function is always a set.

Note that $\ni_{T,S}$ is a symbol of the language. Clearly, $\ni_{T,S}$ is interpreted by the classical ownership of set theory. Indeed, when the types are understood, $\ni_{T,S}$ is simply denoted by $\ni$. A constant of a certain type T is interpreted as an element of dom(T).

TERMS: A constant or a variable is a *term*. If $t_1,...,t_n$ are terms and F is an n-ary data, tuple or set function symbol, $F(t_1,...,t_n)$ is a *term*. (The obvious restrictions on types are of course imposed.) A *closed term* is a term with neither variables, nor data functions.

Example 4.1: The term $[1,\{2,3\},\{7\}]$ is a closed term. On the other, $[1,\{2,3\},F(2)]$ is not closed. These two terms are different, but they may have the same interpretation (if $F(2) = \{7\}$).

LITERALS: Let R be an n-ary predicate, and $t_1,...,t_n$ terms. Then (with the obvious typing restrictions) $R(t_1,...,t_n)$, $t_1 = t_2$, and $t_2 \ni t_1$ are *positive literals*. If ψ is a positive literal, $\neg\psi$ is a *negative literal*. An *atom* is a literal of the form $R(t_1,...t_n)$ or $F(t_2,...,t_n) \ni t_1$. If $t_1,...,t_n$ are closed terms, the atom is said to be *closed*.

Arbitrary well-formed formulas are defined from literals in the usual way. We have defined here the language of a first order logic. One can define a model theory and a proof theory for this language. This is not in the scope of the present paper. We next introduce a clausal logic based on this first order logic.

RULES and PROGRAMS: A *rule* is an expression of the form $A \leftarrow L_1,...,L_n$ where the *body* $L_1,...,L_n$ is a conjunction of *literals*; and the *head* A is an *atom* (and so contains no equality predicate). A *program* is a finite set of rules.

Example 4.2: consider the following program P_0:

R(1,2,3) ← ;
R(1,3,5) ← ;
$F(x) \ni [y,y'] \leftarrow R(x,y,y')$;
$S(x,F(x)) \leftarrow R(x,y,y')$.

In this program, the predicate R is extensionally defined, whereas the function F and the predicate S are intentionally defined.

In datalog, rules are used to specify the extension of derived predicates. Consider the third rule above. The predicate in the left hand side of the rule is $\ni$ which is interpreted by the set membership. In fact, the rule is used to specify the <u>data function</u> F and not the extension of a predicate.

We are interested by Herbrand-like models of our programs. Let P be a program. The *universe* U_p is formed of all the closed terms which can be built from the constants of the program. The *base* B_p is the set of all <u>closed atoms</u> formed from the predicate and function symbols appearing in P and the closed terms of U_p. An *interpretation* of a program P is a finite subset of the base B_p.

Continuing with the example above, we have:

Example 4.2 (continued): An interpretation of the program P_0 is:
$$I = \{ R(1,2,3), R(1,3,5), F(1) \ni [2,3], F(1) \ni [3,5], S(1,\{[2,3],[3,5]\}) \}.$$

It should be noted that elements in the base (and thus, in the interpretation) have very simple form. In particular, literals like $F(2) = \{3,4,5\}$ or $G(2) \ni F(2)$ are not in the base since they are not closed atoms.

In order to define the notion of satisfaction of a rule, and thus of a program, the concept of valuation is introduced. Valuations play here the role of substitution in classical logic programming.

VALUATION: Let θ be a <u>ground</u> substitution of the variables, and I an interpretation. The corresponding *valuation* θ_I is a function from the set of terms to the set of closed terms defined by[2]:

(i) θ_I is the identity for constants, and $\theta_I x = \theta x$ for each variable,

(ii) $\theta_I[t_1,...,t_n] = [\theta_I t_1,...,\theta_I t_n]$, $\theta_I\{t_1,...,t_n\} = \{\theta_I t_1,...,\theta_I t_n\}$, and

(iii) $\theta_I F(t_1,...,t_n) = \{ a \mid [F(\theta_I t_1,...,\theta_I t_n) \ni a] \in I \}$.

The function θ_I is extended to literals by:

(iv) $\theta_I P(t_1,...,t_n) = P(\theta_I t_1,...,\theta_I t_n)$,

(v) $\theta_I(t_1=t_2) = (\theta_I t_1 = \theta_I t_2)$, $\theta_I(t_2 \ni t_1) = (\theta_I t_2 \ni \theta_I t_1)$, and

(vi) $\theta_I(\neg A) = \neg \theta_I A$.

---

[2] The reader has to be aware of a subtlety in (iii). The symbol $\ni$ in $[F(\theta_I t_1,...,\theta_I t_n) \ni a]$ is a symbol of the language COL, whereas the symbol $\in$ denotes the usual membership of set theory.

A valuation in this context depends on the interpretation that is considered. This comes from the need to assign values to terms built using function symbols. As we shall see, this is a major reason for the non monotonicity of the operators that will be associated to COL programs.

Using valuations, we now define the notion of *satisfaction* of rules and programs:

SATISFACTION: The notion of satisfaction (denoted by $\models$) and its negation (denoted by $\not\models$) are defined by:

For each closed positive literal, $I \models P(b_1,...,b_n)$ iff $P(b_1,...,b_n) \in I$; $I \models b_1 = b_2$ iff $b_1 = b_2$ is a tautology; and $I \models b_2 \ni b_1$ iff $b_1 \in b_2$ is a tautology.

- For each closed negative literal $\neg B$, $I \models \neg B$ iff $I \not\models B$.

- Let $r = A \leftarrow L_1,...,L_m$. Then $I \models r$ iff for each valuation θ_I such that for each i, $I \models \theta_I L_i$, then $I \models \theta_I A$.

- For each program P, $I \models P$ iff for each rule r in P, $I \models r$.

MODELS: A *model* M of P is an interpretation which satisfies P. A model M of P is *minimal* iff for each model N of P, $N \subseteq M \Rightarrow N = M$.

Example 4.2 (end): The interpretation I_0 is a model of P_0. Furthermore, I_0 is minimal.

A given COL program may have more than one minimal model. This of course arises because of the use of negation. However, even COL programs without negation may have more than one minimal model as illustrated by the following example:

Example 4.3: Consider the program:

$$F \ni 1; \quad p(F); \quad q(2); \quad q(1) \leftarrow p(\{1\}).$$

Then $\{F \ni 1, p(\{1\}), q(1), q(2)\}$ and $\{F \ni 1, F \ni 2, p(\{1,2\}), q(2)\}$ are two incomparable minimal models.

We want to give the semantics of programs in terms of minimal models. The previous example illustrates a problem that arises for certain program. In the next section, we exhibit a class of programs (the class of "stratified programs") and a choice of minimal models for those programs. Clearly, other classes of programs and other choices may be of interest as well.

5. STRATIFICATION AND FIXPOINT SEMANTICS

The notion of stratification has been used by several authors [ABW, G, N,...] to give a semantics to programs with negations in the body of rules. We present a similar notion for programs allowing complex objects and data functions. We also show how negation can be simulated using sets and data functions.

Some basic notions are first defined.

In a literal $P(t_1,...,t_n)$, the symbol P is the *defined* symbol. Similarly, in a literal $F(t_2,...,t_n) \ni t_1$, F is the *defined* symbol. The *defined symbol of a rule* is the defined symbol of the head of the rule. (This clearly relates to the fact that a rule "$F(t_2,...,t_n) \ni t_1 \leftarrow ...$" does not participate in the definition of the predicate $\ni$, but in that of the function F.)

A symbol which occurs in a rule not as the defined symbol of the head is called *determinant* of the rule.

To define the notion of stratification, we also use the auxiliary concepts of "total" and "partial" determinants of a rule. We say that an occurrence of a determinant predicate P is *partial* in a rule if that occurrence arises in a positive literal. Similarly, the occurrence of a determinant function F in a positive literal $F(t_2,...,t_n) \ni t_1$ is said to be *partial*. A determinant is *partial* (in a rule) if all its occurrences are partial; a determinant is *total* otherwise.

Intuitively, if Y is defined by the rule, and X is a total determinant, then X must be "completely defined" before Y. This is denoted by X < Y. If X is only a partial determinant, then X must be defined no later than Y. This is denoted by X ≤ Y. For each program P, a marked graph G_p is constructed as follows:

* the nodes of G_p are the predicate and function symbols of P,
* there is an edge from X to Y if X ≤ Y, and
* there is a marked edge from X to Y if X < Y.

We are now ready to define the condition for stratification:

Definition: A program P is *stratified* iff the associated graph G_p has no cycle with a marked edge.

If P is stratified, there exists a partition of the rules and therefore of the predicate and function symbols of the program in an ordered sequence of strata such that for each predicate or function symbols X and Y:

* if X ≤ Y, X is in a lower stratum than Y, and
* if X < Y, X is in a strictly lower stratum than Y.

(One can show that for any choice of such sequences, the semantics described below is the same.)

A program is said to be monostratum if there are no symbols X and Y such that $X < Y$, and multistrata otherwise. We illustrate the previous definitions with an example:

Example 5.1:

Consider the following four rules:

$r_1= F(x) \ni y \leftarrow R(x,y);$

$r_2= S(x,F(x)) \leftarrow R(x,y);$

$r_3= F(y) \ni x \leftarrow S(x,Y), Y \ni y;$

$r_4= F(y) \ni x \leftarrow S(y,F(x)).$

The program $\{r_1,r_2\}$ is stratified. For instance, $\{R,F\}$ forms the first stratum and $\{S\}$ the second. The program $\{r_1,r_3\}$ is stratified and is monostratum. On the other hand, $\{r_1,r_2,r_3\}$ and $\{r_4\}$ are not stratified.

We now present intuitively the semantics of stratified programs using a minimal model which is computed using a sequence of fixpoints.

With each program P, we associate an operator T_P. Intuitively, T_P deduces new facts using the rules in P. A crucial aspect is that T_P interprets data functions based on the actual content of the database. These operators are therefore not monotonic in general.

Definition: Let P be a program, and I an interpretation of P. Then a closed term A is the *result of applying the rule* $A' \leftarrow L_1,...,L_m$ *with a valuation* θ_1 if

- $I \models \theta_1 L_i$ for each $i \in [1..m]$, and

- either $A' = P(t_1,...,t_n)$ and $A = P(\theta_1 t_1,...,\theta_1 t_n)$, or $A' = [F(t_2,...,t_n) \ni t_1]$, and $A = [F(\theta_1 t_2,...,\theta_1 t_n) \ni \theta_1 t_1]$.

The operator T_p is defined by: $T_p(I) = \{ A \mid A$ is the result of applying a rule in P with some $\theta_1 \}$.

First suppose that the program P is monostratum. We start with the empty interpretation, apply T_P repeatedly to deduce new facts until saturation. It is proved in [AG] that this yields a model which is the unique minimal model of P. Now consider a multistrata program $\{P_1,...,P_n\}$. Let us start again with the empty interpretation, apply T_{P_1} to derive new facts until saturation, then apply T_{P_2}, etc., until finally, T_{P_n} is applied until saturation. Let I_p be this resulting interpretation. We prove in [AG] that I_p is a minimal model of P. (There may be other minimal models.) We choose that model for semantics of the program P.

This particular choice of semantics may seem arbitrary. However, a similar situation arises in the context of datalog with negation. One can show that the minimal model chosen based on the stratification

* is the least model with respect to some criteria based on priorities among predicate symbols [P]; and

* is a "causal" model [BH].

In our context, similar properties can also be exhibited.

We now illustrate the previous definitions.

Example 5.2:

Consider the following program P:

(a) $R(1,2,3) \leftarrow$;

   $R(1,3,5) \leftarrow$;

   $R(2,2,3) \leftarrow$;

(b) $F(x) \ni [u,v] \leftarrow R(x,u,v);$

(c) $F(x) \ni [u,w] \leftarrow F(x) \ni [u,v], F(x) \ni [v,w];$

(d) $S(x,F(x)) \leftarrow R(x,y,z).$

The program can be stratified in two stratas: $P_1=\{a,b,c\}$ and $P_2=\{d\}$. The following facts can be derived:

T_{P_1} : $R(1,2,3); R(1,4,5); R(2,2,3);$ { using a }

T_{P_1} : $F(1) \ni [2,3]; F(1) \ni [3,5]; F(2) \ni [2,3];$ {using b }

T_{P_1} : $F(1) \ni [2,5];$ { using c }

     --- T_{P_1} cannot derive anything else. ---

T_{P_2} : $S(1,\{[2,3],[3,5],[2,5]\});$ { using d }

     --- T_{P_2} cannot derive anything else. ---

Thus the semantics of this program is described by the following minimal model:

$R(1,2,3); R(1,4,5); R(2,2,3);$

$F(1) \ni [2,3]; F(1) \ni [3,5]; F(2) \ni [2,3]; F(1) \ni [2,5];$

$S(1,\{[2,3],[3,5],[2,5]\}).$

The notion of query is the usual one: a query is a positive literal. Let P be a stratified program and q a query with free variables $x_1,...,x_n$. The answer to query q is defined as:

$$\{ vx_1,...,vx_n \mid v \text{ valuation such that } vq \text{ holds in } I_p \}$$

where I_p is the model of P chosen above. The naive way of computing the answer is to first compute I_p, and then check all valuations. Of course, such algorithm is very inefficient. Techniques have been developed for datalog (see [BR]). Those techniques can clearly be used in our context. New techniques particularly adapted to complex objects have still to be obtained. To illustrate the notion of query, we continue with Example 5.2:

Example 5.2 (end):

Consider the query $F(1) \ni x$?. Then the answers to that query are [2,3]; [3,5]; [2,5]. On the other hand, the answer to the query $S(1,X)$? is {[2,3], [3,5], [2,5]}.

It should be noted that the program in Section 3.1 is not stratified. Indeed, $HOB < R$ because of the statement on employee "Tom", and $R \leq HOB$ because of the HOB defining rule. However, it is clearly possible to give a semantics to such programs. Intuitively, one has to consider a partial order of a set of atoms and terms. For instance, such an order would impose:

$$R(\text{Peter, Max, }\{\text{bridge}\}) < HOB(\text{Peter}) < R(\text{Tom, Peter, }\{\text{bridge}\}).$$

This extension of the stratification is related to the local stratification in the sense of Przymusinski [P]. Furthermore, the definition of boss hobbies is not even locally stratified according to [P]. The complex structure of facts should also be taken into account. For instance, two objects, say A and B, may be both intentionally defined with a subobject of each one of them depending on a subobject of the other. We are currently studying weaker notions of stratification that would capture such situations.

To conclude this section, we present an example to illustrate how negation can be simulated using sets and data functions.

Example 5.3 (negation):

Consider two base unary predicates P and Q, and the following program:

    $R(x) \leftarrow Q(x), \neg P(x)$.

The following equivalent program without negation computes R.

    $F(x) \ni x \leftarrow P(x);$

    $A(x, F(x)) \leftarrow \ ;$

    $R(x) \leftarrow Q(x), A(x,\{\})$.

It should be noted that the literal $A(x,\{\})$ acts here like $\neg P(x)$. Indeed, one can derive the classical stratification requirements for datalog with negation presented, for instance, in [ABW], from the stratification requirements for data functions presented above.

6. CONCLUSION

The paper presents a language to manipulate complex objects based on recursive rules. The novelty is the use of data functions. The semantics of COL programs is defined as a canonical causal and minimal model using a sequence of fixpoint operators. In that sense, the semantics is constructive in nature.

We illustrated the use of the language in various database contexts: heterogeneous databases, semantic modelling, procedural data, and evaluation of datalog queries. This suggested extensions of the language. One of them, namely, single-valued functions, is studied in [AH3]. As mentioned earlier, stratification is a quite restrictive requirement. We are currently considering extensions to stratification. It would be interesting to investigate alternative semantics for COL programs. Besides these issues, important questions are left unanswered such as:

- how to introduce inheritance, and
- how to update COL databases.

Last but not least remains the issue of an efficient implementation. There has been a lot of work on nested relations and complex objects. Few of them have so far been followed by an efficient implementation (e.g., the Verso system at Inria [V], and the Aim project at IBM Heidelberg [D]). We believe that the fixpoint semantics of COL programs makes such an implementation feasible. Indeed, the operators which are described in Section 4 can all be expressed in the algebra of complex objects of [AB]. However, a naive computation of answers to queries is certainly unfeasible. It is therefore crucial to transpose known optimization techniques developed for datalog to the realm of complex objects, and to obtain new techniques tailored to this context. The brief section on datalog evaluation based on COL was meant to suggest that this should not be an impossible task.

ACKNOWLEDGMENT:

The authors wish to thank K. Apt and R. Hull for their suggestions and helpful comments. General discussions on complex objects with C. Beeri also certainly influenced this work.

REFERENCES

[AB]   Abiteboul S., and C. Beeri, On the Manipulation of Complex Objects, abstract in Proc. International Workshop on Theory and Applications of Nested Relations and Complex Objects, Darmstadt (1987)

[ABi] Abiteboul, S., and N. Bidoit, "Non first normal form relations: an algebra allowing data restructuring", in *Journal of Computer Systems and Science* (1986),

[AG] Abiteboul, S., and S. Grumbach, COL: a Logic-Based Language for Complex Objects, Inria Internal Report 714 (1987)

[AH1] Abiteboul S., and Hull, R., "IFO: A formal semantic database model," Proc. ACM SIGACT/SIGMOD Symposium on Principle of Database Systems (1984), to appear in *ACM Transactions on Database Systems.*

[AH2] Abiteboul S., and Hull, R., "Object restructuring in semantic database models," Proc. Intern. Conf. on Database Theory, Roma (1986) to appear in *Theoretical Computer Science*

[AH3] Abiteboul S., and Hull, R., Data Functions, Datalog and Negation, draft

[ABW] Apt, K., H. Blair, A. Walker, Toward a Theory of Declarative Knowledge, Proc. of Workshop on Foundations of Deductive Database and Logic Programming (1986)

[BR] Bancilhon F., R. Ramakrishnan, An Amateur's Introduction to Recursive Query Processing Strategies, ACM SIGMOD Conference on Management of Data, Washington D.C. (1986)

[B+1] Bancilhon F., et al, Magic Sets and Other Strange Ways to Implement Logic Programs, Proc. ACM SIGACT/SIGMOD Symposium on Principles of Database Systems (1986)

[BK] Bancilhon, F., and Khoshafian, S., "A calculus for complex objects, Proc. ACM SIGACT/SIGMOD Symposium on Principle of Database Systems (1985).

[Be+] Beeri, C., et al., Sets and Negation in a Logic Database Language (LDL1), Proc. ACM SIGACT-SIGMOD Symposium on Principle of Database Systems (1987)

[BH] Bidoit, N., R. Hull, Positivism vs. Minimalism in Deductive Databases, proc. ACM SIGACT-SISMOD Symposium on Principles of Database Systems (1986)

[BF] Buneman, P., R.E. Frankel, FQL - a Functional Query Language (preliminary report) proc. ACM SIGMOD conf. on Management of Data (1979)

[D] Dadam, P., History and Status of the Advanced Information Management Prototype, Proc. International Workshop on Theory and Applications of Nested Relations and Complex Objects, Darmstadt (1987)

[FT] Fischer, P., and Thomas, S., Operators for non-first-normal-form relations, Proc. 7th COMPSAC Chicago,(1983).

[GM] Gardarin G., C. de Maindreville, Evaluation of Database Recursive Logic Programs as Recurrent Function Series, proc. ACM SIGMOD conf. on Management of Data (1986)

[G] Van Gelder, A., Negation as Failure Using Tight Derivations for General Logic Programs, Proc. of Workshop on Foundations of Deductive Database and Logic Programming (1986)

[HM]   Hammer M., D. McLeod, Database Description with SDM: a semantic database model, *ACM trans. on Data-base Systems 6,3 (1981)*

[HK]   Hull, R., R. King, Semantic database modeling: Survey, applications, and research issues. U.S.C. Computer Science Technical Report (1986) to appear in ACM computing surveys

[HY]   Hull, R., C.K. Yap, The format model: A theory of database organization. Journal of the ACM 31(3) (1984)

[J]   Jacobs, B., on Database Logic, *Journal of the ACM* (1982).

[JS]   Jaeschke, B., H.J. Schek, Remarks on the algebra of non first normal form relations, Proc. ACM SIGACT/SIGMOD Symposium on Principle of Database Systems, Los Angeles (1982)

[K]   Kuper, G.M., Logic Programming with Sets, Proc. ACM SIGACT/SIGMOD Symposium on Principle of Database Systems (1987)

[KV]   Kuper, G.M., M.Y. Vardi, A new approach to database logic, proc. ACM SIGACT-SIGMOD Symp. on Principles of Database Systems (1984)

[L]   Lloyd, J., Foundations of Logic Programming, Spinger Verlag (1984)

[N]   Naqvi, S.A., A Logic for Negation in Database Systems, Proc. Workshop on Foundations of Deductive Data-bases and Logic Programming ed. J. Minker (1986)

[Pi]   Pistor, P., F. Andersen, Principles for designing a Generalized NF^2 Data Model with an SQL-type Language Interface, IBM Heidelberg (1986)

[P]   Przymusinski, T. C. On the Semantics of Stratified Deductive Databases and Logic Programs, to appear in *Journal of Logic Programming*

[RKS]   Roth, M.A., H.F. Korth, A. Silberschatz, Extended Algebra and Calculus for not 1NF Relational Databases, Technical Report, Department of Computer Science, University of Texas at Austin (1985)

[RKB]   Roth, M.A., H.F. Korth, and D.S. Batory, SQL/NF: A Query Language for ¬ 1NF Relational Databases, Technical Report, Department of Computer Science, University of Texas at Austin (1986)

[SS]   Schek H., and M. Scholl, the Relational Model with relation-valued attributes, in *Information Systems* (1986)

[S]   Stonebraker M., Object Management in Postgres using Procedures, in the Postgres Papers, UCB report (1986)

[Sh]   Shipman, D., The Functional Data Model and the Data Language Daplex, *ACM Transactions on Database Systems.* (1981)

[V]   Verso, J., (pen name for the Verso team), Verso: a Database Machine Based on non-1NF Relations, Inria Internal Report (1986)

A UNIVERSAL RELATION MODEL FOR NESTED RELATIONS

M. Levene and G. Loizou

Department of Computer Science, Birkbeck College, University of London, Malet Street, London WC1E 7HX, U.K.

ABSTRACT

The Universal Relation (UR) model has been researched with the ultimate objective to free the user from logical navigation in a relational database. There have been many different suggestions as to how to implement a UR interface. Nested relations have been recently suggested as a way of extending the applicability of the classical relational model. In this paper we establish a strong connection between the UR model and nested relations. Thus, nested relations are shown to be a suitable internal level for implementing efficiently a UR interface.

1. INTRODUCTION

The Universal Relation (UR) model has been proposed in order to free the user from logical navigation in a relational database. The user views the database as if it were composed of a single relation. Different suggestions have been put forward as to how to implement a UR interface [BB], [MW], [KS], [KKFGU]. Research has been done on comparing these different suggestions [MRW], [MUV], [Ul3], and under what conditions they are similar or equivalent.

Nested relations have been recently suggested as a way of extending the applicability of the classical relational model. Herein we employ the model found in [AB], [OY1] and [RKS] in which nested relations explicitly represent a set of dependencies within their strucutre, and for which an extended algebra allowing null values has been proposed.

In this paper we show a strong connection between the UR model and nested relations. By generalizing the notion of the representative instance [Sa] to nested relations, we get a strong equivalence between a single nested relation and the corresponding UR. We also establish an equivalence between nested relation schemes and γ-acyclic database schemes [Fa2], thus enhancing our results further. This is because γ-acyclic database schemes imply a unique relationship amongst their attributes [BBSK].

We then discuss various extensions of our results. For example, the extension to a nested database at the internal level, which is the topic of another paper. We also extend the UR model to include all three types of null [RKS], and we can further extend it with the representation of functional dependencies in nested relations [OY2].

The remaining sections of the paper are organized as follows. Section 2 introduces the terminology and briefly reviews the UR model and the nested relational model. Section 3 provides the framework within the nested relational model for our main results. Section 4 contains our main results showing that nested relations are a suitable internal level for implementing a UR interface, and in Section 5 we discuss extensions of our model.

2. PRELIMINARIES

2.1. FLAT RELATIONS

Let $U = \{A_1,...,A_p\}$ be the set of universal attributes. Associated with each attribute $A_i \in U$ is a set of atomic values, called the <u>simple domain</u> of A_i, and denoted by $DOM(A_i)$ [Co].

A <u>flat relation</u> (or simply a <u>relation</u>), r, over U is any finite subset of the set of p-tuples in the Cartesian product of the domains.

A <u>flat relation scheme</u> (or simply a <u>relation scheme</u>), R, is a subset of U; R is also said to be in <u>First Normal Form</u> (1NF).

The restriction of $t \in r$ to $X \subseteq U$, denoted by $t[X]$, is a tuple constructed from t by keeping all and only those components that belong to attributes in X.

A <u>flat database scheme</u> (or simply a <u>database scheme</u>) over U is a collection of relation schemes over U, the union of this collection being U. Let $\mathbf{R} = \{R_1,...,R_q\}$ be a database scheme over U, then d = $\{r_1,...,r_q\}$ is a <u>flat database</u> (or simply a <u>database</u>) over $\mathbf{R}$, where each r_i is a relation over R_i, $1 \leq i \leq$ q.

The relational algebra operators [Co] union, intersection, difference, join and projection are, respectively, denoted by $\cup, \cap, -, \bowtie$ and Π. We omit $\cup$ between individual attributes.

2.2. DATA DEPENDENCIES IN FLAT RELATIONS

Let r be a relation over U. We say that r decomposes <u>losslessly</u> onto a database scheme $\mathbf{R}$ if r = $\bowtie_{i=1}^{q} \Pi_{R_i}(r)$. Equivalently, we say r satisfies the <u>join dependency</u> (JD) $\bowtie[\mathbf{R}]$ over U [MMS].

A <u>multivalued dependency</u> (MVD) is a JD with q=2, namely $\bowtie[\{R_1, R_2\}]$ over U [Fa1].

Let $X = R_1 \cap R_2$, $Y = R_1 - R_2$. We use the notation $X \rightarrow\rightarrow Y$ to refer to this MVD. We write X $\rightarrow\rightarrow Y$ (W) to mean $X \rightarrow\rightarrow Y$ in the context of $W \subseteq U$, and, in general, we omit W whenever the context is understood.

Let $W \subseteq U$ and $X \rightarrow\rightarrow Y$ (W), then, if $X \subseteq V \subseteq W$, the <u>projected MVD</u> (PMVD) $X \rightarrow\rightarrow Y \cap V$ (V) holds for V [Fa1].

R is said to be <u>acyclic</u> if $\bowtie[\mathbf{R}]$ is equivalent to a set of MVDs [FMU]. Further characterizations of acyclic database schemes can be found in [BFMY].

Let D be a set of dependencies, and let SAT(D) denote the set of relations over U that satisfy D. We say that D implies a single dependency, d, written in the form of $D \models d$, if and only if (iff) SAT(D) $\subseteq$ SAT(d). A set D_1 of dependencies is equivalent to a set D_2 of dependencies, denoted by $D_1 \equiv D_2$, iff $D_1 \models D_2$ and $D_2 \models D_1$.

A <u>functional dependency</u> (FD) is a statement of the form $X \rightarrow Y$, where $X,Y \subseteq U$. A relation r over U satisfies $X \rightarrow Y$ if every two tuples of r that are equal on X are also equal on Y.

For more details on the theory of dependencies, we refer the reader to [FV], [Ma] and [Ul2].

2.3. NESTED RELATIONS (THE INTERNAL LEVEL)

In this paper we consider a subclass of nested relations, which we call hereinafter simply nested relations.

A scheme tree ,T, defined over a set of atomic attributes $W \subseteq U$, is a tree whose vertices are labelled by pairwise disjoint sets of attributes over W. Following Ozsoyoglu and Yuan [OY1], we can define a nested scheme tree (NRS), R(T), represented by T, and correspondingly an instance of a nested relation, r*, over R(T).

Equivalent definitions of nested relations were given in [AB], [RKS] and [VF], where the corresponding terms format, partitioned normal form and hierarchical nested relation have been used.

We now introduce the notation for scheme trees.

Let T be a scheme tree over a set of atttributes $W \subseteq U$, e = (u,v) be an edge of T, and n be a node of T. Then

(1) ATT(n) is a label for node, n, and is equal to the set of attributes associated with node n;

(2) A(n) is the union of all ATT(v) for all ancestor nodes v of n, including ATT(n);

(3) D(n) is the union of all ATT(v) for all descendant nodes v of n, including ATT(n);

(4) S(T) is the union of all ATT(n) for all nodes n in T;

(5) M(e) is the PMVD represented by the edge e, namely
$A(u) \rightarrow\rightarrow D(v) (A(u) \cup D(u))$;

(6) MVD(T) is the set of PMVDs represented by the edges of T;

(7) ROOT(T) is a function that returns the root node of T.

(Cf. [OY1], [LL1].)

We note that the set of PMVDs represented by the scheme tree, T, is equivalent to a *generalized hierarchical decomposition* [De].

Let $u_1,...,u_m$ be all the leaf nodes of T, then the path set of T, P(T), is given by P(T) = $\{A(u_1),...,A(u_m)\}$.

The following lemma is from [OY1].

Lemma 1. Let T be a scheme tree, then

(1) P(T) is an acyclic database scheme;

(2) MVD(T) $\equiv$ |×|[P(T)].

The following example will be the running example of the paper.

Example 1. Let T be the scheme tree over U = {STUDENT, CLASS, MAJOR, EXAM, PROJECT} shown in Figure 1. Thus S(T) = U, and

$M(e_1)$ = STUDENT $\rightarrow\rightarrow$ MAJOR (U)

$M(e_2)$ = STUDENT $\rightarrow\rightarrow$ CLASS EXAM PROJECT (U)

$M(e_3)$ = STUDENT CLASS $\rightarrow\rightarrow$ EXAM ({STUDENT CLASS EXAM PROJECT})

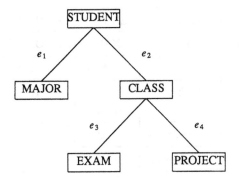

Figure 1

$M(e_4)$ = STUDENT CLASS $\rightarrow\rightarrow$ PROJECT ({STUDENT CLASS EXAM PROJECT}).

The set of PMVDs represented by the edges of T is given by $MVD(T) = \{M(e_1), M(e_2), M(e_3), M(e_4)\}$, and the path set of T is given by $P(T) = \{\{$STUDENT MAJOR$\}$, $\{$STUDENT CLASS EXAM$\}$, $\{$STUDENT CLASS PROJECT$\}\}$.

Let $R(T)$ be the NRS for T of Example 1, then $R(T)$ = STUDENT (MAJOR)* (CLASS (EXAM)* (PROJECT)*)*.

Hereinafter, we let $Z(R(T)) = R(T) \cap U$ denote the *zero order attributes* of $R(T)$, and correspondingly we let $H(R(T)) = R(T) - Z(R(T))$ denote the *higher order attributes* of $R(T)$.

In the sequel, we use the two standard operators, <u>NEST</u> and <u>UNNEST</u> [TF], designated by ν and μ, respectively.

Next we define the <u>UNNEST*</u> operator, denoted by μ^*, which transforms any nested relation into a flat relation; the order of unnesting does not affect the resulting flat relation [TF].

The following algorithm computes $\mu^*(r)$:

```
While H(R(T)) ≠ ∅ Do
    choose (Y)* ∈ H(R(T));
    r := μ(Y)* (r);
    R(T) := (R(T) - (Y)*) ∪ Y
End While;
```

Example 1 (continued). We have for the nested relation, r^*, over $R(T)$ shown in Figure 2, the flat relation $u = \mu^*(r^*)$, shown in Figure 3. Herein we use the notation for representing nested relations found in [RKS] and indicate nulls by empty cells.

2.4. THE UNIVERSAL RELATION (THE CONCEPTUAL LEVEL)

The UR model provides a database with an interface which allows the user to view the database as if it were composed of a single relation. The relational model provides *physical data independence* but does not provide *logical data independence*. The UR model aims at achieving *logical data independence* by freeing the user from navigating among the relations in the database.

STUDENT	(MAJOR)*	(CLASS	(EXAM)*	(PROJECT)*)*
	MAJOR	CLASS	(EXAM)*	(PROJECT)*
			EXAM	PROJECT
Iris	computing	databases	mid final	1NF
		programming	final	
Mark	maths	databases	final	NF2

Figure 2

STUDENT	MAJOR	CLASS	EXAM	PROJECT
Iris	computing	databases	mid	1NF
Iris	computing	databases	final	1NF
Iris	computing	programming	final	
Mark	maths	databases	final	NF2

Figure 3

Several implementations of UR interfaces have been developed in the past few years [Ul3]. Most recent approaches involve the computation of the union of one or more joins, with different assumptions made, see, for example, [BB], [KKFGU], [KS], [MRSSW].

The UR model has also generated controversy [AP], [Ke], [Ul1]. This is due to the variety of proposals put forward, and the arguments that the assumptions made may not be reasonable or desirable in practice.

As before, let U be the set of zero order attributes. At the conceptual level we assume a UR interface over U.

The usual assumptions of the UR model are:

(1) The universal relation scheme assumption (URSA) [MW], [MUV]. The assumption is that each attribute $A \in U$ is assumed to play a unique role. In other words the URSA requires an attribute to mean the same everywhere it appears.

(2) The unique role assumption (URA) [MW], [MUV]. The assumption is that there is a unique relationship among sets of attributes $X \subseteq U$. This assumption is sometimes called the *relationship uniqueness assumption*. The basic relationship on X is denoted by [X] and is called the window for X [MRW].

(3) The one flavour assumption (OFA) [BBSK], [MUV]. Intuitively, the OFA says that the real-world significance of any tuple of a window for X does not depend on the details of its

construction.

There are two basic approaches to the implementation of the UR model.

(1) We assume a UR u, over U, exists and [X] is taken to be the projection of this relation over X.

(2) The UR is not explicit and a computation procedure, in the form of a relational algebra expression, is provided to calculate [X], with respect to (w.r.t.) the internal level. The internal level for flat relations is a flat database.

3. THE NESTED RELATIONAL MODEL

For the extended algebra we use the model of [AB], and also that of [RKS] which incorporates nulls into the said algebra.

3.1. NULL VALUES AND EXTENDED OPERATORS

At this stage we make use only of nulls of type unknown [Co], hereafter denoted by *unk*. The interpretation of *unk* nulls is that the value exists but is unknown at the present moment. When testing for equality between two values v_1, v_2 (possibly values of higher order attributes), if one or both are of value *unk* then $v_1 \neq v_2$. However, if marked nulls were used instead, we would have a less restrictive model but a more complicated one [MUV].

As a result of using this restrictive type of null, we interpret the empty set as being a singleton set of value *unk*. Also, because of the equality rule for *unk* nulls, the operators v and μ need not be modified.

Definition 1. Let r be a nested relation over R(T) and t be a tuple in r. We define DEF(t) (cf. [SM]) recursively by

(1) If T is a single node, n, and ATT(n) = X, then
    DEF(t) = {A | t[A] ≠ *unk* for each A ∈ X}.

(2) If X = ATT(ROOT(T)) and $T_1,...,T_s$ denote its subtrees, then
    DEF(t) = DEF(t[X]) ∪ DEF(t'), where t' ∈ t[R(T_i)], 1 ≤ i ≤ s,
    and there exists no t'' ∈ t[R(T_i)] ≠ t' such that |DEF(t'')| <
    |DEF(t')|. (|S| denotes the cardinality of a set S.)

We observe that t has no nulls iff DEF(t) = S(T).

Let r_1, r_2 be nested relations over R(T).

Definition 2. The extended union of r_1 and r_2 ([RKS], cf. [AB]) is defined recursively by

$r_1 \cup^e r_2 =$
{t | there exists t_1 ∈ r_1 **and** there exists t_2 ∈ r_2 :
  (X = Z(R(T)), for all Y ∈ H(R(T))):
  t[X] = t_1[X] = t_2[X] **and** t[Y] = (t_1[Y] $\cup^e$ t_2[Y]))
  or (t ∈ r_1 **and** (for all t' ∈ r_2 : X = Z(R(T)) : t[X] ≠ t'[X]))
  or (t ∈ r_2 **and** (for all t' ∈ r_1 : X = Z(R(T)) : t[X] ≠ t'[X]))}.

If we remove *less informative tuples* at each stage in the computation of the extended union, then we get the null extended union ($\cup^{el}$) [RKS].

Definition 3. The null extended projection ([RKS], cf. [AB]) of a nested relation, r, over R(T) on the attribute set $X \subseteq R(T)$, is given by $\Pi^{el}{}_X (r) = \cup^{el}{}_{t \in \Pi_X(r)} (t)$.

We next define the extended total projection ($\Pi^e \downarrow$) of r on $X \subseteq R(T)$, which intuitively is the largest subset of the null extended projection that contains no nulls.

Definition 4. Let R(T') be the NRS over X (if $X \cap Z(R(T)) = \emptyset$ then we have a root with the empty set of attributes) and let $r := \Pi^{el}{}_X (r)$. Then

(1) If `T'` consists of a single node, `n`, and `ATT(n) = X`, then
    $\Pi^e \downarrow_X (r) = \{t \mid t \in r$ **and** `DEF(t) = X`$\}$.
    Note that this is equivalent to the standard definition of total projection ($\Pi \downarrow$) for flat relations.

(2) If `X' = ATT(ROOT(T'))` and $T'_1, \ldots, T'_s$ denote its subtrees, then
    $\Pi^e \downarrow_X (r) = \{t \mid t' \in r$ **and** `DEF(t'[X']) = X'` **and** `t[X'] = t'[X']` **and** $t[R(T'_i)] = \Pi^e \downarrow_{R(T'_i)} (t')$, $1 \leq i \leq s$, **and** `DEF(t) = S(T')`$\}$.

Hence for all $t \in \Pi^e \downarrow_X(r)$, DEF(t) = S(T').

$\Pi^e \downarrow$ is faithful [RKS] (i.e. when applied to flat relations it reduces to the standard operator $\Pi \downarrow$) and also precise [RKS] (i.e. $\mu^*(\Pi^e \downarrow(r)) = \Pi \downarrow(\mu^*(r))$).

Example 1 (continued). For r* of Figure 2 we have r'* = $\Pi^e \downarrow_{(CLASS(PROJECT)^*)}$(r*), as shown in Figure 4.

CLASS	(PROJECT)*
	PROJECT
databases	1NF
	NF2

Figure 4

We note that r'*[(PROJECT)*] = {1NF,NF2} as a result of the null extended projection; also, the subtuple t = {programming {}}, which is in $\Pi^e \downarrow_{(CLASS(PROJECT)^*)}$(r*), drops out of the extended total projection, since DEF(t) ≠ {CLASS, PROJECT}.

3.2. EXTENDED DEPENDENCIES

We generalize FDs and MVDs to nested relations in a natural way, i.e. instead of requiring value equality when we have zero order attributes only, we now require set equality for higher order attributes. The following theorem from [FSTV] illustrates this fact.

Theorem 1. Let $XZ \subseteq U$, $X \cap Z = \emptyset$ and r be a relation over U. Then the following statements are equivalent:

(1) $X \rightarrow\rightarrow Z$ holds in r.

(2) $X \rightarrow\rightarrow Z^*$ holds in $r^* = v_Z(r)$.

(3) $X \rightarrow Z^*$ holds in $r^* = v_Z(r)$. $\square$

4. A UNIVERSAL RELATION MODEL FOR A SINGLE NESTED RELATION

We assume R(T) to be a NRS with S(T) = U. When we have a single nested relation at the internal level we interpret this situation as follows: R(T) is a nested universal relation scheme (NURS) at the internal level which supports the UR scheme U at the conceptual level.

We intend to show that under this interpretation the two standard approaches to the UR model, as a view or as a computational method, are equivalent. This can be seen as an extension of the results in [MRW] to nested relations, and a generalization of the results in [AB].

One solution as to how to view the UR model, over U, is to use *weak instances* [Ho],[MUV].

Definition 5. Let D be a set of dependencies for a database scheme **R** with database d. A weak instance for d is any relation u, over U, such that

(1) u satisfies D;

(2) $r_i \subseteq \Pi_{R_i}(u), 1 \leq i \leq q$.

Since there are infinitely many weak instances for d, we assume that the only facts that can be deduced from the UR model, given the relations in the database d, are those that hold in *all* weak instances.

Definition 6. A representative instance (RI) [MUV], [Sa], [SM] for a database d, over **R**, with a set of dependencies D, is a relation u (with nulls), over U, such that

(1) u satisfies D;

(2) $[X] = \Pi\downarrow_X(u)$, where $X \subseteq U$.

Thus the RI is a suitable model of the data as stored in one relation.

4.1. ASSOCIATIONS AND OBJECTS IN A NRS

In [MW] the semantics of the UR model are described in terms of associations and objects. We now review the results in [MW] very briefly. Associations are non-decomposable relationships among attributes and objects are decomposable relationships among attributes over a union of associations.

Let $X \subseteq U$ be an association, then we denote by r(X) the flat relation over X. The tuples in r(X) do not contain nulls, i.e. they are fully defined.

The following three constraints are placed on the said model.

(1) The containment condition for associations (CCA). If X,Y are associations then $\Pi_X(r(Y)) \subseteq r(X)$;

(2) The set of associations is contained in the set of objects for the model;

(3) The set of objects is closed under non-empty intersection.

We note that, under the above assumptions, we can compute [X] by computing the minimum object W containing X, and then projecting the result on X. In order to compute the relation of an object W, designated by $r(W)$, we join the relations for the associations that are subsets of W.

Definition 7. The <u>associations</u> that hold for a scheme tree, T, denoted by **As**(T) (cf. skeleton format [AB]), are defined recursively by

(1) `if T consists of a single node, n, with ATT(n) = X, then As(T) =`
     `{X};`

(2) `if X = ATT(ROOT(T)) and` $T_1, \ldots, T_s$ `denote its subtrees, then`
     `As(T) = {X} ∪ { {XY} | Y ∈ As(`T_j`) for 1 ≤ j ≤ s }.`

Definition 8. Let **Ob**(T) denote the <u>objects</u> that hold for a scheme tree, T, and let $e_1, \ldots, e_m$ be the edges of T with $e_i = (u_i, v_i)$, where i ranges over $\{1, \ldots, m\}$. Then $\mathbf{Ob}(T) = \mathbf{As}(T) \cup \{\cup_{i=1}^{m} \{A(u_i) \cup D(u_i)\}\}$, where $(A(u_i) \cup D(u_i))$ is the context of the PMVD $M(e_i)$.

Example 2. The associations for R(T) of Example 1 are: **As**(T) = {{STUDENT}, {STUDENT MAJOR}, {STUDENT CLASS}, {STUDENT CLASS EXAM}, {STUDENT CLASS PROJECT}}.

The objects for R(T) of Example 1 are: **Ob**(T) = **As**(T) ∪ {{STUDENT CLASS EXAM PROJECT}, {STUDENT CLASS MAJOR EXAM PROJECT}}.

Let the associations and objects of R(T) correspondingly be **As**(T) and **Ob**(T). Then it is easy to show that

Lemma 2. Constraints (2) and (3) above hold for **As**(T) and **Ob**(T). □

Let d = {r(X) | X ∈ **As**(T)} be a database. Then in a similar way to the proof of Theorem 3.2 in [AB], it can be shown that

Proposition 1. The following are equivalent:

(1) $r(X) = \Pi\downarrow_X(u)$ for each $r(X) \in$ d such that u = $\mu^*(r^*)$ for some nested relation r* over R(T);

(2) d satifies CCA. □

Let $\hat{D}$ be the three constraints of Maier and Warren [MW], and let u be a RI for d and $\hat{D}$.

Theorem 2. The following are equivalent:

(1) u is a RI for d and $\hat{D}$;

(2) u = $\mu^*(r^*)$ for some nested relation r* over R(T).

Proof. (Sketch) (1) => (2). Since u is a RI, by Definition 6, [X] = $\Pi\downarrow_X(u)$. Moreover, constraints (2) and (3) imply [X] = r(X) for each X ∈ **As**(T). By Proposition 1 the result follows.

(2) => (1). Let d = {r(X) | r(X) = $\Pi\downarrow_X(u)$, for each X ∈ **As**(T)}. By Proposition 1 u satisfies constraint (1). Also, by Lemma 2, **As**(T) and **Ob**(T) satisfy constraints (2) and (3). □

Example 3. It can be shown that the result of Theorem 2 holds for u and r* given in Figures, 2 and 3, respectively. Let d be the set of total projections of u over **As**(T) of Example 2, and $\hat{D}$ be the three constraints of Maier and Warren, then u is a RI for d and $\hat{D}$, and r* is the nested relation of Theorem 2.

4.2. DEPENDENCIES IN A NRS

Our approach herein is such that the dependencies that hold for the NRS are implied by the scheme tree, T. Thus, if the NRS is flat then there are no dependencies implied by T.

By Theorem 1 and Lemma 1 MVD(T) is equivalent to a set of FDs, which are denoted by FD(T). We consider these FDs as <u>local dependencies</u> that hold for R(T).

Definition 9. Let e = {u,v} be an edge in T and MVD(e) = A(u) $\to\to$ D(v) (A(u) $\cup$ D(u)). The FD, corresponding to MVD(e), that holds for the NRS, R(T), is A(u) $\to$ (D(v))* and is denoted by FD(e).

Example 4. For T of Example 1 we have:

FD(e_1) = STUDENT $\to$ (MAJOR)*

FD(e_2) = STUDENT $\to$ (CLASS (EXAM)* (PROJECT)*)*

FD(e_3) = STUDENT,CLASS $\to$ (EXAM)*

FD(e_4) = STUDENT,CLASS $\to$ (PROJECT)*

We now state the following two facts:

(1) If D(v) is a set of attributes, nesting within the context of D(v) does not effect the FD A(u) $\to$ (D(v))* (See FD(e_2) in Example 4).

(2) ATT(ROOT(T_k)), $1 \le k \le s$, can appear on the left-hand side of an FD, although they may be part of a nesting of attributes (see FD(e_3) and FD(e_4) in Example 4).

Proposition 2. Let u be a relation over U and R(T) be the NRS with S(T) = U. Then the following are equivalent:

(1) u is a RI for d = {r(X) | r(X) = $\Pi\downarrow_X$(u) with X $\in$ As(T)} and $\hat{D}$;

(2) u is a RI for d = {r(X) | r(X) = $\Pi\downarrow_X$(u) with X $\in$ P(T)} and D = |x|[P(T)].

Proof. (Sketch) By Theorem 2, (1) => u = μ*(r*) for some r* over R(T). By Lemma 1, (2) => u = μ*(r*) for some r* over R(T). By the definition of a nested relation the result follows. $\square$

Example 5. Let |x|[P(T)] = |x|[{STUDENT MAJOR},{STUDENT CLASS EXAM},{STUDENT CLASS PROJECT}] be the JD for P(T) of Example 1. Then Proposition 2 holds for u and r* of Example 1.

4.3 THE NESTED RI

Let r* be a nested relation over R(T) with S(T) = U, and let DEPN(R(T)) be the set of dependencies associated with R(T).

Definition 10. r* is a <u>nested representative instance</u> (NRI) for u = μ*(r*) and DEPN(R(T)), if

(1) r* satisfies DEPN(R(T));

(2) [X] = μ*($\Pi^e\downarrow_{(X)^*}$(r*)), where X $\subseteq$ U, (X)* $\subseteq$ R(T) and X = attr((X)*), where attr((X)*) denotes the attributes in (X)* considered as zero order attributes.

Theorem 3. r* is a NRI for u = μ*(r*) and DEPN(R(T)) = FD(T) iff u is a RI for d and $\hat{D}$.

Proof. (Sketch) By using Lemma 1 and Theorem 1, it can be shown that FD(T) is equivalent to the acyclic JD |×|[P(T)], and therefore r* must satisfy DEPN(R(T)). By Proposition 2 and Theorem 2 the result follows, since $\Pi^e \downarrow$ is a precise operator. □

Theorem 3 states that if a database, d, can be represented by a single nested relation (i.e. modelled in the form of a scheme tree), then this is a suitable internal model for implementing a UR interface.

Example 6. Let FD(T) represent the FDs of Example 4. Then it can be verified that the result of Theorem 3 holds for u and r* of Example 1.

With regard to query processing, we note that no joins need to be performed under our internal model, since joins are realized in the nested relation. The window for X, [X], is computed by unnesting an extended total projection over the nested relation (Definition 10), which, by Theorem 3, is the NRI for u.

4.4. SCHEME TREES AND γ-ACYCLICITY

Fagin [Fa2] described γ-acyclic database schemes as possesing a restricted degree of acyclicity and enjoying desirable properties.

Biskup et al. [BBSK] showed that γ-acyclic database schemes satisfy the OFA. By the definition of γ-acyclicity [Fa2], it follows that a γ-acyclic database scheme can provide an optimized UR interface, since there is a unique join that can be used to compute [X]. The ensuing results show that a subclass of γ-acyclic database schemes can also be characterized by scheme trees. Thus, a nested relation is a desirable internal level, since all the joins will be precomputed and redundancy is minimized.

Lemma 3. Let T be a scheme tree, then P(T) is γ-acyclic.

Proof. (Sketch) By induction on the number of paths removed from P(T) we prove that P(T) is γ-acyclic. □

Theorem 4. If **R** is γ-acyclic and ∩**R** is non-empty, then **R** ≡ P(T).

Proof. (Sketch) By Theorem 8.1 in [Fa2] **R** is equivalent to a <u>loop-free</u> <u>Bachman</u> <u>diagram</u> [Fa2]. By using this result, we can prove that **R** ≡ P(T) for some scheme tree T. □

Corollary 1. **R** is γ-acyclic with ∩**R** non-empty iff **R** ≡ P(T). □

Example 7. It can be verified that P(T) of Example 1 is γ-acyclic and that ∩**R** is non-empty.

5. EXTENSIONS TO THE NESTED UR MODEL

5.1. A NESTED UR MODEL FOR A NESTED DATABASE

When we extend our model to handle a nested database (a collection of nested relations) at the internal level, the theory is more complex. We review our results very briefly; the full results appear in [LL2].

We assume at the internal level a <u>nested</u> <u>database</u> <u>scheme,</u> R(F) = {R(T_1),...,R(T_m)}, where F = {T_1,...,T_m} is a scheme forest [OY1] and $\cup_{i=1}^{m} S(T_i)$ = U.

For the join of nested relations to make sense we utilize the notion of <u>compatible nested relation</u> <u>schemes</u> (cf. [AB]). Then we extend the definition of JD to be a dependency over the operators of an extended algebra. Finally, the *Chase* process [MMS] is extended to nested relations.

We assume the only dependencies that hold for $\mathbf{R}(F)$ are implied by the scheme trees in F. By using these dependencies we restructure $\mathbf{R}(F)$ into a <u>compatible nested database scheme.</u> The nested relation scheme over the extended JD [LL2] $|\times|^e[\mathbf{R}(F)]$ (where $|\times|^e$ denotes the extended JD) is an <u>intermediate level,</u> called the NURS.

The main theorem shows that we can create a NRI for a nested database using the extended *Chase*. As in the case of a single nested relation, [X] is an u   ting of an extended total projection over the NRI.

5.2. INCLUDING MORE THAN ONE TYPE OF NULL VALUE IN THE NESTED UR MODEL

Apart from the null value unknown (*unk*) other types of nulls have been studied. The complementary type of null to the *unk* is the null of type value *does not exist* (denoted by *dne*) [Li]. A technique for unifying the *unk* and *dne* interpretation of nulls, by introducing the null of type *no information* (denoted by *ni*), was given in [Za].

The *ni* null is *less informative* [Za],[RKS] than both the *unk* and *dne* nulls and can be used to approximate both. This approach has the disadvantage that some partial knowledge available to the user may be lost.

In extending our results, we still employ the model for nulls in nested relations found in [RKS], in which *dne*, *unk* and *ni* nulls are considered together. Thus, as in the case for *unk* nulls, two attribute values having the value *ni* are *not* considered equal. On the other hand two attribute values having the *dne* value are considered equal, since *dne* can only be interpreted as the domain value that does not exist. The empty set is interpreted as having the value *ni* [RKS].

To modify our results to include nulls of types *unk*, *dne* and *ni*, we have to deal with the semantics of the *dne* null, and modify the definition of DEF(t).

We now present the semantic problems of *dne* nulls, and propose solutions.

The *dne* null is different from the other types of null value in that it is considered as being just another domain value and not as a placeholder for missing information. For this reason we include in the extended total projection of a nested relation, tuples having a value *dne* for one or more of their attributes. For example, the query "List the STUDENTs having no PROJECTs" (i.e. (PROJECT)* = *dne*) will have a defined answer.

The main difference between this approach and the one in [SM] is that we assume an <u>open world</u> (i.e. there may be facts about the world that could be stored in the database but are not). In [SM] a <u>closed world</u> (i.e. *all* the facts about the world are stored in the database) is assumed.

Another semantic problem with *dne* nulls was argued in [RKS].

Assume that the STUDENT with value, "Mark", has no PROJECTs (i.e. (PROJECT)* = *dne*). However, at a later stage "Mark" has a PROJECT as in the running example. It makes no sense at this stage to have two tuples for "Mark", one having (PROJECT)* = {value} (or {*unk*}) and another having $(PROJECT)^* = \{dne\}$. In [RKS] this is called the <u>exclusivity rule</u> for *dne* nulls and is defined as follows.

Let $X \in Ob(T)$, then there do not exist two tuples $t_1, t_2 \in r^*$ (where r^* is the NRI) and $A \in X$ such that

$t_1[A] = dne$, $t_2[A] \neq dne$, and $t_1[X - A] = t_2[X - A]$.

The following modifications need to be made in order to incorporate *unk*, *dne* and *ni* nulls into our model.

(1) Definition of DEF(t) (Definition 1).
   Modify $t[A] \neq unk$ to ($t[A] \neq unk$ **and** $t[A] \neq ni$).

(2) Add the exclusivity rule [RKS] for *dne* nulls.

6. CONCLUDING REMARKS

We have shown a strong connection between the classical UR model and the corresponding nested relation. Under the nested UR model, a nested relation is a suitable internal level for providing a UR interface. The nested relation is a NRI, which satisfies the dependencies induced by the said relation. The advantages of the nested UR model are efficiency, minimal redundancy, and explicit representation of the dependencies. We showed that our results can be extended to handle more than one type of null, and briefly mentioned the extension of the nested UR model when the internal level is a nested database. A further extension, recently achieved, is to include the representation of FDs that hold in the corresponding flat relation of a given nested relation (cf. [OY2]). This provides a better representation of the semantics of the nested relation scheme.

Desai et al. [DSG] propose the use of nested relations to simplify the conceptual level of a UR and thus the specification of document retrieval queries. If a nested relational conceptual level is desired, then the nested UR model would, obviously, be a suitable internal level.

Two important byproducts of the nested UR model are:

(1) No assumption is made w.r.t. disallowing nulls in the database (as in [MUV], where the database has no nulls).

(2) We need not modify our definitions of dependencies due to the presence of nulls.

REFERENCES

[AB] ABITEBOUL S., AND BIDOIT N. 1986. Non first normal form relations: An algebra allowing data restructuring. JCSS **33**, pp. 361-393.

[AP] ATZENI P., AND PARKER Jr. D. S. 1982. Assumptions in relational database theory. Proc. ACM PODS, pp. 1-9.

[BB] BISKUP J., AND BRÜGGEMANN H. H. 1983. Universal relation views: A pragmatic approach. Proc. VLDB, pp. 172-185.

[BBSK] BISKUP J., BRÜGGEMANN H. H., SCHNETGÖKE L., AND KRAMER M. 1986. One flavor assumption and γ-acyclicity for universal relation views. Proc. ACM PODS, pp. 148-159.

[BFMY] BEERI C., FAGIN R., MAIER D., AND YANNAKAKIS M. 1983. On the desirability of acyclic database schemes. JACM **30**, pp. 479-513.

[Co] CODD E. F. 1979. Extending the database relational model to capture more meaning. ACM TODS **4**, pp. 397-434.

[De] DELOBEL C. 1978. Normalization and hierarchical dependencies in the relational data model. ACM TODS **3**, pp. 201-222.

[DSG] DESAI B. C., GOYAL P., AND SADRI F. 1987. Non-first normal form universal relations: An application to information retrieval systems. Information Systems **12**, pp. 49-55.

[Fa1] FAGIN R. 1977. Multivalued dependencies and a new normal form for relational databases. ACM TODS **2**, pp. 262-278.

[Fa2] FAGIN R. 1983. Degrees of acyclicity for hypergraphs and relational database systems. JACM **30**, pp. 514-550.

[FMU] FAGIN R., MENDELZON A. O., AND ULLMAN J. D. 1982. A simplified universal relation assumption and its properties. ACM TODS **7**, pp. 343-360.

[FV] FAGIN R., AND VARDI M. Y. 1984. The theory of data dependencies - A survey. IBM Research Report RJ4321 (47149), San Jose, CA.

[FSTV] FISCHER P. C., SAXTON L. V., THOMAS S. J., AND VAN GUCHT D. 1985. Interactions between dependencies and nested relational structures. JCSS **31**, pp. 343-354.

[Ho] HONEYMAN P. 1982. Testing satisfaction of functional dependencies. JACM **29**, pp. 668-677.

[Ke] KENT W. 1981. Consequences of assuming a universal relation. ACM TODS **6**, pp. 539-556.

[KKFGU] KORTH H. F., KUPER G. M., FIEGENBAUM J., VAN GELDER A., AND ULLMAN J. D. 1984. System/U - A database system based on the universal relation assumption. ACM TODS **9**, pp. 331-347.

[KS] KUCK S. M., AND SAGIV Y. 1982. A universal relation database system implemented via the network model. Proc. ACM PODS, pp. 147-157.

[Li] LIEN Y. E. 1979. Multivalued dependencies with null values in relational databases. Proc. VLDB. pp. 61-66.

[LL1] LEVENE M., AND LOIZOU G. 1987. Project-join constructibility for NF2 relational databases. Bases De Données Advancées, BD3, pp. 143-163.

[LL2] LEVENE M., AND LOIZOU G. 1987. A universal relation interface incorporating nested relations. Submitted for publication.

[Ma] MAIER D. 1983. The Theory of Relational Databases. Rockville, Maryland, Computer Science Press.

[MMS] MAIER D., MENDELZON A. O., AND SAGIV Y. 1979. Testing implications of data dependencies. ACM TODS **4**, pp. 455-469.

[MRSSW] MAIER D., ROZENSHTEIN D., SALVETER S., STEIN J., AND WARREN D. S. 1987. PIQUE: A relational query language without relations. Information Systems **12**, pp. 317-335.

[MRW] MAIER D., ROZENSHTEIN D., AND WARREN D. S. 1983. Windows on the world. Proc. ACM SIGMOD, pp. 68-78.

[MUV] MAIER D., ULLMAN J. D. , AND VARDI M. Y. 1984. On the foundations of the universal relation model. ACM TODS **9**, pp. 283-308.

[MW] MAIER D., AND WARREN D. S. 1982. Specifying connections for a universal relation scheme database. Proc. ACM SIGMOD, pp. 1-7.

[OY1] OZSOYOGLU Z. M., AND YUAN L.-Y. 1987. A new normal form for nested relations. ACM TODS **12**, pp. 111-136.

[OY2] OZSOYOGLU Z. M., AND YUAN L.-Y. 1987. A design method for nested relational databases. Proc. 3rd IEEE Conf. on Data Engineering.

[RKS] ROTH M. A., KORTH H. F., AND SILBERSCHATZ A. 1985. Null values in $\neg$1NF relational databases. Research Report TR-85-32, Department of Computer Science, University of Texas at Austin, U.S.A.

[Sa] SAGIV Y. 1983. A characterization of globally consistent databases and their correct access paths. ACM TODS **8**, pp. 266-286.

[SM] STEIN J., AND MAIER D. 1985. Relaxing the universal relation scheme assumption. Proc. ACM PODS, pp. 76-84.

[TF] THOMAS S. J., AND FISCHER P. C. 1986. Nested relational structures. Advances in Computing Research **3**, JAI Press, pp. 269-307.

[Ul1] ULLMAN J. D. 1982. The U.R. strikes back. Proc. ACM PODS, pp. 10-22.

[Ul2] ULLMAN J. D. 1983. Principles of Database Systems. Rockville, Maryland, Computer Science Press.

[Ul3] ULLMAN J. D. 1983. Universal relation interfaces for database systems. Proc. IFIP, Mason R.E.A. (ed.), North-Holland, pp. 243-252.

[VF] VAN GUCHT D., AND FISCHER P. C. 1986. Some classes of multilevel relational structures. Proc. ACM PODS, pp. 60-69.

[Za] ZANIOLO C. 1984. Database relations with null values. JCSS **28**, pp. 142-166.

MULTILEVEL TRIE HASHING

W. Litwin, D. Zegour, G. Levy

INRIA 78153 LE CHESNAY, FRANCE

ABSTRACT

Trie hashing is one of the fastest access methods to primary key ordered dynamic files. The key address is computed through a trie usually in core. Key search needs then at most one disk access. For very large files, trie size may however become prohibitive. We present an extension of the method, where the trie is split into subtries stored each in a page on the disk. Address computation requires the core for a single page. Two disk accesses may suffice for any key search in a Gbyte file.

I. INTRODUCTION

Trie hashing (TH) manages dynamic and ordered files of records identified by a key. The access function generated by the method is a dynamic trie whose size is usually proportional to the file size. As long as the trie is in a buffer in the main memory (core), any key search takes at most one disk access. This is usually the case, especially for files on personal computers. The method is then among the most efficient. In particular, it is usually faster than B-trees /BAY72/, /BAY77/ because of higher branching factor. Properties of the method are discussed in /TOR83/, /GON84/, /KRI84/, /DAT86/ and /LIT81, 84, 85/.

However, the requirement that the entire trie is in core may be inconvenient for very large files or when several files should be used simultaneously. Below, we describe an extension of the method adapted to these cases. The extension was called *multilevel trie hashing* (MLTH). Its principle is to split the trie into subtries small enough to be fitted in the buffer. Subtries are stored in pages on the disk, organized into a tree. Pages are created through the principle of splitting of overflowing subtries.

Below, Section II recalls at first the principles of TH. The presentation differs from the original one in /LIT81/ by the discussion of properties of the method that appeared in the meantime. Section III defines the MLTH algorithm for trie splitting and Section IV discusses the operations on MLTH file. Section V analyzes the performance of the method. In particular, it shows that two accesses should usually suffice for a key search in Gbyte files.

Section VI shows that MLTH provides a better search performance or is less sensitive to adverse key distributions than the related methods. Section VII concludes the discussion.

II. TRIE HASHING
II.1 File structure

For TH, a *file* is a set of records identified by primary keys. Keys consist of digits of a finite and ordered alphabet, where the smallest digit called *space*. is denoted '_' and the largest digit is denoted ':' . All possible keys constitute the *key space*. Inside a record, only the key is relevant to access computation. Records are stored in *buckets* numbered 0,1,2,...,N that are units of transfer between the file and the core. The bucket number is called its *address*. Each bucket may contain the same number of records called *bucket capacity* and denoted b ; $b \geq 2$.

Fig 1 shows TH file of 31 most used English words /KNU73/. The file is addressed through the trie at the fig 1.c, created dynamically by splits of overflowing buckets in the way shown later on. A trie is classically presented as an M-ary tree whose nodes correspond to digits /FRE60/, /KNU73/. This structure is however inefficient for dynamic files (/KNU73/ pp. 481-485). In TH, the M-ary structure is embedded into a binary structure, as at the figure, called below if needed *TH-trie* and axiomatically defined as *Litwin trie* in /TOR83/. TH-trie is a particular b-tree in the terminology of /KNU73/ (p. 315) that is a single node called *root* plus 0 or 2 disjoint b-trees (not to be confused with the well known B-tree /BAY72/). Each trie has an odd number of nodes and a node usually noted n is either a leaf or an internal node with either 0 or 2 sons. Internal nodes form a binary tree (this is a general relationship between b-trees and binary trees /KNU73/ (p. 315)). An internal node contains a pair of values called *digit value* and *digit number*, usually noted below (d, i). The trie is *empty* when it has no internal nodes. Otherwise, $i = 0$ for the root. A leaf either contains a value noted A that points to bucket A or the value called *nil* that indicates that no bucket corresponds to the leaf. Accordingly, the leaf is called leaf A or node A or nil leaf (node).

To any n corresponds a string called a *logical path* to n noted below C_n and defined recursively as follows :

Let $(c)_l$ be $(l+1)$ - digit prefix of a string c (an empty string for $l < 0$)
- If n is the root, then $C_n = $ ':'.
- Otherwise, let $p = (d, i)$ be the parent of n . If n is the right child then $C_n = C_p$ else $C_n = (C_p)_{i-1}d$.

Fig 1.c shows the logical paths in the example trie.

The logical paths define an M-ary structure on TH-trie called below a *logical structure*, whose internal nodes are digits and leaves are bucket addresses. Fig 2 shows the logical structure of the example trie. All d's with the same i in TH-trie constitute level i in the logical structure. Each node $(d, 0)$ corresponds to a (unique) digit d at the level 0, ordered from left to right according to the digit value order; for instance $(i, 0)$ corresponds to digit 'i' at level 0. The edges link d_i either to d_{i+1} next on the logical path, like 'i' and '_', or to the leaf terminating the path, like 'i' and leaf 3 for instance. This M-ary structure is characteristic to tries (see Fig 31, p. 484 in /KNU73/), except that in TH leaves are pointers to buckets and not the keys themselves.

The basic memory representation of TH-trie is a linked list called *standard representation* /LIT81/. Fig 1.d and 1.e show the standard representation of the example trie. Each element of the list is called a *cell* that consists of four fields. Fields DV (digit value) and DN (digit number) represent an internal node of the trie. The pointer LP represents the left leaf or edge under this node and the pointer RP represents the right leaf or edge. A positive pointer value A, means that the field represents the leaf A. A negative value $-A$, represents an edge and points to cell A representing the child node.

Cell 0 represents the trie root if the root is not leaf 0. The empty trie, corresponding either to the empty file or with bucket 0 only (after the first insertion), is represented as cell 0 with DV = ':', DN = 0 and LP = 'nil' or LP = 0. Otherwise, there is exactly one cell per internal node. The number of cells is also equal to that of the leaves minus one.

The standard representation is not the only one possible. Other representations exist and may have desirable properties /LIT85/.

II.2 Key search

The keys are mapped to the addresses through the logical paths, according to the following rules :

    (i) - all keys are mapped to the root,

    (ii) - let n be a node and S_n the set of keys mapped to n. Let $p = (d, i)$ be some parent with l and r its left and right children. Then, S_l contains all keys c in S_p for which $(c)_i \leq C_l$, and S_r all other keys of S_p.

    (iii) - For any key, its address is the pointer reached through the application of rules (i) and of (ii).

In the example trie, all keys are thus mapped to node (o, 0). Then, only the keys with $(c)_0$ $\leq$ 'o' are mapped to node (i, 0), all others are mapped to (t, 0). From $S_{(i, 0)}$, the keys with $(c)_0 \leq$ 'i' are mapped to $(\_, 1)$, others are mapped to leaf 2. From $S_{(\_, 1)}$, the keys with $(c)_1 \leq$ 'i_' go to (a, 0), others are mapped to leaf 3, etc.

These principles lead to the following algorithm for key search, determining the successive nodes on which the key is mapped :

(A1) TH key search. Let c be the searched key, r the trie root and n the visited node ; $n = (d, i)$ for internal nodes and $n = r$ initially. Let $L(n)$ and $R(n)$ be two operators providing the left and the right child of n. Let C, C' be string variables ; $C = C' = $ ':' initially.

While n is an internal node do :
    set $C' <= (C)_{i-1}d$
    if $(c)_i \leq C'$ then $C <= C'$; $n <= L(n)$ else $n <= R(n)$
    endwhile
    Return n, C

For the example trie, $c = $'s' for instance, returns $n = 1$ and $C = $ 't', while $c = $ 'he' or $c = $ 'gun' return $n = 7$ and $C = $ 'he'. If Algorithm A1 ends up in a nil node, then c is not in the file. The values of C are the logical paths to the successively visited nodes. They are returned for the splitting algorithm A2 below.

While Algorithm A1 is probably the simplest, one may optimize the search. The following algorithm may be faster, as it compares only one digit at the time, skips unnecessary comparisons and does not need C'. It compares at first only the leftmost digit c_0 of c and only to nodes with $i = 0$, until $c_0 = d$ or a leaf is reached. In the case of the matching, the comparison switches to c_1 and to nodes with $i = 1$ only etc. The notation and initial values are basically as in Algorithm A1.

(A1bis) TH key search. Let c_j denote digit j of $c = c_0c_1...c_j...c_k$. Let it be $j = 0$ initially.

While n is an internal node do :
    if $j = i$ then
        if $c_j \leq d$ then
            $C <= (C)_{i-1}d$; if $c_j = d$ then set $j <= j + 1$;
            set $n <= L(n)$;

```
        else n <= R(n)
      else if j < i  then
          set n  <= L(n) ; C  <= (C)_{i-1}d
      else n <= R(n)
   endwhile
   return n, C
```

The search for 'he' for instance, compares at first $c_0 = $ 'h' to digits in nodes with $i = 0$, and to only to such digits. Thus the comparison of 'h' to '_' is skipped. When (h, 0) is reached, the comparison switches to 'e' and to nodes with $i = 1$. TH key search differs thus from the usual key search in a binary search tree or in a usual trie, where the key is compared to each node value. Both algorithms compare indeed only a part of the key either to a value computed from the visited nodes (Algorithm A1) or to selected nodes (Algorithm A2). They apply the idea in hashing that is "to chop off some aspects of the key and to use this partial information as a basis for searching" (/KNU73/, vol 3, p. 507) . Deeper discussion of these aspects of TH is in /LIT85/.

II.3 Range queries

A range query searches all keys c within some bounds c_1 and c_2 ; $c_1 < c_2$; in descending or in ascending order. The rule (ii) above for the key-to-address mapping to implies that the TH file is ordered and thus keys may be searched using only one access per bucket, more efficiently than for a classical hashing. If leaf n points to the visited bucket, then the successor of n in ascending key order is the leftmost leaf in the right subtrie of the (unique) node for which n is the rightmost leaf in the left subtrie. In the trie on Fig 1.b, the successive leaves and buckets are 0, 9, 4, 10, 7, 8, 6, 3, 2, 1, 5.

This order of leaves corresponds to the *inorder* traversal of the trie. It also corresponds to the preorder and postorder traversals, since all these traversals coincide with respect to the leaves order. The inorder traversal is recursively defined as : (1) Traverse the left subtree in inorder, (2) Process the root node, (3) Traverse the right subtree in inorder. Simple algorithms for inorder traversal, as well as for the other traversals are widely known /KNU73/, /TRE85/ etc. The following algorithm is derived from Algorithm T in /KNU73/, Vol 1, p 317. The notation is this from Algorithm A1 and S denotes an initially empty stack.

(T) Inorder traversal of the trie

1. Set $n <= r$.

2. If n is a leaf, go to step 4.

3. Set $S \Leftarrow n$, i.e., push n onto the stack. Set $n \Leftarrow L(n)$ and return to step 2.

4. [$n \Leftarrow$ Stack] Visit n. Then, if S is empty, then return else set $n \Leftarrow S$, i.e., pop n from the stack.

5. Visit n. Then, set $n \Leftarrow R(n)$ and go to step 2.

The leaves in ascending key order are delivered by step 4. To visit them in descending key order, one has to traverse the trie in *converse* inorder (preorder, postorder). The converse orders simply correspond to the interchange of the words "left" and "right" in the original definitions. The corresponding conversion of Algorithm T is trivial.

One way to process a range query is therefore (i) to compute by Algorithm A1 the addresses A_1 and A_2 for c_1 and c_2 and (ii) to read the buckets in the inorder of leaves between these bounds. The Algorithm T will usually visit more leaves, as it starts the traversal from leaf 0 while usually $A_1 > 0$. One may however start the visits directly from A_1. It suffices to put on a stack the nodes whose *left* edges were used while computing Algorithm A1 for c_1. The stack would then contain the same nodes as stack S of Algorithm T when the traversal reaches A_1. The adaptation of Algorithm T is trivial. This strategy may speed up the query processing, though the trie traversal is a memory operation that thus should be anyhow usually much faster than bucket accesses.

To illustrate the range query processing, consider for example the search for keys c starting with 'h', e.g. 'h' $\leq c <$ 'i'. Algorithm A1 would return addresses 7 and 6. If Algorithm T is not modified, it will also compute the traversal for all nodes preceding leaf 7. If Algorithms T and A1 are modified to avoid this part of the traversal, Algorithm T will start with stack S with nodes : (o, 0), (i, 0), (_, 1), (h, 0), (e, 1). The accessed buckets will be in both cases : bucket 7, 8 and 6, in this order .

II.4   File expansion

Insertions expand the file through the splits of the overflowing buckets. Each split usually moves about a half of keys in the overflowing bucket A, into a new bucket, appended to the file end. The move results from the trie expansion, usually by one internal node and one leaf pointing to the new bucket. The effect is that C_A decreases or that it is extended with some digits. If $j + 1$ is the length of new C_A, some prefixes $(c)_j$ in bucket A become then greater than C_A. The moved keys are these with such prefixes.

(A2) TH bucket splitting. Let C result from Algorithm A1 for the key to be inserted. Let N be the last current address in the file. Let B be the ordered sequence of $b+1$ keys to split, including the new key and let c'' be the last key in B. Let c' denote a key in B called the <u>split key</u>, usually near the middle of B.

1. [Determine the split string] Find the shortest $(c')_i$ called the *split string* that is smaller than $(c'')_i$.
2. [Split the bucket] Set $N <= N + 1$. Append bucket N and move to it all keys c in B whose $(c)_i > (c')_i$.
3. [Trie expansion] :
   3.1 [Find the digits of the split string that are already in the trie] If $i > 0$, then cut from $(c')_i$ the largest $(c')_l$; $l < i$; such that $(c')_l = (C)_l$ If $l < i - 1$, then go to step (3.3).
   3.2 [Usual case : expand the trie by one internal node and leaf N] Replace leaf A with node (c'_i, i). Attach leaf A again, as the left child of (c'_i, i). Attach leaf N as the right child of (c'_i, i). Return.
   3.3 [Expand the trie by more than one internal node] Replace leaf A with the the following subtrie :
      - $(c'_{l+1}, l+1)$ is the root,
      - the left child of each (c_j, j) ; $j = l+1, .., i-1$; is $(c'_{j+1}, j+1)$; the right child is a nil node.
      - the left and right children of (c_i, i) are leaves A and N.
   3.4 Return.

The file at Fig 1.b was created by splits generated by insertions of Fig 1.a to buckets with the capacity $b = 4$. For each split, the split key position m in the sequence B was $m = INT(b/2 + 1) = 3$. The initial file consisted of bucket 0 and of leaf 0. The first three splits were as follows :

- key 'a' generated the 1st split. The split key was 'of' and the split string was 'o', as it was the shortest prefix of 'of' smaller than the same length prefix of 'the', the last key in B. Step 2 appended bucket 1 and moved to it keys 'to' and 'the', leaving thus three keys in bucket 0. Step 3 expanded the yet empty trie to node (o, 0) with two children : leaf 0 and leaf 1.

- the insertion of key 'is' generated the 2nd split of bucket 0. The split key was then 'in' and the split string 'i'. Step 2 moved to bucket 2 key 'of', leaving thus key 'is' in bucket 0, unlike it would be the case in a B-tree split. The split resolved the collision, but left bucket 0 full. Step 3 replaced leaf 0 with node (i, 0) and appended to it leaf 0 as the left child and leaf 2 as the right one.

- Key 'i' generated the 3rd split of bucket 0. Algorithm A2 chose key 'i' as the split key. The split string was then 'i_', since the last key of B was 'is', (note that the split string was in this case longer that the split key itself and that 'i' = 'i_' = 'i_ _' = 'i_ _..._'). Step 2 appended bucket 3 and moved there keys 'in' and 'is'. Step 3.1 found, for the first time, that some front digits of the split string are already in the logical path C_0 and thus in the trie, in the occurrence digit 'i'. This digit was then cut off and the split string shortened to the single digit '_'. Step 3.2 replaced leaf 0 by node (_, 1) with leaf 0 as left child and leaf 3 as the right one.

It should appear from these splits that the idea in Algorithm A2 is to minimize the number of nodes created by the split. Step (1) chooses for this purpose the shortest split string $(c')_i$. Step (3.1) removes further all front digits already in C. Usually, this reduces $(c')_i$ to a single digit, leading to a single new leaf that is leaf N and a single new internal node (d_l, l) ; $l \le$ $j+1$; where $(j+1)$ is the current length of C. Otherwise, Step (3.3) creates one internal node and one leaf per remaining digit. Except for the bottom right leaf N, all other right leaves are then nil leaves, as the corresponding buckets would be empty. A nil leaf is replaced with an actual address $N+1$ at the first insertion choosing it. The corresponding bucket is then appended and the key inserted. An example of nil leaf processing is in /LIT81/.

Since a split usually adds only one digit and one address, as long as digits are atomic values, TH-trie is basically the most compact representation in a form of a binary tree of the set of split strings used for the file expansion, (we say basically, since one may optimize Algorithm A2 in a way providing sometimes shorter split strings or even avoiding some splits through a recalculation of the existing node values). To obtain a more compact representation, one has to either break digits to bits, or has to use sequential representations of the logical structure, i. e. without LP or RP /LIT81/, /LIT84/, /TOR83/. These representations are however much less efficient for internal search and dynamic modifications. Another possibility is to avoid to use digit values at all, while calculating the splits using an interpolation like in /BUR83/, but then performance is again less efficient for internal search and more sensible to adverse key distributions. This aspects of TH design are discussed in Section VI.2.

The keys c that move to bucket N are all those whose $(c)_i > (c')_i$. Not only the split key stays in bucket A, but may be some but not all keys above it in B, as it appeared in the example. TH splits have thus a random tendency to load bucket A more than it would be the case of a B-tree with the same position of the split key. If the split key is the middle one, TH splits tend to be on average asymmetric. This asymmetry has no practical effect on bucket load for random insertion, but reveals beneficial to sorted insertions (/LIT85/ and Section II.6). It makes TH splits *half random* /LIT85/ in the sense that if c' is chosen in the middle of the bucket, then bucket A surely keeps each $c \le c'$ and thus at least half of keys. It also situates the method between these using the deterministic splits, like B-trees, and "pure" dynamic hashing methods discussed in Section VI.2 using random splits.

II.5 File contraction

Buckets and leaves A and A' are *siblings* if they have the same parent node. Siblings that after some deletions contain together at most b keys may be merged in the way inverse to splitting, freeing then bucket A' and shrinking the trie. Deletions may also render empty a bucket A that has no sibling, like bucket 6 in Fig 1. Leaf A is then made nil and the bucket disallocated.

II.6 Performance

Performance analysis of TH is in /LIT85/. It mainly concerns the load factor $\alpha = x / (b (N +1))$, where x is the number of keys in the file. The values of α are determined for random, ascending and descending insertions, coming unexpectedly, and noted below respectively α_r, α_a and α_d. It appears that, for the split key near the middle of the bucket, e.g. $m \approx 0.5b$, α_r stays on the average close to 70% as in a B-tree. For the same m, α_a is within $60 \div 70\%$, depending on b. This is substantially better than the well known $\alpha_a = 50\%$ of a B-tree and in particular allow to load the file through the usual insertion algorithm. Finally, the corresponding α_d is $40 \div 50\%$. It increases over 50 % if m is lowered to $m \approx 0.4b$, at the expense of α_a, but for some m, both α_a and α_d are *over* 50 %. The reason for this surprising property that seems unique to TH is that the split asymmetry for the same m and keys is on the average larger for ascending insertions than for descending ones. The value of α_r is almost unaffected when m decreases to $m \approx 0.4b$, though it may slightly improve for some optimal m values under $0.5b$, depending on b. The percentage of nil leaves is negligible, under 0.5% for random insertions. In practice, the trie grows at the rate of one cell per split and there are N cells in the list.

When the trie is in core, any successful search for a key costs 1 disk access. An unsuccessful search costs at most 1 access, as no access is needed to a nil leaf. The practical cell size is six bytes : two bytes per LP and RP and one byte per DV and DN. Therefore, 6K byte buffer suffices for about 1K bucket file, while 64K byte buffer suffices for 11K bucket file. Since typical values of b are between 10 and 200, the corresponding TH files may contain about $10^4 \div 10^6$ records. In particular, if the bucket is the MS-Dos hard disk allocation unit (cluster) that is 4K bytes, then 30K byte buffer suffices for the file covering the 20M byte disk of IBM-AT.

A typical IBM-PC compatible or a Mac has now at least 512K of core or some Mbytes. Macintosh Plus has in particular at least 32K bytes for the cache memory. The assumption that the trie is in core is therefore reasonable, especially for personal computers.

III. MULTILEVEL TRIE HASHING
III.1 The idea

The requirement that the trie is in core may in contrast be inconvenient when the file is very large or many files should be open simultaneously. MLTH is intended for these situations. It keeps TH schema for bucket splitting, but also splits the trie. The subtries are stored in buckets called *pages* structured into an M-ary tree (Fig 3). A page size may be small, usually a few Kbytes. A subtrie splits dynamically when it overflows its page. As for the buckets, page addresses are 0,1,... but they correspond to a distinct physical area. The number of cells per page is called *page capacity* and is noted b'.

III. 2 Trie splitting
III.2.1 Overall principles

Let P be the page that overflows, T the (sub)trie in P and r the root of T. Unless $P = 0$ that is always the root page, there is a parent page P' that points to P. The simplest way to split the trie is to move r to P' or to keep it in page 0 and to make it pointing to two pages containing respectively the left and the right subtrie of r. Node r would become a *split node*. For the trie at Fig 1.b, node $r = (o, 0)$ would become the split node, the subtrie rooted by $(i, 0)$ would enter the left page and the subtrie rooted by $(t, 0)$ would enter the right page. However, as this trie shows, such a *straight split* could be uneven, lowering the page load to some extent for random insertions and largely for adverse distributions. One needs a method making splits usually even. The MLTH split consists of two phases :

1. *Choice of the best split node* noted r', making the number of internal nodes that precede r' in inorder in T the closest to that of nodes following r',
2. *Trie splitting using r'* that is the splitting of the (sub)trie T into two subtries : T'_l whose nodes precede r' in inorder and T'_r whose nodes follow r'.

The inorder keeps the trie splits ordered. The node r' moves to P' or stays in page 0. The pointers in the cell representing r' are set to the addresses of the pages with T'_l and T'_r, becoming *page pointers*. Page pointers are positive, but they cannot be mistaken with bucket pointers, as it will appear. Details of the steps are as follows.

III.2.2 Choice of split node

We call <u>logical parent</u> of node $n = (d, i)$ in T the node p in T mapped to the parent d_p of node d_n in the logical structure of T. For instance, (i, 0) is the logical parent of (_, 1) in the example trie, since node 'i' is the parent of node '_' in the logical structure at Fig 2, as well as (h, 0) is the logical parent of (e, 1). No node $n = (d, 0)$ has the logical parent. For $i > 0$, p is an ascendant of n in T that is the parent of n if n is a left child, otherwise it is the last node on the path E from r to n whose *left* edge is in E. The former case applies to (_, 1), the latter applies to (e, 1).

We further call tries T_1 and T_2 *equivalent* if they have the same logical structure. For instance the tries at Fig 1 and Fig. 4 are equivalent. Equivalent tries provide the same key-to-address mapping, as they have the same logical paths and nodes, but may differ by edges and roots. In particular, if $r'' = (d_{r''}, i_{r''})$ is the root of T_2, then the node $(d_{r''}, i_{r''})$ logically corresponding to r'' in T_1 i.e. mapped to the same digit $d_{r''}$ in the logical structure, cannot have the logical parent p in T_1. Since node p in T_2 would indeed be a descendant of r'' in T_2, as any other node in T_2, p could not be the logical parent of r'' in T_1 and the logical structures would have to differ. For instance, any node (d, i) with $i = 0$ in the example trie may be the root of an equivalent trie, but not a node with $i > 0$. For this trie, there is exactly seven choices for r'', including $r'' = r = (o, 0)$.

The triplet (T'_1, r', T'_r) may be considered as a trie T' rooted by r' and equivalent to T, as will be shown. Let $N + 1$ be the size of T and thus of T' and L the size of T'_1. The best split node r' rooting T' is the node of T that (a) minimizes $|L - N / 2|$, provided (b) it has no logical parent in T. At least one choice of r' always exists, namely $r' = r$. It may happen that it is the only choice.

The test of the condition (a) is trivial, but not this of (b). However, the following properties make it simple and fast :
(i) - if r' is j-th internal node in inorder in T ; $j = 0,1,2,...$; then $L = j$.
(ii) - if the traversal of T uses algorithm T, then the visited node n has a logical parent p in T iff p is in stack S.
(iii) - n has no logical parent if $i_n = 0$ or S is empty and it has a logical parent if $i' < i_n$, where i' is the digit number of the node at the bottom of S. Otherwise, n may have the logical parent or not depending on the trie.

Property (i) results from the definition of the best split node itself. Property (ii) holds since S contains all nodes with the left edge in E which is in particular the case of p. Property (iii) results from the trie expansion principles in Algorithm A2.

The following algorithm applies these properties to find r'. In fact, it computes the whole path E until r', needed for phase 2. The path is computed from stack S produced by Algorithm T assumed slightly modified to contain E. The algorithm already puts on S all nodes with left edge in E. We assume further that each node n stored on S has a flag F that is set to $F <= $ .false when n is pushed onto A in step 3 of Algorithm T. Then, the operation $n <= S$ in step 4 is repeated until n with $F = $ .false. The flag is then set to $F <= $ .true and n is pushed onto A again. Step 5 is then performed for n as presently. The node r' itself is the last in E.

(A3) MLTH split node search. Let it be : $L = -1$, $v = \infty$, $t = N/2$, n the visited node, $i(n)$ the digit number of n, i' the digit number at the bottom of S if S is not empty.

While traversing T in inorder :
  If n is an internal node then :
      set $L <= L + 1$; set $v' <= |L - t|$
  (a)   if $v \le v'$ then return E
      if $i(n) = 0$ or S is empty then set $v <= v'$; set $E <= S$ else
  (b)   if $i' \ge i(n)$ then if S has no node n' with $i(n') = i(n) - 1$ and $F = $ .false
          then set $v <= v'$; set $E <= S$
  endwhile
  return E

The algorithm always terminates, returning E with either a node providing a better split than r or r itself. For the example trie, the execution of Algorithm A3 would be as follows :
  - Node $(r, 1)$ would be visited first. The test of i' would show that $(r, 1)$ has the logical parent and v value would not change.
  - visits to nodes $(a, 0)$, $(b, 0)$, $(f, 0)$ would progressively decrease v.
  - node $(e, 1)$ that could correspond to one of the best values of L that are $L = 4$ and $L = 5$, would not change v,
  - node $(h, 0)$ would further decrease v. Node $(\_, 1)$ would terminate the computation and the algorithm would return $E = (o, 0)$, $(i, 0)$, $(\_, 1)$, $(a, 0)$, $(h, 0)$ with thus $r' = (h, 0)$.

III.2.3 Trie splitting
III.2.3.1 The algorithm

The splitting algorithm is derived from the algorithm for splitting a list into two parts whose concatenation is the original list, in /KNU73/ (p. 466-467). It constructs progressively T'_1 and T'_r while traversing nodes of T in path E from r to r'. Like at Fig 4, it then assimilates the triplet (T'_1, r', T'_r) to a (sub)trie equivalent to T to split in the straight way (with r' as the root).

(A4) MLTH trie splitting. Let P be the page that overflows. Let N' be the last page in the file. Let n be the visited node and n' the child of n in E. Let n_j be a node called a *juncture node* in /KNU73/. In general, if T_1 i s a trie with n_j then we say that one *concatenated* a trie T_2 with T_1 when the root of T_2 replaced n_j, rendering both tries a single one. Initially, T'_1 and T'_r consist each of a single juncture node.

1. [Build T'_1 and T'_r] :
- While visiting successively each $n \neq r'$ in E, starting from $n = r$, do :
- If n' is the left (right) child then concatenate T'_r (T'_1) with n and its right (left) subtrie ; create then the left (right) child of n and set it to current n_j.
- Concatenate T'_r with the right subtrie of r' and T'_1 with the left subtrie of r'.
2. [Write T'_1 and/or T'_r to the disk if they do not overflow] :
- If T'_1 does not overflow then if P is not page 0, then write T'_1 into P else write T'_1 into page N' and set $N' <= N' + 1$.
- If T'_r does not overflow, then write T'_r into page N' and set $N' <= N' + 1$.
3. [Connect r' to the parent of T if any and to T'_1 and T'_r]
- If T has the parent, in page let it be P', then read P'; insert r' value into DV and DN of the first free cell $N'_{P'}$ in the buffer of P'; set $LP(N'_{P'}) <= P$ and $RP(N'_{P'}) <= N''$; set the page pointer that pointed to P within the parent cell to $P <= -N'_{P'}$.
- If P is page 0, then replace the content of P with r' and connect pages $N' - 1$ and N' to '.
4. [Split the overflowing subtrie, if any]. If either T'_1 or T'_r overflows, then apply A4 toT'_1 or to T'_r.
5. If the buffer with r' does not overflow, then write it to page P' or to page 0 and return. Else apply A4 to the subtrie in the buffer.

III.2.3.2 Discussion

Fig 4 shows the split of the example trie. The algorithm worked as follows, from the initial values returned by Algorithm 3 that were : $E = (o, 0), (i, 0), (\_, 1), (a, 0), (h, 0)$ and thus $r' = (h, 0)$.
- Step 1 started with node $(o, 0)$ whose child $(i, 0)$ in E is a left child. Therefore the step

concatenated T'_r with the node (o, 0) and its right subtrie in T. The left child of (o, 0) in T'_r became new n_j.

- Step 1 was then iterated for node (i, 0). Since its child in A is again a left child, this node and its right subtrie in T became the left subtrie of (o, 0) in T'_r. By the same token, the node $(\_, 1)$ and its right subtrie in T became the left subtrie of (i, 0) in T'_r and the left child of $(\_, 1)$ in T'_r became new n_j.

- In contrast, (a, 0) became the root of T'_1 since its child in E is a right child. Also its left subtrie entered T'_1, while n_j became its right child.

- The left subtrie of (h, 0) in T replaced n_j in T'_1 and the right subtrie replaced n_j in T'_r.

- Step 2 wrote T'_1 into page 1 and T'_r into page 2.

- Step 3 replaced the content of buffer of page 0 with cell 0 with values DV = h, DN = 0, LP = 1, RP = 2.

- Step 5 wrote the buffer to page 0 and terminated the algorithm.

The algorithm may generate a multilevel trie, but in practice P' should stay page 0 only. Page 0 should overflow only at the first split of the trie, when the trie becomes bilevel. T'_1 (T'_r) overflows iff the bucket split that triggered the trie split appended more internal nodes to the left (right) subtrie of r than resulted for T'_r (T'_1) from the split. The corresponding recursive call to A4 is very unlikely.

It is also unlikely, although may happen that T'_1 or T'_r consists of a single leaf. This is the case if one chooses (t, 0) as the split node in the example trie. The empty subtrie is represented in the new page by the cell that is a copy of this created for r'. However, the value of the pointer other than this pointing to the new page is set to nil. The cell is replaced with the usual one when the corresponding bucket is split.

The choice of r' did not violate the logical structure. The trie T' produced by the split preserves in addition the inorder. Therefore, all logical paths are preserved as well. The trie T' is thus equivalent to T.

Pages with bucket pointers are called *leaf pages*. Other pages are called *branch pages*. The number of pages that a search examines until it reaches a page is called the *page level*. Leaf pages are all at the same level called the *file level*. MLTH file is in this sense *balanced*, as is a B-tree file. TH file level is of course 0.

Finally, one may observe that the basic action of the algorithms A3 and A4 on T as the whole, may be seen as its transformation into to a better balanced T'. The process balances the respective sizes of T'_1 and of T'_r as equally as possible, but does not attempt to further balance each subtrie. This would have no effect on the page load factor, only on the trie traversal time that is usually anyhow very small compared to the disk access time. Also, experiences show the the subtries are usually already rather good. If one wants nevertheless the best balancing, then the couple A3 - A4 should be applied recursively to the subtries. The corresponding extension is obvious. It may also be applied to the balancing of TH trie as well, as the algorithm proposed in /TOR83/. It remains an open question which algorithm is more efficient. It is however likely that it should be ours, as there is no transformation of T into a canonical form prior to the balancing process.

IV. OPERATIONS ON MLTH FILE
IV.1 Search and insertion.

The search moves to another page when a positive (page) pointer is encountered as long the level of the visited page is smaller than the file level. The page at the file level must be a leaf page and the pointer is a bucket pointer. With respect to insertions, the only new feature consists of page splits.

IV.2 Range query

Range queries that exceed one bucket require the determination of the address of the bucket that follows or precedes the current one with respect to key order. This address may be determined in two manners :

(a) - from the trie. The next bucket to be searched corresponds to the next leaf (in inorder or converse inorder etc.). Usually this leaf is within the same page and sometimes within the sibling leaf page. The general way to find the sibling page is to visit upper level page(s). The root page 0 should be the only such page in practice. The address of the parent page may be found also in stack S.

(b) - from the chain linking logically consecutive buckets, same as this frequently implemented for a B-tree. Accesses to the trie are then no longer needed, except of course for the first key search.

IV.3 Deletions

Deletions may merge sibling pages. Let P' be the page that contains the internal node to be replaced with the value of its left child because of the bucket merge. Let P be its parent page that is the page that contained the split node (thus P' is not the root page). Finally let P'' be the sibling page of P' with respect to P. The following situations may occur :

- The number of cells in P' and P'' is together less than b' and there is no other page at the file level. P' and P'' are then merged into P'. In addition, the split node moves from P into P'. All the corresponding pointers are updated in consequence.
- P' and P'' are the last ones at the current file level and their cells may jointly enter the free space in P. The cells move then to P. The pointers within P are updated in consequence.

Deletions may render the page load uneven, although this phenomena should not have practical importance. In particular, one may rebalance the set of nodes in sibling pages, applying the split algorithm to the set of nodes in both pages and to the parent node. A new parent node may result and a better distribution.

V. PERFORMANCE
V.1 Load factor

The paging does not influence the bucket load factor. Bucket load for MLTH is thus this of TH. The pages themselves are buckets of a dynamic file whose records are cells. For random insertions the load factor α'_r should thus be on the average around $65 + 70\%$, as page splits should be usually even. Fig 5 shows the shape of α'_r as a function of the number of insertions x and its average values obtained by simulations, for three typical values of b'. These values correspond to the page size $p = 0.5, 1, 2$ Kbytes. As one could expect, the average values of α'_r are almost independent of b and b' values, though only $b = 5, 10$ appear at the figure. The split balancing improves the average load by $5 + 8\%$, the load factor for straight splits only, being noted α'_n at the figure. The α'_r curve shape shows the usual periodical behaviour in $\log_2(x)$ and oscillations due to the tendancy of pages to be filled up and to split rather simultaneously. The curve shape for other values of b and of b' is very similar.

For sorted insertions, the average values of α' are between $40 + 80$. Usually, one has $\alpha'_a > \alpha'_d$ but not always. Generally, the actual root was the only choice for the split node for ascending insertions, e.g. split balancing was inoperative. This, because of the structural condition (b) in section III.2.2, despite the existence of nodes better respecting the condition (a) alone. The effect is nevertheless usually positive, as it makes $\alpha'_a \approx 60\%$ and sometimes much higher. The large variation of α'_a values for the same b', but different b values, including $b = 20, 50$ not shown at the figure, was confirmed by several simulations. It seems to indicate a complex relationship between the sorted file size and page and bucket sizes, not yet understood enough.

Unlike for ascending insertions, the split balancing revealed crucial for descending ones. Instead of being stable usually around 45 %, α'_d had tendency to decrease towards almost zero. To obtain higher values of α'_d or of α'_a, for instance for the initial loading, the choice of the split node should enlarge the right or the left subtrie.

V.2 Fanout

We call a <u>fanout</u> of level i ; $i = 0,1,2,...$; the average number of records filling up the file of level i. The fanout will be denoted $x(i)$. For the usual random insertions the fanout of MLTH file is about :

$$x(i) \approx b \ (0.7b')^i {}^{+1}. \qquad\qquad (V.1)$$

Indeed, since $\alpha \approx 0.7$ then the fanout of the root page is :

$$x(0) \approx 0.7b \ b',$$

as this page may contain up to b' cells. Then, the value of $x(1)$ corresponds to the root page full and to the average load of the other pages equal to about 70 %. Thus :

$$x(1) \approx 0.7b \ b' \ (0.7 \ b') = b \ (0.7b')^2$$

etc.

Two byte pointers suffice for files of $2^{15} = 32K$ buckets. The corresponding cell size is six bytes. Let p be the page size in Kbytes. It results from (V.1) that for 32K bucket file, $p \approx 1.3$ usually suffices for two level trie. Indeed, as:

$$32K \approx 0.7 \ b'^{\ 2} = 0.7 \ (Kp)^2 / 36,$$

so :

$$p \approx 1.3.$$

To provide a buffer of this size is generally easy. It also means that a larger page for such a file is unnecessary, unless one wishes to have page 0 only. Assuming the MS-Dos 4K byte clusters for buckets, it furthermore means that the file may span over 130 Mbytes. Finally, assuming b between 10 and 100 as usually, means that the file may grow up to at least 220 000 records and even 2 200 000 records.

For larger files, the pointer size may be three bytes. Such pointers suffice for 1.6M bucket files. This size probably suffices for the largest known files. Cell size is then eight bytes. The fanout becomes about :

$$x\ (i\ ) \approx b\ (90p)^{\ i+1}.$$

Modest $b = 20$ and $p = 10$ suffices thus for a bi-level file of almost 16 million records. A larger page like $p = 32$, leads to such a file of 160 million records. Then, $p = 64$ leads to a more than six hundred million record file etc. In particular, page and bucket sizes equal to the MS-Dos 4Kbytes lead to the file spanning over 0.75G bytes. This size suffices not only for IBM-PC magnetic disks, but also for the current optical disks (about 500M to 1G byte per disk).

V.3 Access performance

The root page may be assumed in core. The successful search for a key needs then $i + 1$ (disk) accesses, in practice two accesses for the largest files, and the unsuccessful one at most $i + 1$ accesses. As nil leaves should be rare, the average cost of an unsuccessful search should be in practice two accesses as well.

In general, the formulae of various access costs to MLTH file in the case of the random insertions are those known, of a B-tree with the same fanout and the same splitting policy. However, they lead to larger pages for a B-tree for the same fanout or to a better performance of MLTH file for the same page size, because of the larger fanout. The reason for that will be discussed.

VI. COMPARISON TO RELATED METHODS
VI.1 B-trees

We will call <u>B-cell</u> data produced by one split within a B-tree file, or within a B*-tree or within a prefix B-tree,... A B-cell contains mainly a record, or a key or a part of a key like a separator /BAY77/, then a pointer and a field indicating the cell length or end, unless the main field is of fixed length. Given the practical sizes of records, of keys and of separators, a B-cell is usually larger than that of the MLTH cell. The cell is largest for a basic B-tree, where it usually contains the whole record, and the smallest for a prefix B-tree.

For random insertions, the load factor α'_r of a B-tree (B*-tree,...) is about the same as that of MLTH, i. e. near 70%. Prefix B-tree is an exception, since the separators length optimization may decrease α'_r. For sorted insertions, the load factor is also usually higher for the ascending case and only a few percent lower for the descending ones. The same choice of page and bucket sizes leads thus for MLTH to a fanout generally larger than this of a B-tree. More precisely, it appears from (V.1) that if B-cell is m times larger than TH-cell, then for the same page size the fanout of MLTH is in general at least m^{i+1} times larger. For a B-tree the keys are usually about 20 - 40 bytes, which means that two level MLTH file may be about 10 to 45 times larger. For a prefix B-tree, $m \approx 2$ should be quite typical, which means that two level MLTH file may be 4 times larger. For smaller files, the disk access costs of MLTH should then be at most those of a B-tree. For larger files, the access costs of MLTH should be smaller by at least one access. Internal search should be faster as well, especially if Algorithm A1bis is applied.

While a prefix B-tree minimizes m among B-trees, it introduces algorithmic constraints with respect to both TH and a usual B-tree. The search is more cumbersome, as the cells are of variable length. The binary search in the page requires the existence of the delimiter noted '*' in /BAY77/ that must not appear inside a separator or a pointer, while modern applications use usually the full ASCII code for separators. Finally, the deletion is complex, as the merge may expand the separators, triggering overflows /BAY77/. Usually, one knows whether the merge is possible only after recalculating the separators. For all these reasons, while B-trees and their basic variants are among data structures most used, as far as we know no commercial system uses prefix B-trees (except might be the new recently announced system Merkur).

B-trees have several variants /KNU73/, /YAO78/, /COM79/, /LOM81/, /ROS81/, /SHO85/,... . Each variant optimizes some performance, usually the value of α_B. However, the ideas in these improvements may also be applied to MLTH and should lead to similar improvements.

VI.2 Dynamic hashing.

Among various dynamic hashing access methods, /LAR78/, /LIT78,80/, /FAG79/,... , some are designed for ordered files. Most known are probably the interpolation hashing (IH) /BUR83/, the grid file (GF) /NIE84/ and the bounded disorder method (BD) /LIT86/. Although IH and GF are basically designed as multikey access methods, one may apply them to primary key ordered files as well.

IH may provide higher load factor than MLTH, as it may attain about 90%. It may also attain a better average search cost, which may be under two accesses. However, while no key search in MLTH may need more than two accesses, keys in overflow chains of IH need several accesses. Finally, IH does not support sorted insertions and is more sensitive to adverse distributions.

GF load factor is similar to that of MLTH. There is no overflow record and so search cost is also two accesses. However, the method is also more sensitive than MLTH to adverse distributions. Insertions may then lead to an exponential growth of the directory.

The nature of BD is different from GF and from IH, since it may be used in connection with any principle of indexing. The principle of BD is indeed to replace in an access method the concept of a bucket pointed by an index cell, with the concept of a multibucket node addressed internally through hashing. The fanout may then increase and so the search costs may decrease. The price to pay is a higher cost of splits and of range queries, since there is no order within the nodes.

One way to compare BD and MLTH is to consider that BD is applied to TH instead of trie splitting. The load factor of BD should therefore be a few percent smaller than this of MLTH, as BD nodes cannot be filled up to 100%. The average search cost may in contrast be smaller, close to one access per search. However, the search cost through overflow chains within nodes may be much higher than with MLTH. When the index attained the maximal size (one page), node sizes grow indeed at least proportionally to the file size.

VII. CONCLUSION

Multilevel trie hashing is a new access method for large ordered and dynamic files. The method applies when the usage of the basic trie hashing is inconvenient. It is based on sophisticated properties of tries, which do not seem to be known yet. Performance analysis shows that two accesses per key search suffice for largest practical files. This makes the method usually faster than a B-tree. As the algorithms are simple to implement and fast, the method should reveal among the most practical known.

A prototype implementation of MLTH in Pascal is presented in /ZEG86/. Present work concerns deeper behavior analysis under various conditions. Future work should concern the concurrent usage of MLTH files and the recovery, on the basis of /ELL83/ and /TRO83/. Also, one should study the design of variants optimizing the load factor, applying the ideas of "overflow", of uneven splitting etc. that worked well for B-trees. Finally, one should extend MLTH to the multikey case.

Acknowledgements

We thank Dr. Vidyasankar for helpful comments.

REFERENCES

/BAY72/ Bayer, R., Mc. Creight, E. Organization and maintenance of large ordered indexes. Acta Informatica, 1, 3, (1972), 173-189

/BAY77/ Bayer, R., Unterauer, K. Prefix B-Trees. ACM TODS, 2, 1,(Mar 1977), 11-26.

/BRI59/ Briandais (de la), R. File Searching Using Variable Length Keys. Proc. of Est. Joint Comp. Conf, 295-298.

/BUR83/ Burkhard, W. Interpolation-Based Index Maintenance. PODS 83.ACM, (March 1983), 76-89.

/COM79/ Comer, D. The ubiquitous B-tree. ACM Comp. Surv. 11, 2 (June 1979), 121-137.

/DAT86/ Date, C., J. An Introduction to Relational Database Systems. 4-th ed., Addison-Wesley, 1986, 639

/ELL83/ Ellis, C., S. Extendible Hashing for Concurrent Operation and Distributed Data. PODS 83. ACM, (March 1983), 106-116.

/FAG79/ Fagin, R., Nievergelt, J., Pippenger, N., Strong, H.R. Extendible hashing - a fast access method for dynamic files. ACM-TODS, 4, 3, (Sep 1979), 315-344.

/FLA83/ Ph. Flajolet : On the Performance Evaluation of Extendible Hashing and Trie Searching. Acta Informatica, 20, 345-369 (1983).

/FRE60/ Fredkin, E. Trie Memory, CACM, 3, 490-499.

/GON84/ Gonnet, G., H. Handbook of ALGORITHMS and DATA STRUCTURES. Addison-Wesley, 1984.

/KNU73/ Knuth, D.E. : The Art of Computer Programming. Addison-Wesley, 1973.

/KRI84/ Krishnamurty, R., Morgan S., P. Query Processing on Personal Computers - A Pragmatic Approach. VLDB-84, Singapore (Aug. 1984), 26-29.

/JON81/ de Jonge, W., Tanenbaum, A., S., Van de Riet R. A Fast, Tree-based Access Method for Dynamic Files. Rapp IR-70, Vrije Univ. Amsterdam, (Jul 1981), 20.

/LAR78/ Larson, P., A. Dynamic hashing. BIT 18, (1978), 184-201.

/LAR82a/ Larson, P., A. A single file version of linear hashing with partial expansions. VLDB 82, ACM, (Sep 1982), 300-309.

/LIT78/ Litwin, W. Virtual hashing : a dynamically changing hashing. VLDB 78. ACM, (Sep 1978), 517-523.

/LIT80/ Litwin, W. Linear hashing : A new tool for files and tables addressing. VLDB 80, ACM, (Sep 1980), 212-223.

/LIT81/ Litwin, W. Trie hashing. SIGMOD 81. ACM, (May 1981), 19-29.

/LIT84/ Litwin, W. Data Access Methods and Structures to Enhance Performance. Database performance, State of the Art Report 12:4. Pergamon Infotech, 1984, 93-108.

/LIT85/ Litwin, Witold. Trie hashing : Further properties and performances. Int. Conf. on Foundation of Data Organisation. Kyoto, May 1985. Plenum Press.

/LIT86/ Litwin, W., Lomet, D. Bounded Disorder Access Method. 2-nd Int. Conf. on Data Eng. IEEE, Los Angeles, (Feb. 1986).

/LOM79/ Lomet, D.,. B. Multi-table search for B-tree files. ACM-SIGMOD, 1979, 35-42.

/LOM81/ Lomet, D. Digital B-trees. VLDB 81. ACM, (Sep 1981), 333-344.

/LOM83a/ Lomet, D. Bounded Index Exponential Hashing. ACM TODS, 8, 1, (Mar 1983), 136-165.

/MUL81/ Mullin, J., K. Tightly controlled linear hashing without separate overflow storage. BIT, 21, 4, (1891), 389-400.

/NIE84/ Nievergelt, J., Hinterberger, H., Sevcik, K., C. The Grid File: An Adaptable, Symmetric Multikey File Structure. ACM TODS, (March 1984).

/ORE83/ Orenstein, J. A Dynamic Hash File for Random and Sequential Accessing. VLDB 83, (Nov 1983), 132-141.

/OUK83/ Ouksel, M. Scheuerman, P. Storage Mapping for Multidimensional Linear Dynamic Hashing. PODS 83. ACM, (March 1983), 90-105.

/RAM84/ Ramamonohanarao, K., Sacks-Davis, R. Recursive Linear Hashing. ACM-TODS, 9, 3, (Sep. 1984).

/REG82/ Regnier, M. Linear hashing with groups of reorganization. An algorithm for files without history. In Sheuermann P. (ed) : Improving Database Usability and Responsiveness, Academic Press, (1982), 257-272.

/ROS81/ Rosenberg, A., L., Snyder, L. Time and space optimality in B-trees. ACM-TODS, 6,1 (1981),174-193.

/SAM84/ Samet, H. The Quadtree and Related Hierarchical Data Structures. ACM Computing Surveys, 16, 2 (June 1984), 187-260.

/SCH81/ Scholl, M. New File Organizations Based on Dynamic Hashing. ACM TODS, 6, 1, (March 1981), 194-211.

/SHO85/ Shou-Hsuan Stephen Huang. Height-Balanced Trees. ACM TODS, 10, 2 (1985), 261-284.

/TAM82/ Tamminen, M. Extendible hashing with overflow. Inf. Proc. Lett. 15, 5, 1982, 227-232.

/TOR83/ Torenvliet, L., Van Emde Boas, P. The Reconstructive and Optimization of Trie Hashing Functions. VLDB 83, (Nov. 1983), 142-157.

/TRE85/ Tremblay, J-P., Sorenson, P., G. An Introduction to Data Structures. 2-nd ed., McGraw-Hill, 1984, 861.

/TRO81/ Tropf, H., Herzog, H. Multidimensional range search in dynamically balanced trees. Agnew. Inf. 2, 71-77.

/WIE83/ Wiederhold, G. Database design. McGraw-hill Book Company, 1983.

/YAO78/ Yao, A., C. On random 2-3 trees. Acta Inf. 18, (1983),159-170.

/ZEG86/ Zegour, D . Implementation du hachage digital multiniveaux. Techn. Rep., (Sep. 1986), INRIA.

(a) the, of, and, to, a, in, that, is, i, it, for, as, with, was, his, he, be,
not, by, but, have, you, which, are, on, or, her, had, at, from, this

(b)

	to	or			you		her			
are	this	on	it	by	with		he			
and	the	of	is	but	which		have		at	from
a	that	not	in	be	was	i	had	his	as	for

| 0 | 1 | 2 | 3 | 4 | 5 | 6 | 7 | 8 | 9 | 10 |

(c)

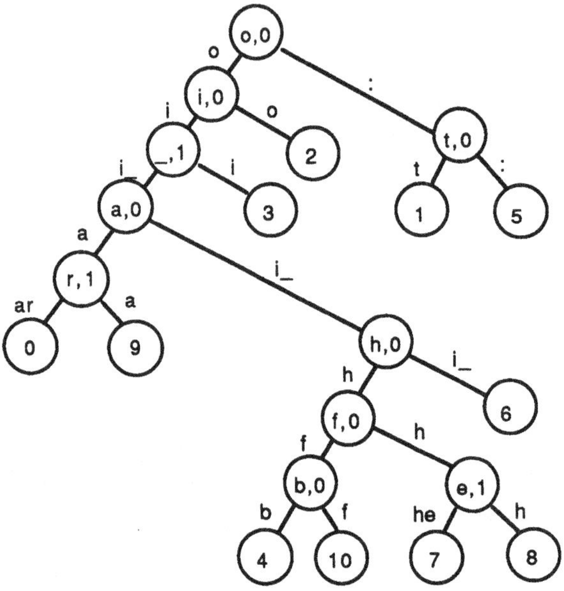

d)

| RP |
| DV | DN |
| LP |

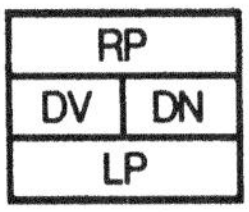

RP - Right pointer
LP - Left pointer
DV - Digit value
DN - Digit number

e)

-4	2	3	-5	5	6	-7	8	9	10
o	0	i	0	_	1	a	0	t	0	h	0	f	0	e	1	r	1	b	0
-1	-2	-3	-8	1	-6	-9	7	0	4

| 1 | 2 | 3 | 4 | 5 | 6 | 7 | 8 | 9 |

Fig 1 : Example file

(a) insertions
(b) buckets
(c) trie with logical paths
(d) cell structure
(e) trie representation

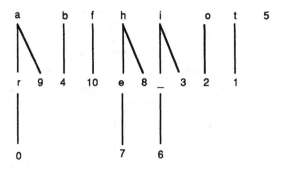

Fig 2 : Logical structure of the trie

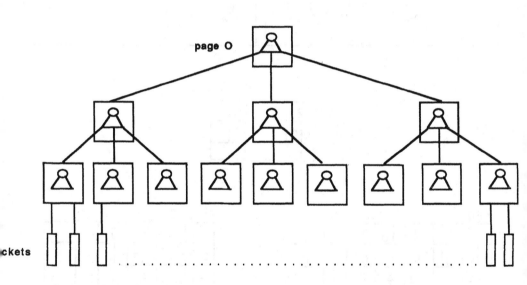

Fig 3 : Multilevel Trie

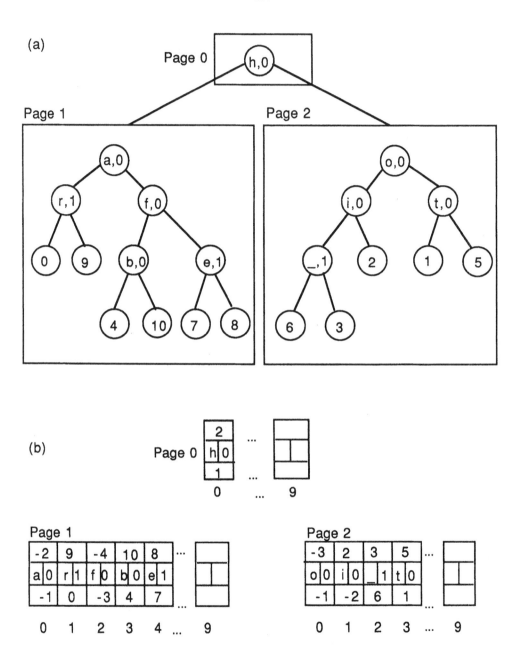

Fig 4 : Trie split

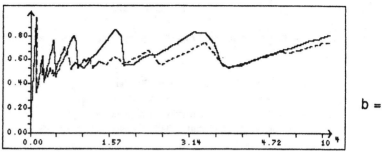

Load factor for random insertions with split balancing (-)
and without (--).

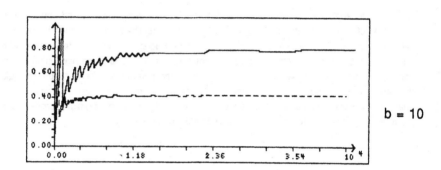

Load factor for ascending (-) and descending(--) insertions.

	p = 0.5 K		p = 1 K		p = 2 K	
	b = 5	b = 10	b = 5	b = 10	b = 5	b = 10
α'_r	67.3	66.4	66.4	66.0	68.0	65.1
α'_n	59.4	61.7	60.4	62.0	60.0	58.0
α'_a	59.9	56.0	46.5	78.4	47.2	43.0
α'_d	46.3	44.0	40.4	42.0	59.3	46.4

Fig 5 : Page load factor

a) curves for p = 1

b) average load factor for random and...

VAR-PAGE-LRU

A Buffer Replacement Algorithm Supporting Different Page Sizes

Andrea Sikeler

University of Kaiserslautern
Erwin-Schrödinger-Straße, D-6750 Kaiserslautern, West-Germany

Abstract

Non-standard applications (such as CAD/CAM etc.) require new concepts and implementation techniques at each layer of an appropriate database management system. The buffer manager, for example, should support either different page sizes, set-oriented operations on pages, or both in order to deal with large objects in an efficient way. However, implementing different page sizes causes some new buffer management problems concerning search within the buffer, buffer allocation, and page replacement. Assuming a global buffer allocation strategy, we introduce a page replacement algorithm which determines several pages stored in subsequent buffer frames to be replaced for a requested page. First investigations prove the algorithm to be a promising solution for buffer management with different page sizes.

1. Introduction

Although several modern operating systems provide a main storage file cache, most database management systems (DBMS) maintain their own database buffer for purposes of interfacing main memory and external storage devices (disks) /St81, CHMS87/. In order to facilitate the exchange of data between main memory and disk storage, the database is commonly divided into pages ("containers") of equal size (generally 512 to 4096 bytes). Typically, the database buffer consists of buffer frames of uniform size /EH84/. Therefore, the unit of data exchange is usually one page requested on demand (FIX operator). For each request (or logical reference /EH84/) the buffer manager has to perform several actions:

- The buffer is searched for the page and the page is located.

- If the page is not in the buffer, a replacement algorithm together with a buffer allocation strategy determines a buffer frame for the page. The "old" page in that buffer frame has to be replaced. Whenever this page has been modified, it has to be written back to disk before the requested page can be located in that buffer frame.

- The requested page is fixed in the buffer, and the address of the buffer frame is returned to the requesting DBMS component, i.e. to the access system.

While the page is fixed in the buffer, the access system may manipulate the contents of that page with simple machine instructions (such as COMPARE, MOVE, etc.). Therefore, replacement for that page is prevented until an explicit UNFIX operation makes the page eligible for replacement.

As a consequence of introducing pages as the unit of data exchange, in most existing DBMS (e.g. SYSTEM R /As76/) the size of objects manipulated by the access system (records or tuples) is limited by the page size of the buffer manager. Thus, modeling of application objects is affected by the page size yielding an unnecessary system restriction. In commercial applications objects are simple, being able to be described by a single record of limited size (less than approximately 2000 bytes). The objects of so-called non-standard applications (such as office automation, geographical data processing or CAD/CAM), however, are generally more complex, and often composed of other simple or complex objects (e.g. the boundary representation of a solid /BB84/). Even a simple object can be described by only a few bytes (e.g. a point in CAD/CAM) or by some Mbytes (e.g. an image or map in geographical data processing). Hence, all new data models for so-called non-standard DBMS (NDBMS), such as NF2 /SS86/, extended relational model /Lo84/, or MAD (molecule-atom data model) /Mi86/, include a data type LONG FIELD, BYTE VAR, etc. for very long attributes. Furthermore, all these models offer the possibility to build complex objects, either in a static or dynamic manner. As a consequence, such concepts have to be supported by all NDBMS components, especially by the access system and by the underlying buffer manager. The access system should be able to handle records spanning two or even more pages. It should cluster all records describing one complex object into one or more pages /DPS86, HR85/. Therefore, it should be possible to define a set of pages. These pages should be treated by the buffer manager as a "single page", i.e. the page set as a whole is transferred to and from the database buffer (e.g. by chained IO). In addition, it seems useful to support different page sizes, as the page size may then be defined in order to approximate the record size, and assuming page level locking in a multi-level concurrency control environment many fictitious synchronization conflicts can be avoided.

In the next section, we describe a possible interface, i.e. the objects and operations, of an NDBMS buffer manager which among other things supports different page sizes. Implementing different page sizes, however, causes some problems discussed in section 3. As a solution to these problems a new page replacement algorithm supporting different page sizes is introduced and investigated (section 4). First quantitative results were gained using slightly modified real page reference strings of CODASYL DBMS applications (section 5). A short summary concludes the paper.

2. Interface of an NDBMS Buffer Manager

The buffer manager described in this section is part of PRIMA (prototype Implementation of the molecule-atom data model), an DBMS-kernel designed and implemented for non-standard applications (for a detailed description see /HMMS87/). PRIMA may be divided into three layers according to the chosen mapping hierarchy (molecules - atoms - pages - disks, Fig. 1). (Atoms are similar to records or tuples, whereas molecules are sets of heterogeneous atoms forming complex objects.) The data system is responsible for the composition and structuring of molecules, i.e. complex objects, which are built dynamically out of atoms. Atoms are mapped by the access system onto the different kinds of "containers" offered by the storage system. Each container may include various atoms which do not belong necessarily to the same molecule. However, molecules may be predefined using atom clusters, which allow for the common storage of several atoms in a single container, perhaps together with other atom clusters. As a consequence, the storage system as the lowest layer has no knowledge about the contents of the containers offered by itself. It solely pursues two major tasks: It manages the database buffer and organizes the external storage devices, thus being responsible for the data exchange between main storage and disk storage. Therefore, the storage system consists of two components: the buffer manager maintaining the database buffer and the file manager of the underlying operating system DISTOS /Ne87/ for data exchange.

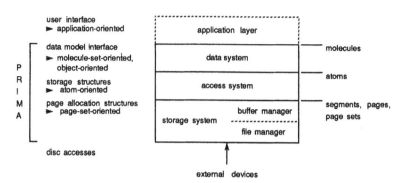

Figure 1: Architecture of a non-standard database system

This file manager offers some nice features regarding the requirements of non-standard applications:

- When creating a file one can choose from among five different block sizes (1/2, 1, 2, 4, and 8 kbytes). The chosen block size is kept fixed during the lifetime of a file.

- Files are dynamic. New blocks may be inserted anywhere and any existing blocks may be deleted.

- Operations on blocks are set-oriented. It is possible to read or write an arbitrary number of single blocks, a sequence of blocks, as well as the whole file.

- Blocks may be clustered. All blocks of a cluster are stored on disk in physical contiguity such that an efficient access to the whole cluster is feasible, e.g. by chained IO. Clusters are dynamic, i.e. they are bearranged whenever they grow or shrink.

Based on the objects and operations of the file manager, the PRIMA buffer manager, by managing the database buffer, provides a number of "infinite" linear address spaces with visible page boundaries. Therefore, the database is divided into various segments consisting of a set of logically ordered pages. Each segment is mapped onto a file and each page to a block. Thus, all pages of a segment are of equal size, which can be 1/2, 1, 2, 4, or 8 kbytes depending on the block sizes of the file manager and which is kept fixed during the lifetime of the segment, i.e. the PRIMA buffer manager supports **different page sizes**. Segments are dynamic. The segment-internal free place administration (FPA), which is integrated into the buffer manager, automatically allocates new pages when space is required which cannot be satisfied by existing pages. Similarly, the FPA automatically deletes empty pages when they reside at the end of the segment. Otherwise, empty pages are reused as soon as possible when space is required.

Hence, two different page types are distinguished within a segment. FPA pages are used only for free place administration. As the FPA is integrated into the buffer manager these pages are not available outside. Data pages, however, are used by the access system to store "user objects", i.e. physical records, address information, access path entries, and so on. They are requested by the FIX-PAGE operator indicating the fix mode, i.e. whether the page is needed for read or write purposes. Moreover, locking is integrated into the FIX-PAGE operator, i.e. the fix mode is used to lock the page in the appropriate mode. Repeated references of the same transaction possibly result in a lock conversion (read to write). Correspondingly, the UNFIX-PAGE operator indicates whether or not the page has actually been modified, i.e. the page has to be written to disk when it is replaced.

The five page sizes, however, do not meet all requirements of non-standard applications. The restriction to a certain page size, even 8 kbytes, is too stringent, especially regarding arbitrary length objects such as complex objects or strings (text, image) which may grow up to some MBytes. Therefore, **page sequences** are introduced as predefined page sets. A page sequence is a set of logical consecutive pages of a segment which contain (from the viewpoint of the access system) one single "user object" spanning these pages /DPS86/. A page sequence consists of a so-called header page and one or more component pages. Page sequences are dynamic since component pages may be added and removed arbitrarily depending on the current length of the "user object". To support physical clustering a page sequence is mapped onto a cluster at the file level. Requesting a page sequence (FIX-PAGE-SEQUENCE operator) causes the buffer manager to fix all pages in the database buffer belonging to that page sequence. These pages, however, are distributed over the buffer, i.e. the page sequence does not build one contiguous linear address space within the buffer, and the access system must be aware of the page boundaries. Correspondingly, the UNFIX-PAGE-SEQUENCE operator releases the whole page sequence, indicating for each page whether or not it has actually been modified.

Additionally, the PRIMA buffer manager offers three operators to handle not only such predefined page sets but also arbitrary page sets. The (UN)FIX-PAGE-SET operator is just a shorthand for a number of subsequent (UN)FIX-PAGE/(UN)FIX-PAGE-SEQUENCE operators. In other words, all specified pages and page sequences are fixed (unfixed) in the buffer. On the other hand, the FIX-ONE-PAGE operator supports access to replicated data fixing only one of the specified pages or page sequences, selecting that page or page sequence with minimum cost, i.e. the buffer manager performs a "page contest" along certain selection criteria (e.g. "already in buffer", page size, lock conflicts).

Regarding the objects and operations of the PRIMA buffer manager the question arises as to whether both *different page sizes* and *predefined page sets* should be supported. In order to answer this question we have decided to implement both concepts thus allowing for a thoroughgoing investigation of the pros and cons of both, e.g.:

- contiguous address space within the buffer versus distribution over the buffer,
- different limited page sizes versus the unlimited size of a predefined page set, and
- support of different block sizes versus support of a flexible cluster mechanism and chained IO by the file manager.

However, the decision as to which concept is best suited strongly depends on the structuring and mapping mechanisms in the application, in the data system, and in the access system (fixed or variable atom sizes, differences in the atom sizes, etc.) Therefore, in this paper we will concentrate on the problem of how to manage the database buffer when implementing different page sizes, whereas first results regarding predefined page sets supported by chained IO are summarized in /WNP87/.

3. Buffer Management Considering Different Page Sizes

Database buffer management includes three major actions which may be influenced using different page sizes: search within the buffer, buffer allocation, and page replacement.

There are different search strategies to locate a page in the buffer (either for a fix or an unfix operator) /EH84/. One of the most efficient is searching indirectly via a hash table. The hash algorithm transforms a segment number and a page number into a displacement in a page table, where an entry describing the page and its current position in the buffer can be found. In conventional DBMS, the current position of the page corresponds to the number of the buffer frame where the page is located. Using different page sizes a page generally occupies a number of subsequent frames depending on how the buffer is divided into frames. Thus, the table entry has to contain the actual number of frames occupied by the corresponding page.

In the case of a fix operation both the buffer allocation strategy and the page replacement algorithm are invoked in order to determine a buffer page to be replaced for the requested page. While the buffer allocation strategy establishes the set of candidate buffer pages from which a "victim" has to be taken, the page replacement algorithm decides which is the "victim". In conventional DBMS, buffer allocation strategies may be classified according to Fig. 2 /EH84/. Using different page sizes, a fourth class of allocation strategies should be considered. Instead of distributing the available buffer frames among the current database transactions or among different page types they are distributed among different page sizes, i.e. the database buffer is divided into different partitions, each containing pages of a single size only /Pa84/. Since once again partition sizes could be either static or dynamic, the same algorithms as in local or page-type oriented strategies may be used (e.g. Denning's working-set algorithm /De68/). Therefore, the same problems and disadvantages arise /EH84/. A static allocation, for example, is very inflexible in situations where the current workload changes frequently, whereas dynamic strategies are sensible regarding the chosen working-set parameters. Moreover, in the case of a dynamic strategy a still unsolved problem is how to reorganize the partitions in an appropriate way. Using a page-size oriented buffer allocation strategy, however, has one major advantage: The same replacement algorithms (and perhaps the same transaction oriented or page-type oriented allocation strategies) as in conventional DBMS can be used within each partition.

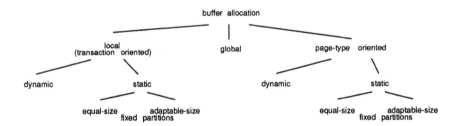

Figure 2: Classification of "conventional" buffer allocation strategies /EH84/

Nevertheless, we have decided to choose a global buffer allocation strategy, i.e. all pages which are not fixed at replacement time can be taken into account by the replacement algorithm, since such a strategy is simple and shows good results in conventional systems /EH84/. As a consequence, the replacement algorithm has to consider different page sizes. Since existing replacement algorithms (such as LRU etc. /EH84/) are only tailored to one page size, we either had to design a new one or to redesign an old one. In PRIMA, we have chosen the second alternative, i.e. the replacement algorithm described in the following section is based on the well-known LRU (least recently used) algorithm. The LRU algorithm was chosen since it has proven well suited in conventional DBMS /EH84/.

4. The VAR-PAGE-LRU Algorithm

VAR-PAGE-LRU was designed for a (database) buffer divided into frames of equal size and for pages of different sizes which are a multiple of the frame size. That is, each page is stored in a certain number of consecutive frames, in order to guarantee relative addressing within the page. As a consequence, VAR-PAGE-LRU has to cope with two problems.

VAR-PAGE-LRU, such as the classical LRU algorithm, initially tries to choose the oldest page (i.e. earliest unfix time) for replacement. However, using different page sizes, two facts have to be considered. On the one hand, pages may be replaced by smaller ones. Thus, free buffer frames arise which results in a **buffer fragmentation** and a perhaps low buffer occupancy. Therefore, VAR-PAGE-LRU has to reuse free buffer frames which are managed in a so-called free-list, in order to minimize buffer fragmentation and to maximize buffer occupancy. On the other hand, in some cases it does not suffice to replace a single page. Rather **multiple buffer pages** have to be replaced in order to achieve enough consecutive free frames for the requested page. These pages, however, should be as old as possible with respect to the LRU property. Therefore, VAR-PAGE-LRU proceeds the LRU-chain backwards starting with the oldest element and marks for each list element those buffer frames as free, which are occupied by the corresponding page until sufficient consecutive buffer frames are marked. Hence, all corresponding pages have to be replaced. However, it may happen that the number of marked buffer frames is too large and that perhaps too many pages are replaced (e.g. when marking combines two regions of already marked buffer frames). Thus, in a second step VAR-PAGE-LRU determines the minimum number of the pages to be replaced. Again the oldest pages should be selected. So, VAR-PAGE-LRU pursues two goals:

(1)   The pages being replaced have to be as old as possible (LRU property).

(2)   The number of pages to be replaced has to be as small as possible (minimizing IO).

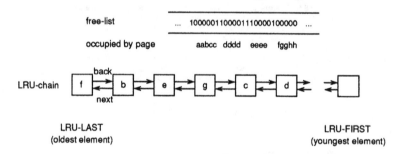

Figure 3: Data structures of VAR-PAGE-LRU

The **data structures** used by VAR-PAGE-LRU are, as already mentioned, an LRU-chain and a so-called free-list. The *LRU-chain* contains all entries of the page table where the corresponding page is unfixed. The entries are sorted according to the time of the last unfix operation on the page. So, "least recently used" is interpreted as "least recently unfixed" and not as "least recently referenced" /EH84/. The beginning and the end of the LRU-chain are indicated by LRU-FIRST and LRU-LAST, respectively. The *free-list* is a bitlist containing one bit for each buffer frame. This bit indicates whether the corresponding frame is free ("1") or occupied ("0"). Occupied means that the frame itself or a consecutive number of frames it belongs to represents a page with a corresponding entry in the page table, whereas free means that the frame may contain a part of a previously replaced page. Fig. 3 shows a corresponding scenario. Additional data structures for buffer management are transaction oriented FIX-chains and a changed-chain. The first contains all entries of the page table in which the corresponding page is fixed by the appropriate transaction, whereas the second contains those entries in which the page has to be written to disk in the case of replacement.

Thus, the first action of VAR-PAGE-LRU (Fig. 4) is to search the free-list for a number of consecutive free frames sufficient for the requested page. If such a sequence exists, no page has to be replaced. Otherwise, the replacement algorithm starts to determine one or more consecutive pages within the buffer which then have to be replaced to get enough free place (perhaps in combination with free buffer frames) for the requested page. Therefore, VAR-PAGE-LRU proceeds in two steps:

```
algorithm:   position := search free-list
             IF   position = 0
                  THEN   copy free-list into work-list
                         actual-page := lru-last
                         range-found := FALSE
                         WHILE NOT (range-found) AND NOT (end of LRU-chain) DO step 1
                         IF   range-found
                              THEN IF   position = 0
                                        THEN   step 2
                              ELSE error

step 1:      IF   actual-page + surrounding free frames of free-list >= #-of-frames
                  THEN   add actual-page to replace-list
                         position := first free frame of range
                         range-found := TRUE
                  ELSE   IF   actual-page + surrounding free frames of work-list >= #-of-frames
                              THEN   free actual-page in work-list
                                     range := first to last free frame of range
                                     range-found := TRUE
                              ELSE   free actual-page in work-list
                                     actual-page := back (actual-page)

step 2:      actual-page := next (actual-page)
             add back (actual-page) to replace-list
             WHILE actual-page <> NIL DO
                  WHILE NOT (actual-page within range) DO actual-page := next (actual-page)
                  IF   left side of range without actual-page >= #-of-frames
                       THEN   range := left side of range without actual-page
                              actual-page := next (actual-page)
                       ELSE   IF   right side of range without actual-page >= #-of-frames
                                   THEN   range := right side of range without actual-page
                                          actual-page := next (actual-page)
                                   ELSE   actual-page := next (actual-page)
                                          add back (actual-page) to replace-list
```

Figure 4: Algorithm VAR-PAGE-LRU

Step 1: Searching for a sufficient range of free frames (Fig. 5)

In a first step the LRU-chain is searched, starting with the oldest page, until enough consecutive pages are found to satisfy the request. For that purpose, a second bitlist, the so-called work-list, is used to simulate the behaviour of the free-list by testing the consequences of freeing more than one page before actually doing so. Hence, the work-list is initialized by the current free-list. The LRU-chain is then searched. For each page, it has to be examined to see if the frames occupied by the page, perhaps in combination with neighbouring free frames from the free-list, are sufficient for the requested page. In this case, this is the only page to be replaced, and the algorithm stops (Fig. 5a). The same check is done with the work-list, and the algorithm turns over to the second step if there is enough space (Fig. 5b). Otherwise, the frames occupied by that page are marked as free in the work-list, and the next page of the LRU-chain is examined.

Step. 2: Searching for a set of pages to be replaced (Fig. 6)

The second step is only necessary when more than one page must be replaced. The space accumulated in the work-list can be larger than the space needed, but replacement should select only a minimum number of pages and should preserve the LRU property. Thus, actual replacement proceeds the other direction through the LRU-chain starting with the last page of the first step. Again each page is examined to see if its frames correspond to the free frames detected in the first step. In this case, it is checked as to whether the page is really needed to build the free frames sufficient for the requested page. If not, the page is deleted from the work-list by marking the corresponding buffer frames as occupied, and the algorithm continues with the remaining number of free frames and the next page of the LRU-chain. Otherwise, the page is put on a list containing all pages to be replaced and the algorithm goes on with the next page.

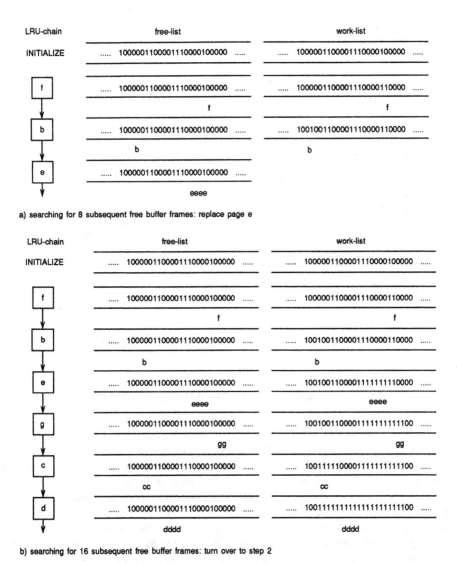

a) searching for 8 subsequent free buffer frames: replace page e

b) searching for 16 subsequent free buffer frames: turn over to step 2

Figure 5: Step 1 of VAR-PAGE-LRU using Fig. 4 as starting scenario

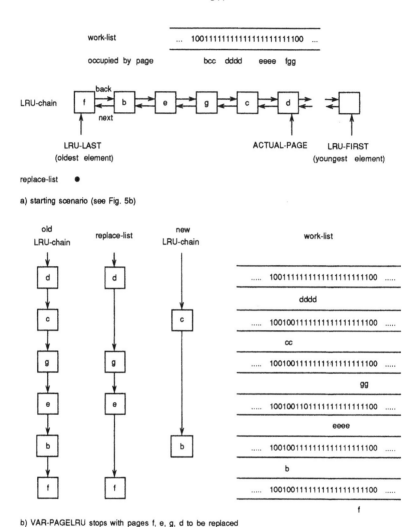

Figure 6: Step 2 of VAR-PAGE-LRU

Fig. 5b and 6 show a complete example of VAR-PAGE-LRU processing. The requested page needs 16 buffer frames. During the first step of the algorithm the pages f, b, e, g, c, and d are added to the work-list in the given order (Fig. 5b). The first step stops with page d, since including this page results in 20 subsequent free buffer frames. During the second step the pages are examined in the opposite direction (d, c, g, e, b, f). Page d is always put on the list containing all pages to be replaced. Page c is removed from the work-list since the remaining number of 17 free frames is still sufficient. As a side effect, page b falls out of the remaining number of examined free frames. Pages g, e, and f are also put on the list. Hence, the number of pages to be replaced is as small as possible and the pages being replaced are as old as possible.

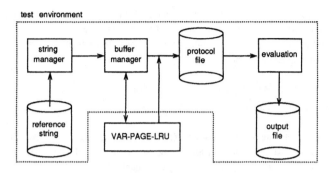

test environment

Figure 7: Test environment for VAR-PAGE-LRU

5. Evaluation and Optimization

Before including VAR-PAGE-LRU into PRIMA, the algorithm was implemented in PL/1 and embedded into a test environment (Fig. 7) in order to gain some information about its over-all behaviour. The test environment allows for the execution of a logical reference string consisting of multiple fix and unfix operations. The test buffer manager implements only those tasks which are necessary in order to estimate VAR-PAGE-LRU. During the execution of a string the buffer manager, as well as VAR-PAGE-LRU itself, write different measurement data on a protocol file which may be prepared in different ways. The most interesting information, however, are data concerning

- buffer occupancy (minimum, maximum, average),
- buffer fault rate,
- the number of LRU pages processed during a page fault, and
- the number of pages to be replaced.

For our investigations we used different real reference strings from CODASYL DBMS applications. Although these reference strings come from conventional applications in a CODASYL environment and therefore might be less realistic for non-standard applications, it was the simplest way to gain large reference strings in order to obtain first results about the behaviour of VAR-PAGE-LRU. For additional investigations, however, it will be necessary to generate synthetic reference strings to obtain more detailed results by varying the reference strings in an appropriate way. Nevertheless, the results illustrated in this section are restricted to the CODASYL reference strings and thus have to be reviewed under these circumstances.

For each of the strings the buffer size was varied from 0.5 Mbytes up to 6 Mbytes (step-width 0.5 Mbytes) using a fixed frame size of 0.5 kbytes. Since the original strings only refer to a single page size, the number of different page sizes, as well as the page sizes themselves, could be chosen randomly. Therefore, we executed measurements for page sizes

(1) which are a multiple of 1, 2, ..., 10 of the frame size and

(2) which are a multiple of 1, 2, 4, 8, 16 of the frame size (according to the page sizes of PRIMA).

VAR-PAGE-LRU demonstrates a very similar behaviour for each of the CODASYL reference strings. Hence, the most important results will be illustrated only for one of the strings. This string consists of 55 560 logical references on 7 different segments and about 7 000 different pages. To generate the page size of a segment the corresponding segment number was used:

(1)   page size = (segment number mod 10) + 1   * frame size

(2)   page size = 2 $^{\text{segment number mod 5}}$ * frame size

Fig. 8 shows the resulting distributions of the logical references on page sizes. For example, about 40 % of the references refer to a page size of 5 frames for (1) and to a page size of 16 frames for (2). As a consequence, the average page size of the alternatives differ from each other (5.4 frames for (1) and 9.4 frames for (2)). However, these distributions might not be realistic at all, but what are characteristic reference strings in a non-standard environment.

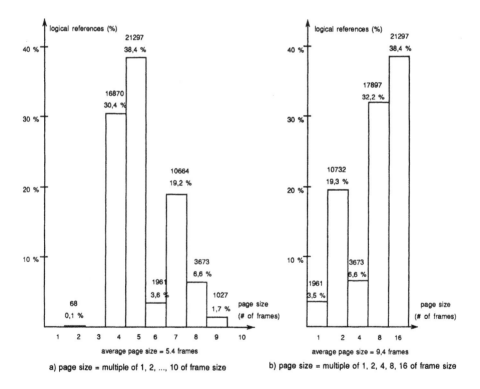

Figure 8: Number of logical references per page size (length of string: 55 560 references)

The results of VAR-PAGE-LRU concerning **buffer occupancy** proved to be very promising (Fig. 9). On the average about 99 % for (1) and 100 % for (2) of the buffer frames are occupied (independent of the buffer size). The minimum buffer occupancy varies between 87.2 % (0.5 Mbytes) and 92.2 % (6 Mbytes) for (1) and between 97.6 % and 99.4 % for (2), whereas the maximum buffer occupancy is always 100 %. The difference between (1) and (2) probably results from the different page sizes. Buffer fragmentation arises when a page larger than the requested one has to be replaced. However, for (2) the page being replaced is at least twice as large as the requested one, i.e. a relatively high number of frames is freed. Therefore, the probability to reuse free frames grows.

For comparison we implemented a straight-forward solution of a static page-size oriented buffer allocation strategy: The buffer is divided into partitions according to the number of different page sizes (10 partitions for (1) and 5 partitions for (2)). Each partition consists of the same number of frames of the appropriate size, i.e. each partition may include the same number of pages. In contrast to VAR-PAGE-LRU, the corresponding results regarding buffer occupancy are substantially worse (Fig. 9). Moreover, buffer occupancy becomes worse as buffer size grows. For instance, using a 6 Mbyte buffer, the minimum buffer occupancy of VAR-PAGE-LRU is about 92 % for (1), whereas partitioning results in a buffer occupancy of 31 %. The reason is that partition sizes are defined independently of the current workload. Hence, some partitions are never or only partially used. This arises in particular for (1) (see Fig. 8).

buffer size			1000	2000	3000	4000	5000	6000	7000	8000	9000	10000	11000	12000
VAR-PAGE-LRU	min	# of frames	872	1806	3633	2724	4515	5439	6367	7339	8204	9160	10088	11067
		%	87,2	90,3	90,8	90,8	90,3	90,7	91,0	91,7	91,2	91,6	91,7	92,2
	avg	# of frames	987	1978	2969	3960	4948	5942	6933	7928	8923	9924	10916	11907
		%	98,7	98,9	99,0	99,0	99,0	99,0	99,0	99,1	99,1	99,2	99,2	99,2
Partitions		# of frames	519	807	1095	1390	1687	1980	2268	2551	2846	3139	3431	3719
		%	51,9	40,4	36,5	34,8	33,7	33,0	32,4	31,9	31,6	31,4	31,2	31,0

a) page size = multiple of 1, 2, ..., 10 of frame size

buffer size			1000	2000	3000	4000	5000	6000	7000	8000	9000	10000	11000	12000
VAR-PAGE-LRU	min	# of frames	976	1969	2970	3970	4969	5969	6970	7968	8953	9948	10959	11926
		%	97,6	98,5	99,0	99,3	99,4	99,5	99,6	99,6	99,5	99,5	99,6	99,4
	avg	# of frames	1000	2000	3000	4000	5000	6000	7000	8000	8999	9999	10999	11999
		%	100	100	100	100	100	100	100	100	100	100	100	100
Partitions		# of frames	891	1731	2571	3405	4245	5085	5925	6761	7601	8441	9281	10115
		%	89,1	86,6	85,7	85,1	84,9	84,9	84,6	84,5	84,5	84,4	84,4	84,3

b) page size = multiple of 1, 2, 4, 8, 16 of frame size

Figure 9: Buffer occupancy

The results concerning the **buffer fault rate** (Fig. 10) also differ for (1) and (2) according to the different average page size. Reference measurements using constant page sizes point out that VAR-PAGE-LRU behaves similarly to the original LRU algorithm (whose behaviour regarding an optimal replacement is known /EH84/). As an example, the buffer fault rate for (1) (average page size = 5.4 frames) is somewhat higher than that for a constant page size of 2.5 kbytes (= 5 frames), whereas the buffer fault rate for (2) (average page size = 9.4 frames) is somewhat lower than that for a constant page size of 5 kbytes (= 10 frames). However, in any case the buffer fault rates of VAR-PAGE-LRU are always smaller than those using different partitions, again for the given CODASYL reference strings.

An important aspect with respect to the time for executing a page fault is the **number of LRU pages processed** during a single page fault. Fig. 11 summarizes the corresponding results which strongly differ for (1) and (2). Whereas for (1) most of the time (86.0 % to 53.4 %) only up to ten pages have to be examined, for (2) in up to 39.9 % of the cases more than 100 pages are touched. This results from the different distributions of the logical references on page sizes as well as from the sequence of the logical references, i.e. the access pattern at the buffer manager interface may strongly influence the number of LRU pages processed. However, synthetic reference strings should be used in order to obtain more detailed results.

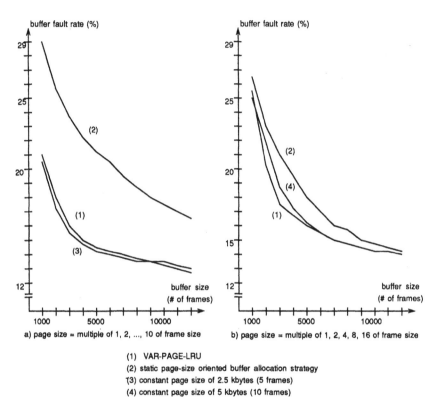

(1) VAR-PAGE-LRU
(2) static page-size oriented buffer allocation strategy
(3) constant page size of 2.5 kbytes (5 frames)
(4) constant page size of 5 kbytes (10 frames)

Figure 10: Buffer fault rate

Consequently, VAR-PAGE-LRU had to be improved with respect to the number of LRU pages processed during a page fault. Therefore, so-called page-size oriented pointers were introduced. Until then step 1 of VAR-PAGE-LRU always started with the last page of the LRU-chain (Fig. 4), i.e. during the execution of a number of subsequent page faults, for the same page size, the same LRU pages are examined again and again although it is obvious that these pages are not sufficient. Thus, the page-size oriented pointers indicate the first page not yet examined for the corresponding page size. Those pointers are the new starting-point of step 1. However, before step 1 all LRU pages from LRU-LAST up to the appropriate pointer are entered into the work-list. As a result, a substantial improvement for (2) as well as for (1) is achieved (Fig. 11), i.e. even for (2) most of the time (88.8 % to 68.2 %) only up to 10 pages are touched.

Moreover, the **number of pages to be replaced** during a page fault influences the time for executing a page request, since IO is the most critical point. However, VAR-PAGE-LRU shows a satisfactory behaviour with regard to this (Fig. 12). Most of the time only one page has to be replaced (92.9 % to 82.8 % for (1) and 82.8 % to 60.7 % for (2)). Additionally, some page faults can be satisfied without replacing any page (3.4 %

to 6.0 % for (1) and 10.8 % to 30.7 % for (2)). Therefore, in only a few of the cases has more than one page to be replaced. Furthermore, for (1) a maximum of 3 pages is affected (3 times), whereas for (2) up to 8 pages have to be replaced (13 times). This difference between (1) and (2) also results from the different page sizes.

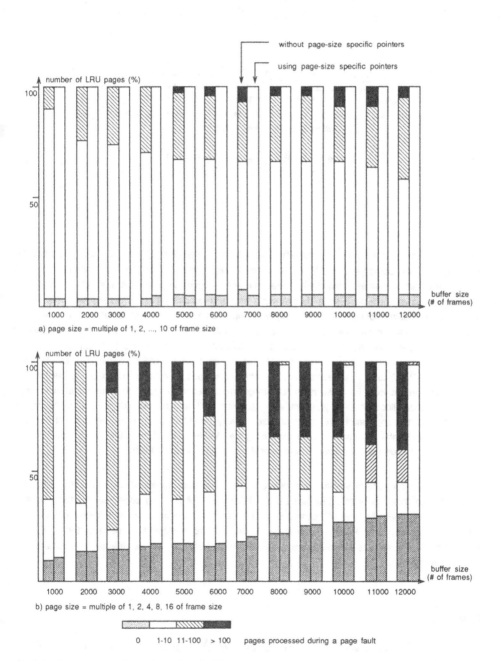

Figure 11: number of LRU pages processed during a page fault

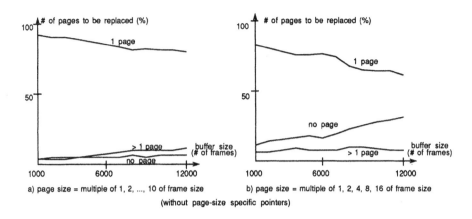

Figure 12: Number of pages to be replaced

6. Conclusions

Non-standard applications require more flexibility with respect to the objects and operations offered at the different layers of an appropriate NDBMS. The buffer manager, for instance, has to support set-oriented operations on pages as well as different page sizes in order to support large objects of variable length. However, implementing different page sizes causes some problems concerning buffer management, i.e. search within the buffer, buffer allocation, and page replacement. Assuming a global buffer allocation strategy we have introduced a page replacement algorithm called VAR-PAGE-LRU. VAR-PAGE-LRU determines one or more consecutive pages within the buffer which have to be replaced in order to create enough free place for a requested page. First investigations using reference strings from CODASYL DBMS applications have proved that VAR-PAGE-LRU is an appropriate and efficient solution. The buffer occupancy as well as the buffer fault rate are, at least for these reference strings, much better compared to those for a static page-size oriented buffer allocation strategy. Moreover, the buffer fault rate corresponds to that of the original LRU algorithm for the appropriate average page size. Hence, the overhead for searching a set of pages to be replaced is accidental. Consequently, we have integrated VAR-PAGE-LRU into the DBMS kernel PRIMA in order to allow for additional investigations with respect to non-standard applications.

However, the question remains whether both different page sizes and predefined page sets should be supported. And if so, how VAR-PAGE-LRU will behave in the case of handling page sets. Certainly, indepth investigations concerning the area of handling page sets /WNP87/ in combination with VAR-PAGE-LRU are necessary. Furthermore, VAR-PAGE-LRU itself has to be analysed in more detail using synthetic reference strings and new ideas such as moving unfixed pages within the buffer have to be reflected and perhaps integrated into the algorithm.

Acknowledgements

I would like to thank M. Michels who implemented VAR-PAGE-LRU and the test environment. Thanks are also due to T. Härder, E. Rahm, B. Mitschang, and I. Littler for helpful commmments and editorial suggestions which helped to improve the presentation of this material. Furthermore, I would like to thank the referees for their fruitful comments and the inspiration of new ideas (e.g. moving pages within the buffer).

References

As76   Astrahan, M.M., et al.: SYSTEM R: A Relational Approach to Database Management, in: ACM Transactions on Database Systems, Vol. 1, No. 2, June 1976, pp. 97-137.

BB84   Batory, D.S., Buchman, A.P.: Molecular Objects, Abstract Data Types and Data Models: A Framework, in: Proceedings of the 10th International Conference on Very Large Databases, Singapore, 1984, pp. 172-184.

CHMS87 Christmann, H.-P., Härder, T., Meyer-Wegener, K., Sikeler, A.: Operating System Support for Database Management Systems, to appear in: Proceedings of the Workshop on "Experiences with Distributed Systems", Kaiserslautern, 1987.

De68   Denning, P.J.: The Working Set Model for Program Behaviour, in: Communications of the ACM, Vol. 11, No.5, 1968, pp. 323-333.

DPS86   Deppisch, U., Paul, H.-B., Schek, H.-J.: A Storage System for Complex Objects, in: Proceedings of the International Workshop on Object Oriented Database Systems, Asilomar, ed.: K. Dittrich, U. Dayal, 1986, pp. 183-195.

EH84   Effelsberg, W., Härder, T.: Principles of Database Buffer Management, in: ACM Transactions on Database Systems, Vol. 9, No. 4, 1984, pp. 560-595.

HMMS87 Härder, T., Meyer-Wegener, K., Mitschang, B. Sikeler, A.: PRIMA - a DBMS Prototype Supporting Engineering Applications, to appear in: Proceedings of the 13th International Conference on Very Large Data Bases, Brighton, 1987.

HR85   Härder, T., Reuter, A.: Architektur von Datenbanksystemen für Non-Standard-Anwendungen (Architecture of Database Systems for Non-Standard Applications), in: Proceedings of the GI Conference on Database Systems for Office, Engineering, and Science Environments, Karlsruhe, ed.: A. Blaser, P. Pistor, Informatik-Fachberichte No. 94, Springer, Berlin Heidelberg New York Tokyo, 1985, pp. 253-286.

Lo84   Lorie, R., et al.: Supporting Complex Objects in a Relational System for Engineering Databases, in: Query Processing in Database Systems, ed.: Kim, W., Reiner, D.S., Batory, D.S., Springer, Berlin Heidelberg New York Tokyo, 1984, S. 145-155.

Mi86   Mitschang, B.: MAD - Ein Datenmodell zur Verwaltung von komplexen Objekten (MAD: A Data Model for Complex Object Management), SFB 124 Research Report, No. 20/85, University of Kaiserslautern, revised in 1986.

Ne87   Nehmer, J., et al.: Key Concepts of the INCAS Multicomputer Project, in: IEEE Transactions on Software Engineering, Vol. SE-13, No. 8, 1987, pp. 913-923.

Pa84   Paul, H.-B., at al.: Überlegungen zur Architektur eines "Non-Standard"-Datenbankkernsystems (Considerations on the Architecture of a "Non-Standard" Database Kernel System), Research Report DVSI-1984-A2, Technical University Darmstadt, 1984.

SS86   Schek, H.-J., Scholl, M.H.: The Relational Model with Relation-Valued Attributes, in: Information Systems, Vol. 2, No. 2, 1986, pp. 340-355.

St81   Stonebraker, M.: Operating System Support for Database Management, in: CACM, Vol. 24, No. 7, 1981.

WNP87   Weikum, G., Neumann, B., Paul, H.-B.: Konzeption und Realisierung einer mengenorientierten Seitenschnittstelle zum effizienten Zugriff auf komplexe Objekte (Concept and Implementation of a Set-Oriented Page-Interface with Efficient Access to Complex Objects), in: Proceedings of the GI Conference on Database Systems for Office, Engineering, and Science Environments, Darmstadt, ed.: H.-J. Schek, G. Schlageter, Informatik Fachberichte No. 136, Springer, Berlin, Heidelberg New York Tokyo, 1987, pp. 212-230.

The Twin Grid File: A Nearly Space Optimal Index Structure *

Andreas Hutflesz
Universität Karlsruhe
Postfach 6980
D - 7500 Karlsruhe

Hans-Werner Six
FernUniversität Hagen
Postfach 940
D - 5800 Hagen

Peter Widmayer
Universität Karlsruhe
Postfach 6980
D - 7500 Karlsruhe

Abstract

Index structures for points, supporting spatial searching, usually suffer from an undesirably low storage space utilization. We show how a dynamically changing set of points can be distributed among two grid files in such a way that storage space utilization is close to optimal. Insertions and deletions trigger the redistribution of points among the two grid files. The number of bucket accesses for redistributing points and the storage space utilization vary with the selected amount of redistribution efforts. Typical range queries – the most important spatial search operations – can be answered at least as fast as in the standard grid file.

1 Introduction

In geographic, engineering, CAD, VLSI and other non-standard database applications, storage schemes are needed that allow for the efficient manipulation of large sets of geometric objects. Especially, proximity queries should be handled efficiently. Index structures for secondary storage have been proposed supporting insertions, deletions, and range queries in a set of multidimensional points (Robinson 1981, Nievergelt et al. 1984, Krishnamurthy et al. 1985, Kriegel et al. 1986, Otoo 1986, Freeston 1987, Hutflesz et al. 1988). The grid file (Nievergelt et al. 1984) has proven to be useful when applied to geometric data (Hinrichs 1985, Six et al. 1988), because it adapts gracefully to the distribution of points in the data space, even if there are clusters (Hinrichs 1985).

However, the grid file suffers from an undesirably low average storage space utilization of roughly 39% only, like many other schemes based on recursive halving (Lomet 1987). Especially if storage space is costly or the set of data points is relatively static, i.e., few insertions and deletions occur after the database has been set up, one might wish to increase space utilization, at the expense of some restructuring, e.g. performed upon insertions or deletions. In contrast, it is usually intolerable to increase the time for answering range queries.

We propose a fully adaptive access scheme, based on the grid file (Nievergelt et al. 1984), that exhibits the following properties:

- storage space utilization is high; experiments show it to be around 90% on the average for two-dimensional points;
- range queries can be answered with at least the same efficiency as in the grid file, for average ranges;

---

* This work was partially supported by grants Si 374/1 and Wi 810/2 from the Deutsche Forschungsgemeinschaft

- the number of accesses to secondary storage per insertion or deletion, including restructuring operations, increases by a small factor as compared with the grid file; experiments show the factor to lie around 2 in a realistic setting.

Our scheme, the *twin grid file*, achieves this performance by using two grid files, both spanning the data space, and by appropriately partitioning the point set between these two grid files. It is similar to recursive linear hashing (Ramamohanarao et al. 1984) or to extendible hashing with overflow (Tamminen 1982) in that primarily one grid file is used to store data points, while the other grid file holds quasi-overflow points. It is different from the above in that a true overflow does not occur, but is instead created artificially for better space utilization. Also, points are quite regularly transferred back and forth between the grid files, as space utilization dictates.

In the next section, we sketch the basic idea of the mechanism of the twin grid file. A precise description of the structure and its operations follows in Section 3. We have implemented the twin grid file and compared its performance with the standard grid file; the implementation is described and the performance evaluation is presented in Section 4. Finally, we draw a conclusion in Section 5.

2 The basic idea

Consider a set of points in the plane, to be stored in a grid file, where each data bucket can hold three points. Let us focus on a series of insertions into the initially empty grid file. To recall the grid file partitioning strategy and compare it with the twin grid file mechanism, consult Figures 2.1 (a) through (f).

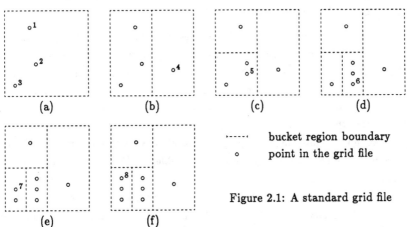

Figure 2.1: A standard grid file

------ bucket region boundary
o   point in the grid file

Figure 2.1 (a) shows three points in the data bucket corresponding to the entire data space. As point 4 is inserted (Fig. 2.1 (b)), the bucket region is split into two, corresponding to two buckets, the minimum number of buckets needed to store four points. After point 5 has been inserted (Fig. 2.1 (c)), we have three buckets, clearly more than the required minimum. Here, the twin grid file idea comes in.

Figures 2.2 (a) through (f) show the insertion of the points under consideration into the twin grid file; it illustrates the basic twin grid file idea and merits careful study.

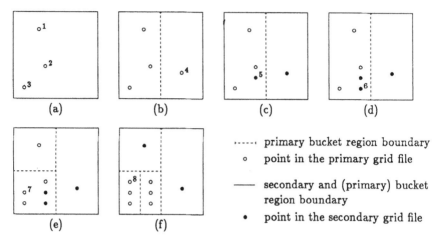

Figure 2.2: A twin grid file

In the twin grid file method, we artificially create an overflow, i.e., we do not store point 5 in the grid file as usual, but instead store it in an overflow bucket. This action alone does not decrease the number of buckets used; however, it gives us the potential to share the overflow bucket among several of the primary buckets. This potential can be exploited immediately by transferring point 4 from its primary bucket to the overflow bucket. Thereby its primary bucket becomes empty and need not be stored explicitly any more. Hence we are able to store the five points in two buckets. For an illustration, see Figures 2.2 (a) through (c).

As long as there is only one overflow bucket, no access structure for overflow buckets is needed. Later on, as the number of overflow buckets increases, we want to perform the operations insert, delete, and range query efficiently for the data stored in the overflow buckets as well. We therefore organize the overflow points in a grid file, the *secondary grid file*. The twin grid file then consists of two parts, the *primary grid file* and the *secondary grid file*. Points will be distributed between the two in such a way that the number of used buckets is small. If a point is to be inserted and falls into the bucket region of a full or an empty primary bucket, the twin grid file examines whether a secondary bucket is available for the insertion point. If this is the case, the point is inserted into this secondary bucket, and hence the use of an extra bucket can be avoided. Otherwise, it is checked whether the number of used buckets can be kept small by means of an extra secondary bucket. To this end, it is examined whether other primary buckets can be emptied by shifting their points into the secondary bucket in question (this holds for point 4 in Fig. 2.2 (c)).

Shifting points from primary to secondary buckets is by far not the only attempt at space optimization in the twin grid file. Whenever it pays off, points are shifted back and forth between the two grid files, triggered by an insertion or a deletion. In Figure 2.2, points 5 and 6 are inserted into the secondary grid file, because in the primary grid file an extra bucket would be needed to store them. Point 7 falls into a region with a full bucket, in the primary as well as in the secondary grid file. Therefore, the corresponding primary bucket is split; no other optimization can be performed. Point 8, again, causes a primary bucket to be split. If nothing else is done, three primary buckets and one secondary bucket are used to store eight points. However, the twin grid file does better. Since points should preferrably be stored in the primary grid file (unless bucket savings are possible), points 5 and 6 are transferred from the secondary to the primary buckets. Still, no bucket has been saved. But now, point 1 can be transferred into the secondary bucket, thereby emptying and saving one bucket. Hence, the twin grid file arrives at storing these eight points in three buckets, whereas the standard grid file needs four buckets. Also note the difference in storage potential of the grid file and the twin grid file at this stage: any next point can be inserted into the twin grid file without the need for an extra bucket, whereas in the grid file an extra bucket may be necessary.

These are just examples of the local restructuring operations performed by the twin grid file. Our proposed set of operations, including the preconditions of their applications, is described in the next section. Note that all restructuring operations are initiated by insertions or deletions of points. Range queries need to be carried out on both parts of the twin grid file, but remain unaffected from the restructurings.

3   The twin grid file mechanism

The twin grid file T consists of two parts, the primary grid file P and the secondary grid file S, both spanning the entire data space. Each grid file partitions the data space into regions associated with data buckets. Dummy buckets, i.e., buckets with empty bucket region, are not stored explicitly; instead, they are represented by a special directory entry.

In order to achieve a high space utilization, we aim at locally minimizing the number of buckets used to store a given set of points. For the purpose of explaining the twin grid file mechanism, let us restrict our attention to two-dimensional points. Locally, i.e., for a (generally small) connected subregion R of the data space, we pursue the following objectives:

1. Minimize the number of buckets used to store the points in region R;
2. Minimize the number of secondary buckets used to store the points in R;
3. Minimize the number of points in R stored in secondary buckets.

These objectives are ordered in decreasing importance. Objective 1 directly translates the overall aim to the considered region R, while Objectives 2 and 3 aim at keeping secondary regions large and secondary buckets rather empty, in order to support future optimization efforts. Clearly, Objective 2 should only be pursued after Objective 1 has been satisfied and similarly for Objective 3 after 1 and 2.

T is restructured to meet these objectives by repeatedly transferring a point from P to S, a *shift down* operation, or from S to P, a *shift up* operation, and carrying out the necessary adjustments within P and S, as prescribed by the standard grid file mechanism. After a sequence of shift operations, a bucket in P or S can be saved in one of two ways. Either it has become empty, i.e., it has not been empty before the sequence of shift operations and is now empty, or two buckets can be merged, according to the grid file mechanism, where the set of points in the two affected buckets fits into one bucket. We call this a *saving* in P or in S, respectively. An additional bucket in P or S may be needed, if a sequence of shifts necessitates a bucket split, or an empty bucket becomes non-empty; we call this a *loss* in P or S, respectively. Any sequence of shift operations that leaves the number of buckets in P or S unchanged is called *neutral* in P or S, respectively.

A *restructuring* operation for T consists of the combined and repeated application of all of the following simple rules.

Rule 1a: If a saving in P or in S is possible without any shift, then perform the corresponding merge operation (see Fig. 3.1 (a)).

This rule directly aims at reducing the total number of buckets used (Objective 1), as do the following Rules 1b through 1d.

Rule 1b: If there exists a sequence of shift down operations leading to one saving in P, neutral in S, then perform these shifts (see Fig. 3.1 (b)).

Rule 1c: If there exists a sequence of shift down operations leading to two savings in P and one loss in S, then perform these shifts (see Fig. 3.1 (c)).

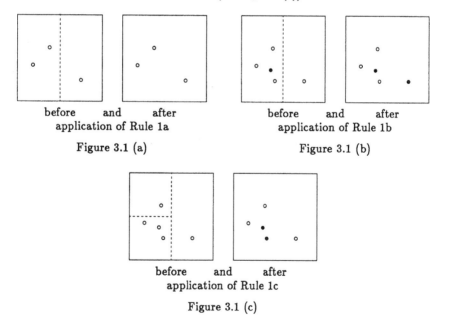

before and after
application of Rule 1a

Figure 3.1 (a)

before and after
application of Rule 1b

Figure 3.1 (b)

before and after
application of Rule 1c

Figure 3.1 (c)

Note that Rule 1c is essential for achieving any savings at all when inserting points into the initially empty twin grid file. Rule 1b affects one bucket becoming empty or two buckets being merged after one sequence of shift down operations; Rule 1c takes a broader view in considering up to four buckets in P. When more and more buckets are considered in this manner, we get the following slightly more general rule that covers Rules 1a through 1c as special cases.

Rule 1d: If there exists a sequence of shift down operations leading to i savings in P and less than i losses in S, for some integer $i > 0$, then perform these shifts.

Objective 2 is pursued by means of Rule 2, as follows.

Rule 2: If there exists a sequence of shift up operations leading to one saving in S and one loss in P, then perform these shifts (see Fig. 3.2).

This rule can also be applied in a more general way, with i instead of one saving in S and loss in P. However, one has to keep in mind that taking a broader view on the optimization region R entails more accesses on secondary storage for testing the preconditions for the application of the rules, without necessarily resulting in a much higher storage utilization.

Finally, Objective 3 is pursued by Rule 3.

Rule 3: If there exists a shift up operation neutral in P and S, then perform it (see Fig. 3.3).

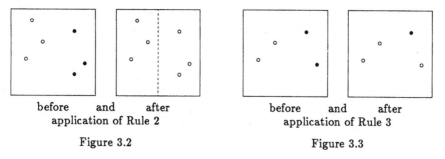

before	and	after
application of Rule 2		application of Rule 3

Figure 3.2   Figure 3.3

As a consequence of the application of Rule 3, all points stored in S lie in bucket regions of full or empty buckets in P.

Even though all of the above rules are simple and their effect straightforward, their combined and repeated application in general may rearrange the association of points with buckets quite substantially (recall Figures 2.2 (e) and (f), where Rules 3 and 1b have been applied).

All restructuring operations are driven by insertions and deletions; range queries do not initiate restructuring operations. In an insertion, the point to be inserted into T is first inserted into P; then, a restructuring operation takes place. Similarly, a point to be deleted from T is deleted from P or S, depending on where it is being stored, and then a restructuring operation follows. Note that an insertion or deletion within P or S may already lead to some reorganization within P or S, as prescribed by the standard grid file mechanism.

In order to keep the restructuring operations reasonably efficient, the set of points to which shift operations may be applied should be limited. On the other hand, this set should not be too small, in order to have an effect on space utilization. In our experiments we restrict the set of shiftable points to lie in a subregion of the data space that is relatively small and simple to find, as follows. At the insertion or deletion of a point, consider the two buckets b_P in P and b_S in S in whose regions the point lies, together with all buckets in P whose regions intersect b_S's and all buckets in S whose regions intersect b_P's. We restrict all restructuring operations to the combined set of these buckets; experimental results for this specific interpretation of the locality of the space minimization efforts are presented in the next section.

4   Implementation and performance

We implemented the standard and the twin grid file on an IBM-AT in Modula-2. Our implementation of the twin grid file for two-dimensional points is based on two separate standard grid files. In addition to the bucket addresses, the directory contains the number of points stored in each bucket. This information greatly reduces the number of bucket accesses in restructuring the twin grid file, without noticeably affecting its space utilization.

Let q be the point to be inserted. Recall that b_P denotes the bucket of the primary grid file P covering point q, b_S the corresponding bucket of the secondary grid file S. Restructuring operations take place in a suitably defined subregion R. To keep R simple, we make sure that any bucket region in P is completely contained in a bucket region in S. To this end, we allow a split in S only if it does not partition a bucket region in P, i.e., the split in S only uses bucket boundaries existing in P. The set B of buckets for restructuring consists of all buckets of P whose regions are completely contained in the region of b_S including dummy buckets. Furthermore, in P only pairs of buckets with both regions lying in one bucket region of S are considered for merge operations.

The effect of the application of our algorithm for a sequence of 100 insertions, as compared with the standard grid file, is shown graphically in Figure 4.1. The standard grid file needs 48 buckets to store the 100 points, whereas the twin grid file uses only 37 buckets.

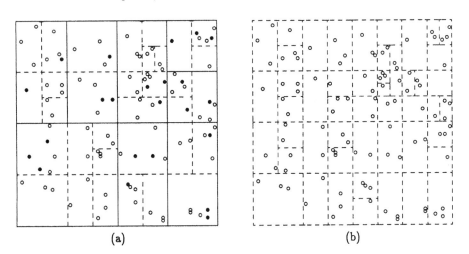

(a)	(b)

Figure 4.1: 100 points in a twin grid file (a) according to our implementation, and in a standard grid file (b), where each bucket can hold 3 points.

Now we describe the procedure to insert point q. We assume that the bucket capacities of P and S are equal. To decide which restructuring operations are to be carried out, we compute the effect of actions (like split or merge) in main memory; these actions are called *tentative* actions in the following description of the algorithm.

Insert q:

If b_P is not full and not empty *then*
>   store q in b_P
else if b_S is not full and not empty *then*
>   store q in b_S
else {an additional bucket in P (Objective 2) is needed}
>   *if* b_P is empty *then*
>>   store q in b_P, shift up all points of b_S lying in the region of b_P (Rule 3)
>   *else* {b_P is full}
>>   *reinsert q.*
>   *Restructure.*

Reinsert q:

Let b_P be the (full) bucket covering q.
Split b_P into b'_P and b''_P with the grid file mechanism, shift up as many points of b_S as possible lying in the regions of b'_P and b''_P.
W.l.o.g., let b'_P be the bucket covering q.
If b'_P is not full *then*
>   store q in b'_P
else if b_S is not full *then*
>   store q in b_S
else {b''_P must be empty, no loss in P}
>   *reinsert q.*

Restructure:

If there is a merge partner b'_S that can be merged with b_S *then*
>   merge b_S and b'_S into b_S (Rule 1a), and update B according to b_S.
If b_S is not empty *then*
>   *if* there is a bucket b_P of B whose region covers all points of b_S *then*
>>   *if* b_P is empty *then*
>>>   shift up all points of b_S into b_P (Rule 2)
>>   *else* {b_P is full}
>>>   tentatively split b_P into b'_P and b''_P.
>>>   *If* all points of b_S can be shifted up into b'_P and b''_P *then*
>>>>   split b_P into b'_P and b''_P, shift up all points of b_S into b'_P and b''_P (Rule 2).
>>>>   *If* there is a merge partner b'_S that can be merged with b_S *then*
>>>>>   merge b_S and b'_S into b_S (Rule 1a), and update B according to b_S.

{Let B' be a subset of the set B of buckets. Let $s_{B'}$ be the maximum number of bucket savings that can be achieved in P by shifting down points from buckets in B' without causing a split of b_S. Let D be such a set of points for shifting down. Let M be a smallest subset of B for which s_M is maximal. Let M_0 be a smallest subset of B for which s_{M_0} is maximal under the restriction that no points may be shifted down.}

Compute M, s_M, D, M_0 and s_{M_0} for b_S.

If b_S is empty and $s_M \leq s_{M_0} + 1$ *then*

> realize s_{M_0} savings in P by merging buckets according to M_0

else

> realize s_M savings in P, and one loss in S if b_S is empty, by shifting down all points in D and merging buckets according to M.

Tentatively split b_S into b'_S and b''_S. Compute M', s'_M, D' for b'_S, and compute M'', s''_M, D'' for b''_S.

If $s'_M + s''_M > 1$ *then*

> split b_S into b'_S and b''_S realizing one loss in S; realize $s'_M + s''_M$ savings in P by shifting down all points in D' and D'' and merging buckets according to M' and M''.

Note that our implementation just represents one specific way of determining the local restructuring region R, and of applying the restructuring rules. We have evaluated the performance of the twin grid file in our implementation and compared it with the standard grid file.

			number of stored points			
			10000	20000	30000	40000
storage utilization		T	90.25271	89.92806	88.54782	90.09009
(in %)		G	69.44444	69.78367	69.83240	69.42034
average storage utilization during		T	89.77570	89.89784	90.05383	88.83731
most recent 10000 insertions (in %)		G	69.58457	69.57880	68.18060	70.84315
number of bucket	Read	T	16873	17619	17170	17555
accesses during		G	9881	9991	9988	9996
the most recent	Write	T	16963	17655	17313	17551
10000 insertions		G	10600	10703	10702	10728
average number of	0.09%	T	4.01	5.31	6.59	7.59
bucket accesses		G	3.16	4.52	5.77	6.74
to answer range queries	1%	T	13.29	21.19	29.22	35.96
with area		G	13.30	22.88	31.88	40.38
(in % of the area	4%	T	35.21	61.54	88.74	112.51
of the data space)		G	39.60	71.87	103.41	134.36

Table 4.1

Table 4.1 shows the results of our performance evaluation. We have inserted 40000 pseudo random two-dimensional points (from a uniform distribution) into the initially empty twin grid file T, in four sequences of 10000 points each. Each bucket holds at most 20 points, a realistic number for many applications. For comparison, we have inserted the same sequences of points into a standard grid file G. After each sequence of insertions, we have measured the actual storage utilization. In addition, we have computed the average storage utilization over each sequence of insertions, as well as the number of read and write accesses to secondary storage. Furthermore, after each sequence of insertions we have carried out 300 range queries with square ranges of three different sizes at pseudo random positions, and we have measured the average number of read accesses to secondary storage to answer these range queries.

The storage space in the twin grid file T is utilized at roughly 90%, which is certainly close to optimal. This exceeds the storage space utilization of the standard grid file G by 20 percentage points. I.e., G needs 29% more buckets than T.

To achieve the high space utilization, the number of bucket accesses during insertions in T is higher than in G, roughly by a factor of 1.7. Note, however, that for simplicity we have kept the entire directory in main memory. Since any insertion or deletion in T leads to an update of the number of stored points in the directory, the affected directory page in T needs to be written to the secondary storage after each insertion or deletion. Therefore, the number of directory accesses in T may exceed those in G by a factor of 4 at most. Experiments show that roughly twice as many external storage accesses are needed in T versus G. This is quite a low penalty in cases where storage space is scarce or the data are changed infrequently. For higher bucket capacity, the insertion cost of points is lower. Our experiments show that doubling the bucket capacity from 20 to 40 points reduces the number of bucket accesses by more than 23%, while space utilization remains at 90%.

It is essential, however, that range queries do not lose their efficiency in T versus G. This is in fact the case for query ranges of at least a small minimum size (a query range intersecting roughly 15 bucket regions, in our setting). As expected, for larger query ranges T performs even better than G, due to the better space utilization.

Other operations than insertion, deletion, and range query are of minor importance in most applications. However, it should be clear that they may be carried out efficiently as well. Let us illustrate this briefly for exact match queries: they cost at most twice as many block accesses as in the standard grid file. Since in our experiments it turns out that 14% of all points are stored in the secondary grid file, successful exact match queries in the twin grid file in our setting cost 1.14 times as many bucket accesses as in the standard grid file, on the average. For unsuccessful exact match queries, the average bucket access factor is 1.56, because non-full and non-empty primary bucket regions cover 44% of the data space, and for query points falling into these bucket regions, no secondary bucket access is necessary. Taking the directory into account, we get 2.28 accesses in a successful and 3.12 accesses in an unsuccessful exact match.

5 Conclusion

We have proposed an index structure for geometric databases, where the efficiency of spatial proximity queries as well as a high storage space utilization are the major concerns. Our structure, the twin grid file, is based on the grid file. By means of distributing the set of points to be stored among two grid files, both covering the entire data space, we achieve a space utilization close to optimal, while preserving the efficiency of range queries.

We have implemented a twin grid file, and compared its performance with a standard grid file. Even though our implementation has used few rules for redistributing points among the two grid files, and these rules have been applied in very limited combinations only, the twin grid file outperforms the standard grid file significantly.

Further optimization can be built into our algorithm easily, thereby enhancing storage space utilization even more, at the expense of more bucket accesses to redistribute points. Figure 5.1 shows that this can even be achieved locally, for an example with three points per bucket.

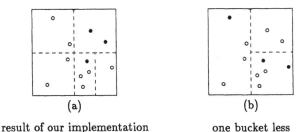

(a)   (b)

result of our implementation   one bucket less

Figure 5.1

The principle of building twin structures can be applied to other index structures as well. One-dimensional index structures, like e.g. extendible hashing (Fagin et al. 1979) and digital B-trees (Lomet 1981), are also suitable for twin structures. However, we expect the beneficial effect to increase with higher dimension. Attractive alternatives to the grid file, like e.g. the BANG file (Freeston 1987), are among the most promising twin structure candidates.

Acknowledgement

We wish to thank Norbert Fels for discussions and valuable suggestions, and Brunhilde Beck and Gabriele Reich for typesetting the paper and styling the layout.

References

R. Fagin, J. Nievergelt, N. Pippenger, H.R. Strong:
Extendible Hashing: A Fast Access Method for Dynamic Files, ACM Transactions on Database Systems, Vol. 4, 3, 1979, 315–344.

M. Freeston:
The BANG file: a new kind of grid file, Proc. ACM SIGMOD-87 International Conference on Management of Data, 1987, 260–269.

K.H. Hinrichs:
The grid file system: implementation and case studies of applications, Doctoral Thesis No. 7734, ETH Zürich, 1985.

A. Hutflesz, H.-W. Six, P. Widmayer:
Globally Order Preserving Multidimensional Linear Hashing, IEEE Fourth International Conference on Data Engineering, 1988.

H.-P. Kriegel, B. Seeger:
Multidimensional Order Perserving Linear Hashing with Partial Expansions, Proc. International Conference on Database Theory, 1986, 203–220.

R. Krishnamurthy, K.-Y. Whang:
Multilevel Grid Files, IBM Research Report, Yorktown Heights, 1985.

D.B. Lomet:
Digital B-Trees, Proc. International Conference on Very Large Data Bases, IEEE, 1981, 333–344.

D.B. Lomet:
Partial Expansions for File Organizations with an Index, ACM Transactions on Database Systems, Vol. 12, 1, 1987, 65–84.

J. Nievergelt, H. Hinterberger, K.C. Sevcik:
The Grid File: An Adaptable, Symmetric Multikey File Structure, ACM Transactions on Database Systems, Vol. 9, 1, 1984, 38–71.

E.J. Otoo:
Balanced Multidimensional Extendible Hash Tree, Proc. 5th ACM SIGACT/SIGMOD Symposium on Principles of Database Systems, 1986, 100–113.

K. Ramamohanarao, R. Sacks-Davis:
Recursive Linear Hashing, ACM Transactions on Database Systems, Vol. 9, 3, 1984, 369–391.

J.T. Robinson:
The K-D-B-Tree: A Search Structure for Large Multidimensional Dynamic Indexes, Proc. ACM SIGMOD International Conference on Management of Data, 1981, 10–18.

H.-W. Six, P. Widmayer:
Spatial Searching in Geometric Databases, IEEE Fourth International Conference on Data Engineering, 1988.

M. Tamminen:
Extendible Hashing with Overflow, Information Processing Letters, Vol. 15, 5, 1982, 227–232.

A Comparison of Concatenated and Superimposed Code Word Surrogate Files for Very Large Data/Knowledge Bases

Soon Myoung Chung   and   P. Bruce Berra

Dep't of Electrical and Computer Engineering
Syracuse University
Syracuse, NY 13244-1240
U. S. A.

Abstract

Surrogate files are very useful as an index for very large knowledge bases to support multiple logic programming inference mechanisms because of their small size and simple maintenance requirement. In this paper, we analyse the superimposed code word (SCW) and concatenated code word (CCW) surrogate file techniques in terms of storage space and time to answer queries in various cases. One of the most important results of our analysis is that the size and the query response time of the CCW is smaller than those of the SCW when the average number of arguments specified in a query is small. It is also shown that most of the query response time is used for the surrogate file processing when the extensional database is very large. Therefore, if we use a special architecture to speed up the surrogate file processing, the total query response time can be reduced considerably.

1. Introduction

Knowledge based systems consist of rules, facts and an inference mechanism that can be utilized to respond to queries posed by users. The objective of such systems is to capture the knowledge of experts in particular fields and make it generally available to nonexpert users. The current state of the art of such systems is that they focus on narrow domains, have small knowledge bases and are thus limited in their application.

As these systems grow, increased demands will be placed on the management of their knowledge bases. The intensional database (IDB) of rules will become large and present a formidable management task in itself. But, the major management activity will be in the access, update and control of the extensional database (EDB) of facts because the EDB is likely to be much larger than the IDB. The volume of facts is expected to be in the gigabyte range, and we can expect to have general EDB's that serve multiple inference mechanisms. In this paper we assume that the IDB is a set of rules expressed as logic programming clauses and the EDB is a relational database of facts.

In order to set the stage for the problem that we are interested in, consider the following simple logic programming problem:

1. grandfather(X,Y) ← father(X,Z), parent(Z,Y)
2. parent(X,Y) ← father(X,Y)
3. parent(X,Y) ← mother(X,Y)
4. father(pat, tiffany) ←
   father(don, louise) ←
   .
   .
   .
5. mother(mary, louise) ←
   mother(lisa, tiffany) ←
   .
   .
   .
6. ← grandfather(X, joan)

The first three clauses form the IDB of rules for this problem, the next two sets form the EDB of facts and the last statement is the goal. To solve the problem (satisfy the goal), we must find the names of the grandfathers of joan. For this we search the father and mother facts on the second argument position, finding values for the first argument position that can be used later. Thus, we need to find joan's mother and father before finding her grandfathers. If we ask a similar but slightly different query

← grandfather(tom, X)

we search the first argument of the father and mother facts in attempting to satisfy it.

Consider the following general goal statement of a logic programming language

$$\leftarrow r\ (X_1, X_2, \cdots, X_n).$$

In this case, values for some subset of the X_i's will be given in the process of trying to satisfy its goal. Since the subset of the X_i's is not known in advance and can range from one to all of the values, this places considerable requirements on the relational database management system that supports the logic programming language. In fact, in order to insure minimum retrieval time from the relational database all of the X_i's must be indexed. With general indexing the index data could be as large as the actual EDB. In order to considerably reduce the amount of index data yet provide the same capability, we have considered surrogate files. Obviously if not all of the X_i's can take part in goal satisfaction then the indexing strategy will change, however in this paper we will assume the most general case in which all of the X_i's are active.

Retrieving the desired rules and facts in this context is an extension of the multiple-key attribute partial match retrieval problem because any subset of argument positions can be specified in a query and matching between terms consisting of variables and functions as well as constants should be tested as a preunification step.

In the context of very large knowledge bases the question arises as to how to obtain the desired rules and facts in the minimum amount of time. Two reasonable choices of indexing schemes to speed up the retrieval are superimposed code word (SCW) and concatenated code word (CCW) surrogate file techniques discussed in [BER87]. Surrogate files are constructed by transformed binary codes where the transform is performed by well chosen hashing functions on the original terms. In [BER87], SCW, CCW and transformed inverted list (TIL) surrogate files were discussed in terms of the structures, updating procedures, performance of relational operations on the surrogate files, and possible architectures to support them. The term "surrogate file" dates back to early work in information retrieval and other terms, such as "signature file" and "descriptor file" have been used to describe similar structures [DU87, FAL84].

Compared with other full indexing schemes such as inverted lists [CAR75], SCW and CCW surrogate file techniques yield much smaller amounts of index data; about 20% of the size of the EDB [BER87] while the inverted lists may be as large as the EDB. This size advantage can yield increased retrieval performance especially when the number of search arguments is greater than one. Inverted lists show advantage in retrieval when a single argument is given since only one list need be processed. Surrogate file technique based on SCW or CCW can be easily implemented with parallel computer architectures because their structures are quite regular and compact [AHU80, BER87].

In terms of maintenance the surrogate file shows considerable advantages. When a new tuple is added to a relation the SCW or CCW is generated and added to the surrogate file. In the case of inverted lists each list must must be processed. Similar operations must be performed for deleting tuples from a relation. When changes to an existing tuple are made, the surrogate file entry must be changed and the proper inverted lists must be changed.

An important advantage of SCW and CCW surrogate file techniques is that they can be easily extended for the indexing of the rules expressed as Prolog clauses, where the matching between constants, variables, and structured terms is required to test the unifiability. [RAM86] and [WAD87] extended the SCW structure for the indexing of Prolog clauses and [SHI87] extended the CCW structure to index the rules and facts in an unified manner.

In this paper, we analyse SCW and CCW surrogate file techniques on the basis of storage space required for the surrogate file and time to retrieve the desired facts from the EDB. We limit our discussion to the EDB because most of the query response time is spent for fact retrieval and relational operations on the EDB, and the proposed structures of SCW and CCW for rule indexing are quite different, so it is difficult to make meaningful comparison at this time.

In the next section we introduce the structures and retrieval procedure of the SCW and CCW surrogate file techniques. We then develop the equations for the surrogate file size and the query response time. The analyses based on the evaluation of those equations are discussed next and finally we close with some thought on the performance improvement with SCW and CCW surrogate file techniques using a special architecture.

2. System Model for SCW and CCW Techniques

2.1. Superimposed Code Word (SCW)

Let a tuple D contain A_r argument values, $D = \{d_1, d_2, \cdots, d_{A_r}\}$. Each argument value $(d_i, 1 \leq i \leq A_r)$ can be mapped into a binary representation (BR) by a well chosen hashing function. The BR can be converted to a binary code word (BCW) with pre-defined length and weight, by using a pseudo random number generator. The weight of a BCW is the number of 1's in the BCW. The process of generating a BCW from an argument value is well described in [ROB79]. The SCW of a tuple is generated by ORing A_r BCW's obtained from A_r argument values. An unique identifier is then attached to the SCW and the tuple. This unique identifier serves as a link between the two and is used as a pointer to the EDB or can be converted to an actual pointer to the EDB by dynamic hashing schemes such as linear hashing [LAR82].

Suppose we have a fact type called borders which is given as follows:

borders (Country_1, Country_2, Body_of_Water).

For a particular instance

borders (korea, china, yellow sea).

we would first hash the individual values to obtain BR's, then the BR's would be converted into BCW's and the SCW would be formed as follows:

H(korea)	$=$	100...01	$\rightarrow$	000...100	
H(china)	$=$	010...00	$\rightarrow$	001...000	
H(yellow sea)	$=$	110...00	$\rightarrow$	100...010	
				101...110	00...01

with the BCW's logically ORed together. The unique identifier is attached as shown and the vertical line shows the boundary. The conversion from a BR to a BCW is necessary to reduce the probability of "false drops" caused by the logical OR operation.

The retrieval process with the SCW surrogate file technique is as follows:

1) Given a query, obtain a query code word (QCW) by ORing BCW's corresponding to argument values specified in the query.

2) Obtain a list of unique identifiers to all facts whose SCW's satisfy

   QCW=QCW .AND. SCW

   that is, obtain a list of all SCW's that have 1's in the same position as the QCW by comparing the QCW with all entries in the SCW file.

3) Retrieve all the facts pointed to by the unique identifiers obtained in step 2 and discard the facts not satisfying the query. These are called "false drops". The facts satisfying the query are called "good drops". The false drops are caused by the non-ideal property of hashing functions and the logical ORing of BCW's which make facts with different

argument values have the same SCW.

4) Return the good drops.

2.2. Concatenated Code Word (CCW)

The CCW of a fact is generated by simply concatenating the binary representations (BR's) of all argument values and attaching the   ie identifier of the fact. With the same example used for SCW, the CCW would be formed as

$$100...01|010...00|110...00|00...01.$$

The retrieval process with the CCW surrogate file is as follows:

1) Given a query, obtain a query code word (QCW) by concatenating BR's corresponding to argument values specified in the query. The portion of the query code word for argument values which is not specified in the query is filled with don't care symbols.

2) Obtain a list of unique identifiers to all facts whose CCW's satisfies
$$QCW=CCW$$
by comparing the QCW with all CCW's in the CCW file. Note in this case the matching is performed on both 1's and 0's.

3) Retrieve all facts pointed to by the unique identifiers obtained in step 2 and compare the corresponding argument values of the facts with the query values to discard the false drops caused by the non-ideal property of hashing functions.

4) Return the good drops.

3. Storage Requirement and Retrieval Performance of SCW and CCW Techniques

Storage requirements can be expressed by the size of surrogate files and retrieval performance can be measured by the query response time for a given query. Notations that are frequently used in this paper are shown in Table 3.1.

Notations	Meanings
A_r	Number of arguments in a fact
R_q	Average number of arguments specified in a query
GD	Average number of good drops per query
FD	Average number of false drops per query
S_{db}	Size of the extensional database in bytes
N	Number of facts in the extensional database
NSB	Number of blocks in surrogate files
NDB	Average number of extensional database blocks retrieved
S	Size of surrogate file in bits
B	Size of a block in bytes
BR	Binary representation
BCW	Binary code word
b_{bcw}	Bit length of a binary code word
QT	Query response time
T_{sp}	Surrogate file processing time
T_{dp}	Extensional database processing time
T_{ba}	A block access time
C_i	Value distribution factor, that is, the average number of facts which have the same value in the i-th argument
C_g	Average of value distribution factor (Average redundancy)

Table 3.1. Summary of Notations Frequently Used

3.1. Size of SCW and CCW Surrogate Files

The equations for the size of the SCW and CCW files are obtained in this section under the assumption, that, if the input values are different from each other, the selected hashing function maps those values into different output values, that is, there are no collisions by the hashing function.

With the above assumption, [ROB79] presented the optimal bit length of a BCW in a SCW in terms of the number of arguments in a fact (A_r), the average number of arguments specified in a query (R_q), the number of facts in the EDB (N), and the average number of false drops (FD). The equation for the bit length of a BCW (b_{bcw}) is given as

$$b_{bcw} = \left\lceil \frac{A_r}{R_q} \frac{[\ln(N) - \ln(FD)]}{[\ln(2)]^2} \right\rceil. \tag{3.1}$$

The SCW also contains its unique identifier which must be greater than or equal to $\log_2 N$, thus the minimal bit length of a SCW (b_{scw}) is

$$b_{scw} = (b_{bcw} + \left\lceil \log_2 N \right\rceil). \tag{3.2}$$

Hence, the minimal size of the SCW file (S_{scw}) is as follows:

$$S_{scw} = b_{scw} \times N. \tag{3.3}$$

For a CCW file, the minimal size can be derived from the fact that the bit length of the hashing function output for an argument in a fact must be at least $\left\lceil \log_2 \frac{N}{C_i} \right\rceil$ where C_i, called the value distribution factor, is the average number of facts whose i-th arguments have the same value. From this fact, we can derive the minimal size of the CCW file (S_{ccw}).

A CCW contains the binary representation of each argument value and its unique identifier. Hence, the minimal size of the CCW file is

$$S_{ccw} = (\sum_{i=1}^{A_r} \left\lceil \log_2 \frac{N}{C_i} \right\rceil + \left\lceil \log_2 N \right\rceil) \times N. \tag{3.4}$$

In this paper, we assumed that the hashing function is ideal and evaluated the minimal storage requirement for surrogate files. However, in actual cases, the hashing function is not ideal and there will be around 30% of collisions if the number of the distinct hashing function output is equal to the number of distinct input argument values [MAR77]. As we increase the length of the binary representation of an argument value, the probability of collisions will decrease: for example, if we assign two more bits to the binary representations in CCW surrogate file, the probability of the collision will be less than 10% and the net increase in surrogate file size will be around 1.5% of the EDB size.

3.2. Query Response Time Using SCW and CCW Surrogate Files

The query response time depends largely on the size of surrogate files and the method of obtaining pointers from the surrogate files. For the size of surrogate files, the equations derived in the previous section are used. Also, it is assumed that a sequential uniprocessor and an I/O channel are available for surrogate file and the EDB processing.

In general, the retrieval process using surrogate files can be divided into several sub-processes as follows:

1. Access to the surrogate files to read the code words from those files.

2. Comparing the QCW of a query with surrogate file code words and obtaining a list of pointers (unique id's) to the EDB.

3. Access to the EDB to read the facts with the pointers obtained in 2.

4. Comparing the query with the facts retrieved from the EDB. This step is to discard the false drops.

3.2.1. Surrogate File Processing Time

Let B be the size of a block in bytes, then there are

$$
NSB = \left\lceil \frac{S_{scw} \ (\text{or} \ S_{ccw})}{8 \times B} \right\rceil \tag{3.5}
$$

blocks in surrogate files and each block contains $\left\lfloor \dfrac{N}{NSB} \right\rfloor$ code words except the final block. Initially, the first block of the surrogate file is accessed in

$$
T_{ba} = \text{Average seek time} + \text{Rotational delay} \tag{3.6}
$$
$$
+ \frac{B}{\text{Transfer rate}}
$$

and the first block will be searched in

$$T_{ss} = \text{the number of bytes in a QCW} \tag{3.7}$$

$$\times \text{ time for byte comparison } / 2 \times \left\lfloor \frac{N}{NSB} \right\rfloor$$

$$+ \frac{(GD+FD)}{NSB} \times (\text{uid collection time})$$

where GD denotes the average number of good drops and FD denotes the average number of false drops per query.

If we assume that the blocks in the surrogate file (SF) reside consecutively in a disk, then the time for accessing the remaining $(NSB - 1)$ blocks is

$$T_{sa} = \frac{B}{\text{Transfer rate}} \times (NSB - 1) \tag{3.8}$$

$$+ \text{Rotational delay} \times (\# \text{ of tracks for SF} - 1)$$

$$+ \text{Minimum seek time} \times (\# \text{ of cylinders for SF} - 1).$$

If sufficient number of buffers are provided, the reading of the last $(NSB - 1)$ blocks can be overlapped with the searching of the first $(NSB - 1)$ blocks. Therefore, the maximum of these two times, i.e, $\max(T_{sa}, T_{ss} \times (NSB - 1))$ will contribute to the surrogate file processing time. For the last block of the surrogate file, the searching time is not overlapped with the block access time. Thus, the total surrogate file processing time is

$$T_{sp} = T_{ba} + \max(T_{sa}, T_{ss} \times (NSB - 1)) + T_{ss}. \tag{3.9}$$

Here we ignore the buffer switching time and the process wake-up time, i.e, the overhead time caused by buffering.

3.2.2. Extensional Database Processing Time

The average number of accesses to the EDB per query is the summation of the average number of good drops and the average number of false drops. If the facts to be retrieved are assumed to be randomly distributed over the EDB, the average number of EDB blocks to be retrieved can be estimated as follows [CAR75]:

$$NDB = \left\lceil \frac{S_{db}}{B} \right\rceil \times (1-(1-\frac{1}{\left\lceil \frac{S_{db}}{B} \right\rceil})^{GD+FD}) \qquad (3.10)$$

where S_{db} denotes the size of the EDB in bytes. If we assume that attributes are independent within a relation, GD can be approximated by using C_i and N.

$$GD = N \prod_{i \in R_q} (\frac{C_i}{N}) \qquad (3.11)$$

Once an EDB block is retrieved, then the facts with matched unique id's will be compared with the query to discard the false drops. The time for this comparison is

$$T_{dc} = \frac{(GD + FD)}{NDB} \times \text{the number of bytes in a fact} \qquad (3.12)$$

$$\times \text{time for byte comparison} / 2 .$$

EDB block accessing and comparison can also be overlapped. So if we assume that the EDB blocks are randomly accessed, the total EDB processing time is

$$T_{dp} = T_{ba} + \max (T_{ba}, T_{dc}) \times (NDB - 1) + T_{dc} . \qquad (3.13)$$

However, since the EDB blocks are randomly accessed, the block access time is much more than the block comparison time. Therefore, the total EDB processing time can be simplified as

$$T_{dp} \approx T_{ba} \times NDB . \qquad (3.14)$$

3.2.3. Query Response Time

The query response time for a given query is the summation of all the surrogate file processing time and the EDB processing time.

$$QT_{scw} \text{ (or } QT_{ccw}) = T_{sp} + T_{dp} \tag{3.15}$$

4. Analysis for SCW and CCW Techniques

Analyses are performed with the equations for the size of surrogate files and the query response time using SCW and CCW techniques assuming that the surrogate files are consecutively stored in a disk, the EDB are randomly stored in a number of disks, and the storage utilization of the surrogate file and the EDB is 1. If the EDB is dynamic, then the storage utilization will be lowered and consequently the number of blocks to be accessed will increase. But once a block is accessed, the time for processing a block will decrease.

4.1. Surrogate File Size

For the analysis of the surrogate file size, it is assumed that the EDB remains at the same size regardless of variation of A_r and 15 bytes are used for each argument value. Therefore, N, the number of facts in the EDB, can be calculated as follows:

$$N = \left\lfloor \frac{S_{db}}{15 \times A_r} \right\rfloor$$

where S_{db} represents the actual EDB size not including the unique identifiers for each fact of the EDB. We also assumed that each argument of a fact in the EDB has the same redundancy value, C_g, which is the average of the C_i's:

$$C_g = \frac{\sum\limits_{i \in A_r} C_i}{A_r}.$$

The results for the size evaluation are shown in Figures 4.1 through 4.3. In Figure 4.1 we plot the size of the SCW surrogate file (S_{scw}) as a function of the number of arguments (A_r) in a fact. The size of the surrogate file is expressed as a percentage of the EDB. The EDB sizes are 10^5, 10^7, and 10^9 bytes while the average number of arguments specified in a query (R_q) takes on the values one and two. Note that S_{scw} increases with the size of the EDB (S_{db}) but decreases with R_q. The reasons for this behavior are readily apparent from equations 3.1 to 3.3.

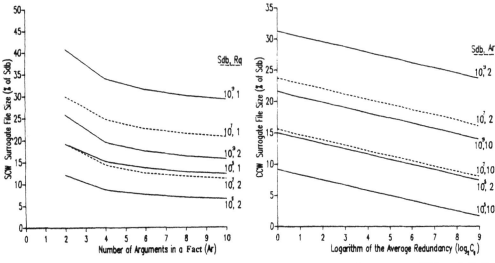

Figure 4.1 Effect of EDB Size and the Average Number of Arguments Specified in a Query on the SCW Surrogate File Size (FD= 1)

Figure 4.2 Effect of Average Redundancy on the CCW Surrogate File Size

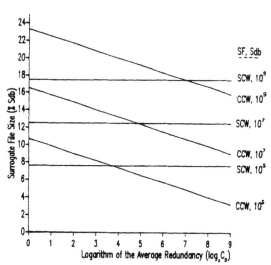

Figure 4.3 SCW and CCW Surrogate File Size Comparison (Ar=6, Rq=2, FD=1)

In the SCW case, if we allow more false drops then the length of the SCW becomes shorter which results in a smaller S_{scw}. However, more false drops leads to more EDB accesses.

In designing the SCW surrogate file one must set the expected number of arguments in a query. In terms of size, the worst case of course is when R_q is 1 and as the value for R_q is set at progressively higher values S_{scw} becomes very small. However, if we assume large R_q in designing the SCW file, we have to allow more false drops than the expected number of false drops, FD, whenever the number of arguments specified in a query is smaller than R_q [ROB79].

In Figure 4.2 we plot the size of the CCW surrogate file (S_{ccw}) as a function of the average redundancy (C_g) in the data. Note that with greater redundancy S_{ccw} becomes smaller because a smaller number of bits can be used for each binary representation. Also note that S_{db} and A_r have significant effects on S_{ccw}.

Finally, in Figure 4.3 we compare S_{scw} and S_{ccw} for various conditions. With regard to the size of surrogate files, we can say that the CCW file technique is better than the SCW technique, even though S_{scw} may be smaller than S_{ccw} when R_q is large, because we assumed that the average number of arguments specified in a query is usually not more than 2. However, in both cases the surrogate file is generally less than 20% of the size of the EDB.

When the size of the EDB is less than 10^7 bytes, the surrogate file size is less than 2 Mbytes, so the whole surrogate file can be stored in a fast memory to speed up the retrieval process.

4.2. Query Response Time

For the query response time, we assumed that the hashing function is ideal, so there are no false drops with the CCW surrogate file technique and the SCW surrogate file technique has only the false drops caused by the logical OR operation on the BCW's. A partial-match query is assumed and the surrogate file code is compared with the QCW by using sequential byte by byte comparison. The query response time results for the SCW and CCW techniques are obtained from the equations developed in the previous section and are shown in Figures 4.4 through 4.12. Table 4.1 shows the values of the parameters used in this analysis. The parameters relating to the disk are obtained from the characteristics of the DEC RA81 disk [DIG82].

Parameter	Value
Average seek time	28 msec
Minimum seek time	6 msec
Rotational delay	8.3 msec
Data transfer rate	2K bytes/msec
Data sector size	512 bytes
Sectors/track	52
Tracks/cylinder	7
Time for byte comparison	3 μsec
Unique id collection time	10 μsec
Block size	2K bytes

Table 4.1. The Values of Parameters

In Figures 4.4 through 4.6 and 4.7 through 4.9, we plot the query response times (QT_{scw} and QT_{ccw}) and corresponding subprocessing times, surrogate file processing time (T_{sp}) and EDB processing time (T_{dp}), for S_{db} of 10^5, 10^7, and 10^9 bytes, respectively. When S_{db} is 10^5 bytes, most of the query response time is spent for EDB access. But when S_{db} is 10^9 bytes, the query response time becomes very large and most of the query response time is spent for surrogate file accessing and searching because of the increased surrogate file size and sequential searching of the surrogate file. The number of arguments in a fact (A_r) has little effect on either QT_{scw} or QT_{ccw} since we assumed that the S_{db} remains constant under the variations in A_r.

When S_{db} is 10^5 bytes, R_q is not a factor which affects QT_{scw}, but QT_{scw} increases as FD increases. However, when S_{db} is 10^9 bytes, the result is reversed, that is, R_q affects the QT_{scw} considerably while FD does not. There are two reasons supporting this result:

1) S_{scw} decreases as R_q increases. However, when S_{db} is small, S_{scw} is also small for any R_q so that the time for accessing and searching the SCW file is almost constant. Therefore, the time for accessing the EDB, which depends on FD, becomes a major factor in QT_{scw}.

2) When S_{db} is large, S_{scw} becomes large so that most of QT_{scw} is spent for accessing and searching the SCW file. Therefore, S_{scw} is a main factor deciding QT_{scw}. Since S_{scw} largely depends on R_q, the change in R_q is directly reflected in QT_{scw}.

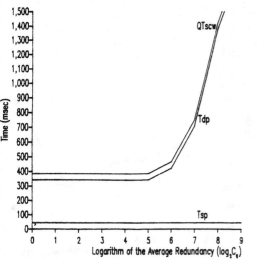

Figure 4.4 Components of the SCW Query Response Time
(Sdb=10⁴bytes, Ar=6, Rq=2, FD=9)

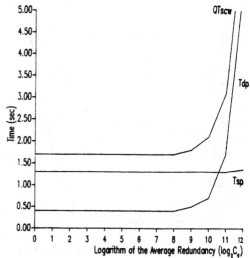

Figure 4.5 Components of the SCW Query Response Time
(Sdb=10⁷ bytes, Ar=6, Rq=2, FD=9)

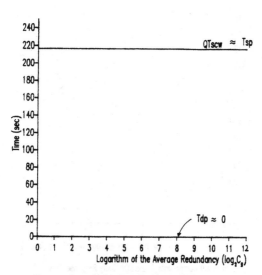

Figure 4.6 Components of the SCW Query Response Time
(Sdb=10⁴bytes, Ar=6, Rq=2, FD=9)

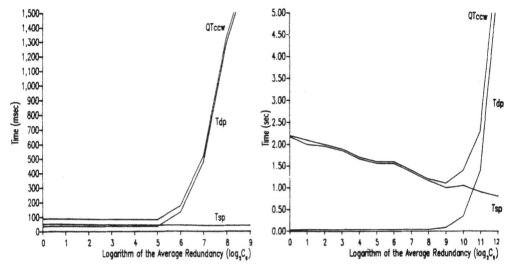

Figure 4.7 Components of the CCW Query Response Time
(Sdb=10⁴bytes, Ar=6, Rq=2)

Figure 4.8 Components of the CCW Query Response Time
(Sdb=10⁶ bytes, Ar=6, Rq=2)

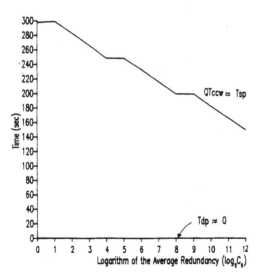

Figure 4.9 Components of the CCW Query Response Time
(Sdb=10⁸bytes, Ar=6, Rq=2)

QT_{scw} and QT_{ccw} are largely affected by C_g when S_{db} is 10^5 bytes and R_q is small. However, as R_q becomes large, the effect of C_g on QT_{scw} and QT_{ccw} decreases. This fact is well explained by the role of R_q and C_g in determining the number of good drops:

1) If R_q is small and C_g is large, then there are so many good drops that a large amount of time is required for accessing the EDB.

2) If R_q becomes large, the number of good drops decrease considerably, and so does the EDB access time, which is the major component of the query response time when S_{db} is 10^5 bytes.

From Figures 4.6 and 4.9, we can see that when S_{db} is 10^9 bytes, as C_g increases, QT_{scw} remains constant while QT_{ccw} decreases. This occurs because a fewer number of bits is required to uniquely identify each attribute value in the CCW case. But when C_g is larger than a certain value, the query response time starts increasing because of the increased EDB access time. Also, we can see from Figures 4.6 and 4.9 that most of the query response time is used for the surrogate file accessing and searching when the EDB is large. Therefore, if we use multiple processors and/or associative memory to speed up the surrogate file processing, we can reduce the query response time considerably. Since the surrogate files are quite regular and compact, they can be mapped into the associative memory. Thus, we can obtain a speed up by the content addressing capability and the parallelism of the associative memory [AHU80, LEE86, BER87]. In addition, we can also obtain a speed up proportional to the number of processors because there is little need for communication among the processors.

Since searching and disk access can be overlapped, if we increase the block size, then the number of disk accesses can be reduced and we can save time as long as the block searching time is less than the block access time. In the case of a multiple disk system, the surrogate file and the EDB are distributed over a number of disks and we can reduce the disk access time by seeking several disks concurrently.

To compare the retrieval performance of the SCW and CCW techniques, we plot QT_{scw} and QT_{ccw} in Figures 4.10 through 4.12 for various parameter values. From those figures we can see that QT_{ccw} is smaller than QT_{scw} when R_q is small, because S_{ccw} is smaller than S_{scw} when R_q is small.

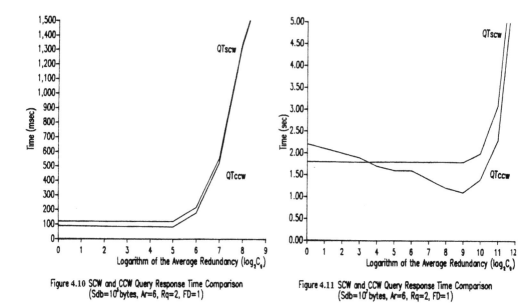

Figure 4.10 SCW and CCW Query Response Time Comparison
(Sdb=10⁴bytes, Ar=6, Rq=2, FD=1)

Figure 4.11 SCW and CCW Query Response Time Comparison
(Sdb=10⁷bytes, Ar=6, Rq=2, FD=1)

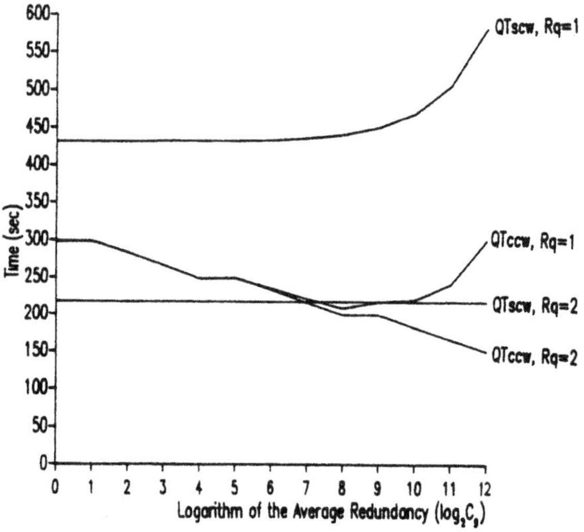

Figure 4.12 SCW and CCW Query Response Time Comparison
(Sdb=10⁷bytes, Ar=6, FD=1)

5. Comparison of SCW and CCW Surrogate File Techniques

As shown by the analysis, the size and query response time of the CCW is smaller than those of the SCW when the average number of arguments specified in a query is small.

It is very easy to update SCW or CCW surrogate files. When a new fact is added to the EDB, the corresponding code word is simply appended to the existing SCW or CCW surrogate files. No other operations are required. To delete a fact, we must find and delete the entry in the surrogate file as well as in the EDB. When one changes the value of a field, SCW requires that a new code word be generated and the old one deleted. For CCW the change need only be made to the portion of the code word in question.

One obvious advantage of CCW over the SCW is that many relational operations can be easily performed on the CCW surrogate file rather than on the relations themselves [BER87]. This offers considerable potential savings in time to carry out those relational operations.

In SCW, the order of argument positions in either query or fact can't be differentiated because a SCW is generated by the logical OR operations on the BCW's. This property of SCW can be a disadvantage when used for rule indexing in the context of logic programming.

SCW surrogate file searching time can be reduced by using the bit-sliced organization to store the SCW files [LEE86]. But in that case, we must read and write back many blocks of SCW surrogate file to update one SCW, which is not tolerable when the EDB is dynamic.

In the SCW surrogate file technique, to reduce the inherent false drops caused by the logical OR operations on the BCW's, one may assign different code weights to the BCW's of argument values depending on the occurrence frequency and query frequency of the argument values. But to do this, the code weights of frequently occurring argument values must be maintained in a table to be looked up whenever generating a binary code word [FAL85, ROB79].

6. Further Research Consideration

The main drawback of the SCW and CCW surrogate file technique is that the whole surrogate file must be read to the main memory and searched. To reduce the searching time, one can produce a block code word for each block of the surrogate file and use the block code words as an index for the surrogate file. A given QCW is compared with the block code words first and only those blocks of the surrogate file whose corresponding block code words match the QCW are retrieved and searched. But the speed up is achieved at the expense of the extra storage space and maintenance cost for the block code words. The performance of the block code words will depend on the following factors:

1) Type of hashing functions used for code generation.

2) Algorithm for generating the block code words.

3) Blocking factor: number of code words blocked together to form a block code word.

4) How frequently the database will change.

[PFA80] introduced the block descriptor generated by logical Oring the disjoint codes of each record and [SAC83] developed two level superimposed coding scheme.

It has been shown that surrogate file processing time is dominant when the EDB is very large. Thus, if we adopt multiple processors and/or associative memory, we can reduce the surrogate file processing time considerably. A general structure of a back end system which contains multiple processors for the management of a very large extensional database of facts is shown in Figure 6.1. We assume that there are gigabytes of data stored on the EDB disks and there are gigabytes of CCW surrogate files stored on the SF disks. Suppose that the user is interested in retrieving fact data given some subset of values from a particular relation. The query code word would be constructed in the Request Processor using the proper hashing function and considering the positions of the values within the relation. The QCW would then be broadcast to all of the Surrogate File Processors (SFP's) to be used as a search argument. One could think of the SFP as a processor with associative memory with the QCW as the search argument. The SFP compares the QCW with each CCW and strip off the unique identifiers of matching CCW's. As soon as any unique identifiers are found by the SFP's they can be sent to the collector and passed on to the Extensional Data Base Manager (EDBM) for processing. The EDBM will retrieve the facts, compare them with the query to insure that a false drop has not occurred, put them in blocks, and send the blocks to the logic programming inference mechanism.

Furthermore, the SFP's can be extended to support complex relational algebra operations such as join. For example, consider a join using the hash join algorithm [BRA84, KIT83]. Since the surrogate files already consist of hash values, we only need to partition the portion of code words that represent the join variable and the associated unique identifiers into SFP's. Then, based on matching within each SFP (which can be done in parallel), pairs of unique identifiers can be sent to the EDBM for final verification.

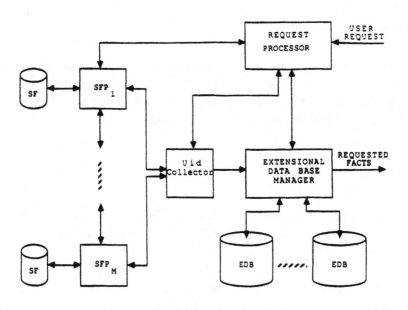

Figure 6.1   Back End System for Fact Management

7. Conclusion

CCW and SCW surrogate file techniques are analysed in terms of storage requirements and retrieval performance. The size and query response time of the CCW is smaller than those of the SCW when the average number of arguments specified in a query is small. Since the size of the CCW and SCW files are generally less than 20% of the EDB and the maintenance of those files is very simple, they are suitable for the applications requiring very large dynamic EDB. Additionally, many relational operations can be performed on the CCW surrogate files rather than on the relations.

CCW surrogate file technique can be implemented easily with multiple processors and/or associative memory to speed up the retrieval process and relational operations in very large knowledge based system. Our future research is towards the development of special architectures supporting the CCW surrogate file technique.

Acknowledgements

This work was supported by the Air Force Systems Command, Rome Air Development Center, Griffiss Air Force Base, New York 13441-5700, and the Air Force Office of Scientific Research, Bolling AFB, DC 20332 under Contract No. F30602-85-C-0008. This contract supports the Northeast Artificial Intelligence Consortium (NAIC).

References

[AHU80]   S. R. Ahuja, C. S. Roberts, "An Associative/Parallel Processor for Partial Match Retrieval Using Superimposed Codes," Proc. 7th Annual Symp. on Computer Architecture, May 1980, pp.218-227.

[BER87]   P. B. Berra, S. M. Chung, N. I. Hachem, " Computer Architecture for a Surrogate File to a Very Large Data/Knowledge Base," IEEE Computer Vol. 20, No.3, March 1987, pp.25-32.

[BRA84]   K. Bratbergsengen, " Hashing Methods and Relational Algebra Operations," Proc. VLDB, 1984, pp.323-333.

[CAR75]   A. F. Cardenas, " Analysis and Performance of Inverted Data Base Structures," CACM, Vol. 18, No. 5, 1975, pp.253-263.

[DIG82]   Digital Equipment Corporation, RA 81 Disk Drive User Guide, 1982

[DU87]   H. C. Du, S. Ghanta, et al.," An Efficient File structure for Document Retrieval in the Automated Office Environment," Proc. Int'l Conf. on Data Engineering, 1987, pp.165-172.

[FAL84]   C. Faloutsos, S. Christodoulakis, " Signature Files: An Access Method for Documents and Its Analytical Performance Evaluation," ACM Trans. on Office Information Systems, Vol. 2, No. 4, 1984, pp.267-288.

[FAL85]   C. Faloutsos, S. Christodoulakis, " Design of a Signature File Method that Accounts for Non-Uniform Occurrence and Query Frequencies," Proc. VLDB, 1985, pp.165-170.

[KIT83]   M. Kitsuregawa, H. Tanaka, T. Moto-Oka, " Application of Hash to Data Base Machine and Its Architecture," New Generation Computing, Vol. 1, 1983, pp.63-74.

[LAR82]   P. -A. Larson, " Performance Analysis of Linear Hashing with Partial Expansions," ACM Trans. on Database Systems, Vol. 7, No. 4, 1982, pp.566-587.

[LEE86]   D. L. Lee, " A Word-Parallel, Bit-Serial Signature Processor for Superimposed Coding," Proc. Int'l Conf. on Data Engineering, 1986, pp.352-359.

[MAR77]   J. Martin, Computer Data Base Organization, second edition, Prentice-Hall, 1977

[PFA80]   J. L. Pfaltz, W.J. Berman, and E.M. Cagley, " Partial-Match Retrieval Using Indexed Descriptor Files," CACM, Vol. 23, No. 9, 1980, pp.522-528.

[RAM86]   K. Ramamohanarao, J. Shepherd, " A Superimposed Codeword Indexing Scheme for Very Large Prolog Databases," Proc. 3rd Int'l Logic Programming Conference, 1986, pp.569-576.

[ROB79]   C. S. Roberts, " Partial Match Retrieval via the Method of Superimposed Codes," Proceedings of the IEEE, Vol. 67, No. 12, 1979, pp.1624-1642.

[SAC83]   R. Sacks-Davis, K. Ramamohanarao, "A Two level Superimposed Coding Scheme for Partial Match Retrieval," Information Systems Vol. 8, No. 4, 1983, pp.273-280.

[SHI87]   D. Shin, P. B. Berra, " An Architecture for Very Large Rule Bases Based on Surrogate Files," Proc. 5th Int'l Workshop on Database Machines, 1987, pp.555-568.

[WAD87]   M. Wada, Y. Morita, et al., " A Superimposed Code Scheme for Deductive Databases," Proc. 5th Int'l Workshop on Database Machines, 1987, pp.569-582.

Filter-Based Join Algorithms on Uniprocessor and Distributed-Memory Multiprocessor Database Machines

Ghassan Z. Qadah

Electrical Engineering and Computer Science Department
Northwestern University
Evanston, IL 60201, USA

Abstract. The hybrid-hash algorithm and its parallel variant have been recently found to outperform all other algorithms in joining disk-based large relations on uniprocessor and ring-interconnected distributed-memory multiprocessor database machines. This paper presents several extensions to the centralized and distributed hybrid-hash algorithms. These extensions are based on the usage of one or more bit-vectors as filters. A comparative performance study to the presented algorithms is carried out. In a uniprocessor environment, this study shows that one of the proposed filter-based algorithms outperforms all of the other ones, including the hybrid-hash algorithm. In a distributed environment, the filter-based algorithms are found to suffer from a serious problem, namely, overloading the interconnection network with the transmission of large size bit-vectors. Different compression schemes are proposed to reduce the size of a transmitted bit-vector. The augmentation of the distributed version of best-performing centralized algorithm with one of the proposed compression schemes have been found to outperform all of the other algorithms and substantially improves the performance of the join operation.

1. Introduction

During the past decade, database machines(DBMs)[Qada85a] have emerged as a distinctive class of computer architectures. Most of these architectures make use of specialized hardware components and/or parallel processing to enhance the performance of the relational database systems[Kim79]. An important subclass is the so called distributed-memory multiprocessor database machines [Baru87, Dewi86,Good81,Hsia81,shu187,Tera84]. A machine in such a class is organized as a set of processing nodes, each of which has a processor, a local high-speed main memory and a mass storage device. A suitable message passing network is used to interconnect the processing nodes of the DBM together. The DBMs, MBDS[Hsia81], GAMMA[Dewi86], Teradata machine[Tera84], the hybercube machine [Baru87] and the hybertree machine[Good81], are examples of such a class. These machines use, respectively, a bus, a token ring, a modified version of the binary tree called the Y-net[Tera84], a hybercube[Seit85] and the X-tree[Good81], as an interconnection structure.

The distributed DBM organization is indeed a desirable one. Not only it permits the processors to operate in parallel (parallel CPU), but it also permits the parallel transfer of data between these processors and the mass storage devices (parallel I/O), thus eliminates the I/O bottleneck encountered in other organizations for DBMs, without substantially increasing the hardware cost of these machines[Bora83]. One of the most important drawbacks of the distributed multiprocessor organization is the fact that an access to a data element residing in a processor's memory by another processor is relatively slow. Therefore, the good choice of algorithms which tend to minimize the amount of data transfer across the interconnection network is very crucial to the cost-effectiveness of such organization.

One of the most important operations of the relational databases and probably the most important limiting factor to their performance is the join.[1] Several algorithms have been proposed to implement the join operation [Babb79,Dewi85,Bitt83,Kits84,Good81,Qada,Vald84]. These algorithms can be grouped into three different classes, namely, the nested-loop, the sort-based and the hash-based. In a recent study, Dewitt et al. [Dewi85,Dewi84] has evaluated the use of a sort-based algorithm, called sort-merge, and a number of hash-based algorithms for joining disk-based large relations on a uniprocessor and ring-interconnected distriuted-memory multiprocessor DBMs. Such a study has revealed that one of the hash-based algorithms, called the hybrid-hash, outperforms almost every other algorithm. In addition, using such an algorithm, the join operation can be carried out in linear time with respect to the size of the relations being joined.

This paper presents several extensions to the hybrid-hash algorithm and its parallel variant. These extensions are generated by augmenting the hybrid-hash and its parallel variant with one or more bit-vectors. The bit-vectors[Babb79] can be used to filter out some of the tuples, from one or both of the relations to be joined, which may not generate any result tuples. Thus, speeding up the processing of the join operation. An intensive study to the performance of the hybrid-hash

---

[1]The θ-join of two relations R and S on attributes A from R and B from S, is the output relation RO, obtained by concatenating each tuple r∈ R and each tuple s∈ S whenever (r[A]θs[B]) is true. is one of the operators "=, =/, <, =<, >, >=." The most frequently used type of the θ-join operation is the equi-join(or simply join), where "θ" is the operator "=."

algorithm and its various extensions on a uniprocessor and a ring-interconnected multiprocessor DBMs is also presented. Such a study uses the performance measure "total execution time(Time)" to compare the various algorithms together. Time for a join algorithm measures the time required to execute that algorithm on a given hardware configuration assuming there exist no overlap between the activities of the various subsystems in such a configuration. In a uniprocessor configuration, this implies that no overlap exists between the processor and the secondary storage device. In a ring-interconnected multiprocessor, the computation of Time assumes non-overlapping activities between the set of processors, the set of secondary storage disks and the ring network. However, the computation of Time takes into consideration the parallel activities of the processing nodes relative to each others.

To compute Time for each of the presented algorithm, we make use of two sets of parameters, namely, the relation-related and the hardware-related. Both of these sets together with their meanings and the values that some of them assume throughout our performance study, are presented in Table 1 and 2, respectively. The relation-related parameters characterize the relations to be joined. Our model of the relations assumes that a tuple from the relations to be joined is equally likely to carry, in its join attribute, any value from the attribute's underlying domain. The size of such a domain is characterized by the parameter ND(refer to Table 1).

Parameter	Definition	Typical Value(s)
R(S)	The two source relations to be joined.	
Rp(Sp)	Number of pages in R(S)	10^4
Rc(Sc)	Cardinality of R(S)[= ceil{Rp*Psize/Ltuple}]	
Ltuple	Length of a tuple from R(or S) in bytes	100
ND	Number of distinguished values in the join domain	Variable

Table 1. Relation-related Parameters

Parameter	Definition	Typical Value(s)
P^*	Number of Processing nodes	Variable
Mp	Number of pages in the main memory of one processing node	Variable
Psize	Size of a page in bytes	4000
Lsearch	Average number of tuples in an entry of a hash table	2
K	Ratio of the number of bits in a bit-vector and that of the tuples being encoded	10
Tcomp	Time to compare two keys	3 microsec
Tor	Time to "or" one byte with another	.3 microsec
Thash	Time to compute a hash function	5 microsec
Tmove	Time to move a tuple in main memory	25 microsec
TIO_seq	Time to perform a sequential disk IO	10 msec
TIO_rand	Time to perform a random disk IO	25 msec
TIO_net	Time to broadcast one page through the token-ring	4-.4 msec

Table 2. Hardware-related Parameters

The hardware-related parameters, on the other hand, characterize the uniprocessor and the ring-interconnected multiprocessor machines. The parameters with an asterisk apply only to the multiprocessor machine whereas the rest of the hardware-related parameters apply to both of the uniprocessor and the multiprocessor machines.

The use of bit-vector filters to speed up the execution of the join operation on a single processor machine was pioneered by Babb[Babb79]. [Qada] and [Vald84] have used the bit-vector filters to speed up the execution of the join operation on shared-memory multiprocessor DBMs. The first to extend the concept of bit-vector filters to the distributed multiprocessor DBMs is probably Goodman[Good81]. He used these filters to speed up the execution of the join operation on an X-tree distributed DBM. Although, such a study showed that a speed advantage is to be gained from using such a system, it did not, however, separate the contribution of the elaborate communication structure and that of the filters to such an advantage. In [Dewi85,Dewi87,Gerb86], Dewitt et al. has also shown (through simulation as well as experimentation with the DBM Gamma[Dewi86]) that indeed speed advantages can be gained by combining the filtering of one of the joined relations with the centralized hybrid-hash(and some other algorithms). In this paper, we try to comprehensively study the algorithms considered by Dewitt as well as some other newly developed serial and distributed filter-based algorithms.

In summary, section 2 describes the processing of the hybrid-hash algorithm on a uniprocessor machine. It also describes the different extensions of such an algorithm using one or more bit-vectors as filters. In addition, section 2 presents the performance evaluation and a comparison between the hybrid-hash algorithm and its various extensions. Section 3 presents the parallel hybrid-hash and its filter-based variants as well as an evaluation and a comparison of the presented algorithms. Section 4 presents some improvements to some of the algorithms described in this paper. Finally, section 5 presents some concluding remarks and briefly outlines our intended future work.

2. The Centralized Hybrid-hash Join and its Filter-based Variants

The hybrid-hash(hh) algorithm belongs to a class of join algorithms, called the hash-based join algorithms[Dewi85,Kiits84,Qada]. A typical algorithm in such a class transforms the join of two large disk-based relations into a number of independent joins, each joins, in memory, a small portion of the original relations. A hash-based algorithm processes the join operation in two distinct phases, namely, the partitioning phase and the join phase. During the former phase, the tuples of the two relations R and S are partitioned into a number of disjointed sets of tuples called buckets, using a suitable hash function. The tuples are assigned to buckets based on the value of the hash function computed on the join attribute value of

The hardware-related parameters, on the other hand, characterize the uniprocessor and the ring-interconnected multiprocessor machines. The parameters with an asterisk apply only to the multiprocessor machine whereas the rest of the hardware-related parameters apply to both of the uniprocessor and the multiprocessor machines.

The use of bit-vector filters to speed up the execution of the join operation on a single processor machine was pioneered by Babb[Babb79]. [Qada] and [Vald84] have used the bit-vector filters to speed up the execution of the join operation on shared-memory multiprocessor DBMs. The first to extend the concept of bit-vector filters to the distributed multiprocessor DBMs is probably Goodman[Good81]. He used these filters to speed up the execution of the join operation on an X-tree distributed DBM. Although, such a study showed that a speed advantage is to be gained from using such a system, it did not, however, separate the contribution of the elaborate communication structure and that of the filters to such an advantage. In [Dewi85,Dewi87,Gerb86], Dewitt et al. has also shown (through simulation as well as experimentation with the DBM Gamma[Dewi86]) that indeed speed advantages can be gained by combining the filtering of one of the joined relations with the centralized hybrid-hash(and some other algorithms). In this paper, we try to comprehensively study the algorithms considered by Dewitt as well as some other newly developed serial and distributed filter-based algorithms.

In summary, section 2 describes the processing of the hybrid-hash algorithm on a uniprocessor machine. It also describes the different extensions of such an algorithm using one or more bit-vectors as filters. In addition, section 2 presents the performance evaluation and a comparison between the hybrid-hash algorithm and its various extensions. Section 3 presents the parallel hybrid-hash and its filter-based variants as well as an evaluation and a comparison of the presented algorithms. Section 4 presents some improvements to some of the algorithms described in this paper. Finally, section 5 presents some concluding remarks and briefly outlines our intended future work.

2. The Centralized Hybrid-hash Join and its Filter-based Variants

The hybrid-hash(hh) algorithm belongs to a class of join algorithms, called the hash-based join algorithms[Dewi85,Kiits84,Qada]. A typical algorithm in such a class transforms the join of two large disk-based relations into a number of independent joins, each joins, in memory, a small portion of the original relations. A hash-based algorithm processes the join operation in two distinct phases, namely, the partitioning phase and the join phase. During the former phase, the tuples of the two relations R and S are partitioned into a number of disjointed sets of tuples called buckets, using a suitable hash function. The tuples are assigned to buckets based on the value of the hash function computed on the join attribute value of every tuple of these relations. In a processor (centralized) environment, the hash function is chosen such that the tuples of one relation which hash to one bucket can fit in the processor's main memory. The join phase consists of a number of steps. During each one of them, the tuples of the two relations which hash to the same bucket are joined using one of the traditional in-memory join algorithm [Dewi84,Qada].

The hash-based class of join algorithms are very powerful for two important reasons, namely, they posses linear time complexities (in terms of the cardinalities of the relations to be joined) and they are suitable for parallel processing. The centralized hybrid-hash (chh) algorithm and its filter-based variants are presented next.

2.1 The Centralized Hybrid-Hash Join Algorithm

The hybrid-hash join algorithm is characterized by the fact that the partitioning phase overlaps the execution of the first step of the join phase(during which the tuples of R and S which hash to the first bucket is joined). A uniprocessor executes such an algorithm as follows[Dewi85]:

1. Choose a hash function which partitions the tuples of relation R into the bucket R_0 of size Rp_0 and equally sized buckets $R_1,...,R_B$ with total size of $(Rp - Rp_0)$, where Rp_0 is the number of pages occupied by the tuples which hash to R_0.

2. Set up in memory one page frame to serve as an output buffer for each of the buckets $R_1,...,R_B$. The remaining free pages in memory is used to store, in a hash table form, the tuples which hash to R_0. Notice that the hash function of step 1 must be chosen such that Rp_0 is equal to the number of free memory pages during the partitioning phase($= Mp - B$).

3. Read relation R from disk. Hash each tuple of R, based on its join attribute value, using the hash function of step 1. If the tuple hashes to R_0, then, store it in the hash table of R_0(HT_R_0). Otherwise, the tuple belongs to the bucket R_i(for $0 < i =< B$), so move it to the ith output page buffer. Whenever an output page is full, store it on disk. When the processing of this step completes, HT_R_0 in main memory will be storing the tuples of R_0, and the sets of tuples which belong to the buckets $R_1,...,R_B$ are separately stored on disk.

4. Repeat step 3 for relation S with the exception that whenever a tuple of S hashes to S_0, it would not be stored in HT_R_0. Instead, it is used to probe HT_R_0 for matches. When the processing of this step completes, the tuples from R and S which hash to bucket #0 (the tuples of R_0 and S_0) would be joined and the sets of tuples which belong to the buckets $S_1,S_2,...,S_B$ are separately stored on disk. That is, the completion of this step signals the completion of the partitioning phase and the joining of the tuples in bucket #0.

5. Repeat the following steps for i=1,2,...,B;

   a. Initialize the hash table HT_R_i in memory to store the tuples of R_i.
   b. Read from disk the tuples of R_i and store them in HT_R_i.
   c. Read from disk the tuples of S_i. Use them to probe the hash table of R_i for matches. Output the result tuples(if any is generated).

Using analysis similar to that of [Dewi84,Qada83], the derivation of a formula to compute the total execution time for the centralized hybrid-hash algorithm, Time(chh), is presented in section 1 of Appendix A. Such a formula can be rewritten as follows:

$$Time(chh) =$$
$$2(B+1)*(TIO\_rand \quad - \quad TIO\_seq) \quad + \quad (Rp+Sp)*TIO\_seq \quad +$$
$$(Rp+Sp)*(1-q)*(TIO+TIO\_seq) \qquad /disk-IO-time/$$

$$+ (Rc + Sc)*(1+C)*Thash \qquad /hash-time/$$

$$+ [Rc + (Rc+Sc)*(1-q)]*Tmove \qquad /move-time/$$

$$+ Sc*Lsearch*Tcomp \qquad /compare-time/$$

Where q is the ratio Rp_0/Rp and 1+B is the number of buckets. B can be computed using the following equation,

$$B = max\{0, ceil[(1-Mp/Rp)/(Mp/Rp - 1/Rp)]\}... \qquad (1)$$

and q can be computed using the following formula;

$$q = 1- B*(Mp/Rp) \qquad ...... \qquad (2)$$

C is 0 if B =0(the hash function partitions the relations R and S into only one bucket) otherwise, C is 1. TIO is TIO_seq if B=1, otherwise TIO is TIO_rand.

2.2 The Filter-based Hybrid-hash Variants

A bit-vector is a vector of bits, each may take the value of "0" or "1." When joining two sets of tuples, the bit-vector in conjunction with a suitable hash function can be used to encode the join attribute values of one set of the tuples[Babb79]. For each tuple of such a set, the hash function is computed using the tuple's join attribute value. The hash function value is used as an address to the bit-vector and the bit with such an address is set to "1." Joining a tuple from the other set starts by applying the hash function to the tuple's join attribute value to compute an address to the bit-vector. The joining of the tuple proceeds only if the addressed bit of the bit-vector is set to "1." In this way, the bit-vector behaves as a filter that eliminates, at an early stages of the processing, some of the tuples that are not needed for forming the join result relation, thus potentially improving the performance of such an operation.

Different versions of the hybrid-hash algorithm can be generated by using one or more bit-vectors to partially or totally filter out some of the tuples of relations S and/or R. These versions are presented below. For each one of these versions, a formula for computing the total execution time, using the derivation method presented in Appendix A, has been developed. These formulas are presented in [Qada87] and will not be repeated here.

Version 1: Partial Filtering of Relation S

The first version of the centralized hybrid-hash algorithm (chh_V1) uses one bit-vector to encode the join attribute values of those tuples of relation R which hash to one bucket. The bit-vector is, then, used to filter out some of the tuples of relation S that hash to the same bucket. chh_V1 proceeds similar to the hybrid-hash with the following additions:

* During the partitioning phase(refer to step 3 of the hybrid-hash), a bit-vector BV_R_0 of suitable length is initialized in memory to encode the join attribute values of the tuples of relation R which hash to R_0.

* During the same phase(refer to step 4 of the hybrid-hash) and whenever a tuple of relation S hashes to S_0, then, such tuple is first checked against BV_R_0. HT_R_0 is checked for matches only if the tuple of S_0 hashes to a "set" bit in BV_R_0.

* During the processing of the ith bucket(for $0 < i = < B$), a bit-vector BV_R_i is initialized in memory. The bits in BV_R_i are set according to the join attribute values of the tuples in R_i. The tuples of S_i are first filtered through BV_R_i. The tuples of S_0 which survive such filtering are then used to probe HT_R_i for matches.

Version 2: Total Filtering of Relation S

The second version of the hybrid-hash algorithm(chh_V2) uses one bit-vector, BV_R, to encode the join attribute values of all the tuples in relation R. BV_R is then used to filter out some of the tuples of relation S that are not needed in the final result. The construction of BV_R and all the filtering of relation S are completed in the partitioning phase of the algorithm(rather than distributed across the various execution steps as in chh_V1). Chh_V2 proceeds exactly in the same way as the hybrid-hash algorithm except in the partitioning phase where the following modifications are made;

* Initialize, in memory, the bit-vector BV_R. As the tuples of relation R are read from disk for partitioning (refer to step 3 of the hybrid-hash algorithm), the join attribute values of these tuples are used to set up the bits in BV_R.

* As the tuples of relation S are read for partitioning(refer to step 4 of the hybrid-hash algorithm), the join attribute values of these tuples are first checked against BV_R. The tuples which hash to bits in BV_R having the value "0" are tossed away. Only the tuples of S which hash to bits having the value "1" are partitioned into S_0 and $S_1, S_2, ..., S_B$. The tuples which hash to S_0 are used immediately to probe HT_R_0 for matches. The tuples which hash to $S_1, S_2, ..., S_B$ are stored on disk. Notice that while the number of buckets in this algorithm is almost the same as that of the hybrid-hash, the number of the tuples in each of these buckets is less due to the filtering process.

* The join of the buckets $1, ..., B$ proceeds exactly as in step 5 of the hybrid-hash algorithm.

Versions 3 and 4: Total Filtering of Relations R and S

The third version of the hybrid-hash algorithm (chh_V3) uses two bit-vectors BV_R and BV_S to encode the join attribute values of all the tuples in relations R and S, respectively. BV_R and BV_S are then used to, respectively, filter out some of the tuples of relations S and R. Both of these bit-vectors are built and used during the partitioning phase of the join algorithm. chh_V3 proceeds similar to the hybrid-hash algorithm with the following added modifications:

* During the partitioning phase, initialize BV_S in main memory. Read the tuples of relation S and set the bits in BV_S according to the tuples' join attribute values.

* Initialize the other bit_vector BV_R in main memory. Read the tuples of relation R from the disk. Filter these tuples using BV_S. Use the surviving set of tuples of R to set the bits in BV_R. Partition, then, such set into R_0 and $R_1, R_2, \ldots R_B$. Store the tuples of R_0 into HT_R_0 and store $R_1, R_2, \ldots, R_B$ on disk.

* Read again the tuples of relation S. Filter these tuples using BV_R. Partition the set of surviving tuples into S_0 and $S_1, S_2, \ldots S_B$. Use the tuples of S_0 to immediately probe HT_R_0 for matches. Store $S_1, S_2, \ldots, S_B$ on disk.

* Read the buckets from the disk, one at a time, and join them as in step 5 of the hybrid-hash algorithm.

The fourth version of the hybrid-hash algorithm(chh_V4) is very similar to chh_V3 except that it avoids the duplicate reading of relation S during the partitioning phase. This is done by storing together with relation S the bit-vector BV_S. Instead of reading the whole relation S to build BV_S, only the pages on disk which store BV_S are read into memory thus saving a considerable amount of disk IO time.

2.3 Performance Comparison of the Centralized Join Algorithms

Using the equations developed for the total execution time(Time) of each of the centralized algorithms and the parameters' setting of Table 1 and 2, we have generated Figures 1 through 3. Each of these figures plots the performance measure Time of the various algorithms versus the ratio Mp/Rp for a given RND and SND Values. Mp/Rp is the ratio of the main memory size(in pages) and that of relation R. On the other hand, RND(SND) is the ratio of the cardinality of relation R(S) and the number of distinct values in the join domain(ND). In our models, the ratio's RND and SND determine the probabilities that a tuple from relation S or R joins with at least one tuple of relation R or S, respectively. To a large extend, these probabilities control the filtering behavior of the bit-vectors. Throughout this performance study, SND is equal to RND(since Sp=Rp). RND may have one of the values {1.(high join probability), .1, .01(low join probability)}.

For a given relation size, there exist a minimum memory size Mp_{min} below which such a memory can not support the processing of the hybrid-hash or the hybrid-hash based algorithms. For example, the memory supporting the execution of the hybrid-hash algorithm must have, during the partitioning phase, enough page buffers to store one page for each of the buckets generated by the algorithm. Mp_{min} in this case is the square root of Rp[Dewi84]. For the filter-based algorithms, Mp_{min} must be large enough, not only to store one page for each bucket, but also to store the

Figure 1. Total Execution Time for the Centralized Algorithms (RND=1.)

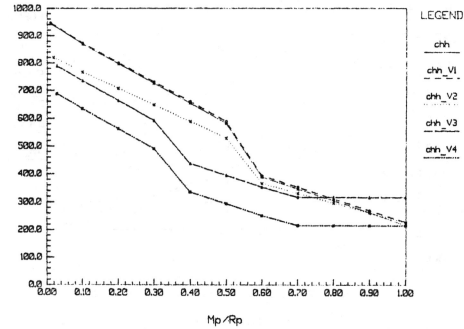

Figure 2. Total Execution Time for the Centralized Algorithms (RND=.1)

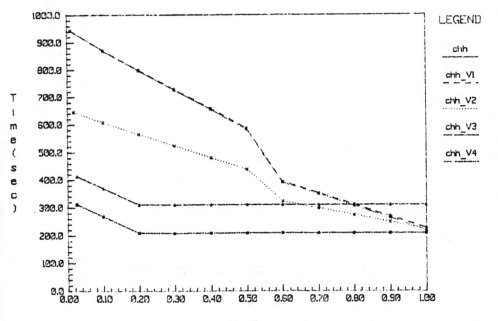

Figure 3. Total Execution Time for the Centralized Algorithms (RND=.01)

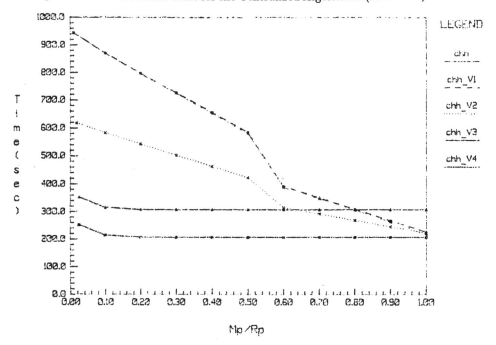

Figure 4. Speed_Ratio for the Centralized Algorithms (RND=1.)

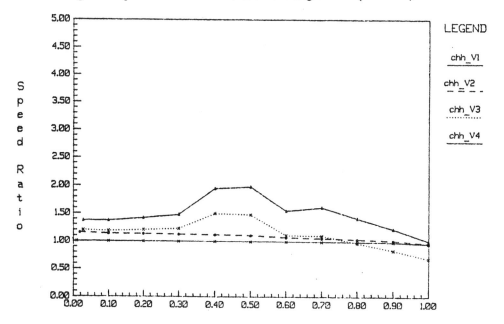

algorithms. These formulas are presented in [Qada87].

Figures 1 through 3 plot Time for each of the centralized algorithms versus Mp/Rp for Rp=10000 pages and RND = 1., .1, and .01, respectively. Mp/Rp is allowed to change from its minimum value all the way up to 1, when all of the tuples in relation R may fit in main memory. A close examination of these figures reveals very interesting observations, namely;

* The algorithms chh_V1 and chh have almost equal execution time over the full range of Mp/Rp , and, therefore no speed advantages can be obtained from chh_V1.

* On one hand, the Time for each of the algorithms chh, chh_V1 and chh_V2 decreases linearly over the full range of Mp/Rp. On the other hand, Time for chh_V3 and chh_V4 decreases linearly as the ratio Mp/Rp increases until a saturation point is reached, beyond which Time stays constant. This can be explained as follows. The saturation point occurs when all of the tuples of relation R which survive the checking of BV_S can be buffered in main memory. Increasing the memory size beyond that point does not help to improve the CPU time or the IO time. The IO time remains constant and equal to the time required to read all of the pages of both of R and S relations.

* The saturation point in the curves of the algorithms chh_V3 and chh_V4 is a strong function of RND. Such a point moves to the left as RND decreases. The reason for this behavior should be obvious.

* Chh_V2 is consistently faster than chh over the whole range of Mp/Rp and for the various values of RND. Chh_V3 is faster than both of algorithms chh and chh_V2 when Mp/Rp is small to moderate. However, when Mp/Rp is large(close to 1), chh_V2 is slower than both of these algorithms. The reason for this is the fact that during the partitioning phase, the algorithm chh_V3 has to read one of the joined relations one extra time. At high value of Mp/Rp and because of the previous fact, the IO time of chh_V3 becomes larger than that of the other algorithms.

* The algorithm chh_V4 is consistently faster than any other algorithm over the full range of MP/Rp.

To measure the relative speeds of the presented algorithms a performance measure, speed_ratio, is used. The speed_ratio of a given algorithm is Time(chh)/Time(algorithm). That is, the reference point in this performance study is taken as chh.

Figures 4 through 6 plot the speed_ratio of the various algorithms versus Mp/Rp for RND = 1, .1 and .01, respectively. The curve representing the speed_ratio of the algorithm chh is a straight line of value "1" and is omitted from these figures. An immediate observation to be drawn from these figures is that the speed_ratio of any algorithm(except chh_V1 which remains constant) is a strong function of the two parameters, Mp/Rp(physical resources available) and RND(data characteristics). As the latter parameter decreases, that is, the join probability gets lower, the speed_ratio of all of the filter-based algorithms improves. This is because, as the join probabilities get lower, more and more tuples are present in both of the joined relations that are not producing any result tuples, and therefore, can be filtered

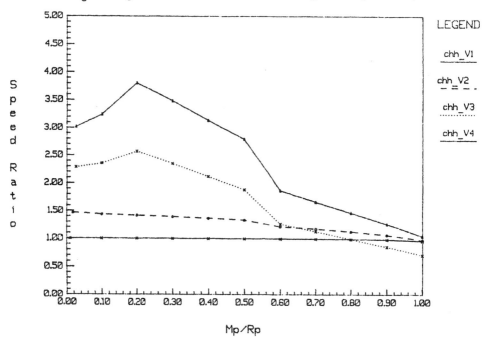

Figure 5. Speed_Ratio for the Centralized Algorithms (RND=.1)

Figure 6. Speed_Ratio for the Centralized Algorithms (RND=.01)

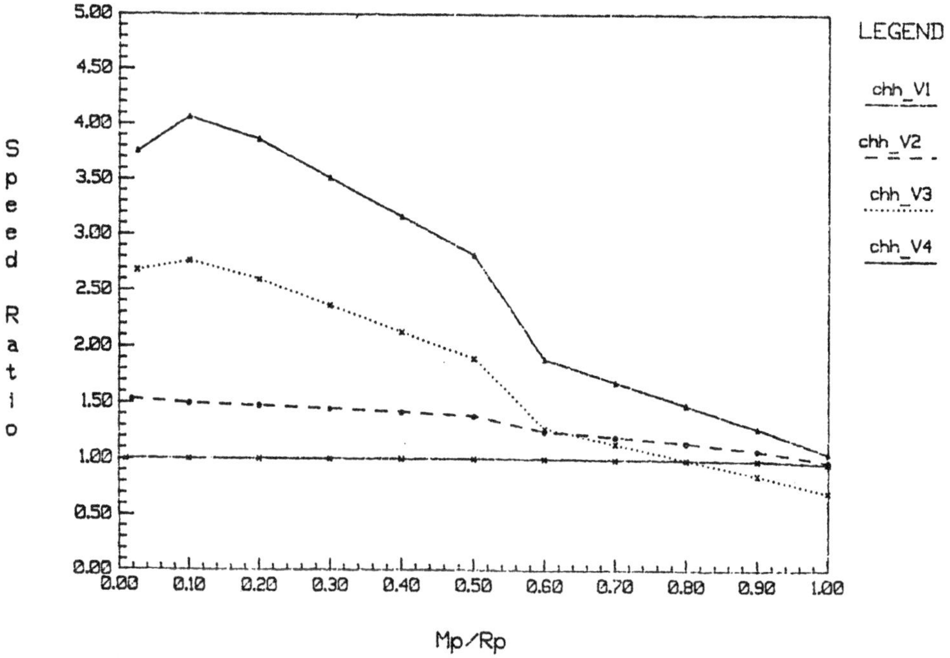

When Mp/Rp is high(close to "1"), all of the algorithms attain a speed_ratio of almost "1," and the best algorithm to be used in this case is chh itself. For small to moderate Mp/Rp, chh_V2 attain moderate speed advantage over chh (at most 1.5 times faster than chh). On the other hand, the algorithms chh_V3 and chh_V4 attain considerable speed advantages over chh(up to a 4 times faster than chh). In such a case, one of the algorithms chh_V3 or chh_V4 is recommended to execute the join operation.

From the above discussion, one may conclude that if a centralized algorithm is to be selected to execute a given join operation, the following rule of thump can be applied. If Mp/Rp(the size of the memory available to execute the join operation relative to that of the relation) is large, chh is the choice. However, if Mp/Rp is small to moderate chh_V4(or chh_V3) is the choice. If only one algorithm is to be selected to handle the join operation, we recommend chh_V4. This algorithm attains such a good performance because it combines the advantage of chh which reads, during the partitioning phase, each of the joined relations only once, and the advantages of the chh_V3 algorithm of being able to filter out from both of the joined relations as much unwanted tuples as possible. one drawback of the chh_V4 is its requirement to maintain a bit-vector for one of the join relations. We believe that the cost of such maintenance is very moderate in terms of storage cost and updating time.

3. The Distributed Hybrid-hash Join and its Filter-based Variants

The algorithms described in this section assume a ring-interconnected multiprocessor system. Each processor has its own disk and local memory which together form what is called a processing node. The two relations to be joined, R and S, are assumed to be horizontally partitioned into equal segments, each of which is stored on a different processing node. Below, the distributed versions of chh, chh_V2, chh_V3 and chh_V4 algorithms are presented. We do not consider the distributed version of chh_V1 because the performance evaluation of section 2.3 has indicated that chh_V1 does not exhibit any speed advantages over the chh algorithm.

3.1 The Distributed Hybrid-hash Algorithm

The distributed hybrid-hash(dhh) algorithm proceeds as follows. Every processing node partitions its share from the relations R and S into buckets in a way similar to that of the chh algorithm. When processing the tuples of a bucket, every processing node hashes, first, its share from the tuples of that bucket to the processing nodes using a suitable hash function. The hash function is computed on the tuples' join attribute values. For a given tuple, the value of the hash function is the address of the processing node where the tuple is to be stored in a hash table form(if the tuple belongs to relation R) or where the tuple is to search for matches (if the tuple belongs to relation S). The tuples generated by a node, each one is augmented with its destination address, are accumulated in the node's output buffer. When such a buffer is full, it is broadcasted over the ring network to all other nodes. A node receiving the broadcast packet selects from such a packet only those tuples whose destination addresses match that of the node. In our performance study, we assume that the size of a packet is one page.

A derivation for a formula for the total execution time of the distributed hybrid-hash algorithm, Time(dhh), is presented in section 2 of Appendix A. Such a formula can be rewritten as follows:

$$
\begin{aligned}
\text{Time(dhh)} = \\
&2(B+1)*(TIO\_rand - TIO\_seq) + (Rp+Sp)*(1/P)*TIO\_seq + \\
&\quad (Rp+\overline{Sp})*(1/P)*(\overline{1}-q)*(TIO\_seq+TIO) \qquad \text{/disk-IO-time/}
\end{aligned}
$$

$$+ (Rp+Sp)*(1- 1/P)*TIO\_net \qquad\qquad \text{/network-IO-time/}$$

$$+ (Rc + Sc)(1/P)*(1+C)*Thash \qquad\qquad \text{/hash-time/}$$

$$+ \{[(Rc+Sc)*(1/P))*(1-1/P)] + (Rc/P)\}*Tmove + [(Rc+Sc)*(1/P)*(1-q)]*Tmove$$
/move-time/

$$+((Sc/P)*Lsearch*Tcomp \qquad\qquad\qquad \text{/compare-time/}$$

Where, C and TIO have the same definitions and values as in the centralized case. B and q are computed using the following formulas,

$$B = \max\{0, \text{ceil}[(1- Mp*P/Rp)/(Mp*P/Rp - P/Rp)]\}$$

$$q = 1- B*(Mp*P/Rp) \qquad\qquad\qquad\qquad (5)$$

3.2 The Filter-based Distributed Hybrid-hash Variants

These algorithms are the distributed version of each of the centralized algorithms chh_V1, chh_V2, chh_V3 and chh_V4, presented in section 2.2. In a distributed environment, the construction of a bit-vector to encode the join attribute values of a set of tuples distributed among different processing nodes is somewhat more complicated than that of the centralized environment. The construction of the bit-vector BV, in a distributed environment, is carried out as follows: Every processing node, say node j for example, initializes, in its local memory, a bit-vector BV^j. The join attribute values of the tuples stored in the jth node are used to set the bits of BV^j. BV^j's are then "ored" to form BV. Such "oring" is performed as follows: initially, each node marks its bit-vector as current, then, in turns, every node in the system broadcasts its current bit-vector to all of the other nodes. Whenever a node receives a bit-vector, it "ors" such a vector with its current one and the result is stored in the current bit-vector. This process continues until every node in the system has broadcast its bit-vector, after which, every node in the system will have a copy of BV stored in its current bit-vector. It is easy to see that such a simple scheme has a linear time complexity with respect to the number of nodes in the system, since it takes P broadcast steps and P processing steps to "or" P

Using the derivation method presented in Appendix A, we have developed a Formula to compute Time for each of the distributed algorithms to be described next. These formulas are presented in [Qada87] and will not be repeated here.

Version 2:Total Filtering of Relation S

This algorithm is the second version of the distributed hybrid-hash algorithm(dhh_V2) , where a single bit-vector BV_R is used to encode the join attribute values of all the tuples of relation R. This algorithm proceeds as follows: during the partitioning phase, every processing node sets the bits in its local bit-vector according to the join attribute values of its share from the tuples of relation R. In addition, the processing node partitions its own share from the tuples of relation R, stores its share from the tuples of $R_1, R_2, \ldots, R_B$ on disk and hashes and distributes its share from R_0 to the other nodes in the system. Every processing node in the system, then, forms a copy of BV_R by receiving and "oring" its local bit-vector with that of every other node in the system, as explained before.

As the partitioning phase progress, every node reads, from its own disk, its share from the tuples of relation S and filter them through BV_R. The surviving tuples of relation S are partitioned and the tuples which belong to $S_1, S_2, \ldots, S_B$ are stored on the local disks, while the tuples of S_0 are hashed and distributed to the other processing nodes of the system to search for matches. During the join phase, the tuples of each of the remaining buckets are processed in exactly the same way as in the corresponding step of the distributed hybrid-hash algorithm.

Versions 3 and 4:Total Filtering of Relations R and S

Version 3 of the distributed hybrid-hash algorithm(dhh-V3) uses two bit-vectors, BV_R and BV_S. This algorithm proceeds as follows: first, the processing nodes read the tuples of relation S and build the bit-vector BV_S according to their join attribute values. The partitioning phase continues by reading the tuples of relation R and filtering them through BV_S. The surviving tuples of relation R are used to build the other bit-vector BV_R. In addition, these tuples are partitioned into buckets and stored on disk(except the tuples of R_0 which are stored in the nodes' main-memory). The tuples of relation S are, then, read again from the disks and filtered through BV_R. The surviving tuples of relation S are, then, partitioned. The algorithm then proceed as in the distributed hybrid-hash algorithm.

The fourth version of the distributed hybrid-hash algorithm(dhh-V4) is similar to dhh_V3 except that it avoids the duplicate reading of relation S as in chh_V4.

3.3 Performance Comparison of the Distributed Join algorithms

The performance of the various distributed algorithms is compared, in this

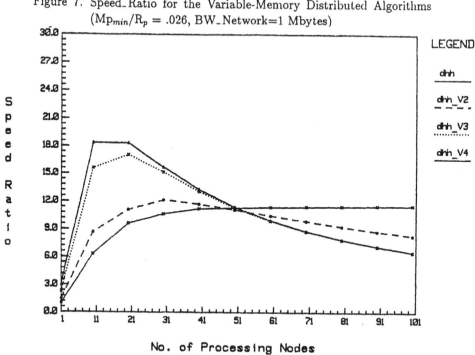

Figure 7. Speed_Ratio for the Variable-Memory Distributed Algorithms
($Mp_{min}/R_p = .026$, BW_Network=1 Mbytes)

No. of Processing Nodes

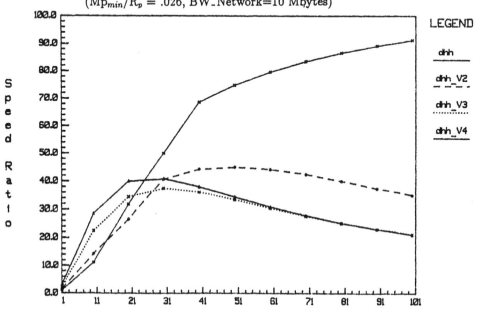

Figure 8. Speed_Ratio for the Variable-Memory Distributed Algorithms
($Mp_{min}/R_p = .026$, BW_Network=10 Mbytes)

No. of Processing Nodes

section, using the measure speed_ratio. Such a measure is defined for a given distributed algorithm as the ratio (execution time ·of· the centralized hybrid-hash/execution time of the given algorithm on the distributed system). The speed-ratio, defined in this way, measures the accumulated effects of the bit-vector filtering and the distributed processing on the hybrid-hash algorithm. Throughout our performance evaluation, we plot the measure speed_ratio for the various algorithms vs. P, the number of nodes in the distributed system. The capacity of the main-memory in each one of these nodes is assumed to be equal to the minimum amount of main-memory required to process the most memory-demanding algorithm(chh_V3 or chh_V4) on a single processing node(Mp_{min}). Therefore, as a new processing node is added to the system, the total main-memory in the system is increment by Mp_{min}(variable memory system).

Figures 7 and 8 plot the speed_ratio vs. P for the various algorithms when processed by a distributed system having a ring network with a bandwidth of 1 and 10 Mbytes, respectively. A close examination of these Figures leads to the following observations:

* Although the speed_ratio of the various distributed algorithms is a strong function of very many parameters, nevertheless, for the current and future ring-interconnection technology, such a speed_ratio is always having a value greater than 1. That is, distributing the join of two disk-based relations among a number of processing nodes is always better than centralizing such processing.

* When the distributed system has a small number of processing nodes(low P), the filter-based algorithms attain speedup advantages over dhh. The amount of such speedup is different from one algorithm to another with dhh_V4 attaining the highest speedup followed by dhh_V3.

* When the system has a large number of processing nodes(high P), the filter-based algorithms are outperformed by the dhh algorithm.

* Beyond a certain value for P(P_d), the filter-based algorithms experience an actual decrease in their speed_ratio's as P is increased beyond P_d. Although, the value of P_d is generally different from one filter-based algorithm to another, nevertheless, such a value is small for all of these algorithms and gets even smaller as the ring bandwidth gets larger(refer to Figures 7 and 8). Such a behavior limits the maximum number of processing nodes that may be used to process any filter-based algorithm to a rather small value. A rather disappointing result!.

4. Discussion and Improvements

The performance evaluation presented in the previous section has pointed out a serious problem with the distributed filter-based algorithms. Increasing the number of nodes in a ring-interconnected system beyond a certain value brings a drop(rather than an increase) in the speed_ratio's (performance) of these algorithms. Such a behavior can be explained as follows: as the number of nodes in the system is increased, the number of the bit-vectors that have to be transmitted across the network will also be proportionally increased. Beyond a certain limit, the network becomes so much overloaded with the transmission of the bit-vectors such that the additional increase in the number of transmitted bit-vectors will offset any speed advantages(or even brings a negative increase in the speed) to be gained from increasing the number of nodes. It is interesting to note that although, the reason behind such a behavior seems intuitive, it has not been pointed out by any previous research in the context of database machines.

To remedy such a situation, one must reduce the time required to broadcast the partial bit-vectors across the ring-network. Such an objective can be accomplished by compressing the size of each of the broadcasted vector. The fact that the number of bits having the value of "1" in a partial bit-vector may not exceed the number of tuples stored in one node(_ Rc/P), and the fact that the total number of bits in a bit-vector is K*Rc(for K >> 1) lead us to conclude that such a vector is sparse, that is, it contains a small number of bits with the value "1" scattered among very many bits having the value of "0." Such a sparse vector can be compressed and only its compressed version needs to be broadcasted across the network. Two compression schemes have been investigated, namely:

Compression Scheme 1. In this scheme, instead of broadcasting its partial bit-vector, a node broadcast only the addresses of those bits in that vector which has the value of "1." A node receiving the broadcast addresses from all the nodes in the system uses them to set up its own bit-vector. In our performance study, we have assumed that an address may use 4 bytes of storage.

Compression Scheme 2: In this scheme, the number of zero's between two adjacent nonzero bits in the partial bit-vector is converted into a binary number of length 4, 8, 12,... bits. The code words generated by a node are collected into pages. The set of code pages generated by all of the nodes in the system is transmitted across the network to a predesignated node. Such a node uses the received code words to set up the bit-vector. When such a vector is complete, it is then broadcasted over the ring-network to all of the other nodes in the system.

The equations developed to compute the performance measure Time for the various filter-based algorithms have been modified to reflect the compression schemes presented above. Figures 9 and 10 present the speed ratio's for the distributed algorithms when the first compression scheme is used, whereas, Figures 11 and 12 present the same measures when the second compression scheme is used. These plots assume a distributed system with a ring-network of bandwidth 1 (Figures 9 and 11) and 10 Mbytes(Figures 10 and 12). A quick comparison between these Figures and Figures 7 and 8, one can see the tremendous improvement in the speed-ratio's (performance) of the filter-based algorithms due to the usage of the compression schemes. In addition, one can see that the curves which represent the speed ratio's

Figure 9. Speed_Ratio for the Variable-Memory Algorithms with the First
Vector Compression Scheme (BW_Network=1 Mbytes)

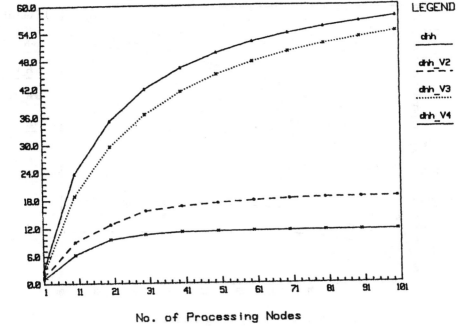

No. of Processing Nodes

Figure 10. Speed_Ratio for the Variable-Memory Algorithms with the First
Vector Compression Scheme (BW_Network=10 Mbytes)

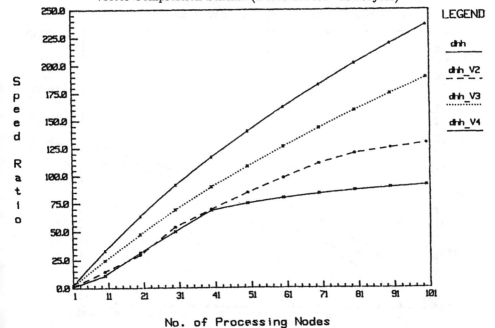

No. of Processing Nodes

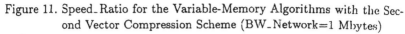

Figure 11. Speed_Ratio for the Variable-Memory Algorithms with the Second Vector Compression Scheme (BW_Network=1 Mbytes)

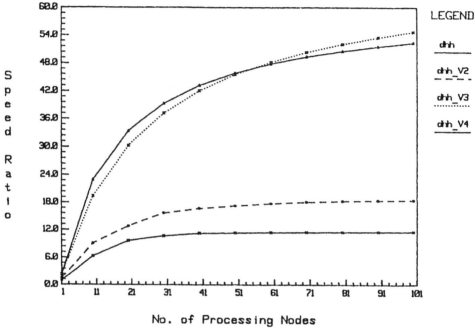

No. of Processing Nodes

Figure 12. Speed_Ratio for the Variable-Memory Algorithms with the Second Vector Compression Scheme (BW_Network=10 Mbytes)

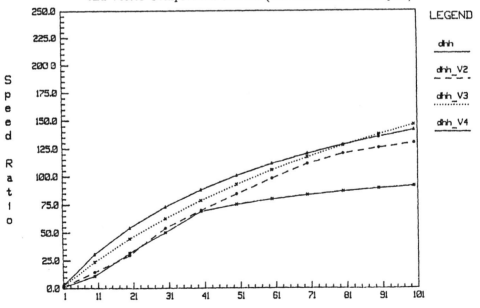

No. of Processing Nodes.

of the compressed filter-based algorithms are always increasing or at worst saturate as P is increased, however, these curves never decrease as in the non-compressed filter-based algorithms. A substantial improvement.

During the analysis of the performance data obtained for both of the compression schemes, we have noticed that for a given filter-based algorithm, the second compression scheme transmit less data over the ring-network than the first scheme, however, it requires from each node much more processing time to generate the code words than the first scheme. Such increase in the processing time required by the second scheme offsets the saving in the time required by the network transmission, thus, the first scheme emerges as the best performing one. The comparison of Figure 9 and Figure 11(or Figure 10 and 12) shows that the first compression scheme indeed outperforms the second one. Because it is simple to implement and it improves the performance of the filter-based algorithms best, we recommend that the first compression scheme be adopted.

5. Conclusions and Further Research

This paper presents several extensions to the serial and parallel hybrid-hash join algorithms. These extensions are based on the usage of one or more bit-vectors to filter out, as early as possible, some of the unwanted tuples from one or both of the relations to be joined. A detailed performance study to the hybrid-hash and the extended algorithms is also presented. Such a study compares the performance of the hybrid-hash algorithm and its various filter-based algorithms. In general, the performance of the filter-based algorithms relative to that of the hybrid-hash has been found to be a strong function of the physical resources available to process the join operation(size of main-memory relative to the size of a relation, number of processing node ...etc) and the characteristics of the relations which participate in the join operation. In a uniprocessor environment, we have found that a certain filter-based algorithm(chh_V4) attains a considerable speed advantages over the hybrid-hash algorithm for a wide range of typical settings of the performance parameters. The winning algorithm makes use of two bit-vectors, each of which is used to filter out the unwanted tuples from one of the relations to be joined.

In a ring-interconnected distributed environment, the filter-based distributed algorithms have been found to suffer from a serious problem, namely, overloading the interconnection network with the transmission of many bit vectors. Different compression schemes are proposed to reduce the size of a transmitted bit-vector. The augmentation of the distributed version of chh_V4(dhh_V4) algorithm with one of the proposed vector compression scheme has been found to outperform all of the other algorithms and substantially improves the performance of the join operation. Thus such a modified algorithm is recommended to be used to process the join operation in a distributed environment.

Appendix A

Derivations of Formulas for the Join Total Execution Time

1. Derivation of a Formula for Time(chh)

Time(chh) = Time(phase$_0$) + Time(phase$_{1...B}$)

Where Time(phase$_0$) =

TIO_rand + (Rp- 1)*TIO_seq	/read in relation R/
+ C*Rc*Thash	/hash the tuples of R to buckets
	C is 0 if B=0, 1 otherwise/
+ Rc*(1-q)*Tmove	/move the tuples of R$_1$,..R$_B$ to disk
	buffers/
+ Rp*(1-q)*TIO	/write to disk R$_1$,R$_2$...R$_B$.
	q = Rp$_0$/R
	TIO is TIO_seq,TIO_rand otherwise/
+ Rc*q*Thash	/hash R$_0$ tuples to hash table/
+ Rc*q*Tmove	/store R$_0$ tuples in Hash table/
+ TIO_rand + (Sp-1)*TIO_seq	/read in relation S/
+ C*Sc*Thash	/hash the tuples of S to buckets/
+ Sc*(1-q)*Tmove	/move the tuples of S$_1$...S$_B$ to disk
	buffers/
+ Sp*(1-q)*TIO	/write to disk S$_1$,S$_2$...S$_B$/
+ Sc*q*Thash	/hash S$_0$ tuples to hash table/
+ Sc*q*Lsearch*Tcomp	/search the hash table of R$_0$/

and Time(phase$_{1...B}$) =

B*[TIO_rand + (Rp$_i$-1)*TIO_seq	/read R$_i$ into memory/
+ Rc$_i$*Thash	/build a hash table for R$_i$/
+ Rc$_i$*Tmove	/store tuples of R$_i$ into hash table/
+ TIO_rand + (Sp$_i$-1)*TIO_seq	/read S$_i$ into memory/
+ Sc$_i$*Thash	/hash S$_i$ to hash table of R$_i$/
+ Sc$_i$*Lsearch*Tcomp	/search the hash table of R$_i$/]

2. Derivation of a Formula for Time(dhh)

$$\text{Time} = \text{Time}(\text{phase}_0) + \text{Time}(\text{phase}_{1...B})$$

where, $\text{Time}(\text{phase}_0) =$

TIO_rand + (Rp/P - 1)*TIO_seq	/read in R^j/
+ C*Rc/P*Thash	/hash the tuples of R^j to bucket
	C is 0 if B=0, 1 otherwise/
+ (Rc/P)*(1-q)*Tmove	/move tuples of R(1,j)...R(B,j) to disk
	buffers, q = Rc_0/Rc/
+ (Rp/P)*(1-q)*TIO	/write to disk R(1,j)...R(B,j)
	TIO = TIO_seq if B=0
	= TIO_rand if B > 1 /
+ (Rc/P)*q*Thash	/hash the tuples of R(0,j) to processors
	and their local hash tables(neglect the
	pointer cost)/
+ (Rc/P)*q*(1-1/P)*Tmove	/move tuples of R(0,j) to net buffer/
+ Rp*q*(1-1/P)*TIO_net	/Transfer the tuples of R_0 across net/
+ (Rc/P)*q*Tmove	/store the tuples of R_0 to the hash
	table of P_j/
+ TIO_rand + [(Sp/P) -1]*TIO_seq	/read in tuples of S^j/
+ C*(Sc/P)*Thash	/hash the tuples of S^j to buckets/
+ (Sc/P)*(1-q)*Tmove	/move the tuples of $S_1,...S_B$ to disk
	buffers/
+ (Sp/P)*(1-q)*TIO	/write to disk $S_1,S_2...S_B$/
+ (Sc/P)*q*Thash	/hash the tuples of S(0,j) to processors
	and their local hash tables/
+ (Sc/P)*q*(1-1/P)*Tmove	/move tuples of S(0,j) to be send to
	other processor, to net buffer/
+ Sp*q*(1-1/P)*TIO_net	/Transfer the tuples of S(0,j) across
	the net/
+ (Sc/P)*q*Lsearch*Tcomp	/search the hash table of R_0/

and $\text{Time}(\text{phase}_{1...B}) =$

B*[TIO_rand + [(Rp_i/P)-1]*TIO_seq	/read R(i,j) into memory/
+ (Rc_i/P)*Thash	/hash the tuples of R(i,j) to the
	processors and their local hash tables/
+ (Rc_i/P)*(1-1/P)*Tmove	/move the tuples of other processors to
	net buffer/
+ (Rp_i)*(1-1/P)*TIO_net	/transfer the tuples across net/
+ (Rc_i/P)*Tmove	/build a hash table for R(i,j)/

$$+ \text{TIO\_rand} + [(Sp_i/P)-1]*\text{TIO\_seq} \quad /\text{read } S(i,j) \text{ into memory}/$$

$$+ (Sc_i/P)*\text{Thash} \qquad\qquad /\text{hash the tuples of } S(i,j) \text{ to processors}$$
and their local hash tables/

$$+ (Sc_i/P)*(1-1/P)*\text{Tmove} \qquad /\text{move the tuples of other processors to}$$
net buffer/

$$+ Sp_i*(1-1/P)*\text{TIO\_net} \qquad /\text{transfer the tuples to the proper}$$
processors/

$$+ (Sc_i/P)*\text{Lsearch}*\text{Tcomp} \qquad /\text{search the hash table of } R(i,j)/]$$

References

[Babb79] Babb, E., "Implementing a Relational Database by Means of Specialized Hardware." ACM Trans. on Database Systems, Vol. 4, No. 6 (June 1979), pp. 414-429.

[Baru87] Baru, C. and Frieder, F., "Implementing Relational Database Operations in a Cube-Connected Multicomputer System." Proceedings of the Third International Conference on Data Engineering, 1987.

[Baru86] Baru, C. K. and Su, S. Y. W., "The Architecture of SM3: A Dynamically Partitioned Multicomputer System." IEEE Transaction on Computers, Vol. C-35, No. 9(September 86), pp. 790-802.

[Bitt83] Bitton, D., et al., "Parallel Algorithms for the Execution of Relational Database Operations." ACM Trans. on Database Systems, Vol.8, No. 3(September 1983), pp. 324-353.

[Dewi79] Dewitt, D. J., "DIRECT- A Multiprocessor Organization for Supporting Relational Database Management Systems." IEEE Transaction on Computers, Vol. C-28, No. 6(June 1979), pp. 395-408.

[Dewi87] Dewitt, D. J., et al., "A Single User Evaluation for the Gamma Database Machine." Proceedings of the 5th International Workshop on Database Machines, 1987.

[Dewi86] Dewitt, D., J., et al., "GAMMA - A High Performance Dataflow Database Machine." Proceedings of the 12th International Conference on Very Large Databases, 1986, pp. 228-237.

[Dewi85] Dewitt, D., J. and Gerber, R., "Multiprocessor Hash-Based Join Algorithms." Proceedings of VLDB, 1985, pp. 151-164.

[Dewi84] Dewitt, D. J. et al., "Implementation Techniques for Large Main Memory Database Systems." Proceedings of SIGMOD, 1984.

[Gard81] Gardarin, G., "An Introduction to SABRE: A Multi-Microprocessor Database Machine." Proceedings of the 6th Workshop on Computer Architecture for Non-numeric Processing, Hyeres, France, June 1981.

[Gerb86] Gerber, R., "Dataflow Query Processing Using Multiprocessor Hash-Partitioned Algorithms." Tech. Report #672, Computer Sciences Department, University of Wisconsin-Madison, Oct. 1986.

[Good81] Goodman, J. R., "An Investigation of Multiprocessor Structures and Algorithms for Database Management." Memo No. UCB/ERLM81(May 81), Electronic Research Lab., College of Engineering, University of California, Berkeley.

[Hsia81]   Hsiao, D. K., and Menon, M. J., "Design and Analysis of a Multi-Backend Database System for Performance Improvements, Functionality Expansion and Capacity Growth (Part I and II)." Technical Reports, OSU-CISRC-TR-81-7 and OSU-CISRC-TR-81-8, The Ohio State University, Columbus, Ohio, 1981.

[Kim79]   Kim, W., "Relational Database Systems." ACM Computing Survey, Vol. 11, No.3, 1979, pp. 185-211.

[Kits84]   Kitsuregawa, et al., "Architecture and Performance of Relational Algebra Machine GRACE." Proceedings of the International Conference on Parallel Processing, 1984, pp. 241-250.

[Qada]   Qadah, G. Z. and Irani, K. B., "The Join Operation on A Shared-memory Multiprocessor Database Machine." to appear in the IEEE Transaction on Software Engineering.

[Qada87]   Qadah,   G.   Z.,   "Filter-based   Algorithms   on   Uniprocessor   and Distributed-memory Multiprocessor Database Machines." Technical Report # 87-06-DBM-03, EECS Department, Northwestern University, 1987.

[Qada85a] Qadah, G. Z., "Database Machines: A Survey." Proceedings of the National Computer Conference, AFIPS Press, 1985, pp.211-223.

[Qada85b] Qadah, G. Z. and Irani, K. B., "A Database Machine for Very Large Relational Databases." IEEE Transaction on Computers, Vol. C-34, No. 11(November 1985), pp. 1015-1025.

[Schw83]   Schweppe, H., Zeidler, H., Hell, W., Leilich, H., Stiege, G. and Teich, W., "RDBM- A Dedicated Multiprocessor System for Database Management." Advanced Database Architecture, Hsiao, D. K.(ed.), Prentice-Hall, 1983, pp. 36-86.

[Seit85]   Seitz, C., "The Cosmic Cube." Communication of ACM, Vol. 28, No. 1 (Jan. 1985), pp. 22-33.

[Shul87]   Shultz, R. and Miller, lla, "Tree Structured Multiple Processor Join Methods." Proceedings of the 3rd Data Engineering Conference, 1987, pp. 190-199.

[Tera83]   Teradata: DBC/1012 Data Base Computer Concepts and Facilities, Teradata Corp. Document No. C02-0001-01, 1984.

[Vald84]   Valduriez, P. and Gardarin, G., "Join and Semijoin Algorithms for a Multiprocessor Database Machine." ACM Trans. on Database Systems, Vol. 9, No. 1(March 1984), pp. 133-161.

PLACEMENT OF REPLICATED ITEMS IN DISTRIBUTED DATABASES

Amir Milo
Ouri Wolfson
Department of Computer Science
The Technion - Israel Institute of Technology
Haifa 32000, Israel

ABSTRACT

We address the problem of determining an allocation scheme for replicated data in a distributed database, with the purpose of minimizing required communication. An allocation scheme establishes the number of copies of each data-item, and at which processors of a given computer network the copies should be located. The problem for general networks is shown NP-Complete, but we provide efficient algorithms to obtain an optimal allocation scheme for three common types of network topologies. They are completely-connected, tree, and ring networks. We also propose a new method by which a processor in a computer network should write all the copies of a replicated data item. This method leads to surprising results concerning the allocation schemes.

1. Introduction

The two main purposes of replicating data in distributed databases are improved performance, and improved reliability. In this paper we concentrate on the performance issue, and only mention how reliability should be addressed in our framework. Replicated data usually improves performance because it enables a data-read to be performed locally or at a "close-by" site. On the other hand, replicated data increases the overhead of a data-write because it has to be transmitted to all processors which store replicas. Therefore, in order to obtain a performance gain the number of data-item copies, and their placement in the computer network should be carefully determined.

In this paper we address the problem of placing replicas of a data-item, i.e. files, relations, or data-blocks, in a given computer-network for minimizing the number of information messages. These are the messages that carry the data-items, and place the bulk of the load on the communication network (control messages such as read-requests, acknowledgments, and subtransaction-initiation are ignored). Our aim is to suggest an algorithm that given a communication network, and read-write ratio for a data-item, will output an allocation scheme that minimizes the number of information messages carrying the data-item. The communication network is modeled by an undirected graph, and we are careful to consider that transmitting the data-item from processor a to processor b requires a number of messages equal to the distance in the network between a and b. The read-write ratio is assumed common to all processors in the network. The allocation scheme output consists of the number of replicas, and at which processors they should be located. We establish that the problem of determining an optimal allocation scheme is *NP–Complete* (even for our simple problem definition), but can be solved efficiently (algorithms are provided) for the following widely-used network topologies: completely interconnected, tree, and ring. Our computer network is homogeneous in the sense that all processors perform similar-type work, and therefore have the same read-write ratio, and the cost of a message on each communication link is equal.

After determining the optimal allocation scheme, the number of replicas should be increased, if necessary, to a minimal threshold required for reliability. We assume that this threshold is known a priori, and determined by means outside the scope of this paper, such as the failure-probability of a processor. For each topology for which we find an optimal allocation scheme, we also discuss how the number of replicas can be raised up to the threshold, such that the "damage" to performance is minimal. This rather simplistic approach (compared to [MR] for example) suffices in a reliable computer network.

This work is distinguished from the previous extensive research on the general file-allocation-problem (see [DF] for a survey) by several features. First, our problem is simple, and the objective function is limited in scope, therefore for specialized topologies we are able to provide optimal solutions in polynomial time. Specifically, the only two parameters to the problem are the network topology, and the read-write ratio. As a consequence, we do not optimize overall performance; we do however optimize one very important factor which determines performance, namely message traffic. In this sense we take what is called in [CMP] the user viewpoint. Namely, we assume a predefined configuration and network topology. Other works attempt to optimize the communication costs as well as storage costs ([C, ML]), communication channels capacity ([MR]), or the communication network topology ([IK]). Additional advantages of our simple model are: independence of many parameters that are hard to estimate or change frequently (such as file-size or storage capacity); and independence of the allocation scheme of one data-item from another, enabling incremental configuration of the system.

A second feature distinguishing the present work is that we assume that the individual-processor algorithm, at run-time, optimizes message traffic. For example, suppose that three processors, a, b and c are connected in a string, namely a is connected by a bidirectional link to b, and b is connected to c. Assume that a writes a data-item which is replicated at processors b and c. In other models a is assumed to transmit the item separately to b and to c. This generates one information message for the first transmission and two for the second. But the transmission from a to c traverses through b anyway, because of the network topology. So a simple message-optimization that we assume a to make at run-time, is to send the item to b, and "ask" b to propagate it to c. This will save one information message. A similar approach was proposed in [SW] to minimize the number of control messages required for transaction commitment. Indeed, it makes sense that if we determine the allocation scheme with the purpose to minimize messages, then each processor does so at run-time. Therefore, we argue that the communication cost of a multicast transmission is not simply the sum of the communication costs between the sender and each one of the receivers. On this subtle point the present paper differs from all other works on the subject, leading to surprising results concerning the allocation schemes. It turns out that the replicas should be clustered in neighboring processors of the network, rather than being "spread out" evenly to allow close access for each processor.

The rest of the paper is organized as follows. The minimal communication cost of a read and a write for a fixed allocation scheme is determined in section 2. The optimal residence set problem is defined and proved $NP-Complete$ for general networks in section 3. In section 4 we present the positive results concerning completely-connected, tree, and ring networks. In section 5 we discuss these results.

2. Read and Write Message-Costs.

Read and write operations for logical entities (or data-items) are issued at each processor in a computer network. Each such operation is eventually translated into zero or more information messages transmitted in the network; they carry the entity to or from the processors storing the physical replicas of the logical entity. In this section we establish the minimal number of network messages required for an arbitrary read and write by a processor. The read case is simple, the write case slightly more involved. We start with some definitions. A *communication network*, or *network* for short, is an undirected graph, $G=(V,E)$. V represents a set of processors, and an edge in the network between processors v and w represents a bidirectional communication link between them. Given a network we define a *residence set* to be a subset of V. It represents the processors where some arbitrary fixed entity is replicated. We assume that reading of an entity by a processor is implemented by transferring the closest replica to it. Therefore, for a given network and residence set the *read cost* of a processor v, denoted r_v, is the length (in edges) of the shortest path in the network between v and a processor of the residence set. It represents the number of information messages required for the entity transfer. Obviously, if v is in the read set the read cost is zero.

Next we establish the write cost for a processor, given a residence set, R. We assume that processor $v \in V$ writes the logical entity, and call it the *writer*; it may or may not belong to the residence set. The processors in $R \cup \{v\}$ are the *participants* in the write protocol, and are denoted by P. A *write instance* is a directed graph, $I = (P, A)$. Each arc of A represents a replica transfer between two participants, and its cost is the shortest path in the network between the processors at its endpoints. Since the entity sent by the writer reaches every other participant we require that there is a path in I from v to each processor in R. The *write–instance cost* is the total cost of its arcs. We are interested in establishing the minimal cost of a write instance. Clearly, for this purpose the only instances to be considered are acyclic. A possible algorithm which sends exactly the messages of a given acyclic instance, I, is the following (assuming I is known to all participants): the writer sends the entity to its sons and each processor after receiving the entity forwards it to its sons and so on, until the entity reaches the leaves of I.

For the next proposition we need to define the *distance graph*, $D_G(\hat{V})$, for an arbitrary subset of processors $\hat{V} \subseteq V$. $D_G(\hat{V})$ is a complete weighted graph with the set of nodes $\hat{V}$. The weight of an edge between j and k in $D_G(\hat{V})$ is the length of the shortest path in G between j and k. Denote by $mst(D_G(\hat{V}))$ a minimum spanning tree of $D_G(\hat{V})$.

Proposition 2.1: Let G be a network, R a residence set, and v a writer. Denote the set $R \cup \{v\}$ by P. Then the necessary and sufficient cost of a write instance is the total weight of $mst(D_G(P))$.

Proof: (necessary) By the definition of a write instance the underlying graph of any write instance is a connected subgraph of $D_G(P)$ that spans all the processors of P. The minimal weight of such a graph is the weight of $MST(D_G(P))$.

(sufficient) Given an $MST(D_G(P))$ we can build the required write instance whose cost is equal to the weight of $MST(D_G(P))$, by directing the edges of the $MST(D_G(P))$ to form a rooted tree, rooted at the writer. $\quad\square$

Therefore we define the *write cost* of processor v, denoted w_v, to be the total weight of $mst(D_G(P))$. The next lemma will be used extensively in our proofs.

Lemma 2.1: Given a network $G = (V, E)$, a residence set R, and a processor $i \in V$, denote by d_i the length of the shortest path in G between i and some processor of R. If R induces a connected subgraph of G then $w_i = d_i + |R| - 1$.

Proof: We prove first that any spanning tree of $D_G(R \cup \{i\})$ is of weight at least $d_i + |R| - 1$.

The $|R|+1$ nodes of the distance graph require $|R|$ edges in order to form a spanning tree. The lightest edge that is connected to i in $D_G(R \cup \{i\})$ is obviously of weight d_i. Each of the other $|R|-1$ edges is at least of weight one, therefore there is no spanning tree whose weight is less than $d_i + |R|-1$.

Now we prove that a spanning tree of such weight exists. R induces a connected subgraph, thus, there are $|R|-1$ edges of weight one, and this set of edges spans the nodes of R in the distance graph. Also, there exists an edge of weight d_i between node i and some node of R. Therefore there exists a spanning tree whose weight is $d_i + |R|-1$.　□

3. The residence set problem

In this section we define the residence set problem, namely the problem of placing the replicas to minimize overall message traffic in a general network. Then its complexity is established. We assume that the ratio of read to write operations is fixed, and equal at all the processors. We denote this ratio by α. Given a residence set, R, and α, the *residence set cost*, denoted $cost(R)$, is defined as $\sum_{i \in V} w_i + \alpha \cdot \sum_{i \in V} r_i$. Intuitively, this expression represents the average cost of an operation when R is the residence set. Given an α, we would like to find the *optimal residence set*, i.e. the residence set with the minimal cost. The *residence set* problem, denoted RS, is defined as follows:

Input: Communication network graph $G=(V,E)$ and two positive real numbers α and C.

Question: Is there a residence set $R \subseteq V$, such that $\sum_{i \in V} w_i + \alpha \cdot \sum_{i \in V} r_i < C$?

Theorem 3.1: *RS* is *NP–Complete*.

Proof Sketch: It is easy to see that $RS \in NP$. Guess a subset $R \subseteq V$, find w_i and r_i for each $i \in V$, and verify that $\sum_{i \in V} w_i + \alpha \cdot \sum_{i \in V} r_i < C$. Obviously, this can be done in polynomial time.

RS is *NP–Hard*. We transform the Steiner Tree (ST) problem to RS. In ST the input consists of a graph $G'=(V',E')$, a subset $X \subseteq V'$ and a positive integer B. The question is whether there is a subtree of G' that includes all the nodes of X and such that its number of edges is no more than B. Without loss of generality we assume that $|X|>1$ and $|X|<B<|V'|$.

Given an instance of the ST problem we construct an instance of the RS problem as follows. The graph G consists of G', with every node $u \in X$ connected to a "crown" of $|V'|^3$ new nodes: $u_1, u_2, \ldots, u_{|V'|^3}$. For example, in fig. 3.1b there is graph constructed from the graph of fig. 3.1a, where $X=\{a,b,c\}$.

Let $\alpha = B$ and $C = 2 \cdot |V'|^3 \cdot |X| \cdot (B+1)$.

It can be shown that there exists a solution to the ST problem if and only if there exists a solution to the RS problem.　□

Although the problem is *NP—Complete* in general, for certain input parameters it can be solved efficiently. It can be shown that if $\alpha > |V|-1$, then the optimal residence set is the whole set of processors, V, regardless of the network topology. In the next section we show that for certain common network topologies the problem can be solved efficiently for any read-write ratio.

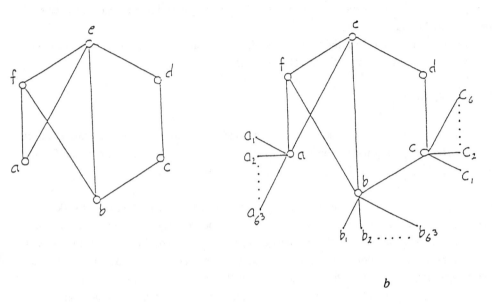

figure 3.1.

4. Special topologies

4.1 Completely Connected Network

Given a residence set, R, in a complete-network (i.e. a clique) we can compute the following costs. For every processor j in R, $r_j=0$; and for every processor k that is not in R, $r_k=1$. Thus,

$$\sum_{i \in V} r_i = |V|-|R|.$$

For every processor j in R, $w_j=|R|-1$ and for every processor k that is not in R, $w_k=|R|$. Thus, $\sum_{i \in V} w_i = (|V|-|R|)\cdot|R|+|R|\cdot(|R|-1) = (|V|-1)\cdot|R|$.

$$\text{cost}(R) = \sum_{i \in V} w_i + \alpha \cdot \sum_{i \in V} r_i = |R|\cdot(|V|-\alpha-1)+|V|\cdot\alpha.$$

We would like to find an $\dot{R}$ which minimizes this expression. Expectedly, the actual residence set is irrelevant, only its size determines the communication cost. If $\alpha < |V|-1$ then the minimum is obtained when $|R|=1$, i.e. any single processor of V constitutes an optimal residence set. If $\alpha \geq |V|-1$ then the minimum is obtained when $|R|=|V|$, i.e. the optimal residence set contains all the processors of V. Therefore, the size of the residence set as a function of α is a step function with *two* values. Interestingly, an intermediate residence set is never optimal (regardless of α).

Adding copies to reach the reliability threshold, if necessary, is trivial since their location is irrelevant, as far as communication cost is concerned.

4.2 Tree Network

We will first prove 4 lemmas, each one of them states a property of an optimal residence sets in tree-networks. Using these properties we will suggest a linear-time algorithm, that finds an optimal residence set for a given read-write ratio, and a given tree-network.

Lemma 4.2.1: An optimal residence set induces a connected subgraph in a tree-network.

Proof sketch: Assume that there exists an optimal residence set, R, which induces an unconnected graph. We construct another residence set, R', such that $cost(R') < cost(R)$. The construction proceeds as follows. Since the induced graph is not connected, there must be at least two processors, i and j, such that on the unique path between them, of length, say $k>1$, there are no copies. To obtain R' we add to R all the processors on this path. The total read cost (i.e. of all the processors) for R' is less than the read cost for R, since we only add copies. The write cost of a processor given R' is equal to its write cost given R, for the following intuitive reason. The distance graph contains an edge of length k between i and j for the residence set R, and k edges of length one for the residence set R'. However, in both cases the weight of the minimal spanning tree of the distance graph is equal. $\square$

Denote the processors of a graph G by $V(G)$.

Lemma 4.2.2: Let R be a residence set that induces a connected subgraph of a tree-network. Assume that processor i is a neighbour of some processor in R, and t_i is a subtree such that $i \in V(t_i)$ and $V(t_i) \cap R = \emptyset$ (see figure 4.2.1). Then, $cost(R \cup \{i\}) > cost(R)$ implies that $cost(R \cup V(t_i)) > cost(R)$.

Proof sketch: Removal of the edge between i and its neighbour in R disconnects the tree to two subtrees: a subtree that contains i, denoted T_i, and a subtree that contains R, denoted T_R. Figure 4.2.1 illustrates the description.

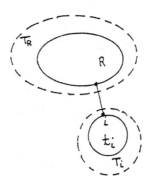

figure 4.2.1.

Adding i to R decreases the read cost of each processor of T_i by one, and does not change the read cost of T_R's processors. Adding i to R increases the write cost of each processor of T_R by one, and does not change the write cost of T_i's processors. So, $cost(R \cup \{i\}) = cost(R) - \alpha \cdot |V(T_i)| + |V(T_R)|$. Since it is given that $cost(R \cup \{i\}) > cost(R)$, then $|V(T_R)| - \alpha \cdot |V(T_i)| > 0$ $\qquad$ (1).

Adding $V(t_i)$ to R decreases the read cost of each processor of T_i by at most $|V(t_i)|$ and does not change the read cost of T_R's processors. Adding $V(t_i)$ to R increases the write cost of each processor of T_R by $|V(t_i)|$ (by lemma 2.1), and does not decrease the write cost of T_i's processors.

Thus, $cost(R \cup V(t_i)) \geq cost(R) - \alpha \cdot |V(T_i)| \cdot |V(t_i)| + |V(T_R)| \cdot |V(t_i)| =$ $cost(R) + |V(t_i)| \cdot (|V(T_R)| - \alpha \cdot |V(T_i)|) >^{(1)} cost(R)$. $\qquad$ $\square$

Lemma 4.2.3: Let R and R' be two residence sets that induce connected subgraphs, and assume that $R \subseteq R'$. Furthermore, assume that processor i is a neighbor of some processor in R, and $i \notin R'$. Then $cost(R \cup \{i\}) \leq cost(R)$ if and only if $cost(R' \cup \{i\}) \leq cost(R')$.

Proof sketch: Removal of the edge between i and its neighbor in R divides the tree-network into two subtrees: a subtree that contains i, T_i, and a subtree that contains R, T_R. Figure 4.2.2. illustrates the description. Adding i to R or to R' changes the costs in the same way: decreases the read cost of each processor of T_i by one, and does not change the read cost of T_R's processors. Increases the write cost of each processor of T_R by one and does not change the write cost of T_i's processors. So, adding i to R decreases $cost(R)$, if and only if adding i to R' decreases $cost(R')$. $\qquad$ $\square$

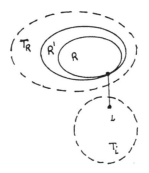

figure 4.2.2.

In the algorithm that will be presented we use the term median of a tree. The median is the node for which the sum of distances to the other nodes is minimal. Note that usually the median of a tree is different than its center. The latter is the node for which the *maximal* distance is minimal. Formally, in a tree let l_{vu} denote the length of the simple path between v and u. A *median* is a node, c, for which $\sum_u l_{cu}$ is minimal. The median can be found in a time which is linear in the size of the tree, by using the following property of a median (see [Z]). A node m is a median of a tree T, if for each one of its neighbors, w, the following is true: if the edge (m,w) is removed, then in the component which contains w there are at most half the number of nodes in T.

It can be shown that in a tree there are one or two medians.

Lemma 4.2.4: For each one of the medians there is an optimal residence set which contains it.

Proof : Omitted and can be found in [M].

Using the properties that have been proven in the above lemmas we present a simple algorithm that finds the optimal residence set. It is given a tree network and a ratio α. The algorithm colors the processors: by blue if the processor is not in the optimal residence set, and by white if the processor has not been checked yet.

TREE-RS: /* Algorithm for finding the optimal residence set */

1. *init*: color all the processors of V by white; initialize R to a median, c.

2.   while there exists a processor in R with at least one white neighbor, j, do:

3.   if $cost(R \cup \{j\}) \leq cost(R)$ then add j to R; else color j by blue.

4.   end while.

5. *output*: R.

Theorem 4.2.1: For any tree-network and any read-write ratio, the residence set, denoted R, output by the algorithm $TREE-RS$, is optimal.

Proof: We will prove that R satisfies the following condition. It is a minimal cost residence set that contains c, with a maximal number of processors. By lemma 4.2.4, a residence set which satisfies the condition is an optimal residence set. Assume that R does not satisfy the condition, and denote by RS a residence set which does so. This obviously implies that $RS \neq R$. The set RS induces a connected subgraph (by lemma 4.2.1), and R induces a connected subgraph (by the way $TREE-RS$ adds nodes to the residence set). We will analyze two cases.

case 1: $R \subseteq RS$. Observe that the graph induced in the network by $RS-R$ is a forest. Consider a tree, t_i, of this forest. It contains a processor, i, that has a neighbor in R. Step 3 of $TREE-RS$ must have been executed for i, but it did not add i to R. In other words, adding i would have increased the cost. From Lemmas 4.2.2 and 4.2.3 we can conclude that by removing the processors of t_i from RS a lower cost residence set can be obtained. Contradiction to the minimality of RS's cost.

case 2: $R \nsubseteq RS$. Let k be the first processor that the algorithm adds, such that $k \in R$ and $k \notin RS$. Denote by R' the residence set that we have before adding k. Note that $R' \neq \phi$ (because at least $c \in R'$), and $R' \subseteq RS$. The algorithm adds k to R', so $cost(R' \cup \{k\}) \leq cost(R')$. k is a neighbor of some processor in R. By lemma 4.2.3 $cost(RS \cup \{k\}) \leq cost(RS)$. If $cost(RS \cup \{k\}) < cost(RS)$ then RS is not an optimal residence set, and if $cost(RS \cup \{k\}) = cost(RS)$ then RS does not have a maximal number of processors. $\square$

In step 2 of the algorithm we check every processors of the tree-network at most once, deciding weather to add it to R, or color it by blue. We perform the comparison of step 3 by using formula (1) in the proof of lemma 4.2.2, which indicates how the addition of a processor to the residence set changes costs. Then the time complexity of finding the optimal RS is linear.

To reach the reliability threshold if necessary, we add copies in the following way. Assume that a residence set, R, is found by the above algorithm. Let processor i be a neighbor of some processor in R. The removal of the edge between i and is neighbour in R disconnects the network. Denote the subtree that contains i by T_i. We iteratively add to R the neighbor, i, for which $|T_i|$ is maximal. The step is repeated until the reliability threshold is reached.

4.3 Ring

We prove 4 lemmas enabling us to conclude that for any size ring, and any read-write ratio, there is an optimal residence set which has at most one hole. Based on this we provide in theorem 4.3.1 a formula to compute the optimal residence set. The first lemma enables us to speak subsequently in more intuitive terms of strings, rather than the distance-graph. We refer to a connected subgraph of a ring network as a *string*. For a residence set, a string without copies is a *hole*.

Lemma 4.3.1: Let G be a ring, R be a residence set, and i be a processor of G. Then w_i equals to the number of edges in the shortest string of G that contains all the processors of $R \cup \{i\}$.
Proof : Omitted and can be found in [M].

Lemma 4.3.2: If the residence set contains more than 2 holes, then it is not an optimal residence set for any read-write ratio.
Proof sketch: Assume that a residence set, R, contains more than two holes. Denote by H the set of processors each of which is not in R, and is not in the two biggest holes of R. Consider the residence set, R', which is $R \cup H$ (we fill all but the two biggest holes). Since R' is a proper superset of R, the total cost of reads for R' is less than for R. Consider an arbitrary processor, i. If i is not in the biggest hole of R, then the length of the shortest string of G that contains all the processors of $R \cup \{i\}$ is the length of the ring except the biggest hole. If i is in the biggest hole of R than the length of the shortest string is the length of the ring except part of the biggest hole, or the length of the ring except the second biggest hole. In both cases w_i for R equals to w_i for R', thus the total cost of writes has not changed. Therefore $cost(R') < cost(R)$ for any α. $\square$

Lemma 4.3.3: If $\alpha > 1$ then in an optimal residence set there is at most one hole.
Proof sketch: Let R be a residence set with two holes. Denote by H_s and H_b the sets of processors of the smaller hole and of the bigger hole, respectively. Consider the residence set, R', which is $R \cup H_s$. It can be shown that $cost(R') < cost(R)$. $\square$

Lemma 4.3.4: If $\alpha \leq 1$ then there is an optimal residence set with at most one hole.
Proof : Omitted and can be found in [M].

By lemmas 4.3.3 and 4.3.4 we conclude that for each ring, and for each read-write ratio, there exists an optimal residence set with only one hole; in other words, there exists an optimal residence-set that induces a connected subgraph of the network. Since the ring is symmetric, the residence set location is irrelevant. Therefore, for each one of the n possible residence set sizes, one can compute the cost, and then choose the minimal. However, we will provide a formula, enabling computation in constant time.

Theorem 4.3.1: Let n be the size of the ring, and α be the read-write ratio. Then the cardinality of the optimal residence set equals to $\dfrac{n \cdot (\alpha - 1)}{\alpha + 1} + 1$.

Proof : Omitted and can be found in [M].

Since the optimal residence set induces a single string, it is obvious how to reach the reliability threshold if necessary; the string is simply extended up to the threshold.

5. Discussion

In this paper we first proposed a new method by which a processor should write all replicas of a data item for minimizing communication. The processor should construct a minimum spanning tree of what we called the distance graph, and then propagate the data item along its edges. The read, as usual, is carried out from the closest replica. Then we showed that determining an allocation scheme, or a residence set, for minimizing overall communication is *NP–Complete* in networks modeled by general graphs. However, we provided constant time algorithms for determining the optimal residence set in completely-connected networks and rings, and a linear time algorithm for determining the allocation scheme in tree-networks.

It turns out that for these special topologies, for any read-write ratio, the data-item should be placed in one connected component of the network. This is counter-intuitive because one would expect that as the read-write ratio grows, the replicas should be spread out throughout the network to allow a close read for each processor, rather than clustering them in one connected component. The reason for this apparent anomaly is the following. Our write policy favors clustering more than other policies. In order to require dispersion the read-write ratio has to grow to such extent, as to make the whole set of processors the optimal residence set - again one connected component.

If the write cost of a single processor were simply the sum of distances to all replicas (namely, a naive write policy), then the optimal allocation scheme would have been different. For example, consider a ring with six processors, and a read write ratio of two (in other words, each processor performs two reads and one write per time unit). If the processors were conducting a naive write policy, then the optimal allocation scheme is 2-symmetric, i.e., place replicas at two processors at a distance of three edges from one another. The cost of this scheme is 26 messages per time unit. For the mst write policy, the optimal allocation scheme is a 3-string, i.e., place replicas on a string of three processors (24 messages). The 3-string is not optimal for the naive write policy (38 messages), and the 2-symmetric is not optimal for the mst write policy (26 messages).

Finally, note that although the optimal residence set for the discussed topologies induces a connected subgraph, this is not necessarily the case in a general network. For example, for the network in fig 5.1 and for $\alpha=1.8$ the unique optimal residence set is {4,8}.

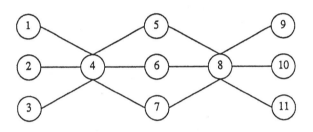

figure 5.1.

References

[C]   R. G. Casey, "Allocation of Copies of a File in an Information Network", Proc. 1972 Spring Joint Computer Conference, AFIPS, 1972.

[CMP]   S. Ceri, G. Martella, and G. Pelagatti, "Optimal File Allocation in a Computer Network: a Solution Method Based on the Knapsack Problem", Computer Networks, **6** :5, 1982.

[DF]   L. W. Dowdy and D. V. Foster, "Comparative Models of the File Assignment Problem", ACM Computing Surveys, **14** :2, 1982.

[IK]   K. B. Irani and N. G. Khabbaz, "A Methodology for the Design of Communication Networks and the Distribution of Data in Distributed Supercomputer Systems", IEEE Transactions on Computers, **C-31** :5, 1982.

[M]   A. Milo, M. Sc. Thesis, The Technion - IIT, Jan. 1988.

[ML]   H. L. Morgan and J. D. Levin "Optimal Program and Data Location in Computer Networks", Communications of the ACM, 20 :5, 1977.

[MR]   S. Mahmoud and J. S. Riordon, "Optimal Allocation of Resources in Distributed Information Network", ACM-TODS, 1 :1, 1976.

[SW]   A. Segall and O. Wolfson, "Transaction Commitment at Minimal Communication Cost", Proc. 6th ACM Symp on Principles of Database Systems, 1987.

[Z]   B. Zelinka, "Medians and Peripherians on Trees", Arch. Math. (Brno), 1968.

OPTIMIZING VOTING-TYPE ALGORITHMS FOR REPLICATED DATA

Akhil Kumar and Arie Segev

School of Business Administration and
Lawrence Berkeley Lab's Computer Science Research Dept.
University of California
Berkeley, Ca., 94720

Abstract. The main objectives of data replication are improved availability and reduced communications cost for queries. Maintaining the various copies consistent, however, increases the communications cost incurred by updates. For a given degree of replication, the choice of a specific concurrency control algorithm can have a significant impact on the total communications cost. In this paper we present various models for analyzing and understanding the trade-offs between the potentially opposing objectives of maximum resiliency and minimum communications cost in the context of the quorum consensus class of algorithms. It is argued that an optimal vote assignment is one which meets given resiliency goals and yet incurs the least communications cost compared with all other alternative assignments. A mathematical model for vote assignment is developed, and optimal algorithms are presented. It is demonstrated that significant cost savings can be realized from these approaches.

1. Introduction

In distributed database systems, data is often replicated at several sites in order to improve responsiveness and availability. However, in order to guarantee serializability and consistency across sites, it is necessary to implement a protocol for concurrency control [BERN87]. In a replicated environment, the usual concurrency control protocols like two-phase locking [GRAY78], or timestamp methods [REED78, THOM79] have to be suitably modified. For instance, two different transactions must not be allowed to simultaneously update different copies of the same file (see [DAVI85] for a survey of replication methods). Several popular methods for replicated data concurrency control are based on the formation of quorums. We refer to such methods as "voting-type" or quorum consensus (QC) class of algorithms. Examples of QC algorithms are: the Quorum Consensus method [GIFF79], the Missing Writes method [EAGE81, EAGE83], and the Virtual Partition method [ELAB85]. Other variants on this theme have been proposed more recently [BARB86, JAJO87, HERL87]. In [GARC85], the notion of coteries is introduced as an alternative to quorums.

This research was supported by the U.S. Army Information Systems Engineering Command via an interagency agreement with the U.S. Department of Energy Applied Mathematics Sciences Research Program of the Office of Energy Research under contract DE-AC03-76SF00098, and by an Arthur Andersen & Co. Foundation Doctoral Dissertation Fellowship.

The common feature in voting-type algorithms is that each site, i is assigned a vote, v_i and in order to perform various operations quorums must be formed by assembling votes. To perform a read (or write) operation, a transaction must assemble a read (or write) quorum of sites such that the votes of all the sites in the quorum add up to a predefined threshold, Q_r (or Q_w). The basic principle behind the algorithm is that the sum of these two thresholds is greater than the total sum of all votes, i.e.,

$$\text{Invariant 1:} \quad \sum_i v_i < Q_r + Q_w$$

Hence a read and a write operation cannot be done simultaneously. Moreover, the write threshold is larger than half the sum of all votes, i.e.,

$$\text{Invariant 2:} \quad \sum_i v_i < 2 \times Q_w$$

Thus, two write operations are prevented from proceeding simultaneously. It is important to note that the above two invariants do not enforce unique values upon Q_r and Q_w. Furthermore, the v_i's do not have to assume unique values. Hence, several alternative sets of solutions for these variable are possible as long as the above two invariants are satisfied. The read-one write-all method is a special case of the quorum consensus method with each v_i and Q_r equal to 1, and Q_w equal to n (assuming there are n copies of the file).

Most previous studies have assigned equal votes to all sites. Weighted voting was suggested in [GIFF79], though no specific vote assignment technique was given. In this paper, we support the argument made in [GARC84] that a non-uniform vote assignment can usually lead to superior performance, and also present two optimal vote assignment schemes. Unlike [GARC84], our optimization metric is communications cost; therefore, an additional contribution of this paper is the integration of communications cost and availability issues as part of optimizing a voting-type algorithm.

An algorithm for replicated data may be evaluated on two criteria: **communications cost** and **failure tolerance**. We define communications cost to be the number of round-trip messages required to handle a certain traffic volume. Failure tolerance is a measure of availability and is defined as the maximum number of site failures that the algorithm can tolerate.[†] The algorithm can tolerate k site failures if a read and a write quorum can be formed in spite of a k-site failure. This implies that the most recent updates are available at one or more sites even if any set of k sites is down.

For instance, it is obvious that the read-one write-all algorithm does not permit write operations if even one site is down because all sites must participate in a write quorum.

[†] Note that the terms resiliency and failure tolerance will be used interchangeably in this paper.

Hence, the failure tolerance is 0. On the other hand, if Q_r is 2 and Q_w is $n-1$ it means that $n-1$ sites must participate in a write quorum, and hence both read and write operations can continue despite one failure. Similarly, a Q_r value of 3 and a Q_w value of $n-2$ make the system resilient to up to 2 failures. It is a simple extension to show that the failure tolerance for the case of each $v_i = 1$ is maximized when both quorums are equal to $(n+1)/2$. Hence, resiliency may be increased by modifying quorum sizes, although this may mean a higher communications cost as we will show in section 2.

In the above discussion we referred only to site failures. However, two types of failures can occur -- site failures and link failures. We will assume that a link failure that does not cause a partition is transparent because every site can continue to access all other sites. On the other hand, if a link failure creates a partition, two sub-partitions will be formed. This situation will be treated as a failure of all the sites in the smaller partition. Consider, for instance, a star network consisting of one central site connected to $n-1$ outlying sites. In such a network, if the link with one of the outlying sites fails, and the site does not have any alternate path to any other site, this situation is equivalent to the site itself having failed. The smaller partition will be defined as the one with fewer total votes. Hence, we translate link failures and partitions into 0 or more site failures for the purpose of our analysis. Finally, we believe that partitions do not occur frequently in well-designed networks because alternative paths are usually provided. Site and link failures are relatively more frequent.

The organization of this paper is as follows. In section 2, we examine the behavior of communications cost for different levels of resiliency in the case of equal vote assignment (i.e., $v_i = 1$, for all sites) and show that lower communications cost and higher resiliency may be conflicting objectives. We also determine the cheapest algorithm for different read-write volume ratios in the absence of availability considerations. In section 3, we illustrate how the votes may be assigned in such a way that the desired level of resiliency is achieved and substantial savings in communications cost are realized in comparison with the case of equal vote assignment. The algorithm for such a vote assignment and the analysis of its cost behavior are presented; an intuitive justification for the superior performance of our algorithm and a qualitative discussion of its pros and cons are also given. Finally, section 4 turns to a general model for vote assignment while section 5 concludes the paper with a summary and discussion of future research.

2. Analysis of QC Algorithms

In this section, we restrict ourselves to voting-type or QC algorithms with equal vote assignments. We will assume, without loss of generality, that all files are completely replicated. First, in section 2.1, we analyze the minimum cost of QC at different values of read-write traffic volumes, disregarding resiliency considerations. Next, the resiliency versus communications cost trade-off is investigated for different values of update-to-query ratio in section 2.2.

The main parameters of interest are:

  n : number of sites where copies of the file exist

  r_i: volume of read (or query) traffic from site i

  w_i: volume of write (or update) traffic from site i

  vol_i: total volume of read and write traffic from site i $(r_i + w_i)$

  V: total read and write traffic volume of all sites $(\sum_i vol_i)$

  Q_r: size of the read quorum

  Q_w: size of the write quorum

The update traffic ratio, ρ_w is defined as:

$$\rho_w = \sum_i w_i / (\sum_i w_i + \sum_i r_i)$$

2.1. Minimum Cost Voting

The communications cost, CC_{qc} for the QC algorithm is the sum of the total traffic resulting from read and write transactions, and is expressed as:

$$CC_{qc} = (Q_w - 1) \times \sum_i w_i + (Q_r - 1) \times \sum_i r_i$$

We will denote the minimum cost by CC_{qc}^*. Notice it is assumed that each site will include its local copy while assembling a quorum and hence it communicates with $(Q_r - 1)$ and $(Q_w - 1)$ additional sites to form read and write quorums respectively. There are two important cases of interest: $\rho_w \leq 0.5$, and $\rho_w > 0.5$. We shall analyze each one separately.

Case 1: $\rho_w \leq 0.5$

Now, since $Q_r + Q_w$ must always be greater than $n + 1$ (see invariant 1 above), and $\sum_i w_i \leq \sum_i r_i$ when $\rho_w \leq 0.5$ (by definition), it follows that CC_{qc} is minimized when Q_r is 1 and Q_w is n . This is exactly the read-one write-all algorithm. Hence, we get the following result:

Result 1: The read-one write-all algorithm incurs the lowest cost when $\rho_w \leq 0.5$.

The minimum communications cost in this case is derived from the general expression by substituting the quorum sizes and is:

$$
\begin{aligned}
CC_{qc}^* \quad &= (n-1) \times \sum_i w_i \\
&= (n-1) \times \sum_i vol_i \times \rho_w \\
&= (n-1) \, \rho_w V
\end{aligned}
$$

For large n, this cost may be approximated as $n\rho_w V$.

Case 2: $\rho_w \geq 0.5$

Reasoning along the same lines as above, it might appear that the communications cost is minimized when Q_r is n and Q_w is 1. However, this is incorrect because invariant 2 is violated. Clearly, Q_w should assume the smallest possible value without violating invariant 2 and this occurs when:[†]

$$Q_w = int(n/2) + 1$$

and, therefore,

$$Q_r = n + 1 - Q_w.$$

Result 2: Hence, when $\rho_w \geq 0.5$, CC_{qc} is minimized at the above quorum values.

For relatively large values of n, we may approximate the quorum sizes as:

$$Q_w = Q_r = n/2$$

Using this approximation, CC_{qc}^* is expressed as:

$$
\begin{aligned}
CC_{qc}^* &= (n/2) \sum_i (r_i + w_i) \\
&= (n/2) \sum_i vol_i \\
&= (n/2) V
\end{aligned}
$$

Note that in this case the quorums are either equal or differ by 1. For example, when n=11, $Q_r = Q_w = 6$. On the other hand, when $n = 12$, $Q_w = 7$ and $Q_r = 6$. The minimum cost is plotted against ρ_w in Figure 1. It should be observed that this cost increases linearly as ρ_w goes from 0 to 0.5 but becomes constant for $\rho_w \geq 0.5$

2.2. Failure Tolerance versus Communications Cost

So far in our analysis, minimum communications cost has been determined without regard to resiliency . Here we will study the implications of increased resiliency on communications cost. Again, there are two cases: $\rho_w \leq 0.5$, and $\rho_w \geq 0.5$.

In the second case, as indicated by Result 2 and the subsequent example above, the two quorum sizes are either equal or differ by 1. This means that the availability is maximum as well. Hence, we may conclude the following:

Result 3: When $\rho_w \geq 0.5$, the failure tolerance is maximized at the least-cost quorum sizes.

[†] int(x) denotes the integer part of x.

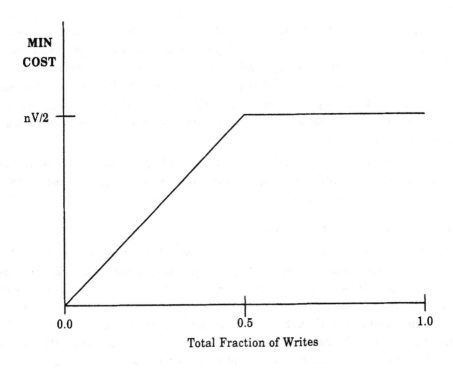

Figure 1: Plot of Min. Cost versus total fraction of writes (ρ_w)

Now we turn to the case of $\rho_w \leq 0.5$. In the least-cost alternative, $Q_r = 1$, $Q_w = n$, and the failure tolerance is 0. Therefore, in order to assure a failure tolerance level of k, Q_w must be reduced by k and Q_r must be correspondingly increased. The resulting incremental cost (IC) is:

$$IC = (\sum_i r_i - \sum_i w_i) \times k$$

This increase is translated in terms of the minimum cost, CC_{qc}^*, and the increase percentage (IP) is computed as:

$$IP = IC \times 100 / CC_{qc}^*$$

After substituting for IC and CC_{qc}^*, and further simplifying, IP may be expressed as:

$$IP = (1-2\rho_w)\times k\times 100/(\rho_w(n-1))$$

In Table 1, IP has been computed for a range of values of ρ_w, with n alternately set at 5 and 10. Note that k is the failure tolerance level. It is evident from this table that for small values of ρ_w, higher resiliency is achieved only by incurring a considerably higher communications cost. For instance, when ρ_w is 0.05 and k is 2, IP is 900 %. This means that in order to make the algorithm resilient to 2 site failures, the communications cost is 9 times larger than its value for 0 failure tolerance. However, as ρ_w approaches 0.5, IP also shrinks and tends towards 0.

In summary, the interesting conclusion to be drawn from this section is that the additional cost of providing failure tolerance is highly dependent on ρ_w. For small values of ρ_w, this cost is very high; however, for $\rho_w \geq 0.5$, it becomes 0.

3. OPTIMAL VOTE ASSIGNMENT

In the previous section it was shown that availability may be improved at the expense of increased communications cost by changing the quorum sizes. The consequent effect on communications cost was expressed analytically. Here we discuss an algorithm for optimally assigning votes to sites so as to minimize communications cost subject to a desired failure tolerance level. As before, failure tolerance, is defined as the number of site failures that can be tolerated. Further, it will be assumed that the inter-site unit communications cost is a constant for all pairs of sites.[†] We first describe the algorithm, then illustrate it with an example and finally present a cost comparison between the

ρ_w	$n = 5$		$n = 10$			
	k = 1	k = 2	k = 1	k = 2	k = 3	k = 4
.05	450%	900%	200%	400%	600%	800%
.10	200%	400%	89%	178%	267%	356%
.20	75%	150%	33%	67%	100%	133%
.30	33%	67%	15%	30%	45%	60%
.40	12.5%	25%	6%	11%	17%	22%
.50	0%	0%	0%	0%	0%	0%

Table 1: Percentage Increase in communications cost for higher resiliency as compared with the minimum cost (for different ρ_w values)

[†] This assumption will be relaxed in section 4.

communications cost resulting from our method and the conventional method in which equal votes are assigned to each site.

3.1. A Vote Assignment Algorithm

This algorithm assumes that there are n copies of the file and the desired fault tolerance level is k. The main steps in the algorithm are listed below and then a brief explanation follows.

Algorithm 1

1. Number the sites as $s_1, s_2, \cdots, s_n$

2. Denote the votes to be assigned as $v_1, v_2, \cdots, v_n$

3. Assign votes to sites $s_{k+1}, s_{k+2}, \cdots, s_n$ such that:

$$v_{k+1} = v_{k+2} = \cdots = v_n = 1$$
$$k \le n/2$$

4. Assign $Q_r = Q_w = n - k$

5. Assign $v_1 = v_2 = \cdots = v_k = int\,((n-k-1)/k)$

6. Let $m = n - k - 1 - \sum_{i=1}^{i=k} v_i$

   If $m > 0$, then assign 1 extra vote to the first m sites, $s_1, s_2, \cdots, s_m$.

Note that in step 1, the sites are numbered arbitrarily in any random order. In step 3, votes of 1 unit are assigned to $n-k$ out of the n sites. These sites are designated as **minor sites**. The basic idea of the algorithm is to assign higher votes to the remaining k sites, which we term as **major sites**. Notice that k can be at most $n/2$. This means that the maximum failure tolerance level is equal to half the total number of sites. The vote assignment scheme ensures that the set of k major sites along with any other minor site can form both a read and a write quorum. Alternatively, if all k major sites are down, then it should still be possible to form both quorums by assembling the votes of all minor sites. This guarantees that no matter which k sites are down, the quorums can still be formed. Consequently, in step 4, Q_r and Q_w are both set to $n-k$, which is the sum of the votes of all the minor sites. In step 5, an amount $n-k-1$ is distributed among the k major sites, thereby ensuring that if the votes of the major sites are added together along with one additional vote, the resulting sum is $n-k$, and hence, both quorums can be formed. The following example illustrates the main steps of Algorithm 1:

Example 1

Say, $n = 8$ and $k = 2$.

Assign $v_3 = v_4 = v_5 = v_6 = v_7 = v_8 = 1$

Therefore, $Q_r = Q_w = n - k = 6$

and $v_1 = v_2 = int(5/2) = 2$

$m = 1$; hence, $v_1 = 3$.

Hence, the final vote assignment is:

$v_1 = 3; v_2 = 2$

$v_3 = v_4 = v_5 = v_6 = v_7 = v_8 = 1$

$Q_r = Q_w = 6$

For the above example, the conventional QC method assigns a vote of 1 to each site and sets Q_r and Q_w to 3 and 6 respectively; these quorum values ensure that the system can tolerate up to 2 site failures.

3.2. Discussion

In this section we present the outline of an informal proof to show that Algorithm 1 chooses an optimal vote assignment. Further, since the algorithm does not distinguish between sites, we discuss ways of assigning the higher votes to specific sites.

Algorithm 1 is based on the following lemma:

Lemma 1: When k-site resiliency is desired, a transaction must communicate with at least k other sites in order to perform a read or write operation.

This is necessary in order to guarantee that even a k-site failure will leave at least one working site with the most recent updates. For instance, if $k+1$ sites have been updated, and k of these sites fail, there will still be one site alive which contains the update. Similarly, a transaction performing a read operation must communicate its intention to at least k other sites. Our algorithm minimizes the total communications cost by ensuring that if all sites are working, any site can form a read or a write quorum consisting of exactly k other sites.

If the desired failure tolerance is k, then higher votes are assigned to k of the n sites, and it is guaranteed that a quorum can be formed if these k major sites and any one other site are included -- a total of $k+1$ sites. Therefore, our vote assignment scheme leads to a least-cost solution if the k major sites are included in all quorums. However, if any of these k sites is down then the transaction must communicate with many more sites in order to assemble a quorum and continue operation. Consequently, with our scheme the total communications cost increases if even one of the major sites is down. In contrast, with an "equal-vote" method this cost is not affected by site failures since all sites have an equal vote. Thus, our method achieves a lower cost under normal operation at the expense of a higher cost when any of the major sites is down. Since the latter situation will occur infrequently, our algorithm is superior to the conventional QC methods.

According to the algorithm as described so far, the assignment of the n votes to specific sites may be done entirely at random. Here we discuss some factors that could influence the choice of the k major sites. If a network is fully connected and site reliability is equal for all sites, then these k sites may be chosen at random. However, this is not usually the case. Two important factors to be considered are site reliability and connectivity. The k larger votes should be assigned to those sites which have greater reliability and are most well-connected with the other sites. (A simple measure of the connectivity of a site is the number of other sites it has direct links with). In a star network, for example, the central site is a good candidate for a higher vote. In such a network, the connectivity of the central site is $n-1$ and that of the others is 1.

One disadvantage with our method is that the communications traffic to the major sites will be very high as compared to the traffic to the minor sites and our analysis does not consider any queuing delays and network congestion. This issue has to be addressed as a part of network design. One way to handle this is to provide high bandwidth lines between all major sites and also ensure fast access to at least one major site from each minor site. With proper network design, this handicap can easily be overcome.

In the next section we present a cost comparison between Algorithm 1 and a QC algorithm which assigns equal votes to all sites.

3.3. Cost Comparison

The cost comparison consists of two cases. First we discuss the case of $\rho_w \leq 0.5$ which is of greater interest. The general expression for the communications cost incurred by the conventional QC method was derived in the previous section. Here we modify it slightly to express this cost as a function of k, the number of site failures which must be tolerated. Therefore, the minimum communications cost in the conventional QC method when k-site resiliency is provided is as follows:

$$CC^*_{qc_k} = k \times \sum_i r_i + (n-k-1)\sum_i w_i$$

The equivalent communications cost incurred in Algorithm 1 is given by the following expression:

$$CC_{opt_k} = k \times \sum_i (r_i + w_i)$$

Therefore, the savings realized from our vote assignment is:

$$CC^*_{qc_k} - CC_{opt_k} = (n-2k-1)\sum_i w_i$$

This savings may be converted into a percentage as follows:

$$\text{Savings \%} = (n-2k-1)(\sum_i w_i)\times 100/(k \times \sum_i (r_i+w_i))$$

$$= (n-2k-1)\times \rho_w \times 100/k$$

Sample calculations of the savings % with n alternately set to 5 and 10 are given in Table 2. In each case, k is varied between 1 and the maximum possible value of failure tolerance (2 and 5 respectively) and ρ_w is varied from 0.05 to 0.5. It is evident from this table that large savings are achievable by using our algorithm.

In the case where $\rho_w \geq 0.5$, the expression for $CC^*_{qc_k}$ is rewritten as:

$$CC^*_{qc_k} = (n/2)\times \sum_i (r_i+w_i)$$

ρ_w	$n = 5$		$n = 10$			
	k = 1	k = 2	k = 1	k = 2	k = 3	k = 4
.05	10%	0%	35%	12.5%	5%	1%
.10	20%	0%	70%	25%	10%	2.5%
.20	40%	0%	140%	50%	20%	5%
.30	60%	0%	210%	75%	30%	7.5%
.40	80%	0%	280%	100%	40%	10%
.50	100%	0%	350%	125%	50%	12.5%

Table 2: Percentage savings achieved from our vote assignment method

The expression for CC_{opt_k} remains the same as before and hence the savings % in this case is given by:

$$\text{Savings \%} = (n/2 - k) \times 100/k$$

When n is 10 and k is 1 this figure is 400%. Again the potential for savings is large.

4. A General Model

In this section we relax the restriction that all inter-site unit communications costs must be equal, and present a general approach for modeling the vote assignment problem. Our approach consists of an integer programming model based on the query and update traffic of each site, and the inter-site communications cost matrix. The following parameters and variables are used in the formulation.

Parameters

c_{ij}: unit communications cost between site i and j

q_i: query volume from site i

u_i: update volume from site i

Variables

v_i: value of vote assigned to site i

Q_r, Q_w: read and write quorums respectively

$$n_{ij} = \begin{cases} 1, & \text{if the read quorum for site i's queries includes a copy at j} \\ 0, & \text{otherwise} \end{cases}$$

$$m_{ij} = \begin{cases} 1, & \text{if the write quorum for site i's updates includes a copy at j} \\ 0, & \text{otherwise} \end{cases}$$

$$w_{ij} = \begin{cases} v_j, & \text{if } m_{ij} \text{ is } 1 \\ 0, & \text{otherwise} \end{cases}$$

$$r_{ij} = \begin{cases} v_j, & \text{if } n_{ij} \text{ is } 1 \\ 0, & \text{otherwise} \end{cases}$$

The integer programming formulation is as follows:

Minimize $\sum_i q_i (\sum_{j \neq i} c_{ij} n_{ij}) + \sum_i u_i (\sum_{j \neq i} c_{ij} m_{ij})$

such that

1) $v_i + \sum_{j \neq i} w_{ij} \geq Q_w$ for *all* i

2) $v_i + \sum_{j \neq i} r_{ij} \geq Q_r$ for *all* i

3) $Q_r + Q_w \geq 101$

4) $2 \times Q_w \geq 101$

5) $100 \times n_{ij} \geq r_{ij}$ for *all* i,j

6) $100 \times m_{ij} \geq w_{ij}$ for *all* i,j

7) $w_{ij} \leq v_j$ for *all* i,j

8) $r_{ij} \leq v_j$ for *all* i,j

9) $\sum_j v_j = 100$

10) $\sum_{i \in s} v_i \geq max(Q_r, Q_w)$ for *all* $s \in S$, *the permutation set of all* $n - k$ *sites*

11) $n_{ij}, m_{ij} \in \{0, 1\}; v_j, w_{ij}, r_{ij} \geq 0$

    The objective function above represents the communications cost incurred in handling the total traffic volume from all sites. The first part of the expression is the cost of the query (or read) traffic of all sites, while the second part represents the cost of update (or write) traffic. Constraints 1 and 2 ensure that each site must form both read and write quorums in order to perform query and update transactions. Constraints 3 and 4 are the two invariants mentioned in section 1. Note that we have set the sum of all votes to 100 in our formulation. This arbitrary selection of the sum of all votes does not affect the model because the relative values are important rather than absolute values. Constraints 5 and 6 ensure that n_{ij} (or m_{ij}) are forced to 1 if r_{ij} (or w_{ij}) assume non-zero values. Constraints 7 and 8 impose upper bounds on the variables w_{ij} and r_{ij}. Finally, constraints 10 are included to guarantee that the votes from any set of $n - k$ sites would add up to both a read and a write quorum.

The above formulation can be solved for the optimal v_i's, Q_r and Q_w by substituting the various parameters in the above system of equations and feeding it into a standard integer-programming package like LINDO [SCHR86]. There are two advantages with the above approach. First, it takes communications costs into account while determining the vote assignment, and is therefore, more general than the Algorithm 1 of section 3. Recall that the algorithm was based on the idea that if all inter-site unit communications costs are equal, then a site should communicate with exactly k other sites in order to provide a failure tolerance level of k at a minimum cost. Upon relaxing the assumption of equal inter-site costs this may not continue to hold because it is conceivable that another quorum with perhaps more than k sites may be formed and yet incur a lower communications cost. Hence, in such a situation, Algorithm 1 may generate a non-optimal vote assignment, and a more sophisticated approach like the one here is necessary in order to achieve optimality.

The second advantage with the general model is that it can be extended to take into account other factors like site reliability and site connectivity. For instance, an additional term can be added to the objective function to represent the cost incurred in situations where one or more site failures lead to a quorum failure, i.e. a quorum can not be formed. The expression can be further augmented with one more term representing the cost of assigning higher votes to sites with poor connectivity. In effect, it is possible to quantify the contribution of these factors and thereby discourage a solution in which a higher vote is assigned to a site with poor reliability or one which is not well connected to other sites. In addition to modifying the objective function, the set of constraints will also have to be appropriately amended. Exact details of these changes are outside the scope of this paper and will be the subject of future research.

5. Conclusion

A novel approach towards understanding and improving voting-type algorithms has been presented. We extended the notion of availability by introducing the concept of failure tolerance. A failure tolerance level of k means that the vote assignment scheme ensures that a quorum can be formed in spite of the failure of any combination of k sites.

Most previous studies did not consider availability in conjunction with communications cost. We have shown that higher failure tolerance and lower communications cost are usually conflicting objectives, and this trade-off has been studied in detail. Analytical results for the performance of QC type algorithms over a range of values of read-write traffic ratios and failure tolerance levels were presented. It has been shown that the particular assignment of votes significantly impacts communications costs.

Two approaches for optimal vote assignment were discussed. First, assuming that the unit communications cost between all pairs of sites is constant, an optimal vote assignment algorithm that minimizes the communications cost for a given failure tolerance level has been described and its performance has been compared with an alternative scheme which assigns equal votes to all sites. This comparison demonstrates that the algorithm proposed in this paper is capable of producing large savings. Furthermore, a mathematical model which allows the inter-site unit communications costs to vary across pairs of sites has been developed.

Our current and future work consist of developing efficient procedures to solve the mathematical programming model of section 4, and also further enhancements to the model in order to take site reliabilities and site connectivities into account.

References

[BARB86] Barabara, D., Garcia-Molina, H., and Spauster, A., "Protocols for Dynamic Vote Reassignment", Technical Report, Department of Computer Science, Princeton University, May 1986.

[BERN87] Bernstein, P., Hadzilacos, V., and Goodman, N., "Concurrency Control and Recovery in Database Systems", Addison Wesley Publishing Co., 1987.

[DAVI85] Davidson, S. B., Garcia-Molina, H., and Skeen, D., "Consistency in Partitioned Networks", ACM Computing Surveys 17(3), September 1985.

[EAGE81] Eager, D.L., "Robust Concurrency Control in Distributed Databases", Technical Report CSRG #135, Computer Systems Research Group, University of Toronto, October 1981.

[EAGE83] Eager, D.L., and Sevcik, K.C., "Achieving Robustness in Distributed Database Systems", ACM Trans. Database Syst. 8(3):354 - 381, September 1983.

[ELAB85] El Abbadi, A., Skeen, D., and Cristian, F., "An Efficient, Fault-Tolerant Protocol for Replicated Data Management", Proc. 4th ACM SIGACT-SIGMOD Symp, on Principles of Database Systems, pages 215 - 228. Portland, Oregon, March 1985.

[GARC84] Garcia-Molina, H., and Barbara, D., "Optimizing the Reliability Provided by Voting Mechanisms", Proc. 4th International Conference on Distributed Computing Systems, May 1984.

[GARC85] Garcia-Molina, H., and Barbara, D., "How to Assign Votes in a Distributed System", Journal of ACM, Vol. 32, No. 4, October 1985.

[GIFF79] Gifford, D.K., "Weighted Voting for Replicated Data", Proc. 7th ACM SIGOPS Symp. on operating Systems Principles, pages 150 - 159. Pacific Grove, CA, December 1979.

[GRAY78] Gray, J., "Notes on Data Base Operating Systems," in Operating Systems: An Advanced Course, Springer-Verlag, 1978, pp393-481.

[HERL87] Herlihy, M., "Dynamic Quorum Adjustment for Partitional Data", ACM TODS, Vol 12, No 2, June 1987.

[JAJO87] Jajodia, S. and Mutchler, D., "Dynamic Voting", Proc. 1987 ACM SIGMOD, San Francisco, CA, May 1987.

[REED78] Reed, D., "Naming and Synchronization in a Decentralized Computer System," Ph.D. Thesis, Department of Electrical Engineering and Computer Science, M.I.T., 1978.

[SCHR86] Schrage, L., "LINDO", Scientific Press, 1986.

[THOM79] Thomas, R. H., "A Majority Consensus Approach to Concurrency Control," TODS, June 1979.

QUASI-COPIES: EFFICIENT DATA SHARING FOR INFORMATION RETRIEVAL SYSTEMS

Rafael Alonso
Daniel Barbara
Hector Garcia-Molina

Department of Computer Science
Princeton University
Princeton, NJ 08544

Soraya Abad

Department of Computer Science
Rutgers University
New Brunswick, NJ 08903

ABSTRACT

Currently, a variety of information retrieval systems are available to potential users. These services are provided by commercial enterprises (such as Dow Jones [Dunn1984] and The Source [Edelhart1983]), while others are research efforts (the Boston Community Information System [Gifford1985]). While in many cases these systems are accessed from personal computers, typically no advantage is taken of the computing resources of those machines (such as local processing and storage). In this paper we explore the possibility of using the user's local storage capabilities to cache data at the user's site. This would improve the response time of user queries albeit at the cost of incurring the the overhead required in maintaining multiple copies. In order to reduce this overhead it may be appropriate to allow copies to diverge in a controlled fashion. This would not only make caching less costly, but would also make it possible to propagate updates to the copies more efficiently, e.g., when the system is lightly loaded, when communication tariffs are lower, or by batching together updates. Just as importantly, it also makes it possible to access the copies even when the communication lines or the central site are down. Thus, we introduce the notion of *quasi-copies* which embodies the ideas sketched above. We also define the types of deviations that seem useful, and discuss the available implementation strategies.

1. INTRODUCTION

In many of today's information retrieval systems (IRS's) all the stored data (e.g., the abstracts of journal articles, the airline schedules) resides at a central node. This central site can be reached by a large number of remote terminals connected via relatively slow communication lines. Users at these terminals do no local processing; they simply send their queries to the central machine and wait for their replies. Data can be added or deleted at the central site, but in many cases it cannot be updated.

A number of developments are slowly changing this IRS model. First, the number of users is growing rapidly. In our "information society" it is becoming increasingly important to have access to timely information. At the same time, the number of personal computers, at home and in the workplace, has grown tremendously, giving more people the hardware necessary to access the IRS's.

The first development implies that the increased IRS services and requirements will tax both the processing and communication capacity of the central site. There are a number of potential solutions to this problem, but the one we will focus on in this paper is *data caching*. This solution is becoming feasible precisely because of the second development, i.e., that the IRS is frequently accessed from personal or mini computers with substantial processing and storage capacity (for example, in 1984, Dow Jones estimated that about 125,000 of its 165,000 customers used personal computers [Dunn1984]). In principle, caching can improve system performance in two ways. First, it can eliminate multiple requests for the same data, eliminating redundant requests to the central IRS site. Secondly, it can improve performance by off-loading work to the remote sites.

However, caching has an associated cost. Every time a cached value is updated at the central site, the new value must be propagated to the copies. Furthermore, the propagation must be done immediately if cache consistency (or *coherency*) is to be preserved. (A cached value for an object is consistent if it equals the value of the object at the central site.) This propagation cost can be significant.

Caching has been successfully used in other environments, but there are some important differences in this case. In a computer hardware cache [Smith1982], it is not expensive to keep the cached and main memory data consistent. This is because updates are small (e.g., a byte is modified), the communication delays are short, and the number of copies is small (e.g, in snooping cache architectures typically there are less than 10 caches connected to a memory system). In an IRS, on the other hand, the communication costs can be much higher. For instance, users typically communicate over telephone lines. Also, the number of caches may be quite large. Finally, the updates can be large (e.g., the abstract of an article or the article itself can be added to a file).

In light of these difficulties, it is important to explore strategies for making update propagation less costly while still retaining the inherent advantages of caching. In this paper we study two such strategies. Both involve taking advantage of the application semantics. The first idea is to let the user explicitly define the information that is of interest and to cache only it. This obviously reduces the need to refresh data that is not going to be used.

The second idea is to allow, whenever possible, a weaker type of consistency between the central data and its copies. For instance, the user interested in the stock prices of chemical companies may be satisfied if the prices at his computer are within five percent of the true prices. This makes it unnecessary to update the cached copy every single time a change occurs. When the deviation exceeds five percent, then a single update can bring the cached copy up-to-date. At a manufacturing company, users may tolerate a delay of one day in receiving the articles of interest. If the system takes advantage of this, it can transmit all the articles during the night when communication tariffs are lower. If a communication or central node failure occurs and its duration is less than 24 hours, then users can continue to access information that is correct by their standards.

We call a cached value that is allowed to deviate from the central value in a controlled way a *quasi-copy*. Quasi-copies have the potential for reducing update propagation overhead and giving the system flexibility for scheduling the propagation at convenient times. Note that the information flow in an IRS with quasi-copies is similar to the flow in many real organizations. The manager of a company is not told every time an employee is hired or leaves. The information is filtered so that he only is informed periodically of personnel changes, or if an exceptional condition occurs (e.g., a mass exodus of employees). Hence, the manager's view of the company (the cached data) deviates from the true state (the central value). Similarly, when a person desires news, he subscribes to magazines and newspapers. The news arrives periodically and there is again a discrepancy between the local and "central" data. In human organizations, people have little control over this process, e.g., Time magazine arrives every week and the New York Times every day, and there is no way to change this. In a computerized IRS, however, we can let users precisely define the limits of divergence of quasi-copies, and the system can take advantage of this to improve performance.

We should point out that quasi-copies are not free either. The reductions in transmission costs are paid for by increases in processing time for bookkeeping, both in the central processor and in the workstations. Hopefully, trading off transmission time for processing time will pay off as workstations become more powerful while transmission costs remain fixed. We will quantify these tradeoffs further in section 5.

Although our ideas could be applied to a system with multiple central sites, we will not consider that case in this discussion. In this paper we will assume that all information is controlled at a single central site. This site executes all updates and hence has the most up-to-date version of all data. Usually remote users only read data. If they want to modify something, they may submit an update transaction to the central site.

Even though quasi-copies seem to be crucial for effective caching in an IRS, very little is known about them. Hence, the objective of this paper is to study data caching and quasi-copies and to attempt to answer some of the basic questions. What types of quasi-copies are most useful? How can they be defined? How can conventional data consistency constraints (e.g., a manager's salary must be greater than his/her employee's salary) be enforced at the cached copies when the individual values can fluctuate?

Quasi-copies can be implemented in a variety of ways. For instance, values that diverge too much can be invalidated or refreshed. Data sent to the caches can include an automatic expiration time and date. The quasi-copy requirements can be enforced at the central or at the remore sites. In this paper we will survey the various implementation strategies and their tradeoffs.

In the following section we define our model more precisely and introduce some terminology. There are two types of conditions that can be specified for quasi-data: selection and coherency. They are discussed in Section 3. The impact of transmission delays and failures, as well as other implementation issues, is covered in Section 4. Performance issues are discussed in Section 5. Section 6 provides a simple example. The final section offers our conclusions, and describes a system that is currently under implementation.

2. THE MODEL

We start by defining more precisely our model and introducing notation that will be used in the rest of the paper. The database is stored at the central node, C, and consists of a set of objects O. Each object $x \in O$ can have a number of values (or fields) associated with it (e.g., object John has name, address, salary values), but for simplicity we assume there is just one value. As is customary, we use the same symbol x to represent both the object and its value. All updates to the database objects are performed at the central site only. As an object is modified, new versions are created. We represent the latest version of object x by $v(x)$. It will sometimes be necessary to refer to the value of an object x at a time t. We represent this by $x(t)$. (Incidentally, we assume that all sites have accurate and synchronized clocks [Lamport1978].)

A set of nodes N $(C \notin N)$ may contain quasi-copies of the objects. The quasi-copy of object $x \in O$ at node $j \in N$ is x^j and is called an image of x. When the identity of node j is not important, we represent the image as x'. The set of objects that have quasi-copies at node j are the objects cached at j. Note that the caches at different nodes can have different objects, and objects can be cached at 0,1,2,... or all nodes.

Users define how quasi-copies are managed by giving two types of conditions: selection and coherency. The selection conditions specify which object images will be cached at the user's site. The coherency conditions define the allowable deviations between an object and its images. In our stock market example, the user issues a selection condition to indicate that he wants copies of the stock prices of chemical companies. His coherency condition would then state that a five percent variation between the central and his site is acceptable. We now discuss these types of conditions in more detail in the next section.

3. SELECTION AND COHERENCY CONDITIONS

In a computer hardware cache, the decision as to what is hold in the cache is made automatically by the system. For example, the system might store every word that is fetched. To make room for the word, it may purge the least-recently-used (LRU) word from the cache.

In an IRS, the same types of automatic strategies could be used to make caching decisions. However, if the system does not know what deviations between the copy and the central object are allowable, then the copy must be kept up-to-date.† A better strategy may be to let the user specify what data is to be cached, and at the same time, define the allowable deviations. Using selection and coherency conditions the user can do this. A selection condition is specified by some or all of the following items:

---

† As discussed in the Introduction, the cost of doing this can be high.

(1) *Selected object(s)*. The condition can explicitly list the objects involved in the selection or can give an expression that evaluates to a set of objects.

(2) *Subscribers*. This is simply a list of nodes (subset of N) that desire a copy of the object (or that no longer want a copy if the condition is turning off the selection).

(3) *Add/Drop*. This item specifies whether the objects are being selected or de-selected. That is, if "Drop" is specified, then the images at the subscriber nodes are removed from the caches (if they existed).

(4) *Static/Dynamic*. If the selection is static, then the objects are selected once when the condition is issued by a user. If it is dynamic, then changes in the data will continuously trigger a re-evaluation of the selection expression, and objects will be added or dropped dynamically.

(5) *Enforcement*. A selection condition can be of two types: compulsory or advisory. If it is compulsory, then the system must guarantee that the selected objects are cached as requested. If it is advisory, then the caching is viewed exclusively as a performance enhancement. In this case, the selection condition is taken as a "hint," and may or may not be followed by the system.

(6) *Triggering Delay*. When a dynamic selection is made, a change to the central database may cause a new object to be added to (or dropped from) the selection list. In some cases, it may be desirable to delay the addition (or deletion) of the object so that changes can be batched together and sent more efficiently.

Once an object has been selected for replication, the coherency condition(s) specify the allowable deviations of the image. The coherency conditions are enforced only when an image exists.

Every image has a default condition which defines the allowable values that it may contain, even if no other conditions are given. This default condition is enforced by the system.

Default Coherency Condition: An image x' must have a value previously held by the object. That is,

$$\forall \text{times } t \geq 0 \, \exists t_0 \text{ such that } 0 \leq t_0 \leq t$$
$$\text{and } x'(t) = x(t_0)$$

Users may specify additional constraints. Actually, any constraint on the values of the objects and images could be defined; however, our goal here is to identify and understand the more useful ones. Three useful constrain types are:

(1) *Delay Condition.* This is similar to the selection triggering delay. It states how much time an image may lag behind its object. For object x, and allowable delay of α is given by the condition

$$\forall \text{times } t \geq 0 \, \exists k \text{ such that } 0 \leq k \leq \alpha$$
$$\text{and } x'(t) = x(t-k)$$

Since this defines a window of acceptable value, we use the notation $W(x) = \alpha$ to represent this condition. Note that, although a quasi-copy with a delay condition may seem similar to a database snapshot, the two concepts are different. A snapshot typically consists of a view of the data as it was at a given time, while a quasi-copy contains information of varying ages, up to the value of the delay condition.

(2) *Version Condition.* A user may want to specify a window of allowable values, not in terms of time, but of versions. For example, if an object represents a VLSI circuit, it may be useful to require a copy that is at most 2 versions old. We represent this condition as $V(x) = \beta$, where x is the object and β the maximum version difference. That is , $V(x) = \beta$ is the condition

$\forall$ times $t \geq 0 \, \exists \, k, t_0$ such that $0 \leq k \leq \beta$
and $0 \leq t_0 \leq t$
and $v(x(t)) = v(x(t_0)) + k$
and $x'(t) = x(t_0)$

(3) *Arithmetic Condition.* If the value of an object is numeric, the deviations can be limited by the difference between the values of the object and it's image. That is, we may state that

$$\forall \text{ times } t \geq 0 \quad |x'(t) - x(t)| < \varepsilon$$

or that

$$\forall \text{ times } t \geq 0 \left| \frac{x'(t) - x(t)}{x(t)} 100 \right| < \varepsilon \%$$

We represent the first condition by $A(x) = \varepsilon$; the second one by $A(x) = \varepsilon \%$. $\bullet$

Yet more conditions can be built out of the three elementary ones we have listed by connecting them with logical "OR", "AND", and "NOT" operators. For example, the condition

$W(x) = 1$ hour AND $V(x) = 2$

specifies that x' can lag one hour behind x, unless x has been modified more than two times within this hour. The condition

$W(x) = 1$ hour OR $V(x) = 2$

means that x' can always log behind x by an hour. It can even log longer if the image is still within 2 versions of x.

As a final point we should point out that so far we have only discussed constraints on a single object and its image. However, there can also be constraints among objects (usually called consistency constraints). For example, if $x_1, x_2, \ldots x_n$ are stock prices in an IRS, and $\bar{x}$ is their average, then we have the constraint $\bar{x} = \text{average}(x_1, x_2, \ldots x_n)$. A user that reads the images of the stock prices and their average cached at his workstation would like to see the condition hold.

We give the user that desires multi-object consistency two choices: the first is to explicitly give the system the constraints that must be satisfied. When a constraint is violated, then the missing updates must be propagated. A second option is to state that a group of objects $x_1,...x_n$ have constraints but not give them explicitly. This option is useful when the users cannot list all their constraints or when it is too expensive to check them. In this case the system must ensure that updates to $x_1,...,x_n$ are applied in order at the copies. That is, let T_0 be the last update transaction whose modifications were applied to one or more of $x_1',...,x_n'$. Let $T_1,...,T_m$ be other updates to one or more of $x_1,...,x_n$ that were not propagated because they did not violate any single object coherency conditions. Finally, let T_{m+1} be an update that does modify one or more of $x_1,...x_n$ and does have to be propagated. Then all the updates of $T_1,...,T_m,T_{m+1}$ must be made on the images $x_1',...x_n'$, to avoid violating any constraints at the remote site.

4. IMPLEMENTATION

In this section we consider a number of issues that arise in the implementation of quasi-copies.

4.1. Transmission Delays and Failures

We now address two complications that may make it difficult to enforce the conditions given by a user: transmission delays and failures. To illustrate, consider the condition $A(x) = \varepsilon$ and assume that an increment of more than 2ε is about to occur at the central site. The condition indicates that the difference between x and x' should "never" be larger than ε, and hence the update to the image must be performed "at the same time" as the object is changed. Strictly speaking, this is not possible. The problem due to failures is similar. For example, if the central site fails just after the 2ε increment is made but before the change is propagated to x', then the condition $A(x) = \varepsilon$ will be violated.

Although a 2-phase commit protocol (or similar strategy) could be used, the update overhead and temporary inaccessibility of data are potential drawbacks. Thus, we propose the following solution. The central site, when operational, will make sure that each remote site receives a message at least every δ seconds. This means that if the central site notices that no message has gone out to a site in $\delta - T_D$ seconds, where T_D is the maximum message delay, then it will send a "null" message. Null messages are numbered just like regular messages, and all messages must be received in order. When a site j notices that δ seconds go by without a message from the central site, it declares the central site failed, and sets a local variable $C\_FAILED(j)$ to true.

Then we interpret every condition $C(x)$ on object x set by a user at node j as

$$C(x) \quad \lor \quad W(x) = \delta \quad \lor \quad C\_FAILED(j)$$

(Condition W is defined in Section 3.) This means that all conditions have an implicit delay window of δ and do not have to be enforced if the central site is down. With this approach, the user can display C_FAILED at the same time he displays his data, and interpret it accordingly. A final point to be made is that the value of δ must be sufficiently large so that the overhead involved in the periodic broadcasts is kept to an acceptable level.

4.2. What to Propagate

When the central site wishes to inform remote sites of an update, it can send the following types of messages:

(a) *Data Message.* A data message contains the new values. These values should overwrite those found in caches.

(b) *Invalidation Message.* An invalidation message identifies the objects that have changed, but does not contain the new values. An invalidation message usually causes the remote node to purge from its cache the referenced images.

(c) *Version Number Message.* This message identifies the objects and provides their new version numbers. The new data values are not included. (The time of update could be included instead of, or in addition to the version number. However, this information can sometimes be inferred from the message arrival time.) The remote node uses the version number to decide if it should purge an image.

(d) *Implicit Invalidation.* In this last case, the central node sends *no* message. Instead, images are automatically invalidated after a certain time (i.e., they are *aged*). That is, when a copy is made, it is sent with a time limit. The remote node then guarantees that it will purge the image at the latest when the limit expires.

In some applications, propagating updates is a reasonable approach. However, in many cases, some of the other approaches may be useful. Implicit invalidation incurs the least overhead and is especially attractive if objects are large or communications faulty. For example, train schedules can be issued, as they are in reality, with an expiration date. When the schedule expires, a new copy must be requested explicitly if there is still interest.

Invalidation and version number messages also have reduced communication overhead, but more than implicit invalidation. They are especially attractive for broadcast environments, where the central node can inform everyone of changes but only those that actually need the new data request it. One application that already uses this strategy is catalogs for department stores. When a new catalog appears, all customers are mailed a postcard informing them. Interested customers must then pick up their copy at the store. Version number messages are desirable when version coherency conditions have been specified. If version number messages are broadcast, the work of checking versions can be off loaded to the remote site. Each remote site can check its own conditions and decide what data must be purged.

4.3. When to Propagate

When an update arrives at the central site, it does not have to be propagated immediately. As a matter of fact, there are several choices:

(a) *Last Minute.* The updates can be delayed up to the point where a coherency or selection condition can be violated.

(b) *Immediately.* Updates could be propagated as soon as they occur.

(c) *Early.* Updates can also be propagated at any other time, after they arrive but before a condition is violated.

(d) *Delayed Update.* A last choice is to delay the installation of an update at the central site. If the update is not installed, the conditions cannot be violated, and the propagation can be delayed.

For example, consider the condition $A(x) = 5$, and the original value of x to be 10, with the cached copy $x' = 10$. Assume that updates begin to increase the value of x to, say 11,12,13,14,15,16. Under last minute propagation, the central site would broadcast the new value of x as soon as the $x = 16$ update comes in.†

Under immediate propagation, every new value of x results in a broadcast. Under early propagation we could schedule a transmission when $x = 13$, for example. And finally, for delayed update, $x = 16$ will not be installed until it is convenient.

---

† Recall that, as it was explained in Section 4.1, there is an implicit window of δ that makes the condition true while the new value is being transmitted.

Immediate propagation should only be used when the selection and coherency conditions require it, or when evaluating the conditions is too expensive. Last minute propagation has the greatest potential for reducing communication costs since it allows as many as possible updates to be "batched" together. However, sometimes early propagation can take advantage of lower communication tariffs or processor idle time. For example, telephone calls are usually more expensive from 8:00 AM to 5:00 PM. Suppose that a delay condition $W(x) = 5$ hours has been defined, and that updates to x have taken place at 7:00 AM. If the telephone is going to be used, it is clearly better not to use last minute propagation (at 12:00 Noon), and to transmit the new data just before 8:00 AM.

Delayed update gives us even greater flexibility and potential for batching together even more updates. However, delaying updates at the central site is an inconvenience since the database there is made to diverge from the "real world." Hence, late propagation is only an option when the applications can tolerate such divergence.

Conceptually, delaying updates at the central site is akin to increasing the delay window $W(x)$ of the objects. However, the advantage of delayed updates is that it can make implicit invalidation work more efficiently. When a remote node requests a copy of object x, the central site can respond with an expiration time t_e in the future. Now, if updates can be put off until time t_e, the copy will not have to be explicitly invalidated.

4.4. Load Balancing

Another issue that need to be considered regarding quasi-copies is that their management is jointly carried out by the central and remote nodes. The work can be done either centrally or remotely, so it is important to distribute the work effectively. The central issue here is who checks the selection and coherency conditions. If the central node checks them, then it must have a model of the state of the remote node. For instance, suppose that a condition is $A(x) = 2$, and x is currently 5. An update $x = 6$ arrives. To know if the condition is violated, the central node must know the value of x'. If $x' = 5$, then the condition still holds; if $x' = 3$ it does not. These models consume storage and processing resources at the central site.

There are, however, conditions which are easy to check at the remote nodes, without imposing any processing load over the central processor. An example is a delay condition in which the value x' is only valid for a window of time. After a period of time, the workstation simply purges the value from its cache, forcing the next request to be directed to the central node. Another type of check that is especially well suited for the remote nodes is the multi-object one. In this case, a constraint like "number of reservations is less than or equal to the number of available seats" must be enforced. As updates arrive at a remote site, these checks can be made. Missing updates can be requested (or data can be purged) if the constraints are violated.

5. A PERFORMANCE MODEL

An IRS with data caching and quasi-copies is a complex system. The performance improvements provided by caching quasi-copies, if any, will be determined by many factors, including processor capacities, transmission speeds, query reference patterns, and update reference patterns.

In an attempt to illustrate the tradeoffs involved, we will present a *simple* performance model and some results. We emphasize that our goal is not to predict the performance of some actual system; rather, it is to exemplify under what circumstances gains can be achieved and what their magnitude might be. Due to our space limitations here, we will include in our model only the essential parameters and will only present two graphs. Clearly, the model can be refined considerably and a thorough analysis of the performance can be done; yet we believe that the fundamental tradeoffs can be observed in our graphs.

In our model, the central site contains the main database copy and receives all updates to it. Update arrivals form a Poisson process with average arrival rate λ_u (Table I contains a list of all parameters and their values). We assume that a fraction h of the database is cached at each workstation. Thus, with probability h an arriving update refers to data replicated at a particular workstation and should be forwarded. However, quasi-copies may reduce the number of updates that are actually forwarded. We let q represent the fraction of the updates that are actually sent out. That is, an update will be sent to a workstation with probability hq.

Queries arrive at each workstation at an average rate λ_q. If the data required by a query were random, the probability that a query could be processed at a workstation would be h. However, we assume that cached data is f times more likely to be accessed by a query. Hence, with probability hf a query can be processed locally; with probability $1-hf$ it is forwarded to the central site. We assume that there are a total of n workstations in the system. (If n is much larger than the value we have used, the central node becomes saturated and caching is even more desirable than what our results will show.)

We model the central and workstation nodes as M/M/1 servers. The average service times for the various types of requests (all exponentially distributed) can be determined from the following parameters:

t_q^w: the processing time for a query executed at a workstation.

t_u^w: the time to install an update at a workstation.

t_q^c: query processing time at central node (20 times faster than a workstation).

t_u^c: update installation time at central node.

t_6: overhead time at central site to propagate an update to a single workstation (the value chosen for this parameter represents the cost of checking the predicate conditions [about 12,000 instructions], plus the processing [not transmission] delay imposed by the network protocols [roughly 1,000 instructions], both on a 10 MIPS processor). If the update is sent to x workstations, the time is xt_6.

Parameter	Value
λ_u	20 updates /second
h	ranges from 0 to 0.2
q	ranges from 0 to 1
λ_q	1 query per second per workstation
f	5
n	150
t_q^w	0.1 second
t_u^w	0.2 second
t_q^c	0.005 second
t_u^c	0.01 second
t_6	0.0013 second

Table I

Finally, the network transmission time is a constant t_r (we are assuming that workstations will communicate with the central database over phone lines; the 0.3 second setting we have chosen for this parameter is approximately the time required to transmit a 40 character message over a 1200 baud line). Since we have no queueing delays at the network, we are assuming for our example that the processors, and not the network, are the potential bottlenecks.

The average query response time is given by the expression

$$R = hf[w_w + t_q^w] + (1-hf)[2t_r + w_c + t_q^c]$$

where w_w and w_c are the average queue wait times at a workstation and at the central site. The wait times can be determined independently from their loads [Kleinrock1975]. At the central site, updates are installed at a rate of λ_u and have an average service time of t_u^c. Propagations to the workstations occur at a rate of $hq\lambda_u$ and each has a combined load (over all workstations) of nt_u^c. Queries arrive at a rate of $n(1-hf)\lambda_q$ and take t_q^c each. Similarly, at a workstation we have queries with a rate of $hf\lambda_q$ requiring t_q^w, and updates at a rate of $hq\lambda_u$ requiring t_u^w.

Figure 1 shows the response time R as a function of h, the fraction of the database at each workstation, for several values of q, the "coherency" index. (Recall that when h is 0, the workstations have no data and all queries are processed at the central site. When h is 0.2, each workstation holds 20 percent of the database. Given our f value of 5, this means that all queries are processed locally.) When $q = 1$ all copies must track the central site closely. In this case caching is not very helpful (for the parameters we selected). As data is cached and h increases from 0 to 0.2, query processing work is offloaded to the workstations. Unfortunately, the savings at the central node are offset by the increased effort of keeping the copies up to date. As h approaches 0.2, the workstations also become saturated with work since they not only must process the queries but must also execute the updates forwarded to them.

As q decreases, the situation changes dramatically. Copies can diverge from the central value, so not every update must be propagated. The effort in update propagation is reduced and all computers can process the queries more quickly. When q is 0.75, a fourth of the updates are not propagated. In this case, the best response time occurs when about 15 percent of the database is cached. The central site has shed enough load to

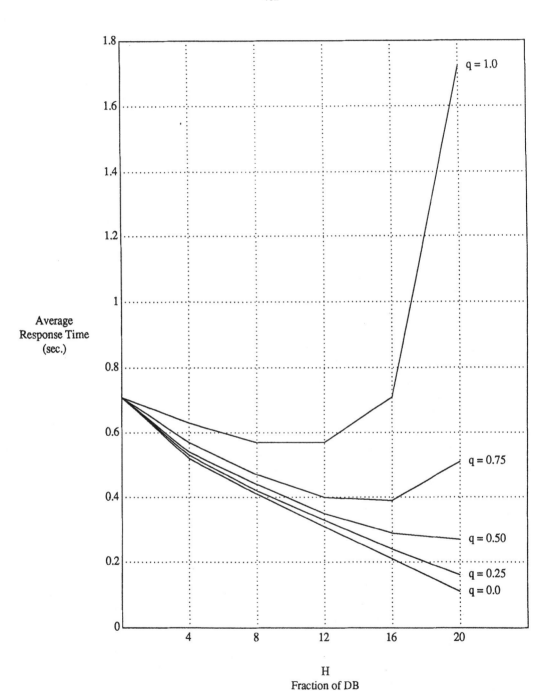

Figure I

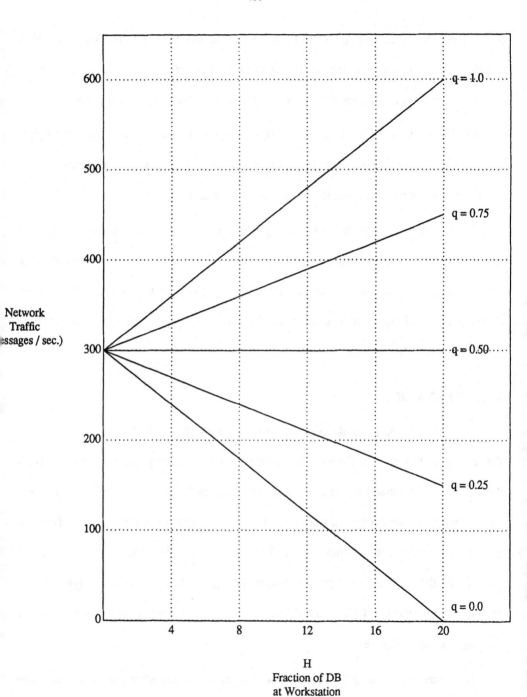

Figure II

make it operate more efficiently, but not enough to overload the workstations. With values of q of 0.5 or less, the workstations never become overloaded, so it becomes feasible to perform all queries locally ($h = 0.2$) and save the transmission costs.

Figure 2 shows the total number of messages transmitted per second. Here again, caching can increase the network load. Quasi-copies (q less than 1) can reduce the network traffic and can even make it less than in the no caching case.

In summary, the objective of caching is to reduce transmission delays for queries and to distribute the query processing load. However, caching may be counterproductive because of updates: updates to cached data generate more messages and processing load. Fortunately, quasi-copies reduce the cost of update propagation and may make caching feasible and very worthwhile.

6. AN EXAMPLE

We feel that the ideas described in this paper can be applied to existing systems. For example, the Boston Community Information System implemented at MIT [Gifford1985] can be studied in the context of quasi-copies.† This system consists of a central site with various databases, with users located throughout the Boston area. The central site is constantly transmitting (via FM radio) the entire database. Users receive and process the data at their personal computers (PC's). Each user selects the type of data that he is interested in. That is, the PC acts as a filter and stores locally the parts of the database that are of interest.

In this system caching is clearly a must. If no local data were stored, a user query could only be answered by waiting for the answer to be transmitted. As of 1985, the time

---

† A second example which illustrates how quasi-copies can be useful in implementing a distributed calendar service is discussed in [Garcia-Molina1986].

to transmit the database was 4 hours. This means that on the average a query would take 2 hours! Selection conditions are also important, for without them the entire database would have to be stored locally. The selection conditions are of type.add, dynamic, and compulsory (see Section 3). The triggering delay is set by the system and is equal to the time it takes to transmit the full database. Objects are dropped from the cache manually by each user.

Multi-object conditions, if they are required, pose an interesting problem. Say for example that there is a consistency constraint that involves objects x and y. At the end of a database transmission the images will satisfy the constraint. Let $x'(a)$ and $y'(b)$ be the images at this time. During the next database transmission, there can be a time when one image has been updated but not the other. Since the values $x'(a+1)$ and $y'(b)$ may be inconsistent, they cannot be read by the same query. The only reasonable choice is to save the old values until the end of a database transmission, at which time they can all be installed atomically. Since it would be costly to save all the old values, it would be desirable to let users define their multi-object constraints explicitly. This way, the system would only save old versions involved in these types of conditions.

In addition to broadcasting the full database periodically, the system also transmits new items with a higher frequency. This in essence defines two types of triggering delays. When a selection condition is first installed, it may take longer to cache data that is old. However, once the initial database transmission delay takes place, new objects that satisfy the condition will be cached more promptly. The ability to broadcast some data at a higher frequency opens the door for a number of additional improvements. For example, the database could be divided into fragments and each fragment could have a different triggering delay defined. Updates do not have to be transmitted as part of the database; they can be broadcast any time after they take place. This shortens the window for the coherency conditions, and again the system can give some fragments shorter windows. All of these improvements will become more important as the size of the database and its full transmission time increases.

The system designers also plan to add a dial-in capability to the system. This can let users define selection and coherency conditions that are stricter than the default ones, and can include non-delay ones like version number or arithmetic conditions. The system would use these conditions to schedule the transmission of data.

7. CONCLUSIONS

In practice, quasi-copies are already in use for all types of information and data. However, they are mostly used in an ad-hoc fashion, outside of computer systems, and without any validity guarantees. In this paper we have suggested that quasi-copies can be useful in a computerized IRS, reducing substantially the overhead of managing replicated data and making data available during failure periods. We have formally defined the notion of quasi-data, presented the types of conditions it can satisfy, and discussed the mechanisms with which a system can take advantage of the added flexibility.

As we have shown in Section 5, caching and quasi-copies can potentially improve performance and availability, however there are also potential problems. This may be so: (1) if there is poor locality of reference, i.e., if it is difficult to predict future accesses, the hit ratio h may be too low and then caching may not pay off; (2) if the selection and coherency conditions are complex, t_6^c and t_6^w may be too high, and then the overhead of the bookkeeping may outweight the savings; all of these things must be kept in mind when considering caching as an alternative.

Caching and quasi-copies also raise a number of challenging questions: How much data should be cached? Which of the mechanisms we have outlined is better suited for a particular application? How does the choice of when to propagate updates affect the performance of the system? What are the breakpoints that make caching and quasi-copies worthwhile? At the user end, there are also open questions: What language is used to define conditions? How does a user determine the delays or deviations that are best suited for him?

We are currently implementing a testbed to empirically answer the above questions. Our prototype implementation is being built on a Massive Memory Machine (MMM) at Princeton University. The MMM processor will be used as the central processor in an IRS. In such a machine, the models of workstation values could be kept in main memory, instead of on the disks, thus reducing the value of t_ξ. The remote workstations will consist of a number of SUN workstations. All the processors will be connected by a local area network, as well as by a number of phone lines. We will consider two types of databases, one a traditional information service, and the other the CSNET netnews database.

References

Dunn1984.

Bill Dunn, "Bill Dunn of Dow Jones: The Data Merchant," *Personal Computing*, pp. 162-176, December 1984.

Edelhart1983.

Mike Edelhart and Owen Davies, *OMNI Online Database Dictionary,* Collier Mac-Millan Publishers, 1983.

Garcia-Molina1986.

Hector Garcia-Molina, Rafael Alonso, Daniel Barbara, and Soraya Abad, "Data Caching in an Information Retrieval System," Technical Report CS-TR-065-86, Department of Computer Science, Princeton University, 1986.

Gifford1985.

David K. Gifford, John M. Lucassen, and Stephen T. Berlin, "The Application of Digital Broadcast Communication to Large Scale Information Systems," *IEEE Journal on Selected Areas in Communication*, May 1985.

Kleinrock1975.

Leonard Kleinrock, "Queueing Systems, Vol. 1: Theory," *Wiley-Interscience*, 1975.

Lamport1978.

Leslie Lamport, "Time, clocks, and the ordering of events in a distributed system," *Communications of the ACM*, vol. 21, no. 7, pp. 558-565, July 1978.

Smith1982.

Alan J. Smith, "Cache Memories," *Computing Surveys*, vol. 14, no. 3, September 1982.

Process Management and Assertion Enforcement for a Semantic Data Model[*]

by

K. Lawrence Chung, Daniel Rios-Zertuche, Brian A. Nixon and John Mylopoulos[†]

Department of Computer Science
University of Toronto
Toronto, Ontario, Canada M5S 1A4

Abstract

The Taxis design language offers an entity-based framework for designing interactive information systems and a data model which supports generalisation, classification and aggregation as abstraction mechanisms. With the aim of balancing expressiveness and performance, this paper describes and discusses design, implementation and performance analysis of the closely related issues of management of long-term activities for Taxis and enforcement of semantic integrity constraints.

1 Introduction

Every model has a *subject matter*. As a model of some slice of the real world or some application domain, a database has, as its *subject matter*, that real world or application domain. The usefulness of the database is to a large extent determined by the degree to which it is perceived by its users to be a natural, direct, complete and accurate model of its intended subject matter. Equipped with expressively powerful tools such as abstraction mechanisms of aggregation, generalisation and classification in an entity-oriented framework, so-called *semantic data models* (see [Borgida, 1985], [Albano, 1985b], [Atkinson, 1985] and [Hull, 1987] for overviews) have been proposed as modelling means for an application domain.

For a database to be useful, however, it must provide more than a faithful model of its intended subject matter. In particular, it must have *performance characteristics* — response time, throughput, robustness and the like — that meet user expectations. These characteristics heavily depend on the computational complexity and the implementation strategies of the semantic data model adopted. Enhancing the expressive power of semantic data models alone without concern for reasonable performance characteristics is obviously not acceptable. Unfortunately, however, expressive power is inversely related to computational tractability and the amenability of efficient implementation.

The main concern of the present paper is the management of long-term processes and the enforcement of semantic integrity constraints for Taxis [Mylopoulos, 1980], a semantic data model intended for the design of interactive information systems. A feature of Taxis, called *scripts* [Barron, 1982], is a powerful tool for the description of long-term activities, and another feature, called *assertions*, for the enforcement of semantic integrity constraints. A companion paper [Nixon, 1987] presents an implementation framework for other features of Taxis. Results presented in this paper are based on two M.Sc. theses by K. Lawrence Chung [Chung, 1984] and Daniel Rios-Zertuche [Rios-Zertuche, forthcoming]. A script is built around a Petri net skeleton of states connected by transition arcs, which are augmented by *activation conditions* and inter-process communication primitives based on Hoare's communicating sequential processes [Hoare, 1978]. Scripts have been completely integrated into the Taxis framework, so that script instances, like all other Taxis entities, are grouped into classes, and classes are organised into a generalisation hierarchy with their states and transitions defined in terms of aggregation. As in other object-oriented languages such as SMALLTALK-80 [Goldberg, 1983] and Actors [Hewitt, 1973], scripts are active entities that have internal states and exchange messages. Unlike objects which adopt a stimulus-response model of behaviour, scripts provide a Petri-net framework for modelling long-term events.

Assertions offer the ability to express semantic integrity constraints declaratively. They are expressed explicitly in terms of entities and attached as invariants on states, global constraints on a script, and as invariants on data classes referred to in the script. Assertions need to be maintained at all times for the database to be well formed with respect to its semantic data model and to be meaningful with respect to its subject matter.

Having provided Taxis with expressively powerful tools for appropriately describing the subject matter of long-term events and semantic integrity constraints, the issue of computational tractability and efficient implementation

---

[*] Parts of this paper are a revision and extension of a forthcoming book chapter [Nixon, forthcoming].

[†] Senior Fellow, Canadian Institute for Advanced Research

of such tools has to be addressed. What also remains is the study of performance of the implementation, which, from the usability point of view, is essential for the description of any implementation.

Section 2 of the paper outlines basic concepts of the Taxis data model. After considering the enforcement of assertions in section 3, the management of scripts is discussed in section 4. Section 5 describes a performance characterisation of the Taxis implementation based on section 3 and section 4. A summary of the paper is presented in section 6 along with future research issues.

2 Review of Basic Features of Taxis

This section sketches the basic features of Taxis to help the reader digest subsequent sections. Unlike traditional record-based approaches that rely heavily on keys among other things, Taxis as a semantic data model offers an entity-based framework in which individuals in the subject matter are modelled as *entities* and inter-relationships between these individuals are modelled as the *attributes* of the entities. Implicit in all entity-based frameworks is *referential integrity* constraint that referenced entities must exist in the database. For instance, for "the department of John" to be meaningful, "John" must exist. Thus, if an entity is removed, it must be confirmed that it is not being referenced in the description of any other entity. This framework leads to a model that corresponds more naturally and directly to its subject matter than the traditional record-based approaches. Entities are grouped into *classes* that are intended to model generic concepts, such as the concept of employee, and describe commonalities of their instance entities by way of attributes, such as salary or employee number, and *constraints*, such as salary being between $10 000 and $100 000. In Taxis, attributes are grouped into *categories*, such as salary being *changeable* or employee number being *unchangeable*, and categories define additional semantics on the attributes. Classes themselves are also treated as entities and in turn grouped into *metaclasses* that enable classes to have their own factual attributes, including aggregate information such as the average salary of the employee class. Furthermore, classes are organised into an *isA* hierarchy where more generic classes are located above less generic classes with the rule that all instance entities of the less generic classes are also instance entities of the more generic classes. For example, the employee class is located above the full-time employee class, and all full-time employees are also employees. A significant consequence of this organisation is that attributes are inherited by less generic classes from more generic classes, and attribute values may be specialised. For instance, the class of full-time employees inherits attributes, such as salary or employee number, from the class of employees, and these attributes may be specialised so that salary of full-time employees may be between $20 000 and $100 000. Transactions describe the way the database changes and model short-term events. By short-term, we mean transient events such as reviewing an employee's salary and changing it. For this reason, transactions are treated as atomic units of execution. Transactions are also treated as entities and grouped into classes. Innovative in Taxis with respect to transactions is that transactions may be organised into an isA hierarchy. For instance, the transaction that reviews the salary of a full-time employee is a specialised version of the one that reviews the salary of an employee.

While assertions and scripts are described in detail in later sections, we present some examples of Taxis class definitions in Figure 1.

The first definition declares the class **Employee** with **unchangeable** attribute **emp#**, **changeable** attributes **salary**, **position**, and **dept**, and **unique** (key) attribute **employeeID** consisting of the **emp#** value.[1]

Attributes are typed. Class definitions induce factual attribute values on their instances. Suppose JohnSmith is an instance of **Employee**. Then the *factual attribute value* JohnSmith.dept (= accounting) must be an instance of the *definitional attribute value* Employee..dept (= Department). The second class declaration describes a transaction which reviews an employee's salary and changes it, provided there is money available in the employee's department. If there is no money available, an instance of the exception class **NoMoneyAvailable** (see the third declaration) will be raised for the problematic employee and his proposed increase, and then a procedure-oriented exception handling mechanism similar to one first proposed in [Wasserman, 1977] will be invoked.

An entity, be it generic (e.g., **Employee**, **NoMoneyAvailable**) or non-generic (e.g., **JohnSmith**, 7, 'John') must be an instance of at least one class. For instance, JohnSmith is an instance of **Employee**, while **Employee** is an instance of the metaclass **AnyDataClass**.

In the generalisation hierarchy of classes, **Any** and **None** are respectively the top and bottom elements. The only instance of **None** is the entity **nothing**, which is therefore an instance of every class.

Unlike other semantic data models such as ADAPLEX [Smith, 1983] [Chan, 1982], GEM [Tsur, 1984] [Zaniolo, 1983] and Galileo [Albano, 1985a], Taxis does not permit *multiple valued attributes*. For example, the class **Employee** can have at most one **dept** attribute and each instance of **Employee** can have at most one attribute value for **dept**.

More complete accounts of Taxis can be found in [Mylopoulos, 1980], [Nixon, 1983] and [Chung, 1984].

---

[1]Not all class definitions are shown; for example, **Department** is presumed to be declared as another class with several attributes, some of which are actually used in Figure 1. Also note that the unique attribute actually defines attribute **employeeID** on **emp#**, with value 0::9999999 ensuring that (non-null) **emp#** values uniquely identify employees.

```
define AnyDataClass Employee with
  unchangeable
    emp#: {| 0::9999999 |}
  changeable
    salary: {| 10000::100000 |}
    position: {| president, secretary, janitor |}
    dept: Department
  unique
    employeeID: (emp#)
endAnyDataClass

define AnyTransactionClass ReviewSalary(e: Employee, incr: Money) with
  prerequisites
    moneyAvailable?: (e.dept.salTotal+incr <= e.dept.maxSalTotal)
                              elseRaiseException NoMoneyAvailable(e,incr)
  actions
    changeSal: e.salary <- e.salary + incr
    report: (e.salary).print
    changeTotal: e.dept.salTotal <- e.dept.salTotal + incr
  postrequisites
    tooHigh?: (e.salary > 75000)
                    elseRaiseException SalaryTooHigh(e,incr)
endAnyTransactionClass

define AnyExceptionClass NoMoneyAvailable with
  unchangeable
    e: Employee
    m: Money
endAnyExceptionClass
```

Figure 1: Sample class declarations

3   Semantic Integrity Constraints and their Enforcement

This section describes the mechanisms offered for the expression of semantic integrity constraints, including temporal ones, and then focuses on the efficient implementation of automatic detection of constraint violations.

3.1   Overview of Semantic Integrity Constraints in Taxis

Semantic integrity constraints (hereafter "assertions") impose constraints on the allowable database states and on the transitions between them [Florentin, 1974] [Melo, 1979]. The former are called *static* or snapshot assertions, and the latter *dynamic* or transition assertions. Assertions can be handled in several ways. One involves periodic auditing. Another uses automatic error detection, either *procedurally*, by specifying the procedures that will do the checking, or *declaratively* by associating assertions, which are to be automatically enforced, with a class definition.

It has been argued that procedural mechanisms do not fully address the needs of database management systems [Hammer, 1975] [Hammer, 1976]. On the other hand, the cost of allowing declarative specifications of assertions will be, in general, high. Two major cost components as discussed in [Lafue, 1982] are selection of assertions for checking after a database update on one hand, and checking of assertions which may no longer hold on the other. In reliable systems handling a large number of long-term entities, these costs will be primarily attributable to secondary storage access. Reducing the cost of assertion checking is, therefore, primarily an exercise aimed at reducing such secondary storage access.

The assertion language is based on a restricted subset of first order logic. The following specialisation of the previous definition of **Employee** illustrates some examples:

```
define AnyDataClass FullTimeEmployee isA Employee with
  changeable
    employmentDate: $Time
    retirementDate: $Time
  assertions
    salHighEnough?: (position not= president) or (salary >= 70000)
                            elseRaiseException SalTooLow(self, salary)
    salIncreasing?: salary.$old < salary.$new ...
    salWithinBudget?: salary <= dept.budget ...
    retireAfterEmployed?: retirementDate after employmentDate ...
    beforeRetirement?: retirementDate after $now ...
endAnyDataClass
```

This definition of the FullTimeEmployee class includes five assertions:

- salHighEnough? requires that every president should earn at least $70 000.[2] If not satisfied, an exception SalTooLow will be called with the violating entity (= self) and the proposed salary as the parameters.

- salIncreasing? is a dynamic assertion which requires that the salary of each full time employee be increasing.[3]

- salWithinBudget? requires that every full time employee earn no more than the budget of his/her department.

- retireAfterEmployed? requires that no full time employee retire before the commencement of his/her employment. Both employmentDate and retirementDate take values that are instances of $Time, a class of temporal entities.

- beforeRetirement? requires that no full time employee work after his/her retirement date. The special variable $now is assigned as value the current system clock time.

For the purposes of enforcing assertions, it is useful to distinguish three categories of assertions: *intra-class*, *inter-class*, and *temporal* assertions. Intra-class assertions are those that constrain attributes of a single class such as salHighEnough? and salIncreasing?, while expressions that relate the attributes of several classes, such as salWithinBudget?, are called inter-class assertions. Finally, temporal assertions, such as retireAfterEmployed? and beforeRetirement?, relate temporal entities. Note that retireAfterEmployed? need only be checked after a database update. On the other hand, beforeRetirement? needs to be checked continuously, at least in principle, since it involves the special variable $now which always has the current clock time as value.

Checking assertions may easily become the bottleneck for the whole system. To avoid this situation, we impose a number of restrictions on the assertion language based on first order logic. Firstly, no explicit quantifiers are allowed in an assertion expression. Moreover, an attribute selection path specified within an assertion for a class (say C_1) is of the form:

$$self.p_1.p_2. \ ... \ .p_n$$

where the first attribute (here p_1) must be associated with the class (C_1) to which the assertion is attached, and p_i $(1 \leq i \leq n)$ is an attribute of class C_i (where $C_i..p_i = C_{i+1}$).[4] The intent of these two restrictions is to associate assertions closely with the existing structure of the model (the structure based on classification, aggregation, and specialisation) and to provide the basis for a linear access to entities on secondary storage. In order to attain linear access, we need another restriction on the form of the selection path, namely, a no-circularity restriction: if $C_i..p_i = C_j$, then we require that $i < j$.[5] With respect to the above selection path, there is at most one path between an instance of C_1 and an instance of C_j $(2 \leq j \leq (n + 1))$, since Taxis does not have multiple valued attributes, and explicit quantifiers are not permitted in assertions. This implies that the maximum number of entities that could be related to any instance of C_i regarding the selection path is the cardinality of C_1 multiplied by $(n - 1)$. This number acts as the upper bound on the detection of assertion failures regarding the selection path, when the attribute p_i of an instance of C_i is updated. In addition, it is also required that the attributes involved in an assertion must not have values which are metaclasses, or very general classes whose extensions vary at run-time (e.g., AnyData, the most general data class): metaclasses may deal with aggregate information, which we do not handle; the use of AnyData may require enforcement for updates to entities in any of several data classes. Secondly, no user-defined transactions can be used in an assertion; otherwise the satisfaction of certain conditions (e.g., if-then-else

---

[2]The assertion can be read (self.position not= president) or (self.salary >= 70000) where self is a free variable ranging over the class being defined (here, FullTimeEmployee); self is implicitly the subject of attribute selections (e.g., self.position).

[3]The built-in attributes $old and $new refer to an attribute value before and after an update respectively.

[4]Therefore, all assertions, when reformulated in prenex normal form, have a prefix consisting of one universal quantifier followed by a number of existential quantifiers. However, the variable bound by an existential quantifier does *not* have to have a value other than nothing, unless stated explicitly that its value should be non-null.

[5]That is, each class involved in the selection path is distinct.

constructs) could invoke other user-defined transactions causing hidden side-effects, which are hard to determine from the selection path. Thirdly, the special attributes $old and $new can only be used to perform comparison on a single selection path so as to avoid the maintenance of attribute histories, which we do not have built-in mechanisms to support for. $now can only be used with the temporal relations **before** and **after**, since some relations such as the equality relation and the inequality relation are too dependent on the load of the environment computer system. Fourthly, we impose the following restrictions on the operators of multiplication and division: (i) these operators take as arguments instances of either **NonPositiveInteger** or **NonNegativeInteger** but not **AnyInteger**, (ii) no nesting of multiplication or division is allowed, (iii) no subtraction may occur within an operand expression. These restrictions permit us to statically determine the sign of an expression involving multiplication or division. Otherwise, determining whether an update violates an assertion is more difficult. For instance, if z is updated, it is in general not possible to determine whether the value of $x/(y - z)$ goes up or not.

Once an assertion is violated, an exception is raised and the procedural exception handling technique mentioned in section 2 is used. When there are multiple assertions associated with a class attribute, the order of checking is assumed to be non-deterministic. The compiler chooses the order depending on the optimisation algorithms used (For instance, a less expensive assertion is checked before more expensive ones). When a violation is detected, only one exception associated with the first violated assertion will be raised (and one exception handler will be invoked).

When are assertions checked and exceptions raised? Unlike the cases discussed in [Stonebraker, 1975] and [Blaustein, 1981] where assertions are treated as **prerequisites** of individual data management operations (creation, removal and modification), Taxis treats intra-class and inter-class assertions as **prerequisites** of Taxis transactions invoked as actions of **transitions** within scripts (For more on this, see section 4).[6] The term **prerequisites** denotes the conditions necessary for the satisfaction of all assertions relevant to the transaction.[7] Thus, temporarily inconsistent states may arise as in System R [Astrahan, 1976] [Chamberlin, 1981], with the resulting advantage of the ability to satisfy requests such as switching flights for two passengers when each of the flights is fully reserved. Temporal assertions that use $now can be enforced by simple periodic checking. For instance, DBALERT [Ribeiro, 1978] for WAND provides a limited form of alerters, where such periodic checking is done. This, however, is both inefficient (because the database is checked even when there is no need) and ineffective (because the database may enter an illegal state). We have opted for an enforcement mechanism that will check only when there is a need. A complication that has to be dealt with concerns the exact times when assertions involving $now are to be checked. Such checks must be done, we feel, in a preventive fashion, rather than in a remedial one. This is achieved by checking such assertions a time unit before they are to change truth value. The length of the time unit is one of the compiler parameters.

3.2   Enforcement of Semantic Integrity Constraints

We first consider intra-class and inter-class assertions. The high cost of enforcing assertions can be illustrated using the **FullTimeEmployee** example plus the following:[8]

```
define AnyDataClass Department with
   changeable
      budget: Money
   assertions
      budgetMaxOK?: budget < 700000 ...
endAnyDataClass
```

Suppose d is an instance of **Department**. When the budget of d is modified from one value to another, we have to go through a two-step process to guarantee the validity of the modification. The first step is to select all the relevant assertions for the update (In this example, not only budgetMaxOK? but also salWithinBudget? specified in the **FullTimeEmployee** class). The second step is to validate the selected assertions with respect to all relevant data. With no guidance, we would have to access all full time employees to enforce salWithinBudget?.

The framework of our compile-time optimisation for checking assertions is based on a proposal presented in [Sarin, 1977]. For each assertion and operation, a set of run-time procedures are compiled to monitor the operation. These procedures are considerably more efficient than naive re-evaluation of the assertion. In the rest of the section, we describe the optimisation techniques in terms of examples and a sketch of the algorithms involved.

In order to select relevant assertions to check after a database update, the compiler generates a list of assertions for each attribute, p, of each class, C. The generation involves finding every assertion in which p of C is used in some attribute selection. For instance, the class **Department** is used in dept.budget of salWithinBudget?.[9] Once all

---

[6]We do not consider the technique of factoring multiple updates. [Hsu, 1985] provides a set of algorithms for efficient enforcement of constraints dealing with multiple updates in a relational database setting, when explicit quantifiers are allowed.

[7]If the **prerequisites** are satisfied, then the transaction will be executed. In an actual implementation, the transaction is first executed (with all its side-effects recorded in some temporary buffer); then, all the side-effects are tested against applicable assertions; if no side-effect violates an assertion, then the side-effects become permanent. Otherwise, no side-effect becomes permanent.

[8]Only some attributes are shown.

[9]Although only one attribute selector is used here, there is no bound on the number of attribute selectors that can be used in an assertion. The compiler should consider all classes and attributes in such an expression.

relevant assertions are collected for each attribute of each class, the second step is to generate efficient procedures to optimise the access to data that are concerned with the assertions. We incorporate techniques from [Bernstein, 1980] and [Blaustein, 1981], and from [Sarin, 1977] for the generation of efficient procedures. Bernstein and Blaustein present a technique utilising aggregate information of maxima and minima of a set of values. Sarin offers a set of heuristics based on the comparison between the values before and after an update.[10]

Before we describe the incorporation of the techniques mentioned above, we consider the possibility of static checking regarding creation and removal. The creation and removal of certain entities do not violate certain assertions [Stonebraker, 1975] [Bernstein, 1980] [Blaustein, 1981]. Creation of an entity requires only that the new entity be checked against the assertions of its own class. With the semantic integrity constraint (see section 2.2) and the restrictions on the assertion language (see section 4.1), we have a stronger result on removal than those in [Stonebraker, 1975] [Bernstein, 1980] [Blaustein, 1981]. Their result is that in the absence of aggregate functions (such as maximum, minimum and average), when no two variables range over the same relations, deletion of universally quantified tuples trivially satisfies the assertion. Our result is that no checking is necessary for the removal of any entity. According to the referential integrity constraint, an entity cannot be removed when any entity refers to it. If the referential integrity constraint is violated, no action will occur and no checking is needed. If it is satisfied (hence the entity is not referenced by any other entity), removal will not violate any assertion.[11] No assertions are allowed on retrieval. Having dealt with creation, removal and retrieval, we henceforth devote ourselves to the enforcement of constraints on modification.

Efficient enforcement of constraints on attribute modification requires the generation of efficient procedures, which avoid accessing non-applicable entities. For instance, when a department's budget is modified, only those full time employees who work for the department should be examined. In addition, these procedures should try to completely avoid iterative checking, whenever possible. This may or may not involve run-time overhead.[12] We first describe Sarin's heuristics which do not require run-time overhead. The assertion `salWithinBudget?` requires that whenever the salary of a full time employee or the department of a full time employee or the budget of a department is modified, this assertion has to be checked. If the salary is decreased (i.e., `self.salary.$old > self.salary.$new`), then `salWithinBudget?` is trivially satisfied and no checking is necessary. Similarly, if the employee's department's budget has not been decreased (i.e., `self.dept.budget.$old <= self.dept.budget.$new`), then again no checking is necessary. But suppose we change the budget of a particular department, without reference to one of its employees. It again suffices to ensure that the budget has been increased, without examining any of the employees.

There are several similar forms of assertions where we are able to statically determine simple conditions which, if satisfied at run-time, will obviate assertion checking. The compiler emits code, based on the sample cases described in the table. In each case, assume we are modifying attribute p. Note that the condition simply compares the old and new values of that attribute, and the comparison operator is called a *guide*.

Assertion Form	Guide	Code Emitted
`self.p (boolean value)`	`not=`	`if self.p.$old    not= self.p.$new` `then Check...`
`self.p       = self.q`	`not=`	`if self.p.$old    not= self.p.$new` `then Check...`
`self.p.$old not= self.p.$new`	`=`	`if self.p.$old    = self.p.$new` `then Check...`
`self.p.r      < 20`	`<`	`if self.p.$old.r   < self.p.$new.r` `then Check...`
`self.p.r      > self.s`	`>`	`if self.p.$old.r   > self.p.$new.r` `then Check...`

Having described an optimisation technique not requiring run-time overhead, we next describe a technique of Bernstein and Blaustein which does require run-time overhead. The idea is to use redundant data such as the (dynamically changing) maxima and minima of a set of data which may reduce the cost of checking assertions. Again, considering `salWithinBudget?`, suppose a department's budget is decreased by a certain amount. Here, the guide is ">" and the comparison of the old value and new value with the guide succeeds. Although this means that iteration is required over all full time employees, if the new budget value is still greater than the maximum of all salaries of all full time employees, then the iteration would not be necessary. A similar observation applies to cases where a new value is less than the minimum of all values (In this case, the guide would have been "<"). When an assertion involves arithmetic operators, it might not be worthwhile to keep extra information for all operands within the assertion. Consider the following:

`assertionWithArithmetic?: x + y > z`

---

[10]See [Chakravarthy, 1984] for efficient processing of queries, but not updates.

[11]If operations such as minimum, maximum and average are allowed in assertions, assertion checking will be needed at removal.

[12]For the purposes of this section, run-time overhead refers to extra processing which is required for run-time operations, even when a particular assertion is not being checked. Examples include maintaining aggregate information such as maxima and minima.

When the value of x decreases, optimisation with the guide would fail and we may want to optimise the checking of:

$$x + minimum(y) > maximum(z).$$

Now clearly, the chance of success with this kind of test is inversely proportional to the number of minimum and maximum values involved, and their ranges. The benefits of maintaining aggregate information in this case probably does not justify the cost. For our purposes, we have chosen to maintain the redundancy only for single operands of <, <=, > or >=.

Thus, at compile time, we want to generate code that optimises the assertion checking for salWithinBudget? when a department's budget is updated:

```
function CheckSalWithinBudget(d1:Department, newBudget:Budget)
                            returns boolean
  testOK? <- true
  /* d1.(budget.$new) <- newBudget  */
  /* Here  >  is the guide  */
  if d1.(budget.$old) > d1.(budget.$new)
    then if d1.(budget.$new)
              < max({x | (e.salary=x) and (e instanceOf FullTimeEmployee)})
           then for each instance e of FullTimeEmployee do
                    if e.dept = d1
                      then begin
                            testOK? <- "evaluate salWithinBudget? for e"
                            if not testOK?
                              then begin
                                    "call the associated exception handler"
                                    exit loop
                                  end
                          end
  return(testOK?)
end CheckSalWithinBudget
```

Here, the maximum value on all full time employee salaries is updated and kept around rather than re-evaluated each time.

With back pointers maintained at run-time (see [Nixon, 1987]), we can make use of them in optimising assertion checking. The optimisation is concerned with the iteration phase after both the test with guide and that using aggregate information fail. The use of back pointers can change the form of the iteration:

```
for each instance e of FullTimeEmployee do
    if e.dept = d1
      then ...
```

once we make use of the fact that we know exactly what instances are relevant by following back pointers. Here, we assume that back pointers are indexed not only with respect to entities but also the classes and attributes involved. The following code checks salWithinBudget? using back pointers:[13]

```
for each inverse attribute selection e.p of d1 do
    if (e instanceOf FullTimeEmployee) and (p = dept)
      then begin
            testOK? <- "evaluate salWithinBudget? for e"
            if not testOK? then exit
          end
```

When multiple assertions are associated with a single attribute we may first evaluate intra-class assertions dealing with a single entity, then inter-class assertions dealing with iteration classes, starting with ones that use guides and aggregate information, then ones that use guides only. Further run-time optimisation could be done by selecting among assertions to iterate over classes with small cardinalities. Yet another optimisation involves factoring out iterations that need to be done over a single class. For instance, the assertion:

bonus < dept.budget and salary < dept.budget

---

[13] In the body of the loop, e ranges over entities and p ranges over attributes, such that e.p = d1.

requires two iterations over **FullTimeEmployee**. These can be combined into a single iteration during which both conjuncts of the assertion are checked.

Having considered intra-class assertions and inter-class assertions, we now shift our attention to describing temporal assertions dealing with **$now**. Temporal assertions require special optimisation techniques. Unlike intra-class and inter-class assertions that need only be checked before an update operation, such assertions need to be checked at designated times. In implementing an enforcement mechanism for such assertions, a special data structure, the *time list*, is used consisting of a list of entities sorted by time whose first entry is the earliest time instance that is after $now. Each time entity in the list indicates the time when an assertion ought to be checked. The list is updated when an entity constrained by a temporal assertion is created. Removal occurs either when $now moves past the first entry or when a temporal assertion is no longer applicable, e.g., when an entity is removed or its time attributes are changed. Each list entry consists of a quadruple with components a time instance, an entity, an attribute, and an assertion. Enforcement uses a trigger mechanism [Eswaran, 1976] and the data structure just described. The trigger mechanism checks the first entry of the list before and after the execution of a transaction (Once checked after the execution of a transaction, T, no checking would be necessary before the execution of another transaction immediately following T). When no transaction remains, the system goes to sleep after setting an alarm to the time indicated by the first entry of the list (For more on this, see the end of section 4). For this trigger mechanism to work well, the time resolution for time entities should be greater than that required to execute any transaction.

A sketch of the assertion enforcement mechanism is presented next. Once all the lists of assertions are compiled for each *attribute* of each *class*, then these assertions are associated with each and every built-in data management operation that could violate them (for non-temporal assertions, if a transaction can satisfy a set of assertions applicable to its operations, then the transaction will be executed; for temporal assertions, if the set of assertions is satisfied, then entries into the temporal list will be created in addition to the execution of the transaction):

```
if AssertionsOKForClassAndAttribute
  then begin
          executeTransaction
          if temporal-assertion
             then create an entry into the temporal list
       end
```

where **AssertionsOKFor***ClassAndAttribute* is a boolean function consisting of a set of function calls, each function checking one assertion. If the current update can satisfy all relevant assertions, the function returns **true**. Otherwise, it returns **false** so that the update operation (hence, its containing transaction) is not performed. For instance, for:

```
d1.budget <- x
```

the following code is emitted:

```
if AssertionsOKForDepartmentAndBudget(d1,x)
  then d1.budget <- x
```

which calls:

```
function AssertionsOKForDepartmentAndBudget(d:Department, b:Budget)
                            returns Boolean
  successful <- CheckBudgetMaxOK(d,b)
  if successful
    then successful <- CheckSalWithinBudget(d,b)
  return(successful)
```

The function **CheckBudgetMaxOK** checks if the update would be valid against the assertion **budgetMaxOK?**. If not, the associated exception handler is called. **CheckSalWithinBudget** checks if the update would be valid against the assertion **salWithinBudget?**. Its optimised code was shown previously.

4 Process Management: Handling Scripts

Efficient management of processes is closely related to efficient enforcement of assertions. This section describes how processes can be efficiently handled in terms of the optimisation techniques described in the previous section.

As we mentioned earlier, scripts model long-term processes such as employment with a company, i.e., the states and state changes a full time employee goes through during employment, such as being hired, getting a pay raise, and retiring. Scripts offer a Petri net-like graphical formalism, inspired by [Zisman, 1978] but incorporate significant extensions, among them (i) the moulding of scripts into the Taxis framework of classes, instances, and attributes, (ii) the addition of inter-process communication primitives based on Hoare's Communicating Sequential Processes

[Hoare, 1978], and (iii) the provision of facilities for communication between the user and the system. Figure 2 is a graphical representation of the Employment script.

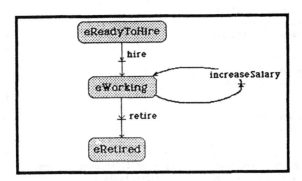

Figure 2: Sample script diagram

The corresponding Taxis declarations are presented in Figure 3. The state eReadyToHire will be an instance of a state class, ReadyToHire, when an Employment script is instantiated. One of the actions of the transition, increaseSalary, is calling ReviewSalary defined in section 2.1. Note that two assertions specific to the FullTimeEmployee script are included: as1 requires that an employee's start date precedes his/her retirement date; as2 requires that full time employees who have worked for the company for more than 3 years earn over $25 000.

As with Petri nets, scripts have two node types, one representing states (indicated by shaded ovals in figure 3) and the other representing transitions from one state to another (and indicated by "->|-"). The description of a state includes assertions which must be true in that state, while the description of a transition includes a list of activation conditions that must be true for the transition to fire and a list of actions that are to be executed in this case.[14] While the same restrictions imposed on assertions apply to conditions, actions can reference any Taxis entity. Actions may also involve calls to Taxis transactions and other scripts, and the raising and handling of exceptions.

The problem addressed in this section is the management of the instances of such scripts. In general, there will be a large number of active script instances, states and transitions at any one time, and it is important to use a strategy for process scheduling that is both fair and efficient. The key to any such strategy is the determination and management of transitions that are eligible for activation or are currently active.

Two requirements must be met for a transition (e.g., retire) to be activated. Firstly, its input (from) states (e.g., eWorking) must be active ("on") and secondly its conditions (e.g., r1) must be true. Once these requirements are met, a transition fires, its actions (e.g., s1) are executed, its input states are deactivated and its output (to) states are activated.

One point to add here is that execution of actions may be suspended for inter-script communication or for communication between the user and the system,[15] and may be resumed upon receipt of a message from another script. To deal with this kind of suspension, we internally split the transition into two contiguous transitions and introduce an intermediate state such that the condition of the second transition is a predicate testing the readiness of the synchronisation. A set of predicates testing the readiness of the synchronisation is available, and adds to the power of the condition language.

To clarify what a transition goes through when it fires, we introduce the possible status values in Figure 4.

---

[14]The basic unit of execution in the Taxis system, for the purposes of process management, assertion enforcement, recovery and concurrency control, is each transaction which is called as a transition action, regardless of the depth of transaction nesting.

[15]Therefore, in contrast to the pure Petri nets and to Zisman's Augmented Petri nets [Zisman, 1978], script transitions are not treated as instantaneous events; rather, they can be active for long periods of time (days or months) in order to synchronise communication between processes or between the user and the system.

```
define scriptClass Employment(e: FullTimeEmployee) with
  locals
    timeToIncreaseSalary: $Time
    tenure: PositiveInteger
    dateToProcessRetirement: $Time
  states
    eReadyToHire: ReadyToHire
    eWorking: NonInitialState
    eRetired: NonInitialState
  transitions
    hire
      from eReadyToHire
      to   eWorking

      actions
        a1: timeToIncreaseSalary <- /* set time to increase salary */
        a2: dateToProcessRetirement <- e.retirementDate
        a3: dateToProcessRetirement.day <- e.retirementDate.day - 1

    increaseSalary
      from eWorking
      to   eWorking

      conditions
        c1: $now after timeToIncreaseSalary
      actions
        b1: tenure <- $now.year - e.employment.year
        b2: incr <-  /*  determine the increment  */
        b3: [e,incr].ReviewSalary
        b4: timeToIncreaseSalary.year <- timeToIncreaseSalary.year + 1

    retire
      from eWorking
      to   eRetired

      conditions
        r1: $now after dateToProcessRetirement
      actions
        s1: /* buy gold watch */
      assertions
        as1: dateToProcessRetirement after e.employmentDate ...
        as2: e.salary > 25000 or tenure <= 3 ...
endScriptClass
```

Figure 9. Sample Script Declaration

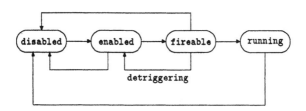

Figure 4. Possible status Values

A **disabled** transition is one whose input states are not all active and an **enabled** transitions is one whose input states are all active but whose conditions are not all satisfied. A **fireable** transition is an enabled transition with all conditions satisfied and a **running** transition is one that is executing actions or testing postrequisites or after all these, deactivating all of its input states and activating all of its output states. For transitions with status **disabled**, **enabled** or **fireable**, we describe briefly a strategy proposed by [Zisman, 1978] and an alternative one we use along with some discussions of relative merits. For related work in the area of active databases, see [Stonebraker, 1986] and [Nierstrasz, 1987].

Zisman's *cyclic checking* strategy maintains an active transition set whose members are enabled transitions, where successive scans are made sequentially and cyclically to find one **fireable** transition all of whose conditions are satisfied. Once the selected one fires, the scan continues.[16] This strategy has several merits. Firstly, it guarantees fairness among transitions and avoids indefinite postponement. Secondly, it is simple to understand and easy to implement. Finally, it has satisfactory performance when the set of transitions is small. However, performance degrades as the ratio of enabled transitions to fireable ones decreases. Suppose the number of enabled transitions is N_e and that of fireable ones N_f, and let R_{ef} be the ratio N_e/N_f. The best situation for this strategy occurs when the value of R_{ef} is always 1, indicating that all the members of the active transition set are actually fireable. The worst case is when R_{ef} approaches infinity indicating that no member is actually fireable or when R_{ef} equals N_e and the number of probes to be made to find one fireable transition is N_e. When R_{ef} is small, the performance of this strategy is favourable but when R_{ef} gets larger, performance degrades.

We expect N_e to be large, say on the order of 10 000 in a real environment and N_f much smaller, say on the order of 100, than N_e with the value of R_{ef} high. Therefore, we propose an alternative strategy which uses a trigger mechanism. The basic idea is to isolate the set of fireable transitions from the enabled transitions and maintain only fireable transitions. Let us introduce a *process queue* whose entries consist of fireable transitions. Treating the conditions of transitions as the *triggering* conditions [Eswaran, 1976] makes it possible to maintain a queue of fireable transitions. That is, a transition is placed in the queue the moment all conditions are detected to be true (provided that all input states are active), hence fireable.[17] This is in contrast to the cyclic checking where a transition is placed in the active transition set when it is enabled (although not fireable).

Note that with cyclic checking, the conditions of each enabled transition are examined only once during each scan of the active transition set in order to see if the enabled transition is fireable. With the trigger mechanism, the conditions of each enabled transition may be examined more than once due to two possible situations: (i) *negative reversal* of the condition, and (ii) *redundant evaluation*.

Negative/positive reversal of a condition means the change in the value of a condition of either enabled or fireable transitions from true/false to false/true respectively. Redundant evaluation means no change in the value of either enabled or fireable transitions, when re-evaluated (i.e., a true/false condition is re-evaluated to true/false respectively, at the cost of one evaluation). An ideal environment for the trigger mechanism to work best regarding the conditions is where only one evaluation is needed per condition, i.e., where neither negative reversal nor redundant evaluation occurs. In another words, only one positive reversal of a condition occurs: a false condition of an enabled transition, once evaluated, becomes true; and it stays true until all other conditions of the transition become true (at this point of time, the transition becomes fireable and is put into the process queue); furthermore, it stays true until the transition is taken out of the process queue and executed.

We first consider the worst adversary, i.e., the repetition of a *mutual cancellation*: a negative reversal of a condition followed by a positive reversal of the condition, whose net effect is nil at the cost of two evaluations. A mutual cancellation of the conditions of both enabled and fireable transitions may occur. A possible mutual cancellation of a fireable transition is as follows. While a fireable transition, say T_f, is waiting within the process queue for its turn to fire, other running transitions may modify the entity or entities referenced in T_f's condition expressions in such a way that T_f becomes no longer fireable and has to be taken out of the process queue. We say that by **detriggering**, T_f becomes **enabled**. If T_f becomes **fireable** again, it has to be put into the process queue again. If changes of status of this sort are frequent for T_f, each time such a change is made, the trigger mechanism has to be invoked to take out T_f (This situation does not apply to cyclic checking). Thus, a mutual cancellation occurring to fireable transitions may not only degrade the system performance but also introduce the possibility of indefinite postponement. We obviate this phenomenon by a simple strategy: a fireable transition *must* fire. That is, no negative reversal is allowed on the conditions of fireable transitions, thus detriggering is prohibited.[18] This strategy has a paramount impact on the performance of the trigger mechanism, since there is no longer any need to evaluate the conditions of any fireable transition (because true conditions persist, the need for redundant evaluation is also eliminated).

Then, the cause of multiple evaluations per condition lies in the presence of negative reversal and mutual cancellations on the conditions of enabled transitions. In our view, this drawback of the trigger mechanism is much milder

---

[16]During each cycle, transitions whose input states are deactivated will be taken out of the active transition set.

[17]A condition tag is maintained for each condition so that, whenever one condition is detected to be true, the other conditions of the transition do not have to be re-evaluated to see if the transition is fireable

[18]If parallel machines are used so that all fireable transitions run concurrently, no negative reversal will take place. On a single machine, if a fireable transition is not fired within a certain time limit (see section 3 on temporal assertions), that may be a signal that the system capacity is exceeded and the database administrator is to be advised to upgrade the system. Thus this strategy is not a far-fetched restriction.

than the drawback of cyclic checking.

Next, we turn our attention to another comparison between the two strategies: the high cost of the trigger mechanism, i.e., the cost involved in the detection of condition satisfaction. This cost can be significantly reduced by employing the optimisation techniques described in the previous section. Note that assertions require a very similar mechanism for their enforcement to the activation mechanism for transitions. As described earlier in this section, Taxis forces condition expressions for transitions to have the same form as assertions with a few minor exceptions. Note, however, that assertion failures raise exceptions while conditions evaluating to **true** trigger transitions when their status changes from **enabled** to **fireable**.

Having decided to use the trigger mechanism, we sketch the overall scheme for the run time assertion enforcement and process control of a Taxis system. The *time list* described in section 3 is used as a main data structure, along with another time list for time entities associated with conditions, a process queue, a queue for inputs and another for outputs. Then, the overall control strategy can be described with an algorithm such as the following:

```
do forever
  for each entry of input queue do
    begin
      CheckTimeLists
      carry out action as requested, triggering a transition if necessary
    end
  for each entry of output queue do
    begin
      CheckTimeLists
      display message to a user
    end
  for each entry of process queue do
    begin
      CheckTimeLists
      run the transition in the first entry
    end
  if empty(input queue) and empty(output queue) and empty(process queue)
    then begin
          set alarm to the earlier of
              (the first entry of the assertion-time-list) and
              (the first entry of the condition-time-list)
          go to sleep, allowing for user input-interrupt
        end
end
```

where `CheckTimeLists` is the following:

```
do while ($now after the first entry of time list for assertions)
  raise the associated exception handler
  remove the first entry
end
do while ($now after the first entry of time list for conditions)
  trigger the associated transition
  remove the first entry
end
```

In addition, `CheckTimeLists` is tested before and after each transaction called by any transition.

The above control is based on a priority scheme. Temporal assertions have higher priority over temporal conditions; next, inputs and outputs are processed before transitions in consideration of user-friendliness. Thus, this scheme views temporal consistency as the most important aspect of the system., i.e., when it is time to check the first temporal assertion or temporal condition, or when there is user input, whichever comes first. Note that different strategies can be used to ensure that entries in each of the three queues are given a fair chance.

5 Performance Characterisation

Based on the implementation strategies and techniques, both for the basic features of Taxis (see section 2 and [Nixon, 1987]), and for assertions and scripts (discussed in sections 3 and 4), this section describes a framework for performance characterisation of Taxis application systems.

Regarding the features of a semantic data model and its implementation strategies and techniques, a major purpose of performance analysis is to answer a series of questions concerning the size and complexity of intended application systems and the capacity and behaviour of the implemented system.

Studies of performance analysis of data processing applications which are based on the traditional data models indicate that the workload characterisation problem is far from being solved for such applications [Ferrari, 1983]. The problem is expected to be much harder for Taxis than for the traditional data models, due to the presence of semantic data model features which enhance expressive power but have not been directly addressed by previous performance analyses. Some of the features that we expect to cause difficulties include:

- an *isA* hierarchy, which skews the distribution of entities among classes, especially in the presence of multiple inheritance (where a class has more than one immediate superclass) making it harder to estimate class cardinalities.

- the referential integrity constraint, which induces additional hidden cost factors, such as the maintenance of back pointers, which must be considered in the computational model and explained to designers.

- communication and synchronisation between scripts, which due to their long term nature cannot be modelled in the same way as operating systems processes [Butler, 1987].

In order to analyse the performance of a Taxis system, we need a workload characterisation. We introduce a set of parameters in section 5.1. We define a computational model for the determination of the workload of the proposed system in section 5.2. In order to parameterise the topology of the schema while minimising the number of parameters in the model, our approach is to restrict the schema to a set of levels, while assuming uniformity of characteristics of classes at each level. Even with this assumption in the performance model, multiple inheritance in the data model complicates matters: it is easy to obtain incorrect load estimates for (iterative) assertion checking, since one cannot "see" the subclasses common to two classes at the same level, resulting in an incorrect count of their common instances.

5.1 Workload Parameters

We require the specification of quantitative aspects of the database entities, and the frequencies of occurrence of different activities [Sevcik, 1981]. Of course, we recognise that the identification of the distribution of values for each attribute, as well as the characterisation of significant correlation among attributes would be very useful [Christodoulakis, 1981], but at this time we leave that for subsequent work.

We start with a parameterisation for Taxis entities and relationships, which has been addressed to a certain extent in [Nixon, 1983] and in [Weddell, 1987]. Following Weddell's model, we consider the variation in cardinalities of class extensions, which is due to the presence of isA hierarchies.

We define the *minimum class* of an entity to be the most specialised class which contains an entity (In Taxis, the minimum class of any entity is unique). In this paper, the *minimum-class cardinality* of a class is the number of entities which have that class as their minimum class, and the *cardinality* of a class is the number of entities which have that class, or one of its specialisations, as their minimum class. Note carefully that for the purposes of this paper, *population* does not have the standard meaning of *cardinality*, but rather a form of cardinality where additional weight is given to entities participating in multiple inheritance; a full definition is given later.

We have the following parameters:

```
L               Levels in the generalisation hierarchy
                Level 1 is the most general level
Count(i)        Number of data classes in each level i
fanUp           The average number of superclasses
                per class.
Vdist           The ratio of number of entities whose minimum
                class is at level (i+1) to that of level i.
                Vdist is assumed to be constant for all i.
N               Total number of data entities
```

Next, we introduce a set of parameters for the behaviour of assertions. To make the modelling process easier, we assume that the cost of checking a set of assertions is independent of the location of the attributes involved, and we allow inter-class assertions only at the same level of generalisation. With these simplifications, one can estimate average values of the distribution of assertions by level, thus simplifying the parameterisation of iterative assertion checking. Optimisation techniques used by the assertion processor minimise the occurrence of those iterations; in order to analyse the remaining iterations, our model must take into account the following abstract parameters [Albano, 1985c].

```
Count AA(i)      Number of intra-class assertions plus
                     temporal assertions at each level i
Count AR(i)      Number of inter-class assertions at each
                     level i
pi               Probability that an inter-class assertion
                     requires iteration
ci               Fraction of the population in the class
                     retrieved in an iteration
```

We identify three types of transactions, each of which can involve precisely one of the four primitive data manipulation operations (insertion, deletion, query, update).

```
Type I       Access an entity by an attribute value and
                 update one attribute.
                 E.g., change the address of an employee.
Type II      Iterate over all the members of a class and update one
                 attribute. E.g., increase by 10% the salaries of the
                 the clerical staff.
Type III     Iterate over a class through a relationship with
                 another class and update one attribute E.g., increase
                 by 10% the salaries of the clerical staff members
                 assigned to the sales dept.
```

We are interested in the frequency of execution of these types of transactions, and introduce the following parameters for the distribution of user-specified data management operations:

```
pInsert    Probability of insertion
pDelete    Probability of deletion
pUpdate    Probability of update
pQuery     Probability of query
```

In our simplified example, we assume that there is only one kind of script in the model, as in the figure. A simple loop was chosen to reflect the "unrolled" execution of more complicated scripts. In the following, "complete one cycle" means a script instance that traverses each of the states in the loop once.

We introduce the following parameters:

```
T            Total number of transitions in the schema
AA           Average number of assertions per state
AC           Average number of conditions per transition
AT           Average number of transaction calls per transition
P            Average time to complete one cycle through
                 the given script
F            Average number of script instances which complete
                 a cycle in time P
TT(j)        Distribution of the three transaction types
```

Let us work out an example with our sample script and the following parameter values:

```
L           = 3        CountAA(i)= 3,5,7      pInsert    = 0.15
Count(i)    = 3,5,7    CountAR(i)= 1,2,4      pDelete    = 0.05
fanUp       = 1.66     pi        = 0.1        pUpdate    = 0.3
Vdist       = 2        ci        = 0.1        pQuery     = 0.5
N           = 1000
```

```
T        = 5        TT(I)    = 0.8
AA       = 2        TT(II)   = 0.15
AC       = 2        TT(III)  = 0.05
AT       = 5
P        = 1
F        = 1000
```

5.2   Workload Model

In order to obtain some acquaintance with what resources we need to handle for an application, we now discuss a small workload model that would provide the number of I/O operations we can expect, and also some idea about the computational demands.

To keep the model simple we need some assumptions: first, we organise the schema in terms of levels, on which the classes are interrelated by assertions only at the same level, and population grows as a particular function (defined below) of hierarchy level; second, at each level, the average fanUp per class is uniformly distributed; third, at each level, not only the population but also intra-class assertions and inter-class assertions are uniformly distributed among classes; fourth, the transactions are shared between the classes in proportion to the population at each level.

We need to distribute the number of data entities by level, based on the assumption that **Vdist** is constant for all levels, to obtain **NL(i)**, the aggregate of the minimum-class cardinalies of the classes at level i.

NL(i) = NL(i-1) * Vdist

$\sum_i$**NL(i) = N**

The **fanUp** parameter captures the existence of multiple inheritance; thus, on average each class can have **fanUp** superclasses. We then combine **fanUp** with the minimum-class cardinalities to obtain (an algorithm for computing) *population*, an indication of cardinality distribution, which is used to solve the multiple inheritance problem mentioned earlier in the paper, by measuring how many entities are involved in checking an assertion on a class at a given level.

```
Population(L) := NL(L)
SNL := NL(L)
for i := (L-1) downTo 1 do
        Population(i) := NL(i) + (SNL * fanUp)
        SNL := SNL + NL(i)
end for
```

Note that Population(i) $\geq$ NL(i). The populations for our three-level example are:

Level i	NL(i)	Population(i)	Population per class i
1	143	1565	521
2	286	1233	246
3	571	571	81

Population by Level.

Also important is the enforcement of inherited assertions. Assertions defined on the upper levels must be inherited by the lower levels. Therefore in our model we need to add to the lower levels the assertions declared in the upper levels.

Level i	IntraClass Assertions At Level (i)			InterClass Assertions At Level (i)		
	defined	inherited	total	defined	inherited	total
1	3	–	3	1	–	1
2	5	3	8	2	1	3
3	7	8	15	4	3	7

Number of Assertions by Level.

We now obtain the average number of assertions per class by dividing the total number of assertions by the number of classes at each level:

level	assertion	
	IntraClass	InterClass
1	3/3	1/3
2	8/5	3/5
3	15/7	7/7

Average Number of Assertions per Class.

The total number of operations in the system is calculated from the abstract parameters. The number of transactions in the system is NTS, and the number of conditions to be fired by scripts is NFS:

```
NTS = T * AT * F       = 5 * 5 * 1000     = 25 000

NCF = T * (AA + AC) * F = 5 * (2 + 2) * 1000 = 20 000
```

We share the number of transactions in the system as previously stated in the fourth assumption in terms of the population per level and the distribution of transaction types to obtain LSTL(j,i), the Load Shared by Transaction Type j and Level i:

level i	type of transaction j		
	I	II	III
1	9200	1725	575
2	7400	1387	462
3	3400	638	213

Untransformed load matrix: Load shared by transaction type and schema level.

The share of this load by type of transaction and by level in the schema gives a clear idea of what our workload is in terms of direct requests. In order to obtain the workload generated by the assertion mechanism, we first need to transform the load matrix into terms of single data management operations. First assume that the relative I/O weight factors for database I/O access are:

`query=1, delete=2, insert=2, update=3`

From the definition of each type of transaction we see that a transaction of type I requires one basic operation to the database; one operation of type II requires iteration over a fraction c_i of the class population, and one type III operation requires two times the number of basic operations that a type II operation does. We then have:

```
Data management operations at level (i)
= LSTL(I,i) + (LSTL(II,i) * ci * populationPerClass(i))
  + (LSTL(III,i) * ci * Pc(i) * 2)

E.g., data management operations at level(1)
= 9 200 + (1 725 * 0.1 * 521)
  + (575 * 0.1 * 521 * 2)
= 158 990
```

Since each insertion and each update causes one assertion to be checked, we can calculate how many assertions we need to check, by means of the parameters pInsert and pUpdate. Each intra-class assertion requires one data manipulation operation, and each inter-class assertion requires iteration over the class with probability pi and iterates over a fraction ci of the class.

```
Workload due to assertions:
    IntraClass load (i) = (pInsert + pUpdate) * intraClassAssertionsAtLevel(i)

    InterClass load (i) = (pInsert + pUpdate) * interClassAssertionsAtLevel(i) *
                 (1  +  pi * ci * populationPerClass(i))
```

kind of	level			total load	relative I/O	total load
operation	1	2	3	by operation	weight factor	in I/O units
USER-REQUESTED DATA MANAGEMENT OPERATIONS:						
insert	23 849	9 638	1 803	35 290	2	70 580
update	47 697	19 275	3 605	70 577	3	211 731
Subtotal: insert + update	71 546	28 913	5 408			
delete	7 950	3 213	601	11 764	2	23 528
query	79 495	32 125	6 009	117 629	1	117 629
DATA MANAGEMENT OPERATIONS INDUCED BY ASSERTION CHECKER:						
for intraClass assertions	71 546	46 261	11 573	129 380	1	129 380
for interClass assertions	146 619	60 023	9 788	216 430	1	216 430
conditions				20 000	1	20 000
				TOTAL I/O LOAD		789 278

The distribution of data management operations by level and type.

As the reader can see, in our example only about half of the total I/O load is due to direct user requests; the other half is data management requested by the assertion checker. This convinces us all-the-more of the need for adequately optimised assertion enforcement mechanisms.

6 Conclusions

We see this work as part of the study of the effects on performance of increasing the expressive power of semantic data models by relaxing restrictions on their assertion languages. The general aim of our approach in the Taxis project has been to allow as much expressive power as possible while achieving reasonable performance characteristics. With this aim in mind, we have discussed the management of scripts used for modelling long-term events, and the enforcement of assertions used for modelling semantic integrity constraints. In order to strike a balance between expressive power and performance characteristics, we have imposed a set of restrictions on the language on one hand, and incorporated a variety of optimisation techniques on the other. By observing the similarity between the detection of assertion failures and the detection of activation condition satisfaction for transitions, a common mechanism, namely a trigger mechanism, has been proposed for the implementation of both assertions and scripts. Our performance analysis quantifies the high cost of management of long-term processes and enforcement of semantic integrity constraints, and shows the results of the optimisation strategies.

As for future work, a compiler to support the two features has to be built as an extension of the compiler described in [Nixon, 1987] which has been implemented. Currently, a partial implementation of a compiler for scripts exists in the form of a parser and a portion of a semantic analyser. Once the compiler is built, it has to be tested in order to prove that its performance characteristics, in fact, abide by the analytical results presented in the paper. In addition, we would like to relax the homogeneity assumptions about the schema in order to handle more general data models. For example, we would like to handle more general population distributions and topological configurations. Our long term goal remains the development of a theoretical framework for the implementation of semantic data models.

Acknowledgements

We acknowledge the contributions of Sun Park in the implementation design, and thank Ken Sevcik and Manolis Koubarakis for their advice. We have had many helpful discussions with David Lauzon and other members of the Taxis project. Marina Haloulos helped prepare the diagrams. This project has been supported by a three-year Strategic Grant from the Natural Sciences and Engineering Research Council of Canada.

Bibliography

[Albano, 1985a] Antonio Albano, Luca Cardelli and Renzo Orsini, Galileo: A Strongly Typed, Interactive Conceptual Language. *ACM TODS*, Vol. 10, No. 2, Aug. 1985

[Albano, 1985b] Antonio Albano, Conceptual Languages: A Comparison of ADAPLEX, Galileo and Taxis. *Proceedings of the Workshop on Knowledge Base Management Systems*, Crete, June 1985, pp. 343–356.

[Albano, 1985c] A. Albano, V. De Antonellis and A. Di Leva, Computer-Aided Database Design: The DATAID Approach. In A. Albano and V. Antonellis (editors), *Computer-Aided Database Design: The DATAID Project*. Amsterdam: North-Holland, 1986, pp. 1–13.

[Astrahan, 1976] M. M. Astrahan, M. W. Blasgen, D. D. Chamberlin, K. P. Eswaran, J. N. Gray, P. P. Griffiths, W. F. King, R. A. Lorie, P. R. McJones, J. W. Mehl, G. R. Putzolu, I. L. Traiger, B. W. Wade and V. Watson, System R: Relational Approach to Database Management. *ACM TODS*, Vol. 1, No. 2, June 1976, pp. 97–137.

[Barron, 1982] John Barron, Dialogue and Process Design for Interactive Information Systems Using Taxis. *Proceedings, SIGOA Conference on Office Information Systems*, Philadelphia, PA, 21–23 June 1982, *SIGOA Newsletter*, Vol. 3, Nos. 1 and 2, pp. 12–20.

[Bernstein, 1980] Philip A. Bernstein, Barbara T. Blaustein and Edmund M. Clarke, Fast Maintenance of Semantic Integrity Assertions using Redundant Aggregate Data. *Sixth International Conference on Very Large Data Bases, Proceedings*, Montreal, October 1980, pp. 126–136.

[Blaustein, 1981] Barbara T. Blaustein, *Enforcing Database Applications: Techniques and Applications*. TR–21–81, Center for Research in Computing Technology, Aiken Computation Laboratory, Harvard University, Cambridge, Massachusetts, 1981.

[Borgida, 1985] Alexander Borgida, Features of Languages for the Development of Information Systems at the Conceptual Level. *IEEE Software*, Vol. 2, No. 1, January 1985, pp. 63–73.

[Butler, 1987] Margaret H. Butler, Storage Reclamation in Object Oriented Database Systems. In Umeshwar Dayal and Irv Traiger (editors), *Proceedings of ACM SIGMOD 1987 Annual Conference*. San Francisco, CA, May 27–29, 1987, pp. 410–425.

[Chakravarthy, 1984] U. S. Chakravarthy, D. H. Fishman and J. Minker, Semantic Query Optimization in Expert Systems and Database Systems. In Larry Kerschberg (editor), *Expert Database Systems*. Proceedings of the First International Workshop on Expert Database Systems, Kiawah Island, SC, Oct 24–27, 1984, pp. 326–341.

[Chamberlin, 1981] Donald D. Chamberlin, Morton M. Astrahan, Michael W. Blasgen, James N. Gray, W. Frank King, Bruce G. Lindsay, Raymond Lorie, James W. Mehl, Thomas G. Price, Franco Putzolu, Patricia Griffiths Selinger, Mario Schkolnick, Donald R. Slutz, Irving L. Traiger, Bradford W. Wade and Robert A. Yost, A History and Evaluation of System R. *CACM*, Vol. 24, No. 10, Oct. 1981, pp. 632–646.

[Chan, 1982] Arvola Chan, Sy Danberg, Stephen Fox, Wen-Te K. Lin, Anil Nori and Daniel Ries, Storage and Access Structures to Support a Semantic Data Model. *Proceedings, Eighth International Conference on Very Large Data Bases*, Mexico City, Sept. 8–10, 1982, pp. 122–130.

[Chung, 1984] Kyungwha Lawrence Chung, *An Extended Taxis Compiler*. M.Sc. Thesis, Dept. of Computer Science, University of Toronto, January, 1984. Also CSRG Technical Note 37, 1984.

[Christodoulakis, 1981] S. Christodoulakis, *Estimating Selectivities in Data Base Systems*. Ph.D. Thesis, Dept of Computer Science, University of Toronto, 1981. Also Technical Report CSRG-136.

[Eswaran, 1976] K. P. Eswaran, *Specifications, Implementations, and Interactions of a Trigger Subsystem in a Relational Database System*, IBM Research Report RJ1820, San Jose CA, Aug 1976.

[Ferrari, 1983] Domenico Ferrari, *Measurement and Tuning of Computer Systems*. Englewood Cliffs, NJ: Prentice-Hall, 1983.

[Florentin, 1974] J. J. Florentin, Consistency Auditing of Databases. *Computing Journal*, Vol. 17, No. 1, 1974.

[Goldberg, 1983] Adele Goldberg and David Robson, *SMALLTALK-80: The Language and its Implementation*. Reading, MA: Addison Wesley, 1983.

[Hammer, 1975] M. M. Hammer and D. J. McLeod, Semantic Integrity in a Relational Data Base System. *Proceedings of the International Conference on Very Large Data Bases*, Framingham MA, 22–24 Sep. 1975.

[Hammer, 1976] M. M. Hammer and D. J. McLeod, A Framework for Data Base Semantic Integrity. *Proceedings, Second International Conference on Software Engineering* San Francisco, CA, 13–15 Oct. 1976.

[Hammer, 1978] M. M. Hammer and S. K. Sarin, Efficient Monitoring of Database Assertions. *International Conference on Management of Data*, ACM SIGMOD, 1978.

[Hewitt, 1973] C. Hewitt, P. Bishop and R. Steiger, A Universal Modular Actor Formalism for Artificial Intelligence. *Proceedings, International Joint Conference on Artificial Intelligence*, Stanford, CA, 1973.

[Hoare, 1978] C. A. R. Hoare, Communicating Sequential Processes. *CACM*, Vol. 21, No. 8, Aug. 1978, pp. 666–677.

[Hsu, 1985] Arding Hsu and Tomasz Imielinski, Integrity Checking for Multiple Updates (Preliminary Version). *Proceedings of ACM-SIGMOD 1985, International Conference on Management of Data*, Austin, TX, May 1985, pp. 152–168.

[Hull, 1987] Richard Hull and Roger King, Semantic Database Modeling: Survey, Applications, and Research Issues. Manuscript, March 1987.

[Lafue, 1982] G. M. E. Lafue, *Management of Database Semantic Integrity: A Survey*. Draft, Rutgers University, Oct. 1982.

[Liskov, 1979] Barbara H. Liskov and Alan Snyder, Exception Handling in CLU. *IEEE Transactions on Software Engineering*, Vol. SE-5, No. 6, Nov. 1979, pp. 546–558.

[Lochovsky, 1985] Fred Lochovsky (editor), Special Issue on Object-Oriented Systems. *IEEE Database Engineering*, Vol. 8, No. 4, Dec. 1985.

[Melo, 1979] R. N. Melo, Monitoring Integrity Constraints in a Codasyl-like DBMS. *Fifth International Conference on Very Large Data Bases*, 1979.

[Mylopoulos, 1980] John Mylopoulos, Philip A. Bernstein and Harry K. T. Wong, A Language Facility for Designing Database-Intensive Applications. *ACM TODS*, Vol. 5, No. 2, June 1980, pp. 185–207.

[Mylopoulos, 1986] John Mylopoulos, Alex Borgida, Sol Greenspan, Carlo Meghini and Brian Nixon, Knowledge Representation in the Software Development Process: A Case Study. In H. Winter (Ed.), *Artificial Intelligence and Man-Machine Systems*, Lecture Notes in Control and Information Sciences, No. 80. Berlin: Springer-Verlag, 1986, pp. 23–44.

[Nierstrasz, 1987] O. M. Nierstrasz, Hybrid — A Language for Programming with Active Objects. In D. Tsichritzis (editor), *Objects and Things*, Centre Universitaire d'Informatique, Université de Genève, 1987, pp. 15–42

[Nixon, 1983] Brian Andrew Nixon, *A Taxis Compiler*. M.Sc. Thesis, Dept. of Computer Science, University of Toronto, April 1983. Also CSRG Technical Note 33, May 1983.

[Nixon, 1987] Brian Nixon, Lawrence Chung, David Lauzon, Alex Borgida, John Mylopoulos and Martin Stanley, Implementation of a Compiler for a Semantic Data Model: Experiences with Taxis. In Umeshwar Dayal and Irv Traiger (editors), *ACM SIGMOD '87, Proceedings of Association for Computing Machinery Special Interest Group on Management of Data, 1987 Annual Conference*, San Francisco, CA, May 27–29, 1987, pp. 118–131.

[Nixon, forthcoming] Brian A. Nixon, K. Lawrence Chung, David Lauzon, Alex Borgida, John Mylopoulos and Martin Stanley, Design of a Compiler for a Semantic Data Model. In J. W. Schmidt and C. Thanos (editors), *Foundations of Knowledge Base Management*. Springer-Verlag, forthcoming. Also Technical Note CSRI-44, Computer Systems Research Institute, University of Toronto, May 1987.

[O'Brien, 1982] Patrick O'Brien, *Taxied: An Integrated Interactive Design Environment for Taxis*, M.Sc. Thesis, Department of Computer Science, University of Toronto, 1982.

[O'Brien, 1983] Patrick D. O'Brien, An Integrated Interactive Design Environment for Taxis. *Proceedings, SOFTFAIR: A Conference on Software Development Tools, Techniques, and Alternatives*, Arlington, VA, July 25–28, 1983. Silver Spring, MD: IEEE Computer Society Press, 1983, pp. 298–306.

[Park, 1985] Sun G. Park, *TAXIED-e: Automation of Scripts and User Interface in an Integrated Interactive Design Environment for Taxis*. M.Sc. Thesis, Department of Computer Science, University of Toronto, 1985. Also Technical Note CSRI-39, 1985.

[Ribeiro, 1978] J. S. Ribeiro, *A Database Interface to Wand for the Network Alerter Service*. M. Sc. Thesis, Dept. of Decision Sciences, The Wharton School, Univ. of Pennsylvania, PA, Nov. 1978.

[Rios-Zertuche, forthcoming] Daniel Rios-Zertuche, M.Sc. thesis, Dept. of Computer Science, University of Toronto, forthcoming.

[Sarin, 1977] S. K. Sarin, *Automatic Synthesis of Efficient Procedures for Database Integrity Checking*. M. Sc. Thesis, Dept. of Electrical Engineering and Computer Science, Massachusetts Institute of Technology, Sep. 1977.

[Schmidt, 1977] Joachim W. Schmidt, Some High Level Language Constructs for Data of Type Relation. *ACM TODS*, Vol. 2, No. 3, September 1977, pp. 247–261.

[Sevcik, 1981] K. C. Sevcik, Database Performance Prediction using an Analytic Model. *Proceedings, Seventh International Conference on Very Large Data Bases*, Cannes, France, Sept. 1981, pp. 182–189.

[Smith, 1977] John Miles Smith and Diane C. P. Smith, Database Abstractions: Aggregation and Generalization. *ACM TODS*, Vol. 2, No. 2, June 1977, pp. 105–133.

[Smith, 1983] John M. Smith, Stephen A. Fox and Terry Landers, *ADAPLEX: Rationale and Reference Manual*, Technical Report CCA-83-08, Computer Corporation of America, Cambridge, MA, May 1983.

[Stonebraker, 1975] M. Stonebraker, Implementation of Integrity Constraints and Views by Query Modification. *ACM SIGMOD International Conference on the Management of Data, Proceedings*, San Jose CA, 14–16 May 1975.

[Stonebraker, 1986] Michael Stonebraker and Lawrence A. Rowe, The Design of POSTGRES. In Carlo Zaniolo (Ed.), *Proceedings of ACM SIGMOD '86 International Conference on Management of Data*, Washington, DC, May 28–30, 1986, *SIGMOD Record*, Vol. 15, No. 2, June 1986, pp. 340–355.

[Tsichritzis, 1982] D. C. Tsichritzis and F. H. Lochovsky, *Data Models*. Englewood Cliffs, NJ: Prentice-Hall, 1982.

[Tsur, 1984] Shalom Tsur and Carlo Zaniolo, An Implementation of GEM — Supporting a Semantic Data Model on a Relational Back-end. In Beatrice Yormark (editor), *SIGMOD '84 Proceedings*, Boston, MA, June 18–21, 1984, *SIGMOD Record*, Vol. 14, No. 2, pp. 286–295.

[Vilain, 1986] M. Vilain and H. Kautz, Constraint Propagating Algorithms for Temporal Reasoning. *Proceedings, American Association for Artificial Intelligence*, Philadelphia, 1986.

[Wasserman, 1977] Anthony Wasserman, *Procedure-Oriented Exception Handling*. Technical Report 27, Medical Information Science, University of California, San Francisco, Feb. 1977.

[Weddell, 1987] Grant E. Weddell, *Physical Design and Query Compilation for a Semantic Data Model (assuming memory residence)*. Ph.D. Thesis, Dept. of Computer Science, University of Toronto, 1987.

[Wong, 1981] Harry K. T. Wong, *Design and Verification of Interactive Information Systems Using TAXIS*. Technical Report CSRG-129, Computer Systems Research Group, University of Toronto, April 1981. Also Ph.D. Thesis, Department of Computer Science, 1983.

[Zaniolo, 1983] C. Zaniolo, The Database Language GEM. *Proceedings, 1983 ACM SIGMOD Conference on Management of Data*, May 1983, pp. 207–218.

[Zisman, 1978] Michael D. Zisman, Use of Production Systems for Modeling Concurrent Processes. In D. A. Waterman and Frederick Hayes-Roth (Eds.), *Pattern-Directed Inference Systems*. New York: Academic Press, 1978, pp. 53–68.

A Uniform Approach to Constraint Satisfaction and Constraint Satisfiability in Deductive Databases

François Bry, Hendrik Decker and Rainer Manthey
ECRC, Arabellastr. 17, D - 8000 München 81, West Germany

ABSTRACT   *Integrity maintenance methods have been defined for preventing updates from violating integrity constraints. Depending on the update, the full check for constraint satisfaction is reduced to checking certain instances of some relevant constraints only. In the first part of the paper new ideas are proposed for enhancing the efficiency of such a method. The second part is devoted to checking constraint satisfiability, i.e., whether a database exists in which all constraints are simultaneously satisfied. A satisfiability checking method is presented that employs integrity maintenance techniques. Simple Prolog programs are given that serve both as specifications as well as a basis for an efficient implementation.*

1. Introduction

Integrity maintenance methods are intended to guarantee that all integrity constraints remain satisfied after an update, provided they have been satisfied before. In general, not all constraints are relevant to an update but only certain instances of some of them. This depends on which relations are updated. It is sufficient to check whether relevant instances are satisfied in order to guarantee satisfaction of the full constraint set after the update. Since this basic principle for efficient constraint checking was first described in [NICO 79] and [BLAU 81], several authors have proposed extensions for the deductive case, e.g., [DECK 86], [LLOY 86], [KOWA 87] and [LING 87]. In the first part of this paper we present a method that is based on principles common to all proposals mentioned, but introduces several new ideas. We propose to perform the computation of relevant constraint instances independently from any access to the fact base. Fact access is entirely delayed to the evaluation phase and may thus benefit from optimization steps performed during query evaluation. Furthermore we propose to simulate evaluation of constraints over the updated database by means of a simple meta-interpreter. This approach permits to handle recursive rules, provided the database query-answering system has this capacity (e.g., [VIEI 87]).

Apart from preventing constraint violations caused by fact or rule updates, one has to detect inconsistencies when updating the constraint set as well. If a newly introduced constraint is not satisfied in the current database, one can try to enforce it by means of further updates to the factual part of the database. However, any attempt to do so will fail, if the new constraint is not compatible with the already existing ones. Such situations can be characterized by the logical concept of finite satisfiability. A set of formulas is finitely satisfiable if there is at least one finite model that satisfies all formulas in the set. Formulas that are not finitely satisfiable either have no model at all, or all models are infinite and thus not suitable for database purposes. In presence of deduction rules, these logical deficiencies may be due to inherent contradictions between rules and constraints as well. Thus constraint violations observed after a rule update possibly indicate that constraints and rules are no longer finitely satisfiable after the modification.

In contrast to constraint satisfaction which is a decidable property, finite satisfiability of constraints is only semi-decidable, i.e., every algorithm for checking this property may run forever if applied to constraint sets that contain certain "axioms of infinity". In [BRY 86] we have discussed this problem in more detail, and have investigated various possible approaches to it. In this paper we propose a method for checking constraint satisfiability that is closely related to the way constraint satisfaction is handled. The method is based on a proof procedure that we have recently presented to the theorem proving community as well [MANT 87a, MANT 87b]. If applied to a given set of rules and constraints, the method systematically tries to construct a finite set of facts such that all constraints are satisfied in the resulting database. If the procedure succeeds in doing so, a finite model of rules and constraints has been found and finite satisfiability has been demonstrated. The construction process can be viewed as a sequence of successive updates, each of them possibly causing constraint violations that can be efficiently checked by means of the techniques mentioned above. The violated constraint instances determined this way are used for deriving the next updates necessary to enforce the violated instance. Only few authors have till now been concerned with constraint satisfiability. In [KUNG 84] a method is proposed that relies on the same basic principle as ours, but is not complete for finite satisfiability and considerably less efficient. The approach of [LASS 87] is efficiently applicable for propositional rules only.

Besides introducing methods for checking both properties, constraint satisfaction as well as constraint satisfiability, we would like to show that Prolog is a very convenient programming language for the implementation of these methods. We therefore include short Prolog programs in the paper, that on the one hand serve as specifications, on the other hand can be efficiently applied in practice. This is particularly important as several Prolog-DBMS couplings are now available (e.g., [BOCC 86]) that allow to use Prolog for database querying as well.

2. Definitions

A deductive database D consists of three finite sets: a set F of facts, a set R of rules, and a set I of integrity constraints. A fact is a ground atom. A rule is an expression $H \leftarrow B$, where the head H is a positive literal and the body B is a literal or a conjunction of (positive or negative) literals. The only terms occurring in a rule are constants and variables. We assume every rule to be range-restricted, i.e., every variable occurring in H, or in a negative literal in B occurs in a positive literal in B as well.

Constraints are function-free, closed first-order formulas with <u>restricted quantification</u>, i.e., quantified (sub)formulas have one of the forms

$$\exists X_1...X_n [A_1 \wedge ... \wedge A_m \wedge Q]$$
$$\forall X_1...X_n [\neg A_1 \vee ... \vee \neg A_m \vee Q]$$

where $A_1, ..., A_m$ are atoms such that every variable X_i occurs in at least one A_j, and where Q is either **true** or **false**, or some formula in which some or all X_i are free. In the Prolog programs quantified formulas are represented as

```
exists([X1,...,Xn], (A1 and...and Am),Q)
forall([X1,...,Xn], (A1 and...and Am),Q)
```

assuming that and and or have been declared as Prolog infix operators. Furthermore we assume that integrity constraints are expressed in the following normalized form:

- Formulas are rectified, i.e., no two quantifiers in a formula introduce a same variable.
- The scope of each quantifier is reduced as much as possible (miniscope form).
- Implications and equivalences are expressed by means of logical connectives $\wedge$, $\vee$, and $\neg$, and negations occur in front of atoms only (negation normal form).
- $\forall$ is distributed over $\wedge$.

These forms are assumed for obtaining more concise definitions throughout the paper. Negation normal form, e.g., allows to speak directly about complementary literals instead of having to use polarities, and in miniscope form governing relationships between variables and scopes of quantifiers coincide. As far as the expressive power is concerned, neither the restricted quantification form nor the above normalization impose significant restrictions. Note in particular that an expression in relational calculus corresponds to a formula with restricted quantification.

The semantics of integrity constraints - as of queries in general - are defined according to a canonical interpretation in which the true atoms are exactly those that are explicit in F or derivable from F and R. In order to be able to uniquely determine the canonical interpretation, we restrict R to be stratified in the sense of [APT 87]. Constraints are satisfied in D if they are satisfied in the canonical interpretation associated with $F \cup R$.

3. Integrity Maintenance

Let single-fact updates be represented by literals, a positive literal indicating insertion, a negative literal indicating deletion. Throughout this chapter, let U denote a ground single-fact update to a database D and let U(D) denote the updated database.

Definition 1:
If U is a positive literal explicit in D, the <u>updated database</u> U(D) is identical with D. If U is a positive literal not explicit in D, U(D) is D augmented with U.
If U is a negative literal $\neg A$ and if A is explicit in D, then U(D) is D without the fact A. If U is a negative literal $\neg A$ and if A is not explicit in D, then U(D) is identical with D.

The truth value of certain formulas - like, e.g., $\forall X\ p(X)$ or $\exists X\ \neg p(X)$ - depends on the database domain as a whole. Evaluation of such formulas therefore requires that the domain is explicitly stored or computed. This can be extremely inefficient. In order to avoid this problem, the class of <u>domain independent</u> or <u>definite</u> formulas [KUHN 67] has been proposed: A formula C is domain independent if and only if its truth value does not depend on any domain element other than those occurring in the relations that are explicitly mentioned in C. For the efficiency of integrity maintenance methods, it is very desirable that all constraints are domain independent. This permits to evaluate only those constraints in which updated relations occur. Formulas with restricted quantifications are domain independent.

Definition 2:
A constraint C is <u>relevant to an update</u> U iff the complement of U is unifiable with a literal in C.

For constraints with restricted quantifications it is even sufficient to evaluate only certain simplified instances of constraints relevant to an update, in order to prove that these constraints are satisfied in the updated database.

Definition 3:
Let C be an integrity constraint relevant to U. A <u>simplified instance</u> of C is obtained as follows:
Let L denote a literal in C unifiable with the complement of U. Let σ denote a most general unifier (mgu) of L and U, and let τ denote the restriction of σ to those universally quantified variables that are not governed by an existentially quantified variable.
  a. partially instantiate C by applying τ
  b. simplify the partial instance $C\tau$ by
     - dropping quantifiers for variables grounded by τ
     - replacing $L\tau$ by **false**, in case $L\tau$ is identical with the complement of U, and eventually applying absorption laws (like, e.g., $\textbf{false} \vee F \equiv F$)
τ is called the <u>defining substitution</u> of the simplified instance.

Consider the integrity constraint:

$$C_1: \forall X \, [\neg p(X) \lor q(X)]$$

The simplified instance of C_1 associated with the update $p(a)$ is $q(a)$. It is indeed sufficient to evaluate $q(a)$ in order to ensure that C_1 remains satisfied in the updated database. The simplified instance of

$$C_2: \forall XY \, \neg p(X,Y) \lor [\exists Z \, q(X,Z) \land \neg s(Y,Z,a)]$$

associated with the update $\neg q(c_1,c_2)$ is

$$\forall Y \, \neg p(c_1,Y) \lor [\exists Z \, q(c_1,Z) \land \neg s(Y,Z,a)]$$

The defining substitution binds X to c_1. Instances of C_1 binding X to anyother constant are not affected by the considered update. Note that the existentially quantified variable Z must remain unbound in the simplified instance. Several examples are discussed in [NICO 79] in which this technique was first described.

More than one simplified instance can be obtained from a same integrity constraint. This happens when the complement of U is unifiable with more than one literal in the constraint.

3.1. Relational Databases

Integrity maintenance for relational databases (i.e., databases without deduction rules) is based on the following result:

Proposition 1: [NICO 79]
All constraints are satisfied in U(D) iff they are satisfied in D and every simplified instance of a constraint relevant to U is satisfied in U(D).

In Prolog, the integrity maintenance principle stated in this proposition can be easily implemented as follows. Assume constraints to be stored as Prolog facts `integrity_constraint(Id,C,V)`, where C is the constraint, `Id` is its unique identifier and V the list of universally quantified variables in C that are not governed by an existential one. Furthermore assume that for every literal L in a constraint C a fact `relevant(Id,L)` has been precomputed, where `Id` denotes the identifier associated with C. Simplified instances of constraints that are relevant to U can be generated through backtracking by means of:

```
simplified_instance(U,SI)  :-
    relevant(Id,U),
    integrity_constraint(Id,C1,V),
    complement(U,UC)
    instantiate(C1,UC),
    integrity_constraint(Id,C2,V),
    simplify(C2,UC,SI).
```

```
complement(not A,A) :- !.
complement(A, not A).

instantiate(forall(_,F1,F2),UC) :-
    !, (complement(UC,U), instantiate(F1,U) ; instantiate(F2,UC)).
instantiate(exists(_,F1,F2),UC) :-
    !, (instantiate(F1,UC) ; instantiate(F2,UC)).
instantiate(F1 and F2,UC) :-
    !, (instantiate(F1,UC) ; instantiate(F2,UC)).
instantiate(F1 or F2,UC) :-
    !, (instantiate(F1,UC) ; instantiate(F2,UC)).
instantiate(L,L).
```

Code for the predicate `simplify` is not given here because it is simple but unsubstantial. The partial instantiation is obtained as follows: Calling `instantiate(C1,UC)` instantiates all variables of C1, particularly those in V. Since variables in V are bound, the subsequent call `integrity_constraint(Id,C2,V)` returns the desired partial instance C2 respecting the bindings given to V before. The set S of instances to be evaluated over the updated database is obtained by calling `setof(SI,simplified_instance(U,SI),S)`.

3.2. Deductive Databases: Principles

In presence of deduction rules, an explicit update may induce further logical changes of the database. Induced updates correspond to facts that are either true after the update but not before, or false after the update but true before. They can be characterized as follows:

Definition 4:

Let L denote a ground literal and A a ground atom.
A ($\neg$A, resp.) is <u>directly induced by</u> L over U(D) iff
- there is a deduction rule A' $\leftarrow$ B such that B contains a literal L' unifiable with L
  (the complement of L, resp.); let τ denote a mgu of L and L'
- A = (A'τ)σ,
  where σ is an answer substitution returned by evaluating (B\L')τ in U(D)
  (B\L' denotes B without L', **true** if B = L')
- A ($\neg$A, resp.) evaluates to false (true, resp.) in D (in U(D), resp.)

A literal is <u>induced by</u> L over U(D) iff it is directly induced by L over U(D) or by a literal induced by L over U(D). Every literal induced by U over U(D) is an <u>update induced by</u> U.

Proposition 1 can be extended to deductive databases by considering all constraints relevant to induced updates too:

Proposition 2:

All constraints are satisfied in U(D) iff they are satisfied in D and every simplified instance of a constraint relevant to U or relevant to an update induced by U is satisfied in U(D).

[**Proof:** (sketched) The property follows easily from Proposition 1 by reduction to the relational case. Consider the canonical interpretation of D as a relational database. Treat the induced updates as explicit updates to this database.]

If integrity maintenance is straightforwardly performed according to Proposition 2 the following would be done: Induced updates are successively computed. As soon as a constraint is relevant to such an update, the corresponding simplified instance is evaluated in the updated database. The methods described in [DECK 86] and [KOWA 87] are of this kind. This approach suffers from two drawbacks. First, all induced updates are computed, even those for which no constraint is relevant. This is for example the case with an update $p(a,b)$ in presence of the deduction rule $r(X) \leftarrow q(X,Y) \wedge p(Y,Z)$ if the predicate r does not occur positively in any constraint. The overhead is considerable if there are a lot of $q(X,a)$-facts. Second, evaluating all simplified instances independently of each other prevents from applying certain optimizations that a global evaluation would permit. Especially the detection of redundant subqueries can be very useful in this context. Consider for example the following constraint:

$$C_1: \forall X \; [\neg student(X) \vee \neg enrolled(X,cs) \vee attends(X,ddb)]$$

Assume that there is a deduction rule $enrolled(X,cs) \leftarrow student(X)$ expressing that all students are enrolled in computer science. The update $student(jack)$ yields the following simplified instance

$$S_1: \neg enrolled(jack,cs) \vee attends(jack,ddb)$$

The induced update $enrolled(jack,cs)$ leads to a simplified instance

$$S_2: \neg student(jack) \vee attends(jack,ddb)$$

Evaluating S_1 and S_2 independently requires to evaluate the subquery $attends(jack,ddb)$ twice. A global evaluation, however, could be expected to avoid this redundancy when simultaneously evaluating both instances. Such redundancies, although a bit artificial in this simple example, appear rather frequently in case of transactions consisting of more than one single-fact update.

Instead of applying Proposition 2 straightforwardly, we propose an alternative approach that does not exhibit the above-mentioned drawbacks. This approach does not interleave generation of induced updates and evaluation of simplified instances, but clearly separates two phases: a preparatory one, that does not access the base of facts, and a pure evaluation phase. In the first phase, potential updates are computed, that represent possible ground induced updates. From potential updates and constraints, expressions called update constraints are generated. In a second stage, all update constraints are evaluated. Facts are accessed only during evaluation.

Definition 5:

Let L be a literal and A an atom (both not necessarily ground).

A ($\neg$A, resp.) <u>directly depends on</u> L iff

- there is a deduction rule A' $\leftarrow$ B such that B contains a literal L' unifiable with L (the complement of L, resp.)
- A = A'τ, where τ is a mgu of L' and L (the complement of L, resp.)

A <u>depends on</u> L if and only if A directly depends on L or on a literal that depends on L. Every literal which depends on U is a <u>potential update induced by</u> U.

Every induced update is an instance of a potential update, depending on the facts stored in the database. If for example the database contains a deduction rule r(X) $\leftarrow$ p(X,Y)$\wedge$q(Y,Z) then r(X) ($\neg$r(X), resp.) is a potential update induced by q(a,b) ($\neg$q(a,b), resp.). Note that potential updates are defined without considering any answer substitution, as opposed to induced updates. There may be potential updates no instance of which is an induced update.

Let 'delta' denote a meta-predicate such that delta(U,L) holds if and only if L is satisfied in U(D), but not in D. Similarly, let new(U,F) denote the evaluation of the formula F over the updated database U(D).

Definition 6:

For every constraint C relevant to a literal L the universal closure of the formula $\neg$delta(U,Lτ)$\vee$new(U,s(C)) is an <u>update constraint for</u> L, where s(C) denotes a simplified instance of C wrt L with defining substitution τ.

Update constraints can be used for integrity maintenance on the basis of the following result:

Proposition 3:

All constraints are satisfied in U(D) iff they are satisfied in D and every update constraint for U or for a potential update induced by U is satisfied in U(D).

[**Proof:** (sketched) By Definitions 3 and 4, all induced updates are instances of potential induced updates. From this remark and from the definition of update constraints, it follows that a simplified instance of a constraint relevant to an induced update is necessarily the right hand side of an instance of an update constraint, the left hand side of which is an induced update. The proposition follows.]

A concept similar to that of a potential update can be found in [LLOY 86]. However, the method proposed in that article does not distinguish between 'new' and 'delta'. Instead of evaluating expressions of the form $\neg$delta(U,L) $\vee$ new(U,s(C)), they evaluate formulas corresponding to $\neg$new(U,L) $\vee$ new(U,s(C)), in our terminology. The resulting loss in efficiency is often considerable. The method described here for single-fact updates has been defined for more general updates, such as transactions and conditional updates [BRY 87]. Rule updates can be treated like conditional updates. However, when defining induced or potential updates one has to respect modifications to the rule set as well.

3.3. Deductive Databases: Implementation

3.3.1. *Computation of update constraints*

According to Definition 5, assume that for every deduction rule A ← B and every literal L in B the facts directly_dependent (L, A, R) and directly_dependent (LC, not A, R) have been computed, where LC is the complement of L and R denotes B\L. The 'dependent' relationship between literals can be represented in terms of directly_dependent through

```
dependent(L,U)  :-
   directly_dependent(L,U,_).
dependent(L,U)  :-
   directly_dependent(L,L1,_), dependent(L1,U).
```

The set P of potential updates induced by U is obtained by calling:

```
setof(L,dependent(L,U),P)
```

In order to stop the generation of potential updates in presence of recursive rules, it is necessary to discard subsumed literals while constructing the set. If the rules are not recursive, this subsumption test is desirable for avoiding redundancies. For every simplified instance SI of C wrt L a Prolog fact update_constraint (L1, (not delta (U, L1) or new (U, SI))) can be computed by backtracking over

```
relevant(Id,L),
simplified_instance(L,SI),
assert(update_constraint(L,(not delta(U,L) or new(U,SI))))
```

The set S of queries to be evaluated on the updated database is now obtained by calling:

```
setof(UC,(update_constraint(U,UC);
          dependent(L,U),update_constraint(L,UC)),S)
```

Since it can be determined without querying the facts, this set can be precompiled as well.

3.3.2. *Simulation of the updated state*

Assume that deduction rules H ← B are stored as meta-facts rule (H<-B). Let the predicate evaluate represent a call to the database query evaluator. Assume in addition that explicitly stored facts can be accessed by means of a predicate explicit. The meta-predicate 'new' permitting to simulate the evaluation of formulas in the updated database before the update is actually performed can be implemented as follows:

```
new(U,true).
new(U,not A)  :-
   !, not new(U,A).
new(U,A and B)  :-
   !, new(U,A), new(U,B).
new(U,A)  :-
   U = not V, !,
   (explicit(A), not (A = V)
          ; rule(A<-B), new(U,B)).
new(U,A)  :-
   not (U = not V), !,
   (explicit(A) ; A = U
          ; rule(A<-B), new(U,B)).
```

Simulating the updated database with new does not require any specific query evaluator. Although new occurs in bodies of clauses defining it, it is worth noting that new is not recursive as long as no deduction rules of the database are recursive. This applies as well to the procedure delta defined below. In presence of recursive rules it is necessary to dispose of a query evaluator able to handle recursion in order to correctly evaluate new and delta. The other solutions proposed in the literature either require the implementation of an additional query evaluator [KOWA 87], or do not handle recursion [LING 87].

3.3.3. Implementation of 'delta'

By definition, delta(U,F) could be implemented by new(U,F), evaluate(not F). However, this direct implementation would in general be extremely inefficient. It would evaluate formulas not relevant to an update twice, once through the meta-predicate 'new', once in the non-updated database. As opposed to that, the following implementation of 'delta' that closely follows Definition 4 exploits that any induced update is necessarily a descendent of the update literal.

```
delta(U,U)  :-
   U = not A,
   not evaluate(U), new(U,U).
delta(U,U)  :-
   not (U = not A),
   not evaluate(U).
delta(U,A)  :-
   A = not B,
   directly_dependent(L,A,R), delta(U,L), new(U,R),
   not evaluate(A), new(U,A).
delta(U,A)  :-
   not (A = not B),
   directly_dependent(L,A,R), delta(U,L), new(U,R),
   not evaluate(A).
```

Instead of completely interpreting every delta-expression inside an update constraint, one can as well imagine various degrees of precompilation or macro expansion of delta-calls. This would result in replacing certain delta-expressions by an expression that consists of calls to new and evaluate.

We point out that it is not necessary to dispose of a coupling between Prolog and the DBMS in order to generate update constraints. The respective program refers to rules, constraints and to the update only, but not to facts. As opposed, the procedures new and delta call the database query-evaluator. Provided the DBMS is efficiently coupled with Prolog, e.g. [BOCC 86], this approach permits to rely on the database query-evaluator.

4. Checking constraint satisfiability

In this chapter we will outline a procedure that, if applied to a set of constraints and rules, systematically attempts to construct a finite set of facts such that all constraints are satisfied in the resulting "database". This sample database is temporary and independent from the set of facts held on secondary storage. The procedure is complete for finite satisfiability as well as for unsatisfiability. If the procedure terminates successfully, finite satisfiability of rules and constraints has been shown, whereas failure indicates unsatisfiability. In case all models of the constraints and rules under consideration are infinite the construction process will not terminate. Because of the semi-decidability of both properties, such cases cannot be avoided. The procedure is based on two main principles:

1. enforcement of violated constraints by means of fact insertions into the sample database so far constructed

2. determination of constraints violated by an insertion by means of techniques introduced in the previous chapter

Initially, the set of facts to be constructed is empty. It is well possible that all constraints are already satisfied in a database without facts. This is the case iff each constraint is a universal formula, i.e., its outermost quantifier is $\forall$. Because of restricted quantification and due to the assumption that $\forall$ has been distributed over $\wedge$, every instance of a universal formula is a disjunction, at least one component of which is a negative literal. In an empty database all negative facts are true, and thus every universal formula is satisfied. This situation arises, e.g., when all constraints are functional or multi-valued dependencies.

The remaining constraints, which are not satisfied in a database without facts, are determined and successively enforced by addition of new facts. Every enforcement step can be viewed as an update in the sense of the previous chapter. Constraint violations caused by these updates can be determined according to the principles discussed and have to be enforced accordingly. Thus integrity checking and database update steps alternate until finally either all constraints are satisfied, or every possible enforcement alternative has led to constraint violations from which no recovery is possible.

As the sample database which is tentatively constructed is comparatively small, it should completely reside in main memory. It is not necessary to take care of separating fact access and update constraint determination as proposed for big secondary storage databases. Thus constraint violations can be determined on the basis of Proposition 2, i.e., by using simplified instances of constraints relevant to actually induced updates instead of potential updates.

Enforcement of violated constraint instances can be achieved by constructively exploiting the inductive definition of the semantics of first-order formulas relative to some interpretation (uniquely represented by a set of positive facts F). In order to satisfy a formula C that is violated in F, do the following:

- if C is a conjunction (disjunction), satisfy all (one of) its immediate subformulas
- if C is $\forall X_1...X_n [\neg R \vee Q]$
  ($\neg R$ representing the disjunction of negative literals that restricts $X_1...X_n$) satisfy each instance $Q\sigma$ such that $R\sigma$ is satisfied in F
- if C is $\exists X_1...X_n [R \wedge Q]$,
  either satisfy at least one $Q\sigma$ such that $R\sigma$ is satisfied in F, or satisfy $[R \wedge Q]\tau$ where τ instantiates each X_i with a new constant not yet occurring in F
- if C is a positive literal, add C to F

Negative literals that are complementary to a fact in F cannot be satisfied without undoing choices made previously.

For completeness reasons we have to assume that for every rule with negative literals in its body an additional constraint has been introduced: For every rule

$$H \leftarrow A_1, ..., A_n \wedge \neg B_1 \wedge ... \wedge \neg B_m$$

involving free variables $X_1, ..., X_k$ a constraint

$$\forall X_1...X_k [\neg A_1 \vee ... \vee \neg A_n \vee B_1 \vee ... \vee B_m \vee H]$$

has to be added. Without this addition certain alternatives that exist for reaching a finite model of the constraint set would never be exploited.

The principle of constructively interpreting the inductive definition of formula semantics is by no means new. It has been proposed independently by several logicians in the early days of automated theorem proving. Their approach has become known as the tableaux method, which has extensively been documented in [SMUL 68]. Our method differs from the original tableaux approach in three points:

1. Instead of fully instantiating universal formulas over the whole domain, we exploit the domain independent-property of restricted quantification that permits to consider only those instantiations that are obtained through evaluation of the restricting literals.

2. In case of existential formulas, the tableaux method considers a single instance only, namely the one obtained through replacing every variable by a newly introduced constant. Consequently, the tableaux method is not complete for finite satisfiability. Only if alternatively the instances obtained through evaluation of the restricting literals are considered too, one can always guarantee that the method stops if finite models exist.

3. Our choice to determine constraints that have to be enforced next in dependence on the most recently introduced facts can be viewed as a special search strategy inside the tableaux approach which may considerably reduce its search space.

While points 1 and 3 are substantial optimizations of the tableaux method, point 2 is an extension of it. This extension is indispensable in the database context, but also leads to a more satisfactory termination behaviour in a theorem proving context. This additional capability has its price: If several constants have to be considered for replacing existential variable, the required case analysis might be fairly expensive. Exploiting domain independence - a property the relevance of which has first been recognized in the database area - can be related to tendencies in theorem proving to exploit typed logic. However, domain independent formulas, especially those with restricted quantification, are less restrictive than the requirement for full typing.

An advantage of our approach is its close affinity to Prolog. Like for integrity maintenance, we give the basic code for a Prolog implementation making use of predicates introduced in the previous chapter. Note that the predicate violated implements the determination of violated constraints wrt to an update according to Proposition 2. The predicate new_constants is assumed to bind each element in a list of variables to a newly generated constant. Fact insertion is implemented through assertions to the Prolog main memory database. Evaluation of constraints is assumed to be done by Prolog. The predicate assume performs these assertions and automatically undoes them when backtracking to a previous choice point.

Like in the tableaux method, one has to organize the generation of new facts in a level-saturation manner. All constraints violated by the most recent update to the sample database are determined before any further updates are initiated. Such an organization is necessary in order to avoid cases where the database under construction is infinitely extended simply because certain constraints that would allow to stop the generation process are never considered. The parameter I attached to most of the Prolog predicates given below indicates the respective generation levels.

```
satisfiable :-
    setof(C, (integrity_constraint(_,C,_), not C),S),
    (S = [] ; enforce_set(0,S),
              satisfiable(1)).


satisfiable(I) :-
    I1 is I - 1,
    setof(C, (generated(I1,A), is_violated(A,C)),S),
    (S = [] ; enforce_set(I,S),
              I2 is I + 1,
              satisfiable(I2)).

is_violated(A,C) :-
    (simplified_instance(A,C) ; delta(A,L), simplified_instance(L,C)),
    not C.


enforce_set(_,[]).
enforce_set(I,[H|T]) :-
    H, !, enforce_set(I,T).
enforce_set(I,[H|T]) :-
    enforce(I,H), enforce_set(I,T).
```

```
enforce(_,true) :- !.
enforce(_,false) :-
   !, fail.
enforce(_,not A) :-
   !, fail.
enforce(I,A and B) :-
   !, enforce(I,A), enforce(I,B).
enforce(I,A or B) :-
   !, (enforce(I,A) ; enforce(I,B)).
enforce(I,exists(Vars,R,Q)) :-
   R, enforce(I,Q).
enforce(I,exists(Vars,R,Q)) :-
   !, new_constants(Vars), enforce(I,R and Q).
enforce(I,forall(Vars,R,Q)) :-
   !, setof(Q,(R and not Q),S), enforce_set(I,S).
enforce(I,A) :-
   assume(A), assume(generated(I,A)).


assume(X) :- assert(X).
assume(X) :- retract(X), !, fail.
```

5. An Example

In this chapter we discuss how satisfiability would be checked by our method if applied to the following example set of rules and constraints:

Rules:
    member(X,Y) ← leads(X,Y)

Constraints:
   (1) $\forall X$ [$\neg$employee(X)$\lor\exists Y$ (department(Y) and member(X,Y))]
   (2) $\forall X$ [$\neg$department(X)$\lor\exists Y$ (employee(Y)$\land$leads(Y,X))]
   (3) $\forall XY$ [$\neg$member(X,Y)$\lor\forall Z$ ($\neg$leads(Z,Y)$\lor$subordinate(X,Z))]
   (4) $\forall X \neg$subordinate(X,X)
   (5) $\exists X$ employee(X)

This example serves at the same time as an explanation of integrity maintenance techniques as described in chapter 3.

Level 0: Initially, only constraint (5) is violated. It is enforced by generating a new constant 'a' and asserting

employee(a)

Level 1: The only constraint violated by this insertion is (1). Enforce its simplified instance $\exists Y$ [department(Y)$\land$member(a,Y)] by generating a new constant 'b' and asserting

department(b)

member(a,b)

Level 2: Insertion of department(b) violates constraint (2); the simplified instance to be enforced is ∃Y [employee(Y)∧leads(Y,b)]. There are two alternative ways how to enforce it:

1st alternative: Evaluate the restricting literal employee(Y) over the available facts. Enforce the resulting instance by asserting

$$leads(a,b)$$

Level 3: Constraint (3) is relevant to this insertion, but two simplified instances of it have to be considered:

$$∀X [¬member(X,b) ∨ subordinate(X,a)]$$
$$∀Z [¬leads(Z,b) ∨ subordinate(a,Z)]$$

the latter because of the induced update member(a,b). Enforcement of both requires to insert

$$subordinate(a,a)$$

which directly contradicts constraint (4). No recovery is possible! Backtrack to the last choice point inside level 2 and retract leads(a,b) and subordinate(a,a) on the way back.

2nd alternative: Generate a new constant 'c' and insert

$$employee(c)$$
$$leads(c,b)$$

Level 3: The only simplified instance of constraint (1) that is relevant to employee(c) is ∃Y [department(Y)∧member(c,Y)]. This instance is satisfied because member(c,b) is derivable from leads(c,b). Insertion of leads(c,b) results in two violated instances like in the first subcase. Both can be enforced by insertion of

$$subordinate(c,c)$$

only, which again is contradictory to constraint (4). No choice remains. On backtracking all facts are retracted and the procedure fails.

The example set has been shown to be unsatisfiable. Finite satisfiability could be achieved by, e.g., transforming constraint (3) into ∀XY [¬member(X,Y)∨leads(X,Y)∨∀Z (...)].

6. Conclusion

An integrity maintenance method and a procedure for checking constraint satisfiability have been proposed. Prolog implementations of both methods have been described.

Our approach to integrity maintenance permits to do more at compile time than other proposals in the literature. Two successive phases, a preparatory one - that does not access the base of facts - and a purely evaluative one are distinguished. Since the constraints are altogether handed over to the database, evaluation can fully benefit from query optimization techniques. We have proposed a meta-interpreter for simulating query evaluation in the updated database before any update is actually performed. This meta-interpreter can rely on any database query evaluator and handle recursive rules, provided the considered query evaluator has this capacity.

The satisfiability checking method extends an original proof procedure with integrity maintenance techniques. It is complete for unsatisfiability and for finite satisfiability. Besides detecting undesirable situations, such as contradicting rules and constraints, it also permits to recognize the acceptable cases, i.e., rules and constraints which admit a finite model. As far as we know, this is the first time that a practicable procedure is proposed, although the need for such a method has been noticed in the literature. Though remarkably short, the Prolog programs given in this paper are fairly efficient. They appear to be useful in the following respect:

- In Prolog-DBMS couplings:
  Such couplings permit to fully implement the approach described in this paper. In particular, the updated database can be efficiently simulated by means of a meta-interpreter.

- In conventional DBMS:
  Indeed, no coupling with Prolog is needed for the phase without fact access. The meta-interpreter written in Prolog can be used as a specification of an extension to the database query evaluator.

- In Prolog main memory databases:
  Experiments made show that the time saved by the reduction techniques of the integrity maintenance method is significant as soon as base relations contain a few dozen of tuples. Conceivable domains of application are single user databases and expert systems.

Promising efficiency has been observed when testing the satisfiability checking procedure on well-known benchmark examples from the theorem-proving literature. However, this has to be completed with further experiments with deductive database applications. Examples of constraints discussed nowadays in the database literature appear to be very simple with respect to satisfiability checking. As far as integrity maintenance is concerned, further work should be devoted to the constraint evaluation phase. Most of the optimization techniques proposed till now are concerned with conjunctive queries. Since constraints have often a more general syntax, optimization methods for general formulas seem to be desirable.

7. Acknowledgement

We would like to thank Hervé Gallaire and Jean-Marie Nicolas as well as our colleagues at ECRC for providing us with a very stimulating research ambience. The work reported in this article has benefited a lot from it.

8. References

[APT 87] Apt, K.R., Blair, H. and Walker, A.
Towards a theory of declarative knowledge.
In Minker, J. (editor), *Proc. Workshop on Deductive Databases and Logic Programming*. Aug., 1987.

[BLAU 81] Blaustein, B.T.
Enforcing database assertions: Techniques and applications.
PhD thesis, Harvard Univ., 1981.

[BOCC 86] Bocca, J.
On the evaluation strategy of EDUCE.
In *Proc. ACM-SIGMOD Conf. on Management of Data*. May, 1986.

[BRY 86] Bry, F. and Manthey, R.
Checking consistency of database constraints: A logical basis.
In *Proc. 12th VLDB Conf.* Aug., 1986.

[BRY 87] Bry, F.
Maintaining integrity of deductive databases.
Int. Rep. KB-45, ECRC, July, 1987.

[DECK 86] Decker, H.
Integrity enforcement on deductive databases.
In *Proc. 1st Int. Conf. on Expert Database Systems*. Apr., 1986.

[KOWA 87] Kowalski, R., Sadri, F. and Soper, P.
Integrity checking in deductive databases.
In *Proc. 13th VLDB Conf.* Sept., 1987.

[KUHN 67] Kuhns, J.L.
Answering questions by computers - A logical study.
Rand Memo RM 5428 PR, Rand Corp., Santa Monica, Calif., 1967.

[KUNG 84] Kung, C.H.
A temporal framework for information systems specification and verification.
PhD thesis, Univ. of Trondheim, Norway, 1984.

[LASS 87] Lassez, C., McAloon, K. and Port, G.
Stratification and Knowledge Base Management.
In *Proc. 4th Int. Conf. on Logic Programming*. May, 1987.

[LING 87] Ling, T.
Integrity constraint checking in deductive databases using the Prolog not-predicate.
Data & Knowledge Engineering 2, 1987.

[LLOY 86] Lloyd, J.W. and Topor, R.W.
Integrity constraint checking in stratified databases.
Technical Report 86/5, Univ. of Melbourne, May, 1986.

[MANT 87a] Manthey, R. and Bry, F.
A hyperresolution-based proof procedure and its implementation in PROLOG.
In Morik, K. (editor), *Proc. GWAI-87 (German Workshop on Artificial Intelligence)*. Sept., 1987.
Springer Verlag IFB 152.

[MANT 87b] Manthey, R. and Bry, F.
SATCHMO: a theorem prover implemented in Prolog.
Technical Report KB-21, ECRC, Nov., 1987.
(submitted to CADE 88).

[NICO 79]   Nicolas, J.-M.
             Logic for improving integrity checking in relational databases.
             Technical Report, ONERA-CERT, Toulouse, France, Feb., 1979.
             Also in Acta Informatica 18, 3, Dec. 1982.

[SMUL 68]   Smullyan, R.M.
             First-order logic.
             Springer Verlag, 1968.

[VIEI 87]   Vieille, L.
             A database-complete proof procedure based on SLD-resolution.
             In *Proc. 4th Int. Conf. on Logic Programming.* May, 1987.

Geo-Relational Algebra: A Model and Query Language for Geometric Database Systems

Ralf Hartmut Güting

Fachbereich Informatik, Universität Dortmund,
D-4600 Dortmund 50, West Germany

Abstract: *The user's conceptual model of a database system for geometric data should be simple and precise: easy to learn and understand, with clearly defined semantics, expressive: allow to express with ease all desired query and data manipulation tasks, efficiently implementable.*

To achieve these goals we propose to extend relational database management systems by integrating geometry at all levels: At the conceptual level, relational algebra is extended to include geometric data types and operators. At the implementation level, the wealth of algorithms and data structures for geometric problems developed in the past decade in the field of Computational Geometry is exploited. - The paper starts from a view of relational algebra as a many-sorted algebra which allows to easily embed geometric data types and operators. A concrete algebra for two-dimensional applications is developed. It can be used as a highly expressive retrieval and data manipulation language for geometric as well as standard data. Finally, geo-relational database systems and their implementation strategy are discussed.

1. Introduction

In various application areas there is a need to store, retrieve and manipulate data with geometric components, for instance in geographic information systems, VLSI- and CAD-databases, pictorial databases etc. We use the general term *geometric database system* for a database system handling any kind of data with geometric properties. In this paper we address what we believe to be the two main problems in the development of a geometric database system:

1. Design a user model of data, including geometric data, and of data manipulation. Such a model should have the following characteristics:
   - It should be *simple*, so that a user can easily learn and understand it and the consequences of actions can be foreseen.
   - The semantics of the model should be *precisely defined* so that there is no ambiguity for the user or implementor of the model.

- It should be *highly expressive* so that it is easy to perform the desired retrieval and data manipulation tasks.
2. Develop an efficient implementation strategy for the user's conceptual model.

Clearly the two problems are closely connected since it makes little sense to develop a data model for which no efficient implementation exists. - For the processing of "business" or "standard" data the relational model of data and relational database systems as its implementation have provided a very successful solution to these problems. In spite of the apparent diversity and complexity of geometric applications we believe that it is possible to proceed in a similar way for geometric database systems. Our approach consists of two parts:

1. Extend relational algebra by including geometric data types and operators. This is possible in a clean and simple way when relational algebra is viewed as a many-sorted algebra, as proposed in [GüZC87] (see the next section).
2. Implement the extended algebra by integrating geometric algorithms and data structures, as developed in Computational Geometry in the last few years, with the standard relational implementation technology.

In the past, the main approaches to the storage and processing of geometric data can be roughly classified as *dedicated geometric systems, non-relational DBMS front-ends*, and *relational DBMS front-ends and extensions*. Systems of the first class usually keep their data in files in either vector- or raster-based formats; they are geared towards efficiently performing a specific collection of functions or commands. A disadvantage is the lack of any high-level data definition facility. Usually the functions offered can only be used in very specific ways; there is little flexibility to perform actions not previously conceived by the system's designers [ChCK81, NaW79]. In the second class, a geometric database or information system is implemented as an application program on top of an existing DBMS. Systems in practical use are often based on non-relational DBMSs in order to achieve reasonable efficiency [Bu84, Fr81]. The disadvantage is again the lack of flexibility, in particular in an interactive environment.

Significantly, as soon as query languages are considered, applications and extensions of relational systems are prevalent (see [ChF81] for a survey), because of their flexibility. Here the main problem is efficiency. For relational systems, several degrees of integrating geometry can be observed. The most basic approach is to force geometric data into a relational format and then to perform operations on these tables with the usual facilities of the relational DBMS [BeS77]. The next step is to augment the relational query language by specific geometric operators [ChF80] which are implemented in terms of the relational operators. Up to this point, no really efficient DBMS can be expected. Recently attempts are being made [ScWa86, LiN87] to implement geometric database systems on top of "kernel" systems supporting nested relations [ScWe86]. This allows to keep the coordinates of a geometric object together within a single hierarchical tuple. However, we feel that this is still not adequate as long as the kernel has no concept of geometric objects as special entities and does not provide specific methods for processing them.

We believe that geometric algorithms and data structures have to be thoroughly integrated with the implementation of relational systems to achieve reasonable performance. It is necessary to stop relying on the standard relational representations and file structures and to introduce specific, efficient representations for geometric objects. This implies that changes have to be made at the conceptual level too, if only to prevent the system from using its standard techniques. Research in this direction has already been reported in [StRG83] where abstract data types are proposed for geometric objects and their operations which at the implementation level have to be supported by geometric file structures. Such file structures have for instance been developed in [NiHS84, Ta82, TiMT83, Gu84]. A similar approach to [StRG83] is described in [Or86] in the context of the PROBE research project [Day86].

In some sense, our model of a geometric database system can be seen as continuing this development and some ideas used are also present in [StRG83], [Or86], and [ChF80]. The choice of geometric data types and operators, as described in the next section, is influenced by [ChF80] (POINT, LINE, PGON) and [MaC80] (AREA) where *maps* (partitions of the plane) are used as the fundamental geometric structure. However, the basic approach to extend relational systems at their foundation by embedding geometric data types and operators into a many-sorted relational algebra and to implement this model using algorithms and data structures from Computational Geometry, is new and much more radical than previous approaches. In the remainder of this paper we describe geo-relational algebra as a user model and query language for a geometric database system (Section 2) and discuss the implementation issues involved in making the transition from geo-relational algebra to a geo-relational database system (Section 3). - Since this paper has a somewhat interdisciplinary content, it may be appropriate to mention standard books on database systems [Da86] and Computational Geometry [PrS85, Me84].

2. The Geo-Relational Algebra

2.1. Basic Concepts and Survey

Geo-relational algebra starts from a view of relational algebra as a *many-sorted* algebra, as (to our knowledge) first described in [GüZC87]. This means that the objects of the algebra are atomic values such as strings, numbers, or boolean values as well as relations. The operators of the algebra include arithmetic operators on numbers (e.g. addition) as well as the relational operators (e.g. selection, join).

Within such a formal framework it is easy to embed geometric data types and operators. The basic idea is the following:

- New data types are introduced for geometric objects, such as POINT, LINE, or REGION. In particular a relation may now have attributes of these new types. Furthermore specific operators are introduced for accessing objects of these data types (geometric objects). The representation of geometric objects is hidden from the user and they are in fact accessible only by the new geometric operators.

- A tuple of a relation describes an object as a combination of geometric and non-geometric attribute values.
- A relation as a whole describes a homogeneous collection of geometric objects, that is, a set of points, a set of lines, etc. (A homogeneous collection of geometric objects is the right kind of input for many geometric algorithms.)

Based on these principles one can design different algebras (that is, collections of data types and operators) for specific applications. In the sequel we describe an algebra which contains rather fundamental data types and operators for the manipulation of two-dimensional geometric data. The choice of data types is perhaps somewhat biased towards geographic applications. For VLSI-design databases, for instance, one would surely add a type RECTANGLE (with specific operators) and perhaps other types. Our specific algebra has the following object classes (or data types):

NUM	numbers	REL	relations
STR	strings		
BOOL	boolean values		

POINT	points in the plane, in a cartesian coordinate system
LINE	lines (a line is a sequence of line segments)
REG	regions in the plane

The geometric object classes are discussed in more detail below. For example, a relation to represent cities might look as follows:

cities	cname	center	cpop
	STR	POINT	NUM

For each city its name, its geographic location with respect to a fixed coordinate system, and its population is given. It is assumed that this relation is to be used in a macro-geographic context such that it is sufficient to describe a city as a point.

A complete list of operators of this algebra is given in Table 2-1. At this point one should only note that each line describes a class of operators with the same functionality and that there are five groups of classes of operators. The first group comprises all the usual operations of a relational database system plus some additional operators. The remaining four groups contain geometric operators. Below we shall discuss each group in detail and illustrate its operators by examples.

1.	NUM × NUM	→ NUM	+, -, *, /
2.	BOOL × BOOL	→ BOOL	and, or
3.	BOOL	→ BOOL	not
4.	REL × REL	→ REL	∪, ∩, −, ×, ⋈
5.	REL	→ REL	σ, π, λ
5.	NUM × NUM	→ BOOL	=, ≠, <, ≤, ≥, >
	STR × STR	→ BOOL	
	BOOL × BOOL	→ BOOL	
7.	REL	→ NUM	count
8.	NUM*	→ NUM	sum, avg, min, max
9.	REL	→ ATOM	extract

10.	POINT × POINT	→ BOOL	=, ≠
	LINE × LINE	→ BOOL	
	REG × REG	→ BOOL	
11.	GEO × REG	→ BOOL	inside, outside
12.	EXT × EXT	→ BOOL	intersects
13.	AREA × AREA	→ BOOL	is_neighbour_of

14.	LINE* × LINE*	→ POINT*	intersection
	LINE* × REG*	→ LINE*	
	PGON* × REG*	→ PGON*	
15.	AREA* × AREA*	→ AREA*	overlay
16.	EXT*	→ POINT*	vertices
17.	POINT* × REG	→ AREA*	voronoi
18.	POINT* × POINT	→ REL	closest

19.	POINT*	→ PGON	convex_hull
20.	POINT*	→ POINT	center
	EXT	→ POINT	

21.	POINT × POINT	→ NUM	dist
22.	GEO × GEO	→ NUM	mindist, maxdist
23.	POINT*	→ NUM	diameter
24.	LINE	→ NUM	length
25.	REG	→ NUM	perimeter, area

Table 2-1: Operators of the geo-relational algebra

The functionality of the operators is basically described in terms of the classes of objects mentioned above. Some additional notations are used to enhance clarity and readability. The notation ATTR* where ATTR represents one of the atomic object classes (admissible as attribute types) is used to refer to a relation of which an attribute of type ATTR is specified. Hence the ATTR* notation determines a column of a relation or, intuitively, a set of objects of class ATTR. This notation is very useful because geometric operators are often applied to a set of geometric objects, given as a column of a relation. In a more formal context, however, one should replace every occurrence of ATTR* by REL. - The notation ATTR* used on the right hand side of an arrow has a slightly different meaning and will be explained below, as well as the generalizations and specializations of object classes denoted by ATOM, GEO, EXT, PGON, and AREA. - Note that Table 2-1 does not yet specify the syntax for writing down algebra expressions nor the parameters that certain operators take. For instance, the projection operator (π) takes the projection attributes as parameters. The distinction between operands and parameters is that operands are objects of the algebra, parameters additional information for the operator. Syntax and parameters are described below.

More formally, the algebra is a collection of sets and functions between these sets; it is described by an S-sorted signature Σ where S is a set of sorts (names for the sets) and Σ a family of sets $\Sigma_{w,s}$ of operator symbols (names for the functions), where $w \in S^*$ and $s \in S$ describe the functionality of operators in $\Sigma_{w,s}$ [GoTW78]. The set of sorts of geo-relational algebra is S = {REL, BOOL, NUM, STR, POINT, LINE, PGON, AREA} and the signature is basically given by Table 2-1. So the algebra consists of a set for each sort in S and a function for each element in Σ. In this paper, due to the limited space, we are only able to sketch the database model, mostly describing it informally. A complete formal model is given in [Gü87] defining the sets and functions of the algebra precisely. (Actually there geo-relational algebra is viewed as one specific extension of a general many-sorted algebra model of an extensible database system and we describe here a slightly simplified version of that model.) [Gü87] in turn develops further the model of [GüZC87].

2.2. The Standard Operators (Classes 1 - 9)

1.	NUM × NUM	→ NUM	+, -, *, /	(_ # _)
2.	BOOL × BOOL	→ BOOL	and, or	(_ # _)
3.	BOOL	→ BOOL	not	# (_)
4.	REL × REL	→ REL	∪, ∩, −, ×, |×|	_ _ #
5.	REL	→ REL	σ, π, λ	_ #
6.	NUM × NUM	→ BOOL	=, ≠, <, ≤, ≥, >	(_ # _)
	STR × STR	→ BOOL		
	BOOL × BOOL	→ BOOL		
7.	REL	→ NUM	count	(_ #)
8.	NUM*	→ NUM	sum, avg, min, max	(_ #)
9.	REL	→ ATOM	extract	(_ #)

The operators of this group allow to perform most of the usual retrieval and data manipulation tasks possible in a relational database system. Classes 4 and 5 contain the standard relational operators union, intersection, set difference, cartesian product, join, selection, and projection. However, in this algebra the σ (selection) and the |×| (join) operator can take an arbitrary algebra expression of result type BOOL as a parameter. Hence it is possible to include arithmetic calculations or aggregate functions in selection or join conditions, to nest further applications of the selection operator into a condition and so forth. These capabilities are also crucial for the extension to geometric objects and operators, as will be shown below.

The λ operator is a powerful facility introduced in [GüZC87]. It allows to dynamically extend an existing relation by a new attribute. For each tuple, a value for the new attribute is computed as the result of evaluating an algebra expression given as a parameter of the λ operator. More generally, the λ operator can take any number of parameter algebra expressions; for each of them it creates a new attribute or replaces the value of an existing attribute.

The **extract** operator is the only new operator in this group with respect to [GüZC87]. It allows to extract an atomic value from a relation in order to make it available for further operations. The **extract** operator takes two parameters: The first parameter is a selection condition, that is, an algebra expression with boolean result, which has to identify a single tuple of the operand relation. The second parameter is an attribute name. If the parameter expression selects more than one tuple the algebra expression containing this **extract** operator is considered erroneous; its evaluation stops and a message is sent to the user.

The listing of operators of classes 1 - 9 has been augmented by a description of the required syntax for writing algebra expressions which allows to use the algebra directly as a query language. The symbols "#" and "_" represent the operator and an operand, respectively. Parentheses have to be put as indicated. Basically the syntax is defined according to the following rules:
- Use postfix notation whenever an operator takes a relation as an operand.
- Put parentheses if the resulting object is atomic.
- Apart from that use the standard notation (infix or prefix) for the respective operator.

Finally, to avoid superfluous parentheses, the outermost pair of parentheses may be stripped from an expression. - Note that the syntax description does not specify the parameters that some operators can take. Parameters appear in square brackets behind the operator symbol. Which parameters an operator takes is in this paper explained only informally together with the operator, but defined formally in [GüZC87] and [Gü87].

We illustrate the use of operators of this group as well as the syntax by a few standard examples. Let *items* be a relation describing the items in a warehouse:

items	item#	qty	desc	s_price	v_price
	NUM	NUM	STR	NUM	NUM

For each item an identifying number, the quantity in the warehouse, a textual description, the supplier price, and the vendor price are given. Here are some example queries:

"Return the names of items of which more than 100 are in stock, and whose vendor price exceeds $ 1000."

items σ [(qty > 100) **and** (v_price > 1000)] π [desc]

The following example illustrates the possibility to put arbitrary calculations into selection conditions: "Find items whose vendor price exceeds the supplier price by more than 20%."

items σ [(s_price/v_price) < 0.8] π [desc]

The next example shows the use of the λ operator and of aggregate functions: "Compute the total value of items in the warehouse."

(items λ [qty * v_price {amount}] **sum** [amount]) {total}

The λ operator extends each tuple of the items relation by a new component whose value is given by the product of the qty and v_price components of this tuple. The new attribute is named "amount" (braces are used universally for introducing names). Hence after application of the λ operator the schema of the resulting relation is:

items	item#	qty	desc	s_price	v_price	amount
	NUM	NUM	STR	NUM	NUM	NUM

The type of the new attribute is, of course, given by the result type of the parameter expression. Finally, let us give an example of a join operation in this framework. Let there be a relation describing articles sold by departments

depts	dept_name	article#
	STR	NUM

assuming the article numbers match the item numbers of the items relation. Then the question "Which departments sell pencils" can be formulated as:

items σ [desc = 'pencil'] depts |×| [article# = item#] π [dept_name].

It should be emphasized that our geometric extension does not start from the classical relational algebra but from the *many-sorted* algebra developed in [GüZC87] which we consider by itself to be a fundamental and significant extension of the classical model. It allows to include domain operations (such as arithmetic operators) and aggregate functions into the formal model, provides a much more general and powerful concept of selection and join, and generally allows *computed* values in result relations. Furthermore [GüZC87] provides a formal treatment of nested and ordered relations (sequences of tuples) and nested algebra expressions.

2.3. Geometric Object Types

We now discuss the geometric objects of the algebra in some more detail. Any geometric object is modeled by *a set of points in the Euclidean plane*. Except for the special case of a POINT object, this set is infinite although it can always be finitely specified. To distinguish between the representa- tion of an object and the object itself we introduce a function *points* which associates with a symbol or representation the set of points represented. Let us start by some geometric preliminaries.

The Euclidean plane is given by the set $P = \mathbf{R} \times \mathbf{R}$ of pairs of real numbers with the usual metric. A *point* is simply an element of P. Of course, for a point $p = (x, y)$ we have *points* $(p) = \{(x, y)\}$. Given two distinct points p_1 and p_2 in P, the set $\{\alpha p_1 + (1-\alpha)p_2 \mid \alpha \in \mathbf{R}\}$ defines a *line*. If we additionally restrict α to lie between 0 and 1, we obtain the set $\{\alpha p_1 + (1-\alpha)p_2 \mid \alpha \in \mathbf{R}, 0 \le \alpha \le 1\}$ which describes a *line segment*, namely the part of the line lying between p_1 and p_2, which are called the *end points* of the segment. A *chain of segments* is a finite sequence of line segments such that any two adjacent segments share an end point and no end point belongs to more than two segments. The set of points associated with a chain is of course the union of the point sets of all segments in the chain. A chain is called *simple* if no point other than an end point is shared by any two segments.

A chain is called *closed* if also the first and last element of the sequence share an end point and in this case is also called a *polygon*. Note that a closed, simple chain divides the plane into two disjoint regions, the *interior* and the *exterior*. A *simple polygon* is thus given by a closed, simple chain and we define its set of points to be the points of the chain together with the points of the interior.

The object types of the algebra can now be defined as follows: A value of type POINT is a point in the sense of the definition above. A value of type LINE is a non-closed, simple chain of segments. A value of type PGON or a value of type AREA is a simple polygon.

In applications, an object of type POINT can be used to model an object whose position, rather than extension, in some plane space is relevant, for instance a city in a geographic application. A LINE object approximates a curve in this space, such as a river or highway. A PGON or AREA object models a simple region (approximating its boundary) without holes, such as a lake or a country. The distinction between the two types PGON and AREA will be explained shortly.

For some applications it would certainly be desirable to admit more complex types of regions, in particular regions with holes. For instance, a lake having an island must now be modeled as if the island's area were part of the lake; the island must be specified as a separate region overlapping the lake. However, we feel that a too high price would need to be paid for generally allowing regions to contain holes. First, these objects are conceptually much more complex which is important when it comes to specifying (and visualizing) the effect of operations. Second, the internal representation is more complex and it is much more difficult to treat these objects algorithmically. So we have restricted the algebra to hole-free regions; this does not preclude the possibility of later extending the algebra by a type for regions with holes.

The distinction between types PGON and AREA concerns the set of polygons occurring as a column of a relation: If the attribute is of type PGON then polygons within the set may intersect each other. If it is of type AREA then essentially all polygons within this set (column) are disjoint. More precisely, we require that two polygons of type AREA belonging to the same attribute are either equal or *their interiors* are disjoint (which means they may share a boundary edge or vertex). Fig. 2-2 illustrates the geometric data objects that can occur as a column of a relation.

Type AREA is motivated by the fact that in applications often subdivisions of some plane space into disjoint regions occur, for instance the area of a continent may be divided into countries, or some land area may be split into regions according to the type of industrial or agricultural use etc. For planar subdivisions special types of operators are applicable, for instance asking for the neighbours of a region, which do not make sense for general collections of polygons.

The restriction imposed on type AREA can be viewed as an integrity constraint on relations. We are forced to allow two polygons in different tuples to be equal because certain relational operators, for instance join, create duplicates. Conceptually we can still think of a subdivision of the plane even when some areas are present more than once. Also the data structures and algorithms for representing and processing subdivisions can handle these duplicates without problems.

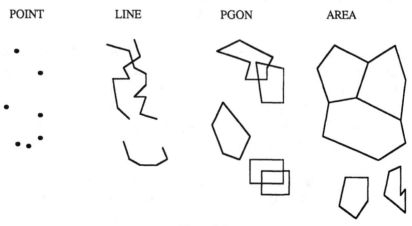

Figure 2-2

Generalizations of the four basic geometric types are REG, EXT, and GEO, referring to any type of region, any extended object (not a point), and any geometric data object, respectively, for instance REG = {PGON, AREA}, EXT = {LINE, PGON, AREA}, etc. A set identifier occurring in the signature listing is to be interpreted as a shorthand for one corresponding line (class of operators) for each element of the set.

2.4. Geometric Predicates

10.	POINT × POINT	→ BOOL	=, ≠	(_ # _)
	LINE × LINE	→ BOOL		
	REG × REG	→ BOOL		
11.	GEO × REG	→ BOOL	**inside, outside**	(_ # _)
12.	EXT × EXT	→ BOOL	**intersects**	(_ # _)
13.	AREA × AREA	→ BOOL	**is_neighbour_of**	(_ # _)

The operators in this group allow to compare two geometric objects in different ways; such a comparison can be part of the parameter expression of a selection or join operation. For instance, it is possible to test whether any geometric object (point, line, or region) is completely inside a region (PGON or AREA). - Here are some examples how the functions associated with operator symbols can formally be defined. Let x, y be the operands.

$$(x = y) \quad := \quad points(x) = points(y)$$
$$(x \neq y) \quad := \quad points(x) \neq points(y)$$
$$(x \textbf{ inside } y) \quad := \quad points(x) \subseteq points(y)$$
$$(x \textbf{ outside } y) \quad := \quad points(x) \cap points(y) = \emptyset$$
$$(x \textbf{ intersects } y) \quad := \quad points(x) \cap points(y) \neq \emptyset$$

Note that the description in terms of the associated point sets frees the definition from unnecessary details about the representation of objects. - Not all operators are quite as simple to define as these geometric predicates. Full definitions of the remaining operators are given in [Gü87].

We illustrate the use of these operators by examples. Suppose besides a relation describing cities of the US there is also a relation describing the states:

cities	cname	center	cpop	states	sname	region	spop
	STR	POINT	NUM		STR	AREA	NUM

We may then ask for a list of cities associating with each city the state it is in:

cities states |×| [center **inside** region] π [cname, sname]

As usual the result of the join is a subset of the cartesian product relation such that for each result tuple the condition "center **inside** region" holds. By projection we obtain the desired list. We introduce a further relation for rivers (and one for highways needed later):

rivers	rname	route		highways	hname	way
	STR	LINE			STR	LINE

We may then determine which rivers are totally or partially in California:

    states σ [sname = 'California'] rivers |×| [route **intersects** region]

Of course it is also possible to change the condition to "route **inside** region" to find the rivers completely inside California. We may also ask for the neighbour states of California:

    states σ [sname = 'California'] states |×| [1.region **is_neighbour_of** 2.region]

Here it is necessary to distinguish between the region attributes of the first and second operand by using a numerical prefix. Sometimes it is easier to formulate a query in a more procedural style by determining intermediate results step by step. For this purpose the query language has been augmented by the possibility to assign a name to the result of an algebra expression and to refer to this result in subsequent expressions. The current example query can alternatively be posed as follows:

    (states **extract** [sname = 'California', region]) {CA};
    states σ [region **is_neighbour_of** CA]

The result of the first expression is the polygonal area describing the state of California which is called "CA". The effect of the semicolon is to remove the current operand. The second expression can now determine the neighbour states of California by a selection instead of a join. - Note that two areas are considered to be neighbours if they have a common edge.

2.5. Geometric Relation Transformers

14.	LINE* × LINE*	→ POINT*	**intersection**	_ _ #
	LINE* × REG*	→ LINE*		
	PGON* × REG*	→ PGON*		
15.	AREA* × AREA*	→ AREA*	**overlay**	_ _ #
16.	EXT*	→ POINT*	**vertices**	_ #
17.	POINT* × REG	→ AREA*	**voronoi**	_ _ #
18.	POINT* × POINT	→ REL	**closest**	_ _ #

The operators in this group take one or more relations (viewed as sets of geometric objects) as operands and produce a result relation. They also, except for the **closest** operator, construct new geometric objects and embed them into the result relation. For instance, the **intersection** operator can be applied to two sets of lines and it constructs all intersection points between lines of the first operand and lines of the second operand, as illustrated in Fig. 2-3.

Figure 2-3

It is important to note that a single line of the first operand can intersect a single line of the second operand in several points. The result relation contains one tuple for each intersection point. This tuple consists of all attribute values of the first operand tuple, all attribute values of the second operand tuple and one additional attribute value of type POINT for the constructed intersection point. This is in fact the meaning of the ATTR* notation on the right hand side of an arrow: the result relation will have a new attribute of type ATTR. - The principle explained here for the **intersection** operator applied to sets of lines is the same for the remaining functionalities of the **intersection** operator and the other operators in this group. So for instance the intersection of lines with regions will result in the construction of new lines and each result tuple will contain all information of the participating line and region plus the constructed intersection line.

The **overlay** operator allows to combine two partitions of the plane into disjoint regions (sometimes called *maps*). The result relation contains one tuple for each new region obtained as the intersection of a region of the first operand with a region of the second operand. Note that our definition of AREA attributes does not require that the plane is covered completely by the regions occurring as attribute values. In this case it is possible that a region of the first operand does not intersect any region of the second operand; it will therefore not be part of any result tuple. The **overlay** operator is illustrated in Fig. 2-4.

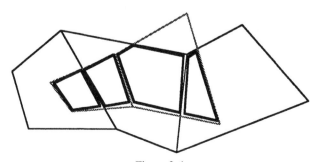

Figure 2-4

The **vertices** operator returns the vertex points of extended objects, for instance, all corner points of a polygon. In the result relation a tuple of the operand relation with a triangular region, say, will appear three times, extended by the different point values of the three vertices. - The Voronoi diagram is a well-known structure in (computational) geometry. For a given set S of points in the plane the Voronoi diagram associates with each point p from S the region consisting of those points of the plane that are closer to p than to any other point in S. Usually some regions of a Voronoi diagram are infinite, namely those belonging to points on the convex hull of the point set. In our framework infinite regions are not allowed. Hence our **voronoi** operator takes as a second operand a polygonal region and constructs the Voronoi diagram for the points inside that region (Fig. 2-5).

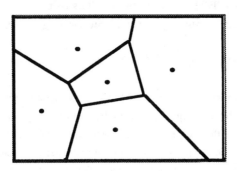

Figure 2-5

Finally the **closest** operator takes a relation, viewed as a set of points, as an operand and returns that or those tuples of this relation whose point component is closest to the point given as a second operand (see Fig. 2-6).

Figure 2-6

We illustrate the use of operators in this group by a few examples. Suppose we want to partition the state of California into "areas of attraction" of big cities (more than 500 000 inhabitants). We can achieve an effect like this by constructing the Voronoi diagram for these cities. We assume that the state area of California has already been determined as shown before and is known as "CA".

cities σ [(center **inside** CA) **and** (cpop > 500000)] CA **voronoi** [center, {attr_area}]

The parameters of the **voronoi** operator are the name of the point attribute of the operand relation and a new name for the Voronoi regions to be constructed. Hence the result relation has the schema:

cities	cname	center	cpop	attr_area
	STR	POINT	NUM	AREA

Here is a somewhat more involved example on the use of the **intersection** operator: "Which city with more than 100000 inhabitants is closest to the point where interstate highway 90 crosses the Mississippi river?"

(highways   σ [hname = 'I90']   rivers   σ [rname = 'Mississippi']
intersection [way, route, {crossing}]   **extract** [**true**, crossing])   {crosspoint};

cities   σ [cpop > 100000]   crosspoint   **closest** [center]

In a first step the intersection point of Interstate 90 with the Mississippi river is determined and called "crosspoint". This is done by selecting the right tuples from the highways and rivers relations and computing the intersections of their respective attributes of type LINE. The query assumes that we know there is only one intersection point (otherwise the verbal question would not make sense). The **intersection** operator will then produce a result relation with a single tuple containing the attribute values of the highway and the river, respectively, and additionally their intersection point in a new attribute called "crossing". The **extract** operator in this case just checks that its operand relation contains indeed only a single tuple and extracts the "crossing" attribute value from this tuple which is then called "crosspoint". - The second part of the query is then a simple application of the **closest** operator to the relation containing cities with more than 100 000 inhabitants.

2.6. Operators Returning Atomic Geometric Objects

19. POINT*	→ PGON	**convex_hull**	(_ #)
20. POINT*	→ POINT	**center**	(_ #)
EXT	→ POINT		# (_)

The first operator constructs the convex hull of a set of points, defined as the smallest convex polygon enclosing all points. The second determines the center of either a set of points or an extended atomic geometric object. Syntactically correct expressions are, for example:

(cities   **convex_hull** [center])
(cities   **center** [center])
center (states   **extract**   [sname = 'California', region])

The geometric meaning of these operators is illustrated in Fig. 2-7.

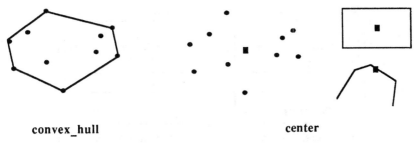

convex_hull   **center**

Figure 2-7

2.7. Geometric Operators Returning Numbers

21.	POINT × POINT	→ NUM	dist	# (_ , _)
22.	GEO × GEO	→ NUM	mindist, maxdist	# (_ , _)
23.	POINT*	→ NUM	diameter	(_ #)
24.	LINE	→ NUM	length	# (_)
25.	REG	→ NUM	perimeter, area	# (_)

The meaning of these operators should be obvious from their name with the exception, perhaps, of the **diameter** operator. The diameter of a set of points is defined as the largest distance between any two points in the set. We give a final example involving the **area** operator: "Which US state has the highest population density?"

$$\text{states} \ \lambda \ [\text{spop}/\mathbf{area}(\text{region}) \ \{\text{density}\}] \ \{\text{xstates}\} \ \sigma \ [\text{density} = (\text{xstates} \ \mathbf{max} \ [\text{density}])]$$

For each state tuple its population density is computed and added as a new attribute, the result relation is named "xstates". From this relation the state tuple with maximal value of the density attribute is selected. Note that it is necessary to introduce the name "xstates" for the intermediate result to be able to refer to it within the selection condition.

3. Remarks on Geo-Relational Database Management Systems

Geo-relational algebra is meant to be the user model as well as the formal foundation for the implementation of a geo-relational database management system. The crucial part of the step from geo-relational algebra to a geo-relational DBMS is the inclusion of efficient geometric algorithms and geometric data and file structures. The relationship between relational algebra, geo-relational algebra, a relational DBMS and a geo-relational DBMS is illustrated in Fig. 3-1.

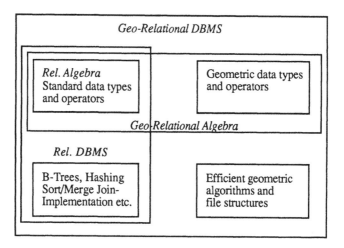

Figure 3-1

A second important issue in the transition to a geo-relational DBMS is the user interface. Clearly the values of geometric attributes cannot be displayed in the usual tabular style nor be entered through a keyboard. In the sequel we first discuss the integration of geometric algorithms into a geo-relational DBMS and then the user interface.

3.1. Implementation

Geo-relational algebra was designed from the beginning with geometric algorithms in mind. The fundamental concept that a column of a relation represents a homogeneous set of geometric objects and that geometric operators of the algebra are applied to such columns harmonizes with the fact that data structures in Computational Geometry are designed to represent such homogeneous sets and that algorithms mostly take one or more such sets as input. Furthermore, relational algebra, rather than the relational calculus, was chosen for the geometric extension, because it is thus possible to establish a direct correspondence between operators of the algebra and well-known geometric algorithms. Here are some examples:

intersection	Bentley/Ottmann, Algorithms for Reporting and Counting Geometric Intersections [BeO79].
overlay	Nievergelt/Preparata, Plane-Sweep Algorithms for Intersecting Geometric Figures [NiP82].
voronoi	Shamos/Hoey, Closest-Point Problems [ShH75]
convex_hull	Graham, An Efficient Algorithm for Determining the Convex Hull of a Finite Planar Set [Gr72].

Of course for some of these operators there exist many published algorithms of which the cited one is only a representative.

Geometric predicates, such as **inside** or **intersects**, occur usually in selection or join conditions. For the implementation two basic principles can be observed:

-    A selection involving a geometric predicate, when applied to a basis relation (not an intermediate result) should lead to a search on a specific geometric file structure.
-    A join involving a geometric predicate is normally executed by a plane-sweep or a divide-and-conquer algorithm.

For instance, suppose the location of the city Baltimore has already been determined and is known as "Baltimore". A selection may then ask for the state containing Baltimore:

states σ [Baltimore **inside** region]

The geometric problem is illustrated in Fig. 3-2 (in principle, no attempt was made to draw a map of the US). If the US states are represented in a specific file structure for geometric subdivision searching (data structures for this purpose are published for instance in [Ki83] and [SaT86]) then this query can be executed efficiently. - The **inside** operator can also occur in a join condition (a previous example), also illustrated in Fig. 3-2:

cities states |x| [center **inside** region]

At least if there is no file structure for geometric subdivision searching available then a plane-sweep through the set of points and regions is probably the most efficient strategy.

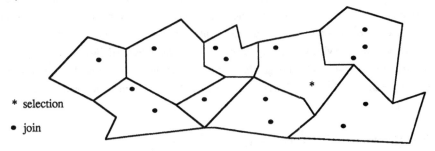

* selection
• join

Figure 3-2

The example queries show a further important point: In general, several strategies could be used to obtain the desired result. The selection of the hopefully best algorithm can depend on many factors. Also depending on the existence of a geometric file structure to support a query (*geometric index*) certain methods may or may not be available in the specific case. For instance, if no geometric file structure is present to support the selection, it is necessary to scan all tuples of the relation. Instead of plane-sweep, the join could be performed by repeatedly searching a geometric index for one operand, if present. It might also be worthwhile to first build a geometric data structure representing one operand set and then to repeatedly search this data structure. If the cardinality of the operand sets is very different, in particular, if one operand set has only a single or a few elements, then again it may not be useful to invest the work for building a data structure for one operand set, but one should rather just scan this operand set comparing with the few elements of the other operand set. And so forth.

Hence it is clear that the "optimizer" component of a geo-relational DBMS has at least a similar importance as its counterpart in a "normal" relational system. It is also obvious that the traditional knowledge used in optimizing has to be extended by a good deal of insight about geometric algorithms.

The approach includes a challenge to the field of Computational Geometry. Namely, the standard assumption that all geometric data and data structures fit into main memory is often inappropriate in a database context. A transition must be made from efficient internal data structures for geometric searching problems to (external) geometric file structures based upon the same principles. Algorithms processing sets of geometric objects must be modified to keep at any time only a small part of their data in main memory. A few papers in Computational Geometry have already addressed this problem [SzVW83, OtW86, GüS87].

3.2. User Interface

We assume that a geo-relational DBMS is accessed through a work station with a bitmap screen and a pointing device (mouse etc.). The hardware may also include a graphics tablet or similar input device for geometric data. The result of a query will usually be displayed in two windows on the bitmap screen: The non-geometric attributes of a relation are shown in tabular format in the first window whereas the geometric attributes are drawn in the second (graphics) window. The two windows may interact with each other, for instance, selecting a row (tuple) in the table will visually emphasize the associated graphic object in the graphics window and vice-versa. Very important is the possibility to define interactively an atomic geometric object (by drawing it in the graphics window) and then to use this object in a query. For instance, it is possible to draw an arbitrary region into a display of a map and then to ask how many people live in this area:

cities σ [center **inside** *] **sum** [cpop]

("*" refers to the currently selected graphical object.) One might measure the size of this area by applying the **area** operator. Or one might draw a projected highway into the map and ask for the roads and rivers intersected by it. And so forth.

To make geometric objects drawn in the graphics window recognizable it should be possible to display as a "background" a predefined map of the area. To support entering the query a third "interaction" window might display the schemas of existing relations. Operators might be selected via menus that offer just the operators applicable to the current operand. There are many more possibilities to design a user-friendly interface.

4. Conclusions

In this paper we have described a conceptual model for a geometric database system. For a user the essential aspects of the model are:

(1) High-level geometric objects are available to model geometric aspects of real life entities and one can perform "calculations" with these objects in a manner similar to writing down simple numerical expressions. For instance, it is as easy to write down a test whether two polygons intersect as whether one number is greater than another. We believe a user does not care to see polygons represented by large collections of numbers stored in relations, nor does he/she want to program the intersection test in SQL, say, based on this representation. Our concept is to hide the internal representation of objects entirely; this representation is defined in the implementation language of the database system which is also used to implement operations efficiently based on this representation.

(2) Writing down a query is conceptually just the composition of functions initially applied to objects known to the system (such as stored relations). Since the domain and range types of functions fit together in many ways a very flexible and expressive query language results, as we hope to have demonstrated by the examples. The underlying mathematical concept is that of a many-sorted algebra.

The choice of geometric operators was motivated by the desire to obtain a practically useful query language and also to show how well-known geometric algorithms, such as constructing the Voronoi diagram, can be embedded into a database system. There was no intention to obtain, for instance, a minimal set. We know of no theoretical criteria for deciding which operators should be present. In practice it will surely happen that an operator appears to be missing for a particular application. The only solution to this problem is to keep the architecture of the database system extensible; that is, to allow further types and operators to be added to the system. Their implementation should be of the same quality as that of the original types and operators.

The implementation of a restricted prototype system called "Gral" (also described in [Gü87]) with such an extensible architecture has been started at the University of Dortmund. The hardware is a SUN work station and the implementation language is Modula-2. At the time of writing, simple storage management and catalog components, a rudimentary user interface, and a facility for managing user-defined types are running. Currently a parser for algebra expressions (independent of specific operators), the general mechanism for evaluating queries, the mechanism for adding operators and their implementation procedures to the system, several fundamental operators, and in particular a plane-sweep algorithm for the "point **inside** region" join have been designed and are being implemented. Of course, there is still a long way to go, for instance no index structures exist yet, optimization has not yet been touched, and almost all geometric operators still wait for implementation.

Acknowledgment. Thanks to Gisbert Dröge for many interesting discussions on geo-relational algebra. He in particular studied geometric operators and helped to shape the collection shown in Table 2-1.

References

[BeO79]   Bentley, J.L., and Th. Ottmann, Algorithms for Reporting and Counting Geometric Intersections. *IEEE Transactions on Computers C-28 (1979)*, 643-647.

[BeS77]   Berman, R.R., and M. Stonebraker, GEO-QUEL: A System for the Manipulation and Display of Geographic Data. *Computer Graphics 11 (1977)*, 186-191.

[Bu84]   Buchmann, A.P., Current Trends in CAD Databases. *Computer-Aided Design 16 (1984)*, 123-126.

[ChF80]   Chang, N.S., and K.S. Fu, A Relational Database System for Images. In: S.K. Chang and K.S. Fu (eds.), Pictorial Information Systems, Springer, 1980, 288-321.

[ChF81]   Chang, N.S., and K.S. Fu, Picture Query Languages for Pictorial Data-Base Systems. *Computer 11 (1981)*, 23-33.

[ChCK81]   Chock, M., A.F. Cardenas, and A. Klinger, Manipulating Data Structures in Pictorial Information Systems. *Computer 11 (November 1981)*, 43-50.

[Da86]   Date, C.J., An Introduction to Database Systems. Addison-Wesley, 1986.

[Day86]   Dayal, U., and J.M. Smith, PROBE: A Knowledge-Oriented Database Management System. In: M.L. Brodie and J. Mylopoulos (eds.), On Knowledge Base Management Systems: Integrating Artificial Intelligence and Database Technologies, Springer, 1986, 227-257.

[Fr81]   Frank, A., Application of DBMS to Land Information Systems. Proc. of the 7th VLDB Conf., Cannes, 1981, 448-453.

[GoTW78]   Goguen, J.A., J.W. Thatcher, and E.G. Wagner, An Initial Algebra Approach to the Specification, Correctness, and Implementation of Abstract Data Types. In: R. Yeh (ed.), Current Trends in Programming Methodology, Vol. IV, Prentice Hall 1978, 80-149.

[Gr72]   Graham, R.L., An Efficient Algorithm for Determining the Convex Hull of a Finite Planar Set. *Information Processing Letters 1 (1972)*, 132-133.

[Gü87]   Güting, R.H., Modelling Non-Standard Database Systems by Many-Sorted Algebras. Fachbereich Informatik, Universität Dortmund, manuscript in preparation, 1987.

[GüS87]   Güting, R.H., and W. Schilling, A Practical Divide-and-Conquer Algorithm for the Rectangle Intersection Problem. *Information Sciences 42 (1987)*, 95-112.

[GüZC87]   Güting, R.H., R. Zicari, and D. Choy, An Algebra for Structured Office Documents. IBM Almaden Research Center, San Jose, California, Report RJ 5559, 1987.

[Gu84]   Guttman, A., R-Trees: A Dynamic Index Structure for Spatial Searching. Proc. of the ACM SIGMOD Conf. on Management of Data, Boston, 1984, 47-57.

[Ki83]   Kirkpatrick, D., Optimal Search in Planar Subdivisions. *SIAM Journal of Computing 12 (1983)*, 28-35.

[LiN87]   Lipeck, U., and K. Neumann, Modelling and Manipulating Objects in Geoscientific Databases. In: S. Spaccapietra (ed.), Proc. of the 5th Int. Conf. on the Entity-Relationship Approach, Dijon, 1986, North-Holland, 1987, 67-86.

[MaC80]   Mantey, P.E., and E.D. Carlson, Integrated Geographic Data Bases: The GADS Experience. In: A. Blaser (ed.), Data Base Techniques for Pictorial Applications, Springer, 1980, 173-198.

[Me84]   Mehlhorn, K., Data Structures and Algorithms 3: Multi-dimensional Searching and Computational Geometry. Springer, 1984.

[NaW79]   Nagy, G., and S. Wagle, Geographic Data Processing. *Computing Surveys 11 (1979)*, 139-181.

[NiHS84]   Nievergelt, J., H. Hinterberger, and K.C. Sevcik, The Grid File: An Adaptable, Symmetric Multikey File Structure. *ACM Transactions on Database Systems 9 (1984)*, 38-71.

[NiP82]   Nievergelt, J., and F.P. Preparata, Plane-Sweep Algorithms for Intersecting Geometric Figures. *Communications of the ACM 25 (1982)*, 739-747.

[Or86]   Orenstein, J.A., Spatial Query Processing in an Object-Oriented Database System. Proc. of the ACM SIGMOD Conf. 1986, 326-336.

[OtW86]   Ottmann, Th., and D. Wood, Space-Economical Plane-Sweep Algorithms. *Computer Vision, Graphics, and Image Processing 34 (1986)*, 35-51.

[PrS85]   Preparata, F.P., and M.I. Shamos, Computational Geometry: An Introduction. Springer 1985.

[SaT86]   Sarnak, N., and R.E. Tarjan, Planar Point Location Using Persistent Search Trees. *Communications of the ACM 29 (1986)*, 669-679.

[ScWa86] Schek, H.J., and W. Waterfeld, A Database Kernel System for Geoscientific Applications. Proc. of the 2nd Int. Symp. on Spatial Data Handling, Seattle, WA, 1986, 273-288.

[ScWe86] Schek, H.J., and G. Weikum, DASDBS: Concepts and Architecture of a Database System for Advanced Applications. TU Darmstadt, West Germany, Report DVSI-1986-T1, 1986.

[ShH75]   Shamos, M.I., and D. Hoey, Closest-Point Problems. Proc. of the 16th Annual IEEE Symposium on Foundations of Computer Science, 1975, 151-162.

[StRG83] Stonebraker, M., B. Rubenstein, and A. Guttmann, Application of Abstract Data Types and Abstract Indices to CAD Data Bases. Proc. of the ACM/IEEE Conf. on Engineering Design Applications, San Jose, 1983, 107-113.

[SzVW83] Szymansky, T.G., and C.J. van Wyk, Space Efficient Algorithms for VLSI Artwork Analysis. Proc. of the 20th IEEE Design Automation Conference, 1983, 734-739.

[Ta82]   Tamminen, M., Efficient Spatial Access to a Data Base. Proc. of the ACM SIGMOD Conf. 1982, 200-206.

[TiMT83]   Tikkanen, M., M. Mantyla, and M. Tamminen, GWB/DMS: A Geometric Data Manager. Proc. of the Eurographics Conf., Zagreb, 1983, 99-111.

AN EXTENSION OF THE RELATIONAL MODEL

TO SUPPORT GENERIC INTERVALS

Nikos A. Lorentzos and Roger G. Johnson

Department of Computer Science,
Birkbeck College, London University
Malet Street
London WC1E 7HX
England

ABSTRACT

A consistent extension of the relational model is defined, which allows the recording and manipulation of generic intervals. Two new relational algebra operations are defined, which are closed. The proposed model has a wide range of applications areas, such as engineering, CAD, cartography, version modelling, temporal databases, soil information systems, mathematics, the management of spatial data and many others.

1. INTRODUCTION

Intervals have often been represented in databases to describe, for example, periods of time and geometric objects. This paper presents, for the first time, the results of research on extending a database to incorporate intervals. The concept of an interval is generalized and an extended relational algebra is proposed. To the authors' knowledge, the formal definition of a generic interval, as a primitive data type, has not been previously addressed. This is one of the topics covered in this paper. In detail, the contributions of the paper are the following.

1. A generic interval is defined formally as a primitive data type.

2. A consistent extension of relational algebra is defined which manipulates both conventional data and intervals in a uniform way. Two primitive operations are also defined which are closed in the model.

3. The model applies to arbitrary alphanumeric domains in addition to the more commonly considered numeric ones.

4. In the context of the management of temporal data, it is argued that a complete solution is provided, in the sense that several weaknesses of other approaches to the manipulation of such data are overcome. In the proposed model, time is treated as data and not as a means of stamping temporal data.

5. Finally, the model has many application areas, including the manipulation of spatial data.

For ease of reference, the relational model, originally defined in [Co], is called *Conventional Relational Model* (CRM). An extension of it, which is defined, in this paper, is called the *Interval-Extended*

Relational Model (XRM). Furthermore, the algebras used in these models are called *Conventional Relational Algebra* (CRA) and *Interval-Extended Relational Algebra* (XRA), respectively.

The paper is divided as follows. Some previous work is referenced in section 2. In section 3 a formalization of an interval is provided, in the context of a computerized database. The XRM is formalized in section 4. Section 5 provides some examples of its application in various areas. In section 6, a special case of its application to temporal databases, is discussed. Some conclusions are drawn in the last section.

2. PREVIOUS WORK

The concept of an interval is known from mathematics. In the context of databases it is used extensively in several areas. In data structures, [NH], intervals are incorporated in indexing techniques for conventional databases. They are used similarly, in [SRF], to index multidimensional objects. In AI, [AI], time-intervals are used in temporal problem solving.

Intervals are also incorporated in data modelling. However, various authors use different approaches to represent an interval. In [RL], an extension of SQL is used which applies to pictorial databases. In this extension, an expression {a±x, b±y} denotes an orthogonal rectangle. It is observed, however, that such a rectangle can be considered as the Cartesian product of two (1_dimensional) intervals.

In the management of temporal data, Navathe, in [NA], represents a time-interval as a pair of attributes (From,To), in which he records the time during which temporal data is valid. A similar approach is used in [Sn]. Various approaches to extending the relational algebra to manipulate temporal data can be found in [Ah], [CC], [GV], [Ta] and [KS1]. An evaluation of nine different temporal extensions of the relational model are provided in [KS2]. A common characteristic of them is that time is seen as a means of stamping data. As a consequence, various primitive relational algebra operations, which are defined in the papers are dedicated to the management of temporal data only and no operations for the manipulation of intervals are defined. One exception is [LJ], where time-intervals are treated like other data.

In the above approaches, the concept of an interval is application dependent. In this paper, however, it is defined as a primitive data type and it is shown that it can be used for a range of applications.

3. INTERVALS IN THE CONTEXT OF DATABASES

Definition 1: A non empty finite set D is called a *1_dimensional space* if it has been supplied with a total ordering, '$\leq$', mathematical relation.

The elements of D are called *D_points*. If D has n points, n>0, it is assumed that $d_1 < d_2 < ... < d_n$.

The points d_i, d_{i+1}, $1 \leq i \leq n-1$, are called *consecutive*. In particular, d_i is the *predecessor* of d_{i+1} and d_{i+1} is the *successor* of d_i.

It should be noted that since D is finite, one element, $d_{n+1} \not\in D$, can always be defined such that d_n and d_{n+1} are consecutive. Alternatively, d_{n+1} is denoted by '$@_D$' or '$@$', if no ambiguity arises.

The underlying domain of every attribute, in the CRM, may be considered as a 1_dimensional space. The authors' justification for this belief, now follows.

Firstly, it is observed that First Normal Form is maintained in the CRM and the underlying domain of every attribute is a non-empty set. Secondly, a system provided default of total ordering is always in effect, for every such domain. Advantage is taken of this in the formation of queries within the SELECT operation, by using the '<' and the other comparison predicates. Finally, because of the computer's restricted representation capabilities, every domain may be considered as finite. For example, if D is the set of integers, only those integers in an interval [-p,q], -p<q, p, q≥0, can be represented in a database. If D is the set of all the lower case strings of exactly three alphabetic characters and '^' denotes the blank character, then the number of strings in {"^^^",...,"zzz"} is finite. A final case is for D to be the set of reals. Although this set is uncountably infinite, only a finite number of the reals can be represented in a computerized system. Assume, therefore, that r_i is one of them and let r_{i+1}, $r_{i+1} > r_i$ be the next representable one. Since, for example, the real $r = (r_i + r_{i+1})/2$ cannot be represented, it can be assumed that, practically, r_i and r_{i+1} are consecutive.

Obviously, in each of the above cases, an element $@_D \not\in D$ can always be defined.

Definition 2: Let D be a 1_dimensional space, $d_p \in D$ and $d_q \in D \cup \{@\}$, $d_p < d_q$. A *(1_dimensional) interval* over D or a *D_interval* is defined as the set $[d_p, d_q) = \{d_i \mid d_i \in D, d_p \le d_i < d_q\}$.

The points d_p and d_q are called the *boundary* points or, conventionally, the *start* and *stop* points of the interval, respectively.

Alternatively, an interval is denoted by the symbol δ, followed by a lower case letter, usually from the end of the alphabet, for example, δx, δy, δz. If δx=$[d_p, d_q)$ then its boundary points are denoted by d_p=start(δx) and d_q=stop(δx).

By definition, δx contains at least one point, its start. If δx contains exactly one point it is called an *elementary* interval. In particular, a predicate *einterval* is defined so that

$einterval([d_p, d_q))$=TRUE ←→ q=p+1.

Definition 3: The set I(D)={δx=$[d_p, d_q)$, $d_p \in D$, $d_q \in D \cup \{@\}$, $d_p < d_q$}, of all the intervals over D, is called the *Interval Domain* (ID) over D.

It is observed that I(D) is finite.

Example : Let ALPHA_3={"^^^", ..., "zzz"}. Then some valid intervals over ALPHA_3 are

  ["car", "cau")={"car", "cas", "cat"}

and ["zzx", "@")={"zzx", "zzy", "zzz"},

where $@=@_{ALPHA\_3}$ has been defined as the successor of "zzz".

An important property of an interval is that it is defined uniquely by its start and stop points. Consequently, equality between them reduces to the following equivalent definition.

Definition 4: Let δx, δy∈I(D). Then δx=δy ←→ start(δx)=start(δy), stop(δx)=stop(δy).

Let E(D) be the set of elementary intervals over D. Then *cinterval*: D ⟶ E(D)⊆I(D) such that $cinterval(d_i)=[d_i, d_{i+1})$ is a one-to-one onto function. Its inverse is denoted by *cpoint*. Therefore, the following property is satisfied.

Every point of a 1_dimensional space is isomorphic to an elementary interval.

This property is referred to, as the *Duality Principle* between points and elementary intervals.

Since D is isomorphic to E(D) and E(D)⊆I(D) then, up to this isomorphism, D⊆I(D).

A 1_dimensional interval is geometrically interpreted as a half-open line segment. Figure 1 summarizes the relative positions of one interval δy with respect to another δx. Thirteen distinct predicates are also

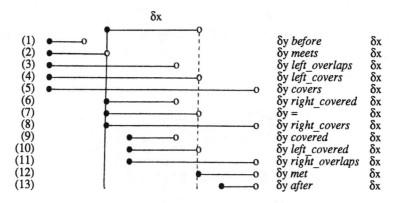

Figure 1: Relative positions of a 1 dimensional
interval δy with respect to another δx.

defined, each of which evaluates to TRUE for exactly one of these positions. They are shown, in infix
notation, in the figure. A formal definition of them, in terms of the start and the stop points of the intervals, is trivial. Some additional predicates are given below. However, instead of defining them formally, which is a simple task, a list of numbers, to the right of each predicate, shows those intervals, in
figure 1, for which it evaluates to TRUE.

δy<|δx ←→ (6 or 9 or 10). (δy is a *pure_subinterval* of δx)

δy≤|δx ←→ (6 or 9 or 10 or 7). (δy is a *subinterval* of δx)

δy|>δx ←→ δx<|δy. (δy is a *pure_super_interval* of δx)

δy|≥δx ←→ δx≤|δy. (δy is a *super_interval* of δx)

δy *overlaps* δx   ←→ (3 or 11).

δy *merges* δx   ←→ (2 or 3 or ... or 12).

δy *common_points* δx ←→ (3 or 4 or ... or 11).

δy *precedes* δx   ←→ (1 or 2 or 3 or 4 or 6).

δy *follows* δx   ←→ (8 or 10 or 11 or 12 or 13).

δy *preequals* δx   ←→ (1 or 2 or 3 or 4 or 6 or 7). (δy *precedes or equals* δx)

δy *folequals* δx   ←→ (7 or 8 or 10 or 11 or 12 or 13). (δy *follows or equals* δx)

δy *adjacent* δx   ←→ (2 or 12).

Some properties, satisfied by these predicates, are omitted, as trivial.

Definition 5: Let $I(D_i)$, i=1, 2, ..., n, be IDs. Then an *n_dimensional interval* or an *interval of degree n*
is defined as every element δx=(δx$_1$, δx$_2$, ..., δx$_n$), δx$_i$∈I(D_i), i=1, 2, ..., n.

The geometric interpretation of δx is an n_dimensional cuboid. In particular, for n=2 it is an orthogonal
parallelogram and for n=3 it is an orthogonal parallelepiped.

4. THE INTERVAL-EXTENDED RELATIONAL MODEL

In this section it is shown how intervals can be represented in the relational model. In addition, two new
primitive operations are defined for their manipulation.

4.1 Representation of N_Dimensional Intervals.

Definition 6: Let I(D_i) be IDs over the 1_dimensional spaces D_i, i=1, 2, ..., n, respectively, not necessarily distinct. Then an *interval relation over* I(D_1)x...xI(D_n) is defined as every subset R⊆I(D_1)x...xI(D_n).

OWNERSHIP

Length	Width	Period
[2,13)	[3,12)	[01.01.52, 04.08.68)
[2,13)	[3,12)	[09.06.74, 22.08.85)
[2,13)	[12,19)	[05.03.74, 08.08.80)
[16,27)	[10,17)	[04.05.72, 03.08.80)

Figure 2: The representation of spatial and
temporal data, in the XRM.

Figure 2 shows how an (interval) relation can be represented in the relational model. The scheme of relation OWNERSHIP is OWNERSHIP(Length=I(INT), Width=I(INT), Period=I(DATE)), where INT={1, 2, ..., 100} is a finite subset of the natural numbers and DATE={01.01.50, ..., 31.12.87} is a finite subset of the set of valid dates.

This relation shows the pieces of land, in metres, owned by a person, John, and the time during which he was their owner.

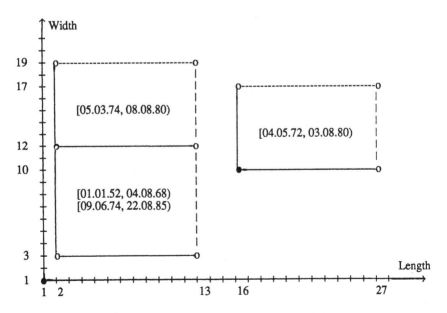

Figure 3: Ground plan of the areas recorded
in the relation of figure 2.

The example shows that, in the XRM, two different but 'hot' research database areas, the management of spatial and temporal data are combined. Indeed, with respect to the former, it is observed that every pair of values for the attributes Length and Width, in OWNERSHIP, represents one of the rectangles, in figure 3. Arbitrarily large rectangles are represented by one pair of attribute values. In [SRF], it is argued that the handling of more complex objects can be reduced to the handling of rectangles in an n_dimensional space. Therefore, the XRM can be used for applications such as geographic databases, [KBK].

With respect to temporal databases, it is observed that the value of every tuple of OWNERSHIP, for attribute Period, shows the time during which John was the owner of the respective land. In contrast to other proposed temporal models, however, time is treated as data and not as a stamp.

MAP

Number	Longitude	Latitude
1	[42, 68)	[1, 13)
2	[21, 49)	[16, 42)
3	[35, 55)	[32, 50)
4	[39, 74)	[54, 77)

Figure 4: A valid relation of the XRM.

Furthermore, pieces of spatial and conventional data are represented uniformly. As an example, consider the relation, in figure 4. Each tuple records a map number and an area of Greece covered by that map. The relation scheme is MAP(Number=INT, Longitude=I(INT), Latitude=I(INT)). The maps are shown in figure 5.

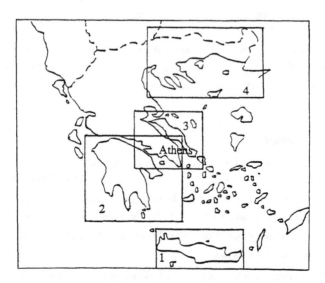

Figure 5: Areas covered by various maps.

Since, up to an isomorphism, INT⊆I(INT), MAP is a valid relation, in the XRM. The fact that INT is defined as the underlying domain of Number acts as an inherent constraint. Its interpretation is that only elementary intervals of the set I(INT) are allowed to be recorded on attribute Number. Furthermore, these intervals are restricted to appear to the user as points.

Finally, if Number=E(INT) is declared at the scheme definition then the inherent constraint is that only elementary intervals are allowed to be recorded and they do appear to the user as intervals. Definitely, the user can convert elementary intervals to points and vice versa by using the *cpoint* and *cinterval* functions, defined previously.

CAR

City	Number
athens	[AA0000, AC0000)
salonica	[AC0000, AD0000)
piraeus	[AD0000, AD5000)

Figure 6: A relation with intervals over
a set of alphanumeric strings.

A final example shows that intervals over arbitrary alphanumeric strings are meaningful in many applications. Figure 6 shows the valid car numbers which the authorities of every city are allowed to provide. The scheme of the relation is CAR(City=ALPHA_10, Number=I(S)), where S={XXNNNN / "AA"≤"XX"≤"ZZ", 0≤NNNN≤9999}.

4.2 Operations

The UNION, DIFF(Set-difference), PROJECT, and CP(Cartesian product) operations of CRA apply directly, in the XRM. For example, if the UNION operation is used to append the tuple

([16,24), [2,8), [04.05.85, 12.12.85))

to the relation, in figure 2, the resulting relation will contain the original tuples of OWNERSHIP plus the new one. For the PROJECT operation it should be noted that if the result of a projection of OWNERSHIP on attributes Length and Width is routed to a graphics monitor then it will appear to the user as in figure 3.

4.2.1 The SELECT Operation

This operation allows the incorporation of any of the predicates, defined in section 3. Normally, the '<', '≤', '=', '≠', '≥' and '>' predicates, of the CRM, are not allowed, in the XRM. This is justified by the following facts. Firstly, because of the Duality Principle, the XRM predicates can also apply to points or to a combination of a point and an interval. Secondly, every CRM predicate is a special case of a respective XRM one. The difference is that the CRM predicates are dedicated to apply only to points. In particular, the following are observed.

(i) When the '=' predicate for intervals is applied to two points, it reduces to the '=' predicate for points.

(ii) When *precedes* applies to two points, it reduces to the '<' predicate.

(iii)When *preequals* applies to two points, it reduces to the '≤' predicate.

The proofs for (i)-(iii) are trivial. Similar remarks apply for the predicates *follows*, *folequals* and '<', '≤', respectively.

Furthermore, it is easy to verify that *preequals* is a partial ordering mathematical relation, when it applies to non elementary intervals whereas '≤', its restriction to points, is a total ordering.

In this way, an important property of the CRM is satisfied, in the XRM, too. Specifically, the CRM predicates apply uniformly to all the attributes of a relation. That is, there is no restriction that some of them do not apply to certain attributes. This uniformity is also inherent, in the XRM but not in other proposed models. For example, the *overlaps* predicate, in [RL] and [NA] cannot apply to pairs of arbitrary alphanumeric strings.

Conventionally, one exception is made. The CRM predicates can be used in the XRM, provided that both of their arguments are points. The only reason which justifies this decision is that users are accustomed to their use.

4.2.2 The EXTEND Operation

Let $R(A_1, A_2, .., A_n)$ be the scheme of a relation. When the EXTEND operation applies to R, on an attribute A_i, $1 \le i \le n$, it results in a relation S of degree n+1. For each tuple $(r_1, ..., r_n) \in R$, S contains a family of tuples $\{(r_{ij}, r_1, ..., r_i, ..., r_n)\}$, where r_{ij} is an elementary subinterval of r_i. Furthermore, if R is the empty relation of degree n, S is the empty relation of degree n+1.

Formally, if the scheme of a relation R is $R(A_1, ..., A_i, ..., A_n)$, and $S = \text{EXTEND}[B_i, A_i](R)$, for some i, $1 \le i \le n$, then

(i) the scheme of S is $S(B_i, A_1, ..., A_i, ..., A_n)$,

(ii) if $R \neq \emptyset$ then $S = \{(r_{ij}, r_1, ..., r_i, ..., r_n) / (r_1, ..., r_i, ..., r_n) \in R, r_{ij} \le |r_i, einterval(r_{ij}) = \text{TRUE} \}$
else $S = \emptyset$.

B_i and A_i have the same underlying domains.

R

A	B	C
[1, 5)	[4, 6)	[2, 9)
[2, 7)	[2, 5)	[4, 8)

S=EXTEND[D,B](R)

D	A	B	C
4	[1, 5)	[4, 6)	[2, 9)
5	[1, 5)	[4, 6)	[2, 9)
2	[2, 7)	[2, 5)	[4, 8)
3	[2, 7)	[2, 5)	[4, 8)
4	[2, 7)	[2, 5)	[4, 8)

Figure 7: An example of the EXTEND operation.

Before an example is given, it should be noted that, from the Duality Principle, an elementary interval can be represented either as a point or as an interval. Without loss of generality it is assumed here, and in the remainder of this paper, that it appears as a point. An example of the application of this operation is given in figure 7.

Furthermore, if R=EXTEND[Town, City](CAR) is issued, where CAR is the relation, in figure 6, then the scheme of R is R(Town=ALPHA_10, City=ALPHA_10, Number=I(S)) and the value of every tuple for attribute City is repeated as its value for attribute Town. Intuitively, this example shows that EXTEND is a closed operation. It is easy to prove that its result is also a uniquely defined relation.

The physical interpretation of EXTEND is that it *extracts* all the elementary subintervals of the i-th component of every n_dimensional interval for some i, $1 \leq i \leq n$.

4.2.3 The UNFOLD Operation

Let the scheme of a relation be $R(A_1, ..., A_i, ..., A_n)$. When UNFOLD applies to R, on attribute A_i, $1 \leq i \leq n$, it replaces each tuple $(r_1, ..., r_{i-1}, r_i, r_{i+1}, ..., r_n)$ of R by a family of tuples $(r_{ij}, r_1, ..., r_{i-1}, r_{i+1}, ..., r_n)$, in the resulting relation, with the property that every r_{ij} is an elementary subinterval of r_i. If R is the empty relation, so is the resulting one.

Formally, if the scheme of R is $R(A_1, ..., A_{i-1}, A_i, A_{i+1}, ..., A_n)$ and $S=UNFOLD[B_i, A_i](R)$ for some i, $1 \leq i \leq n$ then

(i) the scheme of S is $S(B_i, A_1, ..., A_{i-1}, A_{i+1}, ..., A_n)$

(ii) if $R \neq \emptyset$ then $S=\{(r_{ij}, r_1, ..., r_{i-1}, r_{i+1}, ..., r_n) / (r_1, ..., r_n) \in R, r_{ij} \leq r_i, einterval(r_{ij})=TRUE\}$
    else $S=\emptyset$.

Again, as a default, elementary intervals appear as points. Figure 8 shows T=UNFOLD[D,B](R), where R is the relation in figure 7. Since B and D have the same underlying domain, the notation T=UNFOLD[B](R) is used to denote that T retains the scheme of R. Obviously, if only elementary intervals are recorded on B then T=UNFOLD[B](R)=R.

T=UNFOLD[D,B](R)

D	A	C
4	[1, 5)	[2, 9)
5	[1, 5)	[2, 9)
2	[2, 7)	[4, 8)
3	[2, 7)	[4, 8)
4	[2, 7)	[4, 8)

Figure 8: An example of the UNFOLD operation.

UNFOLD is not a primitive operation, since

UNFOLD[B_i, A_i](R)= PROJECT[on all attributes except A_i]oEXTEND[B_i, A_i](R).

The physical interpretation of UNFOLD is that it *splits* the i_th component, $1 \leq i \leq n$, of every n_dimensional interval into its elementary subintervals.

4.2.4 The FOLD Operation

In this paper only a semi-formal presentation of this operation can be given, due to space limitations. The reader can find a formal one in [Lo]. To illustrate the operation, consider relation R, in figure 9(a). It is observed that if the first three intervals of R are *merged* they result in the interval [2,11). This interval satisfies the following properties.

1. Each point of the interval is also a point of at least one of the intervals from which it is derived.

2. Conversely, every point of the intervals [2,5), [5,8) and [7,11) is also a point of [2,11).

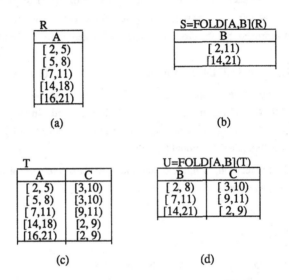

Figure 9: Examples of the FOLD operation.

It is simple to prove that an interval which satisfies these properties is defined uniquely. The same properties are also satisfied by the interval [14,21) and the last two intervals in R. In addition, [2,11) and [14,21) are disjoint. Therefore, the result of the operation S=FOLD[A,B](R) contains just these two intervals and it is shown in figure 9(b).

In general, let $R(A_1, ..., A_n)$ be a relation and assume that S=FOLD[A_i, B_i](R), for some i, $1 \le i \le n$. Then all those tuples of R, whose values for attribute A_j, j=1, 2, ..., n, j≠i, match and whose values for attribute A_i can merge into one interval, δx_i, are replaced, in S, by one tuple r, which satisfies the following properties.

1. The value of r for attribute A_j, j=1, 2, ..., n, j≠i, matches the values of the tuples, from which it is derived, for this attribute.

2. The value of r for attribute A_i is the interval δx_i.

As another example, for the relation T, in figure 9(c), U=FOLD[A,B](T) is shown in figure 9(d).

Because of the Duality Principle, FOLD can also be applied to a relation, on an attribute, in which only points are recorded. Thus, for the relation T, in figure 8, R=FOLD[D, B](T) results in the relation R, in figure 7.

Since B and D have the same underlying domain, the notation R=FOLD[D](T) is used, to denote that R retains the scheme of T.

The physical interpretation of FOLD is that the i-th component, $1 \leq i \leq n$, of two or more n_dimensional intervals *merge* into one interval, whenever this is possible, provided that these n_dimensional intervals match on the rest of their components.

In [Lo] it is proved that this operation is closed and its result is a uniquely defined relation.

It should be noted that the FOLD and UNFOLD operations are different from the NEST and UNNEST operations respectively, of Non-First Normal Form (NF^2) relational algebra, defined in [JS]. For example, the *left_overlaps* predicate, given in this paper, cannot be defined in NF^2. Furthermore, in [Lo] it is proved that the properties of the two algebras are different.

5. APPLICATIONS OF THE INTERVAL-EXTENDED RELATIONAL MODEL

Some examples are now given to show the expressive power of the model in a variety of application areas. In some of these, the algebra, defined in section 4, is used. In some others, the queries are expressed in an SQL-like language, whose definition has not yet been fully completed, in order to illustrate an Interval-Extended Relational Calculus.

Query 1: Consider the relation, in figure 6, and the query *"List the cities whose authorities provide the car numbers in the range [AA5360, AC5920)"*.

This is specified by

   SELECT City
   FROM   CAR
   WHERE Number *common_points* [AA5360, AC5920).

The answer is "athens", "salonica".

Query 2: Consider the relation, in figure 4, and assume that in another relation,

CITY(Name, Longitude, Latitude),

the coordinates of each city are recorded. The query *"List the maps in which Athens appears"* is issued as

   SELECT Number
   FROM   MAP, CITY
   WHERE MAP.Longitude |> CITY.Longitude
   AND   MAP.Latitude |> CITY.Latitude
   AND   CITY.Name = "athens".

The answer is '2', '3'.

Generally, any of the predicates, defined in section 3, can be used.

Query 3: Consider the relation in figure 2 and the query *"Update the OWNERSHIP relation to record that John was, in addition, owner of the area [2,13)x[3,12) during the period [05.04.68, 05.08.78)"*.

Let another relation R, union compatible to OWNERSHIP, contain the tuple

([2,13), [3,12), [05.04.68, 05.08.78))

and assume that the operation S=UNION(OWNERSHIP, R) is used, to append it. Firstly, it is observed that S, the resulting relation, is not semantically correct. Indeed, assume that, subsequently, another query is issued: *"When did John become the owner of the land [2,13)x[3,12)?"* The answer will be the dates 01.01.52, 05.04.68 and 09.06.74. This result gives the user the impression that for some period before 05.04.68 and for some period before 09.06.74, John was not the owner of this land. Clearly, this is not true. However, the user will not realize it, unless he retrieves from S the whole periods during which John owned the land. Secondly, it is observed that if an aggregate function is applied to S, to compute *"for how long, in total, John has been the owner of [2,13)x[3,12)"*, an incorrect result will be derived.

T

Length	Width	Period
[2,13)	[3,12)	[01.01.52, 22.08.85)
[2,13)	[12,19)	[05.03.74, 08.08.80)
[16,27)	[10,17)	[04.05.72, 03.08.80)

Figure 10: The result of appending semantically correct data to an interval relation.

These problems are overcome by the sequence of operations

S=UNION(OWNERSHIP, R)

T=**FOLD** [Period](S),

which result in the relation, in figure 10.

The same operations are used to append the tuple (piraeus, [AD3000, AD9000)) to the relation, in figure 6. This example shows the use of the XRA, to manipulate temporal and non-temporal relations in the same manner.

Query 4: Inversely, assume that a user query is *"Update relation T, in figure 10, to record that John was not the owner of the land [2,13)x[3,12) during the period [04.08.68, 09.06.74)"*.

Let U be another relation, set-difference compatible to T, containing the tuple

([2,13), [3,12), [04.08.68, 09.06.74).

If V=**DIFF**(T, U) is issued, nothing will be deleted from T. The desired result is achieved by the sequence of operations

        T1=**UNFOLD**[Period](T)

        U1=**UNFOLD**[Period](U)

        O1=**DIFF**(T1,U1)

OWNERSHIP=**FOLD**[Period](O1),

which results in the relation, in figure 2.

There are many other application areas for the XRM, for example:

1. The management of soil data, in Soil Information Systems. Typical queries, in these systems, require the retrieval of information about the composition of soil at arbitrary depths.

2. In mathematics, it allows step functions such as

$$F(X,Y)=\begin{cases} f_1 & / \quad x_{11}\leq X\leq x_{12},\ y_{11}\leq Y\leq y_{12} \\ \dots & / \quad \dots \\ =f_n & / \quad x_{n1}\leq X\leq x_{n2},\ y_{n1}\leq Y\leq y_{n2} \end{cases}$$

to be recorded and manipulated as relations.

3. CAD, cartography and version modelling, which are currently being investigated.

6. THE USE OF '@' IN TEMPORAL DATABASES

The use of a special symbol, @, was introduced in section 3. However, since an attribute domain is finite, situations can occur in which the original set of values becomes inadequate. For example, consider the relation in figure 11. It shows the period during which a person was the manager of a department. If the underlying domain of attribute Period is the set I(DATE), where DATE=$\{d_1, d_2, ..., d_{120}\}$ then @=@$_{DATE}$=d_{121}. Hence, it is not possible to record in it, for example, (tom, food, [d150, d180)) since d_{150}>@.

MANAGER

Name	Department	Period
mark	shoes	[d5, d80)
mark	toys	[d80, @)
jane	toys	[d1, d80)

Figure 11: Using '@' in a temporal relation.

To overcome this problem, XRM allows the database administrator to define @ dynamically. In particular, a special variable '*' has been defined which evaluates, every day, to the current day. In addition, one function *eafter* has been defined. Therefore, if the database administrator assigns to @ the value @=*eafter*(*,366), it is possible to record, in the database, data which will be valid during a period, in the future, which does not exceed one calendar year, starting today. In this way, past, present and future data is handled uniformly. The database mirrors the evolution of the enterprise and predictions, which are crucial in making future plans with respect to its current contents, can be supported.

However, one semantic issue has to be addressed. With reference to the relation, in figure 11, assume that today the date *=d_{120} and that @=*eafter*(*,366)=d_{486}. Assume also that a user retrieves the relation MANAGER. If its second tuple were to be displayed as (mark, toys, [d80, d486)) the user would be given the impression that Mark is to cease managing the department on date d_{486}. Clearly, this is not the correct interpretation. Therefore, a '@' is displayed rather than d_{486}. Its interpretation is that *"according to the data, currently recorded in the database, Mark will be managing the toys department, for the indefinite future"*.

This provides the semantically correct interpretation.

7. CONCLUSIONS

An experimental version of the operations defined, in this paper, has been implemented. The prototype uses INGRES for low level data management.

In this paper, an extension of the relational model has been formalized, which allows the recording and manipulation of generic intervals. Two primitive relational algebra operations were introduced, which are closed. The model is applicable to a wide range of applications.

Some of the properties of the operations formalized, in this paper, have been proved and a new functional dependency has been defined. Further research now being undertaken includes the definition of a calculus based language and the incorporation of optimisation techniques.

ACKNOWLEDGMENT

The authors would like to thank the referee for his helpful suggestions.

REFERENCES

[Ah]   AHN I. 1986. Towards an Implementation of Database Management Systems with Temporal Support. Proc. Second International Conference on Data Engineering, IEEE, pp. 374-381.

[Al]   ALLEN J. F. 1983. Maintaining Knowledge about Temporal Intervals. Communication of the ACM 26(11), pp. 832-843.

[CC]   CLIFFORD J. AND CROKER A. 1986. The Historical Relational Data Model (HRDM) and Algebra Based on Lifespans. Internal Report, Graduate School of Business Administration, New York University.

[Co]   CODD E. F. 1972. Relational Completeness of Data Base Sublanguages. Data Base Systems, Courant Computer Science Symposium 6, Ed. Randall Rustin, Prentice-Hall, Inc., Englewood Cliffs, New Jersey, pp. 65-98.

[GV]   GADIA S. AND VAISHAV J. 1985. A Query Language for a Homogeneous Temporal Database. Proc. ACM Symposium on Principles of Database Systems, pp. 51-56.

[JS]   JAECHKE G. AND SCHEK H. 1982. Remarks on the Algebra of Non First Normal Form Relations. Proc. ACM-SIGACT-SIGMOD Symposium on Principles of Database Systems, Los Angeles, California, pp. 124-138.

[KBK] KOLLIAS V. J, BURTON F. W. AND KOLLIAS J. G. 1983. A Soil or Land Information System with Spatial Processing Capabilities. Proc. of the International IASTED Symposium, Athens, pp. 297-300.

[KS1] McKENZIE E. AND SNODGRASS R. 1987. Supporting Valid Time: An Historical Algebra. TR87-008, University of North Carolina at Chapel Hill.

[KS2] McKENZIE E. AND SNODGRASS R. 1987. An Evaluation of Historical Algebras. TR87-020, University of North Carolina at Chapel Hill. Submitted for publication.

[LJ]   LORENTZOS N. A. AND JOHNSON R. G. 1987. TRA: A Model for a Temporal Relational Algebra. To appear in Proc. of Conference on Temporal Aspects in Information Systems, Sophia-Antipolis, France, North Holland Publishing Company.

[Lo]   LORENTZOS N. A. 1987. The Interval-Extended Relational Model and a New Functional Dependency. PhD thesis in preparation, Department of Computer Science, Birkbeck College, University of London.

[NA]   NAVATHE S. AND AHMED R. 1987. TSQL-A Language interface for History Databases. To appear in Proc. of Conference on Temporal Aspects in Information Systems, Sophia-Antipolis, France, North Holland Publishing Company.

[NH]   NIEVERGELT J. AND HINTERBERGER H. 1984. The Grid File: An Adaptable, Symmetric Multikey File Structure. ACM/TODS, 9(1), pp. 38-71.

[RL]   ROUSSOPOULOS N. AND LEIFKER N. 1985. Direct Spatial Search on Pictorial Databases Using Packed R-Trees. ACM-SIGMOD 1985 International Conference on Management of Data, Austin Texas, pp. 17-31.

[Sn]   SNODGRASS R. 1987. The Temporal Query Language TQUEL. ACM/TODS 12(2), pp. 247-298.

[SRF]   SELLIS T., ROUSSOPOULOS N. AND FALOUTSOS C. 1987. The R^+ Tree: A Dynamic Index for Multi-Dimensional Objects. Proc. VLDB 1987, Brighton, England, pp. 507-518.

[Ta]   TANSEL A. U. 1986. Adding Time Dimension to Relational Model and Extending Relational Algebra. Information Systems 11(4), pp. 343-355.

ESPRIT*: Trends & Challenges in DB Technology

Jack Metthey†, José Cotta‡

Abstract

Features concerning DB technology in the R&D Programme ESPRIT are highlighted, both in a perspective way (by looking at ESPRIT 1 projects) and in a prospective way (by looking at the ESPRIT 2 WorkPorgramme).
Then, the ESPRIT Programme is positioned in a global context, including other R&D Programmes from Europe, USA & Japan.
Finally, a provocative discussion about the different approaches taken is opened as conclusion...
Keywords: R&D Programmes, ESPRIT, DB, KB, Architectures, Complex Objects, Object-Oriented Paradigm, Hybrid Systems

Introduction

The ESPRIT insider might have noticed that this paper's title is conveying some kind of paradox, since there is no such thing as a DB Programme in ESPRIT, as opposed to CEC's MAP Programme, which is partly dedicated to **Distributed Databases**. However, this paradox is only superficial, and we shall try to illustrate first how both DBs and KBs are pervading the whole of ESPRIT, without forgetting to mention strengths and weaknesses. Then, some positioning exercise w.r.t other R & D Programmes currently going on around the world will be attempted and last, conclusions will be drawn.

1 ESPRIT: An Industry-Driven Programme

First of all, in its current definition (*WorkProgramme* for **1988** [CEC87a], ESPRIT 2 represents a smooth continuation of ESPRIT 1, at least in the DB field. No major reorientation has happened, although this may evolve in the future, e.g. thru the so-called **"Basic Research"** [1] action. However, as action is still under definition, it is too early to say whether DB and KB research will be significantly addressed there.

Illustrating the Programme's continuity mentioned above, what follows is a synthesis of both the 1988 WorkProgramme contents and the on-going projects, analyzed per section.

*European Strategic Programme for R&D in Information Technology
†SYSECA Consultant, Expert at the Commission of European Communities DGXIII/A/4 (ESPRIT)
‡Project Officer, Commission of the European Communities DGXIII/A/4 (ESPRIT)
[1]The Basic Research action is a new initiative taken in ESPRIT to promote basic R&D. Financial, managerial and monitoring rules of ESPRIT will be relaxed to favor Academia participation. The first call of this subprogramme will be launched during spring 1988.

1.1 Sections Analysis

It is not surprising that the emphasis and the demand which are put on DB technology varies according to sections [CEC87a] (as described in the 1988 WorkProgramme).

1.1.1 Microelectronics & Peripheral Technologies

DB-related concern in this area is mainly about VLSI design and CAD. Typical of this field are the large volume and complex structure of the design data, together with the extensive range of necessary design tools and all their varied interactions, meaning that the requirements of CAD systems for VLSI design are probably among the most challenging of all DBs applications (data types/ time notion/ etc.). This can be best illustrated by the **AIDA** Project (*"Advanced Integrated Circuit Design Aids"* -P.888).

1.1.2 Information Processing Systems (System Design & Knowledge Engineering)

- **System Design**

  Software engineering is particularly permeable to DB & KBs techniques. Broadly speaking, the technology is needed for the so-called *Software Engineering DB* (e.g. the **METEOR** Project -P.432), and future *System Engineering Environment* (Technology Integration Project **ASEE**); the necessity to handle more and more complex systems, where a system view (hardware+software) prevails, requires a **Complex Object Management System** to be available. As such, one can question the potential for evolution of PCTE's OMS, whose granularity is rather coarse, but it should be clear that an OMS forms the core of any environment to be built upon. Another important point currently under investigation (**ALF** -P.1520) is the "initiative taking" KB flavor (triggering mechanisms) such environments should have.

  More restricted themes where KB techniques are particularly influential are reusability (**KNOSOS** -P.974), project management (**PIMS** -P.814), and above all data-intensive applications in **DAIDA** (*"Advanced Interactive Development of Data-Intensive Applications"* -P.892).

- **Knowledge Engineering**

  With some emphasis already put on the development methodology, like in **MDKBS** (*"A Methodology for the Development of Knowledge-Based Systems"* -P.1098), this section is the most active for DB and KB technology innovation, as opposed to the other sections, which are indeed dealing with applications.

  What we see emerging here is mainly the materialization of the Industry concern for the following couple of points:

  - **Optimization**, which is understood in this case to subsume *real-time* aspects, *optimization* per se (of which the *recursive queries* problem is probably the most familiar to everyone), *performance evaluation*; only modest attention is paid to DB & KBs *architectures*, and mostly under the heading of *cooperation* between DBs and KBs, e.g. in **ESTEAM** (*"An Architecture for Interactive Problem Solving by Cooperating Data and Knowledge Bases"* -P.316).

  - **Interfaces** (Natural Language/Text/Graphics), e.g. in **ACORD** (*"Construction and Interrogation of Knowledge Bases Using Natural Language Text and Graphics"* -P.393).

However, some other problems are only marginally addressed (e.g. the incorporation of meta-knowledge aspects, by **ADKMS** (*"Advanced Data and Knowledge Management Systems"* -P.311)). By and large, one could say that two approaches dominate:

* the coupling of *Logic Programming* with relational DBs, e.g. in **LOKI** (P.107), or with distributed heterogeneous DBs, like in **EPSILON** (P.530).

* *complex and complete object-oriented* formalisms for knowledge representation, e.g. in **KIWI** (*"Knowledge Based User Friendly System for the Utilisation of Information Bases"* -P.1117) and **ISIDE** (*"Advanced Model for Integration of DB and KB Management Systems"* -P.1133). These formalisms are likely to constitute the basis for the emergence of object-oriented DBs.

1.1.3 IT Application Technologies (Computer Integrated Manufacturing, Office Systems & Robotics)

Without any possible hesitation, this is the world of **Distributed Multimedia DBMS**, a feature like local area networking being crucial e.g. for the design of *Office Systems* (e.g. **COMANDOS** -P.834). The other aspects are more related to CAD-like problems, whilst the notions of fast access and real-time pop up in *Robotics* or *CIM* (e.g. *"Knowledge-Based Real-Time Supervision in CIM"* -P.932).

Technically related problems worth mentioning are *Multimedia Support, Reliability* and *Safety*, those features being strongly linked to *Distribution*.

1.2 Conclusions (Partial)

As one could expect, ESPRIT turns out to be a rather wide-spectrum and mainly industry-driven Programme, both features reflecting the Programme's roots, as well as the recommendations expressed by the European IT Community during various panels and workshops, the WorkProgramme being nothing more than a tempered trade-off of their requirements. Two major factors can be extracted:

* **DB and KBs architectures** are almost ignored. The explanation for this probably lies in the rather disappointing outcome of all the *Database Machine* projects that were undertaken some years ago: specialized filters or dedicated processors have not proved significantly superior. Clearly, in the DB field, and up to now, ESPRIT has chosen to follow the software road.

* The second factor relates to **Market**: although only *by-products* of KBs work, *Expert Systems* have been privileged (too many projects to quote!), maybe because they are *buy-products*. One may also see there the pernicious consequence of having to-day's DB market already occupied (usually RDBMS marketted by US companies).

2 A Positioning Exercise: Europe vs. US & Japan

The best way of positioning European efforts in this area is to analyze them in the context of international R & D Programmes. It is of course almost impossible to be exhaustive, and only six of these have been selected (sorry for those not mentioned). These are:

- ESPRIT   (CEC)
- ECRC   (D-UK-F)   [NIKO87]

- BD3   (F)   [ADGR87]
- ALVEY   (UK)   [ALVE87]
- MCC   (USA)   [MCC87]
- ICOT   (J)   [ICOT87]

These Programmes provide a good sample of work currently in progress in the areas of the world with the most advanced R&D effort. The existence of industrial participation in the Programmes is a constant, although this participation may vary quantitatively.

Positioning is made along two axis: the first one, ranging from software to hardware, is called "Architecture", and is used to scale the weight of the corresponding components.

The other axis goes from data to knowledge and is entitled "Data Model"; its role is to evaluate the respective weight of DBs and KBs for each Programme.

The outcome of this survey is illustrated by Figure 1, where the balloons size is roughly proportional to the effort allocated to the Programmes.

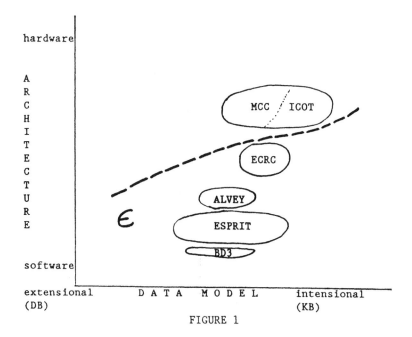

FIGURE 1

The main comment suggested by this Figure concerns the dashed line separating the European endeavors from the Japanese and American ones.

However unfortunate this may be, it is our belief that this is one direct consequence of the fundamental weakness of European hardware manufacturers, clearly illustrating the emphasis put on software solutions in most of the European Programmes.

3 Key Challenges For the Future

Before heading to conclusions, wie would like to highlight some points which we consider important:

- The mastering of *Object Complexity Management* [VALD87] is strategic; along that line, ever increasing attention is being paid to the *Object-Oriented Paradigm* (e.g. **GIP Altair** in France [BANC87], or the **KIWI** project in ESPRIT).

- In the realm of **Hybrid Architectures** (hw+sw), the interest seems now to have shifted from *processors-dedicated* architecture to *plain parallelism* (with the MCC ahead of ICOT). Inherent problems will be the availability of appropriate techniques for assessing performances and provide smart optimizations (distributed algorithms, hot spots detection, etc.).

  That type of move has not been captured in ESPRIT yet, although by and large quite a lot of effort has been put into parallel architectures technologies (e.g. **P.415**, where parallel architectures are developed for supporting object-oriented, logic and functional programming styles).

- DB & KB integrity and consistency are still open problems. Within ESPRIT, several different approaches to this problem are being studied (sometimes within a single project); if this can reveal a fruitful knowledge-generating situation, a synthesis is still needed in order to integrate whatever can be, and to compare alternative solutions.

- The Man-Machine Interfaces of such systems - although beyond infancy - are still adolescent, meaning that an integration among natural language, graphics, etc. is still needed. Next step is standardization, but this is a still later stage of development, where both software and hardware considerations may interfere.

- Last, it would be unfair not to say that in the DB/KB field, some ESPRIT Projects are very innovative: for lack of space and familiarity reasons, only two will be mentioned here, but we insist that they are not the only ones.

  The first one is KIWI, where state-of-the-art work is being done on the treatment of recursion, on the execution of Prolog programs [SACC87] and on the object-oriented approach to DBs; the second, ISIDE, beside developing a dual object-oriented and rule-based approach to the DB programming problem, elaborates on the idea that soon-to-come large core memories will drastically renew DB & KB processing capabilities.

Conclusions (Final)

We would like to conclude our paper by opening a provocative discussion. In fact, two different (probably even contradictory) conclusions can be drawn.

The first one is to say that hardware is progressing faster than software (in general terms), and that this fact will undoubtely open new opportunities, one example being the radical changes that full central memory processing will induce.

More widely speaking, a need has been identified to provide means enabling Hybrid Systems to be coped with. Such capabilities, if available -meaning that the object complexity problem had been given reasonable solutions- would foster the design and development of, for example, highly parallel KB machines, able to deal with ever larger volumes of information of ever more complex nature, coming along with appropriate tools, interfaces and development methodologies.

This is more or less what we can read out of the European R&D Programmes.

The second remark one can make is that the US & Japan seem to favor somewhat more hardware-oriented solutions to the KB problem. Therefore, doesn't a risk exist for Europe to be late, especially when considering that the ultimate goal of a Programme like ESPRIT is to reinforce the position of the European IT Industry in the 90s?

Although one cannot predict the outcome of such a duality, we are sure that it will be challenged by the European IT Community, and that ESPRIT will lead the way in that direction.

References

[ALVE87] ALVEY: ALVEY Achievements, DTI/PUB002/10K/06/87 1987

[ADGR87] Adiba, M., R. Demolombe, G. Gardarin, C. Rolland, and M. Scholl, "Le Programme de Recherches Coordonées Bases de Données (BD3)", *Technique et Science Informatique (TSI)*, Vol. 6, No. 5, 1987

[BANC87] Bancilhon, F., "Objectifs Scientifiques du GIP ALTAIR", *Rapport Technique GIP ALTAIR*, No. 8, 1987.

[CEC87a] CEC ESPRIT WorkProgramme, 22 July 1987.

[CEC87b] CEC, Project Synopses, June 87.

[GS87] Gardarin G., and E. Simon, "Les Systèmes de Gestion de Bases de Données Déductives", *TSI*, Vol. 6, No. 5, 1987.

[ICOT87] ICOT, Research Activities at ICOT 3rd Research Laboratory, *ICOT Journal*, June 1987.

[KMS87] Kiernan G., C. de Maindreville, and E. Simon, "A Production Rule Language for Databases Extended towards the Support of Complex Domains", *ESPRIT '87 Achievements and Impact (Part 1)*, North-Holland 1987.

[MCC87] MCC, Database Program, *MCC* 1987.

[NICO87] Nicolas, J.-M., "Les Bases de Données et de Connaissances à l'ECRC", *TSI*, Vol. 6, No. 5, 1987.

[SACC87] Saccà, D., "Compiling Logic Queries into Prolog Programs", *Università della Calabria*, Rende, Italia, 1987.

[VALD87] Valduriez, P., "Objets Complexes dans les Systèmes de Bases de Données Relationnels", *TSI*, Vol. 6, No. 5, 1987.

Acknowledgment:

We thank our colleagues Cynthia Rees and Brice Lepape for their comments on this paper.

Project Session on

Support for Data and Knowledge-Based Applications

Introduction by Domenico Saccà

Dipartimento di Sistemi, Università della Calabria
Arcavacata - 87030 Rende, Italy

The session on *Support for Data and Knowledge-Based Applications* contains a number of short papers that describe on-going projects aimed at expanding the boundaries of present Database Systems by adapting database technology to new domains of applications (e.g., knowledge-based applications) and to advanced software/hardware environments. The issue of making Database Systems more supportive of new demanding applications by means of innovative technology borrowed from various fields (logic programming, object-oriented systems, programming languages, knowledge representation formalisms, expert systems, etc.) is receiving wide attention these days. (For example, a number of large-scale strategic research programs in Europe, USA and Japan are mainly concerned with the design, development and usage of next-generation Data and Knowledge Base Systems.) The projects presented in this session are examples of how database systems may be made more capable to support data and knowledge-based applications; moreover, they provide an interesting overview of future trends of such systems.

The first two papers give two different answers to the question of whether next generation knowledge base systems will be based on logics (value-oriented) or will rather be object-oriented. (We recall that the term object is presently receiving different definitions; however, aspects such as data abstraction, property inheritance, data persistency, integration of data and operations appear to be common to most definitions.) The first paper *"The ALGRES project"* by Ceri et al. presents an example of advanced "value-oriented" system which extends the relational model to support non-1st-normal form relations and logic programming (particularly, recursion). The system is based on an extended relational algebra that includes a fixpoint operator. On the other hand, the paper *"O_2, an object-oriented data model"* by Lecluse, Richard and Velez describes the features of the data model of new object-oriented database system, where data manipulation, data definition and programming application are done through a unique language. All the above-mentioned object properties are present in O_2; in addition, the type system of O_2 is very well stated and includes recursively defined types. Also methods (operations) are formally defined in O_2 although they are not considered objects so a method cannot be handled as an object by other methods. A rich type system and the definition of methods also belong to other two data models (or database languages), i) Galileo, that supports the abstraction mechanisms of semantic data models and share many of the properties of object-oriented systems, and ii) ATLANT, that is described in the third paper *"Database programming tools in the ATLANT language"* by Zamulin. ATLANT follows the lines of Pascal/R (thus, a full programming language where database objects are persistent data structures completely integrated in the language) but includes many concepts of abstract data types as in the languages CLU and Russel. The fourth paper *"An overview of Sidereus: a graphical database schema editor for Galileo"* by Albano et al. shows that a system with complex objects such as Galileo can be supported by graphical tools that allow the user to handle all abstraction and typing mechanisms of Galileo using simple diagrams (such as Entity-Relationship ones) and graphical editors. Therefore, it seems that simplicity is not any-more a prerogative of value-oriented systems. Nevertheless, the previous question remains: declarativity of value-oriented systems against procedural methods of object-oriented systems (or, perhaps, a synthesis of both).

The fifth paper *"Towards KBMS for software development: an overview of the DAIDA project"* by the DAIDA team addresses a new field of application for Knowledge Base Systems: they may become the basic environment to support not only the usage of software (traditional data-intensive information systems) but also its development (design and implementation). Classical research on database design seems now evolving toward the more general issue of software design. The paper describes the features of a Knowledge Base System that support the main phases of the software life cycle: requirement analysis, design, implementation and usage. The first three phases are equipped with their own languages, respectively, SML, Taxis-DL and DBPL.

The next two papers are concerned with natural languages and databases. This issue is quite familiar in the database community where the term "natural language" has always generated controversy (is the natural language a desirable interface to databases?). The paper *"Entity-Situation: a model for the knowledge representation module of a KBMS"* by Bergamaschi, Bonfatti and Sartori describes the architecture of a system aimed at supporting natural language interfaces. The authors propose to use knowledge base technology to process natural language; to this end, a new data model is introduced that allows to represent the so-called deep structure of the natural language. This model is an extension of the Entity-Relationship model. The other related paper, *"TELL-ME: a natural language query system"* by Himbaut, describes a prototype supporting casual access to databases running in VAX/VMS environment. The prototype is written in PROLOG.

The paper *"ESPRIT: trends and challenges in database technology"* by Cotta and Matthey points out that issues related to the problem of extending database technology (in particular, complex objects, combination of logic programming and databases, novel architectures, integrity constraints, man-machine interfaces, etc.) play a central role in the strategic research program ESPRIT of the European Communities. This program is also compared with similar research programs both in Europe and in the world; finally, some of the projects funded by the ESPRIT program and concerned with the above issues are listed and their major results are discussed.

THE ALGRES PROJECT

S. Ceri(†), S. Crespi-Reghizzi (‡), G. Gottlob (**)
F. Lamperti(*), L. Lavazza (*), L. Tanca (‡), R. Zicari (‡)

(†)   Dipartimento di Matematica, Universita' di Modena
(‡)   Dipartimento di Elettronica, Politecnico di Milano
(*)   TXT-SpA, Milano
(**) Istituto per la Matematica Applicata, CNR di Genova

ABSTRACT

This short paper briefly describes the ALGRES project, an advanced relational programming environment for the specification and rapid prototyping of data-intensive applications. ALGRES is a vehicle for the integration of two research areas: the extension of the relational model to deal with complex objects and operations, and the integration of databases with logic programming. The ALGRES system is intended for the needs of the novel applications in the areas of deductive, engineering, and CAD-CAM databases and of office automation.

1.   OVERVIEW

The ALGRES project, supported by the Esprit project 432 "Meteor" of the ECC and by the italian MPI 40% and CNR, is based on a rigorous formalization of an extended relational algebra ([Abi 84],[Dad 86],[Fis 83],[Gue 87],[Lav 87],[Rot 85]) incorporating two main features: the managemant of complex (non-1st-normal-form) database relations and the use of a fixpoint operator (also called *closure* operator [Aho 79]) to express recursive algebraic expressions. Design goals go beyond the design of a query language, and include full computational completeness.

2.   THE ALGRES MODEL AND THE ALGRES-PREFIX LANGUAGE

The data model incorporates the standard elementary types (character, string, integer, real, boolean) and the type constructors RECORD, SET, MULTISET, and SEQUENCE. The schema of an Algres object consists of a hierarchical structure of arbitrary (but finite) depth built through the above type constructors. The algebraic language ALGRES-PREFIX includes:

1. The classical algebraic operations of selection, projection, cartesian product, union, difference (and derived operators, e.g. join) suitably extended to deal with new type constructors and with multiple-level objects.
2. Restructuring operations (nesting and unnesting) which modify the structure of objects, similar to those defined for non-first normal form relations ([Abi 84], [Rot 85],[Fis 83], [Lav 87]).
3. Operations for the evaluation of tuple and aggregate functions over objects and sub-objects.
4. Operations for type transformations, which enable the coercion of any type constructor into a different one.
5. A *closure* operator which applies to an algebraic expression and iterates the evaluation of the expression until the result reaches a fixpoint [Aho 79].

A goal of the language is to limit the loop complexity and to suppress linked list structures, which are the two major sources of pregramming costs.

3.   FORMAL SEMANTICS OF ALGRES-PREFIX

Due to the complexity and novelty of ALGRES-PREFIX, we have invested efforts in formally defining the semantics of the language by following two alternative ways:

1.   We have given an interpretation of an ALGRES schema as a regular right part, non-recursive context-free grammar; in this way, we define the valid instances of ALGRES objects as the strings generated by the grammar, and algebraic operations as modifications to the grammar and to the generated strings. This approach derives from the theory of syntax-directed translations and provides a very abstract attribute-grammar as foundation for the ALGRES compiler and interpreter.

A difficult aspect of these specifications is modeling ALGRES ability to recursively apply algebraic operations within the specifier of another operator: e.g. the predicate of a selection could involve a join. The formal definition introduces a local environment to model the scope of such inner operators.

From this abstract definition, we have derived a conventional attribute grammar, which is used by the syntax-directed translation. Notice that a similar representation has been implemented in the VERSO database machine [Abi 84].

2.   We have developed an algebraic, axiomatic definition using term rewriting rules for the formal speci-fication of ALGRES-PREFIX [Lav 87]. In particular, for these specifications we have used RAP [Wir 83], a tool for algebraic abstract data type specifications. Since RAP specifications are executable, we have obtained as side effect a first prototype of ALGRES, which for efficiency reasons has been recoded in Prolog [Lav 87]. The Prolog prototype has allowed us to experiment with critical fea-tures of ALGRES-PREFIX, and to revise certain inconsistencies, before availability of the execution environment.

4.   ARCHITECTURE OF ALGRES

ALGRES is interfaced with a commercial relational database system, but is not implemented on top of it. This is for the sake of efficiency: execution of our operations would be expanded into a long chain of database operations, causing very long response times. This danger is particularly serious for operations involving nested loops, or nested relations, or computation of fixpoints for transitive closures. Further, we assume that the ALGRES system will be typically applied to complex data structures of medium size, rather than to very large databases: examples are CAD and engineering systems, knowledge bases, software engineering systems, and some office automation systems. As a consequence of these assumptions, ALGRES objects are stored as main memory data structures, which are initially loaded from an external database, and returned to mass memory after manipulation. The abstract machine supporting the extended data model and its operations, named RA (*Relational Algebra*), reflects these assumptions: only a fraction of the database is supposed to be present in main memory at any time, and speed (rather than memory) is the limiting factor.

The core of the ALGRES environment (fig. 1) consists of the ALGRES to RA translator and RA interpreter. RA instruction set prevides traditional algebraic operations on normalized relations as well as special fea-tures; it has been carefully designed so as to provide instructions that can be efficiently executed over the flat subobjects stored in the main-memory algebraic machine. The translator and RA machine are being implemented on a SUN workstation, with the Informix Database Management System providing permanent storage of objects.

ALGRES run-time efficiency will not compete with traditional imperative Algol-like solutions, but it is intended to compare favourably with other existing productivity tools or high-level languages which have been successfully used for rapid prototyping such as SETL and Prolog.

5.   USER LANGUAGES

ALGRES-PREFIX is not a user-friendly language; it can be considered as the assembler of the extended algebraic machine. In order to provide to traditional database programmers and designers a multi-paradigm, easy-to-use programming environment, we have designed ALGRESQL, an extension of the SQL language which enables a *structured, English-like* query and manipulation language, comparable to other recent pro-posals ([Dad 86], [Rot 85b], [Pis 86]). Programs in ALGRESQL are translated into ALGRES-PREFIX before execution. We are also designing a Datalog [Ull 85] to ALGRES-PREFIX translator, for dealing with recursive queries. DATALOG is a new, Horn clause based logic programming language syntactically similar to Prolog, designed for retrieving information from a flat relational database system. Finally, ALGRESQL s interfaced with the "C" programming language in order to exploit exixting libraries, and to access the acilities of ALGRES from conventional programs.

5. CONCLUSIONS

ALGRES is best described as an operational environment for complex data manipulation, rather than as a query language and database system, which sets it apart from other projects similarly augmenting relational database system with nested relations. A specific run-time support was designed (the RA machine), which s quite different from supports to other dynamical languages (e.g. Lisp), since its basic operations are relational and memory allocation is compact (no lists or garbage collection); in the future we shall report on RA effectiveness.

An attractive development is to graft a logical style (a la Prolog) onto ALGRES: translation of Horn clauses into algebraic expressions has been investigated, and practical algorithms identified, at least for basic recursive queries. Work remains to be done for effectively integrating the two paradigms. We believe that ALGRES provides a novel approach to very high level programming and an open gymnasium for the integration of relational and logical techniques. Research on the execution of Datalog queries using relational algebra and a closure operation is described in [Cer 86],[Cer 87].

The state of advance of the project is as follows: the ALGRES-PREFIX to RA translator and RA interpreter are operational for a large subset of statements, including those for interfacing an external database; the ALGRESQL to ALGRES-PREFIX translator is in progress. Visual programming and interfaces to a conventional programming language (C) are being developed. An exploratory project for introducing recursive Datalog queries into ALGRES is under way. The Prolog prototype of the ALGRES PREFIX interpreter is operational, though rather unefficient, and is being completed and extended to cover error handling. Finally, a treatment of null-valued ALGRES attributes has been developed [Fer 87] (inspired by the one defined in [Gue 87]); its implementation is planned.

A more complete overview of the ALGRES project can be found in [Cer 87b].

ACKNOWLEDGEMENTS

We like to thank M. Dapra' and S. Gatti of TXT for coordination and management of the ESPRIT participation. We also like to thank all students who have completed or are completing their thesis on the ALGRES project, in particular: P. Dotti, M. Ferrario, F. Cacace, M. Giudici, M. Antonietti, P. Buda, P. Nasi, A. Pastori, A. Patriarca, D. Zaffaroni, A. Zavettini.

REFERENCES

[Abi 84] Abiteboul, S. and N. Bidoit "Non First Normal Form Relations to Represent Hierarchically Organized Data", *Proc. of the 3rd ACM PODS*, Waterloo, Ontario, Canada, 1984, and also in *Journal of Computer and System Sciences* 33, 1986.

[Aho 79] Aho, A. and J. Ullman "Universality of Data Retrieval Languages", *Proc. of the 6th ACM SIGMOD*, 1979.

[Ban 86] Bancilhon, F. and R. Ramakrishnan "An Amateur's Introduction to Recursive Query Processing" *Proc. of the ACM SIGMOD*, Washington, D.C., May 1986.

[Cer 86] Ceri, S., G. Gottlob and L. Lavazza "Translation and optimization of Logic Queries: the Algebraic Approach" *Proc. of VLDB 86*, Kyoto, Japan, 1986.

[Cer 87] Ceri, S. and L. Tanca "Optimization of Systems of Algebraic Equations for Evaluating Datalog Queries", *Proc. of VLDB 87*, Brighton, U.K., 1987.

[Cer 87b] Ceri, S., S. Crespi Reghizzi, L. Lavazza and R. Zicari "ALGRES: A System for the Specification and Prototyping of Complex Databases" *Politecnico di Milano, Res. Rep. no. 87-018*, 1987 (submitted for publication).

[Dad 86] Dadam, P. et al. "A DBMS Prototype to Support Extended NF2 Relations: an Integrated View on Flat Tables and Hierarchies" , *Proc. of ACM SIGMOD*, Washington, D.C., May 1986.

[Fer 87] Ferrario, M. and R. Zicari "Extending the ALGRES Datamodel and Algebra to Handle Null Values" *Politecnico di Milano, Res. Rep. n. 88-001*, Nov 1987.

[Fis 83] Fisher, P. C., and S. J. Thomas "Operators for Non-First-Normal-Form Relations" *Proc. of the IEEE COMPSAC*, 1983.

[Gue 87] Gueting, R.H., R. Zicari and D.M. Choy "An Algebra for Structured Office Documents", *Res. Rep. RJ 5559 (56648), IBM Almaden*, S. Jose, March 1987 (submitted for publication).

[Lav 87] Lavazza, L., S. Crespi Reghizzi, A. Geser "Algebraic ADT Specification of an Extended Relational Algebra and their Conversion into a Running Prototype" *Workshop on Algebraic Methods, Theory, Tools and Applications*, Passau, West Germany, 9-11 June 1987 (Springer-Verlag, to appear).

[Pis 86] Pistor, P. and R. Traunmuller "A Database Language for Sets, Lists, and Tables" *Information Systems*, vol.11, no. 4, 1986.

[Rot 85] Roth, M. A., H. F. Korth, and A. Silberschatz "Extended Algebra and Calculus for Non-1NF Relational Databases" *Techn. Rep. TR-84-36 , University of Texas at Austin*, revised version 1985.

[Rot 85b] Roth, M. A., H. F. Korth, and D.S. Batory "The SQL/NF Query Language", *Techn. Rep. TR-85-19 University of Texas at Austin*, 1985 (also in *Information Systems*).

[Sch 86] Schek, H.J., and M.H. Scholl "The Relational Model with Relation-Valued Attributes" *Information Systems*, vol.11:2, 1986

[Ull 85] Ullman, J., "Implementation of Logical Query languages for Databases" *ACM TODS*, 10:3, 1985.

[Wir 83] Wirsing, M. "Structured Algebraic Specifications: a Kernel Language" *Habilitation Thesis, Techn. Univ. of Munchen*, 1983, (to appear in *TCS*, also Univ. of Passau, Techn. Rep. MIP-8511.)

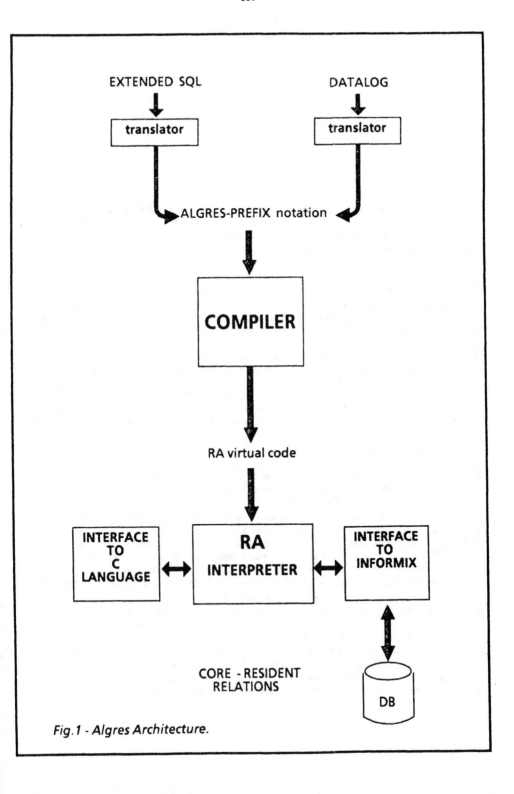

Fig.1 - Algres Architecture.

O₂, an Object-Oriented Data Model

Christophe Lécluse
Philippe Richard
Fernando Velez

Altaïr

January 6, 1988

ABSTRACT

The *Altaïr* group is currently designing an object-oriented data base system called O₂. This paper presents a formal description of the object-oriented data model of the O₂ system. A prototype of the O₂ system is currently running on Sun workstations with a Unix system.

1. Introduction

One of the objectives of the *Altaïr* Group is to develop a new generation database system. The target applications are traditional business applications, transactional applications (excluding very high performance applications), and office applications and its extensions (multi-media and IA-flavored business applications).

The interface between a programming language and a database has traditionally been through subroutine calls or by embedding a data manipulation language into a programming language. This kind of interfaces are awkward because the programmer must learn two different languages. There is both a structural mismatch (the type systems of both languages are different and data is transferred across the interface via variables of a limited set of basic types) and a conceptual mismatch: programming languages being currently interfaced with databases are almost always imperative, whereas query languages are declarative.

Our goal is to design a system such that data manipulation, data definition and programming applications are done through a unique language. The system we are designing is object-oriented. The object-oriented programming paradigm seems us a good way to cope with the goals that we defined above. Its main features are the notion of type [Goldberg & Robson 83] and the subtype hierarchy [Goldberg & Robson 83], [Zdonik 85].

Our approach strongly differs from standard object-oriented ones [Goldberg & Robson 83], [Bobrow & al 86], [Cox 86] , [Stroustrup 86] in that we do not only deal with typed data but also with highly structured one. We use set and tuple constructors to define arbitrarily complex objects. These objects are grouped into types which define a minimal common structure and common behaviour. We want our system to impose strong typing without loosing the advantages of late binding. We think it is necessary for data base applications to have a strongly typed system.

The main contribution of this paper is to propose a data model for an object-oriented data base system. The originality of O₂ is its type system defined in the framework of a set and tuple data model. There already exist data models which deals with inheritance (subtyping) such as [Cardelli 84] and [Bruce & Wegner 86]. There also exist papers which model complex objects [Bancilhon & Khoshafian 87]. Our paper extends to the case of a set and tuple data model, the set theoretic semantics for subtyping as proposed in [Cardelli 84]. Our model differs from that of [Bruce & Wegner 86] in that methods are not objects and that the type system is more permissive. Furthermore, our model allows the definition of recursively defined types. A "person" type may be a record type such that one of its field is itself of type "person".

2. Objects

Intuitively, objects are modeling our (computer) world. We shall consider some basic objects (integers, reals, strings, and so on) and we shall use set and tuple constructors to build structured objects from the basic ones. We shall also use identifiers for objects. These identifiers are necessary to deal with the sharing of objects. Futhermore, we want to be able to model cyclic objects, that is, objects which are components of themselves.

We suppose given: a finite set of *domains* D_1, ..., D_n, $n \geq 1$. , a countably infinite set **A** of symbols called *attributes*, and a countably infinite set ID of symbols called *identifiers*. D denotes the union of all domains D_1, D_2, ..., D_n and we suppose that the domains are pairwise disjoint.

Let us now define the notion of *value*.

Definition 1 :

(i)   The special symbol *nil* is a value, called a *basic value*.

(ii) Every element v of D is a value, called a *basic value*.

(iii) Every finite subset of ID is a value, called a *set-value*. Set-values are denoted in the usual way using brackets.

(iv) Every finite partial function from A into ID is a value, called a *tuple-value*. We denote by $<a_1 : i_1 , ..., a_p : i_p>$ the partial function t defined on $\{a_1, ..., a_p\}$ such that $t(a_k)=i_k$ for all k.

We denote by V the set of all values. □

We can now define the notion of object.

Definition 2 :

(i)   An *object* is a pair o $=$ (i, v), where i is an element of ID (an identifier) and v is a value.

(ii) O is the set of all objects, that is O $=$ ID $\times$ V.

(iii) We define, in an obvious way, the notion of *basic* objects, *set-structured* objects and *tuple-structured* objects (for example, a tuple structured object has a tuple value).

(iv) If o$=$(i,v) is an object then *ident*(o) denotes the identifier i and *value*(o) denotes the value v.

(v)   *ref* is a function from O in 2^{ID} defined as follows :
ref(o) $= \varnothing$ for all basic objects.
ref(o) $=$ value(o) for all set-structured object x.
ref(o) $= \{i_1, ..., i_n\}$ for all tuple-structured object o such that value(o) $= <a_1 : i_1 , ..., a_n : i_n>$. □

Intuitively, *ref*(o) is the set of all identifiers that are referenced in the value of o.

This "tuple-and-set" construction of objects (generally called "complex objects") is similar to that of [Bancilhon and Khoshafian 87], [Bancilhon & al 87], [Abiteboul & Beeri 87] and specially to that of [Kuper and Vardi 84] where identifiers (called addresses) are also introduced.

We now define the consistency of a set of objects.

Definition 3 :

A set Θ of objects is consistent iff :

(i)   Θ is finite,

(ii) The *ident* function is injective on Θ (i.e, there is no pair of objects with the same identifier),

(iii) $\bigvee$ o $\in$ Θ, *ref*(o) $\subseteq$ *ident*(Θ) (i.e every referenced identifier corresponds to an object of Θ). □

In the following, objects belong to consistent set of objects Θ and we denote by Θ(i) the value v such that the object (i, v) is in Θ

3. Type structures

A type is an abstraction that allows the user to encapsulate in the same structure data and operations. In our model, the static component of a type is called a type structure. A type structure is a way of classifying objects with respect to their structure. The operations will be called methods.

As we have basic objects, set-structured objects and tuple-structured objects, we define *basic structures, set-structures* and *tuple-structures*. We first define names for structures.

Definition 4 :

Bname is a set of names for basic structures containing : the special symbols *Any* and *Nil*, a symbol d_i for each domain D_i (we shall note $D_i = dom(d_i)$) and a symbol $'x$ for every value x of D.
Cname is a set of names for constructed structures which is countably infinite and disjoint with *Bname*.
Finally, *Tname* is the union of *Bname* and *Cname* and it is the set of all names for structures. □

Definition 5 :

Basic structures (Btypes) : a basic type is just an element n of *Bnames*.
Constructed structures (Ctypes) : A constructed type is either :

(i) an expression s=t where s is an element of Cnames and t is an element of Tnames,

(ii) an expression $s = <a_1:s_1, ..., a_n:s_n>$ where s is an element of Cnames and "$<a_1:s_1, ..., a_n:s_n>$" is a finite partial function from A to Tnames. We call it a *tuple structure,*

(iii) an expression s={ s'} where s is an element of Cnames and s' an element of Tnames. We call it a *set structure.*

A *type structure* is either basic or constructed. □

The following expressions are examples of type structures:

person $= <$name:string, sex:string$>$
husband $= <$name:string, sex:"'male", wife:wife$>$
wife $= <$name:string, sex:"'female", husband:husband$>$
persons $= \{$person$\}$

This example show that our model allows the definition of cyclic type structures such as "husband" and " wife" which mutually refer. In order to define it formally, we need some technical definitions :

Definition 6 :

A set Δ of constructed type structures is *consistent* (or is a *schema*) iff

(i) Δ is a finite set,

(ii) there is only one type structure for a given name,

(iii) all referenced types are defined by an expression of Δ. □

3.1. Interpretation

An interpretation is a function which associates subsets of a consistent set of objects to type structure names.

Definition 7 :

Let Δ be a schema and Θ be a consistent subset of the universe of objects O. An *interpretation* I of Δ in Θ is a function from Tnames in $2^{ident(\Theta)}$, satisfying the following properties:
Basic Names
1) $I(Nil) \subseteq \{i \in ident(\Theta) / (i, Nil) \in \Theta\}$
2) $I(d_i) \subseteq \{ id \in ident(\Theta) / \Theta(id) \in D_i \} \cup I(Nil)$
3) $I('x) \subseteq \{ id \in ident(\Theta) / \Theta(id) = x \} \cup I(Nil)$
Constructed Names
4) if $s = <a_1 : s_1 , ... , a_n : s_n>$ is in Δ then

$I(s) \subseteq \{$ id $\in$ ident(Θ) / Θ(id) is a tuple structured value defined (*at least*) on $a_1,...,a_n$ and
$\qquad \Theta$(id) $(a_k) \in I(s_k)$ for all k$\} \cup I($Nil$)$

5) if $s = \{$ s' $\}$ is in Δ then
$\qquad I(s) \subseteq \{$ id $\in$ ident(Θ) / Θ(id) $\subseteq I($s'$) \} \cup I($Nil$)$

6) if $s = t$ is in Δ then
$\qquad I(s) \subseteq I(t)$

Undefined Names

7) if s is neither a name of basic type nor a name of the schema Δ, then
$\qquad I(s) \subseteq I($Nil$)$ □

An interpretation I is *smaller* than an interpretation I' iff
$\qquad \forall$ s $\in$ Tnames , $I(s) \subseteq I'(s)$ □

We can now define *the* model of a schema Δ.

Definition 8 :
Let Δ be a schema and Θ be a consistent set of objects. The model of Δ in Θ is the greatest interpretation of Δ in Θ. □

Intuitively, the model M(s) of a constructed type structure of name s is the set consisting of all objects (identifiers of objects) having this structure. For example, if Θ is the following set of objects:

$$o_0 = (i_0, \text{Nil}) ,$$
$$o_1 = (i_1, \{i_2, i_3\}) ,$$
$$o_2 = (i_2, 1) ,$$
$$o_3 = (i_3, 4)$$
$$o_4 = (i_4, <a:i_2>) ,$$
$$o_5 = (i_5, <a:i_2 , b:i_3>)$$

and

$$\Delta = \{ s_1 = <a:\text{Integer}>, s_2 = <a:\text{Integer}, b:\text{Integer}>, s_3 = \{\text{Integer}\}\}$$

then

$$M(s_1) = \{ i_0, i_4, i_5\}$$
$$M(s_2) = \{ i_0, i_5\}$$
$$M(\text{Integer}) = \{i_0, i_2 , i_3\}$$
$$M(s_3) = \{ i_0, i_1 \}$$

This interpretation is derived from an interpretation which was originally proposed in [Cardelli 84]. A proof of the well-foundness of our interpretation can be found in [Lécluse & al 87].

3.2. Partial Order Among Type Structures

Definition 9 :
Let s and s' be two type structures of a schema Δ. We say that s is a substructure of s' (denoted by $s \leq_{st} s'$) iff $M(s) \subseteq M(s')$ for all consistent set Θ. □

For example, if Δ consists of the following type structures :

$$s_1 = <a:\text{Integer}>, s_2 = <a:\text{Integer}, b:\text{Integer}>,$$
$$s_3 = <c:s_1>, s_4 = <c:s_2>,$$
$$s_5 = \{s_1\}, s_6 = \{s_2\}, s_7 = <a:'1>$$

then the following relationships holds among these structures :
$$s_2 \leq_{st} s_1, s_4 \leq_{st} s_3, s_7 \leq_{st} s_1, s_6 \leq_{st} s_5$$

4. Methods

4.1. Definition

We assume that we have a countable set Mnames of symbols that will be used as names for methods.

Definition 10 :

Let Δ be a schema. A *signature* over Δ is an expression of the form:

$$s_1 \times s_2 \times ... \times s_n \to s$$

where s_1, s_2,..., s_n, and s are names corresponding to type structures in Δ or basic names. A *method* m is a pair $m=(n,\sigma)$ where n is a method name (an element of Mnames) and σ is a signature. We shall denote by *name*(m) the name of the method m and by *sign*(m) the signature of the method m. Let $m=(n, s_1 \times ... \times s_n \to s)$ be a method. We say that m *is defined on* s_1. $\square$

We define the model of a signature σ.

Definition 11 :

Let Δ be a schema and σ a signature over Δ ($\sigma = s_1 \times ... \times s_n \to s$). If Θ is a consistent set of objects, then the *model of σ in* Θ is the set of all **partial** functions from $M(s_1) \times ... \times M(s_n)$ in $M(s)$ where $M(s_k)$ is the model in Θ of the structure of Δ identified by s_k. $\square$

4.2. Partial order among methods.

Definition 12 :

Let Δ be a schema and f and g two signatures over Δ. We say that f is smaller than g (or that *f refines g*) iff $M(f) \subseteq M(g)$ for all consistent set Δ. This ordering will be denoted by $\leq_m$. $\square$

This partial order models inheritance of methods, just as the ordering $\leq_{st}$ models inheritance of data structures. In the following section, we put data structures and methods together to define type systems and we use the ordering $\leq_{st}$ and $\leq_m$ to define inheritance of types. The following theorem gives an easy syntactical equivalence to the definition of the partial order $\leq_m$ among signatures.

Theorem 1 :

Let f and g be two signatures over a schema Δ. Then, $f \leq_m g$ iff :

$$f = s_1 \times ... \times s_n \to s$$
$$\text{and} \quad g = s'_1 \times ... \times s'_n \to s'$$
$$\text{and} \quad s_k \leq_{st} s'_k \text{ for } k=1,2,...,n$$
$$\text{and} \quad s \leq_{st} s'. \square$$

Proof : see [Lécluse & al 87]

5. Type systems

We first introduce the notion of *type*. A *type* is a pair $(s, \overline{M})$ where s is a type structure and $\overline{M}$ is a set of methods. We denote by *struct(t)* the structure of a type t and by *methods(t)* the set of methods of a type t.

Definition 13 :

A set of types Π is a *type system* iff
(i) the set of structures associated to Π is a schema.
(ii) for all type t, every method m in methods(t) is defined on struct(t). $\square$

Now, given a type system Π, we must be able to compare two types t and t', with respect to their structures and to the methods they contain.

Definition 14 :

Let Π be a type system and t and t' two types of Π:
we say that *t is a subtype of t'* and we note $t \leq t'$ iff
(i) struct(t) $\leq_{st}$ struct(t'),

(ii) $\bigvee m \in \text{methods}(t)$, $\exists\ m' \in \text{methods}(t')$, name(m) = name(m') and sign(m) $\leq_m$ sign(m'). $\square$

We illustrate this by the following example :

Let Π be the following type system :

Δ = {(person = <age:integer, sex:string>, {(husband, σ_3)})}

(persons = {person}, {(has_parent, σ_1)})

(employee = <age:integer, sex:string, salary:integer>, {(husband, σ_3), (salary, σ_5)})

(employees = {employees}, {(has_parent, σ_1), (managed_by, σ_2)})

(male = <age:integer, sex:"male">, {(hire, σ_4), (husband, σ_3)}) }

σ_1 = persons $\times$ person $\rightarrow$ boolean

σ_2 = employees $\times$ employee $\rightarrow$ boolean

σ_3 = person $\rightarrow$ person

σ_4 = male $\rightarrow$ employee

σ_5 = employee $\rightarrow$ integer

In this type system, the following subtype relationships hold :

employee $\leq$ person, male $\leq$ person and employees $\leq$ persons

In the part concerning methods, our definition differs from the "classical" definitions of data type theory [Bruce & Wegner 86], [Cardelli 84], [Albano & al 85]. Our choice leads to a less restrictive type system, but we give up safety.

6. Concluding Remarks

We have presented the theoretical foundations of the object-oriented data model which we have implemented. The main contribution of this paper is to propose a data model for an object-oriented data base system. The originality of O_2 is its type system defined in the framework of a set and tuple data model. There already exist data models which deals with inheritance (subtyping) such as [Cardelli 84] and [Bruce & Wegner 86]. There also exist papers proposing models for complex objects [Bancilhon & Khoshafian 87]. A prototype implementing this model is currently running in the Altaïr group. The prototype was designed using the Unix system on Sun workstations. We are currently working on some extensions of the model. These are:

(i) Object naming: currently, the only handle that a programmer has on a object is through the name of one of its types. This means that, in order to retrieve an object of the database, the programmer has to send a message to the extension of the type with some key as argument. Such a problem is specific of database object oriented languages: in standard programming languages, we name objects using variables names and manipulate them through those names. Object names seem to be needed, and they have to be introduced in the model.

(ii) Modeling power of the model: a list constructor should be included in order to model ordered collections of data (it could be implemented as a recursive tuple type, but we would lose expressiveness).

(iii) Multiple inheritance: we have to evaluate the usefulness of multiple inheritance in real world applications, and its overall impact on our model, if it turns out to be a useful notion.

(iv) Higher Order Methods: in this model, we made the simplifying assumption that the methods are not objects of the model. So methods can be modeled as first order functions. It should be interesting to extend the model to treat methods as objects and to allow higher order methods.

Acknowledgements

Most of the ideas presented here were generated with F. Bancilhon. This paper also benefits from the careful reading of S. Abiteboul and our colleagues from Altaïr, in particular D. Excoffier. Thanks also go to A. Borgida, P. Buneman, D. Maier and D. DeWitt for the fruitful discussions we had on this model.

7. References

[Abiteboul & Beeri 87] "On the power of languages for the manipulation of complex objects", S. Abiteboul, C. Beeri, *in Int. Workshop on theory and applications of nested relations and complex objects, Darmstadt, 87*

[Albano & al 85] "GALILEO: A strongly typed, interactive conceptual language", A. Albano, L. Cardelli and R. Orsini, *ACM TODS, Vol 10 No. 2, March 85*.

[Bancilhon and Khoshafian 86] "A Calculus for Complex Objects", F. Bancilhon, S. Khoshafian, *ACM Conference on Principles of Database Systems, 86*

[Bancilhon & al 87] "FAD, a Powerful and Simple Database Language", F. Bancilhon, T. Briggs, S. Khoshafian and P. Valduriez, *13th Conference on Very Large Data Bases, Brighton, England, 87.*

[Bobrow & al 86] "CommonLoops:Merging Lisp and Object-Oriented Programming", D. G. Bobrow et al. *OOPSLA 86, Portland, Oregon, Sept 86.*

[Bruce & Wegner 86] "An Algebraic Model of Subtypes in Object-Oriented Languages", K., B. Bruce, P. Wegner, *SIGPLAN notices V21 #40, October 86.*

[Cardelli 84] "A Semantics of Multiple Inheritance", L. Cardelli, *in Semantics of Data Types, Lecture notes in Computer Science, Vol 173 pp. 51-67, Springer Verlag, 84*

[Cox 86] "Object-Oriented Programming, An Evolutionary Approach", B. J. Cox, *Addison Wesley 10393, 86.*

[Goldberg and Robson 83] "SmallTalk-80: The Language and its Implementation", A. Goldberg, D. Robson, *Addison-Wesley, Reading, Mass., 83*

[Kuper and Vardi 84] "A new Approach to Database Logic", G. M. Kuper, M. Y. Vardi, *ACM Conference on Principles of Database Systems, Waterloo, Canada, 84*

[Lécluse & al 87] "O_2, an Object Oriented Data Model", C. Lécluse, P. Richard, F. Velez, Internal GIP *Altaïr* Reasearch Report, Sept 87.

[Stroustrup 86] "The C++ Programming Language", B. Stroustrup, *Addison-Wesley, 86.*

[Zdonik 85] "Object Management Systems for Design Environments, U, S. Zdonik, *"A Quaterly Bulletin of the IEEE Computer Society Technical Committee on Database Engineering,"* Special issue on Object-Oriented Systems, Vol. 8, N.4, December, 85.

DATA BASE PROGRAMMING TOOLS IN THE ATLANT LANGUAGE

A.V. Zamulin
Computing Center of the Siberian Division
The USSR Academy of Sciences, Novosibirsk, 630090, USSR

Abstract

The ATLANT language is designed for the construction and operation of databases supporting various models. The language provides two levels of data definition: local data for a particular program and persistent data maintained for sets of programs. Persistent data are stored in one or several databases. Both local and persistent data are manipulated by the same set of statements. The data model is regarded as a set of data types and therefore the language provides a rich set of built-in specific and generic data types and tools for constructing user-defined types (both specific and generic).

1 INTRODUCTION

The ATLANT (Abstract Type LANguage Tools) [ZAMU86] project is working on the definition and implementation of a database programming language that faclitates the creation of data and knowledge bases according to a variety of models.

The language provides two levels of data definition, creation and manipulation: local data for a particular program and persistent data maintained for sets of programs. Persistent data are stored in one or several databases. Both the local and persistent data are manipulated by the same set of statements. Only one special statement, ON, is provided for connecting programs with selected parts of a specific database.

ATLANT belongs to the PASCAL language family: it uses the same syntactic forms as PASCAL does and has approximately the same sets of built-in data types and statements. It resembles the author's previous language BOYAZ [ZAMU78] but expands it through the mechanism of abstract data types. With respect to data base manipulation, both languages follow the lines of such programming languages as PASCAL/R, PLAIN, TAXIS, PS-ALGOL, GALILEO et al.. The principal feature of ATLANT is the absence of any built-in data model. Instead, it provides a "data type machine" for constructing desired data models by defining an appropriate selection of abstract data types [BW81].

2 DATA TYPE CLASSIFICATION

Every object stored in a database has a type. In ATLANT, such a data type defines a set of values by a set of operations. Any data type consists of two parts: specification and implementation. The specification part lists names and types of operations and the implementation part contains operation bodies in an implementation language. The types whose specification is done in AT-LANT and whose implementation is done in the ATLANT compiler are called built-in types. The

ATLANT language provides the user with an additional possibility of constructing user-defined (abstract) types. Both the specification and implementation of a user-defined type are written in ATLANT using built-in and previously constructed user-defined types. All details of a data type implementation are encapsulated so that objects of a data type may be manipulated only by the operations listed in the specification. The data type module in ATLANT is quite similar to the cluster of CLU [LISK81].

Both built-in and user-defined data types are divided into two classes: specific types and generic (parameterized) types. A specific type characterizes a definite set of values, it does not need any further refinement and is ready for the immediate usage. A generic type is a kind of a data type function yielding data types with the same sets of operations which differ in the types of some operands or/and results. A generic type must be instantiated to produce a specific type.

Any data type may have two classes of operations: constant operations with immutable bodies and variable operations with mutable bodies. The user may assign new bodies to variable operations, changing their algorithms. Failure functions called by constant operations when the latter cannot yield the proper result are examples of variable operations. The possibility of assigning different bodies to failure functions gives the user a convenient mechanism for exception handling. Variable operations may serve also as a database-procedure mechanism for persistent data types.

The set of built-in specific types includes boolean type BOOL, natural type NAT, empty type NONE, identifier type NAME, name specification type SPEC, and type of all data types TYPE.

The set of built-in generic type includes address type, sequence type, enumeration type, array type, record type, union type, file type, stream type and function type.

A specific user-defined type is created by the operation MODULE of the type TYPE. This operation has two arguments: specification and implementation. The specification is introduced as a sequence of name specifications giving names and types of operations. The implementation comprises the representation type which prescribes how to represent the objects of the constructed type and the set of constant declarations and variable initializations giving the algorithms of the data type operations.

The generic type is constructed as a function yielding data types whose specification, representation and implementation depend on the set of parameters. Let

$$T_r = \text{GEN } (p_1 : T_1, \ldots, p_n : T_n)$$
$$\text{MODULE specification}$$
$$\text{BEGIN representation and implementation}$$
$$\text{END}$$

be a generic type then instantiation operation

$$\text{TYPE } T_k = T_r(q_1, \ldots, q_n)$$

yields a specific type, replacing $p_1, \ldots, p_n$ in specification, representation and implementation parts by values of $q_1, \ldots, q_n$.

It is possible to define a subtype for any built-in or user-defined type by specifying additional constraints on the objects of the subtype. One sort of subtypes is built-in: it is the familiar PASCAL-like range type. At the level of built-in types, any subtypes is also a subtypes of type TYPE, subtype defines a subset of data types which has the given subset of operations.

3 DATABASE DEFINITION

An ATLANT database is a set of constants and variables of various types introduced by the data base definition (this set may change with time). Consequently, a database schema is formed by a set of type declarations, constant declarations and variable definitions. A schema composed only of data type declaration represents s specific data model which may be used for the definition of databases.

A data manipulation language is defined by the set of operations of the data types that compose the data model. If a data model contains generic types, the set of their parameters serves as a data definition language. In this case, the definition of the concrete database is the instantiation of the data model.

Thus the language permits two extremes in database definition: either the direct definition as a set of variables and constants of specific types or the instantiation of some data model (mixed strategies are possible, too). The language has also capabilities of redefinition of database constants (including functions, procedures and user-defined data type operations). It can be used for optimization of the database performance.

Any number of overlapping sections can be organized in a database. Each section comprises several variables and/or constants used by some program or a group of programs. Variables included in a given section are marked by the usage mode (access or modification), this helps to prevent the parallel updating of the same variable by concurrent programs.

Each database constant may be equipped with an access lock, and each database variable may be guarded by an access and update lock. The program which deals with locked constants and variables must contain the appropriate access and/or update keys.

4 DATABASE MANIPULATION

An application program binds itself to the selected database section by an ON statement indicating database and section names and a sequence of statements which are to be executed:

```
ON example S1 DO
sequence of statements
END.
```

Any number of ON statements are allowed in one program. When different databases are indicated, the transfer of data among those databases is possible. After the execution of the ON statement, all updated data are automatically returned into the database. In the body of the ON statement the programmer can save updated data by the FIX statement. If the program fails, the database is rolled back to the state fixed by the last FIX statement or by the end of the last ON statement.

In the simplest case the body of the ON statement may consist only of a database procedure call with a particular set of arguments. This provides end-users with the possibilities of easy manipulation of a database. In more complex cases the body of an ON statement may be a program with local data definitions and a sequence of statements processing local and database data.

Any ATLANT statement is considered as an expression of type NONE. The set of statements is quite traditional. There are simple statements (assignment, procedure call, loop exit, function (procedure) return) and compound statements (blocks, conditional, loops, etc.). For processing all or some components of structured variables the scanning statement of the form:

```
IN variable FOR loop-parameter WHEN boolean expression DO statement
```

is provided. It looks like the FOR EACH statement of PASCAL/R [SCHM77] or PLAIN [WASS81] but is applicable to variables of all the types containing the iterator operation. The iterators are defined for such built-in types as sequence, array and file types. The programmer may construct them also on user-defined types (relations, trees, etc.).

5 CONCLUDING REMARKS

In this paper the database programming tools of the ATLANT language are presented. The language is designed for modelling both, the structure and the behavior of data. The data model is defined as a set of (generic) data types. Hence the language does not support any particular built-in data model. Instead, ATLANT provides a data type machinery capable to construct a wide range of data models. The capability of an ATLANT database to store procedures and functions as distinct data objects or as components of structured data which can be activated automatically in response processing user requests allows us to consider ATLANT as a tool for constructing knowledge bases and expert systems.

The ATLANT programming system is being implemented under the UNIX Operating System.

References

[BW81]   Buneman, P., and I. Winston, "The Use of Data Type Information in an Interactive Database Environment", *Proc. Workshop on Data Abstraction, Databases and Conceptual Modelling. SIGPLAN Notices*, Vol. 16, No. 1, 1981, pp. 104-106.

[LISK81]   Liskov, B., et al., "CLU Reference Manual", *LNCC*, Vol. 114, 1981, pp. 190.

[SCHM77]   Schmidt, J.W., "Some High Level Language Constructs for Data of Type Relation", *ACM Transactions on Database Systems*, Vol. 2, No. 3, September 1977.

[WASS81]   Wasserman, A.I., et al., "Revised Report on the Programming Language PLAIN", *SIGPLAN Notices*, No. 5, 1981, pp. 59-80.

[ZAMU78]   Zamulin, A.V., "BOYAZ - A Database Programming Language", *Algoritmy i organizacia ekonomicheskih zadach. Moskva, Statistika*, No. 12, 1978, pp. 40-67, (in Russian).

[ZAMU86]   Zamulin, A.V., "The Programming Language ATLANT (the preliminary communication)", *Computing Center of the Siberian Division of the USSR Academy of Sciences*, Preprint 654, 1986, (in Russian).

AN OVERVIEW OF SIDEREUS:
A GRAPHICAL DATABASE SCHEMA EDITOR FOR GALILEO[1]

A. Albano[2], L. Alfò, S. Coluccini, and R. Orsini

Dipartimento di Informatica, Università di Pisa
Corso Italia, 40 - 56100 Pisa, Italy

Abstract *Sidereus is a workstation based graphical tool to edit a Galileo database schema using a diagrammatic notation. Several tools to manipulate a graphic representation of a database schema exist as commercial products or research prototypes, but the novel aspects of this proposal lie in the fact that the graphical editor is used to model a database using a semantic data model, to deal with complex objects with the values of attributes definable using the rich type system of Galileo, a database language that supports the abstraction mechanisms of semantic data models. Moreover, schemes designed with Sidereus are translated automatically in Galileo code, executable on the same workstation.*

1   INTRODUCTION

The diffusion of workstations and personal computers, with appropriate hardware to support interactive graphics, has promoted a growing interest and demand for graphical tools oriented to database applications. These tools can be classified in two main categories: *Analyst/Designer tools* and *graphical interfaces for DBMSs*. Tools of the first category typically allow the analyst and the designer to work with a graphical editor during the requirements analysis and conceptual design to edit graphical representation of information. Notable examples of these editors are integrated in the Software Through Pictures environment for software development described in [WP87] and distributed by the Interactive Development Environments, Inc. Tools that belong to the second category, graphical interfaces for DBMSs, are designed to facilitate both the design of a relational database schema and the access to the database. The graphical representation of a database schema is a kind of Entity-Relationship diagram that is manipulated to edit a new schema or to modify an existing one. Once the schema is completed, it is translated in a straightforward way to a relational database schema. Examples of such tools are Schema Design of SunSimplify, and EMPRESS/GQL of Empress. When the graphical interface is used also to query or update the database, an SQL statement is formulated by pointing directly to the boxes and connections of the Entity-Relationship diagram. Examples of such tools are EMPRESS/GQL of Empress, and LID (Living in a Database) [FOGG84].

The main limitation of the above proposals is the fact that the expressivity of the adopted data model is limited, since the tools support Entity-Relationship diagrams, or a simplification of them to be easily mapped into relations: For instance, a common limitation is that attributes can be defined only on simple domains. Although semantic data models, and more recently object oriented data models, are widely used to model complex and structured databases and their relevance is thoroughly recognized, the available tools do not offer features to model with the abstraction mechanisms of these advanced data models. For instance, it is not possible to describe structured, derived, and multivalued properties; ISA hierarchies among classes of entities; general constraints. An example of a graphical tool, called Sidereus, to overcome the above limitations is herewith presented. Sidereus is a graphical editor of a database schema in Galileo [ACO85] [AOO87]. Since Galileo supports a semantic data model with the abstraction mechanisms of *classification*, *aggregation*, and *generalization*, and a rich type system to define complex properties, the novel aspect of Sidereus is that the graphical capabilities of the editor permit a complete description of a database schema so that an executable Galileo code, together with the

[1]This work was supported in part by the "Ministero della Pubblica Istruzione"

[2]Present address: Dipartimento di Matematica e Informatica, Università di Udine, Via Zanon, 6 –33100 Udine, Italy

primitive operations to update the database consistently with the specified constraints, can be generated automatically and executed on the same workstation. A prototype implementation of Sidereus has been implemented on a SUN workstation with a bit-mapped display.

2 THE SIDEREUS SYSTEM

Sidereus allows the creation of a full Galileo data schema, since it consists of: a) a diagrammatic editor which operates on a graphical representation of the schema, and: b) a form-based editor for the specification of the attributes of the classes which are not specified with the graphical notation. Once a schema is completed, it is automatically translated into Galileo code, so that the definitions can be type-checked and evaluated by using the Galileo compiler.

Sidereus offers two environments: the *graphical environment* and the *textual environment*. In the former, the user designs the schema graphically. By double-clicking with the mouse on a class, or by selecting a menu command, the user can enter the textual environment, where he can specify the types of the attributes of class elements, either as predefined types or as (user–definable) new types.

The graphical environment A diagram produced with the graphical editor satisfies both a set of semantical constraints, and a set of geometrical constraints. The semantical constraints ensure that the diagram corresponds to a consistent Galileo schema. The geometrical constraints are:

– An arc can be composed only by horizontal and vertical segments connected to their end-points.

– Rectangular, square, or circular nodes can have outgoing and ingoing arcs on every point of their perimeter.

– Diamonds can have only ingoing arcs entering a pair of opposite vertices.

Moreover, a set of automatic and manual facilities are incorporated into the system in order to produce a diagram which satisfies certain aesthetical criteria:

– The outgoing arcs of a class are centered with respect to the edges of the rectangle.

– Class names are centered inside the rectangle representing the class.

– Arcs have at most three connecting segments.

In Figure 1 the workstation screen is shown during database editing in the graphical environment. The palette to the left is a fixed menu which presents the available commands in an iconic or textual form, the bottom window is an area for communications to the user, and the big window, with an example of schema, is the working area. The working area can be scrolled both vertically and horizontally, in order to accommodate a large project.

The user interacts with the system by choosing a command from the palette, and by applying it to some point of the diagram, when necessary. The commands can be classified in the following categories:

Creation Commands It is possible to create: rectangles for classes, arcs from rectangles to diamonds, diamonds with vertical or horizontal connecting "handles", squares for tuple associations, circles for variant associations, arcs for subclass relationship, identifiers for classes and arcs. Moreover, there are two toggle commands: one to insert or remove a cut in an arc (partial associations), and one to change from a single to a double arrow and vice-versa (multi-valued associations).

To apply a command of this kind, the user first clicks with the mouse on the corresponding element of the palette, which is inverted to show the selected operation, then clicks with the mouse on the working area to "stamp" the element on it. While the mouse button is pressed, the object can be freely moved on the screen until a satisfactory position is reached. In all these operations, a continuous feedback is given to the user. Regarding identifiers, the user selects the class or the arc which must be labeled, then writes the identifier with the keyboard. It is also possible to insert comments into any point of the diagram, in order to annotate it.

Geometrical commands The operators available allow the user to duplicate a rectangle, to stretch it, to align the center of two rectangles or a rectangle and a diamond, to center all the arcs outgoing from a rectangle with respect to the edge center, and to move any element of the diagram. An operator also exists which superimposes a grid onto the working area, allowing a more precise placement of the elements.

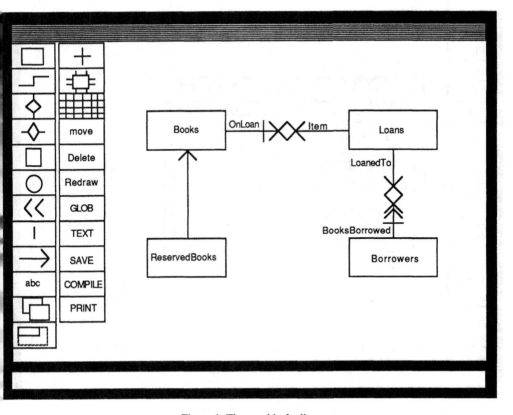

Figure 1. The graphical editor

The graph structure is automatically maintained during the execution of these operations, with redisplay algorithms providing an immediate feedback to the user. For instance, when the user moves a class, all the arcs connected to it are automatically moved. Moreover, all the alignment and centering operations help the designer to produce a neat design with little effort.

Miscellaneous operations Other operations allow deletion of diagram elements, redisplay of the schema, printing of the project and production of the Galileo source file starting from the project. Finally, there is the possibility of switching to the textual environment, independently from the selection of a particular class.

The textual environment This environment is a form-oriented editor for the definition of the class attributes and auxiliary types. The general idea is that it only allows the editing of information which cannot be given in the graphical environment. In particular, the user can specify certain properties of the associations, and give the name and the type of the class attributes which are not associations (*own attributes*), as well as define abstract types which are not class element types and that can be used for the definition of own attributes.

Instead of choosing a text oriented or syntax-directed oriented style of editing, we preferred a fill-in-the-form approach, which is more simple to learn and use. The user is given the possibility of filling the slots of forms which describe the various components of four kinds of entities: a) a class definition; b) a new type definition; c) a tuple type expression; and d) a variant type expression. In Figure 2 an example of the screen is shown during the editing of the attributes of a class.

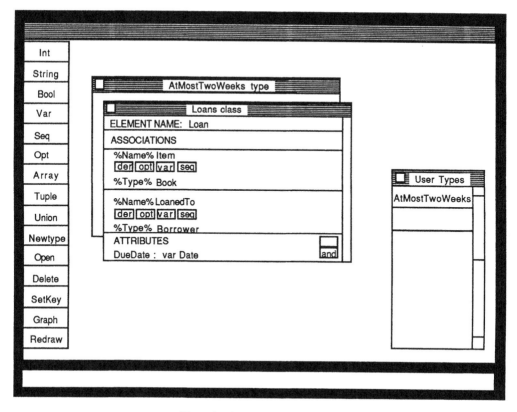

Figure 2. The form-oriented editor

Besides the window which lists all the user-defined types, each window corresponds to a form. A window can be scrolled, moved, resized, and closed. The user can write identifiers for attributes and new types, click on an "and" button to add a new element to a list of items, and click on the left palette to insert a type or specify a command. The palette shows all the primitive types and type constructors available, as well as a set of commands to: a) define a new type; b) open the window corresponding to a certain type; c) delete an element of the form; d) define one or more attributes as the keys of the class; e) return to the graphical environment; and f) redraw the screen.

The most important window is the class window, which describes the class relationships, the own attributes, the keys, and the assertions, which are entered as lines of text and whose control is left to the Galileo compiler.

3   CONCLUSIONS AND FUTURE DIRECTIONS

Sidereus, a graphical tool to edit a Galileo database schema, has been presented. The novel aspects of the proposal are: a) The tool supports a graphical representation of classes, subclasses and relationships between these classes, based on the semantic data model used by the conceptual language Galileo. The definable relationships can be simple, i.e. as those of the Entity-Relationship data model, or compound, using the structuring mechanism of discriminated unions and records; b) Classes can be opened to view a separate window where the names of the attributes and their types can be defined using the Galileo type constructors, together with constraints; and c) The database schema diagram can be translated automatically into Galileo code so that the definitions can be checked using the Galileo typechecker and executed using the Galileo compiler running on the same workstation.

Consequently, Sidereus is not just a graphical editor of database schema using a diagrammatic notation to support database analysis and design activities, as occurs in other proposals, but it is a full graphical editor of database schema for the Galileo language. The present implementation supports only the editing of class, subclasses, constraints, associations definitions (except tuple and variant associations), and data types definitions, but the project will continue to take into consideration the procedural aspects as well, in order to exploit the benefits of the diagrammatic notation to design transactions in Galileo. Another goal to be pursued is the use of the graphical interface as a semantic network database browser to allow queries by examining the contents of classes and by moving from one object to another to retrieve related information.

Sidereus is another achievement of the Galileo Project underway at University of Pisa. The aim of the project is to design and implement a database designer's workbench to design and prototype database applications, and to experiment with advanced features of database programming languages. In this project the role of the Galileo language is twofold: it is a research vehicle both on object oriented database programming languages, and on tools for rapid prototyping of database applications according to a prototype life-cycle model of the development process [AO84]. From our experience, tools such as Sidereus improve considerably both the Galileo programming environment and the usability of the database designer's workbench.

Bibliography

[AO84]
Albano A. and R. Orsini, "A Prototyping Approach to Database Applications Development", *IEEE Database Engineering*, Vol. 7, N. 4, pp. 64-69, 1984.

[ACO85]
Albano A., L. Cardelli and R. Orsini, "Galileo: A Strongly Typed, Interactive Conceptual Language", *ACM Transactions on Database Systems* 10, 2, pp. 230-260, 1985.

[AOO87]
Albano A., M. E. Occhiuto and R. Orsini, "Galileo Reference Manual", Servizio Editoriale Universitario di Pisa, 1987.

[FOGG84]
Fogg D. [84], "Lessons from a "Living In a Database" Graphical Query Language", *Proceedings ACM SIGMOD '84 Conference*, pp. 100-106, Boston, 1984.

[WP87]
Wasserman A. I. and P.A. Pircher, "A Graphical, Extensible Integrated Environment for Software Development", *ACM SIGSOFT/SIGPLAN Software Engineering Symposium on Practical Software Development Environment, SIGPLAN Notices* Vol. 22, 1, pp.131-142, 1987.

TOWARDS KBMS FOR SOFTWARE DEVELOPMENT:
AN OVERVIEW OF THE DAIDA PROJECT

DAIDA Team (*)

Abstract. Esprit project DAIDA investigates a KBMS approach to the development and maintenance of data-intensive information systems. The DAIDA environment manages the multilayered description of an information system (requirements analysis, conceptual specification and design, implementation design and realization) as a knowledge base. This KB is created and maintained under substantial use of (metalevel) knowledge-based tools, including those for mapping higher-level specifications to lower-level implementations. This short paper motivates this concept and sketches DAIDA´s approach to its realization.

1   Project Goals

A large number of projects have addressed the issue of making the production and maintenance of software faster and safer [BALZ85]. Recent attempts include aspects from formal specifications, software databases, and expert systems technology. Unfortunately, despite many good ideas and local improvements, no real breakthrough in productivity has been achieved to date.

In view of these experiences, Esprit project DAIDA [BORG87, JV87], begun in early 1986, decided on several limitations of its scope to increase the probability of success. Firstly, the application domain was limited to *data-intensive information systems (IS)* rather than general software; not only are IS one of the practically most important classes of software, this restriction also allows to bring a lot of specific knowledge to bear in a supporting environment. Secondly, DAIDA concentrates on a set of *well-understood development languages* with which the project partners have substantial experience. Finally, our architecture allows for an *incremental growth* pattern from (almost) manual to (almost) automatic software development, placing the emphasis on support, communication, and gradual knowledge acquisition rather than automation.

In this short note, we first characterize the specific properties that led us to consider the chosen application domain, data-intensive information systems. Then, the architectural and linguistic considerations leading to the DAIDA concept are presented, followed by a more detailed discussion of some of the tools to be included in the DAIDA environment.

(*) This work was supported in part by the Commission of the European Communities under Esprit contract 892 (DAIDA). The DAIDA team consists of: *BIM*, Everberg/ Belgium, prime contractor (Eric Meirlaen, Vera VanHeukelom, Raf Venken -- administrative manager); *Cretan Computer Institute*, Iraklion/ Greece (Alex Borgida, Maria Mamalakis, Manolis Marakakis, John Mylopoulos, Yannis Vassiliou); *GFI*, Paris/ France (Gerard Bonin, Alain Rouge); *Johann Wolfgang Goethe-Universität*, Frankfurt/ F.R.Germany (Henning Eckhardt, Gerhard Ritter, Joachim W. Schmidt, Martin Weigele, Ingrid Wetzel); *SCS Technische Automation und Systeme GmbH*, Hamburg/ F.R. Germany (John Gallagher, Rainer Haidan, Ingo Röpcke, Gernot Ullrich); *BP Research Centre*, Sunbury/ England (Horst Adler, Gerard O´Driscoll); *Universität Passau*, Passau/ F.R. Germany (Matthias Jarke -- technical manager, Manfred Jeusfeld, Thomas Rose). Correspondence address: Matthias Jarke, Faculty of Informatics, Universität Passau, P.O. Box 2540, D-8390 Passau.

2   Support Requirements

Software development environments should provide support for the analysis of requirements, the design of a system, its implementation, testing, and portation to the usage environment. Tools should also aid in the transformation between these different representations. Furthermore, we emphasize the *communication* function of such environments: they must preserve information about the software creation process for purposes such as *maintenance* of systems or *reuse* of existing components.

In general, these problems are far from being solved. However, we claim that data-intensive information systems have unique properties that determine special challenges and opportunities for development support. One important observation is that databases play the double role of storing beliefs about a real world section, and also being used in a real-world section (possibly the same). Special care has to be taken to maintain *validity*, i.e., the relationship between the system specification and (our knowledge of) the real world. Model animation and system prototyping are required to support validation; however, the relationship between the real world and its description in an information system is usually more easily observable than in complex scientific applications.

A second observation is the *longevity* of typical information systems. This places strong requirements on support for systems maintenance over long periods of time, with possibly changing generations of analysts, programmers, hardware, and system software. Again, there is a positive side, too: if properly represented, the application knowledge acquired during initial database design can be exploited in case of error corrections, system enhancements, extensions and new database application programs.

3   Architectural Considerations

Several approaches have been considered in the literature for providing the kind of information system evolution support discussed above:

- *Software databases* allow the organized storage and retrieval of design and software objects but neither provide active support nor decision-oriented documentation in the development and maintenance process. Recent extensions do address the question of multiple equivalent representations but not in the hierarchical form typical for software systems, where requirements determine designs, and designs determine implementations.
- *Expert systems* are well-suited for semi-structured applications in which little theory exists. In software development, this is on the one hand too little, on the other too much: where good formal methods exist, they need a special representation; where they don´t exist, simple rules of thumb do not suffice to replace human intuition.
- *Object-oriented tool kits* provide a simple communication mechanism to access tool objects. While this "open systems" approach appears very effective and flexible, we desire more control over the development process than is traditionally provided.

As a consequence of these deliberations, the *Knowledge Base Management System* approach chosen for DAIDA attempts to include desirable aspects of all the above approaches. This architecture is summarized in fig. 1. Specialized expert system-like tools are embedded into the architecture as extensible "assistants" which can grow with the body of theoretical and practical knowledge about information systems software development. At the physical level, an object-oriented message-passing mechanism is used to facilitate the communication between three conceptually and linguistically specialized environments for requirements analysis, conceptual specification and design, and implementation. At the logical level, this communication is supported and controlled by an enhanced design database, called the *Global KBMS* [JJR87]. The GKBMS contains a uniform abstract representation of the "software world" it controls (namely, versions of design objects and documents, histories of design decisions, and development tools). Inference mechanisms for deductive and direct-manipulation retrieval, consistency control, and reason maintenance [DEKL86] help maintain the complex relationships between objects, decisions, and tools over time. Viewed in a different manner, the GKBMS serves as a medium through which development decisions, their outcomes and rationales can be communicated across people as well as across time. This is seen as a major step towards effective maintenance support in large design teams [DJ85].

All of these components are offered to the developer in an open, window-oriented environment which also includes tools for manual software construction. Language and database sensitive editors play a major role in this context. At a higher level of support, knowledge bases containing standard requirements, designs, and methodologies can be included; at yet a higher level, partial automation of some transformation tasks is offered by so-called mapping assistants.

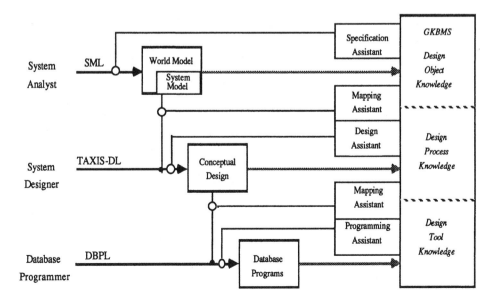

Fig. 1: DAIDA-Architecture

4 Linguistic Considerations

In selecting languages for the four major components of DAIDA (analysis environment, design environment, database programming environment, and GKBMS), two conflicting goals had to be satisfied. On the one hand, the representations offered for each of these tasks should be adapted to database-intensive programming and be as similar to each other as possible, so that the user (developer) will not have to learn several different languages, and transformation tasks can be simplified. Therefore, we chose a set of languages each of which is characterized by constructs for describing complex data objects (and sets of these) and a predicate-logic style of expression.

On the other hand, each of the components stresses different aspects; this would make it difficult to work with a single wide-spectrum language [BAUE76]. In requirements analysis for IS, the analyst needs to give a historical account of his or her knowledge about the system environment, and to relate this account to the description of this environment in the information system model. The language *SML*, evolved from ideas in RML [GBM86] and specialized to IS development from the general conceptual modelling language CML [BGMV85], offers extensible abstraction mechanisms that formalize ideas from semantic networks. An interval-based concept of time embedded in the language can, among other applications, serve as a basis for version management [ALLE83].

At the design level, the language *Taxis-DL* [BMMS87], a non-procedural extension of Taxis [MBW80] expresses the results of important conceptual design decisions which lead to an integrated semantic hierarchy of data object classes (view integration) and the classification of system activities as long-term scripts or short-term database transactions. Taxis-DL does not yet focus on a specific database model or programming language; however, it requires the predicative specification of transactions to a degree of detail that allows rapid functional prototyping in Prolog.

The database programming language *DBPL* [ECKH85] is intended as a tool for producing efficient and safe multi-user information systems software. DBPL is based on a data model supporting the predicative access and control of large sets of shared data and has the programming language Modula-2 as its algorithmic kernel. Important language constructs include selectors [MRS84] and constructors [JLS85] for the abstraction of access expressions; these rule-oriented concepts substantially facilitate the transition from Taxis-DL specifications to their implementation.

Finally, the *GKBMS* needs a knowledge representation language to record a reasoned history of the "software world" consisting of the evolving SML, Taxis-DL, and DBPL descriptions. Since, at first sight, this appears quite similar to the description task at the requirements analysis level, SML was chosen as a starting point for developing a GKBMS model of the evolving software world in CML. This model contains special metaclasshierarchies for the definition and usage of design objects, design decisions, design tools, and their interrelationships [JJR87].

5   Implementation Considerations

To demonstrate the KBMS-controlled open systems approach taken in DAIDA, the system is being implemented for a mixed SUN/UNIX™ and VAX/VMS™ environment, using BIM-Prolog™ with NeWS™-based graphics as a common implementation language.

One of the most challenging tasks relates to the consistent generation and preservation of relationships between the levels of the architecture, in particular, the design of *mapping assistants*. In the mapping from SML to Taxis-DL, at least two issues have to be considered. Firstly, SML allows user-defined metaclasses and property categories, whereas Taxis-DL accepts only a fixed set: entity classes, transaction classes, script classes, and a few more; other SML constructs must be mapped to predicative assertions associated with specific Taxis-DL classes. Secondly, the designer must decide what part of the temporal information in SML should be mapped to Taxis-DL (the rest will be ignored due to destructive update), and how it should be mapped (into transaction definitions, script definitions, or attributes of a historical database [SNØD86]).

In the mapping from Taxis-DL to DBPL, there is one easier and one more difficult task. The former involves the mapping of structures (IS-A hierarchies) of entity classes and transaction classes, to DBPL data set definitions and predicative transaction specifications in a modular software structure. Although several possibilities for this *structural mapping* exist, the options (not the trade-offs!) are relatively well understood [WEDD87] and can be realized rather elegantly with DBPL's access abstraction mechanisms. The second task is the implementation of structurally pre-mapped transaction specifications, i.e., the conversion of preconditions, postconditions, and invariants into efficient programs [HEHN84]. It is hoped that some of the concepts and theorem-proving tools associated with the language Z [O'DR87] can be exploited at least for verifying aspects of correctness, possibly also for partial program generation; this hope is nurtured by the observation that the majority of algorithms in database transactions is relatively simple.

6   Conclusions

We are currently in the middle of designing and implementing the first of two intended DAIDA prototypes. It is fair to say that a host of theoretical and practical questions remain to be addressed along the growth path of the system. For only some of these, experience is available from existing knowledge-based programming environments such as the Programmer's Apprentice [RICH84] or CHI/REFINE [SKW85]. Beyond the specific application, however, the architecture sketched in fig.1 appears to indicate *a new approach to implementing KBMS in general:* embedding time- or space-critical components of some knowledge base ("world model") in a system model, and supporting this system model by implementing it as an information system. This approach extends the well-known coupling and enhancement paradigms for KBMSs in that a tailored information system is *created* (not just accessed) for each knowledge base. Of course, its prerequisite is effective mapping support, as developed in software technology projects such as DAIDA.

References

[ALLE83] Allen, J.F. (1983). Maintaining knowledge about temporal intervals, *Communications of the ACM 26*, 11, 832-843.

[BALZ85] Balzer, R. (1985). A 15 year perspective on automatic programming, *IEEE Transactions on Software Engineering SE-11*, 11, 1257-1267.

[BAUE76] Bauer, F.L. (1976). Programming as an evolutionary process, *Proc. 2nd Intl. Conf. Software Engineering*.

[BMMS87] Borgida, A., Meirlaen, E., Mylopoulos, J., Schmidt, J.W. (1987). Final Version of TDL Design, Report, Esprit Project 892 (DAIDA), Cretan Computer Institute, Iraklion, Greece.

[BORG87] Borgida, A., Jarke, M., Mylopoulos, J., Schmidt, J.W., Vassiliou, Y. (1987). The software development environment as a knowledge base management system, in Schmidt, J.W., Thanos, C. (eds.): *Foundations of Knowledge Base Management*, Springer-Verlag, to appear.

[DEKL86] de Kleer, J. (1986). An assumption-based TMS, *Artificial Intelligence 28*, 2, 127-163.

[DJ85] Dhar, V., Jarke, M. (1985). Dependency-directed reasoning and learning in large systems maintenance, *IEEE Transactions on Software Engineering*, to appear.

[ECKH85] Eckhardt, H., Edelmann, J., Koch, J., Mall, M., Schmidt, J.W. (1985). Draft Report on the Database Programming Language DBPL, Johann Wolfgang Goethe-Universität, Frankfurt.

[GBM86] Greenspan, S., Borgida, A., Mylopoulos, J. (1986). A requirements modelling language and its logic, in Brodie, M.L., Mylopoulos, J. (eds.): *On Knowledge Base Management Systems*, New York: Springer-Verlag, 471-502.

[HEHN84] Hehner, E. (1984). Predicative programming, *Communications of the ACM 27*, 2, 134-150.

[JJR87] Jarke, M., Jeusfeld, M., Rose, T. (1987). A Global KBMS for Database Software Evolution: Design and Development Strategy, Report MIP-8722, Universität Passau, FRG.

[JLS85] Jarke, M., Linnemann, V., Schmidt, J.W. (1985). Data constructors: on the integration of rules and relations, *Proc. 11th VLDB Conference*, Stockholm, 227-240.

[JV87] Jarke, M., Venken, R. (1987). Database software development as knowledge base evolution, *ESPRIT '87: Achievements and Impact*, Amsterdam: North-Holland, 402-414.

[MRS84] Mall, M., Reimer, M., Schmidt, J.W. (1984). Data selection, access control, and sharing in a relational scenario, in Brodie, M.L., Mylopoulos, J., Schmidt, J.W. (eds.): *On Conceptual Modelling*, New York: Springer-Verlag, 411-436.

[MBW80] Mylopoulos, J., Bernstein, P.A., Wong, H.K.T. (1980). A language facility for designing interactive data-intensive applications, *ACM Transactions on Database Systems 5*, 2, 185-207.

[O'DR87] O'Driscoll, G. (1987). Evaluation of program support environments, Report, Esprit project 892 (DAIDA), BP Research Centre, Sunbury-on-Thames, UK.

[RICH84] Rich, C. (1984). A formal representation of plans in the Programmer's Apprentice, in Brodie, M., Mylopoulos, J., Schmidt, J.W. (eds.): *On Conceptual Modelling*, Springer, 239-269.

[SKW85] Smith, D.R., Kotik, G.B., Westfold, S.J. (1985). Research on knowledge-based software engineering environments, *IEEE Trans. Software Engineering SE-11*, 11, 1278-1295.

[SNØD86] Snødgrass, R. (1986). Research concerning time in databases: project summaries, *SIGMOD Record 15*.

[WEDD87] Weddell, G. (1987). Physical Design and Query Compilation for a Semantic Data Model, Ph.D. Thesis, University of Toronto, Canada.

ENTITY-SITUATION:
A MODEL FOR THE KNOWLEDGE REPRESENTATION MODULE OF A KBMS

Sonia Bergamaschi, Flavio Bonfatti, Claudio Sartori

Centro di Studio per l'Interazione Operatore-Calcolatore del CNR
Dipartimento di Elettronica, Informatica e Sistemistica, Universita' di Bologna
Viale Risorgimento 2 - 40136 Bologna, Italy - Tel. +39 51 583660

ABSTRACT

ADKS is an advanced data and management system whose main objective is to couple expressiveness and efficiency in the management of large knowledge bases is described. The architecture of the system and a new semantic model which is the basis of its knowledge representation module is presented.

INTRODUCTION

This paper reports on the research ESPRIT project 311 "Advanced Data and Knowledge management System" (ADKS) started in 1985. The project is carried out by a consortium constituted by Compagnie Bull, Nixdorf Computer, Olivetti SpA, Technische Universitaet Berlin, Universita' di Bologna, Universitaet Dortmund and Universita' di Torino.

The project objective is the development of an advanced Knowledge Base Management System (KBMS) that plays a twofold role:

- it stores large amount of intensional and extensional knowledge, enabling both efficient retrieval of stored data and the deduction of implicit information by taxonomic inference;

- it supports natural language handling, for a high level user interaction.

The ADKS is supported by a relational database system, which provides consolidated and efficient techniques and amenities for storing, accessing and maintaining very large amounts of data. Moreover, the database system is extended with functionalities for the navigation of relations which store concept taxonomies.

Since handling natural language requires a suitable representation and organization of the knowledge base, the knowledge representation model is a key issue in the project.

In this paper, we first give an overview of the system architecture, then describe the Entity-Situation model proposed as the paradigm for knowledge representation. The Entity-Situation integrates ideas from the Entity-Relationship model and from knowledge representation systems based on Structured Inheritance Networks [Brac 85].

SYSTEM ARCHITECTURE

The general system architecture is composed by the four layers visualized in the 3-D representations of Figures 1 and 2. Figure 1 points out the coupling between the Natural Language Handlers (NLH's) and the Knowledge Handler (KH) module. Figure 2 presents the solution adopted to bridge the gap between the knowledge representation and relational levels.

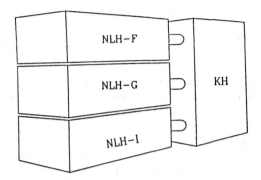

Figure 1 - System architecture: the user interface side

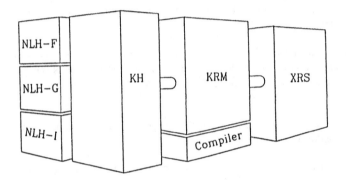

Figure 2 - System architecture: the knowledge base side

The end-user communicates with the system in his/her mother tongue. The natural language handler interprets the end-user sentences and generates a representation of the sentence semantics in terms of the knowledge representation formalism of the knowledge handler. The interpretation is performed by using both linguistic knowledge sources (specific for each language) and the domain knowledge provided by the underlying KH module.

In accordance with the partners' nationalities, it was decided to design three natural language handlers for French, German and Italian, respectively. This led to a neat separation between the surface structure of sentences and their language-independent semantics. The former is managed by the NLH modules while the latter constitutes the knowledge base contents.

The knowledge handler module captures the natural language semantics in terms of both concepts and related facts. This knowledge, which is assumed to be very vast, is managed with the support of a database system. The knowledge handler module is coupled to an extended relational system (XRS) module by the Compiler and the Knowledge/Relations Mapper (KRM) modules.

On the knowledge base side of the system architecture the KH module manages the knowledge necessary both to interpret the user query and answer it. Providing this knowledge is a typical task of the knowledge engineer. Then the system presents two entry levels:

-   the natural language, mainly for issuing end-user queries;

-   the knowledge representation formalism, for building the knowledge base or, at least, its initial kernel.

In both cases the KH module receives statements expressed in the knowledge representation formalism. This formalism must allow computations, i.e. the drawing of inferences from the intensional and extensional information and the control of data consistency.

Since the knowledge base is physically stored in a relational database, the execution of a statement implies issuing operations against the database. In order to achieve complete independence between the KH model and the underlying database system the KRM module is introduced into the architecture.

The KRM module operates on the basis of conversion tables which establish a correspondence between representation of the domain at knowledge formalism level and that at relational level. These tables are produced by the Compiler module, which generates the relational schema for both intensional and extensional knowledge [Berg 86].

The introduction of a compiler is justified by the need to design an efficient relational schema, taking into account the expected large size of the knowledge base and the types of operations to be performed. The compilation process is activated once the intensional description of the application domain has been obtained, or even when it is modified.

Finally, the relational database system is extended to incorporate new graph operators (such as transitive closure of binary relations) to support taxonomic inference.

In conclusion, the ADKS system presents two sides related to natural language user interface and to efficient knowledge base management, respectively. The knowledge representation model which is the basis of the KH module plays a keystone role in the whole system architecture. For this reason it is examined in more detail in the next section.

THE ENTITY-SITUATION MODEL

Different models have been considered for knowledge representation. For example, the Back system has been proposed by the team of the Technische Universitaet Berlin [Luck 87] within the framework of the project. It is based on the well known KL-One model [Brac 85]. Our group developed an alternative solution, the Entity-Situation model, which is more explicitly oriented to represent the natural language semantics. It can be seen as a descendant of the Entity-Relationship model in its original formulation Chen 76], which included the idea of role, and follows the basic approach of the structured inheritance networks [Brac 85, Sowa 84].

The idea of the model derives from the observation that a clause of the natural language has a surface structure and a deep structure [Fill 68]. The clause components (verbs, nouns and so on) are arranged in the surface structure in accordance with the syntactical and morphological rules of the natural language. The deep structure describes the underlying semantics.

The following example shows how the common deep structure of different clauses can be identified. Let us consider three clauses describing the loan of a book:

a library lends books to customers
customers receive books from a library
books are lent to customers by a library

The three surface structures correspond to different views, in that they point out three aspects of the same situation and, from a lexical point of view, also have different verbs. Instead, the deep structure of all three clauses describes the same transfer situation with *library* playing the role of agent, *customers* playing the role of recipient and *books* playing the role of direct object.

The presence of a common kernel of meaning, which is invariant with respect to the different lexical and syntactical aspects of the clauses, suggests the introduction of the **situation** as a new epistemological primitive to represent the semantics of a clause. The situation can be seen as an evolution of the relationship of the E-R model and becomes a higher level object, whose properties are couples <entity, role>. The roles have a semantic meaning and are chosen from a finite set. This set is obtained by classifying the ways an entity participates in a situation.

The problem of defining a complete set of semantic roles is still open, since no general classification has so far been found in the literature. A non-exhaustive list of roles is proposed in [Sowa 84]. It includes the following basic roles: agent or subject, direct object, recipient, instrument, material and some spatial roles.

The features of the Entity-Situation model are thus mainly four:

- a situation is a typed n-ary relationship among entities where the participation of each entity to the situation is characterized by a **role** chosen from those available in the natural language;

- an entity is modelled by the whole set of its properties, i.e. both the structural properties (attributes) and the participation to situations;

- entities and situations are classes, that is they group sets of items which share the same properties; the properties have the meaning of necessary conditions for the classification of an item as an instance of a concept;

- a concept (entity or situation) is marked as **defined** when its properties constitute also sufficient conditions; in this case an item can be automatically recognized as an instance of that concept; a concept is marked as **primitive** when the conditions are not sufficient; in this case an item must be explicitly declared as an istance of that concept, provided that it satisfy the concept necessary conditions.

Situations are organized into a generalization hierarchy with one root (Any_situation) and multiple inheritance. Each situation is represented as the specialization of one or more parent situations from which it inherits attributes and entities in the various roles. The inherited attributes and entities can also be restricted with respect to the parent situations. Moreover, the specialized situations can have additional attributes and roles.

As seen above, a situation contains couples <entity, role>. Then, the description of each involved entity is enriched by its participation to that situation in that role. This means that the definition of a situation affects entities definition.

Entities are organized into a generalization hierarchy with one root (Any_entity) and multiple inheritance. Every entity (with the exception of the root) is represented as the specialization of one or more parent entities from which it inherits both attributes and participation to situations. The inherited attributes and participation to situations can also be restricted with respect to the parent entities. Moreover, the specialized entity can have additional attributes and play additional roles in situations with respect to its parents.

The generation and maintanance of the two hierarchies involves the solution of some non trivial problems, such as computation of specialization links between concepts, classification of items in the proper concept class and definitions consistency check.

From a pragmatic point of view, the situation ensures a bi-univocal correspondence between the deep structure of a clause and the situation. Furthermore, the Entity-Situation model forces the description of all the situations according to the same pre-defined semantic role set, hence the knowledge base organization is more rigid, but it represents the meaning of the participation of an entity to a situation.

CONCLUSIONS

The Entity-Situation model is still under development at the Universita' di Bologna. Up till now we have defined a formal syntax and semantics for the model and are developing a prototype of the KH module which allows automatic classification of entities and situations and consistency checks. The realization of both the Compiler and the KRM module is also in progress and will be ultimated by the end of 1988.

REFERENCES

[Berg 86]   Bergamaschi, S., Bonfatti, F., Cavazza, L., Sartori, C., Tiberio, P., "Logical design of an integrated knowledge and data base", *Workshop on integration of logic programming and databases*, Venezia, Dec. 1986.

[Brac 85]   Brachman, R., Schmolze, J., "An overview of the KL-ONE knowledge representation system", *Cognitive Science 9(2)*, 171-216, 1985.

[Chen 76]   Chen, P., "The Entity-Relationship Model - Towards a unified view of data", *ACM Trans. on Database Systems, 1(1)*, 9-36, 1976.

[D7 86]   *First global system design*, ESPRIT Project 311, Deliverable D7, 1986.

[D9 86]   *Conceptual model for knowledge base*, ESPRIT Project 311, Deliverable D9, 1986.

[Fill 68]   Fillmore, C., "The case for case", in *Universals in linguistic theory*, Bach, E., Harms, R.T. (eds.), Holt, Rinehart & Winston, New York, 1968.

[Luck 87]   von Luck, K., Nebel, B., Peltason, C., Schmiedel, A., *The BACK System*, KIT-Rep. 41, Tech. Univ. Berlin, 1987.

[Sowa 84]   Sowa, J.F., *Conceptual Structures: Information Processing in Mind and Machine*, Addison-Wesley, 1984.

TELL-ME :
A NATURAL LANGUAGE QUERY SYSTEM[1]
Dr. Serge HIMBAUT
Digital Equipment Corporation
Route des Lucioles
BP29 Sophia Antipolis
06560 VALBONNE France
March 14, 1988

abstract : TELL-ME is a VAX/VMS based PROTOTYPE Natural Language Database Query Facility which supports the use of a (limited) subset of the English Language. As a prototype it demonstrates the feasibility of using Natural Language to support casual access to VMS database products.

1 TELL-ME Project

In any sizeable organisation, an increasingly large number of non-computer specialists (users) are expressing a need to retrieve information from a database on an ad-hoc basis. But the act of retrieval requires the availability of suitable tools, e.g. Query By Example, and the appropriate level of training in the use of those tools. These same users can often express their information needs in a native language, which is why we have chosen to create a program which translates information queries written in a subset of English into a logic form suitable for further translation into the appropriate database query language.

As a short term objective we chose to demonstrate the feasibility of a NL Query facility which had some degree of independence of the VMS database product being accessed, and of the particular organisation and contents of that database.

The long term objective of the TELL-ME project is to provide an NL database query facility which includes a capability to perform a detailed semantic analysis of the information request.

To date we have approached the objectives in the following stages :

- Production of a syntactic parser, with some limited semantic analysis, to handle some structures of the English Language and reduce the request to an internal Logic form.

- Production of a User Friendly Human Interface, including error detection and Help, a NL Menu, Synonyms, Adjectives and Saved requests.

- Production of a translator from the internal Logic form to the appropriate database query form.

2 Overview

The TELL-ME syntactic parser has no database dependent elements, i.e. it can be installed on top of a mix of VMS database products (RMS, RDB or DBMS) and allow the user to select, at will from a database menu, the particular database to be accessed. This capability demands that database meta-definitions are accessible to TELL-ME.

Once a database has been selected a user can access the following options :

- Type a request in English form.

- Call the context sensitive help which will display a selection of accepted "next words". One of these can then be selected for automatic inclusion in the request.

---

[1] This Prototype has been developed and tested by the DIGITAL European A.I Technology Group.

- Use a Natural Language menu to build a request (for novice users).

- Use forward and backward paging, plus horizontal scrolling, in order to view the pages of formatted response.

- Use the print facility in order to print all, or a selection, of the pages of formatted response.

- When appropriate, include a keyword in the request for a Graph display with the additional option of printing the displayed graph.

- Create and use a personnal definition of synonyms and adjectives.

- Save one request using a short name, for later retrieval (and use) from a menu of saved requests.

3 Architecture

The core of the program is written in PROLOG II [prologia] with the database and Human Interface making use of VMS layered products. The interface between PROLOG II and the VMS layered products is achieved via the use of the "User Defined Predicate" facility in PROLOG II.

The Prolog program is composed of :

- A grammar : Definite Clause Grammar based on "metamorphosis grammar" [col78].

- A lexicon logically divided into :

    - a common lexicon : composed of **verbs, interrogative pronouns, relative pronouns, and connector definitions.**

    - a temporary lexicon : composed of **common nouns** which are the field names of the database selected by the user.

- A context sensitive help.

- A NL Menu.

- A translator of the internal logic form into a database access language.

4 The Syntactic Parser

The Syntactic Parser applies a top-down and left-associative approach for the analysis of the sentence. Let's follow an example using the Yachts database describing yachts and boats.

Request : Show me the model

4.1 First Pass

The PROLOG code will attempt to find each of the words of the above string (S0 - S3) in the LEXICON and convert each recognised word into a PROLOG Identifier.

The *in-sentence* predicate (with two parameters X_1 and X_2) is used to achieve this and may produce :

X_1 is the first list of the input string, e.g. "show"."me"."the"."model".nil

X_2 is the equivalent list of PROLOG identifiers, e.g. show.me.the.model.nil

In the above example, because all the words are recognised, a transition would be made to the syntactic parser.

4.2 Second Pass

At this point all the words of the request must have been recognised. For example the Grammar used defines a sentence S as :

$$S \longrightarrow Verb\_phrase \; Noun\_phrase$$

In this example X_2 becomes S (a sentence) if it is a verb phrase followed by a noun phrase.

```
        S
      /   \
    vp      np              represented in an internal logic form as :
   / \    / \
show me  the model              show(x,model(x))
```

4.3 Third Pass

This pass translates the Internal Logic Form into the database access language.
The above example *show(x,model(x))* would be translated into

```
        for e in yachts store p using begin p.n1=e.model
```

4.4 Some exception conditions to the above example

4.4.1 Use of plural forms for field names

For this example consider first the following request :

```
Request : show me the models
```

X_1 : "show"."me"."the"."models".nil

X_2 : show.me.the.nil.nil

In X_2 the plural noun models has not been recognised because this noun is stored in the temporary lexicon, as a field name, in the singular form. In this case the Parser would apply some basic rules, resulting in the plural form of the noun being replaced by the singular form. For our example we see now on the screen :

```
Request : show me the model
```

The normal stages of parsing activity (as described in the first example) would then continue, with the resultant Internal Logic form of -

```
show(x,model(x))
```

4.4.2 Incomplete matching on database field names

It is often the case that the field names used in databases may be considered as "unnecessarily long", or have multiple parts (e.g. *this_years_model*), or the user may have some difficulty to remember the exact spelling of a field s/he wishes to access. TELL-ME attempts to overcome these problems by applying a incomplete match on field names.

- Example 1 :

  Let us assume that there are two field names *this_years_model* and *last_years_model*. If we were to make use of the request -

  ```
  Request : show me all models
  ```

  the word models in the request is first replaced by the singular form of the noun model (as shown in the previous example), then on the next pass the incomplete matching facility may replace the word model by *this_year_model*. i.e. the potential choices of field names for the selected incomplete

match database field will be made **arbritarily** from a collection of database field names containing the word **model**.

The request would then be parsed after this point. However the content of the all the database fields established in the collection would be displayed. The request shown on the screen is now :

> Request : show me this_years_model

This would produce the following as the Internal Logic Form :

> show(x,this_years_model(x))

However the translation to the database access language would include the names of all the fields which comprised the **incompletely matched** collection previously established. -

```
for e in yachts store p using
begin p.n1=e.this_years_model; p.n2 = e.last_years_model; end;
```

- Example 2 :

    Let us assume that the user cannot remember exactly how the field name is spelled; if we take a (slightly) modified form of the previous request -

    > Request : show me all mods

    this is not treated as a request on the part of the user for a list of persons who show a liking for one style of music (e.g. as opposed to "rockers"). The request shown on the screen is :

    > Request : show me this_years_model

    which is then translated to the Internal Logic Form

    > show(x,this_years_model(x))

4.4.3 Use of Adjectives

The use of adjectives to qualify a noun, e.g. **expensive models**, is common in database queries. TELL-ME allows a user to create and maintain a file of adjectives which that user would normally use when formulating queries on a particular database. For example:

> Request : show me all expensive models

In this example **expensive** is subsequently recognised as an adjective (via a read reference to the particular users file of defined adjectives for the selected database). The action of the parser is then to verify that the following word is a noun - or an adjective. In this example, following the previously described steps, **models** is replaced by **this_years_model** and **expensive** is translated into a selection expression which reduces the search space for **this_years_model**.

The request which would appear on the screen is

> show me all this_years_models with price > 10000

The Internal Logic Form appears as

> show(x,and(model(x),price((y,greater-than(y,10000)),x)))

The database access language which is then generated appears as

```
for e in yachts with e.price > 10000 store p using
begin p.n1=this_years_model ; p.n2=last_years_model; end;
```

4.4.4 Use of Synonyms.

The use of the word **boats** may be more usual to one particular user than the use of the noun **models**. In this case TELL-ME offers the user the facility to create and maintain a list of synonyms commonly used, by that particular user, in the context of use of a particular database. For example :

Request : show me all expensive boats

will result in boats being replaced by models with the results as previously described.

4.4.5 Use of Constants.

In the previous examples references have been repeatedly made to constants such as price > 10000. i.e. the constant is considered as a possible value of a database field, such as rig = SLOOP.

The Syntactic Parser will check to ensure that the type of constant is consistent with the understood attributes of the database field. e.g. The field price is recorded as a type **integer** - in which case the Syntactic Parser would indicate an error if the user attempted to apply a **string** constant.

4.4.6 Use of Saved Requests.

When a user has formulated a request and obtained a satisfactory response, the user can make use of the facility of saving the request and recalling that same request using a **short name**, or selecting the request from a list (Menu) of saved requests.

4.4.7 Handling of Unknown Words

If the First Pass fails to recognised a word in the request string, then the user is offered the possibility of defining the word as a Synonym, or Adjective. Alternatively the user may re-edit the request or select the context sensitive help which will make use of a Left Associative Grammar to identify the "possible next words" which the syntactic parser would find acceptable.

An error can also occur during the Syntactic Parse (Second Pass), the action taken to correct the request is exactly the same as previously described.

5 Conclusion

The current prototype has been successful in as much as it has enabled us to achieve a better understanding of the technology and of the nature of the problems which are likely to occur.

A significant piece of work remains to be completed in order to achieve the finished product.

Bibliography

[col75]**Colmerauer A**,Grammaire de Metamorphose,internal report, GIA Faculte de Luminy Marseille

[col78]**Colmerauer A**,Metamorphosis Grammar,In l.Bole,editor, Natural Language Communication with Computers,Springer-Verlag 1978

[sab80]**Sabatier P**,Dialogue en Francais avec un ordinateur,Thèse de 3 ème cycle,Faculte de Luminy Marseille

[Pereira83]**Pereira F**,Logic for Natural Language Analysis,SRI Technical note 275

[Winograd83]**Winograd T**,Language as a Cognitive Process,Addison Wesley

[PROLOG II 82]**Khanoui H,Van Caneghem M,Pasero R,Gianesini F**,Prolog II, Addison Wesley

[DE85]/bf Database Engineering oct 85

Project Session on

Distributed Database Applications

Introduction by G. Pelagatti

Dipartimento di Automazione Industriale, Università di Brescia
25060 Brescia, Italy

A Distributed Database is a collection of data which belong logically to the same system but are spread over the sites of a Computer Network. Depending on the degree of logical correlation between the different local databases, the homogeneity or heterogeneity of the local DBMS, the kind and bandwidth of the communication network, and the overall goal of the distributed system, a very wide range of distributed database systems and applications has been built.

These applications range from very tightly coupled homogeneous distributed databases built on top of a high-bandwidth local network to provide the functionality of a "distributed database machine", to very loosely coupled, heterogeneous, transnational database applications providing integrated operations between completely autonomous local systems using different local DBMS.

The projects presented in this session cover this wide range:

- PRISMA is a distributed database machine, homogeneous, tightly coupled, using a high-bandwidth local network;

- SABRINA-RT is a homogeneous, distributed, real-time database application over a wide-area network; the whole system is strongly integrated since it is devoted to a well defined specific application;

- The Multidatabase System for transnational Accounting is built on top of a widearea network which connects autonomous and heterogeneous local systems; site autonomy of each local system is a major requirement and much less integration is desired;

- MULTOS is a document server for building distributed office applications, typically on local networks and with loose coupling between the different sites;

- DURESS defines an "open system environment" for building distributed database applications; a high level of heterogeneity and of site autonomy is provided.

Confronting these very different projects, it seems interesting to investigate to what extent there are common technological problems and solutions for all of them; in other words, whether there exists a "distributed database technology" covering this wide range of applications.

The areas which should be analyzed include:

- System Architecture
- Communication Network Support

- Transaction Recovery

- Concurrency Control

- System Administration

- Query Decomposition and Optimization

- Mapping between Different Data Models

- Linguistic Support for Distributed Database Programming.

Each one of the projects has tackled several of these areas in different environments and with different goals.

PRISMA Database Machine:
A Distributed, Main-Memory Approach *
Research Issues and a Preliminary Architecture

Peter M.G. Apers at the University of Twente

Martin L. Kersten at the Centre for Mathematics and Computer Science

Hans C.M. Oerlemans at Philips Research Laboratories Eindhoven

Abstract

The PRISMA project is a large-scale research effort in the design and implementation of a highly parallel machine for data and knowledge processing. The PRISMA database machine is a distributed, main-memory database management system implemented in an object-oriented language that runs on top of a multi-computer system. A prototype that is envisioned consists of 64 processing elements.

1 PRISMA Project

The long term objective of the PRISMA project is to obtain a flexible architecture for a machine that effectively stores and manipulates both data and knowledge. This long term objective translates into the following goals:

- The construction of a multi-computer system, consisting of a large number of processing elements connected via a message-passing network;

- The definition and efficient implementation of a parallel object-oriented language, called POOL-X;

- The design and implementation of a main-memory database system in POOL-X;

- The design and implementation of an expert system shell in POOL-X that exploits parallelism for inferencing;

- The investigation of using medium to coarse grain parallelism for data and knowledge processing applications, the integration of data and knowledge processing, and the evaluation of the prototype multi-computer, among other things.

The project started in October 1986 and is scheduled until September 1990. The project team consists of members of the Philips Research Laboratories in Eindhoven and the following Dutch academia: Centre for Mathematics and Computer Science, University of Amsterdam, University of Leiden, University of Twente, University of Utrecht. Currently approximately 30 people are directly involved.

---

*The work reported in this document was conducted as part of the PRISMA project, that is partially supported by the Dutch "Stimuleringsprojectteam Informaticaonderzoek (SPIN)."

2 PRISMA Database

2.1 Key Issues in the PRISMA Database Machine

The most important ideas behind the design of the PRISMA database machine are summarized below:

- it aims at performance improvement by introduction of parallelism and by using a very large main-memory as primary storage;

- it is designed as a tightly coupled distributed database system;

- it provides an SQL and a logic programming interface;

- it uses a knowledge-based approach to exploit parallelism;

- it uses a generative approach for data managers;

A comparison with other systems can be found in [1].

2.2 Global Architecture

The PRISMA DBMS consists of centralized database systems, called One-Fragment Managers (or OFM), running under the supervision of a Global Data Handler (or GDH). The architecture of an OFM is explained in section 2.5. The GDH contains the data dictionary, the query optimizer, the transaction manager, the concurrency control unit, and the parsers for SQL and PRISMA-log, a logic programming language like Datalog. Besides these components, there is a recovery component and a data allocation manager.

Parallelism will be used both within the DBMS and in query processing. Within the DBMS this will be obtained by running several instances of components of the DBMS in parallel. Examples of these components are the parsers, the query optimizer, the transaction monitor, and the OFMs for intermediate results. For each query a new instance is created, possibly running at its own processor. This means that evaluation of several queries and updates can be done in parallel, except for accesses to the same copy of base fragments of the database.

2.3 PRISMAlog

The logic programming language that is defined in PRISMA is called PRISMAlog and has an expressive power similar to Datalog and LDL. It is based on definite, function-free Horn clauses and its syntax is similar to Prolog. One of the main differences between pure Prolog and PRISMAlog is that the latter is set-oriented, which makes it more suitable for parallel evaluation.

The semantics of PRISMAlog is defined in terms of extensions of the relational algebra. Facts correspond to tuples in relations in the database. Rules are view definitions including recursion.

2.4 Query Optimization

To exploit parallelism, on a large pool of processors, is a non-trivial task. One dimension of the problem is the grain size of parallelism: coarse or fine grain. In the PRISMA-project the coarse grain approach is taken, because we expect to gain more performance from it in our multi-computer architecture.

A knowledge-based approach to query optimization is chosen to exploit all this parallelism in a coherent way. The knowledge base contains rules concerning logical transformations, estimating sizes of intermediate results, detection of common subexpressions, and applying parallelism to minimize response time.

2.5 Architecture of One-Fragment Managers

The DBMS software is organized as a fully distributed database system in which the components are, so-called, One-Fragment Managers (or OFM). These OFMs are customized database systems that manage a single relation fragment. They contain all functions encountered in a full-blown DBMS; such as local query optimizer, transaction management, markings and cursor maintenance, and (various) storage structures. More specifically, they support a transitive closure operator for dealing with recursive queries.

Several OFM types are envisioned, each equiped with the right amount of tools. For example, OFMs needed for query processing only, do not require extensive crash recovery facilities. Moreover, each OFM is equiped with an expression compiler to generate routines dynamically. In this way the architecture of an OFM is tuned towards the requirements that can be derived from the relation definition and it avoids the otherwise excessive interpretation overhead incurred by a query expression interpreter.

3 PRISMA Machine

The PRISMA machine implements a parallel object-oriented language (POOL-X) on a multi-computer system.

3.1 POOL-X

The programming model of POOL-X is a collection of dynamically created processes. Internally the processes have a control flow behaviour and they communicate via message-passing only, i.e. no shared memory. The computational grain of parallelism is medium to coarse.

POOL-X is closely related to POOL2 [2] a general purpose object oriented language. It is strongly typed and hides the multi-computer details. POOL-X is somewhat tailored to the data- and knowledge-processing applications. At a few specific points it introduces dynamic typing to efficiently support the implementation of relation types. Furthermore POOL-X supports explicit allocation of the dynamically created processes onto processing elements. This allows for a proper balance between storage, processing, and communication, under the control of the implementor of the database system.

3.2 Multi-computer architecture

The multi-computer architecture envisaged in PRISMA encompasses a number of processing elements connected via a high-bandwidth message-passing network. All processing elements have (data)processing, communication and (local) storage capabilities. The various capabilities have to be balanced in such a way that ultimately the processing elements can be integrated in VLSI. In this way a powerful multi-computer can be implemented cost effectively, by simple replication of (cheap) components.

In a first (prototype) setup the multi-computer will consist of 64 processing elements. Each processing element will have four communication links running at 10 Mbit/sec, and a local main-memory of 16 MByte. The topology of the interconnection network will be mesh-like or a variant of a chordal ring [2]. Various simulations show an average network throughput of upto 20.000 packets (of 256 bits) per second for each processing element simultaneously. Given the high communication bandwidth between processing elements, central resource management is feasible and site autonomy problems as appearing in current distributed database management systems do not have to be considered.

Apart from the local main-memory, some of the processing elements will also be connected to secondary storage (disk). Using these, the multi-computer system implements stable storage and automatic recovery upon system failures. This approach leads to a simplification in the design of the database management system.

4 Current Status and Future Plans

Currently the main components of PRISMA, viz. an expert system, database management system and multi-computer, are identified and defined. In the next three years prototypes will be designed and implemented. A prototype implementation of the DBMS is envisioned to be running on an implementation of POOL-X on a sequential computer in the summer of 1988. Subsequently more extended prototypes on the actual PRISMA multi-computer will be realized.

5 Acknowledgement

It is a pleasure to acknowledge the contributions of all PRISMA project members involved; the work described in this document is the result of a stimulating cooperation.

References

[1] M.L. Kersten, P.M.G. Apers, M.A.W. Houtsma, H.J.A. van Kuijk, and R.L.W. van de Weg, *A Distributed, Main-Memory Database Machine*, Proc. of 5th International Workshop on Database Machines, 1987.

[2] W. Bronnenberg, A. Nijman, E. Odijk, R. van Twist, *DOOM: A Decentralized Object-Oriented Machine*, IEEE Micro, October 1987.

SABRINA-RT, A DISTRIBUTED DBMS
FOR TELECOMMUNICATIONS

M. DRIOUCHE (*), Y. GICQUEL (**), B. KERHERVE (*),
G. LE GAC (**), Y. LEPETIT (**), G. NICAUD (**).

(*) INFOSYS, 15 rue A. France, 92800 Puteaux, France
(**) CNET SLC/LSR, BP.40, 22300 Lannion, France

Abstract :

In this paper, we propose an enhancement to the functionalities of an existing database management system for the support of real-time distributed database processing. The main problem in designing such a system is maintaining good performances for processing queries on a given site while the database is being concurrently updated. The system was originally intended for real-time telecommunication applications, but remains open to new classes of applications (CAD/CAM, software engineering, multi-media, distributed systems, etc.). In this paper, we present telecommunication applications and the data management services required to support them. We introduce the architecture of SABRINA-RT which supports the needs of real-time telecommunication database applications.

1.   INTRODUCTION

Using distributed databases in a real-time environment implies important requirements for existing Distributed Data Bases Management Systems (DDBMS), especially for response times. Good response times must be guaranteed for real-time applications on different sites concurrently to database updates. Several approaches have been studied for DBMS real-time applications constraints. Such approaches consists in improving systems performances either in developing sophisticated query processing algorithms [BERN79], or in using adapted file systems [STON83], or in developing a specific memory manager [WEDE86] or also in using parallelism capacities offered by some machines. An other approach consists in building new DBMS with an adapted architecture which corresponds to the needs of real-time applications.

Telecommunications applications are good examples of applications with real-time constraints. To respect such constraints, we chose to build a dedicated DBMS architecture, adapted to specific needs and constructed upon an existing relational DBMS. The purpose of this paper is to present SABRINA-RT a distributed DBMS dedicated to telecommunication applications from the Centre National d'Etudes des Telecommunications (CNET). This DBMS has been built on SABRINA [GARD87] which is a pure relational DBMS prototype developed at INRIA and at University of Paris VI. The main purpose of the collaboration which has been established between CNET, INFOSYS and INRIA is to develop a distributed DBMS prototype, strictly responding to telecommunication applications characteristics, while remaining open to further enhancements.

The paper is organised as follows. In section 2 we present the telecommunications applications. In section 3 we detail the distributed DBMS SABRINA-RT architecture. Finally, we conclude on presenting the advanced state of the prototype.

2. APPLICATION REQUIREMENTS

The main function of a telecommunication system is to manage communication services such as data and image transmission, telephone etc... Such a system is made up of a number of quasi-autonomous physical machines located on various sites. The system is called upon to carry out processing of telecommunication calls and services, and this processing is divided between the various sites. The sites are interconnected by an internal communication network having a high data transfer rate. Transfer between the sites are governed by protocols structured according to the ISO norm [ISO80].

In the practical system, sites fall into two main categories : the local sites and the general site (see figure 1). The local sites provide telecommunication services and constitute the operational part of the system which offers services to the users: calls set up in a switching system, authentifications in a credit card public phone system, network routing in a multiple server system (e.g., 800 servers), etc. On these sites, in order to operate, telecommunication applications need stable data (descriptions of the telecommunications networks, user's rights, logic descriptions of transmission environment...). This data is mainly requested for interrogation with high real-time constraints. On a local site, telecommunication applications both update and query their private data, but global data (shared by the general site and all the local sites) may only be queried. The type of manipulation is mainly simple, the transactions are short but the real-time constraints are important (50 ms per access, 10 transactions per second). Evaluations can be found in [GRAV87]. On this site, the volume of data is very small (5 Megabytes).

The general site is in charge of exploiting the other sites. On this site, the user applications update the stable data from the telecommunication applications, observe and monitor the correct operation of the other sites and draw up statistics. Thus, the main task of this site consists in data management and in maintaining data consistency. On the general site, data processing is complex and the transactions are generally long (a few minutes) and not frequent (10 per hour). On this site, the volume of data is rather large (100 Megabytes).

Facilities provided by relational DBMS respond perfectly to the needs of the general site : easy data administration, flexible schema evolution, high level query languages supporting complex interrogations, tools for physical and semantical integrity management. On the local sites, required services are more restricted. On these sites it is interesting to get sophisticated copies of common data . These copies would contain only locally required data in a way to avoid collecting and computing it each time it is needed. All the possibilities offered by the relational DBMS are not necessary on these sites.

For response time constraints and data availability, we chose a common data replication strategy on all the local sites with a reference copy on the general site which is in charge of managing it. This replication can be partial or total but the replicated part must nevertheless take general updates into account.

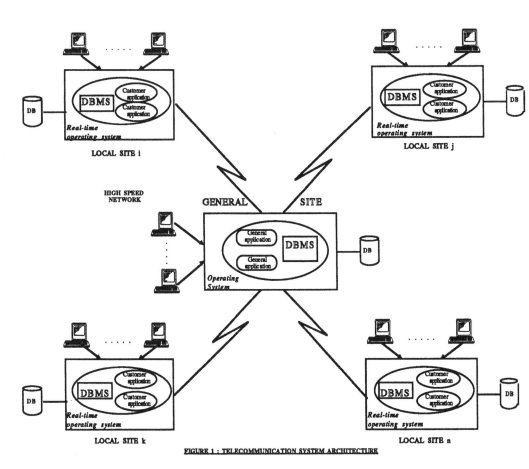

FIGURE 1 : TELECOMMUNICATION SYSTEM ARCHITECTURE

3. THE SABRINA-RT DISTRIBUTED DBMS

Our distributed DBMS is constructed upon SABRINA which presents some particularities well adapted to distribution : the data manipulation protocol, the meta-database manager and view processing. The data manipulation protocol is a translation of all the SABRINA user's commands into messages. This protocol is particularly suited for a distributed context since it constitutes a communication language supporting the dialogue between an interface machine and one or several database machines. In our case, it allows the various sites to exchange data manipulation commands.

SABRINA manages the data dictionary in an integrated way using a relational format. This data dictionary is called the meta-database. In order to take the data distribution into account, we enriched it with new relations. These relations describe all information needed for data localization to perform distributed queries and updates.

In SABRINA, a view extension is computed during the first query on the view. Then, the user's request is processed on this extension. We have proposed in [KERH86], to extend the lifetime of the view's extension beyond the transaction time. Thus, the view is materialized, i.e. a permanent relation is created from the view definition.

concrete views is to constantly reflect the state of the relations from which they have been built. Indeed, a system integrated triggers mechanism carries out the relation updates on the concrete views which depends on them, using a differential update technique. This mechanism is implemented in SABRINA-RT in order to manage the distribution of data in an original way.

We use this approach to distribute data on local sites at update time according to the expected local sites queries. Thus, a concrete view is created on the local site according to the expected requests. This implies distributed view definition and data updates, but local query processing. We then reach a system with distributed updates and local queries without distributed query evaluation. In this system, the local sites are more autonomous. As the concrete view definition corresponds to the expression associated with a query, when knowing the queries expression on a local site, we can decide there to implement the corresponding concrete view. This possibility is especially well adapted to telecommunication needs since the global data querying is repetitive and hence known in advance and since the real-time constraints on local sites doesn't allow distributed query processing.

The SABRINA-RT concrete view mechanism performs the distributed view definition and materialization, local site querying and assures that the basic relation updates are permanently reported to the corresponding concrete views. This mechanism is implemented at the distributed processing level of our architecture (see figure 2).

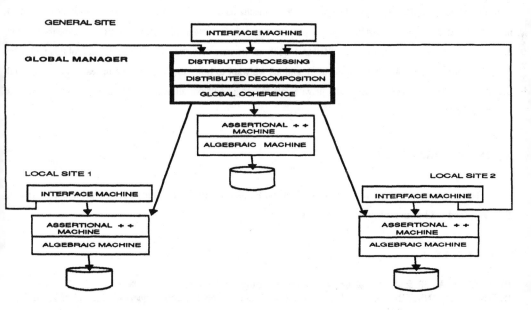

FIGURE 2 : THE ARCHITECTURE OF SABRINA-RT

In the SABRINA-RT architecture the general site software is different from the local ones. The general site is composed of three levels which are implemented on an enhanced version of the SABRINA DBMS. We add new functionalities to SABRINA especially for meta-database management and distributed concrete view processing. On the local sites, the enhanced version of SABRINA is implemented.

The distributed processing level is in charge of driving the global request decomposition and to coordinate the request execution. It also manages concrete views and carries out the global data administration. The role of the distributed decomposition level is to decompose global base requests into a plan which is partly executed on the general site and partly on the local sites. The global consistency level manages the reliability of the system and the coherence of the data. It is based on a concurrency control mechanism which operates on a three state locking protocol [BAYE83] with deadlock prevention using a global wait-for graph. Transaction management is maintained by a two step commit protocol. We chose a three state lock method (read, ready to write, write) in order to favor the reading transactions [GICQ85]. This method allows data to be shared between one writing transaction and several reading transactions, until the ready to write step of the writing transaction. Thus, the number of conflicts is decreased.

4. CONCLUSION

In this paper we presented SABRINA-RT which is a distributed DBMS prototype adapted to telecommunications needs. We first described these applications characteristics : distributed data and processing, real time constraints on local sites and sophisticated data management tools on the general site. These characteristics led us to adapt an existing DBMS with possibilities we could upgrade. We chose SABRINA because its characteristics allowed us to add new functionalities and to define new levels for the SABRINA-RT architecture. In a way to assure data distribution, we implemented the concrete view mechanism which favors local queries without distributed processing. At this time, the SABRINA-RT prototype is at a first stage of implementation. It appears that the alterations we decided to bring to the SABRINA DBMS kernel were easy to realize. A first version of this prototype is now available and we are thinking about alterations we want to bring to the prototype to reach a more general distributed DBMS. It concerns essentially private data interrogation from all available local sites and new real time access methods.

ACKNOWLEDGEMENTS

The authors want to thank Mr Hartmann, Huet and Rodet for their contribution to the project and G. Gardarin, F. Pasquer and J. Kiernan for helpful discussions.

REFERENCES

[BAYE83]   BAYER & all : "Database system Design for high performance", IFIP, 1983.
[BERN79]   BERNSTEIN P.A., CHU D. : "Using semi-joins to solve relational queries", Journal of ACM, V.8, N.1, January 1979.
[BERN81]   BERNSTEIN P.A., BLAUSTEIN B. : "A Simplification algorithm for integrity assertions and concrete views", Proc. of 5th Computer Software and Applications Conf., Chicago, Nov. 1981.
[GARD87]   GARDARIN G. & all : " Sabrina : a relational database system developed in a research environment", TSI, V.6 N.3, 1987.
[GRAV87]   GRAVEY A. : "Evaluation et performances de SABRINA-RT", CNET, Internal report, March 1987.
[GICQ85]   GICQUEL Y., HUET P., LE GAC G., LEPETIT Y. : "Proposition d'une architecture de SGBD pour les Télécommunications", CNET, Internal report, January 1985.
[ISO80]   Information processing systems - Open Systems Interconnection-OSI 7498, Basic reference model, April 1980.

[KERH86] KERHERVE B. : "Vues Relationnelles : Implantation dans les Systèmes de Gestion de Bases de Données Centralisées et Répartis", Thèse de 3ème cycle, Université de PARIS VI, Mars 1986.

[STON83] STONEBRAKER M., WOODFILL J., RANDSTROM J., MURPHY M., MEYER M., ALLMAN E. : "Performance enhancements to Relational Database System", ACM-TODS, V. 8, N.2, June 1983, pp. 167-185.

[WEDE86] WEDEKIND H. AND ZOERNTLEIN G. : "Prefetching in Real-time Database Applications", ACM-TODS, 1986.

A Multidatabase System for Transnational Accounting

Dirk Ellinghaus, Matthias Hallmann,
Bernhard Holtkamp, Klaus-Dieter Kreplin
UNIVERSITY OF DORTMUND, Fachbereich Informatik
Lehrstuhl Software-Technologie, Postfach 500 500
D-4600 Dortmund 50, West Germany

1. Introduction

In a project supported by the CEC in the Multi Annual Program a transaction oriented system is under development that integrates worldwide distributed autonomous databases into a multidatabase system (MDBS) where the constituting database systems might be of different type and are based on different data models. Partners in the project are in Belgium S.W.I.F.T, in France INRIA, and in Germany GMD-FOCUS (formerly HMI-FOCUS) and the University of Dortmund.

2. Organizational Background and Application Requirements

The MDBS under development is aimed at integrating different database systems that are controlled by independent organizations into a single system preserving the autonomy of the different sites. The strong demand of the banks to preserve the autonomy of their databases avoids the adoption of the concepts that are well-known from the research on distributed databases.

The basis for our MDBS for transnational accounting is the current S.W.I.F.T. Network. It can be characterized through the following properties:

The communication discipline is **store & forward.** A bank site submits a message to be transfered to the S.W.I.F.T. network. The message is forwarded in the network towards another site and stored there until the addressed bank fetches it from the network.

The communication is based on **standardized message types** that support the following applications:

- customer and bank funds transfer,
- loan and deposit transactions,
- collections,
- securities,
- documentary credits,
- special payment mechanisms,
- special message transfers.

All message types have a standardized syntax and semantics. The S.W.I.F.T. system is only a message transfer system while most of the connected bank sites maintain their own local database systems.

The most important property of the S.W.I.F.T. system is the **autonomy** of the connected sites. We distinguish between three kinds of autonomy:

- communication autonomy,
- execution autonomy,
- design autonomy.

Communication autonomy means that a site decides on the sending and receiving of messages. This type of autonomy is reflected by the store&forward communication discipline. Execution autonomy means that a site decides in the execution of functions requested from remote sites. There is no way, neither for S.W.I.F.T. nor for another site, to force a site to perform a requested operation. The operations are performed on the bank-own database that is under full control of the local site. Finally, design autonomy means that every bank site desides on the type of database system it uses. It is also up to the bank to implement the operations on their database that realize the functions requested by S.W.I.F.T. message types in accordance with the standardized semantics.

These properties had to be taken into account when developing the MDBS.

The following principal **requirements** for the envisaged MDBS can be identified:

- preservation of the site autonomy,
- move from a pure message oriented system to a transaction oriented system that integrates message transfer and the execution of the requests that are passed within the messages,
- description methods that ease the modification of existing services and the integration of new services,
- OSI based communication,
- a standardized interface to the heterogeneous banks.

3. Systems Architecture

In order to master the complexity of the MDBS it is designed as a **multi-layered** system. The MDBS is composed of a set of sites. The site architecture is modular and hierarchically structured. The gross MDBS architecture is depicted in fig. 1.

The kernel of the MBDS is formed by the **S.W.I.F.T. network.**

Above the kernel we have the **message handling system** or communication layer, resp., that abstracts from the current S.W.I.F.T. message transfer concept in that it provides end-to-end communication between sites. The communication is based on X.400 /CCITT84/. A special user agent is developed.

The autonomy of the sites avoids to adopt traditional transaction concepts in our MDBS environment. Consequently, we have developed

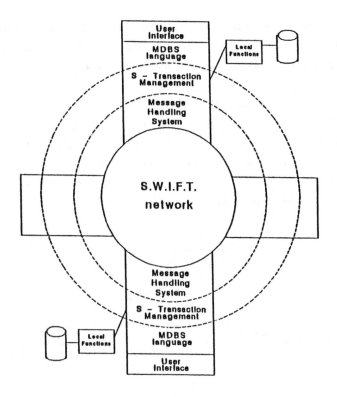

FIG.1: Gross MDBS architecture

a new transaction concept called S-Transactions ('S' stands for 'semi' but can be interpreted too as 'semantic' resp.'S.W.I.F.T.'), that obeys the restrictions and limitations imposed by the decentralization and autonomy of the MDBS. Roughly said an S-transaction consists of a set of requests for functions performed on the local database and of requests for functions to be performed at remote sites. An S-transaction is processed as a unit that has properties of nested transactions /HeRo87/ and of Sagas /GaSa87/. It is the task of the **S-Transaction Management** layer to control the proper execution of S-transactions. To specify S-transactions a language called STDL is developed that contains embedded SQL-statements. D_SQL is mapped on STDL.

The **'Local Functions'** box in figure 1 represents the interface between the MDBS and the local database system. Here the mapping of the requests for local functions as a part of an S-transaction into the corresponding function of the local database system is performed. As a uniform interface to the heterogeneous databases a relational interface in terms of SQL is taken.

The **Application Layer** is located on top of the S-Transaction Management. The user is provided with a uniform MDBS query language called D-SQL which is an extension of SQL. It enables a user either to initiate predefined (canned) S-transactions or free queries described in terms of D-SQL. An overview of the site architecture is given in fig.2.

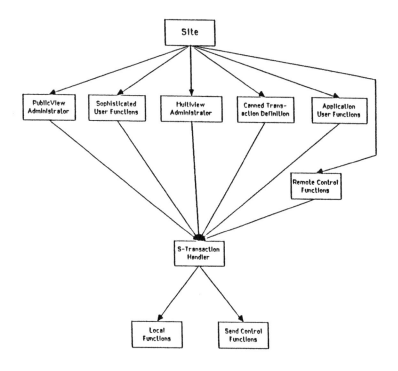

FIG.2: Site architecture

4. State of the Work

The languages of D_SQL /MAP87a/ and STDL /HaHo87/ are specified in detail. Furtheron, a detailed description of S-transactions, an associated recovery concept, and its relation to STDL are provided /MAP87b/. Other reports focus on the overall system architecture /MAP87c/, security /MAP87d/, and the communication subsystem /MAP87e/.

A prototype implementation is under work that includes interpreters for the languages, the specified recovery, communication and security subsystems, and sample databases and application descriptions in D_SQL and STDL for typical applications.

REFERENCES

/CCIT84/ CCITT Recommendations: X.400, X.401, X.408, X.409, X.410, X.411, X.420, X.430. Malaga - Torremolinos, 1984

/GaSa87/ H. Garcia-Molina; K. Salem: SAGAS. Proc. SIGMOD, 1987

/HaHo87/ M. Hallmann; B. Holtkamp: STDL: A Definition Language for Semantic Transactions. GI Conference "Databases for Software Engineering, Dortmund, November 1987

/HaRo87/ T.Haerder; K.Rothermel: Concepts for Transaction Recovery in Nested Transactions. ACM SIGMOD Conference 1987.

/MAP86/ Hahn-Meitner Institut; University of Dortmund: The Formal Definition of S-Transactions. Appendix to the Final Report of MAP 761 (MAP Project 761B) July 1986

/MAP87a/ INRIA: Schema Architecture and Data Language for a Multidatabase System. Deliverable No. 1 (MAP Project 761B), February 1987

/MAP87b/ University of Dortmund: Detailed Description of the S-transaction Concept. Internal Report No. 3 (MAP Project 761B), September 1987

/MAP87c/ Hahn-Meitner Institut; INRIA; S.W.I.F.T.; University of Dortmund: Multidatabase System Architecture. Internal Report No. 4 (MAP Project 761B), July 1987

/MAP87d/ INRIA: Design of a Multidatabase Security Mechanism. Deliverable No. 2 (MAP Project 761B), September 1987

/MAP87e/ Hahn-Meitner Institut: Multidatabase Services on ISO/OSI Networks for Transnational Accounting. Deliverable No.3 (MAP Project 761B), October 1987

MULTOS: a Document Server for Distributed Office Systems

E. Bertino, F.Rabitti, C.Thanos

Istituto di Elaborazione della Informazione
Consiglio Nazionale delle Ricerche
Via S.Maria 46, Pisa (Italy)

ABSTRACT

The features of the query language and the query processing strategy in the MULTOS ESPRIT project are presented and discussed. An extension of the Office Document Architecture to meet the retrieval requirements of a multimedia filing system is also proposed.

1. Introduction

In the last few years, there has been a growing interest in enhancing productivity in the office environments by using computer systems for the automation of routine tasks, for the acquisition, handling and communication of information, and in the intelligent support of decision making. If this is to be achieved, computer systems must be able to process and distribute the type of information that people normally handle and must offer information-processing and communication paradigms similar to that employed manually. Today's computer systems provide comprehensive support for text as a medium and there are a wide variety of text editors, formatters, database systems, and mail systems currently in existence. However, people naturally create, handle, and exchange information by using a wide range of media. Thus, they seek computer-based support non only for text but for graphics, images, voice, and combinations of these media. Consequently, multimedia information systems must be developed to support acquisition/creation/handling/communication of information that expressed in a number of different media.

An essential component of an office computer-based multimedia information system is a multimedia information filing and retrieval subsystem which has to support the storage, searching, retrieval, and updating of multimedia information. The basic building block for this susbsystem is what we call a multimedia document server. By document we mean a structured "office object" such as forms, letters, reports, containing alphanumeric data, text, computer graphics, images and voice.

The use of multimedia office objects introduces integration problems. Therefore, the modelling aspects of office objects play a key role in the design of a multimedia filing and retrieval tool. An Office Document Architecture (ODA) [ISO84] has been proposed by the International Organization for Standardization (ISO). The main goal of this proposal is to facilitate the document communication among document processing tools in a multivendor office systems environment. Thus the modelling concepts have been proposed with the aim of creating a common understanding of the structure of documents, which are exchanged between cooperating tools in office systems. Therefore, although the ODA proposal meets the requirements of one of the components of an office information system (OIS), i.e., the information communication subsystem, the needs of the information filing and retrieval components are not fully addressed. These requirements regard efficient searching and retrieval of stored documents.

In the MULTOS project, which aims at the development of a multimedia document server, the issue of enriching the ODA proposal in order to meet the retrieval requirements has been considered. The extension of the ODA proposal is presented in Section 3 of this paper.

One basic information retrieval requirement of the office application environment is the possibility of retrieving documents by specifying their content since access based on unique identifiers is clearly indequate. In addition, the semantic and syntactical structure of the documents, as they are defined in the ODA proposal and in its extension proposed in Section 3, should be exploited in the query formulation. In Section 4 the query language defined in the MULTOS project is presented and its features are discussed.

The query processing, defined in the MULTOS project, is described is Section 5. Section 2 presents those relevant architectural aspects of a multimedia document server designed in the MULTOS project, which are relevant to the query processing. It should be noted that the first prototype deals with attribute and text data only.

2. The Architecture of a Multimedia Document Server

The design of the multimedia filing system is based on the client-server paradigm [MULT85], [BERT85], [BERT86]. This has been chosen as it leads to an open system consisting of loosely coupled components - the file servers and their clients - and it is thus appropriate for office systems in which flexiblity and extendibility are required. The multimedia filing system consists of a number of autonomous subsystems called document servers and a number of client subsystems.

Let us briefly describe those components of the document server which are relevant to query processing.

Server Controller. The Server Controller coordinates the activities of all the server components in order to execute a query issued by a client. It is also responsible for all the control operations such as authorization control, concurrency control, version control and recovery.

Type Handler. The Type Handler maintains document type definitions and manages all the operations on types.

Collection Handler. The Collection Handler maintains document collection definitions and manages all the operations on collections.

Structure Translator. The Structure Translator handles the conversion between the ODIF representation of documents (exchange format of ODA documents) and their storage format. It also maps document level operations onto the data structures of the Document Storage Subsystem.

Document Storage Subsystem. The Storage Subsystem provides access methods for attribute and text data and allows the storage of large data values. Secondary storage is logically divided into partitions called clusters or volumes. A cluster contains a set of documents plus access information (such as indexes and signature files) for those documents. Therefore clusters are self-contained. In general, a cluster coincides with a disk. However, several clusters can be contained within a single disk. The Document Storage Subsystem consists of a number of modules. The most important of these modules are the following:

a) The Object Handler which allows the storage and retrieval of ODIF document objects.

b) The Index Handler which allows document retrieval based on attribute values. It maintains access structure based on the semantic structure of the documents. It also supports composite indexes that allow document attributes to be indexed across clusters.

c) The Signature Handler which allows document retrieval based on document content. It maintains access structures to the document content based on a signature technique [ROBE79].

3. The Document Model

In MULTOS the representation of documents and operations on them, are based on a formal model. At the beginning, a standardized document presentation was assumed, i.e. the ODA model. The Office Document Architecture (ODA) is a standard defined by ISO [ISO84]. ODA gives a formal description of the document composition (logical structure) and a formal device-independent description of the document presentation/rendition (layout structure).

The logical structure associates the content of the document with a hierarchy of logical objects, whereas the layout structure associates the same content with a hierarchy of layout objects. However, the limits of this standard for retrieval activity were soon apparent, and thus an extension has been proposed within the project. Indeed, in a general office environment, retrieval by name is clearly inadequate whereas retrieval by content is assuming an increasing importance. A document model suitable for supporting retrieval by document content should be, at the same time, as flexible as possible, and should provide as much knowledge as possible about the structure of a given document, in order to assist in the storage and retrieval of these documents.

The proposed modelling approach has three levels in document modelling: conceptual, logical and layout. The logical and layout modelling levels are constituted by the ODA standard. Thus, the extension to the ODA standard is constituted by the conceptual modelling level.

The conceptual structure describes the semantic components of the documents, giving names to these components. The grammar for the conceptual modelling level allows any semantic component to be decomposed hierarchically, giving names to these hierarchical semantic categories. With the name of a conceptual component the user describes the semantic role and semantic composition of that component. The system assumes that a conceptual component with the same name in several type definitions be semantically the same in all these type definitions. The conceptual structure is defined according to the Conceptual Structure Definition (CSD) formalism.

3.1. The Conceptual Structure Definition (CSD)

The conceptual structure defined in CSD is valid for both document instances and document types. In fact, according to our modelling approach, it is not possible to distinguish two disjoint levels of structures, one for document types and the other for document instances. In our model there is a continuum between document types and document instances, ranging from more general weak types to more specific types, obtained by the specialization/instantiation process. Special rules for conceptual structure specialization, which in our case also serve for document instantiation, are also defined.

According to CSD, in the conceptual structure of a document the type name must indicate the type associated to the conceptual structure. For a document type, it must be the name that uniquely identifies the type with this conceptual structure in the system type catalog. For a

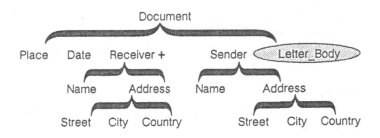

Figure 1.a: *Example of Conceptual Structure of Document Type: GENERIC_LETTER*

document, the name indicates the type in the system type catalog from which the instance was created.

Each conceptual component is labelled by a conceptual name. The name is the only way to uniquely denote the semantics associated to that component, and to the corresponding sub-structure. The naming of conceptual components is very important since the same conceptual component can be recognized in different document types and instances, beacuse the same name is used. Conceptual components with the same name, in different conceptual structures or in different positions of the same conceptual structure, besides having the same interpretation in a document query, must also have the same internal sub-structure, or an equivalent sub-structure.

There are three types of conceptual components: complex, basic or spring. A spring component is a conceptual component for which only the name is specified, while the sub-structure is left unspecified. During the specialization process, the spring component will become either a complex or basic conceptual component.

The complex conceptual components allows components to be structured into simpler ones ("part-of" hierarchy). A conceptual component can either be unexploited or exploited. An unexploited conceptual component indicates a skeleton of other (unexploited) conceptual components, according to which the component is logically structured. When an unexploited component is exploited during the specialization process, its sub-structure of (exploited) conceptual components must follow to the skeleton specified for the original unexploited conceptual component.

A basic conceptual component is constituted by a terminal component. A terminal component refers to a data value, or a data value structure, contained in the document, as specified in the ODIF definition.

In Fig.1.a the conceptual structure of the GENERIC_LETTER type is sketched.

In Fig.1.b the conceptual structure of the BUSINESS_LETTER type is sketched.

The second type is a specialization of the first type since the component LETTER_BODY has been specialized into five new components. In conceptual modelling terms, we can say that BUSINESS_LETTER is-a GENERIC_LETTER.

In the examples of document types, the "+" symbol attached to the component RECEIVER

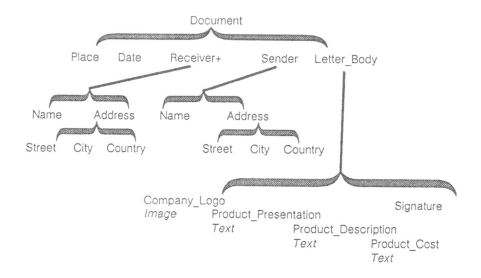

Figure 1.b: *Example of Conceptual Structure of Document Type: BUSINESS_LETTER*

means that it is a multi-valued conceptual component. It should be noted also that the conceptual components NAME and ADDRESS appear in two subtrees having as roots the conceptual components RECEIVER and SENDER respectively.

4. Query Language

Queries may have conditions on both the content and the conceptual structure of documents. Expressing conditions on the document's conceptual structure means asking for documents having the conceptual components whose names are specified in the condition. The query language is fully described in [BERT88]. In general, a query has the following form: (expressions between square brackets are optional)

FIND DOCUMENTS [VERSION *version-clause;*]
[SCOPE *scope-clause;*]
[TYPE *TYPE-clause;*]
WHERE *COND-clause;*

One or more conceptual types can be specified in the *TYPE* clause. The conditions expressed in the query apply to the documents belonging to the specified types. If the types indicated in the query have subtypes, then the query applies to all the documents having as type one of these subtypes. When no type is specified, the query will apply to all possible document types. The conditions expressed in the *COND* clause are a boolean combination of conditions which must be satisfied by the documents retrieved. Conditions on text components and conditions on attribute components, of different types, can be mixed in the *COND* clause. A text condition on the special component named "text" is applied to the entire document.

In order to reference a conceptual component in a document, a path-name must be specified. A path-name has the form:

$$name_1[.|*]name_2[.|*]\ldots name_{n-1}[.|*]name_n$$

where each $name_i$ is a simple name.

The path-name specifies that the conceptual component being referenced is the component having simple name $name_n$ which is contained within the conceptual component whose name is $name_{n-1}$. The conceptual component $name_{n-1}$ is in turn contained in $name_{n-2}$, and so on. Component names within a path-name can be separated by either a "." or a "*". When "." is used, it means that the conceptual component of the left side of the "." contains directly the component of the right. When "*" is used, there may be one or more intermediate components between the component on the left side and that on the right.

In our language, conditions are usually expressed against conceptual components of documents, i.e., a condition has the form:

"*component restriction*",

where *component* is the name (or path-name) of a conceptual component and *restriction* is an operator followed by an expression. This expression may contain other component names.

It should be noted that the component name (or path-name) may refer to a conceptual component which is contained in several conceptual components. For instance, in the example in Fig.1, we could have a condition of the form:

"Name *restriction*".

The restriction applies to both the components whose path-names are Sender.Name and Receiver.Name. The problem is to decide how such a condition is satisfied. There are four possibilities:

(1) Name *restriction* = True if
(Sender.Name *restriction* = True) $\wedge$
($\exists$ (Receiver.Name *restriction* = True))

(2) Name = *restriction* = True if
(Sender.Name *restriction* = True) $\wedge$
($\forall$ (Receiver.Name *restriction* = True))

(3) Name = *restriction* = True if
(Sender.Name *restriction* = True) $\vee$
($\forall$ (Receiver.Name *restriction* = True))

(4) Name *restriction* = True if
(Sender.Name *restriction* = True) $\vee$
($\exists$ (Receiver.Name *restriction* = True))

In this case, the system chooses the fourth solution since it is the most general: the answer to the query (4) contains the answers to queries (1), (2), and (3). This choice reflects our philosophy of giving the user the most general answer, when there are ambiguities in the query. The user who did not have precisely knowledge of the types defined in the document base, can then refine his original query specifying its meaning exactly.

In addition to the previous condition types, the language must allow conditions on the existence of conceptual components within documents. This allows queries to be expressed on the conceptual structure of documents. Therefore, we have defined the operator "with". A condition containing the "with" operator has the form: "with *component*".

This condition expresses the fact that the component whose name (or pathname) is given must be a conceptual component of the documents to be retrieved. To express conditions in which a conceptual component having name $name_i$ must be contained in a conceptual component having name $name_j$ the path-name $name_i * name_j$ is used.

The "with" operator is conceptually very important in our query language. While the other operators allow conditions to be defined on data (ie. document instance) the "with" operator allows the definition of conditions on meta-data (ie. document types).

An example query that will be used throughout this paper is the following:

```
find documents where Document.Date > /1/1/1987/ and
(*Sender.Name = "Olivetti" or
*Product_Presentation contains "Olivetti") and
*Product_Description contains "Personal Computer%" and
(*Address.Country = "Italy" or text contains "Italy") and
with *Company_Logo;
```

5. Query Processing

At more general level the task of query processing can be divided into four main phases. In the first phase, some initial activities are performed such as parsing and catalog access. The query is modified also in light of the type hierarchy. We refer to this phase as the preprocessing phase. In the second phase, the set of clusters that must be accessed is determined. Since document distribution on the various clusters is transparent to the applications using the system, in order to solve a query it must be determined which clusters contain documents which can potentially satisfy the query. We refer to this phase as multi-cluster query resolution. For each cluster involved in the query, a query processing strategy is then defined. We refer to this phase as single-cluster query optimization. Finally, the query is executed following the strategies defined in the previous step. The last two phases i.e. single-cluster query optimization and execution are repeated for all the clusters identified by the multi-cluster query resolution phase.

5.1. The Preprocessing Phase

This phase consists of the following steps.

Parsing

The query is parsed by a conventional parser. The parser verifies that the syntax of the query is correct. The parser output is a query parse tree, which is augmented and modified by the subsequent the query processing steps. In the parse tree, the *COND* clause, i.e. is the boolean combination of predicates, is expressed in Conjunctive Normal Form (CNF).

Catalog Access

During catalog access information concerning the definitions of conceptual types and components is retrieved. This information is stored in several tables (or other data structures) in main memory to be used in the subsequent steps of the query processing.

Component Checking

If a list of types is specified in the query (clause *TYPE*) then a check is made to verify that the conceptual components present in the query belong to that type. Each conceptual component name is also expanded to its complete path name. If there are several paths corresponding to a given name, condition C in which the component appears is substituted by a disjunction of conditions $C_1, \ldots, C_n$, where n is the number of the path names. Each C_i has the same form as C, except that the name of the conceptual component appearing in C is substituted by the i-th path name.

If no type is specified, the catalogs are accessed to determine the document types containing the conceptual components whose names appear in the query conditions (clause $COND$). The list of these types is added to the query tree. If no document type exists containing such conceptual components, the query results in an empty set and query processing stops.

The transformations on the query parse tree include the elimination of all WITH components (in most cases), the reorganization (i.e. addition and/or deletion) of disjuncts in some conjuncts and the possible elimination of certain conjuncts. If the conjuncts have mutually exclusive requirements (i.e. no document type exists containing the required conceptual components), the query results in an empty set and query processing stops. If all conjuncts are eliminated, the answer to the query will be the set of documents belonging to one of the types determined in the Type-Level query processing, and no query optimization is not longer necessary. The algorithms used in this query processing phase are described in [BERT87].

The example query resulting from the transformations performed by the component-checker is the following:

```
find documents type BUSINESS_LETTER; where
DOCUMENT.DATE > /1/1/1987/ and
(DOCUMENT.SENDER.NAME = "Olivetti" or
DOCUMENT.LETTER_BODY.PRODUCT.PRESENTATION contains "Olivetti") and
DOCUMENT.LETTER_BODY.PRODUCT.DESCRIPTION contains "Personal Computer%" and
(some DOCUMENT.RECEIVER.ADDRESS.COUNTRY = "Italy" or
DOCUMENT.SENDER.ADDRESS.COUNTRY = "Italy" or
text contains "Italy");
```

5.2. Multi-cluster Query Resolution

The goal of this phase is to determine the clusters involved in a query. The set of clusters to be accessed is restricted in different ways depending on the query. For instance, if a collection identifier has been specified, the query is restricted to clusters storing documents belonging to that collection only. The conceptual document types specified in the query are also used to restrict the number of clusters to be accessed for query resolution. Finally, the composite indexes can be used if the query contains predicates on such components.

5.3. Query Optimization

For each cluster determined in the previous phase, a query execution strategy is defined. It should be pointed out that each query must be optimized separately for each cluster involved, since the statistics used for query optimization may be different for different clusters.

The result of single-cluster query optimization is a set of basic operations, where basic operations include index access, signature scans (for evaluating text predicates), document accesses, intersection and union of intermediate results. In addition, a schedule is defined stating the order of execution for the various operations. The query optimization algorithm is described in detail in [BERT88].

5.4. Query Execution

Each cluster involved in the query is mounted, if it has not been already mounted, and the query is executed following the strategy defined by the optimizer. Mounting a cluster means mounting the disk where the cluster is stored. The result of the query will be a set of Logical Document Identifiers (*LDI*'s). The result of the original query is the union of the *LDI*'s returned by all the single-cluster queries.

It should be pointed out that several queries from several users may be executed in parallel. This raises the problem of scheduling mounts so that the number of mounts is minimized.

6. Final Remarks

This paper presents the query language and the query processing strategy defined in the first prototype of the MULTOS project. A simplified architecture is presented in order to discuss the query processing. Issues related to query formulation and evaluation, such as the extension of the ODA proposal by adding a semantic structure, are also discussed.

The implementation of the first prototype of a Document Server was completed by September 1987. In this prototype, the query processing is based on data and text components of documents. A second prototype will follow, in which image and audio components will also be considered. In particular, graphics and image components should play an active role in the query processing [MULT87]. Future work will also include possible extensions of query optimization to the case of different signature mechanisms, such as bit-sliced [ROBE79] or S-tree [DEPP86] organizations.

The already existing MULTOS system consists of document servers and clients. The implementation environment consists of several machines, such as DEC Vax-11/780, ATT 3B-2/400 and Sun-3 workstations. The machines are connected by Ethernet, and each machine runs a version of UNIX (1) containing networking software. The MULTOS server software is fairly portable and runs on all these machines (despite some problems of compatibility between UNIX System V and BSD 4.2). The client software was developed specifically for the Sun workstations and relies on the Sun window package.

We think that the importance of this approach to query processing goes beyond the particular application area (i.e. management of multimedia office documents) and the particular implementation (i.e. the MULTOS system). It constitutes one of the first examples of a complete approach to query processing in a system for the *management of complex data objects*. These objects may also include multimedia components.

REFERENCES

[BERT85] Bertino E., Gibbs S., Rabitti F., Tsichritzis D., *Architecture of a Multimedia Document Server*, Proc. 2nd ESPRIT Technical Week, Brussels, Sept. 1985.

[BERT86] Bertino E., Gibbs S., Rabitti F., Tsichritzis D., *A Multimedia Document Server*, Proc. Advanced Database Symposium, Japan, August 29-30, 1986.

[BERT87] Bertino E., and Rabitti F., *An Approach to the Type Management of Complex Objects*, IEEE Data Base Engineering, Vol.10, No.3 (Oct. 1987).

---

(1) UNIX is a trademark of Bell Laboratories.

[BERT88] Bertino E., Rabitti F., Gibbs S., *Query Processing in a Multimedia Document System*, to appear in ACM Trans. on Office Information Systems.

[DEPP86] Deppisch U., *S-Tree: A Dynamic Balanced Signature Index for Office Retrieval*, in Proc. ACM Conference on Information Retrieval, Pisa (Italy), September 8-10, 1986.

[ISO84] ISO DP 8613/2 "Part 2: Office Document Architecture", Information Processing-Text Preparation and Interchange - Text Structures, ISO/TC97/SC18/WG3 N392, 1984.

[MULT85] MULTOS Esprit Project - Report T0: *Global Design*, 1985.

[MULT87] Conti P., Corbo M., Pancaccini G., Rabitti F., Stanchev P., *Second Prototype specifications: Image classification and retrieval by content in MULTOS*, MULTOS Tech. Deliverable OLI/IEI-87-01, March 28, 1987.

[ROBE79] Roberts C.S., *Partial-match Retrieval via the Method of Superimposed Codes*, Proc. IEEE, Vol.67, N.12, pp.63-69, December 1979.

The DURESS Project: Extending Databases into an Open Systems Architecture

W. Johannsen [1], W. Lamersdorf [2], K. Reinhardt [1], J.W. Schmidt [1]

[1] J.W. Goethe-Universität, Dept. of Computer Science, Database and Information Systems
Robert Mayer-Straße 11-15, D-6000 Frankfurt am Main 11, West-Germany

[2] IBM Deutschland, European Networking Center
Tiergartenstraße 15, D-6900 Heidelberg, West-Germany

Abstract

The DURESS (Distributed University Research and Education and Support System) project is a joint effort of the Database and Information Systems Group at the Johann Wolfgang Goethe-University, Frankfurt, and the IBM European Networking Center, Heidelberg, West-Germany. In the DURESS project, the applicability of an integrated database and programming language is extended into an open distributed environment. The extended architecture allows for distributing database 'modules' over separate nodes in a computer network and for accessing components of such modules in a distribution transparent way. In a corresponding prototype, it is demonstrated how the necessary database management and communication system extensions can be realized, exemplarily, based on a centralized DBMS and supported by standard ISO/OSI communication facilities.

1. Introduction

An important tendency in computer system support for data-intensive applications is to adopt to the increasing requirements of cooperative *distributed applications*. Therefore, software engineering environments for such applications (e.g. advanced office information systems [6]) have to be based on an 'open architecture' approach: complex distributed systems can be characterized as consisting of independent components which make all their inter-connections explicitly visible for each other [12].

Traditionally, distributed database systems have been a way to support distributed data-intensive applications by closely integrating data management functions on separate computers under - logically - one compound data management control. Nowadays, the more widespread use of small, decentralized computer systems (up till independent personal workstations) each providing for their own programming and data management support together with increasingly powerful networking functions to interconnect such systems leads to less strict and more flexible ways of cooperation. In many cases, there exists only a loose coupling between independent programming and data management systems. On the other hand, in open distributed computer networks, the effort required for inter-system communication increases considerately, especially in the most general case of a heterogeneous hard- and software environment.

This papers reports on a research and development project which aims at extending existing database and networking technology in order to support distributed data-intensive applications in an open heterogeneous computer network environment. In the 'DURESS' project, the applicability of an integrated database and programming language is extended into an open distributed environment. In a corresponding prototype, it is demonstrated how the necessary database management and communication system extensions can be realized, exemplarily. So, the project proposes, - at the *programming language* interface - a modular language which abstracts from data management and distribution aspects as far as possible. In order to support the *communication* requirements of an open systems environment, the DURESS approach is based on proposals and extensions of the respective ISO/OSI communication standards.

The paper reports on the DURESS programming language interface, the architecture of the underlying extended database and communication system, and the current status of a prototype, respectively.

2. Database Programming in a Distributed Environment

The definition of the DURESS language interface is based on the database and programming language **DBPL** [10] as originally realized on a central computer system [2]. The programming paradigm proposed is centered around a high-level im- and export mechanism for data and other programming language objects to be provided for independent program units (modules) in a centralized as well as in distributed environments. Thus, the basic idea of integrated database programming languages is extended into distributed systems: an abstract language interface for the definition, manipulation, and administration of *all* data objects of an application regardless on which node in a network they reside.

In (relational) database programming languages, relations - as all other data objects - are regarded as typed variables; relation types are constructed orthogonally from types of the database programming language. Database variables are defined in a 'permanently' existing scope and can be 'imported' for manipulation by other program units. Database relations are updated by assignment statements, values are retrieved as expression, and iterators allow for programming loops on (sub-) sets of relation elements.

DBPL consists of Modula-2 [13] as algorithmic language and of a relational extension with first-order predicate expressions for data retrieval and manipulation. DBPL programs are viewed as systems of independent program 'modules' which are related exclusively via well-defined interfaces. A specific type of ('database') module defines the permanent (relational) database which can be imported by other modules. A 'selector' mechanism allows for restricting the database access to a predicatively defined (sub-) relation, a 'transaction' mechanism allows for partitioning database programs for parallel database access as well as for ensuring data consistency.

In the DURESS project, DBPL is extended in such a way that independent program modules can be distributed over *different network nodes* while keeping the basic programming paradigm of im- and exporting modules as communication interface. In the extended DBPL language, the separation of modules over different nodes of a computer network basically allows for im- and export of three different classes of program objects: data types, procedures/transactions, and (database) variables [5]. *Type declarations* can, for instance, be exported in order to generate objects of the same type in different modules (like a central office 'forms' administration). Im- and export of *procedures/transactions* can be viewed as a 'remote procedure call' [1] where the importing module sends a set of parameters to the exporting module where the operation is executed, and possible results are returned to the 'calling' module. Finally, export of a *variable* allows other modules to gain access to the exported variable.

3. Architecture of an Open Communication Support System

Computer architectures suited especially well for data-intensive, distributed, and cooperative office environments are based on local and wide area networks combining end user workstations, specialized I/O-equipment, etc. as well as more powerful host computer systems. Here, application programs include local processing, data manipulation functions as well as 'distributed procedures' describing cooperation of different work units in order to achieve a common goal. In general, cooperation beyond local network boundaries requires communication with heterogeneous partners in 'open' computer networks based on common communication protocols.

In order to realize such an approach, the underlying computer network has to provide a set of basic, commonly accepted communication functions. In a heterogeneous environment of 'open' system interconnections, the required services and protocols are based on standards proposals as issued by the 'International Standards Organization' (ISO) in the layered 'Open Systems Interconnection' (OSI) reference model [7].

Support for the **communication** requirements of heterogeneous networks is based on an ISO/OSI approach both on local area networks and on wide area networks accessed via appropriate inter-net gateway connections. In order to provide access to the services of a remote host computer from a local area network, a dedicated gateway computer transforms the corresponding protocol data units to and from both networks according to the local and 'open system' wide area network conventions. Thus, at a certain layer of the ISO/OSI reference model (e.g. layer 3 or 4), a common user interface is provided which hides the network transport system characteristics from the upper ISO/OSI-layers, i.e. from the development of specific application services.

As a special case of distributed computer networks, **hierarchical** networks consist of a central 'server' node offering services (e.g. data management) to remote 'client' nodes [11] which - in our model - are allowed to import objects from the server.

4. The 'DURESS' Prototype System

The example network architecture for the DURESS prototype system couples a local area (Token Ring) network of IBM PC AT personal workstations via an ISO/OSI based wide area network with a remote DEC VAX host computer system (locally interconnected by a DECNET cluster). Thus, the network hardware configuration provides the prerequisites for realizing hierarchically distributed client/server applications. So, user workstations are enabled to access nodes in remote networks including dedicated servers as, for example, database systems (DBMS), or other service providers via additional wide area networks (as, e.g., 'DFN' in Germany). As shown in Figure 1 the DURESS network configuration can also be viewed as an example of coupling different local (LAN) and wide area (WAN) networks via a public X.25-connection (in Germany offered by the PTT in the packet switching network 'Datex-P').

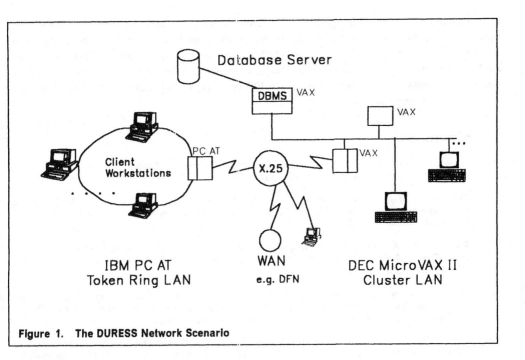

Figure 1. The DURESS Network Scenario

The DURESS prototype realizes the extended database programming language DBPL based on extensions of the corresponding centralized DBPL data management system [4]. As a prerequisite, the DBPL system is transferred to the user workstations and access is provided from there to the remote server node. In a further phase, access to remote objects can be extended to databases on other workstations in the network, thus realizing a 'symmetrically distributed' system.

The additional functions to accommodate the distribution aspects (e.g. distributed query execution, transaction management, etc.) are implemented as extensions to the DBPL runtime system. The synchronization of different modules accessing common data can be implemented with subtransaction including a two-phase-commit protocol ensuring, in addition, controlled error recovery.

The communication support system is realized - in the lower layers of the OSI reference model - as a global 'transport system' using layer-3-gateways to interconnect the corresponding local area networks. The WAN connection between the gateway PC and the VAX systems is based on a public packet-switching network and a realization of an 'internet' protocol to provide a common addressing scheme for all nodes in the combined (sub-) networks [8]. Then, common implementations of OSI layers 4 and above provide the prerequisites for application specific services in the upper layers as, e.g., the client/server database system cooperation (including, e.g., a 'remote operations call' mechanism to invoke server functions from client stations etc.).

In the DURESS prototype development, the communication protocol and service implementations are simplified considerably by using common protocol specification, code generation, and testing **tools** at various layers of the OSI model [3].

Based on the proposed language interface. it shall lateron be demonstrated how the development of specific distributed <u>applications</u>, e.g. in the area of a university office information system environment (supporting university teaching, research, and administration) can be facilitated. Extending the modelling facilities, it seems also interesting to support <u>complex object</u> representations (as, e.g, specified in [9]) applying the distributed DURESS language and implementation approach.

5. References

[1] : Birrel, A. and Nelson, B.: "Implementing Remote Procedure Calls", ACM Transactions on Computer Systems, vol. 2, no. 1, 1984, pp. 39-59.

[2] : Eckhardt, H., Edelmann, J., Koch, J., Mall, M., Schmidt, J.W.: "Draft Report on the Database Programming Language DBPL", DBPL Memo 091-85, Johann Wolfgang Goethe-Universität Frankfurt, Frankfurt, 1985.

[3] : Fleischmann, A.: "PASS - A Technique for Specifying Protocols": Procs. IFIP WG 6.1 7th Intern. Conf. on Protocol Specification, Testing, and Verification, North-Holland Pub. Co., Amsterdam, 1987, pp. 61-76.

[4] : Ge, L., Johannsen, W., Lamersdorf, W., Reinhardt, K., Schmidt, J.W.: "Database Applications Support in Open Systems: Language Concepts and Implementation Architectures", Procs. IEEE Computer Society 4th Int. Conference on Data Engineering, IEEE Press, Feb. 1988.

[5] : Ge, L., Johannsen, W., Lamersdorf, W., Reinhardt. K., Schmidt, J.W.: "Import and Export of Database Objects", Procs. IFIP WG 10.3 Intern. Conference on 'Distributed Processing', Amsterdam, Netherlands, North-Holland Pub. Co., 1988.

[6] : Hewitt, C., "Offices are Open Systems": ACM Trans. on Office Systems, vol. 4, no. 3, July 1986, pp. 271-287.

[7] : IEEE: "Open Systems Interconnection (OSI) - New International Standards Architecture and Protocols for Distributed Information Systems", Proceedings of the IEEE, Special Issue, 71, 12, 1983, pp. 1131-1448.

[8] : Johannsen, W, Lamersdorf. W., Reinhardt, K.: "Architecture and Design of an Open Systems LAN/WAN-Gateway", Proc. IEEE Computer Networking Symposium, IEEE Computer Society Press, April 1988.

[9] : Lamersdorf, W., Schmidt, J.W., Müller, G.: "A Recursive Approach to Office Object Modelling", Information Processing and Management, vol. 22, no. 2, Pergamon Press Ltd., Oxford, U.K., March 1986, pp. 109-120.

[10] : Mall, M., Schmidt, J.W., Reimer, M.: "Data Selection, Sharing, and Access Control In a Relational Scenario", in: Brodie, M.L., Mylopoulos, J., Schmidt, J.W. (Eds.), "On Conceptual Modeling, Perspectives from Artificial Intelligence, Databases, and Programming Languages", Springer-Verlag, New York, 1982, pp. 411-436.

[11] : Svobodova, L.: "Client/Server Model for Distributed Processing", Proc. GI-NTG-Fachtagung "Kommunikation in verteilten Systemen", Karlsruhe, Informatik-Fachberichte, vol. 95, Springer-Verlag, Berlin Heidelberg New York Tokyo, 1985, pp. 485-498.

[12] : Wasserman, A.: "Software Engineering Environments", Tutorial no. 5, Procs. 1st European Conf. on Software Engineering, Strasbourg, France, 1987, pp. 7-24.

[13] : Wirth, N.: "Programming in Modula-2", Springer-Verlag, Berlin Heidelberg New York Tokio, 1982.

Vol. 270: E. Börger (Ed.), Computation Theory and Logic. IX, 442 pages. 1987.

Vol. 271: D. Snyers, A. Thayse, From Logic Design to Logic Programming. IV, 125 pages. 1987.

Vol. 272: P. Treleaven, M. Vanneschi (Eds.), Future Parallel Computers. Proceedings, 1986. V, 492 pages. 1987.

Vol. 273: J.S. Royer, A Connotational Theory of Program Structure. V, 186 pages. 1987.

Vol. 274: G. Kahn (Ed.), Functional Programming Languages and Computer Architecture. Proceedings. VI, 470 pages. 1987.

Vol. 275: A.N. Habermann, U. Montanari (Eds.), System Development and Ada. Proceedings, 1986. V, 305 pages. 1987.

Vol. 276: J. Bézivin, J.-M. Hullot, P. Cointe, H. Lieberman (Eds.), ECOOP '87. European Conference on Object-Oriented Programming. Proceedings. VI, 273 pages. 1987.

Vol. 277: B. Benninghofen, S. Kemmerich, M.M. Richter, Systems of Reductions. X, 265 pages. 1987.

Vol. 278: L. Budach, R.G. Bukharajev, O.B. Lupanov (Eds.), Fundamentals of Computation Theory. Proceedings, 1987. XIV, 505 pages. 1987.

Vol. 279: J.H. Fasel, R.M. Keller (Eds.), Graph Reduction. Proceedings, 1986. XVI, 450 pages. 1987.

Vol. 280: M. Venturini Zilli (Ed.), Mathematical Models for the Semantics of Parallelism. Proceedings, 1986. V, 231 pages. 1987.

Vol. 281: A. Kelemenová, J. Kelemen (Eds.), Trends, Techniques, and Problems in Theoretical Computer Science. Proceedings, 1986. VI, 213 pages. 1987.

Vol. 282: P. Gorny, M.J. Tauber (Eds.), Visualization in Programming. Proceedings, 1986. VII, 210 pages. 1987.

Vol. 283: D.H. Pitt, A. Poigné, D.E. Rydeheard (Eds.), Category Theory and Computer Science. Proceedings, 1987. V, 300 pages. 1987.

Vol. 284: A. Kündig, R.E. Bührer, J. Dähler (Eds.), Embedded Systems. Proceedings, 1986. V, 207 pages. 1987.

Vol. 285: C. Delgado Kloos, Semantics of Digital Circuits. IX, 124 pages. 1987.

Vol. 286: B. Bouchon, R.R. Yager (Eds.), Uncertainty in Knowledge-Based Systems. Proceedings, 1986. VII, 405 pages. 1987.

Vol. 287: K.V. Nori (Ed.), Foundations of Software Technology and Theoretical Computer Science. Proceedings, 1987. IX, 540 pages. 1987.

Vol. 288: A. Blikle, MetaSoft Primer. XIII, 140 pages. 1987.

Vol. 289: H.K. Nichols, D. Simpson (Eds.), ESEC '87. 1st European Software Engineering Conference. Proceedings, 1987. XII, 404 pages. 1987.

Vol. 290: T.X. Bui, Co-oP A Group Decision Support System for Cooperative Multiple Criteria Group Decision Making. XIII, 250 pages. 1987.

Vol. 291: H. Ehrig, M. Nagl, G. Rozenberg, A. Rosenfeld (Eds.), Graph-Grammars and Their Application to Computer Science. VIII, 609 pages. 1987.

Vol. 292: The Munich Project CIP. Volume II: The Program Transformation System CIP-S. By the CIP System Group. VIII, 522 pages. 1987.

Vol. 293: C. Pomerance (Ed.), Advances in Cryptology — CRYPTO 87. Proceedings. X, 463 pages. 1988.

Vol. 294: R. Cori, M. Wirsing (Eds.), STACS 88. Proceedings, 1988. IX, 404 pages. 1988.

Vol. 296: R. Janßen (Ed.), Trends in Computer Algebra. Proceedings, 1987. V, 197 pages. 1988.

Vol. 297: E.N. Houstis, T.S. Papatheodorou, C.D. Polychronopoulos (Eds.), Supercomputing. Proceedings, 1987. X, 1093 pages. 1988.

Vol. 298: M. Main, A. Melton, M. Mislove, D. Schmidt (Eds.), Mathematical Foundations of Programming Language Semantics. Proceedings, 1987. VIII, 637 pages. 1988.

Vol. 299: M. Dauchet, M. Nivat (Eds.), CAAP 88. Proceedings, 1988. VI, 304 pages. 1988.

Vol. 300: H. Ganzinger (Ed.), ESOP '88. Proceedings, 1988. VI, 381 pages. 1988.

Vol. 301: J. Kittler (Ed.), Pattern Recognition. Proceedings, 1988. VI, 668 pages. 1988.

Vol. 302: D.M. Yellin, Attribute Grammar Inversion and Source-to-source Translation. VIII, 176 pages. 1988.

Vol. 303: J.W. Schmidt, S. Ceri, M. Missikoff (Eds.), Advances in Database Technology — EDBT '88. X, 620 pages. 1988.